THE HISTORY OF TREATIES
AND INTERNATIONAL POLITICS

*Storia dei Trattati
e Politica Internazionale*

I

Parte Generale

Introduzione allo Studio della "Storia dei Trattati e
Politica Internazionale": Le Fonti Documentarie e Memorialistiche

The History
of Treaties and
International Politics

ᴗ I

An Introduction to the History of Treaties and
International Politics: The Documentary and Memoir Sources

BY MARIO TOSCANO

The Johns Hopkins Press   Baltimore   1966

to
Chinita
Seeking for Perfection

PREFACE

In the preceding edition of this first volume of the textbook designed to accompany my lectures in the Department of Political Science at the University of Rome, it was emphasized that "the work is in no way definitive, but simply a first endeavor—to be revised and completed later."

In the five years that have elapsed since the publication of the first edition, special effort has gone into making the needed revisions and amplifying those sections that required further detail. The research work of my associates, Professors Gian Luca Andrè, Pietro Pastorelli, Giustino Filippone, and Dr. Franca Avantaggiato Puppo, was directed toward those areas which had only been touched upon in the previous edition. Particular attention was given to suggestions and recommendations made by my distinguished colleagues and an attempt was made to revise the references to the documentary and memoir sources in order to include those published since 1958 and to reorganize the content of the volume, to the extent that it may be considered a complete revision.

In this new edition several initial pages of the preceding one have been omitted because it was found that they were not absolutely indispensable, and these have been replaced with others that better suit the needs of students; the major lacunae have been filled; and attention has been focused on the post-1870 period, with an enlargement of the sections on World War I as a result. Concerning the more recent period, considerable space has been devoted to an analysis of the sources that are generally less well known, such as Scandinavian and Japanese, and the chapters have been restructured. In addition, the bibliographical references have been increased to include those works containing hitherto unpublished source material. These references are extremely brief, and they will be expanded in a later edition.

The present volume is primarily the result of the work of a research team. It expresses my views and those of my collaborators and represents the position of the Institute for the History of Treaties and International Politics of the Department of Political Science of the University of Rome.

In this joint effort, I am particularly indebted to Professors Gian Luca Andrè and Pietro Pastorelli, who did most of the work; to Professor Giustino Filippone, for his research relative to the introductory chapters and the treaty collections; and to Dr. Franca Avantaggiato Puppo, for her bibliographical research.

The list of scholars who have materially aided me in my efforts is a long one, and I desire to omit no one. The Hon. Miss Margaret Lambert, editor of the British and German diplomatic documents collections, contributed to completing the chapter on the Soviet documents, as did her assistant, Miss Eleanor Breuning. Professor Pierre Renouvin, Membre di l'Institut and Dean of the Faculty of Letters at the Sorbonne, has been very generous with his suggestions and useful information, while I am indebted to Professor Jean Baptiste Duroselle of the University of Lille, Director of the Centre d'Etudes des Relations Internationales de la Fondation Nationale des Sciences Politiques, for additional data on the French collection of diplomatic documents for the period following World War I. Minister Kenji Yasuda, chief of the research section of the Gaimusho, and the Italian Ambassador to Tokyo, Maurillo Coppini, made it possible for me, during my visit to Tokyo, to resolve an entire series of problems regarding the Japanese collections of diplomatic documents. Professor Giuliano Bertuccioli has written the paragraphs on the Chinese documentary sources and the section on the Chinese memoir sources which constitute a new addition to the volume, while Minister Plenipotentiary I. N. Zemskov, chief of the research section of the Soviet Foreign Ministry and secretary-general of the commission for the publication of Czarist and Soviet documents, has generously aided my bibliographical and historical research in this area. Professor Angelo Tamborra of the University of Perugia facilitated the investigation of the Yugoslav documents; Professor Fulvio d'Amoja of the University of Florence has added to my work on the Belgian documents; Professor Carlo Giglio of the University of Pavia contributed his special knowledge on the colored books relative to the colonial wars; Dr. Otto Mattei, Secretary to the Italian Embassy in Canberra, is responsible for many of the translations from the Russian, Swedish, and Norwegian; Professor Rodolfo Mosca of the University of Florence and Paolo Vita Finzi, the Italian Minister to Budapest, assisted in developing the details concerning the Hungarian documentary collections. And finally, Professor Anton Maria Bettanini of the University of Padua offered valuable suggestions on the previous edition, while the Italian Ambassadors to Oslo, Silvio Daneo, to The Hague, Raimondo Giustiniani, to Copenhagen, Francesco Lo Faro, and to Stockholm, Benedetto Capomazza di Campolattaro, have greatly facilitated my researches relative to the Norwegian,

Dutch, Danish, and Swedish diplomatic documents. To these, I express my appreciation.

Born in the classroom, this volume was specifically designed to aid students in their preparation for the Italian state examinations, but I also hope that it will be of some use to scholars. While I do not pretend to have definitively resolved all of the problems or to have exhausted every theme considered, I do believe that the revision is a significant improvement over the first venture. Scientific research is without end, and with the help of the readers and of my colleagues, I hope to be able to continue to correct, revise, and improve this text.

MARIO TOSCANO

Rome
March 8, 1963

Note: The spelling of Slavic names has been simplified in the matter of accents to satisfy printing requirements.

PREFACE TO THE AMERICAN EDITION

Although this volume was originally designed to meet the needs of Italian university students enrolled in the International Politics course of the University of Rome, it is sincerely hoped that it will also serve as a helpful compendium to American students enrolled in similar courses. For obvious reasons, from the American viewpoint the space given to Italy's role may appear to be somewhat excessive. Yet it is possible that this very fact will offer advantages that will outweigh any apparent disadvantages. In this translation a number of corrections and revisions have been made in the text. References to recently published materials of particular interest to the subject, as well as an entirely new section on Chinese memoir sources, have been added.

The time-honored word of caution is entirely apropos here. The history of treaties and international politics is a "living science," and, as such, it is constantly subject to further development, to changes, and to revision. Therefore, students should treat this, and all comparable studies, as merely a foundation for their investigations on which they may build toward a mature judgment.

If this introduction to the world of international relations stimulates undergraduates and advanced students to delve more deeply into the problems of international politics, the author's aims will have been well served.

MARIO TOSCANO

Rome
May 1, 1965

CONTENTS

CONTENTS

CONTENTS

THE HISTORY OF TREATIES
AND INTERNATIONAL POLITICS

INTRODUCTION

⟲ SUMMARY: 1. The Teaching of the History of Treaties and International Politics in Italy: a. Origins; b. The Theories of Schiattarella, Gemma, Rapisardi-Mirabelli, Bettanini, and Nava. 2. Contemporary Methodological Practices; the Critics of Diplomatic History and a Definition of the Subject's Field of Investigation. 3. Observations on the Historiography of International Relations in Other Countries: a. France; b. Great Britain; c. The United States

1. THE TEACHING OF THE HISTORY OF TREATIES AND INTERNATIONAL POLITICS IN ITALY.

"History of Treaties and International Politics" is the official title of this course as sanctioned by the legislation of 1938 governing the organization of Italian universities.

Such a title reveals an obvious dualism. On the one hand, there is the "History of Treaties," or, more precisely, the history of that part of international law based on treaties. As legal history, its source and primary objective of investigation are treaties, and it should be considered as an auxiliary science of the study of international law. On the other hand, the author of the legislation used the rather unfortunate label of "International Politics" when he meant "Diplomatic History," that is, that area of general history that has as its specific objective the study of relations between nations. This is political history of a type that finds in treaties only one of the sources to be investigated, and, furthermore, it is a history that considers treaties not in their legal sense but rather as historical documents.

History of treaties and diplomatic history are, therefore, two distinct disciplines, even though, for complex reasons, the differences have not always appeared sharp and clear.

First of all, it should be noted in this context that, principally in

1

nineteenth-century France, the history of treaties was considered—in the wake of a tradition that, despite a somewhat different emphasis,[1] dated back to the previous century—as political history and, more exactly, as a study of the causes that led to the negotiation of the various treaties. So construed, *l'histoire des traités* emerged as a segment of the pattern of general history whose field of investigation was akin to that of diplomatic history, despite the fact that the former remained more narrowly restricted because of its close liaison to the treaties.[2] Second, it must be recalled that for years, in Italy, the history of treaties and diplomatic history have been treated, with rare exceptions, as one subject.

a. Origins.

As a course it was first offered at Florence and at Rome. At Florence at the School of Social Science, established in 1875 by the Marquis Cesare Alfieri di Sostegno as "preparation for public office in politics and administration," a chair in "International Law and History of International Relations" was created for the purpose of teaching the combined subjects. In the same year, the course was incorporated into the program of the School of Law in Rome and offered as an elective under the title "Diplomacy and History of Treaties." Similar courses were introduced in succeeding years in many other universities (Genoa, Bologna, Padua, Naples, Parma, Pavia, Sassari, the Catholic University of Milan), in every case in the School of Law or in specialized institutes attached thereto. The organizational structure remained unchanged until 1925 when the schools of political science were established at the various universities. Offered in the newly created schools, the course became a cornerstone of the academic progam; the title often varied but, in the main, consisted of the binomial

---

[1] In this tradition see Rousset, pp. 65–66, and Gabriel Bonnot de Mably, *Le droit public de l'Europe, fondé sur les traités* (troisième edition, revue, corrigée et augmentée [3 vols.; Geneva: Compagnie des Libraires, 1764]).

[2] See particularly Christophe Guillaume de Koch, *Abrégé de l'histoire des traités de paix entre les puissances de l'Europe depuis la paix de Westphalie* (4 vols.; Basel: Decker, 1796–97); F. Schoell, *Histoire abrégé des traités de paix, entre les puissances de l'Europe, depuis la paix de Westphalie par feu M. de Koch; ouvrage entièrement refondu, augmenté et continué jusqu'au Congrès de Vienne et aux traités de Paris de 1815* (15 vols.; Paris: Gide, 1817–18), of which a four-volume edition was published by Meline, Cans and Co., Brussels, 1837–38; Guillaume Laurent de Garden, *Histoire générale des traités de paix et autres transactions principales entre toutes les puissances de l'Europe depuis la paix de Westphalie; ouvrage comprenant les travaux de Koch, Schoell, etc., entièrement refondus et continués jusqu'à ce jour* (15 vols.; Paris: Amyot, 1848–87).

"History of Treaties—Diplomacy." The new regulations governing higher education, introduced by De Vecchi in 1938, reduced the multiple designations of the course to the single "History of Treaties and International Politics."[3]

These precedents have had a marked influence on the direction taken in the teaching of the subject matter in Italy. Born in the schools of law and usually taught by professors of international law, the subject has long retained a predominantly juridical character. Scholars resorted, therefore, to diplomatic history only to the extent that they believed necessary in order to arrive at a more precise evaluation of the significance and of the importance of the various treaties, to examine their origins, and to study the effect—including the political effect—that these have had. But this historical research has been conducted to serve legal ends. In other words, diplomatic history has been regarded as an auxiliary science in the study of the history of treaties and, not infrequently, as merely a facet of it.

This explains why a precise delimitation of the field of investigation of the history of treaties has on occasion been unsuccessful and why Italian scholars have so often been at variance in their conclusions on the problem of the relation of the history of treaties to diplomatic history.

b. The Theories of Schiattarella, Gemma, Rapisardi-Mirabelli, Bettanini, and Nava.

For Schiattarella,[4] the history of treaties is "the exposition of various aspects of the international community or, as referred to by others, the legal and humanitarian organization of the states as they have evolved over the centuries." A precise distinction does not exist between the history of treaties and diplomatic history as he defines it. However, it is evident from his statement, "the science of diplomacy is a facet of international law," that he ascribes a legal character to both subjects.

Schiattarella adds, nevertheless, that both of the "sciences" must enlist the support of history because they "can only be explained within the framework of the historical facts that provide the mortar, the raw material, and the base." In short, Schiattarella, in ignoring "diplomacy" as an historical subject, assigns to general history that auxiliary function in the history of treaties which other writers attribute to diplomatic history.

[3] See Giuseppe Vedovato, "La storia dei trattati nelle Università italiane," in *Rivista di Studi politici internazionali*, XV, 2 (April–June, 1948), pp. 286–90.

[4] R. Schiattarella, *Propedeutica al diritto internazionale. Lezioni sulla storia dei trattati professate nella R. Università di Siena* (Florence: Pellas, 1881).

The view held by Scipione Gemma[5] emerges—in part—as similar to that held by the school of the *histoire des traités*. He defines the history of treaties as that science which has as its objective "to observe treaties in their subsequent development without extracting them from the socio-political milieu that produced them; to find those causes of which they were the necessary effects, and the effects, in turn, causes; to examine the legal nexus that links one to the other; and above all, to attempt to assemble the reasons for their efficacy, their duration, and their dissolution."

However, the objective that Scipione Gemma poses for himself differs from that of the *histoire des traités* as understood, for example, by Schoell.[6] Gemma, of course, is influenced by the positivism that materialized toward the end of the last century as a reaction to romantic historiography, a positivism that sought to make history a science—from several points of view, analogous to the exact sciences—with its mission the discovery of the general laws that govern the dynamics of history. Thus history must be transformed from a "mass of incoherent facts into a living organism where facts find their reason for being." To reach this goal, history can no longer be limited to the study of the "great man in action, in his passions, and in the manifestations of his genius," but must go beyond to examine the environment in which the man functioned; moreover, it must discover the "laws governing the changes and the development of this environment," since "a multitude united into a society forms a new organism with an autonomy and special and diverse characteristics that are alien to the individuals who compose it." For the study of these social phenomena, continues Gemma, the treaty serves as a precious instrument because it represents one of the most important manifestations of the collective life of a society. "If nothing more," he concludes, "a treaty is a statement of the relation of the power of the states that bring it into being. And by power one does not allude simply to material strength but rather to that entire complex of elements—military, financial, economic, and moral—that contribute to the formation of the might of the state and, therefore, to the relative degree of success in conducting its foreign relations or to the position the state has the right to aspire or to achieve in the international community of nations."

In effect, Gemma represents the historicist's viewpoint of that sphere of history concerned with treaties, but he cannot be considered a precursor of

---

[5] *Storia dei trattati nel secolo XIX* (Florence: Barbera, 1895); *Storia dei trattati e degli atti diplomatici europei dal Congresso di Vienna (1815) ai giorni nostri* (Florence: Barbera, 1941), a revised and enlarged edition of the 1895 publication; 3rd ed., 1949.

[6] See Gemma, pp. 1–2 (Florence: Barbera, 1895); and Schoell, Vol. I, pp. 13–14.

the present approach to the study of treaties, which, as we shall see, has enlarged and developed the traditional scope of the study of diplomatic history. He remains essentially a student of the history of treaties, and his work—as he states—is designed to provide a guide toward understanding "how European public law consistently adjusted to the rapid and profound social and political changes of the 19th century."

A solid methodological definition is advanced by Andrea Rapisardi-Mirabelli.[7] The history of treaties, he states, is "a history of a legal nature and interest," which is, therefore, tied to the history of law. Specifically, it is the history of international law and, even more precisely, of that part of international law that is based on treaties. His field of investigation is the study of the origins, growth, and decline of the international legal institutions that have their roots in treaties.

This investigation, continues Rapisardi-Mirabelli, applying a distinction formulated by Leibnitz, may be conducted from two points of departure, the internal and the external. From the internal point of view, the history of treaties examines the treaty "in the light of its legal significance as well as in the light of its origins, its practical application, its precedents and effects, and its vigor or fraility" and is, therefore, one of the components of international law. From the external point of view, the history of treaties investigates "the events leading to and resulting from certain treaties, or the major consequences of these for the history of an era, of a nation, or of a problem, without which it cannot be said that the treaty is understood in its intrinsic and in its implied importance."

Considered from this point of view, the history of treaties "very closely coincides" with that segment of political history referred to as diplomatic history. The author explains that this discipline, whatever we wish to call it (history of foreign policy, international politics, diplomacy, or international relations) has "as its precise and distinct aim the history of relations between nations whose diversity and variability . . . depend on many events that have their explanation in political history, in collections of treaties, in memoirs, and in diplomatic correspondence and related documents."

Yet the history of treaties, according to Rapisardi-Mirabelli, remains an autonomous discipline with respect to diplomatic history. In fact, he adds, for diplomatic history "international treaties are a category of events and documents pertinent to the political developments to which they are connected while, conversely, for the history of treaties these become the primary aim of the investigation and the political events to which their

[7] *Storia dei trattati e delle relazioni internazionali* (Milan: I.S.P.I., 1940); 2d ed., 1945.

internal and external history is linked are of interest only to the extent
that they serve to cast light upon or explain a particular treaty or to the
extent that these can be explained by it."

Once the relations between these two disciplines are so established, it
follows that, for Rapisardi-Mirabelli, diplomatic history as well as general
history are subjects subordinate to the history of treaties, when such a study
is approached from the external point of view. By the same token, his
assertion that the history of treaties is a part of political history must be
understood in the sense that it is an auxiliary discipline of political history,
to which it contributes in the same manner as do the other special histories
while still remaining an autonomous discipline that is essentially juridical
in character and interest.

An analogous conception of the history of treaties is held by Anton Maria
Bettanini.[8] Treaties, he notes, may be considered from two points of view,
the legal and the historical. From the historical viewpoint, the aim of the
investigation is the search for all of those elements pertinent to the creation
of treaties, a search that can assume a double role: "It can be directed
toward an examination of every historical event and particular circumstance, however remote, which had an influence on the relations between
the nations that prompted the negotiation of a treaty. It may be pointed,
instead, toward the study of specific events surrounding the actual treaty
negotiations, from the immediate origins to the conclusion of the pact."
This investigation into the historical nature of the problem, Bettanini
emphasizes, "must not distort the fact that international treaties by their
very legal nature give birth to situations of a legal character and to legal
institutions." Therefore, the history of treaties "must be specifically directed
toward clarifying the legal aspects of the treaties and toward determining
their historical importance"; thus it is "the history of that facet of
international law that is founded on treaties."

Bettanini adds that the history of treaties bears the same relationship to
diplomatic history as species does to genus; it is the same relationship,
Bettanini specifies, that other subdivisions of diplomatic history, such as the
history of foreign policy or the history of international politics, have to the
whole. This dependence derives from the fact that it is diplomatic history
which furnishes to its various branches "the common source to be attained,
that is, the diplomatic documents." For Bettanini, however, the history of
treaties remains an essentially juridical discipline whose rapport with
diplomatic history is limited to the utilization of common sources.

The scientific formulation given to the history of treaties by Rapisardi-

[8] *Introduzione allo studio della storia dei trattati* (Padua: C.E.D.A.M., 1944).

Mirabelli is, in the main, shared also by Santi Nava.[9] The latter recognizes that to define the history of treaties as a history that is of primary interest to the jurists is only a "happy approximation" of its true nature. From this premise he proceeds to identify more precisely the specific field of inquiry from which the subject draws its autonomy.

As he states, the purpose of the history of treaties is to re-create, in its internal development and within the framework of the facts and ideas in which it came into being, that segment of human activity which regulates the controversies arising between sovereign political collectivities and prescribes the norms of reciprocal conduct—a function that, after all, responds to the "intrinsic needs of those societies for coordinated development" and is "an expression of their vitality and vigor." This discipline, therefore, "scrutinizes the treaties for the purpose of understanding them genetically," at the same time noting the events related to them. Substantially, the discipline examines "the internal development of the treaties as they bind themselves one to the other in space and in time, visualizing them as an organic whole" that reveals "their developed and arrested, derivative and transformative connections, and in seeing them in the succeeding real situations in which they are produced."

2. CONTEMPORARY METHODOLOGICAL PRACTICES; THE CRITICS OF DIPLOMATIC HISTORY AND A DEFINITION OF THE SUBJECT'S FIELD OF INVESTIGATION.

At any rate, in Italy the difficulties raised in determining the kinship between the history of treaties and diplomatic history have lost their significance because of the direction taken by the teaching of the subject matter and by the scientific character of the research in this field of history. Diplomatic history has broken free of the restrictions that once limited it to an auxiliary role in the history of treaties and in the historico-juridical investigations in general.

Today there may be questions concerning the nature of diplomatic history, the definition of its field of inquiry, and the sources upon which it depends—questions, therefore, not only of delimitation but of formulation and of objectives, which raise indirectly the issue of the autonomy of this discipline with respect to history in general.

In reference to these questions, it has been noted by the critics of diplomatic history that a study of relations between nations conducted by

[9] "Note e discussioni sulla specificità della storia dei trattati," in *Studi Senesi*, 1941, fasc. 4–5.

inquiries into governmental actions and diplomatic exchanges cannot produce acceptable results because it ignores vital facets of international politics, that is, economic, social, demographic, geographic, and ideological criteria, etc. Instead, it would be precisely these factors—putting aside an exclusively political approach, insufficient in itself—which would permit an adequate evaluation of events, an understanding of the causes, and a comprehension of the developmental process. Diplomatic history, therefore, should enlarge its scope of inquiry and emerge as a history of international relations so inspired by its wider perspective that it would assume as its basic purpose the identification of those complex forces which are the real actors on the stage of history.

Apart from the relative value that it seems reasonable to assign to the various titles for the subject,[10] that of "history of international relations" appears to be a happy choice. It is especially so when one wishes to call attention to the many factors that affect the relations between states. Still, some clarification appears to be necessary in view of the criticism of diplomatic history as such and, moreover, the direction that some would like to give to the discipline.

First of all, apparently it is possible, especially in recent years, to reject the idea that an interpretation of diplomatic history was ever conceived or effected so narrow as to deny the relevance of the elements of public opinion, economic forces, geographic factors, etc. Fundamentally, of course, diplomatic history is understood to be the history of the relations between nations at the governmental level. But this does not mean that it ignores those factors that directly influence the conduct of foreign policy and, indirectly, the nature of international relations in general. The distinction lies in the fact that diplomatic history, having once identified the elements involved, moves on to scrutinize them as they assume a more "refined" form when acted upon by the governments concerned and by their diplomatic representatives. In defining the field of study, such a formulation appears to

---

[10] In addition to "diplomatic history" and "history of international relations" as denominations, we frequently find "history of international politics" and "history of foreign policy." Only the latter indicates a specific kind of research in the internal affairs of a state to determine the action taken by the state in international affairs, for example, an investigation of the multiple forces at work within a state that contribute to the formulation of a foreign policy and influence its execution. Even in this case, however, we can speak neither of an autonomous discipline nor of a particular direction of study. At best, it is a facet of a wider inquiry leading into the history of international relations. The history of international politics, which, according to Bettanini, would have as its objective "the study of the activities of the individual states in foreign affairs, no longer considered as individual actions but, instead, in the total effect produced by their interaction within specified limits of space and time," suggests a synonym for the history of international relations, but one that is less precise in defining its objective.

adhere more closely to reality and to scientific exactness. For the student of diplomatic history or, if one prefers, of international relations, an examination of these elements cannot in truth be an end in itself but must lead to the disclosure of how and to what extent these factors influence the creation and the realization of a foreign policy.

Second, in assigning a pre-eminent, if not an exclusive role to the so-called complex forces, there is always the risk of ignoring one of the essential elements of a nation's foreign policy, that is, an understanding of the international framework within which foreign policy functions. Without such an understanding, a clear conception of foreign policy is impossible, and the investigation would of necessity deal only in abstractions, which are completely detached from those daily actions and reactions that produce the tangible elements in relations between states.

Finally, and perhaps most significantly, in focusing attention on these complex forces the tendency is to ignore, or at least to underestimate, the role of the individual. Unquestionably, these forces serve as stimuli to, and simultaneously establish the limits of activity for, a government's representatives and their collaborators; they respond to pressures and must adapt their actions to the means available to them. Yet the human element remains of critical importance. Governmental representatives may provide a subjective interpretation of the complex forces at work which in time may prove to be erroneous, but the fact remains that it is precisely this interpretation which has a direct influence on foreign policy. Moreover, it is clear that man does not act solely on the basis of idealistic impulses and within the framework of a vast organic design but very often acts on the basis of immediate needs, convenience, error, and always in response to the pressures of his own personality. These human factors must be kept in mind if the study of international relations is not to be limited to an abstract exercise, detached from reality and implemented by purely imaginary personalities.

Critics of diplomatic history are unanimous in pointing to its inadequacies, but there is no such agreement when they are asked to indicate a more satisfactory approach to the study. In the main, two critical tendencies can be discerned: the one believing the socioeconomic factor to be paramount in importance, accenting material factors such as commercial interests, social organization, population pressures, and economic needs; the other seeking a spiritual explanation for historical events, concentrating its attention on the movement of ideas, sentimental notions, and on the psychology of nations. Of course, both of these schools recognize the validity of the results attained through other approaches to the problems, but usually this is simply a formal concession, granted in passing, after which both return to considering truth exclusively, or almost exclusively, from their respective vantage points. Once they have indicted diplomatic history for providing only an incomplete view of the events, its critics then arrive at even more restricted interpretations of their own, and it is not very difficult to detect in each of these trends an ideological preoccupation which preconditions the outcome of their inquiries and tends to force reality into preconceived patterns.

The limitations inherent in such formulations have been criticized also by Pierre Renouvin, dean of the French school. He emphasizes the importance of structuring the problem as comprehensively as possible without imposing restrictive formats beforehand which are not amenable to variables of time and condition. However, Renouvin, too, assigns diplomatic history a secondary role, a role that does not coincide with its real importance and results in a perversion of the nature of the discipline.

In substance, it does not appear to be possible to accept the idea of international relations as the history of relations between peoples rather than as the history of relations between states. In so doing, the essential realities, which are the actions of governments and their representatives, would be lost. And if it is impossible to ignore the relations between governments without distorting the realities of international relations, it remains a fact that the importance of the so-called diplomatic aspect is unaltered. Furthermore, it becomes the pre-eminent factor because it provides a political analysis of the events, which in itself is an interpretative synthesis.

Insofar as sources are concerned, it is obvious that diplomatic documents, together with memoirs, remain the principal sources upon which our research must be based; this assumption, in turn, contributes to a more exact definition of the subject and ensures its autonomy. This material—as has been noted by Albert Sorel—has certain peculiar characteristics which require the investigator to possess certain talents not usually necessary for the interpretation of an historical document of a different kind. A report, a letter, or the memoirs of a diplomat do not reveal their true significance unless the investigator has a thorough knowledge of the language peculiar to diplomacy, a knowledge of the nature of the environment from which such a document emanates, and a clear understanding of the professional mentality of the writer, etc.

This material, too, has its limitations in the sense that, despite every professional interpretative technique available, the document alone does not reveal the total picture. Thus there is a need to press the investigation beyond the limits of the purely diplomatic sources, yet to be ever aware of the fact that diplomatic history is but a branch of general history, and therefore, like all other specialized histories, it tends to focus on a specific segment of historical reality. From this point of view, it is impossible for diplomatic history to produce anything other than a part of the story; specialized histories—which have their origins in the inability of man to pursue an investigation based on direct experience with every phase of history—presuppose that it is possible to isolate a part of the total reality, despite the obvious fact that all of the aspects of history are so intimately linked that one conditions all of the others and is, in turn, conditioned by them.

In conclusion, the tendency of our discipline to enlarge its field of study in order to put into proper perspective those material and spiritual factors that influence the formulation of a foreign policy and the relations between states is one that can be readily understood. However, this tendency should be kept in check in order to avoid losing sight of the primary objective, i.e., the relations between the states, and therefore those influencing elements should serve only to clarify decisions affecting international relations. Otherwise, the attempt to have our research satisfy every need imaginable may result in our subject's losing the very characteristics that provide the basis for its autonomy and its status as history of a particular kind. Even worse, the result may be its replacement by one or another of the specialized disciplines which, alone, most assuredly can neither explain the complexities of international relations nor achieve the stated objective of writing "history without adjectives."

3. OBSERVATIONS ON THE HISTORIOGRAPHY OF INTERNATIONAL RELATIONS IN OTHER COUNTRIES.

The origins of the various trends in our field of study become clear when the historiography of international relations is examined in the light of its development in several states.

a. France.

In French historiography, international relations initially assumed the character of the *histoire des traités,* that is, the history of relations between states considered on the basis of the treaties, of the negotiations that preceded their consummation, and on the consequences of these accords. So defined, the research objective was more narrowly restricted than that of diplomatic history. Moreover, it was made clear that such historical research was not an end in itself but, rather, sought to reconstruct the origins of a given international situation and to define the rights and obligations of the powers in these particular circumstances. Thus the *histoire des traités* sought practical applications for those actively concerned with politics, government officials, and diplomats; it attempted to assist them either by examining the antecedents of the problems or—according to some authors —by identifying the unchanging elements in the policies of the various powers, or, finally, by ascertaining the historical basis of the existing legal position of the states in the international community.

It is during the nineteenth century in France that the *histoire des traités* is definitely replaced by diplomatic history. The latter, according to Sorel,[11] is a branch of general history and as such loses its meaning and importance if detached from it. But if an adequate grasp of the whole is prerequisite to an understanding of diplomatic history, the study of the latter requires a specific kind of research that has its own peculiar problems of source interpretation. Sources for the study of diplomatic history are divided into two categories: in the first are diplomatic documents as such—treaties, protocols, notes, instructions, dispatches, and reports; in the second are personal documents, private correspondence, and the memoirs of participants and eyewitnesses. Each of the two categories makes a specific contribution to the study. "In the first," Sorel observes, "we find the documents involving the negotiations *per se,* in the second those involving the negotiators . . . in the former we find the affairs of state and in the latter the statesmen. Negotiations, considered apart from the participants, are sterile and incomprehensible. Therefore, our objective is precisely that of providing an understanding of the problem through a reconstruction of the roles of the individuals involved." The objective of "giving meaning to the texts" is reached only through a careful evaluation and integration of the two sources. Of course these criteria are applicable to all historical research, but, Sorel added, in this case they assume particular significance. In fact, it is impossible to interpret this evidence correctly without knowing how it came into being:

> and by this I do not mean simply where, by whom, when, and in what circumstances: these factors are obviously indispensable but they are insufficient. What must be known, through having seen, heard, or lived the experience so that the documents can reveal their true meaning and the testimony assume its proper perspective, is the machinery of diplomacy in action, the way of life of the diplomats, the organization of the

[11] The citations that follow are taken from Albert Sorel, "L'enseignement de l'histoire diplomatique," in *Nouveaux Essais d'histoire et de critique* (Paris: Plon, 1898), pp. 75–84.

chancelleries and embassies, the way in which information is gathered, the preparation of diplomatic correspondence, the techniques employed in diplomatic conversations; in brief, the reasons for and the precise nature of every diplomatic act that we discover formulated and translated in the document itself. It is necessary to have followed diplomatic negotiations step by step as they evolved; to have intimate contacts with embassies and cabinets; to have traveled abroad; to have cultivated foreigners; to have had close contacts with diplomats and at least to have visited this little world apart which is the same in every capital of Europe and nowhere resembles anything else, in order to be equipped with a sense of criticism that penetrates beneath the murky surface of diplomatic waters. It is indispensable to know what transformations take place in the thinking of a statesman before we encounter it at the termination of the process. We must be able to identify the basic desires behind the many nuances of style in the instructions and dispatches. We must be able to recognize the habitual allusions of the writer; we must be aware of the various categories of events reflected in the documentary classifications. It is necessary to understand how a protocol summarizes the work of a conference, especially what is included and what is omitted. These are the only means by which we can reconstruct the event from the document, from the translation to the original text, from the letter to the spirit of the document and, from appearance to reality.

In addition to the subject of the inquiry, it is this dual nature of diplomatic history—the sources and the techniques for their interpretation—that, according to Sorel, gives the discipline its character of a technical investigation, gives it its autonomy, and allows it to make a specific and original contribution to general history.

Critics of diplomatic history accuse it of regarding events exclusively from a political point of view and, therefore, of providing only a partial and incomplete explanation. Criticism of diplomatic history as a subject has been particularly acute in France, where not a few scholars have taken an extreme position vis-à-vis the study, accusing it of considering events exclusively for their political impact and thereby providing only a partial and incomplete analysis. In the first place they reject, or very nearly do, the validity of diplomatic history as a distinct discipline. Second, in insisting on and assigning a pre-eminent role, if not an exclusive one, to other factors such as economics, geography, demography, and social and psychological forces, they seek to restrict validity to one or more of these points of departure. The inevitable result is that they treat the history of international relations from an even more restricted point of view.

This regressive approach has been championed by Pierre Renouvin [12] and by his school, which today must be considered the most representative and scholarly in France. Renouvin himself maintains a critical attitude toward diplomatic history, but, in contrast to other contemporary historians, he does not deny its importance. The diplomatic aspect, he observes, has its own special validity because, better than any other, it opens the way to an evaluation of the role played by statesmen who have guided or who are seeking to guide the political activities of the states. A stateman's political actions

> remain contained within the limits set by economic, financial, and demographic forces and by the moral force of the nation but in certain cases he can modify these forces. Even when his power and authority is circumscribed by the existence of a parliamentary regime, he can, with patient effort and the application of his talents as a political economist, improve the nation's exploitation of its natural resources and increase its war potential; he can impose legislative measures that aid or obstruct migratory movement or encourage an increase in the birthrate; he can convince the citizenry, thanks to the press and the schools, that they should bear the sacrifices demanded by the state; he can seek to maintain the cohesion of the state; he can succumb to the temptation to take advantage of a superiority of armaments which he knows to be momentary; he can be unwise in choosing the diplomatic means and, knowingly or not, provoke, during the course of difficult negotiations, the incident that will arouse passions. How can the influence on the origins of the great wars of modern times be denied of such elements as the concept of national interests, the desire for personal grandeur, or even the temperament of a statesman, from Louis XIV or from Frederick II to Napoleon I, from Napoleon III and Bismarck to Hitler?

Thus, the role of individual initiative, that of the statesman and of his collaborators, remains one of the essential elements to be considered, but of course it does not exhaust the field that the historian should investigate. "First of all," Renouvin emphasizes, "the history of international relations should concern itself with the gradual evolution of the human societies, that is to say, the demographic conditions, the economic conditions and, of course, the psychology of the community," and along with these, "the influence of the great wars that violently accelerated the tempo of evolution

[12] For Renouvin's view see Pierre Renouvin, "L'orientation actuelle des travaux d'histoire contemporaine," in *Atti del X congresso di Scienze Storiche, Rome, September 4–11, 1955, Vol. IV: Relazioni*, pp. 330–88; Pierre Renouvin (ed.), *Histoire des relations internationales* (8 vols.; Paris: Hachette, 1952–58). See also the Italian translation, *Storia della politica mondiale* (8 vols.; Florence: Vallecchi, 1961). Note especially the introduction at the beginning of Vol. I, pp. 1–11, and the conclusion at the close of Vol. VIII, pp. 463–74.

of human societies or of the various civilizations." It is precisely the study of these fundamental forces and of the influence that these have exerted from time to time which, according to Renouvin's conception, constitutes the primary objective of the historian's inquiry in the field of international relations. But Renouvin also warns that such an investigation cannot ignore the decisive role of the state which "stamps its imprint on the basic forces at its command and utilizes them to enhance its own power." This role, he emphasizes, appears most clearly in the origins of international conflicts, in armament policies, in interlocking alliance systems, in the economic pressure applied to other states, and in the appeal to popular passions that often puts other forces in motion which later will be difficult to control.

In this manner, Renouvin places himself in a position which resolves and synthesizes the conflicting points of view. "Foreign policy," he concludes,

in addition to being tied to the personal roles played by the statesmen, is also bound to the entire gamut of activity of human societies and to all of the material and spiritual forces of life. In the search for explanations, which remains the basic purpose of historical inquiry, the major danger lies in isolating one of these factors, assigning to it an exclusive role, or establishing a preconceived scale of values. Economic and demographic forces, the trends in mass psychology and in national spirit, and the activities of governments complete and merge one into the other; the degree of influence varies according to historical periods and from state to state. Historical research must seek to determine the relative importance of each of these. In this way such investigation offers the possibility of reaching the necessary conclusions, but it does not pretend to suggest remedies or, even less, to provide lessons for the future.

b. Great Britain.

The study of international relations in Great Britain is marked by notably different characteristics.[13] First of all, its origins are rather recent. As a subject for scientific investigation or as an academic course (the first chair in international history was established only in 1925), it found acceptance only in the post-World War I era. Various factors contributed to drawing the attention of British scholars to the field: the realization that international events were playing an increasingly important role in the lives of all peoples; the accenting of the tendency toward international co-operation that found concrete expression in the League of Nations; and, finally, the publication of the enormous mass of official documents, which

[13] On this question, see Enrico Serra, "Gli studi di International History," in *Gran Bretagna* (Milan: Giuffrè, 1961).

offered the historian, because of its dimensions, a new tool with which to work.

These beginnings explain how the teaching and study of the history of international relations in Great Britain were, from the start, oriented toward the recent period, despite the fact that some historians such as Namier or Toynbee displayed a tendency to expand their researches chronologically, although for basically different reasons. In reality, British scholars are not particularly preoccupied either by the lack of an historical perspective that is wide enough to view events or derive provisional conclusions (which must be only provisional because objective data are not available), or by the lack of a subjective capacity to consider the recent past from an historical point of view. "To be an historian," affirms Webster, taking the point of view of Croce's historicism, "signifies being an essential part of contemporary life," and, in fact, British historians are agreed in opposing any detachment of international history from the contemporary scene and in considering it to be no more than a living study in constant rapport with contemporary experience. For this reason, above all, international history or diplomatic history or international relations—in Great Britain the different titles have contingent origins and do not indicate differences in methods or structure—differ in character with respect to direction and trend from the course these studies take on the Continent.

Even in the selection of sources, British historiography reveals its individuality. Of course, the diplomatic documents remain basic to every investigation, but memoirs (which in Great Britain are frequently based on vast documentary sources) and authorized biographies drawing from private archives assume a special prominence, along with other sources: the parliamentary papers and newspaper archives, despite the fact they are not peculiar to British political life, are of greater importance in that country than elsewhere.

On the other hand, the tendency to widen the field of research beyond the strictly diplomatic aspect has manifested itself in that country outside of any doctrinal outline and with typical British empiricism. In the main, the research has been concerned with official documents in archives other than those of the Foreign Office, such as the Admiralty: other examples would be the General Staff of the Ministry for the Colonies and the archives for economic affairs. The difficulties in utilizing these sources, which, aside from the quantity involved, are inaccessible for political and security reasons, have been partially overcome by the Official History. The Official History came into existence when the Historical Section of the Committee of the Imperial General Staff entrusted qualified scholars with the task of writing the history of the various campaigns, allowing them, in the process, to see at least a part of the restricted materials. When other ministries took similar steps, the total production was remarkably extensive. If this production can be criticized, from a specific point of view, for the limitations imposed on it by its official character, for the extremely selective criteria established for the use of the material, and for the problems chosen, it has, on the other hand, allowed examination of at least a part of that vast quantity of documentary sources which otherwise would have remained unknown for a long time to come.

c. The United States.

Turning briefly to the characteristics of the historiography of international relations in the United States, we can easily see that it presents certain peculiarities that derive from the need of American historians to keep clearly in mind some of the typical elements of American policy. In this case, too, the attention of scholars has been directed, in general, toward the most recent period, but for reasons that are, by and large, different from those that motivated the British scholars toward the same period. In the first place, there is the fact that the United States has assumed a position of primary importance in world politics only since the turn of the century; second, the study of particular problems having a certain contemporary importance has been prompted by political debate. And even when the research was conducted with scientific objectivity, it was encouraged by a general curiosity concerning the events. It was precisely these debates—for example, the debate on the functioning of the Roosevelt administration—that led to the publication of a wealth of material not only from the archives of the State Department but also from the files of the armed services, which normally maintain an even greater secrecy. Most assuredly, this situation has had its effect on American historians' orientation and selection of problems to be studied. In general, however, it can be said that American historiography of international relations follows, by and large, the traditional lines of diplomatic history, at least in the sense that it assigns a pre-eminent role to the diplomatic phase and, not infrequently, to the exchanges between governments. Nevertheless, American historiography often deviates from traditional outlines in three important respects.

First, influenced by the political reality existing in their country and by the publications noted above, American scholars have been led to base their investigations not only on the archives of the State Department but also on the official files of other departments, in particular those of the military, whose influence on the conduct of foreign policy is probably greater than in other countries. Thus, there emerges something analogous to what occurred in Great Britain with the Official History, the difference being that in the American case the documentation is made available to the scholar directly, rather than indirectly, through the elaboration of an official historical literature.

Second, American historiography has paid a great deal of attention to the influence of public opinion and of "pressure groups" on the conduct of foreign policy. However, this approach is viewed as a device to provide a more exact understanding of the motives that have prompted government decisions and not, as is frequently seen in some European historiographic approaches, as the principal object of a separate and unrelated inquiry.

Finally, the recognition of the importance of the human element in the conduct of international relations has often induced American historians to place special emphasis on this aspect through a detailed examination of the roles played by the statesmen and their immediate collaborators.

In the interest of clarity, it is necessary to note that in the United States courses bearing the title "International Relations" usually have a sociological character,[14] an approach that is so totally foreign to the norms ascribed to the history of international relations with regard to subject, method of inquiry, and objectives that it remains outside of the scope of our study.

[14] For a general introduction to the field of study, see Stanley H. Hoffman (ed.), *Contemporary Theory in International Relations* (Englewood Cliffs, N.J.: Prentice-Hall, 1960).

PART I

THE SOURCES

Chapter I

THE DOCUMENTARY SOURCES

SUMMARY: 1. The Diplomatic Document: a. Definition; b. The Various Types of Diplomatic Documents and Their Interpretation.   2. The Archive: a. The Elements of an Archive; b. Public and Private Archives

1. THE DIPLOMATIC DOCUMENT.

a. Definition.

The field of history investigated by the subject of international relations has, by the very nature of its objectives, a particular species of document as its principal source, that in which the evidence of actions and facts prompting the research is found in largest measure. Any written testimony of an event falls within the scope of the definition of a diplomatic document, whether it be an account of an action completed by an individual, or the simple expression of his thoughts concerning a given problem, or testimony coming from agencies (and often from individuals) who function, either directly or indirectly, in the area of international relations.

Moving from this broad concept to a consideration of the specific methods by which international relations develop, it is imperative that we make a technical distinction between two types of documents: the formal or official document and the informal or "internal" document. In the first category belong those acts which authorized organs of the respective states exchange with each other in their reciprocal contacts in the name of, and on behalf of, the states as members of the international community (for example, the *nota verbale*).[1] The second category includes the entire series of acts that provides the means by which the internal process arrives at the

---

[1] Detailed information on the various kinds of diplomatic documents and on the techniques employed in their preparation, which vary according to period and country, may be found in Sir Ernest Satow, *A Guide to Diplomatic Practice* (4th ed.; London: Longmans, 1958); Anton Maria Bettanini, *Lo stile diplomatico* (Milan, 1933); Adolfo Maresca, *La missione diplomatica* (2d ed.; Milan: Giuffre, 1964).

will of the state, to be reflected ultimately in formal acts (for example, the *report,* the *note*). It should be pointed out that the agencies making these contributions are not exclusively diplomatic ones or ministries of foreign affairs, but also include, depending on the nature of the decision to be made, all bureaus that have a competence in the pertinent area and that can contribute to the formation of the will of the state.

Each of the two categories mentioned above consists of various types of

b. The Various Types of Diplomatic Documents and Their Interpretation.

diplomatic documents. Those of primary importance, along with their particular characteristics according to most recent Italian practice, are noted below.

1. The *treaty,* considered as a diplomatic document, is a formal document testifying to the agreement reached between two or more elements of the international community on one or more problems. In exceptional cases, it is signed by the heads of state or of governments. Usually, however, it is signed in the accepted manner by those representatives or plenipotentiaries authorized to do so.

2. The *exchange of notes.* Generally, this is an exchange of notes, identical in content and written and signed in the traditional form and manner, between a Minister of Foreign Affairs and the head of a mission accredited to that state: such an exchange attests to the will of the two parties and gives substance to a legal agreement in a somewhat less formal and solemn way than by treaty. It must be pointed out that the expression "exchange of notes" when used in this way is a legal one and should not be confused with the same expression as commonly used to indicate simply that one government has dispatched a note (usually a *nota verbale*) to another government and that the latter has replied with a similar document.

3. The *nota verbale* constitutes the most common means of communication between the Ministry of Foreign Affairs and the foreign diplomatic missions, and vice versa. In effect, it is a document which is drawn up according to a precise opening and closing formula and which carries no signature. On the occasion of a meeting, the party that is delivering an official communication of his government submits the document to his interlocutor in order that a written outline of the oral communication may remain as a record of exactly what the former said, or should have said. Thus its content may vary widely. For example, it is also employed in the rapport between the Ministry of Foreign Affairs and the heads of foreign missions.

4. The *memorandum* (*promemoria*) is the document which, in communications between states, is normally used to outline the principal elements of a question; it summarizes the essential points of a government's point of view on the issue. In addition to the more precise nature of its contents, the *promemoria* differs from minutes in that in its preparation it is not subject to a particular form or style.

5. The *memorandum* is also a document used in communicating between states. In general, it is used to explain the position taken by a government on a given issue through a detailed exposition of the precedents and of the historic and legal bases that support and justify such a position. It is comparable to the *promemoria* in that no precise formula need be observed in its preparation. However, while the contents may be similar, the memorandum is usually much more detailed and binding. For this reason, in recent times it has been used also as a document attesting to a provisional agreement between two states. For example, the Italo-Yugoslav accord of 1954 on Trieste was called a *memorandum of understanding* in order to underline its provisional nature, as well as to avoid the necessity for submitting it to the customary procedure (parliamentary ratification) required for a formal accord.

6. The *statement* (*verbale*) is the document that reproduces a conversation in summary form. Once it was customary to edit the summary that each party made of the conversation by the simple expedient of having each party submit its summary to the other for approval and then having the two documents exchanged; or, on the basis of a stenographic record of the colloquy, a single version would be agreed upon and a copy given to each faction. In these cases, the statement assumed the character of a formal document that recorded the official exposition of the respective points of view, and thereby fell into the category of diplomatic documents, which is reserved, in a technical sense, for communications on matters subject to international law.

Today, only on rare occasions are statements submitted to the other party for approval, or otherwise concorded. This is true for two reasons: first, there is a tendency to evade a complete clarification of the respective points of view, and therefore it is important to avoid further discussions on the contents of the statements; second, the increased frequency of meetings in modern times has directly affected the practice. However, it still occurs, despite the fact that today in international meetings and conferences tape recordings are often made of the conversations. However, the exact transcript of the individual statements so recorded is rarely utilized for drawing up a single set of statements; at best, a summary of the remarks of each speaker is submitted, and then only for the approval of the speaker himself, after which the tape, which could constitute an inconvenient proof of what actually was said, is erased.

Generally speaking, statements at present continue to serve as evidences of the position taken by government representatives on a specific situation. Yet to avoid disputes, no party wishes to provide the other with a communication that might be construed as being official and binding. The result is, therefore, that statements are marginal elements to be placed between the category of formal documents and that of informal or "internal" ones, as having the precise characteristics of neither one nor the other.[2]

7. The *memorandum* is also the document employed in written communication within the ministry and is usually addressed by a subordinate to his superior according to the norms of hierarchy. It may or may not be signed, but, in effect, the head of the division from which it originates is responsible for it. Documents of this type form the basis for the decisions reached within a ministry. In practice, there is no restriction as to content: it ranges from an opinion requested and transmitted by an office to the upper administrative and political echelons of the ministry, to the simple transmission of news and information; or it may be the summary of an informal conversation between official or unofficial representatives of two states (agencies or individuals) which is confidential or of an exploratory nature and which is registered in order that a record of the discussion may be preserved.

Finally, it should be noted that this memorandum is, or should be, employed to record the content of a communication transmitted to the ministry via telephone by its representatives abroad, or to record instructions imparted similarly by the ministry or other authority to the former.

8. The *report* is the classic and, historically, the oldest type of document employed by a representative abroad to maintain contact with his ministry in order to discharge his duties properly. It is used: (a) to "refer" to his government any and all news and information of interest and to give the results of contacts with agencies and individuals of the country to which he is accredited, (b) to formulate an opinion and to offer suggestions on the handling of current problems, and (c) to provide objective evaluations of the political climate of the country to which he is accredited. The report which the representative abroad sends to the ministry differs in form and content from all other communications sent by him. Insofar as the report is

---

[2] However, there are exceptions to this practice such as, for example, the official minutes compiled by the offices of international organizations (i.e., the United Nations) or the minutes of official conferences, which, once approved by the parties concerned, become official.

concerned, it is always addressed to the minister personally and is closed with a conventional formula. The content is as detailed and complete as possible; in modern times, frequent reference to the matter has already been made by more rapid means and in summary form (telegraph, teletype, etc.). Until very recently, other representatives abroad— if interested in the same specific issue—were cognizant of the report only if and when it was officially or unofficially disseminated. Today, it is frequently the practice of some of the more important embassies, for well-defined reasons, to transmit copies of the report directly to other interested embassies when it is filed with the ministry.

It should be noted that the report—and this rule applies to every type of document transmitted by a diplomat to his ministry—must be limited to one subject only. Thus a conversation in which several issues are treated should result in a separate report for each topic discussed. Only when this rule is scrupulously observed is it possible to disseminate communications without delay to the appropriate offices of the ministry.[3]

9. The *letter*. In order to meet his obligation to report his personal evaluation of a given situation to the minister, a diplomat may also write a letter. This is not the usual method of communication between an ambassador and the ministry, but it is frequently employed by heads of missions because a personal letter addressed to the minister or another official permits the writer greater freedom of expression in his attempt to convey his thought (which may not yet be completely crystallized) on a given problem, since, theoretically, the letter should not be recorded formally as an official communication. The addition of a letter to the file on a problem under consideration (unless such inclusion is specifically requested) is left up to the discretion of the recipient. Frequently, however, the letter is sent precisely because the writer may subsequently make use of it to support a position, even if the communication is not of an official nature.

10. The *teletype* is another type of document used by representatives abroad. It is addressed impersonally to the ministry, and the text is in the form of a synthesis and is less formal than that of a report. The teletype is also used for dissemination of documents, answering of questions, and transaction of normal business between the ministry and its offices abroad.

[3] Particular importance is attached to the "Final Report" compiled by the ambassador at the termination of a given mission. A number of these final reports, written immediately by ambassadors upon their return home after the declaration of war, have become famous through their inclusion in the colored books. Typical examples are the reports prepared by the British Ambassador to Berlin, Sir Nevile Henderson, which became the British White Book of October 17, 1939, and the highly dramatic report of the Polish Ambassador to Moscow, Brybowski, included in the Polish White Book of 1940.

It is a widely used instrument for these purposes but is employed only rarely for correspondence of a political nature emanating from the embassies.

11. The *urgent teletype* is the means of communication intermediate between the analytical exposition of the report and the conciseness of the commonly used telegram. It consists of a summary exposition written in the style of a telegram; it is employed when the writer chooses not to use or cannot use the telegraph, yet must send an urgent communication to the ministry. In fact, the urgent teletype is sent via air courier and goes directly to the minister's desk. Because six copies arrive at the ministry, it can be distributed promptly to the several offices concerned.

12. The communication referred to as *courier cable* is used when the secret nature of the communication requires that it be consigned in code to the courier. The courier cable is also employed by the ministry for the dissemination in code of secret communications received from a legation abroad, unless urgency, as well as secrecy, demands retransmission by coded telegram.

The urgent teletype and the courier cable are frequently the customary replacements for the outmoded dispatch-in-the-clear and the coded dispatch, from which they stem and whose characteristics, apart from the name, they retain.

13. The *telegram* is the rapid method of communication employed by the diplomatic agent to report important news or the essence of a conversation and by the minister or his office to send instructions to the representative. There are two kinds of telegrams: those *in-the-clear* and those *in code*. Insofar as those in-the-clear are concerned, it is sufficient to say that they serve to transmit information that is nonsecret in character, while a description of the nature of the coded telegram touches on one of the most delicate aspects of diplomatic activity.

The need to guarantee the privacy of communications between a government and its representatives abroad was evident from the moment that nations began to exchange permanent embassies. Despite the fact that the right of a diplomat to correspond freely with his government was universally recognized, diplomatic couriers to whom dispatches were entrusted were often captured: for this reason, diplomats masked the dispatch by changing words to numbers or letters, according to time-tested practices.

Today, if respect for the inviolability of the courier and his "diplomatic pouch" is nearly universal,[4] the need to protect the privacy of communica-

---

[4] This is particularly true for couriers as such, but some problems have arisen and still arise in the matter of the so-called "air pouches" entrusted to aircraft commanders. Given the number of diplomatic legations abroad, it is necessary to entrust aircraft

tions has increased many-fold with the introduction of the telegraph because the dispatch usually must be entrusted to the post and telegraph services of the country to which the diplomat is accredited, and because it is reasonably easy to intercept communications sent by wire or radio. Therefore, the old and relatively simple coding systems gave way to more complicated coding practices such as "double coding," i.e., the employment by the sender of two or more codes keyed to the original. Notwithstanding these protective devices, telegrams continued to be deciphered; not only were code books stolen, but also extremely able cryptographers were capable of discovering the key to a code with the aid of little more than keen intuition and a great deal of experience.

On the eve of World War II, the armed forces—especially the navy—for obvious reasons were particularly concerned with the problem of secrecy and speed of communication. They introduced a new coding device, the so-called "coding machines," which look very much like an ordinary typewriter but which will automatically code a dispatch. This system, in use today, offers three great advantages: it eliminates the time formerly required to code and decode a message; it permits compounding of the code an almost infinite number of times; and it allows frequent key changes, a procedure which formerly was possible only by dispatching a new code book to the sender or receiver of the correspondence. The risk of having a message deciphered would be infinitesimal if the development of electronic devices capable of testing millions of combinations in a few minutes had not materially neutralized the effectiveness of the code machines—at least for the richer and more technically advanced states. Therefore, dispatches continue to be deciphered to the same degree that they were in the past.

The secrecy of the code is also maintained within the ministry, and for this reason the code room, after deciphering the message, substitutes phrases and shifts words about to produce a paraphrase of the original. Normally, it is only this paraphrased text that is disseminated to the various offices.

The number of copies that the code room distributes and the limits imposed on their circulation are usually determined by the recipient, although the sender, on occasion, may indicate precisely those to whom the message should be given. In this context, telegrams arriving in code are divided into four categories: single-copy telegrams, telegrams labeled "secret—no dissemination," telegrams labeled "secret," and ordinary tele-

---

commanders with packets addressed to and from the ministry. However, these normally contain communications of an ordinary nature and are not especially secret. In cases where recourse must be made to foreign airlines, tampering with the pouches or their loss are risks which must still be faced.

grams. Label notwithstanding, two copies of the single-copy telegrams exist, except in rare cases (in addition to the copy for the minister, the code room has one on file), but their circulation is very severely restricted, so much so that as a rule they are not seen outside of the ministry, not even by the personal staff of the head of state or that of the Prime Minister, but the content is usually made known to them by the Foreign Minister personally or by his delegate. Those dispatches labeled "secret—no dissemination" also have an extremely limited circulation, but the minister's most intimate collaborators are usually informed of their content. Logically, those marked simply "secret" have a less restricted circulation; and, finally, the dissemination of ordinary telegrams to the offices concerned is handled by the code room under a directive from the Secretary-General of the Foreign Office.

Telegrams of a highly secret nature leaving the ministry are labeled "personal to the Ambassador—to be decoded only by him." Before the introduction of coding machines, the same tag was applied by the code room to arriving telegrams when the message was in a code known only to the minister.

With the exception of this instance, seen only rarely today, the transaction of Foreign Ministry business is done almost exclusively by paraphrased message, which may be more or less accurately prepared. In general, the historian too has at his disposal in the collections of diplomatic documents only the paraphrased texts; this places him in the same situation as the person who made decisions on the basis of these texts, but it is obvious that the original dispatch would often be not without interest.

Yet if on some occasions it is possible for the researcher who is not content with the published collections to see the original texts by consulting the embassy files preserved in the archives, by an international practice that has allowed very few exceptions, he is deprived of seeing the material that various governments have had at their disposal through deciphering and intercepting foreign communications. The existence of this documentation, which cannot be consulted and yet cannot be ignored because it has often had a significant effect on the decisions made by governments, poses a delicate problem for the historian because he can hardly be in a position to determine how much and to what degree this intercepted material may have influenced the course of events.

On the basis of the evidence provided by known incidents, it can be affirmed that if the deciphering of documents has assuredly had a direct influence on certain decisions, it does not always follow that exact knowledge of another government's point of view has always been advantageous to the state possessing it.

A significant case in point is Mussolini's knowledge, at the beginning of the Ethiopian crisis, of the report of a Cabinet committee meeting presided over by the British Colonial Office Permanent Undersecretary, Maffey, in which it was determined that the Italian expansion program in East Africa would be compatible with Great Britain's Imperial interests if the latter could be guaranteed and an assurance given for an improvement of Britain's position in the Lake Tsana region, which comprises the sources of the Blue Nile. What effect this circumstance may have had on Mussolini's decision to undertake his Ethiopian venture is difficult to ascertain; doubtless, it was of no small importance. However, it must be emphasized that Mussolini's publication of the document when the crisis with Great Britain became more acute would seem to indicate both his resentment of the hostile attitude assumed by London at that time in response to the pressure of British public opinion (an element that the Italian head of state perhaps did not keep in mind when evaluating the Maffey report) and the need to justify his own decision.

Again, with regard to the Ethiopian crisis, certain attitudes of defiance assumed by Mussolini when the British Ambassador, Sir Eric Drummond, informed him of the movement of the Home Fleet to Gibraltar are explained by the interception of dispatches exchanged between the Admiralty and the command of the Home Fleet, from which Mussolini learned that the latter lacked ammunition and was unprepared for immediate action. (Today, these dispatches are used as an explanation of the Admiralty's desire to influence the government to avoid measures that would weaken the British fleet in the Far East, but this explanation does not minimize the impact of these communications on Mussolini's thinking.)

Moreover, it seems that Mussolini's determination to invade Ethiopia was further crystallized after reading a report written by Sir Eric Drummond on the Italian internal political situation during the crisis. In that report the British Ambassador had affirmed that the left wing of the Fascist party was opposed to the Ethiopian venture because such action would definitely postpone certain social reforms it favored; and he concluded that his government should not ignore the possibility that such opposition could bring about the fall of the dictator. London replied that nothing would be more pleasing to the British government. Mussolini reacted to this information by becoming more intransigent and denying the validity of the assertions of Dino Grandi (Italian Ambassador to the Court of St. James) that the major figures in the British Cabinet were well disposed toward the Italian head of state.

Furthermore, it may also be noted that the ineffectiveness of the Anglo-Italian Gentlemen's Agreement of January 2, 1937, was caused by

Mussolini's reaction to the instructions (decoded by the Italian Military Information Service [S.I.M.]) which Eden shortly after the conclusion of the agreement had sent to the British legations in the Balkan capitals, with especial attention to Belgrade, to obstruct the Italo-Yugoslav *rapprochement*.

Finally, Mussolini's resentment against the King of Greece was based on information taken from the British Embassy safe in Rome, a resentment that later had an important influence on the decision to attack Greece. The King had been received by Mussolini in July, 1939, and the Fascist leader was convinced that he had favorably impressed the Sovereign. Instead, on the occasion of a subsequent sojourn in London, the Greek ruler expressed himself about Mussolini in hostile terms. His reading of the summary of these conversations, which was transmitted by the British Foreign Office to the British Embassy in Rome, destroyed whatever illusions the Fascist dictator cherished and drove him further down the road of personal revenge.

Difficulties less serious than those discussed above, but nonetheless significant, are to be found in the evaluation of diplomatic documents defined as informal or internal.

As a matter of fact, diplomats employ a distinct prose which often does not correspond to a linear exposition of the facts and therefore can rarely be accepted literally. Assuming this statement to be almost universally true, two variables must be evaluated in order to grasp the full meaning of all the nuances of diplomatic language: (a) the personality of the writer, and (b) the objective of the communication.

Insofar as the first is concerned, it is obvious that each writer has a tendency to emphasize or de-emphasize the approach characteristic of diplomatic language, depending largely on his temperament, his preparation, his preoccupation with his career, or even his mental and physical state at the actual time of writing.

While not always a simple task, it is possible to determine the nature of the writer's disposition at the time of writing. It is considerably more difficult to comprehend thoroughly the objectives he is seeking via the communication. Of course he is duty-bound to report objectively, but in general some men report objectively and with exactitude and others are more subjective in their statements. Even in the former case, writing a report is not a mechanical process, and it is quite natural for a diplomat to prepare his communication with the personality of the reader in mind.

For example, insofar as a news item is concerned, in the first place it may or may not be transmitted; second, it may be sent for the sole purpose of avoiding criticism at a later date for not having communicated it, and in this case the document may be purely informative in character or it may be vague and obscure; or it may be presented in a manner designed to provoke a specific reaction in the agent's government. Finally, one must not overlook the basic fact that in evaluating a specific item of information the ambassador is often influenced by the political climate resulting from the vantage point of the particular capital to which he is accredited.

The same can be said for the technique of reporting a colloquy. Apart from the case of the individual who reports what he should have said or wanted to say, rather than the actual course of the conversation, a reasonably objective report may, for example, accent one problem instead of another; a conversation may be reported in a very moderate tone, rather than with the violence that characterized the actual exchange, in order to avoid precipitating serious controversy; and, ultimately, the diplomat may attribute certain observations to the spokesman which, in fact, are his own, but which he seeks to impose on his ministry without assuming their authorship. It is difficult to determine the exact content of a colloquy without having access to both versions of what actually transpired. Even with its omissions, such a comparison constitutes the best means of approaching the truth.

This already complex search for the truth has been made infinitely more difficult by the large-scale publication of diplomatic documents, especially after the Nuremberg trials, in which these documents served as a basis for the various accusations. As a result, we now detect a greater tendency on the part of diplomats to avoid taking a definite position, particularly in the matter of comments and recommendations on given situations. Secondly, there has been an increased tendency to report critically on a situation, in certain types of documents, for the sole purpose of protecting oneself in the event of publication of these documents at some future date. It can also be said that outline reporting of political activities which could threaten the peace or sketches concerning projects for military alliances have all but disappeared. Future scholars of contemporary international affairs will have a task infinitely more difficult than those working in the period prior to World War I, when diplomats were convinced that their correspondence would remain jealously guarded in the recesses of the archives for a very long time.

For the diplomat, there also remains the special problem of carrying out the instructions he receives from his government.[5] If he is not in agreement

[5] In this case reference is made to the instructions given by the ministry on a specific issue and not to the general instructions which, at one time, were given to heads of delegations about to begin their missions and which covered the entire gamut of relations between the two countries concerned. Now this practice, to all intents and purposes, has been abandoned, and for the most part instructions are given orally. The work of scholars suffers as a result of this new approach because the earlier practice of providing written general instructions offered an extremely useful over-all picture of the

with the policy lines laid down for him, he is left with three alternatives: he may ignore his instructions, he may resign his post, or he may execute his orders in such a way as to distinguish clearly between his responsibilities and those of his government on the issue in question. The latter course was chosen by Dino Grandi on several occasions during his mission in London (1932–39), while Carlo Sforza, Ambassador to Paris at the time of Mussolini's advent to power, chose to resign in order to avoid sharing responsibility for the policies of the new government (as well as for other reasons having no bearing on this particular discussion).[6]

All of the observations made above are also applicable in large measure to the Minister of Foreign Affairs. An important element of his correspondence merits at least brief comment, namely, instructions which, because of the need to adjust to the personality of the representative to whom they are directed, often may not indicate precisely the objectives to be pursued. Therefore, if the situation requires strong action, the instructions may be phrased in very drastic terms; but if they are to be sent to a diplomat known to be firm, vigorous, and resolute in all of his actions, the instructions may be couched in very moderate terms. For this reason, the same instructions sent to different diplomats may be expressed in different terms.

The combination of these phenomena, which in one way or another contribute to the difficulty of proper interpretation of diplomatic documents, assumes a much greater significance in dictatorial regimes because of the inherent general climate of reciprocal distrust. While subordinates are more inclined to hide certain tendencies and situations that may be disapproved by the regime, the central authorities in turn are led to doubt the veracity of their representatives abroad.

For several reasons the examination of diplomatic documents, notwithstanding the most careful effort at interpretation, does not in itself permit the total reconstruction of the foreign policy of a state. In the first place, because of the particular organization of the state, it may be that foreign policy is not implemented by the Foreign Ministry but, instead, is carried

state of the relations between two countries at a given time and an idea of the plan of action of one government toward another. The general instructions given to French ambassadors from the Treaty of Westphalia to the French Revolution are to be found in *Recueil des Instructions données aux Ambassadeurs et Ministres de France depuis les Traités de Westphalie jusqu'à la Révolution Française* (19 vols.; Paris: Felix Alcan, 1884 *et seq.*).

[6] An interesting analysis of this problem is found in Carlo Avarna di Gualtieri (ed.), *Carteggio Avarna-Bollati* (Naples: E.S.I., 1953). Avarna and Bollati were ambassadors to Vienna and Berlin, respectively, on the eve of Italy's entrance into World War I. The conclusion reached here is that a diplomatic representative is always obliged to carry out his government's instructions.

out by other organs or directly by a specific power bloc within the government. Typical is the example of Nazi Germany, whose foreign policy, fashioned in the Chancellery, was often carried out by bureaus of the National Socialist party and, in particular, by the *Dienst Stelle* Ribbentrop (as we shall observe in a later chapter) rather than by the Wilhelmstrasse.

In the second place, even when the execution of foreign policy is entrusted to the competent ministry, major decisions through which general directives are translated into concrete action are usually made outside the Ministry of Foreign Affairs. Therefore, even in the case where such decisions are the result of a choice made by responsible authorities among the possible alternatives proposed by the Ministry of Foreign Affairs, the diplomatic documents alone seldom reveal the precise reasons that dictated the course of action. For this purpose one must weigh all the other factors that contribute to the process of formulating general directives and major decisions, factors that, while generally known in the broad sense (public opinion, party roles, ideological currents, industrial potential, stage of development, etc.), elude precise schematization because they are extremely variable from period to period and from country to country; they can be clearly understood only through an examination of the politico-constitutional and socioeconomic conditions of a state for a determined period of time.

It is precisely in this sense that one can correctly affirm that diplomatic documents cannot constitute the sole source for the study of international relations. However, if the assertion is pressed to the point of an insistence that investigation must focus almost exclusively on those factors designated as concurrent rather than on the diplomatic documents, one goes to the opposite extreme and inevitably risks losing sight of reality. There are four basic reasons why this is so.

First and foremost, the analyst forgets that the documents emanating from the ministry in the form of instructions already reflect an evaluation of the interplay that such factors as economic, political, military, religious, ideological, and public-opinion pressures have on the point at issue. The upper echelons of the ministry and their chief, the Minister of Foreign Affairs, are extremely sensitive to the pressures created by these forces and seek, more or less successfully, to interpret them correctly, cognizant that if they are not sufficiently well aware of these conditions they may very quickly be replaced with others who are.

Second, in not exploiting diplomatic documents, one ignores completely another determinant in the foreign policy of a state, that is, an understanding of the international scene in which it must operate. Consequently, the foreign policy of a state is seen only in its abstract form, without the indispensable reference to the policy of other states the sum of which produces the history of international relations.

Third, as previously noted, one loses a realistic view of the events as they unfold, and the investigation is reduced to something detached and apart from those almost daily actions and reactions that give substance to international events.

Fourth, it is almost impossible to have a clear conception of the influence exerted by an individual, who may often act on the basis of fortuitous reasoning and thereby lend a subjective interpretation to complex factors of foreign policy.

In effect, this combination of elements, the importance of which needs no further emphasis, is reflected most clearly in the diplomatic documents. Consequently, these emerge as a source of primary importance in understanding the fundamental aspect of international life, as well as that of any other human manifestation—that is, the role played by men.

2. THE ARCHIVE.

a. The Elements of an Archive.

Archives are the primary, fundamental, and indispensable sources for research, the nucleus of our discipline; they are the only tools that make it possible to reconstruct the course of international events with the greatest accuracy.

In fact, the entire complex of documents that are accumulated as a result of the activities of public or private office lays the foundation for creating an archive, thereby constituting the most complete and objective testimony of these activities. In general, completeness and objectivity are two characteristics peculiar to archival material. This is because an archive is not the product of chance or of the arbitrary choices of one individual. The concept of "archive" is the opposite of that of "collection." A collection is always based on strongly subjective criteria imposed by the collector, while an archive is created by the constant and quasi-automatic gathering of all documents that manifest the daily activities of an office or an individual. Even before the documents become of concern to the historian, they serve as an objective and exact record of all that has transpired.

This is the concept of an archive, which, in the technical sense as well, is defined as "that complex of documents gathered by a public office or a private individual in the fulfillment of his duties." In reality, this principle has certain inherent limitations, but however serious these might be, they are never such as to reduce, in the absolute sense, the value of the archive as the primary source for historical research.

b. Public and Private Archives.

From the preceding definition it is apparent that archives are divided into two major categories, public and private, according to their origins.

Public archives are those formed by the collection of documents pertinent to the activities of a central public office (ministry) or a periphery office (prefecture, embassy, etc.) of the state administration.

In conformity with the practice of every modern state, after a prescribed period of time the ministerial archives, with those of their outlying offices (concurrent archives), are merged into the general state archives, which are designed to preserve the archives of the individual administrations. Nevertheless, even after consignment to the general archives, the records of the various offices do not lose their identity because the documents that constitute an archive remain indissolubly bound together by the nature and competence of the office from which they originated. This point of origin, the so-called archivistic link, preserves, for the documents and for the archive which they form, an organic and permanent unity whose importance for historical research has already been amply illustrated.

Two tendencies are to be noted regarding archives of the Ministry of Foreign Affairs: while in many states (Great Britain and the United States, for example) the commonly accepted procedure for depositing documents in the general archives is observed, in others (France and Belgium, for example) the documents continue to be preserved within the Ministry of Foreign Affairs, in an office specifically designated for the purpose. In addition to the particular historical circumstances affecting the manner and time at which the various general archives were established, this separation originates from the necessity, peculiar to the ministries of foreign affairs, in contrast to other central administrative organs, of periodically consulting documents of earlier periods in order to expedite current affairs: thus the need to preserve them in the ministry itself. Further, even where this practice is not observed, the papers of the ministries of foreign affairs are deposited in the state archives only after a much longer lapse of time than is normal for other ministries—usually about ten years.

In Italy, after a period of uncertainty during which the Ministry of Foreign Affairs had clearly revealed a tendency to guard even the most ancient documents, the latter system was adopted, and in 1902 an historical archive for the ministry was established. In this depository are preserved not only the current archives of the central administration, but those of the outlying offices as well (embassy and consular offices abroad).

Consequently, in Italy, ministerial records may be consulted at the central state archives located in Rome, and those of the Ministry of Foreign Affairs, at the historical archives of that ministry.[7] It must be noted that the Ministry of Defense also ignores the practice of depositing its papers in the state archives, as far as the holdings of the General Staff are concerned. With extremely rare exceptions, these records are permanently secret, as is the case in every other nation.

As to the availability of these documents for consultation by individuals not connected with the offices of origin or possession, the archives are split into two divisions, secret and public (in the sense of being open to the public).

The publication of archival holdings is a relatively recent practice, beginning during the second half of the last century and becoming widespread only in recent years. Prior to the mid-nineteenth century, the traditions born of absolute government that were characteristic of nations during the period 1500–1700 dictated that archives should remain closed.[8]

Yet even today the consultation of national archives open to the public (in practice, those of most of the countries of the western world) is subject to precise rules and regulations. In the first place, regulations which permit consulting documents in a public archive are not applicable to recently deposited holdings concerning internal political affairs—and this is true in

[7] The following guides to the historical archives of the Italian Ministry of Foreign Affairs have been published by the Tipografia Riservata del Ministero Affari Esteri (Rome, 1947–59): Vol. I, R. Moscati, *Le scritture della Segreteria di Stato degli affari esteri del regno di Sardegna*; Vol. II, E. Piscitelli, *La Legazione Sarda in Vienna (1707–1859)*; Vol. III, F. Bacino, *Le Legazioni Sarde a Parigi, Berna, L'Aja, Lisbona e Madrid*; Vol. IV, M. Pastore, *La Legazione Sarda in Londra (1730–1860)*; Vol. V, F. Bacino, *La Legazione e i Consolati del Regno di Sardegna in Russia (1783–1861)*; Vol. VI, R. Moscati, *Le scritture del Ministero degli affari esteri del Regno d'Italia dal 1861 al 1887*; Vol. VII, F. Bacino, *Le scritture del "Gabinetto Crispi" e le carte "Sonnino"*; Vol. VIII, R. Mori, *Le scritture della Legazione e del Consolato del Granducato di Toscana in Roma dal 1737 al 1859*.

There are similar guides to the diplomatic papers of other countries. For western Europe, see D. H. Thomas and L. M. Case (eds.), *Guide to the Diplomatic Archives of Western Europe* (Philadelphia: University of Pennsylvania Press, 1959). These guides make it possible for scholars to conduct a rapid preliminary survey of the available source materials for their research, and they aid in locating the materials pertinent to the problems under investigation. It is now possible, using microfilm, to reproduce copies of the documents pertinent to the scholar's research. The technique eliminates the possibility of error in transcription and greatly reduces the time the scholar spends in the archives.

[8] For a history of archives, see Robert-Henri Bautier, "Les Archives," in *Encyclopedie de la Pléiade: L'Histoire et ses méthodes* (Bruges: Librairie Gallimard, 1961), pp. 1120–61.

every country. A decade or so must pass before those papers relating to internal or foreign affairs are available for study. In Italy, for example, by a 1953 law the archives for internal and foreign affairs are open for consultation up to 1900. In practice, these archives remain secret for half a century, despite the fact that they are deposited in a public archive. Recent legislation has rendered this limitation a little less rigid, to the effect that the files are automatically opened for consultation after forty years. In the second place, no citizen or foreign national has the *legal* right to consult these records. A request to examine the files must be submitted, and permission is granted upon proof that the purpose is one of scientific inquiry and that the individual is professionally qualified. If the applicant is a foreign national, the principle of reciprocity, that is, whether or not the country of which he is a citizen grants the same privileges as those for which he has petitioned, is also a contributing factor. Finally, there are certain restrictions on the use of a specific series of documents that the state has decided to publish.

Under special circumstances, documents relating to the foreign policy of a country (therefore, especially those that come from the Foreign Ministry) may be the subject of a special official state publication. Such a publication, which may cover a single problem or an entire period of foreign policy, may appear as one of the well-known "colored books," or in a general collection, or even in guises that we shall examine below.

Despite the fact that these publications, especially the diplomatic document collections (to be discussed extensively in subsequent chapters), are extremely useful working tools, they cannot substitute for actual research in the archives. The collections, even the general ones, cannot be anything more than the selection of documents which, in the judgment of the editor, are the most important; and they are also limited by the exigencies of publishing. Even if it were theoretically possible to publish a collection in its entirety, that is, one which comprised every document on a specific subject, a distinct difference would still exist between the examination of a printed document and the direct perusal of the original preserved in the archive.

The experience of holding in his hand the very papers that were actually involved in the event has a unique effect on the investigator. The sight of the document, often written in the hand of the author himself and marked by erasures and corrections which are at times important indications of his doubts and second thoughts, constitutes an irreplaceable auxiliary instrument in evaluating a personality. For example, upon examining the minute and precise handwriting of Baron Sidney Sonnino, Italian Minister of Foreign Affairs during World War I, we have the immediate impression of a man who, though far from congenial, has a thorough knowledge of the facts and a decidedly firm will. And there is nothing more revealing of the character of the Marchese di San Giuliano, Sonnino's predecessor in the Foreign Office, than the papers prepared with an unsteady hand. Here is the drama of a man gravely ill, who was knowingly exhausting what little energy he could marshal in order to remain at his post during that critical summer of 1914.

In addition to these important aspects of research in the archives, it stimulates new interests in the scholar, providing him with a supply of collateral and auxiliary data that are extremely useful in the research he is undertaking.

Private archives are of great value, especially those containing documents gathered by individuals (statesmen, diplomats, military men) during their active professional lives, and whose private character is retained despite the fact that for various reasons they may be preserved in state archives.

Theoretically, private archives are less important than public ones (the collections of public offices), but for specific problems they are frequently a unique and irreplaceable source. Their importance is explained by the motives that prompt the creation of private holdings, and these motives may also account for the fact that they are often very extensive. In addition to purely personal correspondence, which may or may not be of interest to the historian, these archives frequently include a portion, or even the greater part, of the official correspondence transmitted by or to these individuals. According to procedures established in almost every country, when their term of office expires, public officials, or those who function temporarily in such capacities, are obliged to surrender all official documents that were made available to them in the performance of their official duties, or, in any event, to consign them to their respective ministries.

In practice, for two reasons these norms are rarely observed. First, and especially significant in our field, there is the type of document consisting of the personal letter, which, as we have seen, is incorporated in or omitted from the files at the discretion of the recipient, although its contents may be of fundamental importance to an understanding of specific events. Second, there is a tendency among those whose primary duties involve analysis and exposition to retain possession of the pertinent documents to assist them in recalling accurately actions taken and, when necessary, to defend themselves against criticism of their actions. This practice would not be detrimental to the public archives if only copies of the aforementioned documents were retained; instead, for specific reasons, such as a hurried transfer from one post to another, the original documents are frequently kept by the representative.

This tendency was particularly prominent in the period preceding World War I. For example, a large part of the political correspondence of the foreign ministers Visconti-Venosta, Minghetti, and Crispi, along with that of many other diplomats, formed the basis of their respective private archives.

The losses sustained by the Italian central state archives and by the historical archives of the Ministry of Foreign Affairs as a result of this practice are very significant. As a case in point, there is preserved in the private archives of Prime Minister Vittorio Orlando, in addition to numerous letter books from the office of the Prime Minister and copies of the most important telegrams relating to foreign policy for the period 1917–19, the original of the official letter sent to him by the Chief of the General Staff of the Army, General Luigi Cadorna, dated November 3, 1917, written after the disaster at Caporetto and evaluating the military situation. "The most obvious and profound significance," Orlando states in his memoirs, where the letter is published, "was to urge the civil government to surrender."[9]

In summary, it can be said that private archives serve to complement public archives often in a useful and occasionally in an indispensable way, in much the same fashion that the scholar integrates the archives of several countries during the course of research leading to the reconstruction of the history of a problem or of a phase of international relations.

[9] Rodolfo Mosca (ed.), *Vittorio Emanuele Orlando, Memorie 1915–1919* (Milan: Rizzoli, 1960), p. 571. For the text of the letter, see pp. 501–3.

Chapter II

MEMOIRS AS SOURCES

⌒ Summary: 1. Definition. 2. Positive and Negative Aspects of Memoirs as Sources

1. DEFINITION.

The recollections and diaries of participants in given events or of those who can provide testimony on the events to serve the needs of historical research may be considered to be memoir sources.

Theoretically, the importance of these sources ought to be decisive because in these one should be able to discover the true and unqualified thoughts of the writer, so as to make reconstruction, not only of the facts, but also of the forces that created them and of the objectives they pursued, an extremely simple task. In reality, however, a combination of factors contribute to making memoir sources very difficult historical tools to use.

2. POSITIVE AND NEGATIVE ASPECTS OF MEMOIRS AS SOURCES.

First, it is important to keep in mind the inherent distortion of perspective arising from the tendency of every individual to consider himself and his actions at the center of activity. This very human approach leads the author, perhaps unconsciously, to alter the facts, often to a very marked degree.

Second, when considerable time has elapsed between the events and the actual writing of the memoir, the author may in good faith err in referring to them. Errors of this kind more frequently occur when the memoir is written long after the event, without the aid of notes or other reference material. Naturally, diaries are not subject to these pitfalls because they are essentially day-by-day notations.[1]

Aside from unconscious distortions of the truth, frequently the author of a memoir intentionally presents an inexact account of the facts. Here, too, the range between truth and fiction is very wide: it is inevitable for a person writing of himself or of his actions to seek to put one or the other in the best possible light, emphasizing positive aspects and ignoring negative ones. However, it often happens that memoirs are written for the specific purpose of replying to criticism launched against the author's activity. In this case, these assume the character of an instrument of self-defense and must be so considered and interpreted. This is even more true if we limit our discussion to memoirs of the most recent years.

At one time it was the practice to publish one's recollections only after many years had passed between the actual events and the publication of the memoir (they were usually published posthumously). However, since the end of World War I, the interval has been so reduced as to be inconsequential. This practice has the advantage that the author is writing while events are still clear in his mind, but it also gives rise to several problems of no mean importance: first and foremost, for personal reasons or political timeliness a complete exposition of the facts may be precluded; then too, human passions have a tendency to color any realistic account.

In this context, it should be noted that in recent years the reading public has increased enormously as a result of an intensified interest in international affairs. A person writing his memoirs in the first half of the nineteenth century was appealing to a narrowly restricted audience which was capable of comprehending—often through personal experience—the difficulties involved in a specific political maneuver. The author could address this audience with the knowledge that he would not be misunderstood. Today, a statesman or a diplomat in referring to his own activities must bear in mind that many of his readers have little understanding of—or ability to justify—the uncertainties, the compromises, and the errors that are inevitable in the conduct of affairs by one who bears the burden of public responsibility. Further, the writer cannot ignore the weight of public opinion even when he knows it to be misguided. He is obliged to justify not only a political action but a human and moral experience as well, often at the cost of distorting his own personality. On the other hand, it must be

---

[1] It should be carefully borne in mind that it is not unusual to come upon a work which, despite the fact that it is compiled as a diary in order to give the reader the impression of spontaneity and immediacy, was in fact written, or at least amply modified and corrected, at a much later date.

recognized that the historical significance of modern memoir-writing has greatly increased because of the enormous number of memoirs published, which facilitates comparison in the interest of accuracy, and because of the basic objectivity of the content.

Up to this point we have examined factors contributing, in varying degree, to the reduction of the value of memoirs as sources for historical research. Turning to the positive aspects, especially of those memoirs concerned with the most recent period, it must be noted that not all diplomatic negotiations are carried on via official channels, that is, through the respective diplomatic missions or through the offices of the ministries of foreign affairs. For example, specific circumstances may prompt an unofficial approach, particularly when it is important to avoid a violent reaction or when, for good reason, it is necessary to avoid involving the government directly. Other cases stem from personal initiative, a very common approach when there are divergencies between the Ministry of Foreign Affairs and other organs of the state. In this connection, it is important to recall the phenomenon that appeared with much publicity during and immediately after World War I, whose influence was felt to some extent in all countries but most keenly in the Anglo-Saxon world. We speak of the reaction against "secret diplomacy," considered by many as one of the principal causes of the war. The almost universal aversion to certain "secret" techniques of diplomacy had, for a number of years, such an impact on the functions of the ministries of foreign affairs as to reduce the prestige of these organs to the point where, for all practical purposes, the most important negotiations were carried on outside of these traditional channels and, not infrequently, without their knowledge. Another factor contributing to this state of affairs was the concentration of power in superorgans (for example, war cabinets), whose creation was justified as a war measure; these could easily by-pass the authority of the Ministry of Foreign Affairs.

As a case in point, during the preparatory phase of the Paris peace conference, this combination of circumstances made it possible for many negotiations, among them those of the greatest importance, to be conducted by individuals totally unconnected with the diplomatic corps. The consequences of this practice, from the standpoint of historical research, were that little or no trace of these negotiations can be found in the archives, and in order to reconstruct them it is necessary to use the memoirs and diaries of the participants as primary sources. In other cases, too, memoirs are equally irreplaceable as primary sources: it is sufficient to note how important these are to the study of American foreign policy, on which the President exercises such a decisive influence. At this point, the recollections of his collaborators become vitally significant, directly associated as they are with the most important episodes and the weightiest decisions.

Another instance illustrating the increased importance of memoirs is the widespread use of modern means of communication, primarily the telephone. It is obvious that there is no record of a telephone conversation in an archive unless a written note is made of it: it is only through the testimony of the speakers that it is possible to reconstruct episodes that occasionally may be of considerable importance. The Ciano-Ribbentrop conversations during the heyday of the Axis are examples of important telephonic exchanges; once the conversation was terminated, it would have been good procedure to make written notes of what had transpired. But this did not normally occur, and if a record exists of such dialogues, it is because of Ciano's diary or the testimony of some other individual who happened to be present during those conversations.

If the importance of memoir material is sometimes unequaled for the reconstruction of events, it does not necessarily mean that the research process is made easier, for the fact remains that the negative aspects noted earlier always play a part in determining the value of memoirs.

Ideal conditions for research are present when it is possible to establish a rapport between the two categories of sources so as to integrate one into the other conveniently. In this way the origins and content of the documents are explained in greater detail, and the facts to which the memoirs refer are confirmed by the documents. Without seeking to establish a preconceived preference for either of these two types of sources, the fact remains that the document, in addition to those values already ascribed to it, usually has a unique importance for the historian because the evidence it contains leaves the author's possession very soon after its preparation and therefore is not subject to change at a later date. In the case of memoirs, this is true only when there is absolute certainty that the diary, for exceptional reasons, has been published without the author's having had the opportunity to effect substantial changes or corrections.

PART II

PUBLICATION OF THE SOURCES

Chapter I

COLLECTIONS OF TREATIES

SUMMARY: 1. The Earliest Collections of Treaties: Chifflet and Peller.   2. The Great Collections of the Close of the Seventeenth Century: Léonard, Leibnitz, the *Grand Recueil,* Rymer.   3. The Dumont Collection and Its Continuators, Barbeyrac and Rousset; the Works of Saint Prest and Lamberty.   4. The post-Dumont Eighteenth-Century Collections: Abreu y Bertodano, Wenck, Martens.   5. The Private Collections of the Nineteenth and Twentieth Centuries.   6. The Modern Official Collections

1. THE EARLIEST COLLECTIONS OF TREATIES: CHIFFLET AND PELLER.

As has been noted, one of the sources for the history of international relations is treaties. If, in the legal sense, treaties constitute the principal source of international law insofar as our field of study is concerned, in essence they are considered as historical documents that reflect a particular relationship between the existing forces of the contracting parties at the time the signatures are affixed.

The original texts of the treaties are normally preserved in the archives, but they are not always easily accessible to scholars. Normally, archival materials of recent date may not be consulted. Then too, the most ancient documents have often been lost over the centuries, and it is only through copies that the texts may be known. To track down the original is not always possible or convenient. Therefore, the advantage of finding them in collections devoted to international treaties is obvious.

This genre of publication makes its first appearance in the sixteenth century and subsequently changes in purpose and form. It may be divided into (a) *general collections,* when they include all of the treaties signed in a given period; and (b) *special collections,* when they are limited to a particular type of treaty (i.e., commercial treaties) or when they concern only the treaties concluded by one state.

47

Of greater importance, partly because of the connection with the historical development of this kind of undertaking, is the distinction between (a) *official collections*, those assembled by individual states or, in recent years, by international organizations such as the League of Nations or the United Nations; and (b) *private collections*, where the collecting and publishing of the material has been the work of private individuals or groups.

In some instances, this distinction may appear to be overly subtle because it is evident that consultation and publication of materials contained in a state archive may be undertaken only with the consent of the proper authorities. Thus the publication of these collections is often a private endeavor with official sanction. However, the distinction remains valid in this case because the responsibility of the state is not directly involved.

In examining this type of publication, two limitations must be kept in mind that are basic when one seeks to restrict the discussion to true treaty collections. The first is that the publication of single treaties, a practice introduced with the invention of movable type but whose antecedents, especially with regard to treaties of peace or commercial accords, may be traced to much earlier times, is alien to the discussion.

The Papal Bulls *In apostolicae sedis specula* and *Cum nos hodie* of August 21, 1461, published the same year at Mainz, may be considered to be the first printed documents concerning international relations. In these, Pius II prohibited Diether von Isenburg from exercising the right of franchise in the election of the Emperor and also divested him of the archbishopric of Mainz and of the office of Archchancellor of the Empire. Shortly thereafter, the Treaty of Arras was published, signed by Louis XI and Maximilian of Austria on December 23, 1482, and printed in April, 1483; and the Treaty of Picquigny of August 29, 1475, between Louis XI and Edward IV, was published in England in 1485 or 1486. The publication of these two treaties sought to clarify the respective positions of the two sovereigns in the face of the conflicting matrimonial obligations assumed by Louis XI in the name of the Dauphin. There followed the Concordat of 1448 between the Emperor and the Pope, printed at Strasbourg in 1513; the text of the Capitulations treaty entered into by France and the Sublime Porte and published in Paris in 1570; the treaty between France and Savoy of 1569, also published in Paris in 1597; and still others demonstrating the progressive development of the tendency to make known, via the printing press, those treaties that aroused the greatest popular interest.

These publications constitute an historical fact: in order to understand clearly the origins of the first treaty collections, they should not be ignored.

As early as the end of the fifteenth century, the need to present to the public those political acts that had the greatest repercussions or to justify, by reference to established precedents, an action taken was clearly shown.

The second limitation in our examination of treaty collections is this: the distinction between collections of treaties as such and collections of the *acta publica* in which treaties are only one of the species of documents included must be made clear. However, a precise distinction is possible only for those collections limited to the recent period. In the seventeenth-century collections and in most of the eighteenth-century ones, it is normal to find, along with treaties, other documents (edicts, proclamations, unilateral affirmations or rejections of rights, testaments of sovereigns, and acts of various kinds from which the public law of Europe is derived). The latter are of interest to our field of study to the extent that they influenced the course of international relations, but they cannot be classified as treaties. Reference will be made to these collections when they are, in the main, composed of treaties.

Its title notwithstanding, the work published by Jean Tillet[1] in 1577 cannot be considered to be a collection because the author supplies only a summary of the treaties without including the texts, although reference is made to the royal archives where the originals were to be found. In contrast, true collections are those for which Melchior Goldast is justly famous:[2] the documents are given in their entirety, though these are not collections of treaties but rather of *acta publica* concerning the internal affairs of the Empire.

The popularity of these collections of *acta publica*, in any event, confirms the growing interest in political affairs. And it is precisely to satisfy this growing curiosity that with increasing frequency, at the beginning of the seventeenth century, works begin to appear having the characteristics of chronicles, such as the *Theatrum Europaeum*[3] or Vittorio Siri's *Mercu-*

---

[1] *Recueil des guerres et des traités de paix, de trêve, d'alliance d'entre les Rois de France et d'Angleterre depuis Philippe I.er, roi de France, jusqu'à Henri II* (Paris: Dupuis, 1577). The work is to be found with the author's other writings and those of his brother, the Bishop of Meaux, under the title, *Recueil des Roys de France.*

[2] Among Goldast's publications, the first is most noteworthy. Melchior Goldast, *Imperatorum, regnum et electorum S. R. I. statuta et rescripta a Carolo M. ad Carolum V et a Carolo V ad Rudolphum II* (3 vols.; Frankfurt: 1607). Other editions appeared in 1615, 1625, 1673, and 1713.

[3] *Theatrum Europaeum, oder, Aussfürliche und warhafftige Beschreibung aller und jeder denckwürdiger Geschichten, so sich hin und wieder in der Welt, fürnemblich aber in Europa und Teutschlanden, so wol im Religion als Prophanwesen, vom Jahr Christi 1617 biss auff das Jahr 1629 exclus. bey Regierung deren beyden. . . . Römischen Keysern Matthiae und Ferdinandi dess Andern. . . . zugetragen haben etc. . . . Mit vieler fürnehmer Herrn und Potentaten Contrafacturen, wie auch berühmter Städten, Vestungen Pässen, Schlachten, und Belägerungen eygentlichen*

rio,[4] in which a great quantity of material can be found, including many treaties.

The first true collection of treaties we find, compiled in 1643 by Jean Jacques Chifflet[5] and comprising the treaties of 1526 and 1611 negotiated by the crowns of France and Spain, was made public for a very different reason. It was created to provide a ready reference book to be used by the Spanish plenipotentiaries charged with concluding peace with France at Münster. This publication was not planned for the general public but rather for a team of "experts." Careful consideration should be given to this development, for similar requirements are the basis of virtually all subsequent publications of this genre. It should also be noted that the Chifflet collection went through two more editions, in which the material was brought up to date to include the Peace of the Pyrénées of 1659.[6] The number of copies printed was increased with each edition, an evidence of growing public interest.

At the time of the negotiations leading to the Treaties of Westphalia, public curiosity had become sufficiently widespread to induce private publishers to print the text drafted at Osnabruck in July, 1648, even before it was signed, along with that of Münster of October 24, 1648.[7] Immediately after Westphalia, numerous collections of treaties appeared in print, the majority, however, limited to special cases and interests.

A small collection was published in 1650 and contained those treaties concluded by Louis XIII from 1628 to 1644.[8] The same year marked the appearance of an analogous collection,[9] probably edited by Jean Jacques Chifflet, that included the treaties signed by the kings of France between 1621 and 1648. A third collection, published in Amsterdam in

---

Delineationen und Abrissen gezieret, und jetzo zum drittenmahl, nach beschehener Revision und Verbesserung, an Tag gegeben und verlegt, durch weyland Matthaei Merians seel (Erben in Franckfurt. Mit Röm. Keys. Mayestät sonderbarer Gnade und Privilegio, 1635–1738), 32 parts in 21 vols. The first volume concerned the years 1618–28. The twenty-first volume concerned the years 1716–18.

[4] Vittorio Siri (ed.), *Mercurio overo historia de' correnti tempi.* The first volume appeared in 1644, the fifteenth and last in 1682. These concern the years 1635–55.

[5] *Recueil des traittez de paix, trêves et neutralité entre les couronnes d'Espagne et de France* (Antwerp: Imprimerie Plantinienne, 1643), 2d ed., 1645; 3d ed., 1664.

[6] The text of the Treaty of Aix-la-Chapelle of May 12, 1668, ending the War of Devolution was later inserted in a number of copies of the last edition.

[7] Three editions were published, two in Germany and one in Holland.

[8] *Traictez de confédération et d'alliance entre la Couronne de France et les Princes et Etats estrangers,* 1650.

[9] Jean Jacques Chifflet [?], *Recueil des traictés de confédération et d'alliance entre la Couronne de France et les Etats et Princes étrangers depuis l'an 1621 jusques à present avec quelques autres pièces appartenantes à l'histoire* (Amsterdam: Pierre van Dyck, 1650).

1664,[10] was in all likelihood a second edition of the latter brought up to date. In 1672 still another edition appeared with further adjuncts.

Undoubtedly, the best known among these collections is the *Theatrum pacis*, edited by Christoph Peller[11] and published in Germany in 1663, which comprised all the treaties signed in Europe from 1647 to 1660 (Peace of Oliva). Despite the fact that the collection consists of only seventy documents, the publication is of fundamental importance because it was the first general collection to appear up to that time and, secondly, because it contained only treaties and excluded memoirs, letters, and other acts. A second volume,[12] published in 1685 at Nuremberg, added to the collection by including treaties negotiated up to 1685.

2. THE GREAT COLLECTIONS OF THE CLOSE OF THE SEVENTEENTH CENTURY: LÉONARD, LEIBNITZ, THE *GRAND RECUEIL*, RYMER.

By the end of the seventeenth century the practice of publishing treaty collections had become commonplace. There are a number of possible explanations of this phenomenon, of greater or lesser importance, depending on the circumstances. However, all contributed toward whetting the interest of private publishers and inducing governments to allow scholars easier access to archival materials.

The first reason for the new practice was the desire to furnish diplomats and government officials with a practical instrument that would provide data on the background of a given problem and eliminate the need for

[10] *Recueil des traictés de confédération et d'alliance, entre la Couronne de France, et les Princes et estats estrangers, depuis l'an M.DC.XXI jusques à present, avec quelques autres pièces appartenantes à l'histoire* (Amsterdam: Pierre van Dyck, 1664). A second edition was published in 1672.

[11] Christoph Peller von und zu Scheppershof, *Theatrum pacis, hoc est: Tractatuum atque instrumentorum praecipuorum ad anno inde MDCXLVII ad MDCLX usque in Europa initorum et conclusorum collectio* (Nuremberg: 1663–85). Peller also published, in 1666, a more limited collection relative to the years 1647–66 that includes the texts of the treaties of Münster and Osnabruck, the Peace of Westminister of September 15, 1654, which brought the first naval war to a close, the Treaty of Roskild between Denmark and Sweden of March 8, 1658, the Peace of the Pyrénées, and the Treaty of Oliva. See Peller, *Collectio praecipuorum tractatuum pacis ab anno 1647 ab annum 1664 utpote Hispanorum et Belgarum, Osnabrugensis, Monasteriensis, Cromwellio-Hollandicus, Dano-Suecicus, Pyrenaicus, Polono-Suecicus* (Nuremberg, 1666). A second edition appeared in 1684.

[12] *Theatri pacis pars altera, hoc est tractatuum atque instrumentorum pacis praecipuorum ab anno inde MDCLX ad annum MDCLXXXV inter Europaeos atque aliis cum nationibus initorum et conclusorum collectio secunda* (Nuremberg, 1685). Another edition of the two volumes of the *Theatrum pacis* was published in 1702.

extensive archival research—not always an easy task, given the chaotic state of the holdings. It was possible to locate the originals only of those acts signed by a prince or by a state, although for the conduct of negotiations it was often useful to know the details of the accords signed by other rulers. In this context, it should be noted that even earlier it had become a frequent custom to compile small, handwritten collections of certain papers, when ready availability of specific documents was deemed necessary, in order to facilitate the work of the negotiators. It was common practice then as now to refer in one treaty to the text of another in order to reconfirm, modify, or abrogate certain clauses. This explains why acts of a much earlier date are often found inserted in these collections. With these texts readily available, negotiators could resolve many editorial problems simply by referring to formulas used in earlier agreements.

Along with this practical technical aim, the collections sought to satisfy other needs, among them the desire to assuage public curiosity about events that today would be called developments in international relations. This interest had become clearly evident by the end of the sixteenth century and had progressively deepened during the course of the seventeenth, particularly after the end of the Thirty Years' War, when the European chessboard was active with complex power gambits that attracted increasingly greater public attention. By the second half of the seventeenth century, interest in international affairs was no longer limited to the professional statesman: politics—as Bernard notes in the introduction to his collection—is "the fashionable science," and there are no longer any persons disinterested in it.

The diffusion of Grotius' theories also constituted a potent impulse toward research and publication of the texts of treaties. When Grotius published his *De jure belli ac pacis* in 1625, only a very limited documentation was available to him, which explains his repeated reference to examples drawn from ancient history. But his theories stimulated the interest in the study of public law and in research into those acts that are the basis of conventional law. In modern times, too, it is the need to satisfy a similar demand that prompts the inclusion of the most recent materials, arranged according to scientific criteria, in collections of treaties.

In these early collections we note the ever-increasing desire to provide a more secure documentary basis for historical studies and to draw a clear distinction between these studies and the enormous output of material of a pretentious and controversial nature that, at the least, seems to fall short of satisfying the scientific mind of the age. The collections of treaties, so popular in the years bridging these two centuries, were thus absorbed as part of the historiographic tendencies of the erudite school whose exponents in France are the Benedictines of the Congregation of St. Maurice. Putting aside the empiricism of the humanistic period, which was watered down by literary embellishments, research into and criticism of the sources began to provide each historical treatment with an indispensable solid documentary base.

These changes influenced the attitude of both princes and governments, who were encouraged to open their archives more freely. It is necessary to keep in mind the growing public interest in political problems, but to do so according to the new spirit that guided the culture of the age. As has been noted, pamphlet literature of a philosophico-literary nature had lost much of its influence: it had to change its base; it had to "document itself," and governments had to provide the indispensable materials. Thus there comes to light, scattered throughout a host of publications of various kinds, a complex of documents that had no precedent. Logically, statesmen and scholars alike were most anxious to see these assembled in an organic way. Many of the collections of treaties and of *acta publica* appearing in this period were the result of these requests, and they themselves were instruments of high-level political controversy.

Frédéric Léonard was probably inspired in his role as editor by the official post he held and by his business instincts. Appointed royal printer to Louis XIV in 1668, he obtained in 1678 the exclusive right to publish all treaties concluded with or without French participation for twenty years, a privilege that also gave him access to the royal archives. One of his documentary collections appeared in 1683,[13] relating to the Dutch war from its declaration by the United Provinces, on April 6, 1672, to the conclusion of the Treaties of Nijmegen in 1678, along with annexes concerning the deliberations of the Royal Chamber of Metz on the question of the feudal dependencies in the bishoprics of Metz, Toul, and Verdun up to the annexation of Strasbourg in 1681. The collection had an obvious official character, and in all probability Léonard had been commissioned to publish it in reply to the reaction provoked in all of Europe by the policies of the "Chambers of Reunion" inaugurated by Louis XIV.

In any event, the publication was a huge success, to such an extent that shortly thereafter Léonard conceived the plan of assembling in one large collection all of the treaties signed by the kings of France, beginning with the Treaty of Arras of 1435. In contrast to the earlier work, this one appeared to be designed to exploit public interest commercially, even

---

[13] *Recueil de tous les traités modernes conclus entre les potentats de l'Europe: de tous les mémoires qui ont servi à faire la paix de Nimégue: et de tous les arrests de la Chambre Roiale de Metz, relatifs aux traités de Nimégue et de Münster* (Paris: Frédéric Léonard, 1683).

though, at the time of its preparation, Léonard enjoyed the widest privileges that were the prerogatives of his office. That it was edited for profit is proved by the manner in which it was published. In fact, the collection,[14] which appeared in 1693, did begin with the Treaty of Arras, and the first volumes covered the period up to 1600 in chronological order. However, in the succeeding volumes, the carelessness with which the material was assembled is clearly evident. The absence of organization is noted: some documents are presented chronologically and others by country. Proper page numbering is also missing because in many cases Léonard simply bound together a series of documents that had been printed separately some time earlier. As for the sixth and last volume, it shows the least organization of all: it covers the years 1632–90, the period covered, in the main, in other volumes, and it contains, in addition to the treaties signed by the kings of France, those concluded by the anti-French coalitions, along with other materials pertinent to the negotiation of treaties and to the formulation of the political acts of the Chambers of Reunion up to the Truce of Ratisbon, on August 15, 1684.

Obviously the criteria of selection adopted by Léonard varied from time to time. In all probability, he sought to satisfy the interest of the public by including documents which could have been considered of a contemporary nature; it is also possible that he had to take into account certain pressures from above. It was very likely the pressing need to put the greatest number of volumes on sale as quickly as possible that induced him to abandon his original organic plan.

Despite these negative aspects, the Léonard collection must be regarded as of prime importance, not for its size alone (*ca.* nine hundred treaties, in addition to numerous other documents), but also because the author was in a position to gather materials from primary sources such as the Trésor des Cartes, the royal library, the Chambres des Comptes of Paris, Lille, Nantes, etc. In fact, later compilers had to make wide use of this collection, particularly the publishers of the *Grand Recueil* of 1700, who, while criticizing Léonard's work, utilized *in toto* what the French publisher had been able to uncover. Therefore, Léonard gives to research a vast original contribution, which is lacking—at least to a degree—in later compilations, but it is to the latter that scholars today refer in order to avoid the difficulties inherent in using the Léonard collection (despite the existence of a Table of Contents at the end of the last volume).

Also rich in hitherto unpublished material is the *Codex juris gentium*

[14] *Recueil des traitéz de paix, de trêve, de neutralité, de confédération, d'alliance et de commerce, faits par les rois de France, avec tous les princes et potentats de l'Europe, et autres, depuis près de trois siècles* (6 vols.; Paris, 1693).

diplomaticus, published in the same year, 1693, by Leibnitz.[15] Appointed by the House of Brunswick to conduct geneological investigations in Germany, Italy, England, and elsewhere, Leibnitz, during the course of his journeys, assembled the documents for his compilation, a collection of acts dating from 1096 to 1497, among which there are a number of treaties pertaining to the public law of Europe. The collection differs from Léonard's not only in its general nature but also in its conception. It is obvious that Leibnitz sought to investigate and bring to light a complex of historical sources according to the pattern suggested by the erudite school, whose criteria Leibnitz followed with rigorous scientific exactitude. In substance, it is a collection of *acta publica,* and this characteristic is even more clearly evident in the addendum (*Mantissa*), published by Leibnitz in 1700.[16]

The author left the *Mantissa* without a title because it contained a wide variety of data designed to be used in separate booklets and not intended for insertion in a chronological series. In it Leibnitz included materials collected during his investigations at the English court and at the courts on the Continent—materials extraneous to his research on the House of Brunswick. Particularly important were the findings at the court of the Elector of Brandenburg. The *Mantissa* consists of two parts: the first contains tracts, dissertations, and other items of this genre on various questions such as the concordat between Leo V and Francis I, the pontifical ceremony during the vacancy of the papal throne, etc.; the second contains the material more properly defined as documentary, such as the statutes of the major royal orders and a number of public acts concerning, for the most part, the internal problems of the Empire or ecclesiastical questions, always divided, however, according to subject.

[15] Gottfried Wilhelm Freiherr von Leibniz, *Codex juris gentium diplomaticus, in quo tabulae authenticae actorum publicorum, tractatuum, aliarumque rerum majoris momenti per Europam gestarum, pleraeque ineditae vel selectae, ipso verborum tenore expressa ac temporum serie digestae, continentur; a fine saeculi undecimi ad nostra usque tempora aliquot tomis comprehensus* (Hanover, 1693).

[16] *Godefridi Guilielmi Leibnitii, Mantissa Codicis juris gentium diplomatici, continens statuta magnorum ordinum regiorum, acta vetera electionum regis Romani, manifestationes jurium inter Franciam, Angliam, et Burugundiam olim controversorum; concilia item Germanica, ceremoniale sedis Romanae vacantis, concertationes imperium regnaque inter et ecclesiam Romanam praesertim Bonifacii VIII tempore et circa concordata Galliae cum Leone X, scissionem Bohemicam, saecularisationes ditionum episcopalium a pontificibus factas, absolutionem Henrici IV Gall. r., praeterea Austriaco-Luxenburgica, Anglo-Scotica, Helvetico-Novo-Castrensia, etc., ac tandem complures foederum aliorumve publice gestorum tabulas; ex manuscriptis praesertim Bibliothecae Augustae Guelfebytanae codicibus, et monumentis regiorum aliorumque archivorum, ac propriis denique collectaneis* (Hanover, 1700). This collection was reprinted in 1747.

His contemporaries, while complimenting Leibnitz as an investigator and praising his collection for the quantity of unpublished material that it contained, criticized its lack of homogeneity. Nevertheless, subsequent collections drew heavily from it.

Aside from the intrinsic value of Peller's *Theatrum pacis* or that of the Léonard and Leibnitz collections, these were very profitable publication ventures, arousing more than usual interest among the publishers of that era. No single collection appeared to be entirely satisfactory—the *Theatrum pacis* and the Leibnitz collection because they were too restricted, the Léonard collection because it lacked organization and was limited almost exclusively to those acts signed by the kings of France. On the other hand, there was a real need for a collection that would gather into a single large and well-organized work the vast mass of documentary material recently brought to light, not only in these collections but also in the works of an historical nature such as that of Aitzema on the United Provinces[17] or that of Guichenon on the House of Savoy;[18] in the political newspapers such as the *Mercure historique et politique* of The Hague, the *Europaische Mercurius*, and *Les Lettres Historique*; or in the numerous publications that the various sovereigns were commissioning official historians to produce in order to justify their policies or to advance their claims in the most favorable light.

Toward the end of the century, two groups of publishers from Amsterdam and The Hague conceived the idea of publishing a large new collection that would surpass all previous efforts in periods embraced and richness of materials. Jacques Bernard, a French theologian who had taken refuge in the Netherlands and who was already well known for his literary and historical work,[19] was entrusted with the task. However, the research was done, in large measure, by one of the publishers of the Hague group,

---

[17] Lieuwe van Aitzema, *Saken van staet en oorlogh in ende omtrent der Vereenigde Nederlanden beginnende met het jaer 1621* (7 vols.; The Hague, 1669–71). A French translation was published in London under the title, *Histoire civile, politique, militaire, et ecclésiastique des Provinces-Unies, et de tous les états voisins*. And, by the same author, *Historia pacis a foederatis Belgis ab anno MDCXXI ad hoc usque tempus tractatae* (18 vols.; Leyden: Elzevir, 1654).

[18] Samuel Guichenon, *Histoire généalogique de la royale maison de Savoye. Justifiée par titre, fondation de monastères, manuscripts, anciens monuments, histoires et autres preuves autentiques* (4 vols.; Lyons: Guillaume Barbier, 1660; Turin: Jean Michel Briolo, 1780). The documents are in Vols. III and IV.

[19] From 1692 to 1698 Jacques Bernard published "Les Lettres Historiques," compiled Vols. XX–XXV of the *Bibliothèque Universelle* begun by Le Clerc, and from 1699 to 1710 replaced Bayle as publisher of the *Nouvelles de la Republique des lettres*. In 1699 he published *Actes et mémoires des négociations de la paix de Ryswick* (4 vols.; The Hague: Moetjens). A second enlarged edition in five volumes appeared in 1707, and in 1727 a third edition was issued by the Van Duren publishing firm.

Moetjens, the name often used in referring to the collection ultimately published in four volumes in 1700.[20]

It comprised treaties concluded in all parts of the world, beginning in 536 A.D., and whether in the length of the period covered or in the vast quantity of material included (1,625 documents), it surpassed by far anything done previously. It was an extraordinary work, above all because of the precision with which it was done: where possible the text was reproduced in its original tongue, leaving intact the misspellings and the archaic words, and the source of each document was noted, along with an indication of the lacunae, if any. The technical format turned out to be singularly impressive: a bibliographical essay on the sources at the beginning of the compilation, a chronological table in each volume, and a subject index at the end of the last volume.

As is the case in nearly all of the collections of the period, even the *Grand Recueil* (as it was called by contemporaries) included, along with treaties as such, a certain number of other documents such as declarations of war, marriage contracts, wills, etc.; but this material, in addition to being reasonably limited, was directly pertinent to the relations between sovereigns or between states. For this reason, this collection differed markedly from those of *acta publica*.

The originality of its contribution must be judged to be modest because the *Grand Recueil* was first and foremost a compilation, a summation of the results achieved by other researchers up to that time.

Of greater importance, in this sense, is the collection published in England between 1704 and 1717 by Thomas Rymer and, after his death, by his collaborator, Robert Sanderson. Appointed royal historiographer early in 1693, some months later Rymer was directed to publish all of the treaties concluded by the kings of England with other princes and states, beginning with the year 1101. In all likelihood, the undertaking had two aims: first, to prepare a working instrument for the conduct of the foreign affairs of the state, and second, to illustrate with this monumental work the glories of the

---

[20] Jacques Bernard, *Recueil des traitez de paix, de trêve, de neutralité, de suspensions d'armes, de confédération, d'alliance, de commerce, de garantie, et d'autres actes publics, comme contracts de mariage, testaments, manifestes, declarations de guerre, etc. faits entre les empereurs, rois, républiques, princes, et autres puissances d'Europe, et des autres parties du monde; depuis la naissance de Jesus-Christ jusqu'à présent; servant à établir les droits de princes et de fondement à l'histoire. Rassemblez avec soin d'un grand nombre d'ouvrages imprimez, où ils étaient dispersez, et de divers recueils publiez ci-devant, auxquels on a ajouté plusieurs pièces, qui n'avaient jamais été imprimées. Le tout redigé par ordre chronologique, et accompagné de notes, de tables chronologiaues et alphabetiques, et des noms des auteurs dont s'est servi* (4 vols.; Amsterdam: Henry and the widow of T. Boom; The Hague: Adrian Moetjens, Henry van Bulderen, 1700).

crown, affirming at the same time the legitimacy and prestige of the new dynasty. Moreover, it assumed the role common to English historiography of that era, that is, it became an instrument of political controversy—and one of its most effective tools—in the internal struggles of the kingdom. Historical writings that found expression in the works of Burnet and in those of Clarendon, both extremely partisan and representing opposite ends of the political spectrum, had one point in common, the search for new materials on which to base their respective theses on the events of the past.

The first volume of the collection[21] appeared in 1704 and was followed by sixteen others, the last appearing in 1717. Rymer died in 1713, and his assistant, Robert Sanderson, completed the sixteenth and seventeenth volumes, which contain name and subject matter indexes for the entire collection. Sanderson continued the work, publishing three more volumes between 1726 and 1735, bringing the collection down to 1654.[22]

Certain peculiar characteristics can be ascribed to this collection. First, it differs from it predecessors in the extent and quantity of the material it embraces: and if a criticism is to be made—and contemporaries did so—it is that a uniform criterion of selection was not maintained. Various acts were inserted whose content was foreign to the interests and limits established by the compilers themselves, even if the concession is made that Rymer's purpose was to produce a collection of *acta publica* limited, in general, to the problems of primary interest to the foreign policy of the crown. Second, it must be observed that the texts of the *Foedera* offer a guarantee of accuracy which, of necessity, is lacking in the majority of the other collections of the period, whose authors, unlike Rymer, did not have the good fortune to have free access to the secret archives. Not only was Rymer able to compare the known texts with the originals, but he was also able to gather new material in a measure unequaled in any of the earlier collections. In effect, if the various collections of the period have an unofficial character, Rymer's, in contrast, can be considered to be an official

---

[21] Thomas Rymer, *Foedera, conventiones, literae, et cujuscunque generis, acta publica, inter regis Angliae, et alios quosvis imperatores, reges, pontifices, principes, vel communitates, ab ineunte saeculo duodecimo, viz. ab anno 1101, ad nostra usque tempora, habita aut tractata; ex autographis, infra secretiores archivorum regiorum thesaurarias, per multa saecula reconditis fideliter exscripta. In lucem missa de mandato reginae* (17 vols.; London: Churchill, 1704–17).

[22] The first edition was limited to 250 copies, evidence that the publication was originally intended for a very restricted reading public. A few years after publication it had become a bibliographical rarity. A second edition, revised, was published by George Holmes in 1727. In 1739 the Hague publishers began publication of a third edition, which, in ten huge volumes, incorporated the twenty volumes of the first and second editions. A number of documents were added in the third edition, and the English documents were translated into French.

one, whether because of his post or because he had the precise mandate of the crown to assemble and publish the collection.

Rymer's collection inspired the analogous but very inferior one published by Johan Christian Lünig between 1710 and 1722 in Germany.[23] This work contained acts concerning the internal affairs of the Empire, relations between member states, and relations with other states. Despite the fact that, in contrast to Rymer, Lünig did not have free access to the archives for this and his other works,[24] he did gather a conspicuous quantity of material—some unpublished—without, however, a sufficiently acute sense of criticism and following a questionable criterion of selection.

3. THE DUMONT COLLECTION AND ITS CONTINUATORS, BARBEYRAC AND ROUSSET; THE WORKS OF SAINT PREST AND LAMBERTY.

As all of this new material was being rushed into print, the Dutch publishers of the *Grand Recueil,* spurred on by the remarkable success achieved by their undertaking (the edition was exhausted in a very short time), brought out a limited collection in two volumes in 1707. It was edited by Moetjens[25] and included a selection of the more important

[23] *Das Teutsche Reichs-Archiv* (24 vols.; Leipzig, 1710–22). The collection was enlarged by Lünig with the *Codex Germaniae Diplomaticus* (2 vols.; Frankfurt and Leipzig, 1732–34). While the pertinent part of the first of these works was incorporated in the Dumont collection, the second, published after the *Corps Diplomatique,* was not exploited by Rousset in the first two volumes of the supplement to the Dumont. However, only a small part of the proceedings published by Lünig—the section concerning the hereditary lands of the Hapsburgs—could have been properly included in these supplements.

[24] See especially Lünig, *Codex Italiae diplomaticus quo non solum multifariae investiturarum literae, ab augustissimis Romanorum imperatoribus Italiae principibus et proceribus concessae atque traditae; verum etiam alia insignia varii generis diplomata, tam edita, quam multa anecdota, ipso concernentia continentur* (4 vols.; Frankfurt and Leipzig, 1725–35); Lünig, *Die teutsche Reichs-Cantzely, worinn zu finden auserlesene Briefe welche von Käysern, Königen, Chur-und Fürsten, Praelaten, Grafen und Herren, auch Rittern, Edlen und Enedlen, ingleichen freyen Republiquen, Reichs-, Cräyss-, und Land-Ständen, Geist- und Weltlichen Collegiis, der freyen Reichs-Ritterschafft, auch Reichs- und andern Städten, sowohl in frölichen als traurigen Begebenheiten, denn in Religions, Staats-, Kriegs-, Justiz-, Müntz-, Zoll-, Post-, Commercien-, und andern Sachen, seit dem Westphälischen Friedens-Schlusse de a. 1648, und zwar von Jahren zu Jahren, bis auf den zwischen Ihro Käyserl, Majestät dem Heil. Röm. Reiche und der Cron Franckreich dieses 1714. Jahr zu Rastadt praeliminariter geschlossenen und zu Baaden in der Schweitz vollends zum Stande gebrachten Frieden, in teutscher Sprache abgelassen worden* (8 vols.; Leipzig: Gledisch, 1714).

[25] *Recueil de divers traitez de paix, de confédération, d'alliance, de commerce, etc., faits depuis soixante ans, entre les rois, princes, et états souverains de l'Europe, et qui font les plus importants, les mieux choisis, et le plus convenables, au temps present* (2 vols.; The Hague: Moetjens, 1707).

documents of the *Grand Recueil,* beginning with those of 1648 and with the addition of post-1699 materials. Three years later the same Moetjens published a new collection, edited by the French scholar Jean Dumont,[26] who had also begun his work with the materials of 1648; but it differed from its predecessors in that a large body of unpublished material was added. At first Dumont, a refugee in the Netherlands at the time, had sought to interest the Amsterdam and The Hague publishing groups in a plan that he had been considering for some time: the publication of a second edition of the *Grand Recueil,* revised and enlarged by the addition of material he had been collecting personally. His proposal was ignored, and he had to be satisfied with the publication of what he had assembled.

The vast quantity of material that appeared in Rymer's volumes and, to a lesser extent, in the Lünig compilation, coupled with the success achieved by the brief Dumont collection, very soon prompted the Dutch publishers to give serious consideration to Dumont's proposal for a second edition of the *Grand Recueil.* Reaching an agreement with Dumont was not an easy matter because in the interim he had moved to Vienna, where he had been appointed official historiographer to the Emperor. Moreover, he meanwhile had developed and enlarged his original plan to contemplate a vast and systematic collection that would include treaties and public acts from the time of Charlemagne. These would "serve to establish, limit, preserve or abolish the rights of princes or of states either in reference to their dominions, their rank, and their possessions or in relation to the public constitution" of the kingdoms and of the states: a "corpus" that would embody and serve as a basis for public law, as envisaged by Grotius and patterned after the work produced by Tribonian for Roman law in the Justinian *Corpus juris civilis.*

This ambitious project did not coincide with the more limited objectives of the Dutch publishers. However, this difference of opinion on the structure of the collection was not very serious because, probably in 1716, the two parties reached an agreement that allowed Dumont's plan to take shape and form as the work progressed; convinced of the soundness of his undertaking, he was not alarmed that the work was assuming proportions far greater than those originally estimated in the contract.

The new sources that Dumont was able to tap included a large number of documents spontaneously sent to the publishers by the Royal Berlin

---

[26] *Nouveau recueil de traités d'alliance, de trêve, de paix, de garantie, et de commerce, faits et conclus entre les rois, princes, et états souverains de l'Europe, depuis la paix de Münster jusques à l'an M. DCC. IX, lesquels pour la plupart n'ont point encore été imprimés et sont très utiles pour les negotiations de la paix prochaine* (2 vols.; Amsterdam: Moetjens, 1710). It seems that Dumont may have collaborated in the preparation of the preceding collection.

Library of the King of Prussia (the library also collected manuscripts), documents he was able to collect from the archives of the United Provinces at The Hague and from the Spanish Embassy in that city, and selections from the more than one thousand documents placed at his disposal by the Archchancellor of the Empire, his immediate superior. Dumont also contacted almost every court in Europe to urge these to contribute to the collection, but the returns from this request fell far short of what he had anticipated. Nevertheless, in six years of research, he succeeded in gathering almost fifty thousand documents, from which he made a most careful selection—either in an attempt to avoid burdening the collection with material of little significance, or in order to provide only the best copies available, or, finally, to avoid including nonauthentic documents.

The results of this scholarly work were noteworthy, but Dumont, in an annotation that reveals the degree of his scientific scrupulousness, warns that he assumes responsibility only for the faithful reproduction of the text of the source indicated or that of the source which he considered to be the most accurate, but not for the authenticity of the documents themselves, particularly those which he was forced to copy from other publications in the absence of the originals.

When the collection was completed, the Dutch publishers were not satisfied with the results; they viewed it as something entirely new and not a revision of the *Grand Recueil,* and demanded that Dumont modify it. In order to preserve the essential lines of his project, Dumont undertook to divide the material into two separate collections. In the first, he assembled all of the treaties and other documents most closely identified with the relations between princes and between states, according to the general outline established by the *Grand Recueil.* The second collection, which he promised to publish subsequently, contained a preliminary section devoted to the treaties and *acta publica* of the period from Constantine to Charlemagne, a second section containing the material omitted from the first collection—material that, in general, concerned the public acts and the internal relations of the Empire—and a third section devoted to diplomatic ceremonial.

Despite the fact that this new arrangement more or less satisfied the wishes of the publishers, they insisted on other changes—primarily of a formal nature—to give the collection more of the character of a second edition of the *Grand Recueil* of 1700 rather than that of the first part of the *Corps universel diplomatique* as conceived by Dumont.

However, if the publishers were now assured of being able to offer the collection promised to and expected by the public, statesmen, historians, diplomats, and jurists, whose needs Dumont had attempted to satisfy with his work, also had at their disposal what they desired, a collection founded on a solid scientific basis.

Dumont lived to see only the first four volumes of his opus published (he died in 1727), but the material for the other four volumes that comprise the collection was already in the hands of the publishers, who, without noting the author's death, continued its publication, aided by the collaboration of the noted French publicist Jean Rousset, who was also a political refugee in the Netherlands.[27] The eight volumes cover the years 800–1730 and contain over ten thousand documents.

The importance of this collection appears obvious from what has been noted concerning the criteria employed by Dumont in its preparation: its major virtues are to be found in the disciplined method of selection, in the tremendous quantity of original documentary material presented by Dumont through his archival research, and in the critical examination of those documents appearing in earlier collections. His is the most comprehensive product of erudite historiography in the area of source study of materials pertinent to relations between states, and the value of the Dumont collection is confirmed by the fact that it is still regularly consulted by scholars.

The task of continuing Dumont's work, the publication of the material that he had, in large measure, already gathered for his second collection, or Part Two of the *Corps universel diplomatique,* was entrusted by the publishers to two individuals, Barbeyrac and Rousset.

Jean Barbeyrac, professor of law at the University of Groningen and a learned scholar of great fame, was engaged to develop the preliminary section originally planned by Dumont to deal with the pre-Charlemagne

---

[27] Jean Dumont, *Corps universel diplomatique du droit des gens; contenant un recueil des traités d'alliance, de paix, de trêve, de neutralité, de commerce, d'échange, de protection et de garantie, de toutes les conventions, transactions, pactes, concordats, et autres contrats, qui ont été faits en Europe, dépuis le regne de l'Empereur Charlemagne jusques à présent; avec les capitulations impériales et royales; les sentences arbitrales et souveraines dans les causes importantes; les déclarations de guerre, les contrats de mariage des grands princes, leurs testaments, donations, renonciations, et protestations; les investitures des grands fiefs; les erections des grandes dignités, celles des grandes compagnies de commerce, et en général de tous les titres, sous quelque nom qu'on les désigne, qui peuvent servir à fonder, établir, ou justifier les droits et les intérêts des princes et états de l'Europe; le tout tiré en partie des archives de la très auguste Maison d'Austriche et en partie de celles de quelques autres princes et états; comme aussi des protocolles de quelques grands ministres; des manuscrits de la Bibliothèque Royale de Berlin; des meilleures collections, qui ont déja paru tant en Allemagne, qu'en France, en Angleterre, en Hollande, et ailleurs; sur tout des Actes de Rymer; et enfin les plus estimés, soit en histoire, en politique, ou en droit* (8 vols.; Amsterdam: P. Brunel, R. and G. Wetstein, les Janssons Waesberge et l'Honoré et Chatelain; The Hague: chez P. Husson and Charles Levier, 1726–31).

period. He decided that the best results could be obtained by going well beyond the age of Constantine, as planned by Dumont, back to the point in time where history could first be distinguished from legend, in order to present a more complete picture of the creation and development of the norms governing coexistence among politically organized civilized groups.[28]

The increase in the chronological compass of the project required that certain corrections be made in the criteria established for the composition of the work. If one went back beyond a certain point in time, one could seldom find the complete text of a treaty or other act fundamental to the rapport between states, empires, or political communities, and thus the task of compiling a collection of documents of the same genre as that of a more recent period was rendered well-nigh impossible. Research usually uncovered summaries of treaties or other acts, perhaps only a few clauses or parts of these, or even mere references to these fragments in the works of the Greek and Latin writers, or on inscriptions, monuments, etc. Therefore, Barbeyrac structured his volume on the basis of brief and separate narratives (which he defined as "articles"), presented in chronological order, in which, in addition to what he had found of each treaty or act, he sought to provide its history; that is, he attempted to "explain the occasion, motives, circumstances, consequences, in a word, to include everything that appeared to be necessary or useful to the understanding" of the document. Observing this procedure, "this work may be considered in some ways to be a kind of universal history based on treaties," adds Barbeyrac. There is little that is new in the volume that covers the period 1496 B.C.–813 A.D., but it is important, nonetheless, as a first offering of extremely fragmentary and diverse materials appropriately annotated and carefully organized into one organic whole.

The task of preparing the second volume for publication was considerably easier for Rousset because the material left by Dumont, although poorly organized—Dumont was engaged in the last phases of his research at the time of his death—was copious and very nearly complete. Rousset had only to make a few additions, eliminate a certain number of acts having too restricted a nature, provide the over-all organization, and update the collection to 1739. As soon as the editorial work was completed, the

---

[28] Jean Barbeyrac, *Histoire des anciens traitez ou Recueil historique et chronologique des traités répandus dans les auteurs Grecs et Latins, et autres monuments de l'antiquité, depuis les tems les plus reculez jusques à l'empereur Charlemagne* (Amsterdam: chez les Janssons à Waesberge, Wetstein and Smith, and Z. Chatelain; The Hague: chez P. de Hondt, the widow of Ch. Le Vier, and J. Neaulme, 1739). Barbeyrac's work constitutes the first supplemental volume to the Dumont.

volumes appeared in print.[29] A group of collaborating experts added a general alphabetical Table of Contents for Dumont's eight volumes, as well as for the two volumes printed under Rousset's direction.

The section dedicated to diplomatic ceremonials was ultimately included in parts four and five of the supplement.[30] However, Rousset modified Dumont's original plan on this point. The latter had proposed to follow the practice established for the other volumes, in this instance, to assemble all of the documents pertinent to the diplomatic ceremonials in effect at the courts of Europe and to publish them in chronological order. Instead, Rousset preferred to group the documents by courts or by states to which reference was made and to add completely new data, such as that on the ceremonial at the Sardinian court, so as to present a complete picture of the practices in effect in each country. This was a change that produced something of greater practical value, despite the fact that it modified the nature of the work to the extent of giving a quasi-descriptive form to the straightforward collection of acts that it was originally intended to be.

Two other publications are normally considered to be complementary to the Dumont collection, even though they have substantially different characteristics from those of the latter. The first of these comprises in four volumes important documentary materials—instructions, negotiators' dispatches, letters, etc.—on the negotiations that preceded the Peace of Münster and the Treaty of Osnabruck.[31] We are not concerned in this case with a collection of treaties or *acta publica* but with a collection of

[29] Jean Rousset, *Supplément au Corps universel diplomatique du droit des gens, contenant un recueil des traitéz d'alliance, de paix, de trêve, de neutralité, de commerce, d'échange, de protection et de garantie, de toutes les conventions, transactions, pactes, concordats, et autres contracts, capitulations impériales et royales, donations, renonciations, protestations, testaments, investitures, et en général de tous les titres, sous quelque nom qu'on les désigne, qui ont échapé aux premmières recherchez de Mr. Du Mont. Continué jusqu'à présent* (2 vols.; Amsterdam: chez les Janssons à Waesberge, Wetstein and Smith, and Z. Chatelain; The Hague: chez P. de Hondt, the niece of Ch. Le Vier, and J. Neaulme, 1739). These two volumes constitute the second and third supplements to the Dumont.

[30] Jean Dumont and Jean Rousset, *Le cérémonial diplomatique des cours d'Europe, ou collection des actes, mémoires, et relations qui concernent les dignités, titulaires, honneurs, et prééminences; les fonctions publiques des souverains, leurs sacres, couronnemens, mariages, batêmes, et enterremens; les investitures des grands fiefs; les entrées publiques, audiences, fonctions, immunités, et franchises des ambassadeurs et autres ministres publics; leurs disputes et démêles de préséance; et en général tout ce qui a rapport au cérémonial et à l'etiquette* (2 vols.; Amsterdam: chez les Janssons à Waesberge, Wetstein and Smith, and Z. Chatelain; The Hague: chez P. de Hondt, the widow of Ch. Le Vier, and J. Neaulme, 1739).

[31] *Négociations secrètes touchant la paix de Münster et d'Osnaburg; ou Recueil général des preliminaires, instructions, lettres, mémoires, etc., concernant ces négociations, depuis leur commencement en 1642, jusqu'à leur conclusion en 1648. Avec les depêches de Mr. de Vautorte, et autres pièces au sujet du même traité jusqu'en 1654 inclusivement* (4 vols.; The Hague: L. Neaulme, 1725–26).

diplomatic sources of various types, which are of great value for the study of the international relations of that era.

The second source, published in 1725 by Jean Yves de Saint Prest[32] and presented as an introduction to the Dumont collection, is in reality, a history of peace pacts of the seventeenth century down to Nijmegen, based on treaties.

Its distinguishing characteristic lies in the fact that the texts of the treaties are not cited *in toto* but are summarized and are preceded by an historical account of the negotiations, a very common practice in the first half of the eighteenth century and one that was to be widely imitated. The work is divided by geographical sectors, and, within these limits, by states. The titles of sovereigns are listed, followed by an account of their origins. The pattern clearly reveals the purpose for which it was undertaken. The reasons which induced Saint Prest to circumscribe his treatment of the more recent period, limiting himself to noting the preceding treaties only when reference was made to them or when they proved to be indispensable to the clarification of later accords, were obviously practical ones—the author himself declares that he has attempted to provide a work useful to "public ministers and other negotiators."

A formulation analogous in certain respects to Saint Prest's is found in the well-known work of Guillaume de Lamberty,[33] where documents of various kinds and of varying degrees of importance for the period 1690–1718 are assembled, with frequent references to problems of an internal character, juridical questions, ceremonials, etc. Similar, also, is the equally famous work of Jean Rousset,[34] the author of the two supplemental volumes to the Dumont collection, who, in twenty-three volumes in twelve

[32] *Histoire des traités de paix et autres negotiations du dix-septième siècle, depuis la paix de Vervins jusqu'à la paix de Nimegue: où l'on donne l'origine des prétentions anciennes et modernes de toutes les puissances de l'Europe, et une analyse exacte de leur negotiations, tant publiques que particuliers* (2 vols.; Amsterdam: J. F. Bernard; The Hague: frères Vaillant and Prevost, 1725). The appendix includes: "Histoire des traités de Westphalie"; "Histoire des traités de paix faits par le Roi depuis ceux de Westphalie" (incorporates the negotiations conducted by De Lionne in Madrid leading to the Treaty of the Pyrénées in 1656); "Histoire des traités de paix entre Louis XIII et XIV et Charles IV de Lorraine depuis 1630 jusqu'en 1663."

[33] *Mémoires pour servir à l'histoire du XVIII siècle, contenant les négociations traités, résolutions, et autres documents authentiques concernant les affaires d'etat; liés par une narration historique des principaux événements dont ils ont été précédés ou suivis, et particulièrement de ce qui s'est passé à la Häie, qui a toujours été comme le centre de toutes ces négociations* (14 vols.; The Hague: Henri Scheurleer [Vols. I–X]; Amsterdam: Pierre Mortier [Vols. XI–XIV], 1724–40).

[34] *Recueil historique d'actes, négociations, memoires, et traités, depuis la paix d'Utrecht jusqu'au second congrès de Cambray inclusivement* (23 vols.; The Hague, Amsterdam, Leipzig: Henri Scheurleer, Pierre Gosse, Meynard Uytwerf, Arkstée & Merkus, 1728–55). Beginning with the twenty-first volume the last words of the title are changed to *jusqu'à celle d'Aix la Chapelle.*

tomes, has traced, through documents, a history of the relations between the sovereigns of Europe in the period between the Treaty of Utrecht of 1713 and the Treaty of Aix-la-Chapelle of 1748. Even the selection criteria used by Rousset may be open to question, especially with regard to the material included in the last volumes, where a number of documents relating to German internal affairs are to be found. Nevertheless, his work merits the attention of scholars, not so much for the value of the documentary material it contains, but rather for the effort of the compiler to provide a logical and coherent pattern for the apparently contradictory policies of the Great Powers and of the principal instigators of their actions.

4. THE POST-DUMONT EIGHTEENTH-CENTURY COLLECTIONS: ABREU Y BERTODANO, WENCK, MARTENS.

Dumont's contribution marks one of the several high points in the history of the publication of treaty collections. After his, no other general collection appeared for a long time. There was the conviction that Dumont's work could not be surpassed and that, in any event, the lacunae in his work were not such as to warrant another equally imposing publishing effort. Furthermore, public interest was shifting towards the issues dear to the culture of the Enlightenment, and the historiography of the second half of the eighteenth century, which regarded past events merely as instruments for polemics, was not particularly concerned with a critical evaluation of the sources because ascertaining historical truth, the principal objective of the erudite school, did not interest historians of the Enlightenment.

With Dumont, the heyday of treaty collections comes to a close, a trend that found its finest expression in the *Corps universel*. Collectors' interests now take a different turn. For all practical purposes, the succeeding collections may be grouped according to three concepts: (a) special collections relating to single states, (b) summaries or outline manuals to provide the reader with less expensive and more manageable works than Dumont's, and (c) chronological continuations of Dumont's volumes.

Among the specific collections devoted to a single country, perhaps the most important is the one commissioned by Philip V and directed by the Spanish scholar Abreu y Bertodano. After the volumes edited by Chifflet for the Spanish plenipotentiaries at Münster, no other publication of its kind had appeared in Spain. At the turn of the eighteenth century, the Marquis de Santa-Cruz had initiated a project to gather materials for a collection of treaties concluded between the Spanish crown and other

European powers, but the work was interrupted by his death. Perhaps by the use of this material and a considerable expansion of the chronological limits, Abreu assembled a collection[35] that was intended to serve to illustrate the glories of Spain from the time the Phoenicians reached Spanish soil. However, practical requirements subsequently dictated a reduction of the scope. More precisely, publication was to begin with 1598, with Abreu reserving the right to return to the earlier period at a later date. Thus, between 1740 and 1752 twelve volumes were published embracing the reigns of Philip III (1598–1621), Philip IV (1621–65), and Charles II (1665–1700), along with a general Table of Contents at the end of the collection. Abreu's official position did not preclude his acquiring materials from sources other than the crown's archives. In the main, these were garnered from earlier collections, and only rarely is there a noteworthy contribution to an already known text. Yet Abreu's original contribution remains of some significance, even if it is much less than what might have been expected from an official collection.

Nearly half a century later, Charles IV took the initiative in adding to Abreu's collection. This resulted in the publication of a three-volume compilation of the treaties of Spain with other countries for the period 1701–1801,[36] with the style and format similar to the Abreu volumes and the criteria employed almost identical.

---

[35] José Antonio de Abreu y Bertodano, *Colección de tratados de paz, alianza, neutralidad, garantía, protección, tregua, mediacción, accesión, reglamento de límites, commercio, navegatión &c. hechos por los pueblos, reyes, y principes de España con los pueblos, reyes, principes, repúblicas, y demás potencias de Europa, y otros partes del mundo; y entre si mismos, y con sus respectivos adversarios: y juntamente de los hechos directa, o indirectamente contra ella, desde antes del establicimiento de la monarchia Gothica, hasta el feliz reynado del rey N.S.D. Phelipe V. En la qual se comprehenden otros muchos actos públicos y reales concernientes al mismo asunto, como declaraciones de guerra, retos, manifiestos, protestas, prohibiciones, y permissiones de comercio, cartes de creencia, plenipotencias, &c. y assimismo ventas, compras, donaciones, pérmutas, empeños, renuncias, transacciones, compromissos, sentencias arbitrarias, envestiduras, homenages, concordatos, contratos matrimoniales emancipaciones, adopciones, naturalizaciones, testamentos reales, &c. y las bulas, y breves, y breves pontificios, que conceden algun derecho, privilegio, ó preeminencia à la corona de España: con las erecciones de las compañias, assientos, y reglamentos de comercio en las Indias orientales, y occidentales, &c. Fielmente sacados le los originales, ó copias autenticas de la secretaria de estado, archivo de Simancas, y demás archivos, y libererias reales, y particulares como también de libros, y papeles impressos; dispuestos en orden chronológico, y por reynados, y traducidos en castellano los que se hicieron en otros idiomas* (12 vols.; Madrid: Diego Peralta, Antonio Marin, y Juan de Zuñiga, 1740–52).

[36] Antonio de Capmany y de Montpalau, *Colección de los tratados de paz, alianza, comercio, &c., ajustados por la corona de España con las potenzias extrangeras desde el reynado del Señor Don Felipe Quinto hasta el presente* (3 vols.; Madrid: Imprenta Real, 1796–1801).

The collection edited by Mathias Dogiel for the treaties concluded by Poland[37] also has an historical character. The project was initially planned as eight volumes in which the material was to be organized by countries involved in the pacts, but only the first, fourth, and fifth volumes[38] appeared between 1759 and 1764. In its incomplete state it has real value only for the earlier period. Despite area restriction, it includes a significant number of documents that do not appear in the Dumont collection or in Rousset's supplements. It should also be noted that the Dogiel collection, in addition to treaties, contains a number of other documents—the collectors based their efforts on Rymer's experience—making it a collection of *acta publica*.[39]

A different approach is to be found in many special collections that appeared in the second half of the eighteenth century and with increasing frequency toward the close of the century. They focus on the more recent period and have much more restricted chronological limits, an observation that leads to the conclusion that the political aims they were meant to serve were more important than the goals of historical research.

Of particular note are those published in the northern European states because it is in this area that the Dumont and other collections showed the most serious omissions. Among these, the one for the treaties signed by Sweden, edited by Modée and published after his death in 1761,[40] merits

---

[37] *Codex diplomaticus regni Poloniae et magni ducatus Lituaniae, in quo pacta, foedera, tractatus pacis, mutuae amicitiae, subsidiorum, induciarum, commerciorum, nec non conventiones, pactiones, concordata, transactiones, declarationes, statuta, ordinationes, bullae, edicta, rescripta, sententiae arbitrales, infeudationes, homagia, pacta etiam matrimonialia et dotalia, literae item reversales, concessionum, libertatis, immunitatis, donationum, oppignorationum, renuntiationum, erectionum, obligationum, emptionum, permutationum, cessionum, protestationum, aliaque omnis generis publico nomine actorum et gestorum monumenta, nunc primum ex archivis publicis eruta ac in lucem protracta exhibentur* (3 vols.; Vilna: ex Typographia regia et Reipublicae Collegii C.C.R.R. Scholarum Piarum, 1758–64).

[38] These volumes refer to the following countries: Vol. I: Bohemia, Hungary, Austria, Denmark, Bavaria, Brandenburg, Republic of Venice, Saxony, France, Brunswick, Holland, Transylvania, Silesia, Pomerania, Moldavia, Wallachia; Vol. IV: Prussia; Vol. V: Livonia.

[39] A number of treaties concluded by Poland may be found in *Constitutiones Poloniae seu Prawa Konstytucye y Przwilcie Krolestwa Polskiego y Wielkiego Kiestwa Litewskiego y wszystkich Prowincyi* (8 vols.; Warsaw, 1732–90), concerning the period 1347–1780. There is a small collection comprising the treaties concluded between 1618–1775. However, in this compilation only briefs or extracts of the treaties are published: Sacek Jeziersky, *Traktaty Polskie z sasiednemi mocartstwy zawarte od Roku 1618* (Warsaw, 1789).

[40] Gustaf Reinh Modée, *Utdrag af de emellan hans konglige Majestaet och cronan Sverige a ena, och utrikes magter a andra sidan sedan ar 1718 (intil 1751) slutne alliance-tractater och afhandlingar* (Stockholm: Gresing, 1761).

special mention. Although limited to only thirty-five years (1718–53), it contains a great deal of new material. The Danish collection published in 1796 by Clausen[41] is definitely unofficial in character. Thanks to the patronage he enjoyed, the author was in a position to draw from primary sources and to include many unpublished documents, even if for political reasons he could not make public a number of treaties, such as those with Russia of 1769 and 1773. But, like the preceding one, it remains extremely limited chronologically—it covers only the period 1766–94 and cannot, therefore, fill the gaps that exist for the earlier period. New material of minor importance is found in the collection published at Warsaw in 1791.[42] It embraces the treaties signed by Poland between 1764 and 1791, some in Latin and others in French.

A second category of collections that gained in popularity after the appearance of the Dumont was what was referred to as "manuals of treaties." Normally, they were collections of a general nature, containing only the most important acts. Without doubt the most noteworthy of these is the one published by Schmauss in 1730,[43] when the Dumont collection was still in press. It begins with the year 1096 but it is only with the sixteenth-century documents that the work acquires any real consistency: the oldest treaties are presented only in summary, that is, only the principal articles are printed in their entirety. The more recent documents—the collection includes those of the Congress of Soissons—are faithfully reproduced except for the ratifications and the full-power clauses. In its entirety, the work includes 418 documents, among these a certain number of treaties that do not appear in the Dumont or in the Rousset supplement, illustrative of the fact that this is not an ordinary compilation.

A much inferior work is the three-volume collection appearing anonymously in Warsaw in 1774 and comprising the treaties concluded between

[41] Heinrich Friedrich Christian Clausen, *Recueil des tous les traités, conventions, mémoires, et notes conclus et publiés par la couronne de Dannemarc depuis l'avénément au throne du roi régnant jusqu'à l'époque actuelle, ou dés l'année 1766 jusqu'en 1794 inclusive* (Berlin: Jean Frédéric Unger, 1796).

[42] Daniel Gralath, *Traktaty, konwencye, handlowe y graniczke, wszelkie publiczne, umowy, miedzi rzeczapospolita Polska y obcemi panstwami ad Roku 1764 dotad to jest do roku 1791 za panowaria Stanislawa Augusta Zawarle swych oryginal nich iezykach zebrane i ella wygody powszechny podane do drucka* (2 vols.; Warsaw, 1791).

[43] Johann Jacob Schmauss, *Corpus juris gentium academicum, enthaltend die vornehmsten Grund-Gesetze, Friedens- und Commercien-Tractate, Bündnüsse und andere Pacta der Königreiche, Republiquen, und Staaten von Europa, welche seither zweyen Seculis biss auf den gegenwärtigen Congress zu Soissons errichtet worden* (2 vols.; Leipzig: John Friedrich Gleditschens seel. Sohn, 1730).

1648 and 1763.[44] The texts of the documents are almost always in extract form, but a few are reported in their entirety, among them the Russo-Polish treaty of 1786, which is one of the altogether new elements in the collection. Another Polish collection, one published by Jeziersky,[45] has the same format as that noted above. Although it covers a longer period (1618–1775), it is limited to the treaties signed by Poland. La Maillardière's manual has very little value[46] and bears mention here only because it is a good example of the type of publication that frequently appeared in the second half of the eighteenth century. It is simply a summary of the texts of selected documents, and therefore cannot be utilized in a scientific study.

A third type of collection of the 1700's, appearing after Dumont's, is made up of the works complementing the *Corps universel* and is best represented by the works of Wenck and Martens. The Wenck collection[47] in three volumes is, without doubt, a notable production and includes the treaties signed between 1735 and 1772. The fact that nearly half a century had elapsed before something was done to update the *Corps universel* seems to indicate the lack of interest in this type of publication among both scholars and the public. The Wenck collection seems to support this contention, its general character notwithstanding, in that the tendency to publish only the most recent documents is clearly evident, a tendency that became commonplace toward the end of the century.

Wenck was proceeding at a snail's pace with the publication of his collection—ten years were to elapse between the publication of the first and second volumes. The delay induced Georg Friedrich Von Martens, professor at the University of Göttingen, to assume the task of providing a supplement to the Dumont and to Wenck's own collection. In order to avoid interfering with Wenck, who had announced the publication of the third volume of his opus as imminent, Martens began his collection with the preliminaries to the Peace of Fontainebleau (November, 1762), leading to the termination of the Seven Years' War—which he introduced with the text of the Family Compact of 1761—and in a very short time he

[44] *Traktaty miedzy mocarswami Europeyskiemi od roku 1648 Zaszle do roku 1763 Podlug lat porzadku z przymaczona potrzebney historyi wiadomoscia opisane* (3 vols.; Warsaw, 1774).

[45] See p. 68, n. 39.

[46] Charles François Lefèvre de la Maillardière, *Abrégé des principaux traités conclus depuis le commencement du quatorzième siècle jusqu'à présent entre les différentes puissances de l'Europe, disposés par ordre chronologique* (2 vols.; Paris: the widow Duchesne and Valade, 1778). A new edition appeared in 1783.

[47] Friedrich August Wilhelm Wenck, *Codex juris gentium recentissimi, et tabulariorum exemplorumque fide dignorum monumentis compositus* (3 vols.; Leipzig: apud. haer. Weidmann. and Reich, 1781–95).

published four volumes comprising pertinent data up to 1790 and another three volumes that completed the collection up to the Peace of Lunéville of 1801.[48]

Meanwhile, he continued to gather material on the preceding period that for various reasons had failed to find a place in the Dumont, the Rousset supplements, or the Wenck collection. Martens included this documentation in the first volume of a four-volume supplement that completed his collection up to and including 1807.[49] His last effort was the preparation of a second edition,[50] which involved a reorganization of all of the documents he had assembled in his collection, excluding those relating to the period prior to 1761, as well as a complete reclassification of the treaties in proper chronological order, which order had been upset by the supplements.

The Martens collection is the last great private general collection. To the author goes the merit of having continued the work of Dumont and Wenck. Martens was favored by the considerable assistance furnished him by his university; that is, unlike Dumont, he was able to avoid the necessity of depending on the patronage of the powerful publishing groups of Amsterdam and The Hague and did not receive an official appointment, such as was held by Rymer. On the other hand, the limitations of the collection may also be traced to this factor. Martens was forced to limit the scope of his work for financial reasons, and, most important of all, he was restricted to publishing only those documents that had been made public by the various governments, without being able to collate the texts with the originals because, as a private individual, he had no right of access to them. From all this it is evident that the Martens collection cannot offer an original contribution comparable to that found in previous publications.

[48] *Recueil des principaux traités d'alliance, de paix, de trêve, de neutralité, de commerce, de limites, d'échange, etc., conclus par les puissances de l'Europe tant entre elles qu'avec les puissances et états dans d'autres parties du monde depuis 1761 jusqu'à présent. Tiré des copies publiés par autorité, des meilleures collections particulières de traités, et des auteurs les plus estimés* (7 vols.; Göttingen: Jean Chrétien Dieterich, 1791–1801).

[49] *Supplément au Recueil des principaux traités d'alliance, de paix, de trêve, de neutralité, de commerce, de limites, d'échange, etc., conclus par les puissances de l'Europe tant entre elles qu'avec les puissances et états dans d'autres parties du monde dupuis 1761 jusqu'à présent. Précédé de traités du XVIIIème siècle antérieurs à cette époque et qui ne se trouvent pas dans le Corps universel diplomatique de Mrs. Du Mont et Rousset et autres recueils généraux de traités* (4 vols.; Göttingen: Henri Dieterich, 1802–8).

[50] *Recueil de traités d'alliance, de paix, de trêve, de neutralité, de commerce, de limites, d'échange, etc., et plusieurs autres actes servant à la connaissance des relations étrangères des puissances et états de l'Europe tant dans leur rapport mutuel que dans celui envers les puissances et états dans d'autres parties du globe, depuis 1761 jusqu'à présent. 2e édition revue et augmentée* (8 vols.; Göttingen: Dieterich, 1817–35). The last four volumes were edited by Karl Martens.

Nevertheless, despite the ground gained by the official publications, the Martens series is still widely consulted by scholars both in the original volumes and in the various supplements that have since appeared, edited by Martens' heirs and others.

Un Nouveau Recueil de traités[51] was published in sixteen volumes between 1817 and 1842 and comprised the treaties concluded in the period 1808–39. At the same time Murhard[52] published three volumes of *Nouveaux Suppléments,* in which are to be found those post-1761 treaties that Martens had omitted from his initial collection. Hitherto unpublished treaties and public acts dating from 1559 are included in the appendixes. This work is supplemented, in turn, by a *Nouveau Recueil général*[53] in twenty volumes, published between 1843 and 1875 and covering the years 1840–74, and by a second *Nouveau Recueil général*[54] in thirty-five volumes, for the years 1876–1908. A third *recueil* begun in 1909[55] brought the collection up to 1942.

The consultation of a work of such magnitude is certainly not easy because the compilers have often not been able to place the treaties in exact chronological order—the case, for example, with those treaties whose texts had to remain secret. Tables of Contents, published from time to time,[56] help to make up for this difficulty, but unfortunately they do not

[51] *Un Nouveau Recueil de traités d'alliance, de paix, de trêve, de neutralité, de commerce, de limites, d'échange, etc., et plusieurs autres actes servant à la connaissance des relations étrangères des puissance et états de l'Europe tant dans leur rapport mutuel que dans celui envers les puissances et états dans d'autres parties du globe depuis 1808 jusqu'à present* (16 vols.; Göttingen: Dieterich, 1817–42).
[52] Friedrich Wilhelm August Murhard, *Nouveaux suppléments au Recueil de traités et d'autres actes remarquables, servant à la connaissance des relations étrangères des puissances et états dans leur rapport mutuel, depuis 1761 jusqu'à présent, fondé par George Frédéric de Martens. Suivi d'un appendice contenant des traités et actes publics importants d'une date antérieure* (3 vols.; Göttingen: Dieterich, 1839–42).
[53] *Nouveau Recueil général de traités, conventions, et autres transactions remarquables, servant à la connaissance des relations étrangères des puissances et états dans leurs rapports mutuels* (20 vols.; Göttingen: Dieterich, 1843–75).
[54] *Nouveau Recueil général de traités et autres actes relatifs aux rapports de droit international. Continuation du grand recueil de G. Fr. de Martens. Deuxième série* (35 vols.; Göttingen: Dieterich, 1876–1908).
[55] Heinrich Triepel, *Nouveau recueil général de traités et autres actes relatifs aux rapports de droit international. Continuation du grand recueil de G. Fr. de Martens. Troisième série* (Leipzig: Dieterich, 1909–42).
[56] *Table général chronologique et alphabétique du Recueil des traités, conventions, et transactions des puissances de l'Europe et d'autres parties du globe, servant à la connaissance des relations étrangères des états dans leur rapport mutuel. Commencé par Geo. Fr. de Martens et continué jusqu'à nos jours* (2 vols.; Göttingen: Dieterich, 1837–42). This table includes the material incorporated in the second edition edited by G. F. Martens, in the *Nouveau Recueil* to 1839, and in the *Nouveaux suppléments* edited by Murhard. It is divided into two parts, one chronological and one alphabetical. Much more detailed is the table prepared by

exist for all of the volumes. Two small collections containing the principal treaties were published, covering, however, only the years 1761–1885.[57]

5. THE PRIVATE COLLECTIONS OF THE NINETEENTH AND TWENTIETH CENTURIES.

In addition to being the most important, the Martens is also the last of the great general collections. With the spread of constitutional governments, treaty collections increasingly have become state enterprises, and private collections, by and large, tend to be restricted to specific subjects or to specific historical periods.

Among the many nineteenth-century private collections, the one edited by Carlos Calvo[58] for Latin America from 1493–1823 is worthy of special note. The sixteen-volume collection was published between 1862 and 1868 (the documentation is not restricted to treaties) and is especially rich in data pertinent to the revolutionary and early independence periods in Latin American history.

The collection of treaties negotiated by the Ottoman Empire from 1536 (treaty of alliance and commerce between Suleiman the Magnificent and Francis I) to 1910, begun by Ignatz von Testa and continued by his sons,[59] is a particularly significant one. It varies from the usual format in

---

Julius Hopf, *Table général du Recueil des traités de G. F. Martens et de ses continuateurs. 1494–1874.* (Ière éd.), 7 volumes; *Suppléments,* 4 volumes; *Recueil* (2ème éd.), 8 volumes; *Nouveau recueil,* 16 volumes, *Nouveaux suppléments,* 3 volumes; *Nouveau recueil général,* 20 volumes (2 vols.; Göttingen: Dieterich, 1875–76).

[57] Karl von Martens and Ferdinand de Cussy, *Recueil manuel et pratique de traités, conventions, et autres actes diplomatiques, sur lesquels sont établis les relations et les rapports existant aujourd'hui entre les divers états souverains du globe, depuis l'année 1760 jusqu'à l'époque actuelle* (7 vols.; Leipzig: F. A. Brockhaus, 1846–57); Friedrich Heinrich Geffcken, *Recueil manuel et pratique de traités. Deuxième série* (3 vols.; Leipzig: F. A. Brockhaus, 1885–88)

[58] *Recueil complet des traités, conventions, capitulations, armistices, et autres actes diplomatiques de tous les états de l'Amérique latine compris entre la golfe du Mexique et le cap de Horn, depuis l'année 1493 jusqu'à nos jours, précédé d'un mémoire sur l'état actuel de l'Amérique, de tableaux statistiques, d'un dictionnaire diplomatique, avec une notice historique sur chaque traité important* (11 vols.; Paris: Librairie de A. Durand, 1862–68). Calvo, *Amérique latine. Recueil historique complet des traités, conventions, capitulations, armistices, questions de limites, et autres actes diplomatiques de tous les états* (*Annales historiques de la révolution de l'Amérique latine, accompagnées de documents à l'appui. De l'année 1808 jusqu'à la reconnaissance par les états européens de l'indépendance de ce vaste continent*) (5 vols.; Paris: Librairie Espagnole de Mme. Denné-Schmitz, 1864–67).

[59] Ignatz von Testa, *Recueil des traités de la Porte Ottomane avec les puissances étrangères depuis le premier traité conclu, en 1536, entre Suléyman I et François I jusqu'à nos jours* (11 vols.; Paris: Amyot, Muzard, Ernest Leroux,

that the texts of the treaties are followed by a selection of documents pertinent to the diplomatic negotiations leading to the accords. Like the preceding collection, it is unusually large, especially for this period, for a private collection that is limited in subject matter and areas of interest.

Two collections of documents designed to provide the antecedents to problems of major importance at the time of publication were produced in France, the first in 1859 and the second in 1862, by the refugee Polish scholar Leonard Borejko Chodzko, writing under the pseudonym of Count d'Angeberg. The first collection concerned Austro-Italian relations beginning in 1703,[60] the second, the treaties, from 1762 on, concluded by Poland or having to do with Polish territory.[61] These collections are reasonably large and comprise various kinds of texts, such as speeches and declarations, whose inclusion was obviously dictated by criteria of a polemical nature and which therefore are not always of great interest from the historical point of view.

A rather large Italian collection was edited by Count Luigi Palma[62] in the years 1879–90 and published in three volumes; it embraced the treaties and conventions then in force between Italy and other states.

The two collections published by Edward Hertslet have somewhat unique characteristics. The first of these[63] seeks to account for the territorial changes in Europe in the period 1815–91 through the texts of treaties and other international accords. However, the documentation is not always restricted to the subject suggested by the title because declarations of war, treaties of guarantee, declarations of neutrality, and, in the last volume (1876–91), official declarations and diplomatic documents are to be found here. The second collection[64] concerns Africa and traces the territorial changes from the Hispano-Portuguese treaty of March, 1878 (the cession

---

1864–1911). For the Ottoman Empire treaties, see also Gabriel Effendi Noradounghian, *Recueil d'actes internationaux de l'Empire Ottoman. Traités, conventions, arrangements, déclarations, protocoles, procès-verbaux, firmans, bérats, lettres patentes, et autres documents relatifs au droit public extérieur de la Turquie* (4 vols.; Paris, Librairie Cotillon, F. Pichon, Successeur; Leipzig, Breitkoff and Haertel; Neuchâtel, Attinger Frères, 1897–1903).

[60] Comte d'Angeberg, *Recueil des traités, conventions, et actes diplomatiques concernant l'Autriche dans ses rapports avec l'Italie, depuis 1703 jusqu'en 1859* (Paris: Amyot, 1859).

[61] Comte d'Angeberg, *Recueil des traités, conventions, et actes diplomatiques concernant la Pologne, 1762–1862* (Paris: Amyot, 1862).

[62] Luigi Palma di Cesnola, *Trattati e convenzioni fra il Regno d'Italia ed i governi esteri* (3 vols.; Turin: Unione tipografico-editrice, 1879–90).

[63] *The Map of Europe by Treaty; Showing the Various Political and Territorial Changes since the General Peace of 1814* (4 vols.; London: Her Majesty's Stationery Office, 1875–91).

[64] *The Map of Africa by Treaty* (3 vols.; London: Her Majesty's Stationery Office, 1895); 2d rev. ed., 1896; 3d ed., rev. and enlarged, 1909.

of Fernando Po) down to 1909. The data in the first compilation are organized chronologically (with subject indexes at the end of the third and fourth volumes); the second is organized by states (with the addition of a chronological index). Hertslet's contribution is especially important for those acts subscribed to by Great Britain because the author, who was employed in the archives of the Foreign Office, was able to see the originals. Particular attention should be paid to the many little maps reproduced from those attached to official acts and incorporated into the collection.

In Italy, Amedeo Giannini edited significant collections of treaties and documents dealing primarily with eastern Europe and the Balkans.[65] More recently, interesting documents have appeared in a collection of treaties and other agreements concluded by the Soviet Union between 1917 and 1939, edited by Leonard Schapiro.[66]

For the post-World War I period, despite the updating of the Martens collection and the appearance of the League of Nations series (see below), the best general collection of political treaties by far is the one edited by Gretschaninow under the general editorship of Viktor Bruns.[67] The collection was designed to provide scholars with a convenient reference source and includes all European and non-European alliance treaties, treaties of guarantee, friendship, nonaggression, etc., beginning with the Treaty of Versailles (the first document is the Anglo-French treaty of guarantee of June 28, 1919). Other pertinent documents are incorporated, such as official declarations, communications, and speeches, that serve to

[65] *Trattati ed accordi per l'Europa danubiana* (Rome: Edizioni di politica, 1923); 2d ed.: *Trattati ed accordi per l'Europa danubiana e balcanica* (Rome: Istituto per l'Europa Orientale, 1936). *Trattati ed accordi per la pace adriatica* (Rome: Edizioni di politica, 1924); 2d ed.: *Documenti per la storia dei rapporti fra l'Italia e la Jugoslavia* (Rome: Istituto per l'Europa Orientale, 1934). *Trattati ed accordi per la pace con la Germania, 1918–1924* (Rome: Edizioni di politica, 1929). *Trattati ed accordi per l'Europa Orientale* (Rome: Istituto per l'Europa Orientale, 1934). *Documenti per la storia della pace orientale, 1913–1934* (Rome: Istituto per l'Oriente, 1934).

[66] *Soviet Treaties Series. A Collection of Bilateral Treaties, Agreements and Conventions, etc., Concluded between the Soviet Union and Foreign Powers* (2 vols.; Washington, D.C.: The Georgetown University Press, 1950–55).

[67] Viktor Bruns, *Politische Verträge. Sine Summlung von Urkunden* (*Traité politiques. Recueil de Documents*), tome I: *Garantiepakte, Bündisse, Abkommen über politische Zusammenarbeit, Nichtangriffs-und Neutralitätsverträge der Nachkriegszeit* (*Traités de Garantie, d'alliance, de collaboration politique, de Non-Agression et de Neutralité conclus après la guerre*); tome II: *Materialen zur Entwicklung der Sicherheitsfrage im Rahmen des Völkerbundes* (*Documentation relative au développement de la question de la sécurité dans le cadre de la Société des Nations*), *1920–1935;* tome III: *Garantiepakte, Bündisse, Abkommen über politische Zusammenarbeit, Nichtangriffs- Neutralitäts- und Abrüstüngverträge der Nachkriegszeit* (*Traités de Garanties, d'alliance, de Collaboration politique, de Non-Agression, de Neutralité et de Désarmement conclus après la guerre*) *1936–1940* (Berlin: Carl Heymanns Verlag, 1936–42), 3 tomes in 5 volumes.

clarify the texts of the treaties reproduced in their entirety. The collection is organized chronologically, the first and third volumes (the latter in two parts) incorporating materials up to and including the Hungarian-Yugoslav treaty of friendship of December 12, 1940. The second volume is also in two parts and deals exclusively with the problem of security within the framework of the League of Nations and includes, in addition to the various treaty projects, a rich and imposing documentation consisting of reports of the preparatory and study commissions, the recommendations of the Assembly, government memoranda, etc. Given the nature of the subject matter, this volume is arranged topically rather than chronologically. The Bruns collection is the most recent major undertaking of its kind, and its great virtue lies in the fact that it is an enormously useful tool even for a period systematically covered by the official collections.

The early years of this century saw "treaty manuals" become extremely commonplace. While the analogous publications of the eighteenth century were, in essence, planned to provide inexpensive and manageable compendiums for statesmen and the educated public, the more recent ones, in the fields of international law and history, are largely didactic in nature.

The most outstanding manual published in the nineteenth century is that of Friedrich Ghillany,[68] published in 1855, which includes the principal treaties beginning with Westphalia. Despite its limitations, this collection was realized according to rigorous scientific standards, with the texts reproduced in their entirety and in their original tongues. The Ghillany collection was very popular in its day and was partly translated into French;[69] that is, those treaties in languages other than French were translated. Thus in order to have the complete collection in French, it is necessary to have both editions.

Henri Vast's collection of the treaties of the reign of Louis XIV[70] is of great value, but it is something more than a collection of documents. Vast wrote a long historical narrative as an introduction to the collection, so that basically the work is a diplomatic history of the reign of Louis XIV. Each treaty text is accompanied by a bibliography indicating the collections wherein the text is published, the archival sources on the negotiations that preceded the conclusion of the treaty, the literature on the question, and references to the archival originals.

---

[68] *Diplomatisches Handbuch, Sammlung der wichtigsten europaeischen Frieden-schluesse, Congressacten, und sonstigen Staatsurkunden von Westphaelischen Frieden bis auf die neueste Zeit. Mit kurzen geschichtlichen Einleitungen* (3 vols.; Nördlingen: Beck, 1855–68).

[69] *Manuel diplomatique, recueil des traités européens les plus importants, depuis la paix de Westphalie jusques et y compris le traité de Paris de 1856* (Paris and Brussels, 1856).

[70] *Les grands traités du règne de Louis XIV* (3 vols.; Paris: Picard, 1893–99).

The famous Albin collection[71] aims primarily to meet the needs of statesmen and journalists and is designed only incidentally to fulfill didactic ends. This explains why the editor concentrated his attention on the most recent period (the collection begins with the treaties of 1815), adopting what is essentially a "political" yardstick as a basis for selection, that is, weighing the collection in favor of those documents dealing with questions of current interest. The material is organized by regions (western Europe, eastern Europe, etc.) and then by countries. Each documentary paragraph is preceded by a brief introductory note.

Mowat's first collection of treaties and other documents[72] begins with 1815 and is intended to provide a clear picture of the changes that have taken place in the European state system after Westphalia. In his second collection, edited a few years later in collaboration with Oakes,[73] Mowat incorporated only those treaties relative to the most important European diplomatic problems of the century 1815–1914. Each treaty is preceded by a detailed historical note.

Ettore Anchieri's collection[74] is clearly a teaching aid. It, too, begins with 1815, and the selection of the documents is designed to allow the student to see the period in perspective, while at the same time considerable space is devoted to World War II documents. In addition to treaties, the texts include diplomatic papers, official declarations, etc. In Part I (1815–1945) these are arranged chronologically; in Part II (post-1945), according to subject. A chronological index completes the volume.

The volumes published by Colliard are also planned to meet classroom needs, although they are of somewhat greater interest to law students than to historians. The first volume[75] is in two parts, of which the first is of primary importance for the study of international law and is arranged topically, and the second is arranged chronologically (1815–1950) and is of major interest to students of diplomatic history. Along with treaties other acts are included that are of significance in the development of international relations, such as the Franco-German declaration of December 6,

---

[71] Pierre Albin, *Les grands traités politiques. Recueil des principaux textes diplomatiques depuis 1815 jusqu'à nos jours, avec des commentaires et des notes* (Paris: Alcan, 1911); 2d ed., 1912; 3d ed., 1923; reprinted in 1932 with the addition of a chronological list of the principal treaties concluded after 1919.

[72] Robert Balmain Mowat, *Select Treaties and Documents To Illustrate the Development of the Modern European States-System* (Oxford: Clarendon Press, 1915); 2d ed., enlarged, 1916.

[73] Mowat and August Henry Oakes, *The Great European Treaties of the Nineteenth Century* (Oxford: Clarendon Press, 1918); 2d ed., rev., 1921.

[74] *La diplomazia contemporanea. Raccolta di trattati e documenti diplomatici* (2d ed.; Padua: C.E.D.A.M., 1959).

[75] Claude Albert Colliard, *Droit international et histoire diplomatique. Documents choisis* (Paris: Editions Domat Montchrestien, 1948); 2d ed., 1950.

1938, the first and second Vienna arbitrations, the Churchill-De Gaulle accord of August 7, 1940, etc. In the second volume[76] the material of the preceding volume is revised and updated to 1956. The two-part arrangement of the first volume is abandoned in the latter one in favor of a division by geographical areas and, within each area, by subject matter. Thus it appears that its original design as a teaching device has given way to one with greater appeal to political interests.

The collection begun by Garcia de la Vega[77] in 1850 for Belgian treaties is illustrative of one that bridges the gap between official and private collections in that the author received permission to check his texts against the originals without receiving an explicit authorization for his work. The twenty-one-volume collection begins with 1831 (however, the acts relative to Belgian affairs concluded between 1814 and 1830 are incorporated as a preface to the fourth volume) and terminates with 1913. The last five volumes were edited by Alphonse de Busschère.

The collection of treaties entered into by the Netherlands in the period 1813–1915 begun by Lagemans and continued by Brenkelman[78] is analogous in many respects to the Belgian collection. These editors also had access to the archives, which permitted them to collate the texts and to add numerous unpublished documents to the collections.

6. THE MODERN OFFICIAL COLLECTIONS.

At the beginning of the last century, with the emergence of parliamentary governments, as already noted, the official collections gradually assumed a dominant position.

In Great Britain, the practice of publishing an official collection of treaties at regular intervals was developed by private initiative. It was Lewis Hertslet, the librarian at the Foreign Office, who, in 1825, began collecting the published treaties entered into by Great Britain beginning with the year 1812 and republished them for the use of government officials and members of Parliament. Despite their limited circulation, these volumes attracted an increasingly wide circle of readers, and in 1832 Hertslet was authorized to republish the materials he had already issued (a fifteen-

---

[76] *Actualité internationale et diplomatique* (Paris: Editions Domat Montchrestien, 1957).

[77] Desire Garcia de la Vega and Alphonse de Busschère, *Recueil des traités et conventions concernant le royaume de Belgique* (Brussels: Greuse, 1850 et seq.).

[78] Evert Godfried Lagemans and J. B. Brenkelman, *Recueil des traités et conventions conclus par le royaume des Pays-Bas avec les puissances étrangères depuis 1813 jusqu'à nos jours* (The Hague: Belinfante, 1815 et seq.).

volume collection). In addition, Hertslet was commissioned to publish on an annual basis those treaties entered into by Great Britain beginning in 1832.[79]

The collection edited by Sir Charles Aitchinson concerning India,[80] the first edition of which was published in Calcutta in 1862, is official in character. The systematic arrangement of the documents (the treaties are divided according to geographical areas to which the individual principalities belonged, or by states, in the instance of the major principalities such as Hyderabad) is especially helpful to the scholar in facilitating research among the myriads of accords through which the East India Company, and later the office of the Governor-General, extended their control on the Indian subcontinent and which, in general, continued to regulate the relations between Great Britain and the so-called "India of the Princes." Successive editions of the collection were published in which the material was increased and brought up to date, the 1909 edition consisting of thirteen volumes. It should be noted that those treaties concluded by the government of India with its territorial dependencies and the treaties with those countries whose relations were properly the affairs of the Indian Office are also included (Persia, Afghanistan, the Persian Gulf protectorates, Arabia, East Africa, etc.).

A private undertaking was also responsible for the publication of the Austrian government's collection of treaties. In 1855 Leopold Neumann[81] started a collection of treaties signed by the Austrian crown and assembled the data for the period 1763–1856 in six volumes. Beginning in 1877, the project was reactivated by Neumann with official sanction, and carried down to 1912 by Plason de la Woestyne.[82]

In 1864, Alexandre de Clercq, under the auspices of the Ministry of

[79] *British and Foreign State Papers. Compiled by the Librarian and Keeper of the Papers, Foreign Office* (London: Harrison, 1832 *et seq.*).

[80] Sir Charles Umpherston Aitchinson, *A Collection of Treaties, Engagements and Sunnuds Relating to India and Neighbouring Countries* (Calcutta, 1862); *A Collection of Treaties, Engagements and Sunnuds Relating to India and Neighbouring Countries. Revised and Continued up to the Present Time by Lieut. A. C. Talbot* (7 vols.; Calcutta and Foreign Office Press, 1876); *A Collection . . . Revised and Continued up to the Present Time* (Calcutta: Superintendent of Government Printing, 1892), 11 volumes plus a volume of maps; *A Collection . . . Revised and Continued up to the 1st of June, 1906, By Authority of the Foreign Department* (13 vols.; Calcutta: Superintendent of Government Printing, 1909).

[81] *Recueil des traités et conventions conclus par l'Autriche avec les puissances étrangères depuis 1763 jusqu'à nos jours* (6 vols.; Leipzig: Brockhaus, 1855–59).

[82] Neumann and Adolphe Plason de la Woestyne, *Recueil des traités et conventions conclus par l'Autriche avec les puissances étrangères depuis 1763 jusqu'à nos jours. Nouvelle suite* (Vienna: Imprimerie I. et R. de la Cour et de l'Etat, 1877 *et seq.*).

Foreign Affairs, initiated a collection of treaties for the French government, and it was continued by Etienne de Clercq.[83] The collection begins with the treaties of 1713 and includes a number of tables and ample indexes for very convenient reference. In this connection Basdevant's collection[84] should be mentioned, in which all of the treaties in effect between France and the other states at the close of World War I are included.

In Italy the first official collection was commissioned by Charles Albert's Secretary of State for Foreign Affairs, Count Solaro della Margarita, in 1836, and it was completed in 1861.[85] The eight volumes comprise all of the treaties concluded by the House of Savoy between 1559 (Treaty of Câteau-Cambresis) and the creation of the Kingdom of Italy in 1861. This was followed, in 1862, by a collection of treaties and commercial conventions then in effect with other states, consisting of 157 documents dating from 1751 to 1862.[86]

Solaro della Margarita's collection was continued by the Ministry of Foreign Affairs in 1865 under a new title[87] and modified again with the appearance of the forty-sixth volume dealing with 1940.[88] It continues to be published, and the sixtieth volume has appeared, relating to the affairs of 1946.

With the idea of gathering together the most important papers regarding African political affairs, which were either scattered throughout various collections or still unpublished, the Italian Ministry of Foreign Affairs in 1906 published a collection of documents concerning Africa for the period 1825–1906.[89] Two other official collections, one containing the treaties of

[83] Alexandre de Clercq and Etienne de Clercq, *Recueil des traités de la France, publié sons les auspices du ministre des affaires étrangères* (Paris: Amyot, 1864 et seq.).

[84] Jules Basdevant, *Traités et conventions en vigueur entre la France et les puissances étrangères* (Paris: Imprimerie Nationale, 1918 et seq.).

[85] Clemente Solar de la Marguerite, *Traités publics de la royale maison de Savoie avec les puissances étrangères depuis la paix de Câteau-Cambresis jusqu'à nos jours publiés par ordre du Roi et présentés à S.M.* (8 vols.; Turin: Imprimerie Royale, 1836–44; Turin: Favale, 1852–61).

[86] Ministero degli Affari Esteri di S. M. il Re d'Italia (ed.), *Raccolta dei trattati e delle convenzioni commerciali in vigore tra l'Italia e gli stati stranieri* (Turin: Favale, 1862).

[87] Ministero degli Affari Esteri (comp.), *Raccolta dei Trattati e delle convenzioni concluse tra il Regno d'Italia ed i Governi esteri* (Turin: Paravia, poi Tipografia riservata del Ministero degli Affari Esteri, 1865 et seq.).

[88] *Trattati e convenzioni tra l'Italia e gli altri stati* (Tipografia riservata del Ministero degli Affari Esteri, 1951 et seq.).

[89] *Trattati, convenzioni, accordi, protocolli ed altri documenti relativi all'Africa, 1825–1906* (3 vols.; Rome: Tipografia riservata del Ministero degli Affari Esteri, 1906). A supplementary volume bringing the material up to 1908 was published in 1909.

commerce and navigation concluded by Italy between 1914 and 1929[90] and the other dealing with the Consular Conventions,[91] were published in 1929 and 1932, respectively. During World War II, a project was launched for a collection of treaties and accords relating to Africa for the period 1684 to the present, but the work was interrupted with the completion of the third volume, which covered the period up to 1873.[92]

The official Russian collection is of a much earlier date. Undertaken by Feodor Fedorovich Martens in 1874,[93] it opens with the documents relative to the Peace of Westphalia and closes with 1906. In addition to the documents, it includes a short narrative, based on archival materials, on the negotiations that preceded each treaty. The text is printed in both French and Russian.

The Swedish treaty collection begun in 1877 by Olaf Rydberg is even broader, with documents dating back to 1822.[94] The work was continued by others and includes treaties relative to Norway for the period 1815–1905.[95] After the separation of the two states, the Norwegian Foreign Minister in 1907 published a collection of the treaties then in effect between Norway and other states,[96] and the Stockholm government followed suit in 1910 with a similar collection for Sweden.[97] In 1888 the Rumanian Minister of Foreign Affairs published a collection of the same type,[98] obviously designed to define more clearly the obligations assumed by the Rumanian

---

[90] *Trattati di commercio e Navigazione tra l'Italia e gli altri Stati per il periodo 1914–1929* (3 vols.; Rome: Ministero dell'Economia Nazionale, 1929).

[91] *Convenzioni consolari tra l'Italia e gli altri Stati* (Rome: Tipografia riservata del Ministero degli Affari Esteri, 1932).

[92] *Trattati, convenzioni e accordi relativi all'Africa* (3 vols.; Rome: Tipografia riservata del Ministero degli Affari Esteri, 1940–43).

[93] Feodor Fedorovich Martens, *Recueil des traités et conventions conclus par la Russie avec les puissances étrangères, publié d'ordre du Ministère des Affaires Etrangères* (15 vols.; St. Petersburg: Imprimerie du Ministère des Voies de Communication, 1874–1909).

[94] Olaf Rydberg and Carl Jacob Hallendorf, *Sverges traktater med främmande magter jemte andra dit hörande handlingar* (Stockholm: Norstedt, 1877 *et seq.*).

[95] Olaf Rydberg, Oscar Josef Alin, and Carl Johan Sandgren, *Sverges och Norges traktater med främmande magter . . .* (Stockholm: Norstedt, 1896 *et seq.*).

[96] *Recueil des traités de la Norvège. Publié à l'usage des représentants diplomatiques et consulaires de Norvège, par les soins du ministère des affaires étrangères* (Christiania: Grondahl, 1907).

[97] Carl Johan Sandgren, *Recueil des traités, conventions et autres actes diplomatiques de la Suède entièrement ou partiellement en vigueur le 1 janvier 1910* (Stockholm, 1910).

[98] Trandafir Djuvara, *Traités, conventions et arrangements internationaux de la Romanie actuellement en vigueur publiés d'ordre de M. le Ministre des affaires étrangères, d'après les textes originaux avec notes explicatives et index suivis des tarifs douaniers et de notices statistiques sur le commerce extérieur précédés d'une introduction à l'étude du droit conventionnel de la Roumanie* (Bucharest: Degenmann, 1888; Paris: Rousseau. 1888). The texts are in French and Rumanian.

government in the ten years of its recognized existence as a sovereign state.

The well-known Olivart Spanish collection was preceded by other similar, and sometimes private, projects, so that the panorama of Spanish collections is quite extensive. After those already mentioned (the Chifflet, the Abreu y Bertodano, and the Capmany collections, together embracing the period 1559–1801), the first to appear in the nineteenth century was Cantillo's private collection,[99] which once again emphasized the eighteenth century, beginning with the year 1700 and terminating with 1842. It was continued anonymously for the period 1842–67[100] and officially for the same period under the editorship of Florencio Janer,[101] and it continued officially for the years 1868–74;[102] finally toward the end of the century, Olivart was engaged for the task by the Minister of State, Marquis de la Vega. Olivart picked up where Cantillo had stopped and published the treaties for the years 1842–1904,[103] adding two supplementary volumes which brought the work up to 1911.[104]

Viscount Borges de Castro edited the official Portuguese collection of treaties concluded by the Portuguese crown beginning in 1400. The eight-volume collection covered the years to 1858[105] and was soon enlarged by the addition of an imposing supplement for the years 1829–40, edited by

[99] Alejandro del Cantillo, *Tratados convenios y declaraciones de paz y de comercio que han hecho con la potencias estranjeras los monarcas españoles de la casa de Borbon. Desde el año 1700 hasta el dia. Puestos en orden e illustrados muchos de ellos con la historia de sus respectivas negociaciones* (Madrid: Imprenta de Alegria y Charlain, 1843).

[100] *Tratados de España. Documentos internacionales que han sido publicados después de la Colección del Cantillo* (n.p., n.d.).

[101] *Tratados de España. Documentos internacionales del reinado de Doña Isabel II desde 1842 a 1868. Colección publicada de orden del ministro de estado con un discurso preliminar* (Madrid: Ginesta, 1869).

[102] *Tratados de España. Documentos internationales que corresponden a la época intermedia de los gobiernos constituidos desde el mes de octubre de 1868 hasta fin del año 1874. Collección oficial publicada por el ministro de estado con los datos auténticos de su archivio* (4 vols.; Madrid: Ginesta, 1875–87).

[103] Ramon de Dalnau y de Olivart, *Collección de los tratados, convenios y documentos internacionales celebrados por nuestros gobiernos con los estados extranjeros desde el reinado de Doña Isabel II hasta nuestras dias acompañados de notas historico- criticas sobre su negociación y cumplimiento, y cotejados con los textos originales. Publicada de real orden con la autorización del excmo, Sr. ministro de estado Marqués de la Vega di Armijo* (14 vols.; Madrid: El Progreso Editorial, 1890–1911).

[104] *Tratados y documentos internacionales de España publicados en la Revista de derecho internacional y política exterior* (4 vols.; Madrid: Alvarez, 1905–12); *Tratados 1908–1910. Cuaderno I: Tratados de 1908* (Madrid: Revista de derecho internacional y politica exterior, 1911).

[105] Josè Ferreira Borges de Castro, *Collecçao dos tratados, convençoes, contrados e actos publicos celebrados entre a corõa de Portugal e as mais potencias desde 1640 até ao presente* (8 vols.; Lisbon: Imprensa Nacional, 1856–58).

Biker,[106] and then continued directly by the Ministry of Foreign Affairs.[107]

In 1908 the United States, following the example of the British, brought out a *Treaty Series*,[108] an annual publication in which all treaties concluded by the executive branch of government appear. The series begins with number 489 in order to avoid having to alter the chronological order of the agreements previously concluded, which had appeared in volumes published at various intervals either at the request of the Senate, who subsidized them, or by the government directly, or by individuals holding official authorization (Davis,[109] Cadwalader,[110] Haswell,[111] Malloy[112]). However, the definitive edition of the treaties concluded by the United States down to 1863 remains the one in eight volumes edited by Miller.[113]

[106] Julio Firmino Biker, *Supplemento a Collecçao dos tratados, convençoes, contratos e actos publicos celebrados entre a corõa de Portugal e as mais potencias desde 1640* (22 vols.; Lisbon: Imprensa Nacional, 1872–80).

[107] *Nova collecçao de tratados convençoes, contratos e actos publicos celebrados entre a corõa de Portugal e as mais potencias compilados por ordem do ministerio dos negocios estrangeiros em continuçao da Collecçao de Josè Ferreira Borges de Castro* (Lisbon: Imprensa Nacional, 1890 *et seq.*). A collection of major importance to Portuguese colonial policy was edited by Biker, comprising the treaties and accords entered into by Portugal beginning with the sixteenth century: *Collecçao de tratados e concertos de pazes que o estado da India Portuguesa fez com os reis e senhores com quem teve relaçoes nas partes da Asia e Africa Oriental desde o principio da conquista até ao fim do seculo XVIII* (14 vols.; Lisbon: Imprensa Nacional, 1881–87). Despite the title, the collection comprises material up to 1887.

[108] *Treaty Series, Nos. 489 et seq.* (Washington: U.S. Government Printing Office, 1908 *et seq.*).

[109] John C. B. Davis, *Treaties and Conventions Concluded between the United States of America and Other Powers since July 4, 1776* (Washington: U.S. Government Printing Office, 1873).

[110] John L. Cadwalader, *Treaties and Conventions Concluded between the United States of America and Other Powers since May 1, 1870* (Washington: U.S. Government Printing Office, 1876).

[111] John H. Haswell, *Treaties and Conventions Concluded between the United States of America and Other Powers since July 4, 1776. Containing Notes with References to Negotiations Preceding the Several Treaties to the Executive, Legislative, or Juridical Construction of Them and to the Causes of the Abrogation of Some of Them, a Chronological List of Treaties and an Analytical Index* (Washington: U.S. Government Printing Office, 1889). This collection, which is much more complete than the earlier ones, was enlarged by three supplements between 1894 and 1897.

[112] William M. Malloy, *Compilation of Treaties in Force* (Washington: U.S. Government Printing Office, 1904). The first collection edited by Jonathan Elliot was private in character: *Diplomatic Code of the United States of America Embracing a Collection of Treaties and Conventions between the United States and Foreign Powers from the Year 1778* (Washington: Elliot, 1827). The collection was reprinted in 1834 in two volumes with the addition of recent materials.

[113] David Hunter Miller, *Treaties and Other International Acts of the United States of America* (8 vols.; Washington: U.S. Government Printing Office, 1931–48).

A useful guide to the treaties, indicating the collections containing the published texts, was assembled by Tétot[114] and embraces the period 1493–1867. Ribier[115] enlarged the guide to extend the coverage to 1897. For the succeeding period, the *Catalogue of Treaties*[116] published by the U.S. Government Printing Office is a very useful tool. The latter covers the years 1814–1918 and is especially rich in detail for the post-1897 period, largely because the editors gave proper consideration to the Tétot and Ribier guides and avoided excessive duplication.

Finally, reference should be made to the Myers guide to treaty collections.[117] It is an invaluable manual and the best of its kind. The Myers manual is not limited to treaty collections as such but also refers to various publications in which the texts of treaties, as well as other materials pertinent to treaties and international agreements, may be found. Its only limitation is the fact that over forty years have passed since its publication, and it has not been brought up to date.

Immediately after the founding of the Chinese Republic in 1912, the Foreign Ministry published a multivolume collection of treaties concluded by China during the last imperial dynasty, the Ch'ing, 1648–1911.[118] No official collection exists for the period 1912–27, making it necessary to refer

---

[114] Tétot, *Répertoire des traités de paix, de commerce, d'alliance, etc., conventions et autres actes conclus entre toutes les puissances du globe, principalment depuis la paix de Westphalie jusqu'à nos jours. Table générale des recueil de Dumont, Wenck, Martens, Murhard, Samwer, de Clercq, Léonard, Angeberg, Lesur, Hertslet, Neumann, Testa, Calvo, Elliot, Cantillo, Castro Soutzo, State Papers, etc. etc., donnant l'indication du recueil où se trouve le texte de chaque traité* (2 vols.; Paris: Amyot, 1866–70). The material is listed chronologically in the first volume and alphabetically in the second.

[115] Gabriel de Ribier, *Répertoire des traités de paix, de commerce, d'alliance, etc., conventions et autres actes conclus entre toutes les puissances du globe depuis 1867 jusqu'à nos jours. (Faisant suite au Répertoire de M. Tétot.) Table générale des principaux recueils français et étrangers donnant l'indication du volume et de la page du recueil où se trouve le texte de chaque traité* (2 vols.; Paris: Pedone, 1895–99).

[116] *Catalogue of Treaties, 1814–1918* (Washington: U.S. Government Printing Office, 1919).

[117] Denys Peter Myers, *Manual of Collections of Treaties and Collections Relating to Treaties* (Cambridge, Mass.: Harvard University Press, 1922).

[118] Wang I and others, *K'ang-hsi, Yung-cheng, Ch'ien-lung, Tao-kuang t'iao-yüeh* [Treaties of the K'ang-hsi, Yung-cheng, Ch'ien-lung, and Tao-kuang Reigns] (5 vols.; Peking: Ministry of Foreign Affairs, 1915); *Hsien-feng t'iao-yüeh* [Treaties of the Reign of Hsien-feng] (6 vols.; Peking: Ministry of Foreign Affairs, 1915); *T'ung-chih t'iao-yüeh* [Treaties of the Reign of T'ung-chih] (10 vols.; Peking: Ministry of Foreign Affairs, 1915); *Kuang-hsü t'iao-yüeh* [Treaties of the Reign of Kuang-hsü] (34 vols.; Peking: Ministry of Foreign Affairs, 1915); *Hsüan-t'ung t'iao-yüeh* [Treaties of the Reign of Hsuan-t'ung] (5 vols.; Peking: Ministry of Foreign Affairs, 1912). A photolithographic copy of these collections was issued in 1964 in four volumes by the Kuo-feng publishing firm of Taipeh.

to private collections[119] or to the bulletins published by the Ministry of
Foreign Affairs.[120] An incomplete collection of treaties negotiated by
Nationalist China from 1927 to 1957 was published in 1958 by the
Ministry of Foreign Affairs of Nationalist China in Taipeh.[121] In turn, the
Ministry of Foreign Affairs of the Chinese People's Republic in 1957 began
publication of the treaties concluded by that government, beginning with
1949.[122] It should also be noted that the Peking government has announced
its decision to publish a major collection of international treaties, starting
with those of 1814.[123]

In addition to these collections in Chinese, there are others in English of
a private nature, such as those of Mayers,[124] Rockill,[125] Murray,[126] and Yin
Ching Chen.[127]

The Japanese Foreign Ministry began publication of a collection of
treaties in 1922,[128] of which thirty-eight volumes had appeared by December, 1964.[129] There are two collections for the preceding period: one begun

---

[119] For example, the Hsieh Tien-Ts'eng and others, *Chung-kuo ts'an-chia chih
kuo-chi kung-yüeh hui-pien* [Compendium of International Treaties to Which China
Was Signatory] (Shanghai: Commercial Press, 1937); or the Wang T'ieh-
Yai, *Chung-wai chiu-yüeh chang hui-pien* [Compendium of Ancient Treaties
between China and Other Countries] (2 vols.; Peking: San-lien, 1957, 1959).

[120] For example, the *Wai-chiao kung-pao* [The Diplomatic Gazette] published
monthly beginning in 1921.

[121] *Treaties between the Republic of China and Foreign States (1927–1957)*
(Taipeh: Ministry of Foreign Affairs, 1958).

[122] *Chung-hua jen-min kung-ho-kuo t'iao-yüeh chi* [Collection of Treaties of the
Chinese People's Republic] (Peking: Shih-chiai chih-shih, 1957 *et seq.*). Twelve
volumes were published between 1949 and 1963.

[123] *Kuo-chi t'iao-yüeh chi* [Collection of International Treaties] (Peking: Shih-
chiai chih-shih, 1959 *et seq.*). To date volumes have been published for the following
years: 1917–23, 1924–33, 1934–44, 1945–47, 1948–49, 1950–52, 1953–55,
1956–57.

[124] W. F. Mayers (ed.), *Treaties between the Empire of China and Foreign Powers*
(Shanghai and London, 1877); 5th ed. published in Shanghai, 1906.

[125] W. W. Rockill, *Treaties and Conventions with or concerning China and Korea,
1899–1904* (Washington: U.S. Government Printing Office, 1904).

[126] J. V. A. Murray, *Treaties and Agreements with and concerning China,
1894–1919* (2 vols.; Washington: Carnegie Endowment for International Peace,
1921).

[127] Yin Ching Chen (ed.), *Treaties and Agreements between the Republic of
China and Other Powers, 1929–1954* (Washington: Sino-American Publishing
Service, 1957).

[128] *Jōyaku shu* [Treaty Collection], Ministry of Foreign Affairs, Treaties Office
(Tokyo, 1922). The first volume, published in August, 1922, contains the first treaty
of the series: *The Washington Treaty, 1921–1922.*

[129] Treaty No. 1,566 of the series appears in Vol. XXXVIII, published in
December, 1964; it was signed in New York and is the Narcotics Convention of
March 30, 1961, effective December 13, 1964.

in 1925, containing the treaties of 1918,[130] and a second begun in 1930, containing treaties from 1854.[131]

Official treaty collections published by international organizations form a separate and distinct category. An example of these appeared following the convention of October 18, 1907, for the peaceful settlement of international conflicts, in which Article 43 obliged the contracting powers to transmit copies of all arbitration treaties subscribed to by them to the International Office of the Permanent Court of Arbitration at The Hague. The International Office of the Permanent Court published six series of these accords between 1911 and 1938,[132] beginning with the treaty between Argentina and Uruguay of June 8, 1899, and ending with the Denmark-Yugoslav accord of December 14, 1935.

In contrast, the collection published by the League of Nations is general in character. According to Article 18 of the pact, the member states were obliged to register with the Secretariat of the League every international treaty or agreement concluded by them, and the Secretariat provided for their publication. The registration requirement existed not only for treaties as such but also for all international commitments containing obligations of a legal nature. The obligation was not limited to agreements concluded between League member states alone, but also extended to those concluded between member and nonmember states. In addition, provision was made for nonmember states to register voluntarily with the League Secretariat all international accords subscribed to by them.

The intent of these provisions was to provide the wherewithal to facilitate the creation of a clear and indisputable international political system, to encourage public control over foreign policy, and, last but not least, to give the League of Nations the means to lend moral sanction to contractual obligations.[133] It should be noted that, according to the provisions of Article 18 of the League pact, no treaty or international

---

[130] Jōyaku isan [Treaty Compendium], Japanese Ministry of Foreign Affairs, Treaties Office, new edition (Tokyo, 1936).

[131] Kyū jōyaku isan [Compendium of Ancient Treaties], Japanese Ministry of Foreign Affairs, Treaties Office. Part 1 of vol. I begins with the treaty concluded with the United States, March 31, 1854.

[132] Traités généraux d'arbitrage communiqués au Bureau International de la Cour Permanente d'Arbitrage (The Hague: van Langenhuysen, 1911–38), 6 series in 7 volumes. The third series consists of two volumes. For arbitration treaties, see also Williams R. Manning, Arbitration Treaties among the American Nations to the Close of the Year 1910 (New York: Oxford University Press, 1924); Max Habicht, Post War Settlement of International Disputes. A Compilation and Analysis of Investigation, Conciliation, Arbitration and Compulsory Adjudication Concluded during the First Decade following the World War (Cambridge, Mass.: Harvard University Press, 1931).

[133] On this issue, see the memorandum approved by the Council of the League of Nations meeting, Rome, May, 1920.

convention was considered to be binding until registered with the League, an obligation that was discussed at length on a theoretical plane but which was rarely observed in practice.

Nonetheless, article 18 did lay the groundwork for a large and important collection,[134] published in monthly booklet form beginning in September, 1920, and ending in 1946 with Volume CCV, when the registration service was permanently terminated. The material is not organized chronologically but rather by date of registration, a factor that can render research a bit difficult. In order to offset this weakness, a Table of Contents was published, beginning in 1927, for the first thousand documents. Subsequent Tables of Contents were compiled for every five hundred documents published. The last of these, the ninth, lists Document No. 4,834, which terminates the collection. The texts are published in their original languages, along with French and English translations.

Article 102 of the United Nations Charter requires the registration with the Secretariat of the United Nations of every international treaty or agreement, and the Secretariat provides for its publication in the *United Nations Treaties Series*.[135] Contrary to what was provided by the League pact, failure to register an act does not affect its validity: it remains binding on the contracting parties, but it may not be invoked before an organ of the United Nations.

In order to visualize the content of the collection, it is necessary to keep in mind that the terminology used in Article 102, "treaties or international agreements," has been broadly interpreted to include the unilateral obligations of an international character that have been accepted by the state in whose interests these obligations have been assumed. The collection also includes the treaties or international agreements concluded by the United Nations or by one or more of its dependent institutions, as well as those subscribed to by a state prior to the effective date of the Charter and which had not been included in the League of Nations collection but which were subscribed to by nonmembers of the League before or after the Charter was in force and voluntarily transmitted to the Secretariat by such nonmembers.

The United Nations collection also publishes the texts in the original languages, followed by English and French translations. The documents are catalogued in order of registration or classification. The volumes are published monthly.

---

[134] *Recueil des traités et des engagements internationaux registrés par le Secrétariat de la Société des Nations* (205 vols.; Geneva, 1920–46).

[135] *United Nations Treaties Series. Treaties and International Agreements Registered or Filed and Recorded with the Secretariat of the United Nations.*

Chapter II

THE COLORED BOOKS

⌇ SUMMARY: 1. Definition: Origins and Historical Evolution of the Colored Books. 2. Evaluation of the Importance of the Colored Books as Sources

1. DEFINITION: ORIGINS AND HISTORICAL EVOLUTION OF THE COLORED BOOKS.

The "colored books" are limited collections of diplomatic documents that a government or a head of state publishes, usually during an international crisis, to inform the parliament of the action taken in that contingency. The label derives from the fact that the covers of these booklets are traditionally always the same color: thus we have the Italian Green Books, the British Blue Books, the French Yellow Books, etc.

The historical origin of these publications is to be found in English parliamentary practice. During the second half of the seventeenth century, the first collections of diplomatic correspondence (Blue Books) appeared in England and were distributed by the government to members of both houses of Parliament for the express purpose of providing a documented rebuttal to the criticism of the opposition. However, throughout the eighteenth century Blue Books were published only very infrequently, and then only in those exceptional cases when the government's foreign policy aroused a particularly violent reaction in Parliament. Usually the British followed the practice common in all other states of entrusting the defense of government policy to official reporters, who informed the public, by means of pamphlets published for the occasion, of the actions and objectives of the ministers in a given situation.

It was only during the Napoleonic wars that the publication of the Blue Books assumed the aims and objectives that characterize the colored books today. The series of defeats suffered at the hands of Napoleon and the great sacrifices demanded of the people by the war forced the British government to reveal some of the behind-the-scenes diplomatic negotiations in order to demonstrate that any compromise with the French Emperor was impossible. It was George Canning, Minister of Foreign Affairs in the Portland Cabinet from 1807–9, who, more than any other British statesman, understood the need to inform the country of international developments in order to avoid the excesses and uncertainties provoked by military failures. Under his direction, the Blue Books appeared with a frequency and a detail unequaled in the past.

Undoubtedly, the innovation introduced by Canning was dictated by the particular circumstances in which Britain found herself, and therefore it cannot be considered to be a new practice initiated by the government. In any event, it was an important landmark, perhaps a decisive precedent, to which successive ministers of foreign affairs very often had to refer.

On the other hand, it must be pointed out that the Napoleonic wars had greatly increased the interest of the public in foreign affairs, and this interest was reflected in parliamentary debate, where the opposition was inevitably drawn to focus its criticism precisely on foreign policy issues.

Thus, even after the victory over Napoleon, the British government found itself pressed to publish Blue Books with an ever-increasing frequency.[1] During the course of the negotiations at Vienna, Lord Castlereagh, whose temperament and political views differed markedly from Canning's, also decided to make public a portion of the documents concerning the most critical issues of the day in order to reply to the criticism that his Continental policy had provoked in Great Britain. Circumstances and the political needs of the moment determined the degree to which his successors followed his example.

As the practice became increasingly commonplace in Great Britain, it was inevitable that the other European governments would reply in kind. During the first half of the nineteenth century, the publication of colored books gradually became more widespread, especially because the growth of parliamentary regimes in Europe created conditions similar to those in Great Britain.

During this same period, an interesting evolution took shape in the objectives of these publications. While continuing to be "presented to Parliament," in reality, the colored books tended to influence public opinion directly and to arouse responses that the government deemed favorable to its policy. As a result, the colored books were no longer limited exclusively to the parliamentary world, and in many states (in 1830, Great

---

[1] A complete catalogue of the British Blue Books published between 1814 and 1914 is to be found in Harold V. Temperley and Lillian M. Penson, *A Century of Diplomatic Blue Books, 1814–1914* (Cambridge: Cambridge University Press, 1938).

Britain) they were placed on public sale; this factor greatly influenced the choice of materials to be included, since, as will become apparent, they were now intended to satisfy propaganda needs first and foremost.

Thus, beginning with the last half of the nineteenth century, a second phase in the history of the colored books was initiated, a period during which they flourished and played a major political role. On the one hand, increased public interest favored their growth and diffusion; on the other, parliaments elected on the basis of a restricted suffrage benefited by the election of particularly well-qualified men, able to discuss and evaluate the important issues of foreign policy. And so, as the norms governing their publication became firmly established, the colored books increased in size as well as in number, and they were no longer limited to exceptional cases. They tended to appear, especially in certain countries, with increasing regularity to illustrate the government's conduct of foreign policy. In the matter of norms governing publication, the most interesting innovation was the practice of requesting permission of the other country or countries involved in a particular issue before publishing those notes, messages, etc., coming from their governments.

At the turn of the century, a change was discernible and was attributable to several factors. First, the extension of suffrage opened parliamentary posts to men much less qualified to discuss and evaluate issues requiring a specific kind of knowledge. Second, even if it could be easily proved that there was a greater public participation in the affairs of state, the attention of the masses, and therefore of their representatives, was drawn primarily to internal problems because of the growing importance of the social question. Insofar as foreign policy was concerned, it usually became a matter of secondary importance, and the least qualified element of the electorate ignored it almost entirely. Meanwhile, the idea became ingrained that the conduct of foreign policy should be entrusted to specialists and that it should be above partisan politics. In the years just prior to World War I the colored books tended to appear less and less frequently, and it was only when war broke out that the powers turned out colored books on a grand scale.[2]

Following the 1914–18 conflict, world public opinion regarding international problems seemed to be profoundly changed. The illusions of the earlier period were dissipated, and the public was convinced that the primary responsibility for the catastrophe could be placed on the shoulders

[2] The colored books relative to World War I were assembled under the auspices of the Carnegie Foundation by J. B. Scott (ed.), *Diplomatic Documents Relating to the Outbreak of the European War* (2 vols.; New York: Oxford University Press, 1916).

of a restricted number of technicians. Now it insisted on public control of foreign policy to prevent the involvement of the masses against their will in a war. Obviously, such control was to be exercised primarily by parliaments, and in practice, the most important decisions relative to foreign policy were preceded by ample public debate in which the government's foreign policy aims and methods to accomplish those aims were minutely detailed. As a result, the publication of colored books became superfluous, and they were issued only in exceptional circumstances: for example, in instances when public debate of a problem could not be quickly arranged. In fact, a great many colored books reappeared only on the eve of World War II, and these were primarily designed to serve propaganda ends.

However, colored books were published in the period between the wars, and their contents differed widely from what had appeared in these publications prior to World War I. First, several governments decided to present to their respective parliaments (and, therefore, each in its own "color") identical collections of documents relating to agreements concluded between them. This was especially true for international conferences (for example, the Lausanne Conference of 1923). Second, during World War II the German government, reverting to a precedent dating back to the Napoleonic era, published a number of White Books containing not only its own documents but also enemy documents captured during the course of military operations.[3]

In summarizing these brief comments on the origins and evolution of the colored books, it is possible to distinguish between three sufficiently clear and distinct phases. The first phase, ending roughly in the middle of the nineteenth century, is characterized by the growth of the practice of issuing colored books, in direct relation to the increase in the number of constitutional and parliamentary regimes established in the period. In the second phase, beginning approximately at mid-century and terminating shortly before the outbreak of World War I, the publication of colored books reached its apogee, prompted by parliamentary requirements and also (the elements are closely connected) by the increase in public interest in problems of this nature. In the third and last phase, the decline of this

---

[3] *The German White Books on the Origins of the War: German White Book No. 3* (Polish documents on the origins of the war); *No. 4, No. 5, No. 6* (documents on Anglo-French policy aimed at enlarging the conflict), 1st, 2d, and 3d series, 1939–40. The unofficial character of the following precludes its being cited along with the colored books. Nevertheless, its contents require that it be noted here: Fritz Berber, *Europäische Politik, 1933–1938 im Spiegel der Prager Akten* (Essen: Essener Verlagsanstalt, 1940). This volume includes 182 Czechoslovak documents captured by German troops. The utility of this source is limited by the fact that the documents are severely mutilated and are often mere extracts.

practice was clearly evident and colored books appeared only in exceptional cases.[4]

2. EVALUATION OF THE IMPORTANCE OF THE COLORED BOOKS AS SOURCES.

Turning now to an evaluation of these "books" as sources for historical study, it is obvious that they have unique characteristics, derived essentially from the fact that they are issued very soon after the event to which they refer. Consequently, their publication is determined exclusively by political rather than by scientific criteria, and their preparation is designed to satisfy a series of immediate needs—factors which oblige historians to use them with special caution.

In the first place, because they are designed to justify government policy, they do not include those documents reflecting adversely on the government, nor do they include those documents publication of which is held to be inopportune at that particular moment for reasons of domestic or foreign policy.[5] These characteristics become even more evident when the colored books are especially designed to influence public opinion. For example, in the case of a diplomatic negotiation, it is inevitable that concessions be made by both sides in order to reach an accord: this is a fact well known to all who have had any experience whatsoever in such matters. Yet the

[4] For purposes of illustration, it is recalled that between 1871 and 1914 the French published 107 Yellow Books. Among them there were several very large ones, such as the Yellow Book for 1877 on the Eastern question and the one for 1886 on Greek and Rumelian affairs. Between 1914 and 1939 only 16 Yellow Books were issued. In Italy, from 1860 to 1914 only 107 Green Books were presented to Parliament; from 1915 to 1923 only 9 were issued.

[5] The telegram sent by Crispi to the Italian Chargé d'Affaires in London, Catalani, on April 28, 1888 (Telegram No. 592, in *Archivio Storico del Ministero dell'Africa Italiana*, position 3/1–5) is of interest here:

Confidential. The situation in Parliament demands that I issue the Green Book on Massawa without delay, precluding the possibility of submitting the galley proofs to the British government according to the obligations assumed by my predecessors and which, on this occasion, I would prefer to scrupulously observe. Nevertheless, you may reassure Salisbury that the infraction is purely superficial and without consequence. In fact, we have not hesitated to suppress everything that, directly or indirectly, implied the existence of any accord or understanding whatsoever with England or with Egypt. We say no more than what has been revealed in the Blue Book: perhaps even less. We chose to err on the side of caution rather than to give Salisbury the slightest cause for dissatisfaction and I prefer to be accused of omissions rather than of indiscretion. I authorize you to read this telegram to Lord Salisbury and to beg His Lordship to overlook this exception made necessary by circumstances and to advise him that every precaution has been taken in the matter to satisfy him.

masses find it extremely difficult to comprehend, especially when questions debated violently and emotionally, such as those normally covered in colored books, are involved, and they adopt a position of absolute intransigence. In the interest of avoiding strongly negative reactions, it is often necessary to ignore certain aspects of the negotiations that would reveal the concessions made to the other side, with the result that reality is altered more or less profoundly. Furthermore, every effort is made to conceal anything that would openly reveal errors of judgment and conduct committed on the part of the government issuing the material.

In addition, there remains the need to preserve the secrecy of the codes, and governments resort to strategems of various kinds, such as the publication of reports instead of telegrams or extensive paraphrase of the documents. The latter presents serious obstacles to a precise reconstruction of historical facts because once changes in the text are initiated, the end result is often also substantially altered, and therefore such changes distort the real meaning of the document. A comparison of an original document with the paraphrased version in a colored book has repeatedly revealed curious distortions brought about by this practice. Nonetheless, it can open up an interesting area of investigation because with the original document at hand it is possible, through a study of the motives that prompted the alterations in the paraphrased texts, to single out certain positions taken and to understand the goals pursued.

A case that caused a sensation in its day was that of the Orange Book on the origins of the war of 1914, published by the Russian government.[6] The omission of parts of certain documents and the suppression of others distorted many vital aspects of the diplomatic situation on the eve of the conflict; it pictured the attitude of the Central Powers from the beginning of the crisis as being one of complete intransigence, in contrast to the conciliatory position taken by Russia and France. A comparison of the documentation given in the Orange Book with the originals in the archives revealed a previously unsuspected amount of tampering and it also made it possible to rectify judgments made on the basis of the documentation publicized in the Orange Book. For example, for the purpose of historical accuracy the dispatches of Izvolski, Russian Ambassador to Paris, are especially significant. Reported in these dispatches is the encouragement given by French statesmen to the Russians to proceed secretly with mobilization plans, along with repeated assurances that France was firmly determined to fulfill to the letter her obligations as an ally in the event of

[6] Ministère des Affaires Etrangères, *Recueil de documents diplomatiques. Négociations ayant precédé la guerre, 10/23 Juillet–24 Juillet/6 Août 1914* (Petrograd: Imprimerie de l'Etat, 1914); English translation in Scott, II, 1331–82.

a conflict. Now, there is little doubt that these dispatches—omitted in the Orange Book—had a significant influence on the decisions taken by the Czarist government. On the other hand, the attitude of responsible Frenchmen seems to confirm the impression that almost from the beginning of the crisis, and certainly long before the crucial July days, Paris was convinced that war was now inevitable, a fact that must be weighed properly in order to evaluate the significance of the several attempts to find a satisfactory compromise in order to avoid the holocaust.

Frequent serious alterations are also evident in the colored books published by other countries during the crisis of 1914. The French Yellow Book[7] includes a telegram sent on July 31, 1914, by Paléologue, French Ambassador to St. Petersburg, reporting the news of Russian mobilization, ordered *as a reply to Austrian mobilization* and to the German military preparations. This document is a forgery. Paléologue had dispatched a telegram consisting of a single line to advise of the Russian mobilization order: the longer version appearing in the Yellow Book had been "created" to demonstrate that Austrian general mobilization had preceded the Russian or, at least, that the French had acted on the basis of that conviction. Nevertheless, neither of these facts corresponds to the truth. The same documents, published later in the Quai d'Orsay's general collection, reveal that mobilization was ordered first by the St. Petersburg government, and not by Vienna, and that the French government knew of the exact sequence of events, thanks to the information sent to Paris by the French military attaché in Vienna.

It is also true that in the colored books that appeared with the outbreak of World War II a comparison of the published documents with the originals—when this has been possible—has revealed serious distortions of the truth. German White Book No. 2[8] includes the minutes of the meeting between Von Ribbentrop and the Polish Ambassador, Lipski, of March 21, 1939, in which several anti-Soviet statements made by the Nazi Foreign Minister are deleted—statements intended to illustrate on what grounds a German-Polish understanding was possible, that is, on a common anti-Soviet policy. These utterances had been deleted because after the conclusion of the Nazi-Soviet Pact of August 23, 1939, they were politically inopportune. However, their suppression prevented historians from grasping the real significance of the step taken by Von Ribbentrop, a step which,

[7] Ministère des Affaires Etrangères, *Documents diplomatiques, 1914. La Guerre Européenne, I, Pièces relatives aux négociations qui ont precédés les déclarations de guerre de l'Allemagne à la Russie (1er Août 1914) et à la France (3 Août 1914). Déclaration du 4 Septembre 1914* (Paris: Imprimerie Nationale, 1914). English translation in Scott, I, 531–767.

[8] *German White Book*, No. 2 (documents on the origins of the war), 1939.

in effect, represented a last-ditch attempt to come to an agreement with Poland before embarking on a dynamic eastern policy. Equally serious are the alterations contained in the minutes of the Ribbentrop-Lipski meeting of March 26, 1939, also included in German White Book No. 2. As reported here, the text makes the Polish position appear to be extremely rigid, almost menacing, thereby giving the reader the impression that the breaking off of negotiations was fully justified in view of the obvious impossibility of reaching an accord.

The White Book published by the Polish government in exile in March, 1940,[9] also reveals serious omissions. This White Book contains a telegram sent on August 31, 1939, by the Minister of Foreign Affairs, Beck, to the Polish Ambassador, Lipski, in Berlin, in which the Ambassador is directed to tell the Wilhelmstrasse that the Warsaw government was ready to give favorable consideration to the British suggestion that direct negotiations between Poland and Germany be reopened, in order to arrive at a peaceful solution of the Danzig question and all other pressing problems affecting the relations between the two powers. However, the same telegram, as deciphered by the German Information Service,[10] emerges as something quite different in that it also contains a directive prohibiting Lipski from accepting or discussing any German requests. It may be true that this directive was included (as Colonel Beck stated to the British Ambassador, Kennard) because it was feared that the Germans would present their demands in the form of an ultimatum, but keeping in mind the slowness with which the Warsaw government responded to the British suggestion to reopen negotiations, the hypothesis may be advanced that the Poles at this late date were not about to reopen discussions which would inevitably lead to the cession of vast territories to the Germans.

Neither are the Italian government's Green Books free of these weaknesses, but, like their British counterparts, they contain omissions—occasionally extensive omissions—rather than outright alterations. The effects, from the point of view of historical research, are equally negative. We will have occasion to refer to these again when we discuss the volumes published by the Ministry of Foreign Affairs on Italian undertakings in Africa.[11]

Despite the serious limitations noted above, the importance of the colored book is enhanced in the case where a country that has been issuing such

[9] République de Pologne, Ministère des Affaires Etrangères, *Les relations polono-allemande et polono-soviétiques au cours de la période 1933–1939. Recueil de documents officiels* (Paris: Flammarion, 1940).

[10] The episode is revealed in Dahlerus' memoirs. See pp. 633–35.

[11] See pp. 285–87.

books for a given period has not published a general collection of an historical nature. To illustrate: the British Blue Book on the origins of World War I[12] has been superseded by the appearance of the Foreign Office collection for the period 1898–1914,[13] the last volume of which contains the same documents as the Blue Book but without omissions or paraphrases. On the other hand, the two Gray Books published by the Belgian government in 1915[14] retain their general interest because the Belgian government has not published a general collection since these appeared.

For the same reason, the Orange Book on Bulgaria's intervention in the war, published by the Stambulinski government in 1920–21,[15] retains its value. This collection is unique in that it appeared a considerable time after the events to which it refers, and its character is substantially the same as that of the colored books published by the revolutionary governments of Germany and Austria immediately after the collapse of the imperial regimes,[16] that is, it levels accusations against Stambulinski's opponents, including King Ferdinand and his collaborators, for their wartime policies which had been violently criticized by Stambulinski. It is not an easy task to determine to what extent the selection of material was influenced by the desire to emphasize the errors committed by the members of the previous regime. In any event, the contribution made by the Bulgarian Orange Book is of vital importance to an understanding of the negotiations conducted by Sofia with both the Entente and the Central Powers in the summer of 1915. Especially significant is the section referring to the negotiations with Belgrade, on whose outcome, in effect, the

[12] Miscellaneous, No. 10 (1915), *Collected Diplomatic Documents Relating to the Outbreak of the European War. Presented to Both Houses of Parliament by Command of His Majesty, May, 1915* (London: His Majesty's Stationery Office, 1915); also reproduced in Scott, II, 863–1054.

[13] See p. 139 *et seq.*

[14] Royaume de Belgique, *Correspondance diplomatic relative à la guerre de 1914 (24 juillet–29 août)* (Paris: Hachette, 1915). English translation is in Scott, I, 349–416, 419–530.

[15] *Diplomaticeski Dokumenti po namĕsata na Bŭlgarija v evropejskata vojna* [Diplomatic Documents Relative to Bulgaria's Entrance into the European War] (2 vols.; Sofia: State Publishing House, 1920–21). A German translation, "Die Bulgarischen Dokumente zum Kriegsausbruch 1914," appeared in *Die Kriegsschuldfrage* for March, 1928. This article contains only a partial translation of the documents relative to the July crisis. A French translation, "L'entrée en guerre de la Bulgarie d'après les documents diplomatiques bulgares," appeared in *Revue d'histoire de la Guerre Mondiale,* Vols. III and IV (1931), and represents only a partial translation of the documents relative to the last phase of Bulgarian neutrality, August–September, 1915.

[16] See pp. 126–31.

prospects of an agreement with the Entente powers depended. The absence in the Orange Book of documentation concerning the contacts between the Bulgarian and German General Staffs—contacts that had a strong influence on the choice made by Bulgaria on September 6, 1915—should also be noted,

Comparable cases for World War II are much more numerous because many governments found it impossible to publish a general collection concerning the prewar period, either because of damage suffered by the archives or because of the political changes that occurred at the close of hostilities. For example, until recently, as a result of the damage suffered by the archives of the Quai d'Orsay, no general collection of French diplomatic documents for the prewar period had been published, giving the Yellow Book published shortly after the start of the conflict a position of prime importance.[17] That publication contains 370 documents, devoted principally to the attempt at a Franco-German *rapprochement* culminating in the declaration of December 6, 1938; the occupation of Czechoslovakia by Hitler on March 15, 1939, in violation of the Munich agreement; and the negotiations between Paris, London, Warsaw, and Berlin during the summer crisis of 1939.

For analogous reasons, the above-mentioned Polish White Book of 1940 is also of basic importance. Although it embraces a much longer period (1933–39), the bulk of the documentation deals with the final crisis preceding the outbreak of war from the point of view of relations with Germany and the Soviet Union.

Perhaps of even greater significance are the two Finnish Blue-White Books that appeared during World War II. The first[18] is an essential source for the study of the negotiations that preceded the Soviet aggression against Finland, while the second[19] was published to explain motives prompting the Helsinki government to join Germany in the war against the U.S.S.R. and is limited to the period between the Peace of Moscow (March 13, 1940), which terminated the so-called "Winter War," and June 26, 1941, when hostilities between Finland and the Soviet Union were renewed.

---

[17] Ministère des Affaires Etrangères, *Le livre jaune français, Documents diplomatiques 1938–1939. Pièces relatives aux événements et aux negociations qui ont precédé l'ouverture des hostilités entre l'Allemagne d'une part, la Pologne, la Grand-Bretagne et la France d'autre part* (Paris: Imprimerie Nationale, 1939).

[18] Finnish Blue-White Book, *Documents on the Russo-Finnish Controversy and on the Outbreak of Hostilities between Finland and the Soviet Union, November 30, 1939.*

[19] Finnish Blue-White Book, No. 2, *The Attitude of the Soviet Government toward Finland after the Peace of Moscow.*

The Belgian Gray Book devoted to events preceding the German attack of May, 1940,[20] and the Greek White Book on relations with Italy[21] are of minor importance. The value of the former lies in its introduction—an overview of Belgian policy and the action taken by the Brussels government during the first phase of the conflict—rather than in its content, which is limited to 22 documents, for the most part already known. The latter is more consistent (183 documents). However, since it focuses on Italian policy prior to the Italian attack against Greece, it has been largely superseded by the published German and Italian collections. Nevertheless, it should be noted that the information possessed by the Greek government was exact. Not only were the Greeks *au courant* of Mussolini's and Ciano's intentions, they were also well informed of the repeated efforts of the Wilhelmstrasse to prevent an Italian action in the Balkans.

The Swedish and Norwegian White Books, published after the close of World War II, are unique in character. These are collections that appeared long after the date of the events to which they refer and in an atmosphere profoundly changed from the one in which they occurred. This time interval permitted a greater choice in the selection of the materials to be included, and the documents pertinent to Swedish and Norwegian affairs published or in the course of publication in other countries forced the editors to observe much more rigid criteria of objectivity in the matter of reproducing the documents selected. While these volumes are technically colored books, they have most of the characteristics of historical collections.

In addition, it should be mentioned that a close liaison exists between the Swedish and Norwegian White Books. They were published according to a plan developed by both governments, and the work of the Oslo and Stockholm commissions was carried on in close collaboration in order to avoid publishing any document that would arouse negative reactions in either country. The method of approach, unique at least in scope, has undoubtedly resulted in the suppression of certain data whose nature is impossible to determine.[22]

From the creation of the kingdom to the present, Italy has published 119 Green Books:

(1) Notes exchanged between the French and Italian governments relative to the recognition of the Kingdom of Italy (Ricasoli), June 27,

[20] Belgium, *The Official Account of What Happened, 1939–1940* (London: Evans, for the Belgian Ministry of Foreign Affairs, 1941).

[21] Greece, Ministry for Foreign Affairs, *The Greek White Book. Diplomatic Documents Relating to Italy's Aggression against Greece* (London: Hutchinson, for the Greek Ministry for Foreign Affairs, 1942).

[22] For an analysis of the contents of these White Books, see the section on the Scandinavian documentary sources below, pp. 316–22.

1861. (2) The Roman question. Documents and proposals (Ricasoli), November 20, 1861. (3) Documents relative to the dispute between the Spanish and Italian governments concerning the disposal of the Neapolitan archives (Ricasoli), December 3, 1861. (4) Diplomatic documents concerning several Italian problems (Durando) (brigandage, the Roman and Venetian questions), July 12, 1862. (5) Diplomatic documents concerning the Roman question (Durando), November 18, 1862. (6) Diplomatic documents (Visconti Venosta) (the Roman, Polish, and Serbian questions, etc.), May 29, 1863. (7) Diplomatic documents relative to the arrest carried out at Genoa on board the French packet "Aunis" (Visconti Venosta), July 23, 1863. (8) Diplomatic documents for the year 1865 (Lamarmora), December 12, 1866. (9) Diplomatic documents for the year 1866 (Visconti Venosta), December 21, 1866. (10) Documents relative to the negotiations conducted with the court of Rome (Di Campello) (Tonello mission), July 15, 1867. (11) Diplomatic documents concerning the Luxemburg questions (Di Campello), June 5, 1867. (12) Diplomatic documents concerning the Antibo Legion (Menabrea), December 9, 1867. (13) Diplomatic documents on the Roman question (Menabrea), December 9, 1867. (14) Diplomatic documents concerning Roman Affairs (Menabrea), March 20, 1869. (15) Documents relative to the murder of Count Alberto Boyl, secretary of the Italian Legation in Greece, and of Cavaliere Lorenzo Chapperon, former Italian Consul at Asunción (Visconti Venosta), May 3, 1870. (16) Documents relative to the murder of Count Alberto Boyl, secretary to the Italian Legation in Greece, second series (Viscount Venosta), May, 1870. (17) Diplomatic documents relative to the Roman question (Visconti Venosta), December 29, 1870. (18) The Treaty of London of March 13, 1871, and the protocols of the conferences (Visconti Venosta), May 23, 1871. (19) Diplomatic documents relative to the Geneva arbitration of 1871–72 (Visconti Venosta), November 30, 1872. (20) Diplomatic documents concerning the negotiations with Greece on the "Laurium" affair (Visconti Venosta), November 30, 1872. (21) Diplomatic documents concerning judicial reforms in Egypt (Visconti Venosta), January 26, 1875. (22) Diplomatic documents concerning Far Eastern affairs (Melegari), March 3, 1877. (23) Diplomatic documents concerning the Protocol of London of March 31, 1877 (Melegari), April 12, 1877. (24) Diplomatic documents concerning Far Eastern affairs (Cairoli), June 21, 1878. (25) The Treaty of Berlin of July 13, 1878, and the Protocol of the Congress of Berlin (Cairoli), December 9, 1878. (26) Diplomatic documents concerning Egyptian affairs (Depretis), July 2, 1879. (27) Documents relative to Eastern affairs (Cairoli). First series: I. The ratification of the Treaty of Berlin; the Russo-Turkish peace treaty; evacuation and surrender of the respective territories. II. Turkish reforms. III. Ottoman finances. IV. The Bulgarian arrangement. V. The disposition of Eastern Rumelia. Second series: VI. Frontier delimitations: (a) Serbia, (b) Bulgaria, (c) Eastern Rumelia, (d) Montenegro. Third series: VII. Delimitation of the Greco-Turkish frontier. VIII. Recognition of Serbia. IX. Recognition of Rumania, June 5, 1880. (28) Diplomatic documents of the Conference of Madrid relative to the protection of Morocco (Cairoli), November 15, 1880. (29) Diplomatic documents. Conference of Berlin on the Greco-Turkish question (Cairoli), November 15, 1880. (30) Diplomatic documents relative to the war between the Republic of Chile and the republics of Peru and Bolivia (Cairoli), February 1, 1881. (31) Diplomatic documents. Greco-Turkish question (1881) (Mancini), First series, September 15, 1881. (32) Diplomatic documents. The Beilul and Raheita (Assab) incidents (Mancini), First series, December 7, 1881. (33) Diplomatic documents relative to the war between the Republic of Chile and the republics of Peru and Bolivia (Mancini), Second series, December 7, 1881. (34) Diplomatic documents concerning Assab (1870–82) (Mancini), June 12, 1882. (35) Diplomatic documents. The Egyptian question (1881–82) (Mancini), December 14, 1882. (36) A report on the judicial reforms in Egypt (Mancini), December 23, 1882. (37) Diplomatic documents relative to the war between the Republic of Chile and the republics of Peru and Bolivia (Mancini), Third series, January 23, 1883. (38) Diplomatic documents concerning the indemnities for the damages suffered by Italians during the recent Egyptian incidents (Mancini), First series, February 28, 1883. (39) Diplomatic documents relative to the Turco-Hellenic question (1882) (Mancini), Second series, March 13, 1883. (40) Diplomatic documents relative to the Tripoli incidents (Mancini), March 13, 1883. (41) Diplomatic documents. The second Beilul investigation (Mancini), Second series, March 13, 1883. (42) Diplomatic documents. The Danubian question 1881–83 (Mancini), April 11, 1883. (43) Diplomatic documents relative to the suspension of Italian consular jurisdiction in Tunis (1882–84) (Mancini), February 28, 1884. (44) Diplomatic documents relative to the indemnities for the damages suffered by Italians during the recent Egyptian incidents (Mancini), Second series, April 5, 1884. (45) Diplomatic documents. Equatorial Africa and the Berlin conferences (1882–85) (Mancini), March 26, 1885. (46) Diplomatic documents. Negotiations with Austria-Hungary on fishing rights in the Adriatic and the Conference of Gorizia (Mancini), April 28, 1885. (47) Diplomatic documents. The Egyptian question (1883–85) (Mancini), First series, April 28, 1885. (48) Diplomatic documents. The war between the Republic of Chile and the republics of Peru and Bolivia (Mancini), Fourth series, June 16, 1885. (49) Diplomatic documents. Negotiations and convocation of a diplomatic conference in Rome relative to the conventional norms of private international law and to the execution of judgments granted abroad (1881–85), June 28, 1885. (50) Diplomatic documents. The Egyptian financial question (Di Robilant), Second series, November 25, 1885. (51) Diplomatic documents. Eastern Rumelia (Di Robilant), First series, November 25, 1885. (52) Diplomatic documents. Eastern Rumelia (Di Robilant), Second series, January 18, 1886. (53) Diplomatic documents. Eastern Rumelia and Greece (Di Robilant), Third series, June 12, 1886. (53a) Memorandum on the politico-administrative organization and on the economic conditions of Massaua (Di Robilant), June 30, 1886. (54) Diplomatic documents. Protests of the Italians in Colombia (Di Robilant), November 23, 1886. (55) Diplomatic documents. Bulgaria (Di Robilant), November 23, 1886. (56) Diplomatic documents. The war between the Republic of Chile and the republics of Peru and Bolivia (Di Robilant), Fifth series, January 17, 1887. (57) Diplomatic documents. Negotiations and correspondence relative to the renewal of the Treaty of Trade and Commerce with France (Crispi), First series, February 4, 1888. (58) Diplomatic documents. The Suez Canal (Crispi), First series, February 27, 1888. (59) Diplomatic documents. Negotiations and correspondence relative to the Treaty of Trade and Commerce with France (Crispi), Second series, February 29, 1888. (60) Diplomatic documents. Massaua (Crispi and Bertolé Viale), First series, April 24, 1888. (61) Diplomatic documents. Negotiations and correspondence relative to the Treaty of Trade and Commerce with France (Crispi), Third series, November 8, 1888. (62) Diplomatic documents. The Suez Canal (Crispi), Second series, November 8, 1888. (63) Diplomatic documents. Massaua (Crispi), Second series, November 8, 1888. (64) Diplomatic documents. Italo-French declaration (December 8, 1888) on the inviolability of consular archives (Crispi), February 9, 1889. (65) Diplomatic documents. The occupation of Keren and Asmara (Crispi and Bertolé Viale), December 17, 1889. (66) Diplomatic documents. Ethiopia (Crispi), First series, December 17, 1889. (67) Diplomatic documents. The slave trade (Crispi), December 17, 1889. (68) Diplomatic documents. Candia (Crispi), December 17, 1889. (69) Diplomatic documents. Bulgaria (Crispi), December 17, 1889. (70) Diplomatic documents. Ethiopia (Crispi), Second series, May 5, 1890. (71) Diplomatic documents. The Berlin International Conference for the Protection of Laborers (Crispi), June 7, 1890. (72) Diplomatic documents. The Antonelli mission to Ethiopia (Crispi), April 14, 1891. (72a) Protocols 24/3 to 15/4, 1891, relative to the delimitation of areas of influence between Italy and England in the northern and southern regions of Ethiopia and in Eritrea (di Rudinì), April 16, 1891. (73) Diplomatic documents. The New Orleans incident (di Rudinì), April 30, 1891. (74) Diplomatic documents. The interview of the Governor of Eritrea with the chiefs of the Tigre (di Rudinì), January 14, 1892. (75) Diplomatic documents. The New Orleans incidents (di Rudinì), May 4, 1892. (76) Diplomatic documents. Aigues Mortes (Brin), November 23, 1893. (77) Diplomatic documents. Aigues Mortes (II) (Blanc), February 20, 1894. (78) Diplomatic documents. Measures agreed upon with the government of the United States of North America in the interest of Italian emigration (Blanc), July 7, 1894. (79) Diplomatic documents. The Melilla incident (Blanc), December 6, 1894. (80) Diplomatic documents. The Melilla incident, Second series (Blanc), December 6, 1894. (81) Diplomatic documents. The Sherif succession (Morocco) (Blanc), December 6, 1894. (82) Diplomatic documents. Venezuela (Italian protests), First series (Blanc), December 6, 1894. (83) Diplomatic documents. Venezuela (Italian protests), Second series (Blanc), December 6, 1894. (86) Diplomatic documents. Agordat and Kassala (Blanc), July 25, 1895. (87) Diplomatic documents. Halai Coatit and Senafe (Blanc), July 25, 1895. (88) Diplomatic documents. The civil administration of the colony of Eritrea (Blanc), July 25, 1895. (89) Diplomatic documents. Italian Somaliland (Blanc), July 25, 1895. (90) Diplomatic documents. Correspondence between the central government and the government of Eritrea (di Rudinì), March 20, 1896. (91) Diplomatic documents. African developments (January, 1895–March, 1896) (Caetani), April 27, 1896. (92) Diplomatic documents. African developments (January, 1895–March, 1896) (Caetani), April 27, 1896. (93) Diplomatic documents. African developments (March–April, 1896) (Caetani), April 27, 1896. (94) Diplomatic documents. Amba Alagi (Macallè) (Caetani), April 27, 1896. (95) Diplomatic documents. Treaty of peace between Italy and Ethiopia (Visconti Venosta), May 24, 1897. (96) Diplomatic documents. Crete—the Turco-Hellenic conflict (Visconti Venosta), December 1, 1897. (97) Diplomatic documents. Crete (Canevaro), November 29, 1898. (98) Diplomatic documents. Developments in China, Part I (Prinetti), July 10, 1901. (99) Diplomatic documents. Developments in China, Part II (Prinetti), September 8, 1901. (100) Diplomatic documents. Incident between Comm. Silvestrelli, Royal Minister to Berne, and the Federal Council of Switzerland (Prinetti), April 15, 1902. (101) Diplomatic documents. Anglo-Italian accords (Prinetti), December 10, 1902. (102) Diplomatic documents. Conditions and administration in the Benadir (Morin), March 21, 1903. (103) Diplomatic documents. Italian Somaliland (Di San Giuliano), January 30, 1906. (104) Diplomatic documents. Macedonia (Di San Giuliano), January 30, 1906. (105) Diplomatic documents. Supplementary agreement between Italy and England of March 19, 1907, relative to northern Italian Somaliland (Tittoni), May 15, 1907. (106) Diplomatic documents. Crete (Di San Giuliano), May 20, 1911. (107) Diplomatic documents. Morocco (Di San Giuliano), May 20, 1911. (108) Diplomatic documents. Austria-Hungary (Sonnino), May 20, 1915. (109) Diplomatic documents. Franco-Italian agreements (1900–2) (Scialoja), January 2, 1920. (110) Diplomatic documents. The Pact of London of April 26, 1915 (Scialoja), March 4, 1920. (111) Diplomatic documents.

Direct negotiations between the Italian government and the government of the Serbs-Croats-Slovenes in the interest of peace in the Adriatic, June 20, 1921. (112) Diplomatic documents. Inter-Allied conferences of London and Paris on German reparations (minutes and documents) (Mussolini), February 26, 1923. (113) Diplomatic documents. The Lausanne Conference (the peace treaty with Turkey) (Mussolini), Tome I, April 20, 1923. (114) Diplomatic documents. The treaty of peace with Turkey (Mussolini), Tome II, June 1, 1923. (115) Diplomatic documents. The treaty of peace with Turkey (Mussolini), Tome III, December 7, 1923. (116) Diplomatic documents. The treaty of peace with Turkey (Mussolini), Tome IV, December 7, 1923. (117) Documents concerning Italy's African problems before the United Nations (Sforza), autumn, 1949. (118) Alto Adige (Segni), September 16, 1960. (119) Alto Adige (Segni), September 19, 1961.

Chapter III

THE COLLECTIONS OF DIPLOMATIC DOCUMENTS RELATIVE TO THE ORIGINS OF WORLD WAR I

⟅ SUMMARY: 1. The Collections of Diplomatic Documents Published prior to the Outbreak of World War I.   2. The Collections Drawn from the Russian Archives.   3. The Special Austrian and German Collections.   4. The German General Collection.   5. The British Collection.   6. The French Collection.   7. The Austrian Collection.   8. The Boghicevic (Boghitschewitsch) and Schwertfeger Collections.

1. THE COLLECTIONS OF DIPLOMATIC DOCUMENTS PUBLISHED PRIOR TO THE OUTBREAK OF WORLD WAR I.

The publication of organic collections of diplomatic documents sponsored by governments reached unprecedented levels at the end of World War I. These publications were prompted mainly by the controversies that arose over the issue of war responsibility and by the extraordinary importance acquired by propaganda as an instrument of political conflict. Such collections, precisely because they were designed to influence world public opinion and to explain the activities of governments during the crises that led to 1914, have relatively well-defined chronological limits and normally do not extend beyond the period from the end of the Franco-Prussian War to the beginning of World War I.

It is interesting to recall, nevertheless, that in the years just prior to World War I there already were several published collections of documents in existence. To be exact, the French government in 1910 started the publication of a collection concerning the origins of the Franco-Prussian War, which included a vast quantity of material for the period from December 23, 1863, to the declaration of war.[1] This undertaking,

[1] *Les origines diplomatiques de la guerre de 1870–1871* (29 vols.; Paris: Ficker, later Lavauzelle, 1910–30).

comprising twenty-nine volumes and completed in 1930, is also interesting from a technical point of view: the documents are arranged chronologically, according to a plan which was to be followed by the French in subsequent collections. To facilitate research, each volume is prefaced by a Table of Contents.

It is not easy to explain how the Quai d'Orsay, usually very reticent about opening its archives, arrived at the decision to publish the documents. It is probable that there was nothing particularly dramatic behind the decision, and it was made simply in response to the repeated requests of French scholars, who were anxious to have at their disposal material which was of great scientific interest, although of little political value. On the other hand, these requests may have stimulated a favorable reaction on the part of Foreign Ministry officials, who were interested in demonstrating that the direction of foreign policy under the Second Empire had been the personal prerogative of Napoleon III and that therefore only he was responsible for the errors that led to the disaster of 1870.

In any event, the French collection is a splendid achievement, not only from the point of view of content, but also because it set the pattern for successive publications of the same genre. It can justly claim to be the first great collection of diplomatic documents in the modern sense, even though it was preceded by several German documentary collections of importance. In fact, the latter do not fit the strict definition of general collections, being limited exclusively to the activities of a single individual, albeit a major figure. Furthermore, they are not official collections, i.e., they are not published directly by the government but are instead private collections or, at best, semiofficial compilations.

The first of these collections appeared between 1882 and 1884[2] and concerns Bismarck's activities as Prussian representative at the Frankfurt Diet. It is of value only for a study of the relations between the German states.

The collection devoted to Prussian policy for the period 1850–58, published by Poschinger in 1902,[3] has a much wider scope and includes the dispatches of Manteuffel, Prussian Minister of Foreign Affairs during those years.

To complete the identification of the principal collections of diplomatic documents relative to the years preceding the outbreak of the Franco-Prussian War, attention should be called to three other collections, which,

---

[2] H. von Poschinger (ed.), *Preussen im Bundestag 1851–1859* (4 vols.; Leipzig: Hirzel, 1882–84). It should be noted that the materials contained herein are reprinted, along with important additions, in the complete works of Otto von Bismarck.

[3] H. von Poschinger (ed.), *Preussen auswärtige Politik 1850–1858* (Berlin: Mittler, 1902).

however, were published *after* World War I and are, therefore, expressions of the postwar tendency to rush archival materials into print.

The first of these, published in 1926 by Professor Hermann Oncken,[4] focuses on Napoleon III's Rhineland policy and consists of three volumes of which the first is essentially a critical introduction, while the second and third contain a wide selection of documents taken from the Austrian archives. The period covered is 1863–70, with special emphasis on the events following the Austro-Prussian War of 1866. From the Italian standpoint, the most interesting subjects treated are the negotiations for the projected Italian-French-Austrian alliance directed against Prussia—negotiations which resulted in no more than an exchange of noncommittal letters between sovereigns.

The collection published under the direction of Professor Heinrich Srbik, beginning in 1934,[5] is larger but is limited exclusively to Austrian relations with the German states. It assembles, in five large volumes, a mass of documents drawn from the Austrian archives for the period 1859–66 and is evidently designed to provide as complete a picture as possible of the origins of the Austro-Prussian War of 1866. However, the fact that several important problems, such as the Italian and Polish questions, are all but ignored and Austrian Balkan policy is, for the most part, not discussed stimulated some criticism on the part of scholars. The documents are arranged chronologically, but the inadequacy of the Tables of Contents makes consultation of the materials especially burdensome.

Publication of a collection on Prussian foreign policy for the years 1858–71 was begun in 1932 as an answer to the French collection.[6] It was designed to include the Treaty of Frankfurt, but publication was interrupted by the outbreak of war, and the ten-volume set ends with February, 1869. No other volumes have appeared since that time, though it is possible that the project will now be reactivated and completed. An interesting facet of this collection is the inclusion of a small number of unpublished documents drawn from the archives of other countries (principally Great Britain and Russia), but it does not include Bismarck's dispatches, published in the general collection devoted to his work. It is regrettable also that this collection lacks an adequate Table of Contents to facilitate consultation. The lacuna left by the omission of the last volumes

[4] H. Oncken (ed.), *Die Rheinpolitik des Kaisers Napoleon III 1863–1870 und der Ursprung des Krieges von 1870–1871* (3 vols.; Stuttgart: Deutsche Verlag Anstalt, 1926).

[5] H. Srbik (ed.), *Quellen zur deutschen Politik Osterreichs 1859–1866* (Berlin: Verlag Gerhard Stalling, 1934–38), 5 volumes in 6 tomes.

[6] *Die Auswärtige Politik Preussens, 1858–1871* (Berlin: Verlag Gerhard Stalling, 1932–45), 10 volumes in 11 tomes.

of the collection has been filled, in part at least, by Robert H. Lord's publication on the origins of the Franco-Prussian War,[7] in which 263 documents from the Prussian archives are reproduced, preceded by an excellent introduction.

Recently, 307 other documents relative to Prince Leopold's candidacy for the Spanish throne, drawn from the holdings of the German archives captured at the close of World War II, have been published in Great Britain by Georges Bonnin.[8] This material had been kept in strict secrecy until its publication here. While it is important because it makes possible an accurate reconstruction of the negotiations surrounding this episode, apparently it does not substantially alter the judgments on the question rendered earlier by scholars.

2. THE COLLECTIONS DRAWN FROM
THE RUSSIAN ARCHIVES.

Apart from the exceptions noted above, all of the great collections of diplomatic documents appeared, as observed earlier, after the end of World War I. It should be remembered at the outset that these publications do not stem from any desire on the part of governments to satisfy the needs of scholars, but rather from the degree of importance that wartime propaganda assumed as an instrument to be used against the enemy. During the 1914–18 conflict direct civilian participation in warfare for the first time reached such a proportion as to constitute a major implement of war for the states involved. It was to eliminate or at least neutralize this potential threat that this new tool was devised—an instrument that proved so efficacious as to astonish even those who employed it on a grand scale.

The importance of this new implement of war was readily grasped by the Bolsheviks, who, once they had attained power with the November Revolution, promptly employed it extensively to strengthen their internal position, to hasten the end of the war, and, finally, to discredit the so-called capitalist governments in the eyes of the masses and to incite the latter to world-wide revolution, believed by them to be the inevitable consequence of the war.

In order to bolster its propaganda thesis that the war had been plotted by the capitalist-imperialist powers, as well as to enlighten the Russian people on the blunders of the Czarist regime, the Soviet government began the

[7] Robert H. Lord, *The Origins of the War of 1870* (Cambridge, Mass.: Harvard University Press, 1924).
[8] Georges Bonnin (ed.), *Bismarck and the Hohenzollern Candidature for the Spanish Throne* (London: Chatto and Windus, 1957).

publication of a series of documents taken from the Ministry of Foreign Affairs in St. Petersburg—documents that included, among others, the Treaty of London concluded between Italy and the Entente powers on the eve of the Italian intervention in 1915, the agreements granting the Straits to Russia, and the British-French-Russian-Italian negotiations for a partition of the Middle East.

In the initial phase of publication, the material was printed, without the slightest regard for organization or order, in journals, newspapers, and especially in the *Krasny Archiv*,[9] a specialized journal that continued to publish these documents for twenty years and is, therefore, the most important source for them.

Of particular significance in these revelations is the fact that the Soviets, in addition to making public the Czarist documents, also published a number of diplomatic documents of other countries which had been deciphered by the famous "Black Cabinet" in St. Petersburg and preserved in the archives of the Russian Ministry of Foreign Affairs. When it was possible to compare these with the originals, the Russian version proved to be genuine, thus confirming the reliability of the source as well as the exceptional efficiency of the Czarist decoding service.

Nevertheless, even if the doubts regarding the authenticity of this material must be considered without foundation, it is equally probable that the Soviet editors selected the documents to be published on the basis of political and propagandistic criteria and that not all of the historically valid material has appeared.

Naturally, it is impossible to determine what portion of the total documentary holdings was published in this manner. In any event, note should be taken of the enormous importance of the documentation published by the Soviets on the activities of the western powers in the Far East in order to underline, for the benefit of the Chinese people, the aims of the imperialistic, "bourgeois" governments and to point out what really lay behind their political and economic penetration of China. This propaganda effort by the Soviets was closely linked to the new attitude of the revolutionary government, which, while pursuing the objectives of domination of Czarist Russia, intended to arrive at these goals by totally different means. Thus, the Kremlin began its campaign of denunciation of the policies of the previous Russian government by renouncing concessions

[9] An abridged edition in English of the first thirty numbers of the *Krasny Archiv* is available: Louise M. Boutelle and Gordon W. Thayer, *A Digest of the Krasny Archiv* (Cleveland: The Cleveland Public Library, 1948). A selection of documents drawn from the *Krasny Archiv* and concerning the history of Russia for the period 1915–18 is to be found in Colwyn Vulliamy, *The Red Archives* (London: Bles, 1929).

in China, along with extraterritorial rights. They hoped to win the sympathy and support of the Chinese public in order to aid the revolution then under way in South China and destined to end only in 1949. This unquestionably audacious move was to have profound consequences in China, as well as a tremendous effect for years to come on the shape of events in the Far East.

Simultaneously, the Soviets achieved the important objective of placing White Russians, who had taken refuge in China in large numbers, in a particularly disadvantageous position. The majority of these refugees were forced to emigrate because with the loss of extraterritorial rights their condition became extremely precarious. The publication of these documents by the Soviets was also to have a certain influence on the negotiations then under way in Paris. From time to time, they were referred to in memoranda published by the Chinese on the Shantung question and on the problem of the German islands in the Pacific, and these memoranda were repeatedly referred to during the peace conference sessions.

In Italy, too, the Soviet revelations echoed loudly. In 1917, *Pravda* published a text of the Treaty of London containing a clause obligating the Entente powers "to support Italy in her opposition to any proposal that might be made to seat a Vatican representative at the peace table at the close of the present conflict" (Article 15). In reality, the text made public by the Soviet newspaper was very different from the original, and it had the effect of accentuating the anti-Vatican statements that the original actually contained. Understandably, a violent polemic broke out between the Holy See and the Italian government, an argument which was taken up by Catholic forces in other countries as well. The revelations made public in *Pravda* concerning the territorial advantages conceded to Italy by the Treaty of London intensified the violence of the arguments over the new Adriatic frontier, strengthened the belief of Italians that the Entente powers were jealous of Italy, and, finally, added fuel to nationalist and Fascist forces in their sharp critical attacks on the democratic Italian government.

However, this mass of material could not be expected to have wide circulation in the western world: the Russian language was not generally understood, and, furthermore, it was difficult to follow documentation presented in such a disorganized manner. To offset these inconveniences, numerous volumes containing the most important materials that had appeared in Soviet newspapers and journals were published, in the period immediately after the war, in France, Great Britain, the United States, and especially in Germany. These volumes, even as summarized in the press, were to have the double effect of stimulating both public curiosity and scientific interest in the study of the problems associated with diplomatic activities of the prewar period.

Among the early publications that should be noted is the Cocks collection,[10] which appeared in Great Britain in 1918. It was small in size but crammed with important disclosures; for example, it contained the text of the Treaty of London and the accords reached for the partitioning of the Ottoman Empire. Of particular interest were the minutes of the meeting of the Russian Crown Council on February 8, 1914, during which plans for the conquest and occupation of the Straits in the event of war were discussed and approved. A short time later an abridged edition of these minutes appeared in French, edited and translated by Emile Laloy,[11] which added some fifty new documents that the Soviets had published in the interim.

An important contribution toward the reconstruction of the negotiations preceding Italy's intervention in the war is a little volume published in 1923 and entitled, "The Italian Intervention in the Secret Papers of the Entente."[12] This publication—another example of Soviet skill in selecting propaganda subjects—was designed to exploit the discontent and disillusionment rampant in Italy after the Paris conference; it revealed, among other things, the extent to which the western powers had opposed the expansion of Italy in the Adriatic from the moment negotiations leading to the Treaty of London were begun. It was through this little book that the Italian public first learned how trying the negotiations leading up to intervention had actually been. Only then was it possible to understand that the myth that Italian intervention was something decisive, a thing feared and desired by all powers concerned, in fact did not at all correspond with reality. Neither the Entente, which was seeking to draw Italy into its camp, nor the Central Powers, which were working to block the intervention of Italy on the side of the Allies, had indicated anything more than a willingness to make well-defined and limited concessions—a revelation that laid bare the actual value ascribed by both sides to Italian intervention.

It is important to observe that in the interim the Soviet publications were gradually changing their pattern, abandoning their practice of publishing diplomatic documents in newspapers and journals, and turning instead toward the compilation of collections limited to a single question and issued

[10] Samuel Cocks, *The Secret Treaties and Understandings* (London: Union of Democratic Control, 1918).

[11] *Les documents secrets des Archives du Ministère des Affaires Etrangères de Russie* (Paris: Bossard, 1919).

[12] *L'intervento in guerra dell'Italia nei documenti segreti dell'Intesa* (Rome: Rassegna internazionale, 1923).

in book form. If this change reflected a greater ability to organize in the Soviet state, it also offered evidence of a shift in Soviet aims and objectives. Initially, the Soviets were primarily concerned with defeating their enemies at home, bringing the war to a quick end, and combating on a psychological plane the intervention of the armed forces of foreign powers in the affairs of the U.S.S.R. However, once it became clear that efforts to topple the revolutionary regime had failed, the Soviets then concentrated their propaganda attack on the capitalistic system, accusing it of being the source of international conflict.

This new course taken by the Soviet propaganda machine does not appear as a clear-cut, progressive development. First of all, the collections are not all of the same consistency or on the same level: some are designed to present exhaustive documentation on one well-defined subject, while others contain heterogeneous material, albeit of equal importance. The negative aspects of this practice are shown in the publication of many of the same documents over and over again. Yet the technique has undoubtedly contributed to greater diffusion of the papers emerging from the Russian archives and has encouraged, in a most dramatic way, production in the field of diplomatic history.

Among the numerous publications of this kind, Baron von Romberg's work is worthy of note.[13] It was designed to reveal the extent to which the Czarist government was guilty of the gravest kind of falsification in the publication of the Orange Book on the origins of the war. Von Romberg published the Russian Orange Book along with the original texts of the dispatches made public by the Soviets, and, in this way, proved that the Czarist government had suppressed over half of the telegrams exchanged with its embassy in Paris, among them several of decisive importance for an exact evaluation of specific events. As for the telegrams they had published, these had been severely amputated or contained insertions deliberately contrived to change the meaning of the original dispatch. The effect of this volume was sensational: not only did it demonstrate the absolute unreliability of the Orange Book as a source, but it also cast serious doubts on the authenticity of the documents published in similar fashion by the other Entente governments. Von Romberg's work constituted a potent incentive for a critical re-examination of the whole question of war responsibility on the basis of more precise documentation.

And finally, to add to the bewilderment of a public already shaken by

---

[13] G. von Romberg (ed.), *Die Fälschungen des russischen Orangebuches* (Berlin and Leipzig: de Gruyter, 1922). The English translation is *The Falsifications of the Russian Orange-Book* (London: Allen and Unwin, 1923; New York: Huebsch, 1923).

these revelations, *Un livre noir* appeared, beginning in 1922. This was a collection in three volumes (six tomes).[14] Because it appeared in French translation, it was destined to be widely read and to become an instrument of intense anticapitalist propaganda throughout the world.

The publisher of *Un livre noir*, who was linked to the Communist party in France, planned the publication as a popular and informative contribution. For this reason the volumes lack summary Tables of Contents and scientific notes, but the material they contain is extremely significant, even if difficult to use. The collection is based mainly on a Soviet publication dealing with Franco-Russian relations in the period 1910–14,[15] with important adjuncts, as well as some omissions (for example, the documents relative to the Liman von Sanders mission are not included). The correspondence between the Russian Ministry of Foreign Affairs and the Russian Embassy in Paris forms the nucleus of the collection. It lacks basic unity because the subjects treated are extremely varied. But in addition to the dispatches exchanged between St. Petersburg and Paris, the collection includes documents relative to other embassies, conference minutes, memoranda of ministry officials, etc.

The first volume is devoted to the correspondence of 1911–12 between the Russian Ambassador to Paris, Izvolski, and the Ministry of Foreign Affairs. The second volume is a continuation of the first to August 5, 1914. It also includes sixteen telegrams from Benckendorff, Russian Ambassador to the Court of St. James, sent between February, 1913, and July 26, 1914, in addition to the protocols of the Franco-Russian military conferences of August, 1913. Other documents refer to specific problems such as the negotiations for the loan to Russia, the Straits question, etc.

The third volume is divided into four tomes. The first contains Izvolski's telegrams for the period August 5, 1914–April 21, 1915, and is especially useful for the reconstruction of the negotiations between Italy and the Entente powers. The second tome concerns Balkan policies, with special reference to the Anglo-French-Russian efforts to induce the Greeks to enter the war. Here, too, the documentation is based on the correspondence of the Embassy in Paris and, except for an unexplained five-month lacuna in the correspondence, covers the period September 25, 1915–April 11, 1916. The third tome is the least well organized of all because it treats widely different subjects, ranging from the negotiations to draw Rumania into the war to the discussions on the partitioning of the Otto-

---

[14] *Un livre noir. Diplomatie d'avant guerre d'après les documents des Archives russes* (Paris: Librairie du Travail, 1923–32), 3 volumes in 6 tomes.

[15] *Materialy po Istorii Franko-Russkich Otnošenisza 1910–1914* [Data for the History of Franco-Russian Relations, 1910–1914] (Moscow, 1922).

man Empire into spheres of influence. The documentary base is also much larger and includes telegrams to and from the Russian embassies in Paris, London, Rome, Berne, and Bucharest for the period April–September, 1916. Of somewhat minor interest is the fourth and last tome, which brings the collection up to March 22, 1917, and is useful for an understanding of the peace proposals launched during that period.

To repeat, the importance of *Un livre noir* lay not only in the documentary content it offered to scholars, but also in the fact that it was widely read and influenced public opinion all over the world.

The public was shocked by the disclosures concerning secret subsidies paid to French journalists and politicians[16] by the Czarist government. However, perhaps the most significant point brought to light by *Un livre noir* is the proof of the very strong Russian spirit of revenge against Germany for the humiliation and loss of prestige suffered at its hands, especially during the Bosnian crisis. These *revanchist* tendencies appear almost to have been stronger in St. Petersburg than in Paris, and the picture would be incomplete if we failed to remember that Izvolski, Czarist Ambassador to Paris, was then the ex-Minister of Foreign Affairs—Izvolski, one of the protagonists in the Bosnian affair.

Less well known to the general public but of extraordinary significance to historical research is Baron Schilling's diary, which appeared in German translation in 1924. Schilling was Sazonov's Chief of Cabinet in the Foreign Ministry and the latter's closest collaborator. His diary deals with the last days of the July crisis of 1914 and makes possible a detailed reconstruction of the activities in St. Petersburg just before the conflict. More important, perhaps, is the fact that the diary provides the key that enables us to pinpoint the exact time at which the order for general mobilization of the Czarist armies was given, the element upon which rests the entire thesis of those who seek to put the immediate responsibility for the war on the Russians.

In this context it must be remembered that before World War I all European military experts were in agreement that in the event of Russian general mobilization the German government would counter with a declaration of war within twenty-four hours. It was known that, given the numerical superiority of the Russian armed forces, if the Russians were permitted to mobilize their forces completely, the Germans would find

---

[16] On this point see the documents published in "L'abominable vénalité de la presse," in *D'apres les documents des Archives russes, 1897–1917* (Paris: Librairie du Travail, 1931). The majority of the documents contained in this volume were published by the newspaper *L'Humanité* in the period December, 1923–March, 1924.

themselves in an inferior position and would be deprived of any strategic initiative. Moreover, since Russian general mobilization took a long time because of the vastness of the Empire and the shortage of rail transport, the Germans had a margin of about three weeks in which to launch a decisive offensive that would turn the military situation in their favor. As a logical consequence, the idea developed that a Russian announcement of general mobilization was tantamount to a declaration of war; therefore, the ability to reconstruct the exact moment at which the decision to mobilize was made assumed vital significance in ascertaining responsibility for the war.

In Baron Schilling's diary all of Sazonov's meetings are reported, including his conversations, not only with foreign diplomats, but also with the Czar and with the Minister of War. In addition, Schilling gives texts or summaries of many telegrams hitherto unknown and of major importance for the re-creation of the action taken and the objectives sought by the Czarist government. On the whole, it seems that the Russian military did not intend to provoke a conflict. Rather, they urged mobilization to prevent a surprise attack. As a matter of fact, they received the decree for general mobilization from the Czar, who, a short time later, changed the order to one for partial mobilization. At the time no one knew that the Russian General Staff had made no provision for partial mobilization. The military was therefore forced to insist on general mobilization, the only measure for which technical preparations had been made. When they obtained still another decree from the Czar authorizing general mobilization, the military avoided all further contact with him, so that they could present the government with a *fait accompli*. In connection with these documents, it bears noting that Baron Schilling, who fled to London after the Revolution, confirmed, in the Introduction to the English edition of his diary,[17] the complete authenticity of both the diary and the other documents included.

New elements of fundamental importance to the comprehension of Czarist diplomacy during the war came to light a year later in the collection published in Leningrad in 1925 and translated into German in 1927.[18]

Perhaps the major significance of this collection lies not in the information revealed by the documents, but in the fact that it enables the scholar to obtain a real grasp of the characteristics of Czarist diplomacy and thereby provides the means for arriving at an over-all evaluation of Russian

[17] Baron Schilling (diary), *How the War Began in 1914* (London: Allen and Unwin, 1925).

[18] *Carskaja Rossija v Mirovoj vojne* (Leningrad: State Publishing House, 1925). The German translation is *Das zaristische Russland im Weltkriege* (Berlin: Deutsche Verlagsgesellschaft für Politik Geschichte, 1927). There is a severely abridged edition of this work available in French: *Documents diplomatiques secrets russes 1914–1917* (Paris: Payot, 1928).

diplomatic methods. An examination of this material (a part of the collection concerns the Italo-Russian exchanges relating to the Balkans) confirms the impression of the extreme complexity of Czarist diplomacy—traditionally regarded as the most intricate in Europe—but it also reveals how uncertain and hesitant the St. Petersburg government was when situations demanded prompt and decisive action. Apart from the difficulties inherent in the relations between the Balkan states, Russian diplomacy, as revealed by these documents, proved to be anything but positive. The indecision characterizing Russian diplomacy appears to have been a major cause of the Entente's serious diplomatic failures in the Balkans.

The unique nature of the relationship of the Balkan states to each other complicated the already critical situation even further. The ties that linked them to one or another of the belligerent camps were not such as to restrict their freedom of action. Each nurtured claims to portions of the territories of almost every one of its neighbors, and as long as the outcome of the war was in doubt, they were disposed to join one side or the other on the basis of the compensation offered. So, from the beginning of the war, the Balkan capitals became scenes of bitter diplomatic contests, during which the various negative aspects of Czarist diplomacy were clearly revealed. While the Russians were pursuing the impossible objective of trying to bring all of the Balkan states into the Allied camp, their activities manifested their complete inability to press negotiations to a prompt and successful conclusion, hesitant as they were to make decisions and utterly incapable as they were of making acceptable concessions until forced to do so by circumstances.

The collection is divided into four sections, dealing with Turkey, Bulgaria, Rumania, and Italy, respectively. The most important disclosure in the Turkish section is of a proposal advanced by the Turkish government on August 5, 1914, for an alliance with the Entente powers. The offer is all the more astonishing when one realizes that just three days earlier Turkey had secretly signed an alliance with Germany. It is rather difficult to decide whether the offer was a delaying action to allow the Turkish army sufficient time to complete its preparations, or whether it was simply the product of the adventurous mind of Enver Pasha, who with this gambit may have sought to neutralize the Russian threat to the Straits. In either case, the proposal was an interesting one, both for the effect an Ottoman alliance with the Entente would have had on the policies of the other Balkan states, and because it offered the prospect of opening the Straits to Allied material aid to Russia, thereby eliminating a thorny problem which the Allies tried vainly to resolve by force of arms some months later. But on this occasion, too, Sazonov was incapable of making a prompt decision, torn as he was between the desire not to surrender his claims to the Straits and the knowledge of the advantages to be gained by a Turkish alliance. In the end, he decided to postpone any decision until such time as the military situation was clarified, with the result that Enver Pasha brought Turkey into the war on the side of the Central Powers.

It has often been observed that Turkey committed a fatal blunder in allying herself with the Central Powers because it meant war against Russia, the power that coveted Turkish territory. In reality, the Turkish position was desperate: it was impossible for the Ottoman government to escape from German influence on Turkish affairs, which increased markedly at the outbreak of the war with the arrival of two German heavy cruisers in Turkish waters formerly based at Messina, in accordance with a provision of the Triple Alliance; they moved to Constantinople after the Italian declaration of neutrality. Furthermore, had Turkey chosen to join the Entente, it is more than likely that the government would have had to contend with the same problems of nationalism that beset the Empire at the close of the conflict. In contrast, during World War II Eduard Beneš followed exactly the opposite policy in allying Czechoslovakia with the Soviet Union—the very power claiming portions of Czechoslovak territory—with much the same results: Czechoslovakia had to renounce the planned Polish-Czechoslovak confederation, cede sub-Carpathian Ruthenia to the Soviets, and open her doors to Soviet penetration.

The scene of the most violent diplomatic encounter was, undoubtedly, the Bulgarian capital. Sofia was determined to use the world war as a means to avenge the defeats suffered during the second Balkan war and to obtain Macedonia, but no definite plan to achieve these goals had been formulated by the late summer of 1914. Perhaps in no other case are the defects of Russian diplomacy so clearly apparent. Influenced by the bitter Serbian opposition to concessions to the Bulgars and fearful of the effect that a Bulgarian attack on Constantinople would have, Sazonov could not bring himself to make a clear and satisfactory offer to the Bulgarians regarding Macedonia. His dilatory tactics permitted the Bulgarians to extract concessions from him piecemeal, to which they added various conditions. The end result was that Russian delay and ambiguity drove Bulgaria into the arms of the Central Powers—one of the most serious setbacks suffered by Entente diplomacy of the entire war.

Something similar was to happen in the case of Rumania. A Rumanian intervention—whose military importance seems to have been exaggerated by the Entente—was considered a serious possibility the moment war was declared. Rumania was tied to Austria by the alliance of 1883, subscribed to by the Germans later the same year and joined by Italy in 1888. Yet during the second Balkan war Rumanian policy was definitely anti-Austrian. Moreover, Bucharest coveted the Austro-Hungarian territories of Transylvania and Bukovina. In all likelihood, a prompt offer of territories, including Bessarabia, would have induced the Rumanian government to come into the war immediately on the Entente side. But Sazonov hesitated to sacrifice Russian territory, and the opportunity was lost, although the Rumanian decision not to intervene was obviously also conditioned by the first resounding German military victories. Negotiations with Bucharest were reopened in 1915, when new German military successes on the eastern front made a pressure-relieving attack on the lines of the Central Powers particularly desirable. This time the Czar was quick to accept Bratianu's demands; but the latter, impressed by the Entente's difficult military situation, avoided concluding the alliance.

New and difficult negotiations finally brought Rumania into the war in August, 1916, too late for it to have the political and military effects desired by the Allies. Rumanian forces, benefiting from the element of surprise, won some initial victories but were soon put on the defensive by the combined Austrian-German-Bulgarian counterattacks. When the Russian front was breached, the Rumanian position became desperate, and they were forced to accept the terms imposed by the Central Powers in the separate peace of Bucharest in May, 1918.

Finally, the same methods were employed by the Russians in their negotiations with Italy, and the documentation included in the last section of the collection permits a step-by-step examination of the details. However, in this case the influence of the governments of London and Paris on St. Petersburg was far greater because the two western powers were not in the least disposed to surrender control of these negotiations to the Russians, whether because of the greater importance attached by the West to the Italian intervention or because of the vital character of the related Adriatic problems, in which the British and the French had paramount interests. The fact that a vote of the majority decided that London would be the principal scene of the negotiations precluded the prospect of the Russian collection's being the principal source of information on these deliberations. Nevertheless, it does clarify many important aspects of the negotiations, such as the constant Russian pressure to guarantee Serbia a dominant position in the western Balkans; the British reaction to these maneuvers, which was designed to assure the Russians a *longa manus* toward the Mediterranean; and, once again, Sazonov's tenacious resistance to concessions and his clashes with the Allies, especially with Lord Grey, down to the final resolution—the controversy over the date to be set for Italy's intervention.

Some unpublished materials regarding the relations between the western powers and Russia before, during, and after the war are to be found in the volume published in 1926.[19] This is not a compilation of diplomatic documents as such, but rather a collection of essays, purely propagandistic in character, written by Russian officials and bureaucrats who had transferred their allegiance to the new regime. The most important of these is the essay written by General Zaiontchkovsky, which examines the evolution of the Franco-Russian Alliance as modified by the military agreements between the two countries. Zaiontchkovsky seeks to demonstrate that from the moment the alliance was signed the Paris government considered it to be an instrument of war against Germany, and that the Czarist regime betrayed the real interests of the state by surrendering its freedom of action vis-à-vis Austria in order to support the anti-German policy of France.

The tendency of Soviet publications to assume a more organic character, uniting in one volume all of the documents pertinent to a single issue, finds its clearest expression in three collections edited by E. A. Adamov and published between 1922 and 1926.

The first of these is devoted to the relations between the European powers and Greece during the war[20] and constitutes an essential source for the study of the problem either from the point of view of international relations or from that of the internal affairs of Greece, as illustrated in detail in the dispatches of the Russian Ambassador to Athens. In general, it is not a very edifying page in the book of Entente diplomacy. France, Great Britain, and Russia were guarantors of Greek neutrality and territorial integrity, but they did not hesitate to violate this neutrality in the interest of dragging her into the war against the Central Powers and resorted to methods that violated the very principles that their war propaganda was blatantly expounding. The Allied occupation of Salonika resulted in changes in the Athens government and in the monarchy. In effect, it obliged Greece to abandon its policy of neutrality and was directly responsible for the postwar catastrophe in Greece. Greek intervention on the side of the Allies was justified on the basis of Greek territorial claims, and it was precisely for this purpose that Venizelos plunged Greece into a war with Turkey—a war that resulted in the forced exodus of all Greeks living in Anatolia and provoked a crisis whose consequences are still felt.

[19] *Kto dolžnik?* (Moscow: Arioizda-Telstvo, 1926). French translation: Victor Margueritte (ed.), *Les Alliés contre la Russie, avant, pendant, et après la guerre mondiale* (Paris: Delpeuch, 1926).

[20] *Evropejskie Deržavy i Grecija v epochu Mirovoj vojni* (Moscow: State Publishing House, 1922). German translation: *Die europäischen Mächte und Griechenland während des Weltkrieges* (Dresden: Reissner, 1932).

The second collection is limited to the negotiations between the Entente powers for the partition of Turkish territories in Asia Minor[21] and is based on an especially large documentation, in which the material taken from the French Embassy archives in St. Petersburg plays a conspicuous role. Obviously, the object of this collection was to influence the Arab states, demonstrating that if they were reasonably well satisfied with the decisions taken at the peace conference these results were reached only after extensive haggling and a series of deals not always in the best interests of the people most directly concerned. The behind-the-scenes bargaining and the contents of the Sykes-Picot Accords, the negotiations with Russia to provide adequate compensation for the gains contemplated for the British and the French, the efforts of these powers to limit or prevent Italian participation in a division of the spoils—these were all elements which served to illustrate that the old colonial spirit was still very much alive. Behind the façade of solemn declarations of principle, the Entente powers looked upon the Turkish territories strictly in terms of their utility to the occupying powers. The propaganda import of this collection aside, the material contained herein is of inestimable value to the historian. For instance, it permits the reconstruction of the negotiations that led to the agreements of St. Jean-de-Maurienne, which assigned to Italy a vast sphere of influence and control in Asia Minor in the territories of the three vilayets of Smyrna, Adalia, and Konia.

The documentation relating to these problems is completed by a collection on Constantinople and the Straits which appeared in Russian in 1925 and in German and French translation in 1930.[22] This collection is a particularly accurate one; the material is organized systematically, and certain documents published earlier but reprinted in order to give the reader a more complete view of the problem are included. An explanatory introduction, along with notes and a Table of Contents, facilitates the use of the compilation.

This publication was also designed for a specific purpose, that is, to focus the attention of Mustafa Kemal's nationalist government on the threats that

[21] *Evropejskie Deržavy i Turcija vo vremja Mirovoj vosny. Razdel Aziatskoj Turcii* (Moscow: Litisdat, 1924). German translation: *Die europäischen Mächte und die Türkei während des Weltkrieges. Die Aufteilung der asiatischen Türkei* (Dresden: Reissner, 1932).

[22] *Evropejskie Deržavy i Turcija vo vremja Mirovoj vosny. Konstantinopol i prolivy* (2 vols.; Moscow: Litisdat, 1925–26). German translation: *Die europäischen Mächte und die Türkei während des Weltkrieges. Konstantinopel und die Meerenger* (4 vols.; Dresden: Reissner, 1930–32). French translation: *Constantinople et les Détroits* (2 vols.; Paris: Editions Internationales, 1930). The Adamov and Grimm studies found at the beginning of the first and second volumes of the Soviet edition have been omitted in the French edition.

existed to Turkish territorial integrity. By so doing, it increased the value of Soviet friendship in Turkish eyes, a tendency that had already found expression in the Soviet-Turkish accords of 1921. Of course, it was a well-known fact that more than one power coveted control of the Straits, but this collection, like the preceding one, found its *raison d'être* in the Soviet's Near Eastern policy. The latter was designed to weaken the position of the victorious western powers by constantly exposing them to the public as nothing more than champions of traditional colonial imperialism. The right of colonial peoples to independence had been proclaimed at the Congress of Batum, and now it was to be supported by a scientific study of Near Eastern problems, a proposal that the Soviets sought to encourage by placing the necessary materials at the disposal of scholars. Thus, this collection is singularly important, making it possible to re-create the Czarist plans and directives for the acquisition of the Straits through a study of the minutes of the Russian interministerial conferences, the negotiations that led to the Anglo-French-Russian accords of March, 1915, and the behind-the-scenes activities of the Allied military operations in the Gallipoli peninsula.

As may be inferred from the documents, the fact that the St. Petersburg government, on the eve of the war, considered it possible to realize its Straits aspirations in short order has been interpreted as proof that the Russians had planned and precipitated the conflict in order to achieve these aims. However, the documents in question indicate a tendency (hardly new), rather than a hard and fast directive for action; moreover, this interpretation is borne out by the evidence that the Czar's ministers were fully aware of Russia's military weakness. Once war was declared, the Russians had to consider the enormous difficulties involved in realizing their ambitions in the Straits area.

The Gallipoli campaign—launched ostensibly to open a line of supply to Russia and Serbia, but in reality prompted by the desire to apply greater pressure on Greece to enter the war and, above all, to extend British influence eastward—aroused such strong suspicions in St. Petersburg as to induce the Czarist government to insist on broad negotiations to decide the future of the entire Near East. Long and complex negotiations were begun and resulted in the recognition of Russia's pre-eminent interests in the Straits and in the partition of the Ottoman territories between England and France, as agreed upon in the Sykes-Picot agreements of May, 1916.

The documentary material published in this collection also covers the period immediately following the fall of the Czarist government. It illustrates the Russian government's progressive adjustment to the realities of the situation, to the point of the Communist regime's advocacy of "peace without annexations or indemnities." It may be interesting to compare this documentation with the Soviet demands on Turkey advanced in 1945, demands that appear to have been inspired by expansionist tendencies analogous to those of the imperial governments. However, publication of this fundamental collection foreshadowed a third phase, to be marked by the appearance of a vast general compilation, which, under the title "International Relations in the Age of Imperialism,"[23] was able to include all of the documents contained in the Russian archives from the Congress of Berlin to the Bolshevik Revolution.

The collection was begun in 1931 but remains largely incomplete. According to the initial plan, it was to be divided into three series, but no volume of the first series has appeared, and only Volumes XVIII–XXI of the second series have been published, covering the period from May 1, 1911, to November 20, 1912. Volumes I–X of the third series have been issued; these span the period January 1, 1914–March 31, 1916. An edition of this collection has been published in German translation,[24] in which the material has been reorganized along different lines and useful notes have also been added.

Certain peculiarities characterize this compilation and set it apart from similar publications discussed below. First of all, it includes a wide selection of materials relative to the war period, in contrast to almost all official publications of other governments, which terminate with the outbreak of the war. This contrast is readily explained by the fact that the Soviet government had no compunction about revealing the behind-the-scenes activities of the Czarist government, while the French and the British, for example, had solid reasons for keeping secret those activities of an exceptional nature that occur in wartime.

The demands of war give birth to procedures that deviate widely from the norm. Frequently, the most unorthodox techniques are employed, and programs are proposed (often highly theoretical ones) which, even if justified by the needs of the moment, are open to serious criticism if studied apart from their historical perspectives. In fact, these proposals often clash with the moral and legal principles of a sensitive public. Factors such as these, along with the obligation of protecting foreign collaborators who give

[23] *Mezhdunarodnye Otnosenija v epochu imperializma* (Moscow-Leningrad, 1931 et seq.).
[24] *Die internationalen Beziehungen im Zeitaler des Imperialismus* (Berlin: Hobbing, 1933 et seq.). In this edition the material has been divided as follows: Series I, Vols. I–IV; Series II, Vols. V–VIII (these eight volumes correspond to the first eight volumes of the third series in the Russian-language edition); Series III, Vols. I–IV (these correspond to the four volumes published in the second series of the original).

their assistance to the government in such unique activities, induce governments to maintain archival secrecy regarding wartime documents. For the Soviets, these considerations were not only inconsequential but were valid reasons for publication, an excellent incentive to reveal, in accordance with a predetermined propaganda line, those hidden maneuvers that appeal to popular fantasy.

The second characteristic of the large Soviet collection, and a trait common to almost all of the other collections published by that government, is the practice of including numerous documents of other governments deciphered by the "Black Cabinet." Actually, the quantity of such material is so vast as to have made possible the completion of a series of scholarly studies relative to the activities of the Entente powers. Insofar as Italy is concerned, it permitted a reconstruction of the negotiations leading to the Treaty of London, the accords of St. Jean-de-Maurienne, etc., on the basis of Italian materials long before the Rome government decided to publish its own collection of diplomatic documents.

Nonetheless, from the technical standpoint the compilation reveals some serious weaknesses. It is very inconvenient to use because of the absence of adequate Tables of Contents, which would permit the reader to establish a sense of direction so as to avoid a long and involved search for pertinent documents. According to the publishers, this inconvenience was to have been eliminated by the Table of Contents found at the beginning of each volume, but these have proved to be inadequate because they do not list all of the major questions and the numbers of the corresponding documents.

A negative judgment must also be rendered on the character of the notes accompanying the texts: in effect, these notes satisfy purely propagandistic ends and maintain no scholarly standards whatsoever. They are repeatedly slanted, to the point and beside the point, to underline the war plots of the capitalist powers and the imperialistic aims of their actions. On the other hand, the facility with which the editors arrive at certain conclusions leaves the reader somewhat perplexed, especially in the apparent absence of any doubt in their minds as to the objectivity of their assertions. As a case in point, several notes concerning Asia Minor blithely refer to an Italo-Turkish accord of March, 1914, for the restoration of the Aegean Islands (the Dodecanese) to Turkey in exchange for railroad concessions in Asia Minor—an accord which, in fact, never existed.

The German edition is by far superior to the original and for this reason is the most widely used by scholars. In fact, not only is the translation extremely accurate, but the notes which have propaganda overtones have been replaced with notes edited according to the most exacting standards of objectivity, together with excellent bibliographical references. Further,

Tables of Contents have been appended to each volume, which greatly simplifies a search for documents by subject.

Along with the official Soviet publications, mention must also be made of several private collections of documents coming from the Russian archives, whose importance is surely not inferior to the official collection. The first of these is Count Benckendorff's papers, published by authority of the German government and edited by the ex-Counsellor to the Russian Embassy in London, Siebert.[25]

The importance of this collection becomes readily apparent when it is recalled that Count Benckendorff had been the Russian Ambassador to London from 1903 to his death in 1917 and that during his long mission he found himself in the very midst of events destined to revolutionize the alliance arrangements of the major European powers. He arrived at his post on the eve of the Russo-Japanese War and had to face that particularly critical period in Anglo-Russian relations, brought on by developments in the Far East as well as by the traditional rivalries existing between the two countries regarding Central Asia. Once past the critical phase, he was instrumental in the *rapprochement* between London and St. Petersburg, so warmly encouraged by Paris, whose success was crowned by the 1907 accords relative to Persia, Afghanistan, and Tibet. From this time on, Anglo-Russian relations became openly friendly, and Benckendorff labored successfully to win British support for Russian policy during the course of the Balkan wars. He participated in the London Conference of Ambassadors for the preliminary peace as the Czar's emissary, and he also took part in the negotiations leading to Italy's intervention in the war, which, as already noted, took place in London. His correspondence is, therefore, a prime source for the study of the conflict that raged between Sazonov and Lord Grey over the extent of the territorial compensation to be awarded to Italy.

The opportunity to examine the archives of the Czarist Embassy in London also led to the publication of Baron de Staal's papers several years later. Baron de Staal had been Benckendorff's predecessor in London from 1884–1902. In spite of the excellent edition of these papers produced by Alexander Meyendorff, Baron de Staal's nephew,[26] the material is of relatively minor importance because the years of the Staal mission coincide

---

[25] Benno Siebert (ed.), *Diplomatische Aktenstücke zur Geschichte der Ententepolitik der Vorkriegsjahre* (Berlin-Leipzig: De Gruyter, 1921). An American edition was published in New York in 1921 by G. P. Putnam's Sons. A second German edition, considerably enlarged, edited by Benckendorff, appeared under the title *Diplomatischer Schriftwechsel* (3 vols.; Berlin-Leipzig: De Gruyter, 1928).

[26] Alexandre Meyendorff (ed.), *Correspondance diplomatique du Baron de Staal, 1884–1900* (2 vols.; Paris: Rivière, 1929).

with the period in which Anglo-Russian rivalries in Asia lent a certain static quality to the relations between the two powers, a situation stemming from the acknowledged impossibility of resolving the fundamental antagonisms that separated them.

However, much information on the major themes of European diplomacy for those years is provided by these papers. Among others worthy of mention is the proposal made by Lord Roseberry in 1894 to Czar Alexander III for the convocation of a European conference to study the arms problem and to formulate proposals for the limitation of land forces. The indecisive reply from St. Petersburg, followed by the Czar's death, shelved the British suggestion. Four years later, Czar Nicholas II was to reopen the entire issue. It is significant to note in this context that Great Britain championed the forces favoring disarmament at the very time that the Franco-Russian Alliance was being concluded, and that the Russians took the lead in the disarmament proposal when the limits of French power were revealed during the Fashoda crisis.

Another private collection has contributed a great deal to our knowledge of the diplomatic events leading to World War I. It was published by the German diplomat Fritz Stieve, and includes the papers of Alexander Izvolski,[27] Russian Foreign Minister from May, 1906, to September, 1910, and then Ambassador to Paris until his resignation in June, 1917. Stieve's collection is limited to the period January 1, 1911–June 30, 1914, with one volume for each calendar year. The material is organized chronologically, and a table at the beginning of each volume listing the documents, their dates, and the identity of the sender and the recipient simplifies research to a degree. Despite the fact that most of the material contained in these volumes was already known through earlier Soviet disclosures (particularly Un livre noir), the collection, which in all probability is based on the archives of the Russian Embassy in Paris, remains a major source for the study of the relations between Paris and St. Petersburg. This is particularly true for the re-creation of many episodes relating to the origins of the war and is even more important when it is recalled that Izvolski, thanks to his personal contacts, was in a position to exercise a great deal of influence on the decisions taken by his government and by his sovereign.

Having neatly assembled in one convenient set the complete file of the principal documents concerning Izvolski's activities during the period in

[27] Friedrich Stieve (ed.), *Alexander Petrovic Iswolski. Der Diplomatische Schriftwechsel, 1911–1914* (4 vols.; Berlin: Deutsche Verlagsgesellschaft für Politik und Geschichte, 1926). Stieve added a volume of commentary based on the German defense thesis regarding war responsibility: *Iswolski und der Weltkriege* (Berlin: Deutsche Verlagsgesellschaft für Politik und Geschichte, 1926).

question, the reader is free to subject his character and personality to a remarkably close scrutiny. In general, the impression gained is one of a man of inexhaustible activity—often confused and lacking in judgment, to be sure, but nevertheless driven by an indestructible will to create a diplomatic situation that would permit Russia to avenge the defeat suffered at the hands of Germany during the Bosnian affair.

Stieve also published a kind of supplement, which united Izvolski's correspondence of the period 1914–17 in one volume,[28] except that notwithstanding the title, the documents included end, for all practical purposes, with May, 1915. The few documents referring to the later period are of very minor importance. Despite the fact that the worthwhile documents are essentially limited to the first ten months of the war, their level of usefulness is very high, particularly for the war aims issue and for information concerning the Entente's diplomatic activity vis-à-vis the neutrals, whom it hoped to inveigle into the war against Germany.

An understanding of Izvolski's activities during the years in which he was at the helm of the Ministry of Foreign Affairs is provided by the two volumes containing his private correspondence.[29] They include a complex of letters written between 1906 and 1910 by the Russian ambassadors accredited to the five most important European capitals (Berlin, Vienna, Paris, London, and Rome), which, with few exceptions, had been unpublished. The practice, already very common in that era, of carrying on a personal correspondence outside of and complementary to the official one allows the historian, when such correspondence is available, to examine with greater precision the state of mind and views held by the writer. There is a latitude of expression in these letters that cannot be found in the official correspondence. The two volumes are of some significance, although it is very probable that the selection was strongly influenced by a desire to present Izvolski's policy in the best possible light.

Among the Soviet publications, a place apart is reserved for the minutes of a special commission of investigation, nominated after the abdication of Nicholas II to inquire into the illegal activities of the old regime.[30] In essence, the documentation contained herein concerns the internal aspects

---

[28] F. Stieve (ed.), *Iswolski im Weltkriege. Der diplomatische Schriftwechsel Iswolskis aus den Jahren 1914–1917* (Berlin: Deutsche Verlagsgesellschaft für Politik und Geschichte, 1926).

[29] Alexandre Iswolski, *Au service de la Russie. Correspondance diplomatique 1906–1911* (2 vols.; Paris: Les Editions Internationales, 1937–40).

[30] French translation: *La chute du Régime Tsariste: Interrogatoires des Ministres, Conseillers, Géneraux, Haut Fonctionnaires de la Cour Impériale russe par la Commission Extraordinaire du Gouvernment Provisoire de 1917* (Paris, 1927). The French edition consists of a selection of the materials from the original seven-volume Russian edition.

of Czarist policy and touches only occasionally upon diplomatic affairs. On the other hand, the interrogation of high officials reported in these minutes, conducted in an atmosphere that was anything but serene, shows such clearly defensive characteristics that their historical accuracy is open to serious question. The importance of this publication lies in the fact that it illustrates the kind of source that soon afterwards was given the widest kind of dissemination and markedly influenced the reconstruction of the diplomatic and military events relating to World War II.

3. THE SPECIAL AUSTRIAN AND GERMAN COLLECTIONS.

Within months, the example set by the Bolsheviks was followed by the revolutionary governments established in Germany and in Austria after the fall of the monarchies. The new governments planned the publications to serve internal propaganda needs, that is, to demonstrate to their respective publics that the masses had been dragged into the war through the machinations of the emperors and by certain military and political cliques within the old ruling castes.

A three-volume collection was published by the new Austrian government in 1919 as a supplement to the 1914 Red Book; it comprises the documents for the period between the assassination of Archduke Francis Ferdinand at Sarajevo (June 28, 1914) and the outbreak of the world war (August 3, 1914), in addition to several telegrams that extend the period to August 27, 1914.[31]

The value of this collection becomes evident when it is recalled that Vienna was the very center of the war crisis and that now for the first time archival material was brought to light which made it possible to reconstruct the events of those decisive days with greater objectivity than had been the case when only the colored books were available.

Finally, it was now possible to understand clearly two elements characterizing the policies of the Austrian Foreign Minister, Count Berchtold, during the entire July, 1914, crisis: on the one hand, his firm determination to take advantage of the situation in order to square accounts with Serbia, and on the other, his inability to control the situation once he had taken the first retaliatory steps. Furthermore, with the new documentation available, scholars were able to trace the evolution of the Austrian government's determination, on the day after the assassination, to liquidate the Serbian problem once and for all.

[31] *Diplomatische Aktenstücke zur Vorgeschichte des Krieges 1914* (3 vols.; Vienna: Staatsdruckerei, 1919).

The documents contained in the collection confirm the fact that two essentially diverse currents existed within the policymaking echelons of the Austro-Hungarian governments. The Hungarians were primarily preoccupied with Rumania, which, despite its adherence to the Triple Alliance, gave indications of being a doubtful ally. Therefore, the Magyars planned to offset the danger of a Rumanian defection by bringing Bulgaria into the Triple Alliance and by coming to terms with Turkey and Greece, acts which would have completely transformed Rumania's role within the Alliance system. In Vienna, the primary interest instead was in implementing an anti-Serbian policy, and the conclusion had been reached that only force would serve to eliminate the threat of the Pan-Serbian ideal. Thus in the summer of 1914 relations between Vienna and Budapest were strained by a substantial difference in point of view, not only with regard to objectives but also (in view of the persistent Magyar objections to the use of force to resolve the problems facing the Dual Monarchy) with regard to methods.

In this instance, the documentation contained in the supplement to the Red Book reveals the essential factors determining the course of events. First of all, Germany, which in the preceding year had been able to exercise a moderating influence on the Austro-Hungarian government, now granted Vienna carte blanche. Kaiser William and the German military experts held it to be highly improbable that Russia would risk war to protect Serbia, but they were also of the opinion that in the event of war Germany was now at the peak of her power and could face a test of arms with confidence of success. In effect, the German position was very similar to that taken by the Nazi leaders twenty-five years later, during the crisis of 1939: faith in their ability to localize a conflict with a small power, but, at the same time, conviction that if a general war had to come, that particular moment offered Germany the greatest chance of success.

Conversely, Berchtold, who was not noted for his energy, reacted psychologically to the assassination of the Archduke; that is, he reacted with violence, fearing that conciliatory approaches would lower the prestige of the Dual Monarchy in the eyes of Germany and of the world. As confirmed by the evidence in this compilation, Berchtold took advantage of the support given to him by Berlin to overcome Hungarian opposition to the plan to attack Serbia. Moreover, he expressed himself in such a way as to leave the impression that it was Germany who insisted on a military solution of the Serbian problem. After this maneuver and throughout the rest of the crisis, Berchtold maintained a very reticent attitude toward Berlin, toward the President of the Hungarian Council, Tisza, and toward his own Emperor, Francis Joseph.

The most revealing evidence of Berchtold's attitude is to be found in his dealings with the Italian government. Berchtold refrained from communicating his intentions to them, as he feared a demand for compensation on the basis of the provisions set forth in Article VII of the Triple Alliance agreement. Moreover, it is necessary to recognize that Berchtold's reticence, insofar as Italy was concerned, was greatly abetted by San Giuliano's attitude. The latter, despite his awareness (thanks to several indiscretions) of what Vienna was contemplating, refrained from taking the initiative to clarify the entire situation in order to avoid jeopardizing any possibility of eventual Italian territorial growth.

Other documents of exceptional importance coming from the Vienna archives appeared the following year in a semiofficial collection edited by Professor Alfred F. Pribram, which contained the principal treaties subscribed to by Austria-Hungary between 1879 and 1914.[32] This work made available for the first time the complete texts of such agreements as the Austro-German Treaty of Alliance of 1879, the Triple Alliance treaties, the Three Emperors' League accords, concluded in 1881 and renewed in 1884, and the Austro-Serbian treaty of 1881, renewed in 1889. This massive documentation simplifies the task of putting a large portion of European diplomatic activity into proper perspective with reasonable accuracy, something that Pribram himself accomplished in the second section of his work, using the materials contained in the Vienna archives. In the last edition Pribram also made use of the first volumes of the German general collection, about which further comment will be made below.

It was learned that the Austro-German Alliance remained in effect even after the conclusion of the Triple Alliance, a factor that explained why the *casus foederis* of the Triple Alliance provided only for the eventuality of an unprovoked attack by France or by two or more great powers, but not for an attack by Russia alone, a situation provided for in the alliance of 1879. This fact must be kept in mind in order to understand the peculiar position in which Italy found herself within the framework of the relationship of the Triple Alliance to the Central Powers, for whom the alliance of 1879 constituted the real basis of mutual solidarity.

Perhaps the most interesting part of the Pribram collection deals with the Triple Alliance and the evolution of that treaty of alliance on the occasions of its periodic renewals. Inevitably, the content of the agreement signed in 1882 reflected the difficult position in which Italy found herself at that time. In substance, it may be said that neither Berlin nor Vienna was disposed to assume precise obligations. The Austrian government, pre-

[32] *The Secret Treaties of Austria-Hungary 1879–1914* (2 vols.; Cambridge, Mass.: Harvard University Press, 1921–22).

occupied by the tension existing between Rome and Paris, feared being drawn into a war with France. The Germans, despite the fact that they evaluated the Italian position with greater accuracy, particularly Italy's probable role in the event of an Austro-Russian conflict, had little faith in Italian military capability and even less in the serious intentions of its political leaders. And so Italy found itself subscribing to an alliance which offered very little.

Within five years, Italy's position in the alliance clearly improved. The intensification of the Austro-Russian clashes in the Balkans and the crisis in Franco-German relations contributed to increasing Italy's value as an ally, and in 1887 the Italians were able to obtain two significant concessions from their allies as the price for renewing the agreement. The first of these, an Italo-Austrian accord annexed to the alliance treaty, now obliged the two contracting parties to respect the *status quo* in the Near East or, in the event that the situation was altered to the advantage of one, to grant compensation to the other. This was the first time that the interests of the Italian Kingdom in the Balkans were recognized by an international agreement, and this recognition was conceded by the very country that had consistently refused to do so in the past. The concession is all the more significant when it is understood that the Austrians were fully aware that such a concession created obstacles to their own plans for expansion and at the same time posed threats to Austro-Hungarian territorial integrity because of Rome's tendency to seek compensation in Austrian crown lands inhabited by Italians.

Second, Italy also obtained a guarantee of her interests in the Mediterranean, by means of an Italo-German convention annexed to the pact that widened the *casus foederis* to include the eventuality of French occupation of Tripoli or Morocco. Clearly, the provision was designed to maintain the *status quo* in North Africa, and therefore, being purely defensive, it received German support.

In the subsequent renewal of the treaty in May, 1891, Rudinì's efforts resulted in the addition of still another article, in which Germany agreed, subject to a formal accord, to support any action Italy might undertake to re-establish the equilibrium in North Africa in the event of its upset by another power. Pribram's publication permitted students to examine, for the first time, not only the real content of the Triple Alliance but also the very important periodic changes which had substantially modified Italy's position with respect to the Central Powers. These changes converted the Alliance from an essentially static document to a dynamic one, at least for the period from 1891 to the Italo-French accords of 1902.

At the same time the Germans published a collection of diplomatic documents covering the period from Sarajevo to the declaration of war,[33] adding a few documents that expanded these limits slightly (the first document is dated June 15, 1914, and the last is dated August 6, 1914). Published shortly after the war, this publication is also known simply as the Kautsky documents or the Kautsky collection, so called for the Socialist editor-statesman responsible for the work. Certain characteristics of this work reappeared again and again in subsequent German collections and also influenced the publications of other countries. When compared with the Bolshevik collections, the differences are profound: the polemical introductions and the notes designed for propaganda effect so common in the Soviet collections are replaced in the Kautsky documents by scholarly notes, which record the original texts of many telegrams or the contents of important telephone conversations and contribute to a more precise understanding of the events in question. The only omission is the military documents, whose interest must be considered significant and, in some instances, definitive.

It must be emphasized that the conclusions reached through a study of the materials do not appear to support the contentions of the German revolutionaries that William II and his government cold-bloodedly exploited the Sarajevo incident to unleash the world war. Undoubtedly, the personality of the Kaiser lent itself to serious criticism. His famous marginal comments on documents (whose historical importance has, perhaps, been exaggerated, since they do not appear to have seriously affected the conduct of foreign affairs) reveal a rather volatile temperament, an unfortunate trait for a man in his position. It might also be admitted that William II did not find the idea of war completely abhorrent. But all of these conjectures do not amount to the slightest proof that either he or his advisers harbored a preconceived plan to precipitate a general war. Instead, the major blunder of the German government during the crisis was that of having failed to restrain its Austrian ally from following a course that was inevitably destined to bring on Russian intervention and a general war. This was the central point of the German political drama and the central point of the drama of all great powers, whose foreign policies are influenced, far more than is normally supposed, by those of their less powerful allies. Germany was strong, but she was also isolated, and nowhere was this fact more clearly understood than in Berlin, where there was complete awareness that Germany had only one sure ally, Austria-Hungary. Therefore, it was a mistake to give *carte blanche* to Vienna in its

[33] Karl Kautsky (ed.), *Die deutschen Dokumente zum Kriegsausbruch* (4 vols., Charlottenburg: Deutsche Verlagsgesellschaft für Politik und Geschichte, 1919–20); 2d ed., enlarged, 1927. English translation: *The Outbreak of the World War* (Washington, D.C.: Carnegie Endowment for International Peace, 1924).

controversy with Belgrade. But it must also be pointed out that at this time a German refusal to do so would have involved great risks, particularly after the veto of the previous year. Such a refusal might well have broken the ties between Germany and Austria-Hungary, leaving Germany to face the Franco-Russian menace alone.

Generally, it can be affirmed that the material contained in the Kautsky collection only partially fulfilled the aims of the Socialists who had sponsored it. In truth, the criteria employed for the selection of the documents does not appear to have been consistent. One has the distinct impression that the initial strong anti-Hohenzollern character of the collection became progressively weaker as the compilation developed, and that the opening document (a report from the German Ambassador to St. Petersburg, in which Russia's bellicose policies are illustrated) was added after the collection had taken shape. In other words, it seems that, in the process of gathering material, the desire to focus war responsibility on the Imperial government was replaced by a desire to bring about an admission of complicity on the part of the other powers. Besides, the polemical nature of the German historical literature, so evident immediately after the war, was beginning to change. If, as a result of Socialist prodding, violent criticism of the previous regime had prevailed in the beginning, it was not long before scientific studies turned to an examination of the problems relative to the origins of the war, with the avowed purpose of discrediting the thesis advanced by the victors that the Central Powers were solely and exclusively responsible.

Because of its importance, this element requires clarification. Before the 1914–18 conflict, the idea of war responsibility had never entered the thinking of peacemakers and, therefore, had never exercised any influence on the framing of a peace treaty. To be sure, normally the vanquished state was called upon to pay an indemnity, but this fact should not lead us to the wrong conclusion: the defeated nation was obliged to pay the indemnity because it had lost the war, not because it was judged guilty of provoking it.

In contrast, during World War I, the question of war responsibility became the target of the propaganda machines on both sides. The accusation leveled by the Allies against Germany of having provoked the war could not help but have certain consequences: if the war was Germany's responsibility, it was simple justice that Germany should pay for the material damage her actions had caused. From this emerged the concept of reparations, to which Germany was condemned by the Treaty of Versailles.

Consequently, the question of who precipitated the conflict became an issue of absorbing interest. If Germany had been condemned to pay reparations because she was in fact responsible for the war, it follows, then, that in the event that it could be demonstrated that she was not guilty of the charge, or that the victorious powers shared the responsibility, the reparations system would collapse—at least on moral grounds.

Therefore, a potent political impulse with eminently practical ends drove the Germans to publish numerous collections of documents, designed to furnish scholars with the raw material necessary to destroy the official thesis of the Entente, which had been sanctioned by the Versailles pact.

With this motivation, a major contribution toward an understanding of the events of the last days of the crisis was made: the publication of the dispatches sent by the representatives of the German states in Berlin—dispatches that constitute the subject of two collections, one taken from the Bavarian archives[34] and the other, which appeared much later, comprising materials from Baden, Saxony, and Württemberg.[35] The information that these provide is indeed valuable. Through the confidential comments of the Prussian Chancellor, officials, and Prussian political leaders, the statements made to diplomats—since they were Germans also, a greater freedom of expression was permitted—present an accurate picture of conditions in Berlin during the critical days of July, 1914, and permit conclusions concerning some of the problems relative to the immediate responsibility for the war. Thus it can be seen that, despite the existence of warmongers (particularly among the military, who held the situation to be extremely favorable from a strategic point of view), the prevailing opinion was that the Austro-Serbian crisis should be exploited to permit the Austro-Hungarian Empire to strengthen its weakened prestige, which was beginning to cause serious concern in German circles. This attitude would almost certainly bring on an Austro-Serbian war, but it was believed that such a conflict could be localized because Russia was bluffing and Great Britain was not about to go to war to "pull others' chestnuts out of the fire."

The reports of the *Reichstag* Commission of Inquiry, created in 1919 to look into the various aspects of the war,[36] contribute a great deal to historical knowledge for that period. The Commission was divided into four subcommittees, each to study one of the following topics: (1) the

[34] Pius Dirr (ed.), *Bayerische Dokumente zum Kriegsausbruch und zum Versailler Schuldspruch* (Munich and Berlin: Oldenbourg, 1922); 2d ed., enlarged, 1923; 3d ed., enlarged, 1925.

[35] August Bach (ed.), *Deutsche Gesandschaftsberichte zum Kriegsausbruch 1914* (Berlin: Quaderverlag G. m. B. H., 1937).

[36] *Beilagen zu den stenographischen Berichten über die öffentlichen Verhandlungen des Untersuchungsausschusses* (Berlin: Norddeutsche Buchdrückerei und Verlagsanstale, 1921). English translation: *Official German Documents Relating to the World War* (2 vols.; New York: Oxford University Press, 1923).

causes of the war, (2) the factors that prevented the conclusion of an earlier peace, (3) the acts of disobedience and disloyalty committed against political authority, and (4) cruel and inhuman acts committed during the conflict. While the reports of the last two subcommittees contribute very little of interest to students of diplomatic history, the data collected by the first two subcommittees furnish important and interesting information for the diplomatic historian. By means of a questionnaire submitted to responsible officials in service during the period in question, the first subcommittee was able to gather together a group of statements about such hitherto obscure phases of the July crisis as the real meaning of the Austro-German conversations at Potsdam, the activities of the German Ambassador, Tschirschky, whose personal initiative was reported to have gone beyond his instructions, and so on. The second subcommittee conducted an exhaustive inquiry into the impediments to attempts to negotiate a peace treaty during the winter of 1916–17; in contrast to the first subcommittee, it arrived at the conclusive judgment that it would have been possible to initiate peace negotiations except for the decision to renew unrestricted submarine warfare made by the Germans at that precise time. This conclusion must be taken with a grain of salt since, given the peculiar mental characteristics of the British, it is extremely doubtful that Great Britain would have agreed to a compromise peace.

Finally, three official collections were published on the armistice and the peace, and they are of primary interest to students who wish to study the particular details that brought the conflict to an end.

The first of these[37] covers a discussion that took place between the German High Command and the political leaders in Berlin on the need of requesting an armistice. In essence, the collection was aimed at clarifying for the German public various facets of the debates then raging on the war responsibility issue.

The second collection,[38] in three volumes, assembles rich material relative to the armistice period and the activities of the Armistice Commission. It throws light on the work of the German delegates, who were obliged to labor in an atmosphere of extreme difficulty, created by the intransigence of Foch and his collaborators and by the numerous violations of the armistice clauses that were perpetrated by the Allied representatives, particularly in Alsace-Lorraine and in the eastern territories. The failure to lift the blockade and the continuous flow of new demands by the Entente

[37] *Amtliche Urkunden zur Vorgeschichte des Waffenstillstandes* (Berlin: Reimar Hobbing, 1919); 2d ed., 1924. English translation: *The Preliminary History of the Armistice* (New York: Oxford University Press, 1924).

[38] *Der Waffenstillstand, 1918–1919* (3 vols.; Berlin: Deutsche Verlagsgesellschaft für Politik und Geschichte, 1928).

amounted, in effect, to a continuation of the war and reduced Germany to a state of total collapse. While such behavior may have facilitated the acceptance of the Versailles *Diktat,* it also created deep resentments, which would color the attitudes of the German government and public for a very long time.

The third collection[39] concerns the peace treaty, and its emphasis is mainly on the correspondence exchanged between the German delegation at Versailles and the Allies. Other previously published documents also find a place in the collection, such as "The German White Book concerning the Responsibility for the War,"[40] published for the first time in 1919, and Brockdorff-Rantzau's official declarations.

4. THE GERMAN GENERAL COLLECTION.

All of these publications were received with great interest by scholars and by the general reading public. However, if they had great value for the comprehension of developments on the eve of the war, or of several aspects of the war itself, or of its conclusions, they cast little light on the long-range origins of the war. As researchers tended to penetrate ever deeper into the causes, their tendency was toward widening the scope of their investigations; that is, toward inquiring into the major events in international politics of the decades preceding the war, for only through these could be found the long-range causes of the catastrophe.

The emergence of this new field of investigation gave the German government the opportunity to develop further its defensive thesis of the origins of the war and to advance, in the eyes of world public opinion, the German case for a revision of the Treaty of Versailles based on the recognition of the principle of general co-responsibility for the war. It was with this goal in mind that Berlin decided to undertake the publication of a vast general collection of diplomatic documents, drawn from the archives of the Ministry of Foreign Affairs, dealing with the entire period, from the preliminaries to the Peace of Versailles (February 26, 1871) to the start of the crisis in 1914.[41]

[39] *Materialen betreffend die Friedensverhandlungen* (Charlottenburg: Deutsche Verlagsgesellschaft für Politik und Geschichte, 1919).
[40] *Das deutsche Weissbuch über die Schuld am Kriege mit der Denkschrift der deutschen Viererkommission zum Schuldbericht der Alliierten und Assoziierten Mächte* (Charlottenburg: Deutsche Verlagsgesellschaft für Politik und Geschichte, 1919); 2d ed., enlarged, Berlin, 1927.
[41] *Die Grosse Politik der Europäischen Kabinette* (Berlin: Deutsche Verlagsgesellschaft für Politik und Geschichte, 1922–26), 40 volumes in 54 tomes. The

The project had no historical precedent, and it was destined to create a sensation not only in Germany but also in the rest of the world. As expected, there were those who opposed the gesture because its results would be largely negative. These criticisms triggered off varied polemics in Germany, particularly on the part of conservatives, who feared that the documentary evidence would strengthen the existing criticisms of the old regime, as had been the case when the supplement to the White Book was published in 1919. In this view, Kautsky and the other Socialist writers who had exploited the diplomatic documents for the purposes of internal propaganda had done little more than to damage seriously Germany's international position and to undermine the German government's "claim to innocence" in the question of war responsibility. Conservatives predicted that the Socialists would use the material published in the general collection in much the same way. Other critics of the proposal were quick to point out that the time was not right for such a publication, that there existed a real danger of inflaming passions even further, and that it was certainly an inopportune time to make public a huge documentary collection which, limited exclusively to the diplomatic story, was hardly sufficient in itself to produce an accurate picture of events.

In Entente circles the German announcement was greeted with a certain dismay. In fact, it was estimated that once the Germans had published their documents and they had been studied, along with the contents of the Soviet collections, very few diplomatic secrets would remain inviolate and particulars would be brought to light which, for political reasons, should best be kept out of the public domain for the time being. But the German decision was made with precisely this intention; that is, in order to foil all attempts by other states to keep their previous activities secret, in this way obliging the victors to publish the documents contained in their archives. The Germans were convinced that these documents would demonstrate that by their policies all of the Great Powers contributed to bringing on the war.

The commission, which selected the material with surprising speed, completed its task in four years and published the forty volumes (fifty-four tomes) of the collection between 1922 and 1926. The vastness and importance of the data assembled was without precedent. What was most striking was the organization of the project, conditioned by highly scientific

---

collection terminates with the beginning of the Sarajevo crisis because the post-June 28, 1914, material had been published in the supplement to the White Book. There is also a French edition, *La politique extérieure de l'Allemagne* (Paris: Costes, 1928 *et seq.*), but it is incomplete, and, for the moment, the edition ends with the thirty-second volume and the year 1908. In the French edition, the documents are organized chronologically.

criteria which found expression in the wide selection of documents and the rich scholarly notes. Even if the German collection was designed to fulfill clearly defined political aims, it brought the debate to a level where only scholars and others equally well qualified were capable of authoritative comment, and this comment could be given expression, in general, only in serious scholarly writing. On the other hand, the objections of those who were prepared to doubt the authenticity or the completeness of the documentation were muted by the evidence, which seemed to exclude the possibility of falsifications or omissions of any consequence, certainly those that could materially alter the meaning of events.

From the technical viewpoint the great German collection stands as a model of its kind, even if its editors cannot entirely avoid criticism. In the first place, the collection is based almost exclusively on reports, an approach that offers the advantage of permitting greater exposition of the various situations it describes and of eliminating the chance of errors in deciphering telegrams. On the other hand, the almost exclusive use of reports precludes the possibility of following the exact order of events and/or reconstructing the action of the Berlin government in all of its details.

The commission has also been criticized for the way the material is organized. Instead of adhering to a chronological system and listing the documents according to the date sent or received, the editors chose to assemble in separate chapters all of the data relevant to a specific question. It was affirmed that this system was adopted to aid the research efforts of those interested in studying a particular problem. In reality, it is likely that the system of division by subject matter was chosen primarily to accelerate the publication date by taking as a starting point the contents of the various storage files of archival materials. In any event, if at first glance the organizational plan appears to offer certain advantages, a closer examination reveals that its negative aspects more than outweigh the positive.

It must be noted that the rule that each document must deal with a single issue is not always strictly observed, and, as a consequence, it sometimes happens that data concerning subjects other than the principal one appear in a telegram or a report. However, its greatest disadvantage is that this artificial division creates a series of separate impressions, makes it difficult to re-create the atmosphere of the scene in which the reaction to the reports occurred, and blocks a clear view of the nexus existing between the various issues and a quick grasping of the influence of one on the other. In conclusion, the organizational plan adopted by the German commission is only an apparent simplification of the work of the historian. In order to see the panorama of the period in all of its detail, he must study other chapters of the collection in addition to those which pertain to his research problem, so as to reconstruct the natural links between the various questions which the artificial division by subject destroyed.

Insofar as the documents themselves are concerned, it should be mentioned that the editors observed selection criteria that are definitely perspective in nature. The Bismarckian period seems to be covered in broad strokes, while documents are included in increasing abundance as progress is made toward more recent times (and thus those of greater political interest).

The scientific merits of the collection remain to be evaluated. As has been stated earlier, when it appeared, it created the impression that it had no important omissions, and it was this fact that gave the publication its authoritative stature. Such a positive evaluation is equally valid today. To be sure, when the opportunity arrived of examining the archives of the Wilhelmstrasse, which were captured by the Allied troops during the last phase of World War II, it became apparent that a portion of the unpublished material was of real historical importance. Yet in general the omissions of the collection remain without vital significance. Of course, it should come as no surprise that certain selection criteria were observed which contributed to political ends. The degree may vary, but almost every collection of the genre is tainted by this practice. It is not difficult to understand how the editors of the German collection—who were subject to strong political pressures—may have sought to temper the requirements of historical accuracy with the desire to avoid doing great damage to their country.

Nevertheless, the reception given to the great German collection and the effects that the work had on the nature and course of scholarly research proved the judgment of the sponsors of the project to be absolutely correct. On the basis of a documentary collection unrivaled to date, German and foreign scholars have been able to reconstruct events accurately and in such detail as to demonstrate that they did not support the German "war guilt" thesis affirmed in the Treaty of Versailles: many went so far as to apply the Entente thesis in reverse and to assert that it was France and Russia who, by their policies and actions, made war inevitable; the more moderate elements concluded that the most plausible hypothesis associated all of the Great Powers, including Great Britain, in co-responsibility. It is evident that this mass of literature,[42] in part inspired by scholarly goals, in part by political interest, but in every case destined to have an enormous impact on

[42] For an overview of the historical writing on this subject see Federico Curato, "La storiografia delle origini della prima guerra mondiale," in Ettore Rota (ed.), *Questioni di storia contemporanea* (Milan: Marzorati, 1952), I, 393–530.

world public opinion, could not but cause grave concern in responsible London and Paris circles. Be that as it may, the fact remains that the *Grosse Politik* was and is the foundation stone upon which all of the literature relative to the diplomatic origins of World War I is based.

The capture of the German archives by Allied troops during World War II[43] brought other data to light which, in a sense, make it possible to bring the German collection up to date.

The first publication incorporating the new material was edited by Zeman and deals with the relations between the Berlin government and the Russian revolutionary movement from 1915–18.[44] The new documentation permits a closer study of the German wartime diplomatic activity, only imperfectly understood until now, which was to label Germany as the "mother of the Russian Revolution." In fact, the idea that the war would be a long one with the outcome uncertain and that Germany would have to fight it on two fronts became accepted as early as November, 1914. The German government and General Staff were thus presented with the problem of finding a way to bring the war on one of the two fronts to a victorious conclusion. The attempts to negotiate with France and with Russia to this end are too well known to warrant more than mention in passing. However, in the case of Russia, German diplomacy was not limited solely to negotiation with the Czarist government. Russia's internal situation offered the possibility of pursuing another course, that of supporting the opponents of the Czarist regime, an action that would have the immediate effect of weakening the internal structure of the St. Petersburg government and the later effect of favoring the emergence of a new ruling class with which it would be possible to arrange a separate peace under advantageous conditions.

The Zeman collection offers an insight into this attempt, even if it can only be an indication of what went on—given the nature of the action, it was not to be expected that the archives would contain an abundance of material. From the available evidence it is possible to document the origins and aims of the policy of aiding the Russian revolutionaries, the contacts between them and the German government, particularly those made through the Russian emissary, Helphand, and the Wilhelmstrasse official, Von Bergen, and the substantial role played by this policy in bringing the Bolsheviks to power. The documentation is extremely rich for 1917 but tapers off sharply, in amount if not in importance, for the succeeding months because the editor purposely ignored the material on the already

[43] On the German archives during World War II, see p. 162.

[44] Z. A. B. Zeman (ed.), *Germany and the Revolution in Russia 1915–1918. Documents from the Archives of the German Foreign Ministry* (London: Oxford University Press, 1958).

sufficiently well-known negotiations at Brest Litovsk. It is unnecesary to emphasize the importance of this collection, given the nature of the documents and the problems to which they refer—problems hitherto only vaguely understood and without documentary support.

A significant contribution is being made by a collection now in the process of publication, whose aim is the clarification of the German attitude on the peace issue during World War I.[45] This question has been examined many times on the basis of countless testimonies, so that the collection does not and cannot offer any especially sensational revelations, but it does enlarge our knowledge and is very useful for the purpose of checking, completing, and correcting what is already known. Moreover, the editors did not limit themselves to a consideration of the peace overtures in a narrow sense but have also included a rich documentation on the negotiations between Vienna and Berlin to determine war aims in view of a possible compromise peace. This simplifies the task of reconstructing the position assumed by the Central Powers on several questions, such as the Belgian and Polish issues, and clarifies certain aspects of the dissension in Germany over the political and military conduct of the war effort. When completed, this compilation will amount to three volumes, containing nearly 1,500 documents. To date only the first volume, which covers the period August, 1914–January, 1917, has appeared. The major issues treated are the attempt to arrange a peace with Russia through Denmark in 1915, immediately after the colossal defeats suffered by the Russian armies, and the Austro-German negotiations of March–June, 1916, to resolve the Polish question. In addition, it provides very important data on Belgian contacts with King Albert during the winter of 1915 and the peace offer of December, 1916, especially with regard to the exchange of views on this occasion between the Chancellor and the general staffs of the army and the navy. The collection, which presents the documents in their original languages, is edited in accordance with the most exacting scholarly criteria and is accompanied by faultless summary tables, Tables of Contents, and explanatory notes.

5. THE BRITISH COLLECTION.

The British government was the first to react to the sensation created by the German general collection. Following the publication of the Kautsky

[45] André Scherer and Jacques Grunewald (eds.), *L'Allemagne et les problèmes de la paix pendant la première guerre mondiale. Documents extraits des archives de l'Office allemand des Affaires étrangères*, Vol. I: *Des origines à la déclaration de la guerre sous-marine à outrance* (*août 1914–31 janvier 1917*) (Paris: Presses Universitaires de France, 1962).

documents, the historian Headlam-Morley, consultant to the Foreign Office, was charged with preparing a similar collection drawn from the Ministry's archives and, like the German one, covering the period between Sarajevo and the British declaration of war on Germany. While Headlam-Morley was at work selecting the documents, news reached London of the decision taken by Berlin to publish the great general collection; in addition to clearly revealing the inadequacy of a collection limited to the final days of the crisis, this news led to the obvious conclusion that British policies would not always appear in a favorable light if major prewar diplomatic secrets were revealed to the public.

These considerations prompted the Labourite Ramsey MacDonald, Britain's Prime Minister, to authorize, in the summer of 1924, the publication of an analogous general collection of documents taken from the archives of the Foreign Office and covering the period 1898–1914 (that is, from the time Britain abandoned her policy of "splendid isolation" to the declaration of war on Germany). The project was entrusted to two well-known scholars, George P. Gooch and Harold W. V. Temperley; they in turn asked Headlam-Morley to continue his collection, already well under way, and to include it as the last volume of the general collection.[46] This explains why the volume which chronologically should have been the last to appear was the first to be published, and it also accounts for the marked differences that exist in the organization of Headlam-Morley's volume in comparison to the others in the series.

The British editors adopted the system of organizing the material into chapters according to subject. In this decision they were evidently influenced by the pattern set for the German collection. However, the British editors sought to eliminate the inconveniences inherent in such a scheme of organization by prefacing each volume with a summary outlining its contents in some detail and by adding a subject matter index and a name index containing references to the pertinent documents. Despite these precautions, it appears that the negative aspects inherent in the system were not eliminated. From this point of view, the chronological system adopted by Headlam-Morley for his volume is much more satisfactory.

The usefulness of the collection is somewhat reduced by the extremely restrictive criteria adopted in the selection of documents, particularly in the initial volumes, where the documentation is, on the whole, insufficient. This insufficiency is due in part to failure to consult private archives such as those of Joseph Chamberlain and Lord Salisbury, which contain materials

[46] *British Documents on the Origins of the War, 1898–1914* (London: His Majesty's Stationery Office, 1926–38), 11 volumes in 13 tomes.

of the greatest importance for the study of negotiations carried on outside of official channels, such as, for example, the Anglo-German *rapprochement* discussions in 1890.

However, it must be mentioned that the position of the British editors was substantially different from that of their German or Soviet counterparts. The fact that the latter dealt with materials referring to regimes which had ceased to exist and with the secrets and reputations of individuals who required no particular protection gave them much greater freedom of choice in selecting their material. For the British editors the task was not so simple. Notwithstanding their unquestioned scholarly integrity, they were faced with the necessity of giving due consideration to the political implications of each selection, whether for Britain or its friends and allies, in order to avoid domestic or foreign repercussions not directly pertinent to historical research.

It is hardly possible to determine accurately to what degree this factor may have influenced the choice of materials. Yet it must be recognized that on more than one occasion the editors demonstrated a remarkable broadmindedness in their choices; for example, the republication of the August 6, 1914, report by Sir Edward Goschen, British Ambassador to Berlin, containing Chancellor Bethmann-Hollweg's famous phrase referring to the treaty guaranteeing Belgium's neutrality as a "piece of paper." As a result of the work of the Allied propaganda machines, this phrase, taken out of context and published in such a way as to imply its exact opposite, became a slogan around the world for the cynicism that characterized German diplomacy. The truth is that as uttered by Bethmann-Hollweg and reported by Goschen the phrase had an entirely different meaning. It had no disparaging implications whatsoever. On the contrary, it expressed the distress of the German Chancellor, who, taken by surprise by the British declaration of war, saw his entire policy, which had been dedicated to bringing about a new era in Anglo-German collaboration, culminate in an unforeseen disaster. It is true that this document had been included in the first British Blue Book, published in 1915, but it is equally true that its distorted interpretation had been accepted by the public, thanks to the work of the Entente propagandists. The republication of this document—not absolutely necessary, since the text included in the Blue Book was substantially correct—testifies to a high degree of objectivity.

Nevertheless, the Foreign Office collection has some unique characteristics, which contribute to its striking individuality and greatly increase its scientific value. In the first place, in general, and unlike the German general collection, telegrams rather than reports form the documentary base of this work. The result is that a more precise reconstruction of events is possible, beginning from the moment and the manner in which certain information reached the Foreign Office for the first time.

Of exceptional importance is the fact that the minutes referring to certain documents, in which the opinions of the Foreign Office officials are recorded, are also included. As a matter of fact, it is the practice of the Foreign Office, when instructions have to be prepared, to use a four-column sheet of paper: in the first column the competent office chief writes the text of the communication in black ink and initials it; in the second column the division head either expresses his complete approval of the text by simply affixing his signature in blue ink, or introduces modifications by writing them out, or may suggest that the document not be transmitted; in the third column the Permanent Undersecretary (a post equivalent to that of Secretary General in the Italian Foreign Ministry) in turn makes his observations, using a different color of ink; in the fourth and final column the Minister for Foreign Affairs, using red ink, introduces the final changes and affixes his signature.

This procedure, which removes the document from the anonymity of the Minister's signature and preserves the individuality of the staff, is of exceptional interest to historians in that it permits the internal formative process of British foreign policy to be traced in the opinions of the upper echelons in the Foreign Office, expressed in writing, reflecting the impressions of the moment, and in the complete belief that they would never be published.

Thus, for example, the telegram sent by the British government to Tokyo on August 6, 1914, requesting Japanese intervention in the war on the basis of the terms of the Anglo-Japanese Alliance as renewed in 1911, was commented on negatively by the Permanent Undersecretary. This negative comment confirms the existence of two different points of view in the Ministry: one opposed Japanese intervention for fear of the complications that it would cause in the Far East and the repercussions it would have on the policies of the United States and of the Dominions, while the other subordinated everything to the immediate need to find support for an effort against Admiral von Spee, whose naval units were menacing the British lines of communication in the Pacific and Indian oceans.

Other valuable elements in the study of the reactions of the Foreign Office and the attitudes of its officials are the marginal notes inserted by these officials on arriving documents, which, very appropriately, have been included by the editors where they were considered to be of real historical value.

Finally, it should be indicated that a number of documents coming from the military have been included in the collection. The most important are the *promemoriae* from the Admiralty because of the influence they had on more than one occasion on British foreign policy.

As a case in point, the origins of the crisis in Anglo-Italian relations during the Libyan war must be searched for in the completely negative position taken by the British Admiralty toward the Italian occupation of the Aegean islands (the Dodecanese), which the Admiralty considered a threat to the Straits and to the life line to India. The Admiralty's opposition in this case provides the key to several problems which would otherwise be incomprehensible. For instance, it explains the uncertainties that beset the Foreign Office. Although Britain sought an early end to the Italo-Turkish conflict, fearing that a weakened Turkey would face complications in the Balkans, and wished to maintain a friendly attitude toward Italy in order to avoid compromising the results of the Franco-Italian *rapprochement,* it could not, on the other hand, ignore the pressures of the Admiralty and its strategic requirements. Therefore, the Foreign Office was induced to follow a policy destined to produce a negative reaction in Rome, where, as a result of this shift in British attitude, it was decided to anticipate the renewal date of the Triple Alliance.

The British collection was completed in eleven volumes (thirteen tomes) within twelve years, 1926–38. The first volume refers to the end of "splendid isolation" and is limited almost exclusively to the negotiations for the resolution of several extra-European problems (the Far East, the question of the Portuguese colonies, the Anglo-German negotiations on Samoa, Anglo-French negotiations relative to African territories, the Fashoda affair, the Boer War, etc.), while British relations with other European powers are also observed from this particular angle of vision.

Such an approach is perfectly understandable when it is recalled that British foreign policy was largely conditioned by these issues. Even more, the end of "splendid isolation," a policy whose greatest proponent was Joseph Chamberlain, was the result of the need to arrive at some permanent arrangements with the other Great Powers in order to have greater freedom of action in the colonial field.

This approach is also taken in the second volume, which is essentially limited to two major questions: the negotiations for the Anglo-Japanese Alliance of 1902, Britain's first formal written alliance with another Great Power in this period, and the negotiations with France which produced the *Entente Cordiale* in April, 1904, and marked the definite abandonment of the policy of "splendid isolation." Other chapters concern British activity in the Far East, with particular reference to Manchuria. Twenty-two documents also deal with the attempted Anglo-German *rapprochement* of 1901, the possibilities for the success of which, at that moment, appeared to be extremely good, thanks to the presence of Lord Lansdowne in the Foreign Office in place of Lord Salisbury.

The third volume covers, by and large, the period 1904–6, and documents are provided for the development of the entente with France and its first test in the Moroccan crisis, beginning with the negotiations with Spain and terminating with the Algeciras Conference. The last chapter is devoted to the relations with Germany following the crisis and includes, in addition to the summary account of the meeting between Edward VII and William II at Kronoberg, the important Haldane diary on the mission to Berlin. The Appendix contains a significant report by Sir Eyre Crowe on Anglo-German relations and Lord Sanderson's reply to it, inspired by an entirely different point of view.

The fourth volume is more compact in that it seeks to present a complete picture of Anglo-Russian relations from 1903 to the 1907 agreement. It contains a wealth of documents relating to British policy during the Russo-Japanese War, with particular reference to the Dogger Bank episode, which was provoked by the Russian Baltic fleet at the beginning of its long journey to the Far East, and to the Portsmouth treaty negotiations conducted under the auspices of Theodore Roosevelt. The other chapters deal with the policy of *rapprochement* with Russia, tenaciously pursued by Sir Edward Grey after he took over the foreign affairs portfolio in 1905, and treat separately the three issues (Tibet, Persia, and Afghanistan) which were to form the basis of the 1907 accords. It is to be noted that, unlike the Chamberlain and Salisbury papers, the editors here made full use of Sir Edward Grey's correspondence and the material made available by Sir Arthur Nicolson.

In the fifth volume the system of division by subject matter is employed most effectively. The British editors usually sought to have the volumes follow a chronological order, but Volume V is an exception to that rule. It was obviously planned this way to permit a more complete and unified picture of the policy of the Foreign Office toward Turkey and the Balkan peninsula. The opening and closing dates 1903 and 1909, chosen by the editors for the documents comprising this volume, encompass a period sufficiently homogeneous that, if a division by subject matter had to be followed, they could not have been altered without serious damage.

The volume opens with several long reports on the organization of the Ottoman Empire, its internal situation, and the general course of its foreign policy. Successive chapters include documentation concerning the Macedonian question and the action taken by the Great Powers to oblige the Porte to concede reforms, several documents on the origins of, and what transpired at, the Reval meeting between Edward VII and Nicholas II (the

only documentary source extant on this event), the diplomatic correspondence concerning the Young Turk revolution, and, finally, the
documentation on the Bosnian crisis, more complete than in previous
collections.

Volume VI is much more compact because it is entirely devoted to the
development of Anglo-German relations in the period 1907–12. The
documentation covers, item by item, all of the major problems that served to
reinforce the rivalry between the two countries in these years. Particularly
detailed is the material concerning the naval armament controversy, and
the documentation concerning the Berlin-Baghdad railway and the Anglo-
German negotiations over the Persian Gulf is also very extensive. The last
part of the volume deals with the Haldane mission and the fruitless
conversations that stemmed from it.

All of the data pertinent to the Agadir crisis of 1911 has been taken from
the general framework of Anglo-German relations and incorporated into a
separate volume, numbered VII in the series. In this case, too, the
documentation goes beyond the narrow limit of the crisis because data are
supplied for the Anglo-French-Spanish Accords of 1907. Documents are
included which enable one to follow the developments of the Moroccan
situation to the outbreak of the crisis and beyond, to its solution. The last
chapter is of considerable interest. It includes extracts of comments on the
crisis in the international press, which were transmitted to the Foreign
Office in the dispatches from the heads of missions abroad, a rather unusual
inclusion in a collection of diplomatic documents.

The title of Volume VIII is *Arbitration, Neutrality, and Security,* and it
embraces a complex of totally unrelated questions. Evidently, they were
included here because there was no appropriate place for them in the other
volumes.

The first chapter, concerning relations with Italy, includes a melange of
documents, beginning with the Mediterranean Agreements of 1887 and
ending with 1908. Subsequent chapters deal with Portugal, Norway, the
status quo in the Baltic, and, in greater detail, with the Second Hague
Peace Conference. The most interesting questions seem to concern the
London Naval Conference of 1908–9 (about which the German collection
reveals little or nothing) and the negotiations for the renewal of the
Anglo-Japanese Alliance, which was successfully concluded without arousing the reaction in Washington that had been feared.

Volume IX (in two tomes) is of infinitely greater importance and deals
with the Balkan area from the end of the Bosnian crisis to the Treaty of
Bucharest, August 10, 1913, which terminated the second Balkan war. This
material is also of direct interest to Italy in that it includes about two

hundred documents on British policy during the Libyan war and, as has been noted, describes some of the behind-the-scenes activities by which it is possible to comprehend the policy followed by London on that occasion.

The documentation on the Balkan wars is especially rich and of particular importance to a comprehension of the diplomatic activity of the Great Powers, who, under these circumstances, effectively achieved for the last time prior to World War I the "concert of Europe," succeeding first in localizing the war and then in terminating it.

Volume X is also in two tomes. In the first of these, concerning the Near East, the opening section deals with the emergence of Albania as a sovereign state; it documents the Vienna-Belgrade controversy over the removal of Serbian troops from Albania and the London Conference of Ambassadors, called to decide the territorial limits of the new state and also the question of the dynasty. A great deal of space is devoted to relations with Russia, particularly in relation to the Persian question, toward which the British revealed very great sensitivity, an observation also confirmed by the long negotiations over the Baghdad railway, which are reported in the second tome of Volume X.

Special mention should be made of the documents referring to the transfer of the British fleet from the Mediterranean to the North Sea, discussed in the Grey-Cambon letters of November, 1912. The London government, while "half-promising" military support, proposed to preserve a certain freedom of action in order to protect herself in the event of any foolhardy French *démarche*.

It is common knowledge that this exchange of letters forms the basis of the accusation against Grey that he had compromised Britain's freedom of action. Supporters of this thesis insist that, over and above the literal meaning of the words employed in the letters, what really mattered was the fact that London and Paris had agreed on a common course of action, from which there was no retreat.

Simultaneously, other negotiations were under way between London and Rome to reach an understanding that would oblige the two contracting parties to respect the *status quo* in North Africa. The aim of the discussions was to conclude an agreement similar to the Italo-French agreement of 1902; it was not realized, although the conversations did lead the British to conclude that they could transfer the Home Fleet from the Mediterranean to the North Sea without fear of danger from the Italian quarter.

The Appendix contains several most interesting documents concerning Japan's entry into the war, as well as the much-discussed Kitchener rapport with the leaders of the Arab movement.

The eleventh and last volume deserves separate treatment. As has been pointed out, this volume was the first of the series to be published, in 1926, and was edited by Headlam-Morley, whose criteria differed from those of Gooch and Temperley.

In the first place, here the documents are organized chronologically, making it possible to follow the crisis development in all of its ramifications—day by day, and, in some instances, hour by hour. Moreover, the range of the documentation (which, it should be emphasized, touches an extremely sensitive area) appears to be comprehensive, leading to the conclusion that omissions were reduced to a minimum and, in any case, were not such as to compromise appreciably an accurate reconstruction of the principal events. Therefore, it is possible to conclude that during the decisive days of the crisis the policy of the British government was not as sure or as certain as had been stated. Instead, there was a great deal of hesitancy and doubt among the ministers, even if certain high officials such as Sir Eyre Crowe (whose famous strongly worded memorandum of July 31, 1914, to Grey is also included) appear finally to be committed to a course of action.

Furthermore, in addition to the value these documents have for the re-creation of British policy, they are enormously significant for the information they contain concerning the events taking place in the other capitals of Europe, which is reported by the British diplomats in detail and, above all, honestly. A clear illustration of this point is the episode of the presentation of the note to Serbia following the assassination at Sarajevo, an event which the British Minister to Belgrade was able to communicate to his government before any of his Entente colleagues accredited to that post had received the information. At the same time, he did not fail to inform his superior in London that this momentous information had been given to him by the Italian Chargé d'Affaires (the present Ambassador Cora, then a young Second Secretary of legation), who, because of the excellent rapport between these two diplomats, actually helped the British minister code the telegram containing the news to be transmitted to London.[47]

6. THE FRENCH COLLECTION.

Of the Great Powers entering the war in August, 1914, France was the last to publish a large general collection relative to the prewar period. At the close of the conflict the French government had published, in Yellow Book

[47] On this episode see the article written by Ambassador Cora, cited below, p. 353.

form, three collections concerning, respectively, the Franco-Russian Alliance,[48] the Franco-Italian Accords of 1902,[49] and Balkan affairs, 1912–14[50]—collections which, particularly in the case of the first two, constituted a documentary contribution of no mean importance. They were to create considerable astonishment in London, where, for the first time, the British learned the exact nature of Franco-Russian commitments and the extent of the Prinetti-Barrère Accords.

However, after this promising beginning, the Quai d'Orsay proceeded no further, and while Germany and Great Britain were producing two great general collections, France issued no other official documentary publication, despite the pressure on the Ministry, applied by scholars and statesmen, to do so.

It is very likely that the negative effect of this attitude was not fully appreciated in responsible French circles. If the Quai d'Orsay's failure to publish diplomatic documents can be construed as a blunder which, from a political point of view, placed French scholars at a serious disadvantage with respect to their German and British counterparts, that decision would also prove to be so particularly inopportune as to force the French government to reverse its position some time later.

In the first place, the Quai d'Orsay's silence was eventually rather generally interpreted as an indirect confirmation of the validity of the accusations, leveled by German historians and spread by one school of American historians, that France was in large measure responsible for the war.

In the second place, scholarly studies, which of necessity had to use the German collection as their primary source, were profoundly influenced by it and became largely revisionist in nature, while French historians were helpless in countering the accusations heaped on their country. Therefore, the impression was created that the official thesis placing the responsibility for the war squarely and exclusively on German shoulders was no longer tenable, and the result was serious damage to France. On the international plane, for example, French intransigence on the reparations issue no longer appeared to be justified by the premise inserted in the Versailles treaty, at least to a growing body of world opinion. On the domestic front, the extreme left took advantage of this changing opinion to accuse the

[48] *L'alliance franco-russe. Origines de l'alliance 1890–1893. Convention militaire, 1892–1899, et convention navale, 1912* (Paris: Imprimerie Nationale, 1918).
[49] *Les accords franco-italiens de 1900–1902* (Paris: Imprimerie Nationale, 1920).
[50] *Les affaires balkaniques 1912–1914* (Paris: Imprimerie Nationale, 1921).

ruling classes of having voluntarily led the country into a war that, though won, brought mourning and unprecedented ruin.

By 1928, when the French government finally decided to publish its diplomatic documents, the situation was already compromised, and the announcement that a large collection was about to appear did not create a stir comparable to that caused by the *Grosse Politik*. Once published, the French collection never exercised a decisive influence on world historiography, simply because scholars continued in most cases to base their work on the German documents and limited themselves to adding to them those new facts divulged by the French collection.

The first volume of the Quai d'Orsay's collection appeared in 1929, and the publication was completed thirty years later, although interrupted during the war period. Prior to World War II twenty-nine of its forty-two tomes had been published.[51]

From a technical viewpoint the collection presents several new and important approaches, important because they were to have a real influence on the character of the publications appearing at the close of World War II. For the first time a division by series was introduced, for the purpose of accelerating the publication of those volumes of greater political interest. In fact, the commission decided to divide the entire collection into three series, to be published simultaneously and independent of each other in order to produce the volumes on the crisis of July, 1914—of course, the volumes of greatest interest—within a reasonable period of time.

The first series begins at the same point as the German collection, that is, with the preliminaries to the Peace of Versailles of February 26, 1871, which brought the Franco-Prussian War to a close, and terminates with December 31, 1900. It consists of sixteen tomes, of which nine (1871–August, 1892) had appeared prior to 1940.

The second series starts with January 2, 1901 (the official date of the Visconti Venosta-Barrère Accords) and ends with November 4, 1911, i.e., the Franco-German Accord on Morocco. Only the first eight tomes of this series (1901–January, 1906) had been completed by the beginning of World War II. The series was completed in 1955 and consists of fourteen tomes (the ninth is in two parts).

Series III carries the documentation down to the outbreak of World War I, and publication was completed in 1936 and comprises eleven tomes.

The commission published the documents in chronological order, according to the system adopted for the French collection on the origins of

[51] *Documents diplomatiques français, 1871–1914* (Paris: Imprimerie Nationale, 1929–59), 42 tomes.

the war of 1870, thereby eliminating division into chapters, which the British and German editors had preferred but which, in practice, turned out to be inconvenient. To simplify the research of those studying a specific problem, subject matter tables were incorporated in each volume, wherein the documents are grouped according to the subject treated. Beside each document there is an indication of the content (the so-called *regesti*), a novel approach adopted by almost every subsequent collection.

Insofar as the notes are concerned, they are less numerous and extensive than those in the other general collections, and, as in the *British Documents,* their function is purely explanatory, in contrast to the argumentative nature of the notes in the *Grosse Politik.*

The scholarly value of the collection requires some comment. No doubt exists as to its fundamental importance as a primary source for the study of the diplomatic events leading to World War I, and it can be favorably compared to the collections published by other governments; nevertheless, it has not fully satisfied the expectations of scholars, and, in truth, the majority of the criticisms of the collection are not entirely unjustified.

Meanwhile, scholars were somewhat perplexed by the manner in which the commission was formed. On the commission, scholar-specialists were joined by a large number of diplomats whose assignment it was to clarify, by bringing their own personal experiences into play, the exact meaning of the documents, the real aims they were seeking to accomplish in given circumstances, etc. If from a theoretical point of view the scheme was a good one, the mere sight of the names of Paléologue, Jules Cambon, Barrère, and other ambassadors who played important roles in the shaping of the events in question leaves the reader somewhat dubious as to the effectiveness of their contribution. Their actions had been, in a manner of speaking, *sub-iudice,* even when they were not actually accused outright, as in Paléologue's case, of having contributed by their attitudes toward precipitating the catastrophe.

A clarification which places this reservation in its proper perspective was recently offered by the last secretary-general, a member of the commission from its inception. He has stated that in fact these diplomat-members were present only at the inaugural session of the commission, that only one diplomat participated in the working sessions, and that the latter had never held a major diplomatic post.[52]

This important observation aside, the fact remains that for various reasons, and not all of these attributable to the commission, the French collection contains lacunae of some significance. To begin with, it has been

[52] P. Renouvin, "Les documents diplomatiques français 1871–1914," *Revue Historique,* July–September, 1961, pp. 139–52.

possible to ascertain that French statesmen have been very reticient about putting in writing the most confidential aspects of their activities. The result is that the documentation contained in the archives appears to be inadequate on those very points on which the collection should have brought clarification. Thus, very little has emerged concerning Poincaré's and Viviani's visit to St. Petersburg in July, 1914, during the period that the crisis between Vienna and Belgrade was moving toward a climax. It is very nearly certain that these Franco-Russian talks had a marked effect on the subsequent attitude of the Czarist government. The reticence evident in the Poincaré and Paléologue memoirs, references found in Schilling's diary, Poincaré's attitude during his official speeches, and his comments during his encounters with the Austrian Ambassador all lead one to believe that on this occasion the Russians were encouraged by their allies to maintain an attitude of the most rigid intransigence. It was natural for scholars to expect to find some precise information in the French collection on the content of the talks which Poincaré had with Sazonov and with the Czar, but it appears that nothing was found that would enlighten readers on this issue of great significance in the debate on war responsibility.

A second challenge to the completeness of the French collection is its limited utilization of the private archives, which the British editors, in contrast, used generously in their collection. The omission is rather serious when it is recalled that the practice of carrying on extensive personal correspondence, common during this period, had assumed extraordinary proportions in the French case. This was partially due to the personalities of the ministers of foreign affairs: chosen from a restricted number of qualified statesmen, they remained at their posts for comparatively long periods of time and were able, therefore, as a result of personal preparation and knowledge of foreign affairs, to discuss the issues of the moment directly with the heads of mission. However, it must be emphasized that the failure to utilize the private archives of such statesmen as Delcassé and Hanotaux is not due to the negligence of the researchers charged with the task of assembling the collection. It is due, instead, to the refusal of the statesmen themselves, or of their heirs, to release the archival materials in their possession. This refusal was possible because, after a careful investigation, it was proved that French legislation did not give the state any claim to private papers, that is, to letters and notes sent or received by a minister outside of official channels during his tenure of office.

Other omissions may be noted in the volumes published after World War II. After the liberation of Paris an examination of the archives revealed the loss of documents having a certain importance, a loss that could not always be offset by drawing upon ambassadorial archives. Such losses include the files on the Fashoda affair and the Dreyfus case (it was said that important revelations were contained in the latter) and the correspondence concerning Italy, Spain, Turkey, and the United States for the period 1911–12.

As to the criteria of selection adopted by the commission, these consisted, essentially, of the inclusion of an abundant documentation relative to major issues, by means of which it is possible to reconstruct the general lines of French foreign policy, and, conversely, of ignoring minor issues almost entirely. Moreover, these criteria permitted the exclusion of the documents concerning colonial expansion and the extension of French influence in China and elsewhere. Thus the collection includes relatively little data concerning extra-European problems. For these questions, then, the numerous Yellow Books published periodically retain their fundamental importance, since the Yellow Book documents were not included in the general collection.

Despite the omissions that have been noted, the data revealed by the French publication not only contribute to a clear and precise understanding of the Quai d'Orsay's position in all of the major prewar issues, but, as has already been observed, are of fundamental importance to all scholars for a study of the relations between the Great Powers from 1871 to 1914. Insofar as the question of war guilt is concerned, the French collection has made a major contribution, not always favorable to the French government or to French diplomacy. It can now be verified beyond all doubt that the French, too, shared responsibility for the crisis of 1914.

In this context, the role of the Paris government in encouraging Russian intransigence during the decisive days, as illustrated by Poincaré's visit to St. Petersburg or Paléologue's subsequent actions guaranteeing the Czar, on repeated occasions, full and unqualified support, is of vital significance. Paléologue's role in the development of the crisis deserves the severest censure: he did nothing to prevent the Russian government from taking the fatal step of ordering general mobilization, although he knew full well that this move would inevitably result in a declaration of war by Germany. Moreover, once he became aware of the steps being taken by the Russians, he failed to inform his government accurately or quickly, thus precluding any possibility of a moderating action which might have had decisive results.

It must be further stated that the French government during the July crisis failed to give the slightest encouragement to those few initiatives which might have prevented the war. On July 26, Sir Edward Grey proposed a conference to find a compromise solution to the problem; the following day—prompted by suggestions from Belgrade—the Italian Foreign Minister advanced the idea of a joint action by the other four Great Powers, demanding that Serbia accept the Austrian note in its entirety, while privately and separately the four Great Powers would pledge themselves to make every effort to block any infringement of Serbian sovereignty. Both of these overtures were received by Paris with noticeable coolness and, in effect, were allowed to lapse without the slightest effort being made to utilize them to stem the rush of events toward catastrophe by containing the Russians.

7. THE AUSTRIAN COLLECTION.

Several years later the Austrian government also decided to publish its diplomatic documents concerning the prewar period in order to complete the *Supplement to the Red Book,* which, as already noted, was released in 1919, shortly after the fall of the monarchy.

On the basis of period covered (from the beginning of the Bosnian crisis to the outbreak of the war) and criteria used for selecting material, the Austrian collection is much more limited than comparable collections by other states. The Austrian publishers maintained that Hapsburg Balkan policy had played the major role in the Empire's international activities and, therefore, that they were justified in their decision to publish exhaustive documentation on the Balkan issues that had dominated the European international scene in the years just prior to the war and on which the Austrian archives possessed exceptionally rich holdings.

For this reason the Austrian collection is of a unique nature, something less than a true general collection and something more than a monographic one. From this publication it is a bit difficult to obtain a comprehensive view of Austria-Hungary's relations with Europe because all documents not directly or indirectly related to the Balkans are excluded. Offsetting this weakness is the inclusion of a vast quantity of special data on relations with Serbia and on various aspects of Austro-Russian rivalry in the Balkans, and such new elements as to permit an even more thorough examination of the question of war responsibility.

The nine-volume collection was published as a unit in 1930[53] and was patterned on the French system of chronological order, although without the Table of Contents at the beginning of each volume, a device which proved itself very useful in the Quai d'Orsay's collection. The last volume

[53] *Oesterreich-Ungarns Aussenpolitik von der bosnischen Krise 1908 bis zum Kriegsausbruch 1914* (9 vols.; Vienna and Leipzig: Oesterreichische Bundesverlag für Unterricht, Wissenschaft und Kunst, 1930).

contains an index of persons cited in the documents, but despite its great detail it is not completely satisfactory for easy consultation.

Among the many pieces of new information worthy of note included in the collection, special reference should be made to the first volume, which contains the Austrian minutes of the Buchlau meeting between Aehrenthal and Izvolski on September 16, 1908. The importance of this document is greatly enhanced by the fact that the Soviets have not published the corresponding Russian notes. According to these minutes, Izvolski's later assertion that he was surprised by the annexation of Bosnia-Herzegovina proves to be only partly true. At Buchlau he was informed of Austria's intentions, and he agreed not to oppose such action by the Vienna government in exchange for Austrian support of a future Russian demand for the free passage of individual Russian ships through the Straits.

Therefore, Izvolski's "surprise" was limited to the fact that Aehrenthal, contrary to what had been established at Buchlau, did not give the St. Petersburg government sufficient advance notice before proceeding with the annexation. This would explain the initial reaction of Izvolski, who, up to the time that he hoped to obtain modifications in the agreements governing the use of the Straits, abstained from taking a position opposing the Austrian action. Only when he realized the impossibility of overcoming British opposition to a change in the status of the Straits did he launch a counteroffensive.

This document, which touches upon one of the most controversial questions of the entire prewar period, has not ended the debate. Keeping in mind that the document in question is an undated office copy, more than one historian has questioned this version of the facts, which in effect contradicts the policy line followed by Izvolski and which, if true, would reveal an astonishing degree of naïveté on the part of the Russian Foreign Minister. Without going into the relative merits of the arguments, it bears emphasizing that the publication of the Austrian minutes is an event of exceptional importance and remains basic in any investigation of this episode, which was destined to have such a decisive influence on Austro-Russian relations.

The five following volumes are devoted to Count Berchtold's policy. Berchtold succeeded Aehrenthal in the Foreign Office after the latter's death in February, 1912, and he directed Austro-Hungarian foreign policy until January, 1915. The documents reveal him to be much less brilliant than his predecessor and to have neither Aehrenthal's authority nor his clarity of ideas.

To be sure, in judging Berchtold's work one must be mindful of the particular difficulties presented by the Balkan situation during these years—difficulties which he had in part inherited from Aehrenthal. The latter's surrender of the Sanjak of Novi Bazar, for example, was proving to be increasingly damaging to Hapsburg interests. However, Berchtold was certainly not equal to his task: on the one hand, on more than one occasion his limited ability permitted the consolidation of situations to the point of getting out of hand; on the other, he never succeeded in establishing a clear-cut course for Austro-Hungarian foreign policy. Consequently, foreign policy was left to the tender mercies of the Ballplatz officials, who were in anything but unanimous agreement on a course of action and who soon fell under the growing influence of the military cliques supporting the extremist views of Conrad von Hotzendorff.

The glaring light cast on this state of affairs by the Austrian documents makes it possible to correct a number of judgments previously expressed by historians on the policies of the Vienna government, which were largely founded on what it had been possible to learn from the material contained in the German general collection.

Through a study of the Austrian documents, it is possible to place in its proper perspective the influence exercised by Germany on the Hapsburg Empire attitude during the Balkan wars, also a matter of some importance in the question of war responsibility.

In effect, it has been confirmed that Germany, which in 1912–13 had taken the necessary steps to block an Austrian attack on Serbia, during the July, 1914, crisis shifted positions and gave carte blanche to her ally in the controversy with Belgrade, and in so doing facilitated the outbreak of hostilities. It is undoubtedly true that during the course of the Balkan wars Berlin repeatedly intervened to counsel moderation and prudence, and it is clearly demonstrated by the German documents that both Bethmann-Hollweg and Von Moltke opposed an eventual Austrian intervention in support of Bulgaria, which was under attack by its former allies. However, in the light of the evidence provided by the Austrian collection, it does not appear certain that Berchtold had definitely decided to attack Serbia. Therefore, it may be concluded that the German pressures were not decisive. At best, they served to eliminate any uncertainty in the choice of policies to follow.

In conclusion, the evolution of the crisis of 1914 along lines different from those of the previous years may be explained by the Austrian decision to pursue a policy of maximum risk in its conflict with Belgrade (a decision that was not reached during the Balkan wars) rather than by any change of policy in Berlin.

8. THE BOGHICEVIC (BOGHITSCHEWITSCH) AND SCHWERTFEGER COLLECTIONS.

A complete documentation of the immediate origins of World War I lacked only the contribution of the Serbian government files. The importance of these files cannot be overestimated because the actions of the Serbian government during the July, 1914, crisis had left many questions unanswered, even for scholars who supported the thesis that war responsibility was exclusively limited to the Central Powers.

Despite numerous requests to do so, the Yugoslav Ministry of Foreign Affairs continued to refuse to publish its prewar diplomatic documents, and this position remained unchanged even after the appearance of the large general collections published by other states. As expected, this attitude aroused the suspicion that the Belgrade archives contained materials of a compromising nature for the prewar Serbian governments. The hypothesis was strengthened by the fact that at the war's end the Yugoslav government threatened to renew hostilities with the Austrian Republic if the latter did not promptly turn over to Yugoslav authorities all diplomatic documents concerning Serbia.

It must be added that the Yugoslav government has not yet seen fit to publish its prewar holdings. Consequently, the collection published by the former Serbian Minister to Berlin, Boghicevic, translated into German and containing rich documentation concerning Serbian foreign policy from 1903–14, becomes particularly significant.[54]

The Boghicevic collection differs markedly from those already examined. This is neither an official nor an unofficial publication. It is simply the private general collection of a Serbian ex-diplomat, whose editorial efforts reveal a strong bias against the policies of prewar Serbian statesmen.

The first volume contains numerous official documents either in Boghicevic's possession or copied by him at an earlier date. It begins in 1903, a decisive year in Serbian history, with Peter Karageorgevic's ascension to the throne and precipitation of a Serbian diplomatic revolution. The ties that linked Serbia to Austria were severed, and the Balkan kingdom was taken into the Russian orbit. The documents concerning this period are relatively few in number and of limited importance. The material becomes plentiful and extremely significant only with the

[54] Milos Boghitschewitsch (ed.), *Die auswärtige Politik Serbiens 1903–1914* (3 vols.; Berlin: Brückenverlag, 1928–31).

beginning of the Bosnian crisis, during the course of which a number of important conversations took place between St. Petersburg and Belgrade concerning positions to be taken in the light of the new situation brought on by the Austrian coup. These documents confirm the previous impression that Izvolski, despite his energetic diplomatic maneuvers, never seriously considered plunging Russia into a war with Austria-Hungary over the Bosnian question, and that he was fully aware of the fact that for the moment war was to be avoided because of Russia's military unpreparedness. On the other hand, the Czar's Minister, while pressing Serbia to refrain from taking any reckless steps, did not conceal his intentions of seeking revenge at the first favorable opportunity, thereby encouraging the Serbian government to persist in its new and dangerous Pan-Slav policy while awaiting future developments.

As for the material for the years immediately following the crisis of 1908, undoubtedly it is of great interest insofar as it concerns Serbia's relations with the other Balkan states. However, its primary importance is that it permits an appreciation of the extent to which Serbian policy was stubbornly directed toward realizing its anti-Austrian ambitions, as well as the constant menace that this policy constituted for the Dual Monarchy.

The disclosures in the second volume are much less important. The documents "taken from the archives of Russia, Montenegro, and other states" are, in the main, reprints of previously published materials.

In general, the new data found herein confirm the impression gained in the first volume and read like a bill of indictment against Pasic's policies. The latter was accused by many, including King Nicholas of Montenegro and his Foreign Minister, Plamenatz, of wanting war at any cost in order to realize his dream of a Greater Serbia.

The third and last volume is a history of Serbian foreign policy, written by Boghicevic and based on the documents published by him.

In the use of this documentation, which is of singular interest because it is the only Serbian source available, very special care is required. The clearly polemical character given the collection by Boghicevic, whether in his choice of documents, or in the editorial notes, or, finally, in the account provided in the last volume, obliges the scholar to submit the work to a minute critical study that even then does not always produce clear and precise results. The charges and countercharges by Balkan statesmen are, in most cases, impossible to check. Therefore, while this material might be considered adequate as an outline of the general scheme of Serbian policy, it is very nearly impossible to use in determining the roles played by individuals and in delegating responsibility.

Finally, it should be recalled that in 1941, after the occupation of

Belgrade, the German government sent a special commission to the old Serbian capital to examine the contents of the local archives, with the idea of eventually publishing the most important documents on the origins of World War I. However, this project produced no practical results, and nothing has been published.

Another collection of a semiofficial character was assembled from the Belgian archives captured by German troops after the fall of Brussels in 1914. The German government began publication of this material in the *Norddeutsche Allgemeine Zeitung* to support its thesis that prior to the war Belgium violated its obligations as a neutral by coming to terms with the Entente powers in the event of an attack against Germany. This attempt to justify the violation of Belgian neutrality found little to sustain it in the documentation, but the German publication launched a debate, which, spreading rapidly to encompass prewar relations between the Great Powers, opened up the entire question of war responsibility.

In 1916 the German government considered the possibility of publishing an organic collection of the holdings in the Belgian archives and for this purpose sent a professional historian, Bernard Schwertfeger, to Brussels to examine the captured material. In Schwertfeger's opinion there was no concrete evidence on which to build a case against Belgium, and he recommended that the documentation be used instead to publicize the judgments favorable to Germany and the negative criticisms of Entente policy that were contained in the Belgian diplomatic dispatches. Subsequently, the project was shelved, at least in its original form, but Schwertfeger was authorized to publish selected documents that he had been able to consult in Brussels. A five-volume collection appeared in 1919,[55] and it was followed in 1925 by a considerably expanded second edition.[56]

The selection criteria adopted and the method employed in presenting the material clearly reflect the revisionist approach then current in Germany. The first five volumes are the most interesting, and essays at the beginning of each explain the historico-diplomatic setting for the documents contained therein. These essays openly seek to justify German action against Belgium and to accuse the Entente of having planned aggression against Germany. The importance of this collection would have been very

[55] Bernhard Schwertfeger (ed.), *Zur europäischen Politik 1897–1914: unveröffentlichen auftrage* (5 vols.; Berlin, 1919).

[56] Schwertfeger, Alfred Doren, and Wilhelm Köhler (eds.), *Die belgischen Dokumente zur Vorgeschichte des Weltkrieges, 1885–1914. Amtliche Aktenstücke zur Geschichte der europäischen Politik 1885–1914* (9 vols.; Berlin: Deutsche Verlagsgesellschaft für Politik und Geschichte, 1924 et seq.).

much greater if the editors had set out simply to reconstruct Belgian foreign policy. Instead, they chose Entente policies, as reflected in the diplomacy of a neutral state, as the central theme. Consequently, this documentation has been largely superseded by the collections on the origins of the war which subsequently appeared in other countries.

Insofar as the criteria of selection are concerned, these were constantly influenced by a desire to emphasize the aggressive policies of the former enemy powers and to focus attention on the positive evaluations of Belgian diplomacy vis-à-vis Germany. It must also be added that the editors frequently omitted portions of documents without indicating the nature of the content of the deleted sections. Considering the decidedly propagandistic tone of the collection, not a few doubts are raised as to the reliability of this documentation, or at least, as to its real scientific value.

In the first five volumes the documents are reproduced in the original French text, together with a German translation, and are divided as follows:

Volume I: 104 documents, from July, 1886, to December 3, 1893, with special reference to the French government's policy of revenge and to the formation of the Franco-Russian Alliance. This is the only volume containing a significant number of dispatches sent from Belgian missions abroad to the Foreign Office.

Volume II: 52 ministerial circular letters sent to Belgian missions abroad in the period September, 1897–December, 1902, and 19 re-transmitted dispatches coming from various offices abroad, which bring the collection up to 1904. The material principally concerns the action taken by the Dual Alliance to block the *rapprochement* between Germany and England.

Volume III: 101 circular letters dating from January, 1905–December, 1907, primarily concerning British policy and the development of the Moroccan crisis of 1905–6.

Volume IV: 140 ministerial circular letters for the period January, 1908–January, 1912, relative to Balkan problems (the Bosnian crisis, Albania) and the Agadir crisis.

Volume V: 97 circular letters for the period January, 1912–July, 1914. It is to be noted that, in contrast to the 42 documents for 1912 and the 38 for 1913, only 17 documents are included for the first six months of 1914. Only two circular letters are included for the period following the assassination at Sarajevo, one of July 3 and the other of July 13. These refer to two dispatches of very minor importance from Paris and Berlin.

The sixth and seventh volumes are supplementary and contain no new material. Volume VI contains 119 selected Belgian documents published in

1915 by the German Ministry of Foreign Affairs in reply to the colored books published by the Entente.[57] The documents are preceded by seven syntheses and comments that had appeared in the *Norddeutsche Allgemeine Zeitung* in 1915.[58] Volume VII includes the first Belgian Gray Book and the first part of the Second Gray Book, both published in Paris by the Belgian government.[59] The last two volumes include two studies on Germany's Belgian policy, patterned along the lines of the German revisionist theses.

From a technical viewpoint, it should be noted that the collection does not have Tables of Contents referring to individuals or events. Instead, there is a simple list of selected documents at the close of each volume, but there is no indication of the nature of their content.

---

[57] *Belgische Aktenstücke 1905–1914* (Berlin: Mittler, 1915). The collection was published simultaneously in English and French.

[58] "Die Belgischen Gesandtschaftsberichte 1905–1914," *Norddeutsche Allgemeine Zeitung,* July 29–August 25, 1915.

[59] See note 14, p. 96.

Chapter IV

THE COLLECTIONS OF DIPLOMATIC DOCUMENTS RELATIVE TO WORLD WAR II AND ITS ORIGINS

SUMMARY: 1. The Collections Drawn from the German Archives. 2. The British Collection.   3. The State Department Collection and Other American Documentary Collections.   4. The Soviet Collections. 5. The Italian Collection and Other Italian Documentary Sources.   6. The Hungarian and Yugoslav Collections.   7. The Portuguese and Polish Collections.   8. The French Documentary Sources.   9. The Scandinavian, Dutch, and Belgian Documentary Sources.   10. The Japanese Documentary Collection.   11. The Chinese Documentary Sources.

1. THE COLLECTIONS DRAWN FROM THE GERMAN ARCHIVES.

At the close of World War II, the condition of European archives was immeasurably worse than it was in 1919. During World War I the capitals of only a few secondary states were occupied by enemy troops, and moreover, destruction by aerial bombings was minimal. During the second conflict, in striking contrast, the capital of *every* Continental state involved in the war was occupied by the enemy, with the exception of the Soviet capital.

In the face of the enemy's advance, each government naturally took steps to safeguard its archives, but the transfer often occurred under dramatic circumstances and with inadequate facilities. As a consequence, losses and dispersions were not uncommon, and were usually the result of transportation difficulties and the prevailing state of disorder. However, often such losses were the work of those who, for personal reasons or to serve party ends, took advantage of the occasion to contrive the disappearance of material deemed compromising. When the rapid approach of the enemy made transfer impossible, the archives were simply destroyed, as happened in the case of the archives of the Quai d'Orsay, burned in May, 1940, just before the Germans entered Paris.

The vicissitudes affecting the destiny of the German archives are singularly interesting, and the importance of these archives for a study of international relations between the two wars does not need to be underscored. In view of the increased intensity of the bombings, the German Ministry of Foreign Affairs began, as early as 1943, to decentralize its archives, keeping in Berlin only the current files and transferring the rest to less exposed outlying districts. Toward the end of 1944, when the Soviet advance threatened a sweep into Germany, a second transfer was arranged to move the archives to the safety of western Germany. Finally, in the spring of 1945, the order was given to burn the most important papers concerning the period following Hitler's rise to power. The arrival of the American troops prevented the execution of the order, and, except for a small part (including, however, nearly all of Von Ribbentrop's archives), the material was recovered intact, even if partially damaged by previous transfers and with some losses, which were inevitable under the circumstances.

Some of the German diplomatic documents also fell into Soviet hands. It is impossible to establish their exact content (not considered to be especially noteworthy) and equally impossible to know to what extent they will be published.

Every attempt has been made to fill the existing lacunae by utilizing the archives of the German embassies, especially those in Rome and Tokyo, but the procedure, even if of indubitable value, has only partially filled the gaps in the ministerial archives. In the embassy files, in addition to copies of arriving and departing telegrams, can be found the informative dispatches; that is, copies of telegrams and reports sent by other heads of mission, which the ministry then re-transmits to its embassies in order to keep them informed or to check on the accuracy of certain information. However, the material brought to light in this manner only partially fulfills the demands of historical research. Normally, this material lacks certain details (date and time of arrival or departure of the original document) that are often of great importance. At the same time, it is often the case that the informative dispatches are only excerpts from the original text. Above all, it is impossible to reconstruct the formative process of a country's foreign policy from these documents because it usually is not the practice to send to embassies such notes as the minutes of meetings within the ministry or documents pertaining to the relations between the ministry and other state organs.

Almost all of the available German diplomatic documents have come to light in a most unusual way. Their publication—with the exception of a very recent little volume concerning the Locarno Pacts, published by the Pankow government[1]—has not been effected by a German government but, instead, by the governments of other states or by international bodies—a new approach, or, at least, one differing from the usual practice.

The first important information on the contents of the archives of the Wilhelmstrasse was supplied by the United States government in 1946, when it published in *The Department of State Bulletin*[2] a long series of German documents concerning the relations between Germany and the other members of the Tripartite Agreement. The Nuremberg trials against key Nazi figures were then under way, and the International Tribunal for the Far East was getting ready to hold its hearings for Japanese statesmen and military men accused of war crimes. By publishing these documents, the American government intended to give the widest coverage possible to this material, which constituted the proof of German and Japanese aggressive policies, in order to influence the American public, which was already giving indications of being somewhat perplexed regarding the juridical basis for the Nuremberg and Tokyo trials.

The fact that the publication was designed to serve clearly defined political aims is demonstrated by the selection of the documents. Germany's aggressive intentions are illustrated in the minutes of the many Italo-German conferences, such as the Berlin meeting of September 28, 1940, between Hitler, Von Ribbentrop, and Ciano; the conference at Palazzo Venezia of March 1, 1941, between Mussolini, Hitler, Von Ribbentrop, and Ciano; and the meeting on April 29, 1942, between these four at Schloss Klessheim. Other documents refer to German plans for the invasion of Norway and to Hitler's plans for the reorganization of Denmark. A great deal of space is also devoted to Japanese-German relations (Hitler and Von Ribbentrop's conferences with Ambassador Oshima) and to Spain's relations with the Axis. The documentation for the latter was included to bolster the American position toward the Franco government, the latter having been excluded from membership in the United Nations on the basis of the Potsdam Agreements, and to support the Polish-French initiative of April, 1946, to induce the members of the United Nations to break diplomatic relations with Spain.[3] The bulk of this material is also included in the general collection referred to below, but some documents

---

[1] See below, pp. 173–74.

[2] *The Department of State Bulletin*, XIV (Washington: Department of State Printing Office, 1946).

[3] Fifteen documents concerning Spanish-Axis relations assembled in a small collection: *The Spanish Government and the Axis* (Washington: Department of State Printing Office, 1946).

were not reprinted elsewhere and may be found only in *The Department of State Bulletin*.

At almost the same time, scholars received a windfall of significant material pertinent to German foreign policy from the Nuremberg trials, where Hitler's principal political and military collaborators appeared as defendants. Punishment of war criminals had been foreseen at the close of World War I, and all of the treaties of peace ending the 1914–18 conflict included clauses obliging the vanquished states to deliver, upon request of the victors, those individuals responsible for the conflict or those guilty of atrocities during the war. These clauses in the Versailles treaties, which had been perplexing even at the time,[4] in practice were never enforced because at the request of the German government the war criminals were not extradited, but were tried under the special jurisdiction of the Leipzig Supreme Court. The few trials held resulted either in acquittals or in sentences that were very light in proportion to the crimes committed.

During World War II, the need to punish those guilty of war crimes was emphasized from the beginning and led, by agreements between the Allied Powers (Moscow Tripartite Declaration of October 30, 1943, and the Anglo-French-Soviet-American Pact of London of August 8, 1945), to the creation of an International Tribunal whose legal character was determined beforehand. This tribunal claimed jurisdiction over three categories of crimes: in addition to war crimes as such, "crimes against peace" and "crimes against humanity"—two categories whose legal interpretation is still the subject of debate—were added.

This expanded jurisdiction required investigation into a wide range of data, which, in practice, led to an examination of all National Socialist policies, beginning with the events leading to Hitler's rise to power and terminating with the end of the war. It was also necessary to conduct a minute inquiry into every phase of activity of the Nazi regime, in internal as well as external affairs, in such areas as diplomacy, military developments, occupation of enemy territory, and racial persecutions.

The prosecution based its arguments on a vast documentation, which had been gathered by the victorious powers during the war and during the occupation of Germany. But one must clearly recognize that this material, gathered especially for the trials, is extremely heterogeneous and not always of interest to the student of international relations. It should be remembered that, in addition to the diplomatic documents captured by the Allies, the prosecution was able to utilize the tape recordings of intercepted

[4] In this regard see Vittorio Emanuele Orlando, *Il processo del Kaiser* ("Vita e Pensiero"; Milan, 1937), an extract.

telephone conversations, many German General Staff documents, minutes of the secret meetings presided over by Hitler, the diaries of Halder, Jodl, and Frank, the Rosenberg correspondence, and many other sources. Directly or indirectly, this new mass of information contains much which is of interest to the historian.

An illustration of the importance of this material is the minutes of the meeting convoked by Hitler at the Chancellery on November 5, 1937, at which, for the benefit of the military leaders and the Minister of Foreign Affairs,[5] he outlined his future plans. According to Hitler, the first objectives of Nazi expansion were Czechoslovakia and Austria (in inverse order to what was later adopted), and these objectives were to be realized between 1943–45, by which time, according to Hitler, German military strength would surpass that of the Anglo-French coalition. This time limit might be anticipated in the event of serious internal disorders in France or the outbreak of war between Italy and the western democracies over the Spanish situation—an eventuality which, again according to Hitler, was anything but improbable. Obviously, this revelation of Hitler's projects does not come from the Ministry of Foreign Affairs and is largely military in character. However, its importance for an evaluation of Nazi foreign policy is fundamental.

Italo-German relations were illustrated at Nuremberg by an abundance of very interesting documents. Among the most important are the minutes of the meetings of Mussolini and Ciano with Hitler, Von Ribbentrop, and Goering; the letters exchanged by the two dictators; many telegrams and reports from Von Mackensen, the German Ambassador to Rome, and from the Italian Ambassador in Berlin, Bernardo Attolico; and the famous "Cavallero Memorial" on the Pact of Steel. The material concerning Japan is particularly noteworthy, especially the summary of the Hitler-Matsuoka conversations of March–April, 1941, during which Hitler exerted every effort to block the signing of a Soviet-Japanese nonaggression pact by clearly stating the possibility of a Soviet-German conflict.

All of this material was made available to scholars during the trials in the form of booklets, distributed daily to the press, which contained the minutes of the sessions, the texts of the interrogations, and some of the documents offered in evidence by the prosecution. This system of distribution, while satisfying journalistic needs, was inadequate from the scholar's point of view, particularly since serious omissions were evident in the documentation distributed.

[5] "Promemoria Hossbach of November 10, 1937," in *Trial of the Major War Criminals before the International Military Tribunal* (Nuremberg, 1947–49), XXV, Doc. PS-386, 402–13.

Therefore, scholars welcomed the appearance of an imposing work published by the American government in 1946, comprising the most significant parts of the material presented at the trials by the Anglo-Saxons.[6] Notwithstanding the fact that it was an indisputable step forward, this collection, too, has some serious defects, at least from the viewpoint of historical research. In the first place, it contains no descriptive Table of Contents, a fact of no small importance when it is recalled that the material is organized to meet the court's needs. Thus the search for a specific document is made extremely difficult, especially since the collection is published in sections according to the use the prosecution made of its contents during the trials. A page-by-page examination of the collection is required—an imposing task, given its dimensions. It should also be noted that the published material varies greatly in importance. Items of major significance are found side by side with items which, if not of little or no value, at least are well known and easily found in other sources such as newspaper articles, Nazi legislation, or Hitler's speeches. Finally, many documents are reproduced only in part, and the translation is not always accurate.

It should also be noted that the second volume of the supplement includes the minutes of the interrogations of the Nazi leaders conducted by the Americans prior to the trials and that not all of the material contained in this collection was presented at Nuremberg. Therefore, this work cannot be considered to have been superseded by the proceedings of the trials.

A larger and better-organized collection of the proceedings of the trials was compiled and published by the Attorney General of the United Kingdom.[7] The twenty-four-volume collection contains the stenographic text of the interrogation of the accused and the depositions of the prosecution and the defense. In general, the interrogations are disappointing, although a few new details emerge. Of some interest, for instance, is Goering's declaration that he only learned at Nuremberg of the existence of a secret protocol attached to the Anti-Comintern Pact signed by Germany and Japan on November 25, 1936, and that it was not revealed to the Italians when they signed the pact the following year.

The textual depositions are much more interesting. The summary of the Moscow negotiations in 1939 provided by the Wilhelmstrasse's legal

[6] *Nazi Conspiracy and Aggression* (Washington: U.S. Government Printing Office, 1946), 8 vols. and 2 supplement vols.

[7] *The Trial of 14 German Major War Criminals: Proceedings of the International Military Tribunal Sitting at Nuremberg, Germany* (24 vols.; London: His Majesty's Stationery Office, 1946–49).

counsellor, Gaus, is particularly exciting, as is the deposition of Ambassador Schmidt, who, in his role of interpreter, participated in almost all of the important meetings.

Publication difficulties, involving problems of paper supply, delayed the appearance of this collection, so that even before it was completed, a definitive edition was published under the auspices of the International Military Tribunal. The latter, in forty-two volumes, is by far the most complete, and scholars refer to it as a matter of course. It was published in two editions, one in English[8] and the other in French.[9] Both have subject matter and proper name indexes, which are a great help in research, even if they are not entirely satisfactory. Documents in French, English, and German are reproduced in the original language.

The so-called "Nuremberg Little Trial," held concurrently with that of the major war criminals, was, in effect, twelve trials of minor war criminals held between October, 1946, and April, 1949.

The proceedings of these trials, published in fifteen volumes by the American government, include materials of varying importance.[10] Only a few of the proceedings concern the conduct of German foreign policy and diplomatic-military events of World War II.[11]

[8] *Trial of the Major War Criminals before the International Military Tribunal* (42 vols.; Nuremberg, 1947–49).

[9] *Procès des grands criminels de guerre devant le Tribunal Militaire International* (42 vols.; Nuremberg, 1947–49).

[10] *Trials of the War Criminals before the Nuremberg Military Tribunals under Control Council Law N. 10* (15 vols.; Washington: U.S. Government Printing Office, n.d.). Given their vast bulk, the trial proceedings are not published in their entirety. Complete documentation may be found in the Library of Congress.

[11] The list of trials is as follows:

Case 1: against Karl Brandt and others (Medical Case) accused of medical experiments on human beings (in Vols. I and II).

Case 2: against Fieldmarshal Erhard (Milch Case), accused of war crimes (in Vol. II).

Case 3: against Josef Altstoetter and others (Justice Case); against fourteen officials of the Reich's Ministry of Justice or members of the special courts or of the Peoples' Courts (in Vol. III).

Case 4: against Oswald Pohl and others (Pohl Case); against eighteen officials of the S.S. financial or administrative service (in Vol. V).

Case 5: against Friedrich Flick and others (Flick Case); against six officials of the Flick industrial complex (in Vol. VI).

Case 6: against Carl Krauch and others (I. G. Farben Case); against twenty-three officials of the Farbenindustrie (in Vols. VII and VIII).

Case 7: against Wilhelm List and others (Hostage Case); against twelve generals accused of atrocities especially in Greece, Yugoslavia, and Albania (in Vol. XI).

Case 8: against Ulrich Greitfelt and others (Rusha Case); against fourteen S.S. members attached to the Race Section (in Vols. IV and V).

Case 9: against Otto Ohlendorf and others (Einsatzgruppen Case); against twenty-

One of these was the Ministries Case (Case No. 11), involving, among others, the Secretary of State of the Wilhelmstrasse, Von Weizsäcker; a number of diplomats, such as the ex-Director for Political Affairs, Ernst Woermann, the ex-Minister to Budapest, Otto von Erdmannsdorff; economic experts Karl Ritter and Wilhelm Keppler; and the head of the *Auslandorganisation* of the Nazi Party, Ernst Bohle.

The material made public during this trial is of real value to the scholar, even though it was selected to prove or disprove the responsibility of the accused and not to reconstruct German foreign policy. Because the material was drawn largely from archives other than those of the Ministry of Foreign Affairs, it retains its high level of importance even after the publication of the general collection of German diplomatic documents.

Insofar as the German occupation of the Balkans is concerned, important revelations came to light from the files of the Hostage Case (Case No. 7), involving the trial of twelve generals of the Wehrmacht accused of atrocities. Significant data emerged concerning the action taken by the German troops against the Italian forces in the Balkans after the armistice of September 8, 1943. Finally, the last trial, the High Command Case (Case No. 12) dealing with high-level military personnel, provides some important information about military strategy.

While the Nuremberg trials were still under way, the British and American governments agreed to the joint publication of the captured German diplomatic documents housed near Oxford, there to be studied and microfilmed. This project, with which France associated herself in April, 1947, was designed to produce a large organic collection similar to those that appeared at the end of World War I, the difference being that in this case the collection would be edited and published by ex-enemy countries instead of by the government to whom the documents belonged.

Before publication of this collection was begun, the American government published a number of the German documents concerning Soviet-German relations for the period April, 1939–June, 1941, in a volume entitled *Nazi-Soviet Relations, 1939–1941.*[12]

---

four S.S. officers accused of atrocities in occupied territories of the U.S.S.R. (in Vol. IV).

Case 10: against Alfred Krupp and others (Krupp Case); against the industrialist Krupp and twelve directors of the Krupp complex (in Vol. IX).

Case 11: against Ernst von Weizsäcker and others (Ministries Case); against twenty-one high officials in various administrative offices (in Vols. XII, XIII, and XIV).

Case 12: against Wilhelm von Leeb and others (High Command Case); against three marshals, nine generals, and one admiral (in Vols. X and XI).

[12] *Nazi-Soviet Relations, 1939–1941. Documents from the Archives of the German Foreign Office* (Washington: U.S. Government Printing Office, 1948).

Once again, we find a political motive prompting a publication. By 1948, that particular international situation known as the "Cold War," characterized by antagonism between the United States and the Soviet Union, the two strongest powers in the war against Nazi Germany, had already crystallized. Of necessity, this development left the American people somewhat bewildered, attuned as they were to wartime propaganda directed toward the development of a certain sympathy for the Soviet Union and characterized, above all, by lavish praise of the Red army's contribution to the common victory. Now, on the heels of the emergence of the "Cold War," the American government had been obliged to ask for new sacrifices by the public to support high military expenditures and to underwrite the Marshall Plan, and this at the very time when the government was taking an unprecedented step in American history by committing the United States to a peacetime alliance, the Atlantic Pact, that would involve it directly in European affairs.

Acceptance of these historic changes required adequate preconditioning of public opinion. In the first place, it was necessary to dismantle the entire propaganda apparatus created during the war to support the Soviet Union and to demonstrate that if the Soviet Union had fought side by side with the Anglo-Americans, it was simply because the U.S.S.R. had been attacked by Germany. It would be shown that before this attack took place, the Soviet government had shown no particular sympathy for the Allied cause and even less revulsion for Nazi Germany. Even more, she had maintained a policy of close collaboration with the Nazis, beginning in August, 1939, that is, from the signing of the Nazi-Soviet Pact, a step which gave Hitler strong encouragement to take the road to war.

It was with the intention of producing a strong impression on the American and European public that the American government decided to publish the documents contained in *Nazi-Soviet Relations*—not a particularly large collection, but destined, nevertheless, to have a profound world-wide effect because of the importance of the revelations it contained.

The German documents clearly demonstrated the magnitude of the Soviet contribution to Germany's war potential, both in the enormous consignments of materials delivered to Germany with scrupulous punctuality over a period of almost two years, and in the diplomatic assistance Russia gave to Germany on repeated occasions, such as in the course of the Moscow conversations with Saracoglu or during Hitler's "Peace Offensive," launched in October, 1939. Above all, these documents exposed, with singular clarity, the hammer-like characteristics of Soviet diplomacy, especially after the failure of Litvinov's League policy and the humiliations suffered at the hands of the western powers. The cynicism displayed by

Molotov on the occasion of Hitler's attack on Poland and the techniques employed to absorb the Baltic states provided sufficient evidence upon which to base a judgment of Soviet policy for that period. This judgment appeared to reduce Soviet policy to the same level as that of Nazi Germany.

Propaganda value aside, the documents were of inestimable value to the historian. All of the most important behind-the-scenes Soviet-German negotiations undertaken during the summer of 1939 were brought to light: the particulars of the Moscow conversations between Stalin, Molotov, and Von Ribbentrop; the economic negotiations between the two countries; the minutes of Molotov's conversations in Berlin; and the negotiations to include the U.S.S.R. in the Tripartite Agreement. This complete and valuable collection makes it possible to reconstruct the origins of Nazi-Soviet friendship and the various steps that led to the final break between the two powers.

Among other items of interest, the complete text of the secret protocol attached to the nonaggression pact of August 23, 1939, was brought to light—a document that, in effect, provides the key to subsequent Soviet policy. On the basis of that accord, Germany and the U.S.S.R. divided eastern Europe into two spheres of influence, the Soviet Union acquiring a free hand in much of Poland, in Estonia, Latvia, Finland, and Bessarabia. Accordingly, this allocation became the premise on which the new dynamics of Soviet policy were founded, and it explains both the subsequent Soviet moves and the attitude of Berlin towards the Kremlin on those occasions.

The psychological effects derived from the publication of *Nazi-Soviet Relations* forced the Moscow government, in order to provide a factual base for its thesis, to reply at the propaganda level with an analogous publication. In substance, the Soviets affirmed that the Nazi-Soviet Accord of August 23, 1939, became necessary as a direct result of Anglo-French policy: the attitude of Britain and France on the occasion of the *Anschluss* and the two Czech crises had convinced the Soviet government that it was highly unlikely that the two western powers would ever resort to arms to contest the German advance. Above all, however, the Nazi-Soviet Accord was made indispensable by British attempts to arrive at an understanding with Berlin during 1938 and 1939, with the objective of channeling German dynamism toward the Ukraine. Faced by this reality, the Soviet government was forced to take steps to avoid disaster and, therefore, signed the nonaggression pact, which, if it accomplished nothing else, postponed the Soviet-German conflict and gained for the Soviets the time necessary to complete preparations for resisting a German attack.

Obviously, this theory contained weaknesses: for example, it failed to justify the multiple aggressions of the U.S.S.R. against Poland, the Baltic states, Finland, and Rumania. However, in order to support this thesis, the Soviet government in 1948 published a small, two-volume collection concerning several aspects of international politics on the eve of the war.[13]

The first volume contained documents from various sources—some German diplomatic documents captured by the Soviet army, some Czechoslovak documents that the Soviets had found in the archives of the Wilhelmstrasse, and, finally, some documents whose origins are not indicated. Not all of this material was unpublished (some of these documents had already been presented at Nuremberg, and others had appeared in colored books or in the publications of scholars authorized to use them), but the publication continues to be of major importance for the study of particular aspects of Anglo-German relations. The second volume is based on the papers of Ambassador Herbert von Dirksen, papers which the Soviets found in the latter's residence at Groeditzberg. Von Dirksen had been German Ambassador to Moscow, Tokyo, and London, but the material published in this volume concerns only the last of these missions, or, more precisely, the period from May 5, 1938, to August 25, 1939. This collection contains copies of official documents that Von Dirksen had saved for his own use, his correspondence with other diplomats, and, finally, a memorandum written by Von Dirksen in September, 1939, in which he summarized the events of his mission to London.

One of the most interesting documents consists of the British offer to discuss the restitution of the ex-German colonies. This fact, while it provides ample evidence of the seriousness of Chamberlain's efforts to arrive at a *modus vivendi* with Germany, assumes major significance in a study of Hitler's "colonial policy"; the offer merits the most careful consideration in that it played a primary role in the formation of German foreign policy following the advent of Hitler to power. In this context it

---

[13] English-language edition: *Documents and Materials relating to the Eve of the Second World War* (2 vols.; Moscow: Foreign Languages Publishing House, 1948).

The publication of these volumes was preceded by the appearance of an "historical note" in: Bureau d'Information Sovietique, *Falsificateurs de l'Histoire, Notice historique,* Supplement to *Temps Nouveaux,* No. 8, February 18, 1948 (editions of the Moscow journal, *Trud*). In this note the Soviet government promptly denied the validity of the contents of *Nazi-Soviet Relations* and, at the same time, accused the democracies of having attempted to negotiate a separate peace with Germany in 1941, 1942, and 1943, stating that German documents in Soviet possession confirmed this accusation. However, the documents offered as proof of the validity of the accusation have not been published.

should be noted that the Berlin government, at the very moment when it was signing the alliance with Japan, negotiated with the latter for the restitution of the ex-German islands in the Pacific; the Japanese, recognizing the need to offer the Germans adequate compensation, agreed to return these islands to Germany despite the fact that Japan was then at the very apogee of its "Greater East Asia Policy."

All of this leads to a consideration of the importance (as shown in the developments of the international situation between the two world wars) of the fact that the peacemakers at Versailles refused to grant Italy a mandate over ex-German colonies. If Orlando's request for a mandate in Togoland had been satisfied, undoubtedly Italy and Germany, whose relations were already somewhat strained by the Alto Adige question, would have encountered greater difficulty in forming an alliance.

To complete the references to German material published by the Soviets, it should be noted that in 1946, that is, prior to the publication of *Nazi-Soviet Relations,* Moscow had published a small collection in three volumes,[14] devoted to Turkey, Hungary, and Spain, respectively.

The first of these volumes, limited to the period 1941–43, illustrates the attempts of the German Ambassador to Ankara, Von Papen, to conclude the nonaggression pact of June 18, 1941, and his subsequent efforts to consolidate further the already favorable German position in Turkey. This material clearly indicates the state of mind dominant in Ankara on the eve of the German attack on the Soviet Union and the nature of the evolution of the Turkish attitude in the light of the development of military operations on the eastern front.

The second volume, which concerns Hungary, contains the minutes of several of the most important meetings between Hitler and Von Ribbentrop and the Magyar leaders in the years 1937–39. Several dispatches from the German Ambassador in Rome clarify the Italian position on the Danubian problems, while the last documents in the volume throw some light on the maneuvers for a separate peace under way in 1942 in Budapest and Bucharest.

Perhaps of even greater interest is the volume concerning Spain, in which numerous documents concerning Italian activities during the Civil War are also to be found. Included are the text of the Italo-Spanish Accord of November 28, 1936, the minutes of the Ciano-Von Neurath meeting of October 25, 1937, and those of the Mussolini-Bülow-Schwante colloquy of October, 1937, data so extremely valuable that the smallness of the

[14] *La politique allemande (1936–1943): Documents secrets du Ministère des Affaires Étrangères d'Allemagne* (3 vols.; Paris: Dupont, 1946–47).

collection is regrettable. In this case, also, the publication was designed to serve political ends by discrediting the Ankara government, against which Moscow, at the close of the war, had formulated precise claims concerning the Straits; the Madrid government, at that moment boycotted by the United Nations; and, finally, that Magyar political element which, according to the results of the postwar elections in Hungary, continued to enjoy a large following throughout the country.

In 1959, more than a decade after the publication of these collections, the Soviets published a volume of documents on the Locarno Conference[15] in support of the thesis, upheld by Soviet historiography, that the pacts of 1925 had constituted an attempt by the western powers to create a capitalist united front against the U.S.S.R. In this case, too, the source is a German archive captured by the Soviets and, although it is not so indicated, is presumed to be part of Ambassador von Dirksen's archive, the latter having been secretary to the German delegation at the Locarno Conference.

This material, a great part of it unpublished, also includes the preliminary negotiations, limited, logically, to the diplomatic actions of the Berlin government. The heart of the volume consists of the minutes of the Locarno meetings, edited by the secretaries of each delegation. In fact, the conference, on a motion by Austin Chamberlain, agreed not to compile a duly approved single set of minutes. Therefore, each delegation proceeded to compile its own minutes but, apparently, with the understanding that pertinent documents would be exchanged.

This procedure, while it can lead to certain inconveniences on a practical plane, proves to be extremely useful to the historian, providing him with more details of the conversations, for the very understandable reason that each delegation seeks to focus its report on those points of major interest to the country it represents. Furthermore, the inevitable differences that are found between the various minutes offer an opportunity to make comparisons which are useful in clarifying the positions of the individual delegations. In order to underscore the importance of this collection, it should be noted that no copy of this material was found in the archives of the Wilhelmstrasse captured by the Allies.

The East German government has recently published a volume on the same question,[16] covering the period January, 1925–February, 1926. This publication supports the Soviet thesis on the meaning of the Locarno Conference; however, it is not simply a copy of the Soviet volume, but is

[15] *The Locarno Conference, 1925* (Moscow: Gospolitizdat, 1959), in Russian.
[16] Ministry of Foreign Affairs of the German Democratic Republic, *Locarno-Konferenz, 1925* (Berlin: Rütten and Loening, 1962).

based on a broader documentation drawn from archival sources (the archives of the German Embassy in Moscow) now in possession of the Pankow government.

In any event, the largest and most complete source of German documentary materials is the great general collection, which, as has been noted, was to be edited by an Anglo-French-American commission from archives captured by the Allied troops. When the commission initiated its labors, it found the archives in a chaotic state, occasioned by the repeated transfer of the material by the Germans during the war, and by the Allies later. In both cases, the haste with which the material was gathered and transported contributed to worsening a situation already made difficult by the dimensions of the Wilhelmstrasse archives, which contained documents for the period 1867 to the end of World War II. Since reorganization of the material would have required many years of work, the commission decided to proceed with the publication of several volumes, establishing, in the process, the basic criteria to be observed in preparing the entire collection for publication.

It was decided, in the first place, that the collection would cover the period 1919–45, since the aim of the publication was to provide "a complete picture of German foreign policy before and during the second World War."

Furthermore, the selection and presentation of the material was to be on the basis of purely scientific criteria: the members of the commission were not limited in their activities by any restrictions whatsoever. In addition to the diplomatic documents, every official document contributing to a clearer understanding of the events was to be utilized, and, except in rare cases, every document was to be reproduced in its entirety, avoiding summations or deletions which might arouse suspicion in the reader's mind that such suppressions might have been dictated by political motives.

Finally, following the system adopted in the French collection on the origins of World War I, the collection was divided into four series to permit the rapid publication of the volumes relating to the last period, which, naturally, were those most eagerly awaited. However, these plans were to be substantially modified in later years.

As soon as the Bonn government was recognized by the western powers, it initiated discussions about the return of the German archives, and, after long negotiations, an agreement was reached with the Allied commission in which the commission undertook to continue the publication of the collection but would limit its efforts to the C and D series, the series covering the Hitlerian period. The German government agreed to handle the publication of the A and B series, covering the period 1919–32.

Once the material was reorganized, it was noted that it reached proportions far greater than had been envisaged at the outset. Therefore, the commission, under pressure from the British because of cost, decided to reduce its area of activity still further and deal only with the years 1933–41. In summary, the publication plan presently in effect is as follows: Series A and B (from 1919 to January 29, 1933) to be edited by the German government; the number of volumes in these series has not yet been established. Series C (from January 30, 1933, to August 31, 1937) to be edited by the Allied commission in six volumes. Series D (from September 1, 1937, to December 8, 1941) to be edited by the Allied commission in thirteen volumes.

It is likely that the German government at a later date will want to complete Series D and will publish the remaining material for the period up to the end of the war.

It bears noting here that the German archival material captured by the Allies was microfilmed before its restitution to the Bonn government. Therefore, scholars may make use of it with relative ease by requesting copies from the Public Records Office in London or the National Archives in Washington.[17] It is less easy to consult the unpublished materials taken from archives other than those of the Wilhelmstrasse, such as those of the navy (on the period 1865–1945), the Wehrmacht, the General Staff, and the Nazi organizations. Despite the fact that these archives were taken to Great Britain and to the United States, as yet they have not all been microfilmed.

The volumes published by the Allied commission appear in four editions, two in English (one American[18] and one British[19] and identical in every respect), one in German,[20] and one in French.[21] The German edition differs from the others in that the documents are printed in the original language, whether it be German or another. The French edition, instead, is a selection, albeit a very ample one, of the most important documents.

[17] A catalogue of the archival materials of the German Foreign Ministry for the years 1867–1920 was published in 1959: *A Catalogue of Files and Microfilms of the German Foreign Ministry Archives, 1867–1920* (The American Historical Association, 1959). For the period following 1920, the publication of a catalogue is in progress: Department of State and the Hoover War Library, *A Catalogue of Files and Microfilms of the German Foreign Ministry Archives, 1920–1945*.

[18] *Documents on German Foreign Policy 1918–1945 from the Archives of the German Foreign Ministry* (Washington: U.S. Government Printing Office, 1949 et seq.).

[19] *Documents on German Foreign Policy, 1918–1945, from the Archives of the German Foreign Ministry* (London: Her Majesty's Stationery Office, 1949 et seq.).

[20] *Akten zur deutschen auswärtigen Politik 1918–1945* (Baden-Baden: Imprimerie Nationale, 1950 et seq.).

[21] *Les Archives Secrètes de la Wilhelmstrasse* (Paris: Plon, 1950 et seq.).

However, because it is incomplete, it is not recommended as a source for scientific study.

The first volume of the collection appeared in 1949, and publication continues: thus far the Bonn government has not published a single volume of the material entrusted to it, while four volumes of Series C and twelve volumes of Series D have been published.

The first volume in Series C begins with January 30, 1933, that is, with the advent of Hitler to power, and terminates with October 14, 1933, the date of Germany's resignation from the League of Nations. The bulk of the documentation is devoted to two issues, namely, the disarmament negotiations and the negotiations for the Four-Power Pact. In both cases, it appears that the material published does not substantially modify the general historical outlines reconstructed earlier. Nevertheless, it makes it possible to follow with greater precision the development of the discussions that took place, and, insofar as the disarmament problem is concerned, it touches on an issue—albeit in somewhat different terms—that is still very much with us. Therefore, the study of past experience can constitute a useful lesson and an effective means of avoiding the pitfalls that led to failure in earlier negotiations.

Of particular interest in this volume are the minutes of the Cabinet meetings presided over by Hitler. These are an especially valuable source, despite the fact that they are extracts, limited to material directly pertinent to foreign policy, and the data that might serve as a means of understanding the effect of internal developments on the conduct of foreign affairs are omitted.

The second volume is of even greater interest; it deals with the period from October 14, 1933, to June 13, 1934, that is, the eve of the first Hitler-Mussolini meeting, which took place in Venice. It includes documentation concerning the German-Polish negotiations for the nonaggression declaration signed on January 26, 1934. The efforts of Hitler to demonstrate the peaceful nature of German foreign policy and to weaken the Franco-Polish Alliance were already known, but the documents establish that Berlin considered the agreement to be purely a matter of contingency. This is further confirmed by the form adopted: a simple declaration instead of a nonaggression pact, in which it would have been difficult to avoid reference to a mutual respect for each other's territorial integrity. A pact could easily have been interpreted as an indirect acceptance of the permanence of Germany's eastern frontiers.

The material concerning relations with Austria has importance even if this topic cannot be studied solely on the basis of diplomatic documents, since Austro-German relations were also affected by the actions of organs of the Nazi party operating outside of the control of the Ministry of Foreign Affairs. The documents prove that toward the close of 1933 the German government hoped to achieve a rapid Nazification of Austria by applying heavy pressure on Vienna, but that the signing of the Italian-Austrian-Hungarian Protocols of Rome (March 15, 1934) persuaded Hitler to follow a more cautious approach and to attempt first of all to reach an agreement with Mussolini. It is precisely in this shift in tactics that an explanation can be found for the repeated German attempts to resolve the differences existing between Germany and Italy, and it provides the background for the Venice meeting between the two dictators.

A great deal of space in this volume is devoted to relations with the Soviet Union, which markedly deteriorated during the winter of 1933–34, a deterioration aggravated by Berlin's refusal to subscribe to a joint accord recognizing the independence and territorial integrity of the Baltic states. Pointedly significant is the documentation relative to Far Eastern affairs, especially with regard to German-Japanese relations. It is interesting to note in this context that a strong difference of opinion existed in Berlin concerning the position to be taken by Germany toward Japan. From Tokyo, Ambassador von Dirksen—pursuing a course that Hitler himself had approved—insisted that his government recognize Manchukuo and take advantage of Japan's isolation to strengthen, as far as possible, the bonds of friendship with the Japanese. Such a friendship could assume great importance as a potential threat to the Soviet Union. However, the prevailing opinion at the Wilhelmstrasse was that it was vital to avoid increasing the tension already existing between Berlin and Moscow and that closer ties to Japan, whose policies had aroused violent reactions throughout the western world, were not in Germany's best interests, in that they would increase its isolation. This negative attitude—caused also by pressures from German business interests, preoccupied as they were by Japanese competition—prevailed, an apparent demonstration that early in 1934 the Wilhelmstrasse was able to act, at least in certain areas, independent of, and often in opposition to, the Nazi party's point of view.

The third volume of Series C concerns the period June 14, 1934–March 31, 1935, months that were crammed with events of major importance, especially for a Germany faced with international repercussions from the assassinations of Captain Roehm and General Schleicher and from the abortive *Anschluss* of July, 1934. The significant portion of the documentation obviously concerns the Austrian question and its impact on the relations between Rome and Berlin. The details of the Venice meeting between Hitler and Mussolini are not yet entirely clear. Of course, no agreement was reached on that occasion. Hitler presented five points which, in his judgment, were to form the basis for a resolution of the Austrian question, but it is not absolutely certain whether Mussolini accepted these points, as the Wilhelmstrasse maintained, or whether he limited himself to taking note of them without committing himself, as the Italians maintained. In any event, there is no doubt that the meeting ended without producing any concrete results. In fact, it created certain misunderstandings in Berlin and in Rome. After a brief respite, Italo-German relations once again worsened, not only because of the disagreement on the Austrian question, which was to culminate in the crisis of July, 1934, but also because of the conflict of interests in the Danubian basin. These documents, first published in this volume, finally permit a reasonably accurate analysis of this aspect of Italo-German relations.

The fourth volume of Series C, the last to be published to date, covers the period April 1, 1935–March 4, 1936, bringing the account to the eve of the remilitarization of the Rhineland. This is a period during which Europe experienced an evolution which was decisive in many ways, particularly after the progressive crumbling of organized resistance to German designs. The recently published material makes it possible to comprehend this evolution clearly, as well as to examine, precisely and in detail, key events which, together, constituted the origins and development of the process.

An important observation derived from these documents is that they confirm the extremely close ties existing even then between German minorities abroad and the Nazi party. This relationship had considerable bearing on the conduct of German foreign policy, despite the protests of Von Neurath, who was preoccupied with the effect such ties could have on Germany's relations with Poland, the only country that maintained a cordial rapport with Germany at the time. But they were protests that apparently had little effect: in June, Hitler himself encouraged the Nazi leaders in Danzig to violate the constitution and to maintain a position of absolute intransigence on every issue. Moreover, in this and in other cases, all advice recommending prudence and caution was destined to lose its efficacy because the evolution mentioned above led to the collapse of European resistance.

In this context, the satisfaction produced in Berlin by the Anglo-German Naval Accord of June, 1935 (ample documentation on this point is provided in this volume), is striking—even if not altogether surprising. In fact, the reaction might be even better described as one of relief than of satisfaction, almost as if German foreign policy had suddenly been released from an awful incubus. Technical aspects aside (naval circles emphasized that it would take ten years or more to achieve the 35 per cent limit established by the treaty), its political consequences were considered to be of major importance. In the first place, it was noted in a *promemoria* of August 28, 1935, that Great Britain had rendered null and void one of the most important sections of the Versailles treaty. Secondly, the Stresa Front, marking the climax of Italo-French-British solidarity against Germany, was irreparably damaged by the Anglo-German Accord, and, above all, the isolation that until a few months earlier had kept Germany on the margins of European politics was eliminated.

The most important documentation contained in this volume concerns Italo-German relations during the Ethiopian war. It is a well-known fact that during this period Rome-Berlin relations still continued to be characterized, if not by outright coolness, certainly by persistent distrust, which had been engendered by the Austrian question as well as by the conflict of interest in southeastern Europe. This recent publication, while it confirms this state of affairs, permits a more exact identification of its causes.

First, it is clearly evident that the German government was obsessed by the fear that, once the Ethiopian crisis had been resolved, Italy would again align herself with the Stresa Front. It appears that, at least for some time, Berlin underestimated the extent of the break between Italy and the western democracies. The hypothesis held most valid was that, once the latter had arrived at some compromise with Italy on Ethiopia, Rome would realign itself with London and Paris more closely than ever because, weakened by the inability to achieve a complete victory, it would be in no position to pursue a totally independent course.

This error in evaluation, if partially justified by the repeated Franco-British attempts at compromise (attempts that often appeared to find some response in Rome) was also arrived at by an underestimation of Italy's military possibilities in Ethiopia. In effect, at least until February of 1936, the Germans seemed to consider it impossible for the Italian forces in East Africa to win a decisive victory, and they deduced that Italy, in order to escape the blind alley in which it found itself, would be forced to follow a policy dictated by Britain and France without being able to establish a new base for European policy.

The mixed reception given to an important compromise on the Austrian problem offered by Mussolini in January, 1936, can be understood only within this framework. On two occasions, January 6 and January 27, Mussolini informed Ambassador von Hassell that he would not object if Berlin and Vienna concluded a friendship and nonaggression pact, a pact which, he emphasized, "would in effect bring Austria into the German orbit" and would oblige the former to align her foreign policy to that of Germany. Italy, continued Mussolini, had no objection to Austria's becoming a satellite of Germany, retaining only the outward character of independence.

The episode was, in part, already known. Von Hassell had reported it casually in a telegram of July 11th, subsequently published in the first volume of Series D. Now that it is put in its proper perspective, however, it demonstrates that as early as January, 1936, Mussolini was ready to accept the solution which, in effect, would be realized in the Austro-German Accords of July 11, 1936. The fact that he had referred to the problem on two separate occasions and later, at Von Hassell's request, confirmed and clarified his views on the matter excludes the possibility that his statement was only of passing importance—that it represented simply a momentary reaction to the Anglo-French attitude on the Ethiopian problem and, therefore, should be dismissed as one of his bombastic utterances, devoid of any serious content.

It should be noted that while Von Hassell considered Mussolini's offer to be a decisive step toward the solution of the Austrian question in favor of Germany, Von Neurath's reactions were completely negative. He considered the proposal as a device to weaken the Anglo-French Front and an attempt to limit Germany's freedom of action in the sphere of Austria's internal politics. Therefore, he advised that action on the suggestion should be entirely dilatory until the matter was dropped.

On the other hand, it was evident early in February that Berlin's attention was being focused elsewhere. As revealed in Von Hassell's *promemoria* of February 14th, Hitler on that date told his collaborators that he had decided, as a reply to the imminent ratification of the Franco-Soviet Pact, to denounce the Locarno Pacts and to proceed with the remilitarization of the Rhineland. He told them that this move had been originally planned for the spring of 1937 but that it had been necessary to move up the date to take advantage of the difficulties confronting the western powers following the Ethiopian crisis.

It should also be noted that by this maneuver the German Chancellor appeared to aim not only at a substantial strengthening of Germany's military position, but also at creating a situation that would make it easier to achieve a policy of *rapprochement* with Italy. To this end, Von Hassell was directed to suggest to Mussolini that Italy be the first to denounce the Locarno Pacts. In the recent past, Italy had often expressed the intention of denouncing the 1925 agreements in retaliation for Belgium's action in aligning herself with the western democracies. It appears that on the spur of the moment Mussolini was not completely adverse to acting on the suggestion, but after some second thoughts it was ignored.

The first volume of Series D contains the documents for the period September, 1937–September, 1938, and is divided into seven chapters, each limited to German foreign policy in a particular area. The organization of this material is as follows:

Chapter I: Relations with the western Great Powers, September 30, 1937–March 11, 1938.

Chapter II: Relations with Austria, July, 1936–July, 1938.

Chapter III: Relations with the United States, August, 1937–September, 1938.

Chapter IV: Relations with the Far East, July, 1937–September, 1938.

Chapter V: Relations with the Soviet Union, November, 1937–July, 1938.

Chapter VI: Relations with the Holy See, March, 1937–September, 1938.

Chapter VII: Relations with the Great Powers of western Europe, March–August, 1938.

It may readily be observed that the chronological limits of this volume are rather elastic because the commission had to consider the particular requirements of each of the issues involved. For example, in the case of Austria it was necessary to begin with the July 11, 1936, accord, which clearly marks a turning point in the relations between the two countries and was the beginning of the policy that was to lead to *Anschluss* in March, 1938. For the Far East, however, it was logical to take the beginning of the war in China as the point of departure. On the other hand, the commission's decision to place in separate volumes the documents relating to certain issues of specific importance leads to the omission of the documentation on the Czechoslovak crisis of 1938 and on the Spanish Civil War from the chapters dealing with the western powers. This material is to be found in Volumes II–III of the series. In effect, this technique creates a certain degree of confusion that could have been avoided by the adoption of a chronological structure. Furthermore, for reasons which are not entirely clear, the documents containing the proposals for an Italo-German understanding that were exchanged between Ciano and Von Ribbentrop in Rome on the occasion of Hitler's visit to the Italian capital were also omitted. These important documents were published only several years later by the British historian D. C. Watt.[22]

Such defects are not as glaring in the second volume, which, limited to the Czechoslovak question, has a purely monographic character. The

[22] D. C. Watt, "An Earlier Model for the Pact of Steel. The Draft Treaties Exchanged between Germany and Italy during Hitler's Visit to Rome in May, 1938," *International Affairs*, XXXIII (1957), fasc. 2.

documentation covers the period October 1, 1937–September 30, 1938, but the bulk of the material deals with the various aspects of the Sudeten crisis which followed the *Anschluss* and culminated in the Munich Agreements.

This volume is of primary importance, however, despite the fact that not all the questions posed by historians are given satisfactory answers. The contacts that Henlein had with Hitler and with Von Ribbentrop in March, 1938, prove conclusively that he operated on the basis of orders received from Berlin and that the Sudeten leaders' repeated declarations of their desire to seek an accord with the Prague government were nothing more than tactical expedients hiding their real intent, i.e., the destruction of the unity of the Czechoslovak state.

On the other hand, the documents appear to be inadequate on another problem, namely, the real intentions of Hitler in the event that France and Great Britain clearly demonstrated their preparedness to go to war to defend Czechoslovakia's integrity. The German documents prove that this eventuality had created grave apprehensions in the Wilhelmstrasse, where, for example, Von Weizsäcker had repeatedly emphasized the dangers of a general war and advocated a policy of caution in order to avoid this calamity. However, this does not throw much light on Hitler's thinking on the matter, and it was on his will, in the final analysis, that the ultimate decision depended. For this purpose, the military documents included by the commission are also insufficient, since by their very nature these have well-defined limitations as sources.

The third volume in the series is also limited to a single issue, the Spanish Civil War. It provides an extremely interesting picture, in part new, of the relations between Germany and Franco's nationalist government. Various aspects of Franco's long struggle to resist German pressure to acquire control of Spain's mineral resources are revealed here. The documents on relations with Italy are also important, but those dealing with Germany's role on the Non-Intervention Committee are few in number and of minor value. The committee, because of limitations of space, perhaps selected them by a too rigid criteria.

Those who hoped to find confirmation in this volume of an understanding between German and Spanish military men dating back to the period prior to the Civil War were greatly disappointed: not a single document appeared in the volume to prove this thesis, which had been supported by many. Instead, the published documents make it clear that in the days immediately following outbreak of the Civil War, a strong difference of opinion existed between the Wilhelmstrasse and the General Staff. The Ministry of Foreign Affairs was inclined to maintain a certain reserve while awaiting a clarification of the situation, but the military, spearheaded by Goering, were urging prompt military assistance to Franco.

This dualism in German policy was to affect subsequent events, giving rise to many doubts and hesitations and to some conflicting undertakings. It was only in the fall of 1936 that a clear-cut decision was made to throw Germany's full weight behind the Falangist movement—a decision stimulated in part by the desire to offset the large-scale aid sent to the Madrid government by the Soviet Union. Later on, the German Foreign Ministry tended to follow a more cautious policy in the Spanish conflict. The Italo-Spanish Accord of November 26, 1936, further increased the doubts entertained by the staff at the Wilhelmstrasse regarding the Spanish question. Von Hassell, the German Ambassador to Rome, gave voice to these doubts when he observed that as a result of the Italo-Spanish Accord Italy might succeed in eliminating the Reich's influence in Spanish affairs, and that this premise raised serious questions as to the wisdom of a policy involving Germany in an undertaking from which it could expect only limited gains, or gains not at all commensurate with its sacrifices. These considerations, which in substance faithfully reflected prevailing opinion in the Wilhelmstrasse, must be construed to have been the key factors behind the decision by the German government early in 1937 to surrender the leading role in Spain's Civil War to Italy, while continuing the economic penetration of Spain that had been begun earlier.

The fourth volume covers the period from the Munich Pact (September 30, 1938) to the German occupation of Prague (March 15, 1939) and is divided into eight chapters, on Czechoslovakia, Great Britain, France, Italy, the Holy See, the Soviet Union, the United States, and the Far East, respectively; they are preceded, as usual, by a general analytical Table of Contents in which the documents are listed chronologically.

Without a doubt, the events referred to in this volume are among the most interesting of the entire period preceding World War II. The relations between Germany and the western powers had not yet reached the point where it was manifest that peaceful coexistence had been rendered impossible. On the contrary, the desire to avoid a conflict with Hitler was extremely strong among at least some of the responsible French and British leaders, and this feeling might have led to unforeseeable results if Germany had been satisfied with the gains she had made in the east (that had brought within the confines of the Reich almost all of the German-speaking peoples), or, in continuing her dynamic policy, if she had come to an agreement with the Poles and directed her expansion even further eastward. In this context the documents pertinent to Germany's relations with the western powers assume a special significance, as do, in the light of subsequent events, the documents concerning the Soviet Union, in which several indications leading to the *coup de théâtre* of August, 1939, may be seen.

To complete the documentation for the period September, 1937–March, 1939, the commission has assembled the material relative to relations with the minor powers in the fifth volume. Divided into ten chapters (Poland and Danzig, southeastern Europe, the Baltic states, northern Europe, Belgium and Holland, Switzerland, Turkey, the Near East, Latin America, and the Jewish question), this volume's major appeal lies in the 140 documents concerning Polish-German relations. In this period they are particularly significant because the conclusion of an accord between Berlin and Warsaw might have brought about a substantial change in German foreign policy, assuming the definite anti-Soviet manifestations referred to above. The documents also reveal the extent of the tension reached in German-Polish relations in the winter of 1938–39 and point an accusing finger at the government in Warsaw for keeping the seriousness of the situation hidden from the British and French, leading those powers to draw the erroneous conclusion that the country under immediate threat was Rumania.

In the sixth volume (covering the period March 16–August 8, 1939, that is, from the occupation of Prague to the reopening of Polish-German negotiations) the commission judged it necessary to adopt a chronological order for the documents because it was impossible to separate the various intimately connected issues without making an exact comprehension of the facts extremely difficult. The documents are of exceptional importance. Suffice it to note that the period includes the Italo-German-Japanese negotiations for the Tripartite Pact and the Rome-Berlin negotiations leading to the signing of the Pact of Steel at the same time that Soviet-German negotiations, which would ultimately lead to the agreement of August 23, 1939, were developing.

The seventh volume of the series, entitled *The Last Days of Peace*, covers the period August 8–September 3, 1939, that is, to the Anglo-French declaration of war on Germany. Essentially, the importance of this volume lies in the information it provides on the question of immediate responsibility for the war, a problem which, in the case of World War II, until now has prompted very few debates.[23] The documentation does provide some clarification, particularly of the course of the Polish-German negotiations on the eve of the conflict. In this connection, a comparison of the German documents with those published earlier in the Polish White Book is of real interest. From these two sources it may be concluded that if the Warsaw government maintained an extremely rigid position, encour-

[23] The recent volume by A. J. P. Taylor, *The Origins of the Second World War* (London: Hamish Hamilton, 1961), has, in effect, opened debate on previously unchallenged theses.

aged also by the security offered by the British guarantee, an agreement between Germany and Poland was, nevertheless, impossible because Hitler was not seeking a solution to the Danzig problem but, rather, the dismemberment of Poland.

The volume also contains a large number of documents concerning German-Soviet relations and the negotiations leading to the nonaggression pact of August 23, 1939. This collection includes nearly one hundred documents on this particular question that are not found in *Nazi-Soviet Relations,* but this additional information does not alter the story to any appreciable degree.

Volume VIII covers the period September 4, 1939–March 18, 1940, the latter being the date of Mussolini's meeting with Hitler at the Brenner Pass, which marked a turning point in Italy's march toward war. Here, too, a great deal of space is devoted to Nazi-Soviet relations, but, in contrast to the previous volume, there is considerable new material, particularly concerning Nazi-Soviet economic relations and the German reaction to the Soviet absorption of the Baltic states. However, the most important part of the documentation concerns Berlin's relations with Rome and Tokyo, where German diplomacy was taxed to the limit in its attempt to offset the confusion and consternation provoked by the news of the Nazi-Soviet Pact.

The ninth volume of Series D ends with June 22, 1940, the date of the French armistice, and is of special interest because it contains all of the material on the Italo-German negotiations on the eve of Italy's intervention in the war, the minutes of the Hitler-Mussolini meeting in Munich where the clauses of the armistice with France were drawn up, and an extremely rich collection on the actual armistice negotiations. Equally important is the material on the German invasion of Denmark and Norway and the numerous documents on German-Soviet relations not published in *Nazi-Soviet Relations.*

The next volume, the tenth of the series, covers the weeks between the conclusion of the armistice with France and the signing of the second arbitration agreement in Vienna (August 30, 1940), an extremely limited period but one of major significance because of the variety of problems facing German diplomacy and the consequences these problems were destined to have in the immediate future.

The interests of the three major Continental powers meet and clash in southeastern Europe. The acquisition of Bessarabia and northern Bukowina by the Soviet Union marked the first rift in the Nazi-Soviet collaboration and induced Bulgaria and Hungary to rush forward with their claims to Rumanian territory. The Axis powers were obliged to intervene with the Vienna arbitration proposal, an agreement realized without Soviet participation and without prior consultation between Berlin and Moscow, as had been stipulated in the August 23, 1939, accord. Germany's offer of a guarantee to Rumania emphasizes the anti-Soviet character of the Axis action and brings to a striking close a documentation of fundamental importance for an understanding of the origins of the Nazi-Soviet conflict.

Volume XI of Series D concerns the period August 31, 1940–January 31, 1941. Among the more significant issues covered are the long negotiations undertaken to draw Spain into the conflict, which reached their decisive phase during the last four months of 1940. These negotiations were to be considered from the viewpoint of a proposal for the concentration of the German war effort in the Mediterranean in order to take over Gibraltar and the Suez, a project warmly supported by Admiral Raeder and, once the plan for the invasion of Britain was determined to be impractical, by Hitler as well. It is very probable that, if these plans had been realized, the war would have taken a different turn: such a major undertaking in the Mediterranean might have prevented Hitler from attacking the Soviet Union a short time later. On the one hand, if the continued resistance of the British made Spain's entry into the war a matter of the greatest urgency for the Germans, on the other, it also induced the Madrid government to stay out of a conflict that promised to be a long one; especially since that nation was still exhausted from three years of civil war, was facing an extremely critical internal situation, and was exposed, by the nature of its geography, to British attacks that it would find difficult to sustain. Therefore, the negotiations of the last months of 1940 were characterized by desperate Spanish attempts to cancel the obligations Spain had assumed with the Axis, while at the same time avoiding a total break in relations. This was an extremely dangerous alternative because the German armies were poised on the Pyrénées.

The papers pertinent to Italo-German affairs are also of considerable importance. Italo-German relations underwent a profound change following Italy's military defeats in Greece and in North Africa. Moreover, Mussolini's and Ciano's unfortunate Balkan military enterprise convinced the German Chancellor that it was necessary to take over complete control of the direction of the war, eliminating the autonomy enjoyed by his ally up to this time, which had been synthesized in the concept of "parallel war." The apogee of this evolution was reached at the Hitler-Mussolini meeting on January 19–20, 1941, and this new relationship between the Axis powers was confirmed in the military and political fields.

If the material concerning German-Soviet relations adds little to what had already been published in *Nazi-Soviet Relations*, the documents on the Balkans are of major importance, particularly those on the negotiations undertaken to draw Bulgaria and Yugoslavia into the Tripartite Agreement. The section reserved for Berlin-Vichy relations is also noteworthy, even if a number of these documents were already known from the volumes of Ambassador Otto Abetz and the collection dealing with the French delegation to the German Armistice Commission.[24]

Volume XII covers the period February 1–June 22, 1941. The most revealing data concern the negotiations to draw Yugoslavia into the Tripartite Pact. The German documents now permit the drawing of some firm conclusions and put an end—at least in part—to the many uncertainties arising from the contrasting versions offered by Yugoslav statesmen.

On the basis of evidence provided by these documents, it may now be affirmed that both Cvetkovic and the Regent did everything possible to avoid adhering to the Tripartite Pact, and that when forced to bow to heavy German pressure, they fought to reduce Yugoslavia's Tripartite Treaty obligations to the absolute minimum.This resistance was prompted by fear of the reaction a policy of close collaboration with the Axis would provoke in Yugoslavia, especially among the Serbs. The new facts furnished by the Wilhelmstrasse documents tend to show that, at least to the end of February, 1941, Yugoslav leaders banked on playing upon the latent Italo-German rivalry in order to avoid meeting Hitler's demands. In this maneuver they were encouraged by the favorable reception given to the Stakic mission by Mussolini. In this instance, Mussolini's adroit maneuvering bears noting. In notifying Berlin of these contacts, the Italian head of state hastened to emphasize how an Italo-Yugoslav accord would break Greek morale, thus rendering German military intervention in the southern Balkans superfluous. However, these unofficial negotiations were brought to a halt by a veto from Berlin which, at the end of February, "advised" Palazzo Chigi against pursuing them any further.

Insofar as the long-debated question of Yugoslav plans for the acquisition of Salonika are concerned, the documents contained in this volume include the exchange of notes with the Axis powers in which Yugoslav aspirations for an outlet on the Aegean are recognized. However, in view of the way in which the negotiations were conducted, it may be concluded that the prospects of acquiring Salonika did not play the decisive role (as had been believed previously) in the decisions taken by Prince Paul and his collaborators. The decision to adhere to the Tripartite Pact was not made as a necessary preliminary step to an alliance with the Axis, but because

[24] See pp. 311–13.

German pressure had become unbearable and adherence to the Tripartite Agreement seemed to be the only way to preserve Yugoslav neutrality. For these reasons, the Yugoslav leaders did everything possible to reduce Yugoslavia's obligations in the agreement, and finally succeeded in achieving a position of considerable autonomy within the framework of the alliance. As a case in point, the Axis powers agreed not to ask for the right of transit of Axis troops through Yugoslav territory and also recognized that the application of the principle of *casus foederis* was possible only upon Yugoslav request. So circumscribed, Yugoslav adherence to the Tripartite Pact was little more than a formality. Yet it did allow Yugoslavia to survive a particularly critical period (shortly after, the beginning of the Russian campaign would completely alter the situation); it protected Yugoslavia against unilateral Italian action, thanks to the Axis guarantee of its territorial integrity; and, in effect, it made involvement of Yugoslavia in the conflict somewhat more difficult. These various facts should be kept in mind in order to evaluate properly the foreign policy of the Belgrade government—a complex of factors that tends to support strongly the criticism launched by the supporters of the old regime against the authors of the *coup d'état* of March 27 and, in general, against the champions of an even greater intransigence.

In accordance with the plan adopted in 1958, the thirteenth and last volume of Series D published by the Tripartite Commission covers the period June 23–December 11, 1941, the date of Germany's declaration of war on the United States. While the documentation is particularly detailed, there are no surprising revelations. However, the evidence does show that the German government was reluctant to accede to the Japanese request that the two other major powers (Germany and Italy) immediately declare war on the United States. The second Japanese request, presented simultaneously with the first, was much more favorably received by the Wilhelmstrasse. In the latter, the Japanese indicated that they were anxious to sign a pact guaranteeing that the Tripartite Powers would not sign separate armistice or peace pacts with Great Britain and the United States. In September, 1941, Von Mackensen reported to Berlin from Rome that, on the basis of confidential information received from persons very close to Palazzo Chigi, Ciano, believing an Axis victory to be impossible, was seeking the opportune moment to end the war by a compromise peace. It should be noted, however, that it was Japan who made the first attempt to violate the obligations she had requested her allies to assume.

The growing German distrust of the Italian Minister of Foreign Affairs must be kept in mind because it directly affected Italo-German relations. For example, the discussions that took place concerning the status of

Italian workers in Germany degenerated into a controversy that threatened to undermine the rapport between the two powers, rather than merely to clarify a delicate and difficult situation between two allies united in a common cause.

The deterioration of Italo-German relations was arrested in November, when the German Foreign Office undertook to implement the new slogan "European solidarity," proclaimed by Hitler in his speech of November 8, 1941. The failure to realize the objectives of the Russian campaign had warned Germany of the necessity of obtaining maximum co-operation from all European forces in the struggle with the Soviet Union. This volume reveals the extent of the German effort to this end, culminating in the solemn ceremony of November 25, 1941, in which Bulgars, Danes, Finns, Croatians, Rumanians, and Slovaks signed the Anti-Comintern Pact while the original signatories solemnly renewed their pledge.

While the documents concerning relations with the Vichy government do not contain anything startlingly new, careful attention should be paid to them, especially those concerning the sections of the May Protocols referring to the use of the Tunisian ports for supplies destined for Libya. Toward the end of the year Italy was able to insert herself in the dialogue between Berlin and Vichy and obtained better results than did German diplomacy.

From observations of the individual volumes published thus far, it is evident that the collection of German documents is of exceptional scholarly value. It would be facetious, however, to believe that the entire story of Nazi foreign policy could be re-created from these records alone. This statement is equally true of all collections of documents, which, alone, are not adequate to explain all of the aspects of a state's foreign policy, and this inadequacy should be particularly emphasized in the case of this collection.

For example, the German collection has important lacunae created by the war, the extent of which has not yet been—and perhaps may never be—clearly determined. In addition to the Von Ribbentrop papers, a large part of the archives of the Division of Economic Affairs apparently has been lost, a loss which in this instance deprives us all of the documentation relating to the economic aspects of Germany's Far Eastern policy.

On the other hand, one must praise the commission's decision to include certain documents that, although they did not form part of the Foreign Ministry's archive, are, nevertheless, of major importance to diplomatic studies. Illustrative of this contribution are the minutes of the Cabinet meetings, the minutes of Hitler's meetings at the Reichschancellery, and the military documents (Hitler's directives, operational orders, the war diary of the Wehrmacht's operations headquarters, etc.), whose decisive importance has been demonstrated on many occasions.

Furthermore, the hypothesis was advanced—particularly in the early stages of the project—that the commission's selection of the documents to be included was conditioned by political considerations. The very fact that the editors were drawn from three countries aroused the suspicion that the suppression of pertinent documents had reached noteworthy proportions because each editor, in insisting on certain omissions, had forced the others to do the same, "do ut des." Whatever basis may have existed for these initial suspicions, they cannot be sustained today.

The most serious deficiency is caused, instead, by a peculiar, yet characteristic, aspect of foreign policy in modern times, and one that reached a high level of development in Hitler's Germany; that is, a nation's entire foreign policy is no longer the exclusive prerogative of the Ministry of Foreign Affairs. This phenomenon, at least since the end of World War I, is noted everywhere to some degree, but it reached major proportions in Germany,[25] where the rivalries existing between the various organs of the state (Ministry of Foreign Affairs-General Staff) and among the exponents of National Socialism (Von Ribbentrop-Goering, for example) gave rise to frequent unofficial undertakings which have a decisive importance because of the authoritative character of their initiators. Not infrequently, a scholar is faced with a baffling problem whose explanation can be found in the personal action of an individual or in the activity of the military as it tended to usurp the prerogatives of the Foreign Ministry.

There are numerous examples of this development: on October 19, 1937, the German Ambassador to Rome was informed that the Wilhelmstrasse, in complete agreement with Tokyo, preferred that Italy's adhesion to the Anti-Comintern Pact be effected via a bilateral Italo-Japanese agreement. The following day, Von Ribbentrop's personal representative called on Ciano to suggest that Italy instead subscribe directly to the German-Japanese agreement; and this was done on November 6th. This episode is sufficiently indicative, but it must be stressed that it is only one of many to be found in the collection. Suffice it to recall the many unofficial undertakings involved in the German maneuvers leading to the *Anschluss*, or the activities of the military during the initial stages of the Spanish Civil War, or finally, Goering's probings to arrive at a compromise peace during the early months of the war.

The major difficulty seems to come from the fact that effective control of Nazi foreign policy always remained in Hitler's hands, and he, in the final

[25] See Gordon A. Craig, "The German Foreign Office from Neurath to Ribbentrop," *The Diplomats* (Princeton: Princeton University Press, 1953).

analysis, made the decisions. At this point, the establishment of the exact moment at which decisions in matters of foreign policy were made and the process by which the decisions were reached is highly problematical, all the more so when it is recalled that not infrequently German diplomats were not informed of what was happening in *alto loco* because of Hitler's often-expressed lack of faith in his diplomats.

Insofar as the technical aspects of the collection are concerned, it should be noted that, in the beginning, the commission chose to assemble the material by subject. Subsequently, this technique was abandoned in favor of publishing the documents in chronological order with a Table of Contents according to subject, which includes a brief summary of the content of each document. This system produces very satisfactory results because, while it facilitates a superficial investigation by noting the key documents for each subject, it also provides the best possible organization of the material for detailed research. An index of proper names is appended to each volume but without page references, however. And finally, it is observed—and this concerns Italy particularly—that the collection of German diplomatic documents includes explanatory notes. These notes are especially significant in that they document the existence of mysterious channels linking Palazzo Chigi to Villa Wolkonski (the German Embassy) and also provide interpretations of the policies of the Fascist regime. Several of these interpretations are unique, and, were it not for the fact that they were probably bits of gossip circulated to damage the reputation of an important figure, they would be the bases for an entirely new explanation of the origins of certain decisions taken by the Fascist dictator. However, these pages are not particularly edifying.

In addition to the collections referred to thus far, special mention should be made of the seven minute books published in 1947 by the British Admiralty, containing the minutes of the conferences held by Hitler with the naval High Command.[26]

This source is essentially limited to the military aspects of the war. However, it is also of great value to the study of German foreign policy in this period because at these conferences Hitler often expressed his views on the political-military situation and laid down the general lines of future action in such detail as was possible only when he was talking to his closest collaborators.

---

[26] *Fuehrer Conferences on Naval Affairs, 1939, 1940, 1941, 1942, 1943, 1944, 1945* (London: Admiralty, 1947), 7 fascs. This source was reprinted in *Brassey's Naval Annual* for 1948 with some addenda. An American edition includes additional Raeder *promemoria: Führer Conferences on Matters Dealing with the German Navy, 1939 to 1945* (9 vols.; Washington: U.S. Navy Department, 1946–47).

Through these, it is possible to reconstruct the origins of many of Hitler's plans, the precise moment in which he decided to put them into effect or to abandon them, and his reactions, along with those of his intimates, to the course of the war.

This material partially fills an important gap in the German collection, a gap that is characteristic of German documentation for this period because of the absence of an organ comparable to a Ministerial Cabinet in which problems of major importance might have been discussed. It must be added that Hitler was not in the habit of making notes on political questions, nor was he prone to write personal letters to his collaborators. Therefore, the minutes of the military conferences are the best sources on which to base a reconstruction of the real thoughts of the German Chancellor.

Among the most interesting details to be found in the minutes are those relative to the planning of the Norwegian campaign, these take on a decisive importance when it is noted that Wilhelmstrasse documents provide little specific information on this matter. As is commonly known, the preparations for this campaign were made by Rosenberg and Admiral Raeder, and the Ministry of Foreign Affairs was not informed of them. In this instance, too, the fact that the left hand did not know what the right hand was doing led to characteristically conflicting actions, especially in the negotiations with the Norwegian government following the invasion.

The material concerning the projected invasion of Britain is also extremely rich. The documents show that following the collapse of France Hitler considered the surrender of Great Britain imminent and that he was disposed, under the circumstances, to offer the British relatively favorable peace terms. Not until mid-July did it become clear that it was impossible to arrive at a compromise peace with the British, and only then did Hitler begin to consider the possibility of a landing on Britain's southern coasts, an operation for which the German High Command had not made even preliminary feasibility studies. Because of the overwhelming superiority of the British fleet, an invasion was, from the outset, dependent on absolute control of the air over the Channel. The desperate defense mounted by the Royal Air Force blocked the German attempt to dominate the air over Britain and, as a result, the German invasion plans went awry.

These documents are also essential to the reconstruction of various other phases of German foreign policy during World War II, at a time—as in all conflicts—when the closest possible ties link diplomatic activity to military operations. The minutes of the conferences held during the closing months of 1940, for example, are indispensable to an understanding of the origin and development of the negotiations conducted in that period to draw Spain into the war. No less important are the documents relative to Italo-German relations after Italy's attack on Greece, which reveal that, from that time on, Hitler and his advisers lost all faith in Italy's military capability. It was this fact, together with Spain's refusal to enter the war, that induced Hitler to change his Mediterranean strategy from offensive to defensive. Hitler's attitude toward the French is illustrative of other important elements found in the collection. In one instance, it is confirmed that Weygand's presence in North Africa had a determining influence on Hitler's relatively moderate policy toward Vichy. And again, in reference to Italo-German relations, the minutes of Hitler's conferences of July 17, 1943, on the eve of the Feltre meeting, and those following the fall of Mussolini (July 26 and August 19), when measures were taken to meet the new developments in Italy, are particularly noteworthy.

Recent publications in Germany devoted to the military history of World War II are also of interest to the study of the diplomatic activities of the period. The publication of the first six volumes of the Wehrmacht's "War Diary,"[27] covering the years 1942–45, merit special recognition.

This source was already known in part through the published proceedings of the Nuremberg trials (documents of series PS and C) and through the collection of German diplomatic documents wherein numerous extracts of the "War Diary" appear, along with the memoirs of Helmuth Greiner, the first compiler.[28] The "War Diary" has been reorganized and is being republished under the editorship of Professor Percy Ernst Schramm, who replaced Greiner. Despite the fact that it is incomplete (approximately 25 per cent of the material was destroyed), it remains an important source for diplomatic studies. In this sense, its value will be augmented as the volumes relative to the years preceding 1945, which contain more detailed references to the political aspects of the conflict, are published.

In using this source, one must remember that, while the material was gathered day by day, it was edited after a certain lapse of time—about two months. Therefore, some *post factum* corrections were probably made to render errors of judgment less evident or to minimize delays in planning and execution. Professor Schramm advises that he sought to avoid reporting words or actions that would be damaging to specific individuals and that this practice was even more strictly observed after the abortive attempt on Hitler's life on July 20, 1944, when surveillance of German military leaders became much more severe. However, these observations are of special interest to military historians or to those interested in evaluating the existing friction between Hitler and the Wehrmacht generals; they are

[27] Percy Ernst Schramm (ed.), *Kriegstagebuch des Oberkommandos der Wehrmacht (Wehrmachtführungsstab)* (6 vols.; Frankfurt am Main: Bernard and Graefe, 1961–64).

[28] Helmuth Greiner, *Die Oberste Wehrmachtführung* (Wiesbaden: Limes, 1951).

of only peripheral interest insofar as they affect the political references made in the diary. On this point, special note should be taken of the numerous "reports in retrospect" included, which provide a complete picture of a given phase of an operation—reports that often examine the political factors that influenced the operation or led to its planning in the first place.

The collection of Hitler's fifty-two operational orders issued between August 31, 1939, and November, 1943, may be considered a supplement to this source. This collection was recently published by Walther Hubatsch,[29] who, together with Felix Hartlaub,[30] collaborated with Schramm in compiling the official Wehrmacht operational diary.

To a great extent, this material came to light during the Nuremberg trials, and it is reprinted in the German diplomatic document collection limited to the period covered by the collection. However, the publisher has added a certain number of documents concerning the execution of the operations and numerous operational plans. These offer the opportunity of identifying with greater accuracy the factors motivating German foreign policy during the war period. The following examples may be cited: the project outlines on May 19, 1943, for the defense of the Balkans without the participation of Italian troops, a plan that appears to have provided for the imminent collapse of Italy; and the documentation concerning German plans for the control of Italian territory after July 25, 1943.

A large number of documents pertinent to military history were published by several German specialists. In addition to the collection of a general nature edited by Jacobsen,[31] the following should also be noted: Walther Hubatsch's volume on the German attack on Denmark and Norway,[32] and Jacobsen's collection concerning the planning and execution of the attack against France,[33] based on the diaries of the various units

[29] Walther Hubatsch (ed.), *Hitlers Weisungen für die Kriegsführung 1939–1945. Dokumente des Oberkommandos der Wehrmacht* (Frankfurt am Main: Bernard and Graefe, 1962).

[30] Felix Hartlaub, *Im Sperrkreiss. Aufzeichnungen aus dem Zweiten Weltkrieg* (Hamburg: Rowohlt, 1955). A summary based on the personal recollections of the author.

[31] Hans-Adolf Jacobsen, *1939–1945. Der zweite Weltkrieg in Chronik und Dokumenten* (Darmstad: Wehr and Wissen, 1959).

[32] Walther Hubatsch, *"Weserübung". Die deutsche Besetzung von Dänemark und Norwegen 1940* (Göttingen: Musterschmidt, 1960). See also the official British publication: T. K. Derry, *The Campaign in Norway* (London: Her Majesty's Stationery Office, 1952).

[33] Hans-Adolf Jacobsen (ed.), *Dokumente zur Vorgeschichte des Westfeldzuges 1939–1940* (Göttingen: Musterschmidt, 1956); Jacobsen, *Fall Gelb. Der Kampf um den deutschen Operationsplan zur Westoffensive 1940* (Wiesbaden: Steiner, 1957); Jacobsen, *Dunkirchen. Ein Beitrag zur Geschichte des Westfeldzuges 1940.*

of the Wehrmacht and on the personal diaries of the Wehrmacht generals. Other documents of exceptional military interest are Von Bock's and the work of Karl Klee on Operation SEA LION,[34] although the extensive documentation in the second volume of the latter is generally already well known. No less significant are the fragments of Hitler's conversations with his military leaders, previously edited in part by Felix Gilbert[35] and more recently published in the original German by Helmuth Heiber,[36] and the Wehrmacht's reports on the military situation, published by Erich Murawski.[37]

General Halder's well-known war diary deserves special comment. This document was in part made public at the Nuremberg trials. Subsequently, the Historical Division of the U.S. army brought out an English translation.[38] It has recently been republished in its original German by Jacobsen,[39] who added an index of names and numerous explanatory notes that clarify frequent obscure passages in the text.

Halder's diary is factual in character and consists of notes recorded by him in order to recall accurately events that occurred and statements made to him. Thus, the diary contains little in the nature of personal opinion;[40] at best, an expression of his astonishment or disappointment may be indicated by an exclamation mark at the end of a sentence. Written in the terse style of a telegram, it is difficult to read, and the meaning is not always clear. However, for the patient scholar, the diary is often irreplaceable for the reconstruction of the political and military conduct of the war.

A typical illustration is the meeting of August 31, 1940, during which

---

[34] Karl Klee, *Das Unternehmen 'Seeloewe'. Die geplante deutsche Landung in England 1940* (2 vols.; Göttingen: Musterschmidt, 1958). See also Ronald Wheatley, *Operation Sea Lion. German Plans for the Invasion of England, 1939–1941* (Oxford: Clarendon Press, 1958); Walter Ancel, *Hitler Confronts England* (Durham, N.C.: Duke University Press, 1960).

[35] Felix Gilbert, *Hitler Directs His War. The Secret Records of His Daily Military Conferences* (London: Oxford University Press, 1950).

[36] Helmuth Heiber (ed.), *Hitlers Lagebesprechungen. Die Protokollfragmente seiner militarischen Konferenzen 1942–1945* (Stuttgart: Deutsche Verlagsanstalt, 1962).

[37] Erich Murawski, *Der deutsche Wehrmachtbericht 1939–1945. Ein Beitrag zur Untersuchung der geistingen Kriegführung. Mit einer Dokumentation der Wehrmachtberichte vom 1.7.1944 bis zum 9.5.1945* (Boppard: Boldt, 1962).

[38] *The Halder Diaries* (7 vols.; Washington: Infantry Journal, 1950).

[39] Hans-Adolf Jacobsen (ed.), *Generalobertst Halder. Kriegstagebuch,* Vol. I: *Vom Polenfeldzug bis zum Ende Westoffensive* (14.8.1939–30.6.1940); Vol. II: *Von der geplanten Landung in England bis zum Begin des Ostfeldzuges* (1.7.1940–21.6.1941)(Stuttgart: Kohlammer, 1962–63). The third volume will appear shortly.

[40] On this issue see, instead, Fritz Halder, *Hitler als Feldherr* (Munich: Dom, 1949), and Peter Bor, *Gespräche mit Halder* (Wiesbaden: Limes, 1950).

Hitler discussed two key issues with his military leaders: the plans for the invasion of Britain and the plans for a campaign against the Soviet Union. We have a detailed summary of the former in the *Fuehrer Conferences on Naval Affairs* collection. Halder's diary dwells particularly on that part of the conference devoted to plans for the Soviet Union, and also notes the political considerations which, according to Hitler, made imperative an attack toward the east even before the defeat of Great Britain.

It should further be mentioned that, on the basis of Halder's notes, many scholars have concluded that Hitler decided on an attack against the U.S.S.R. at this meeting. This conclusion does not seem warranted. In this, as in other analogous circumstances, it is necessary to distinguish between the project and its execution. To be sure, it is a fact that in the course of that meeting Hitler outlined, for the first time in a precise and concrete manner, the idea of attacking the Soviet Union without waiting for the conclusion of war with Britain, but the successive course of Soviet-German relations clearly establishes that such a decision was made much later, that is, only after the failure of the Berlin talks with Molotov of November, 1940.

2. THE BRITISH COLLECTION.

In March, 1944, Foreign Secretary Anthony Eden announced to Commons the government's decision to proceed with the publication of the diplomatic documents contained in the archives of the Foreign Office for the period between the two world wars.

The compilation was entrusted to two well-known scholars, Professors Rohan Butler and E. L. Woodward, each to edit one of the two series proposed: the first, for the period 1919–29; the second, for the years 1930–39. Following the publication of the German documents, it was decided to divide the second series into two parts in order to hasten the publication of the volumes covering the very last period. Consequently, the collection appears as follows: Series I, from June 29, 1919, to May, 1929; Series II, from May, 1929 (the beginning of the preliminary talks for the London Naval Conference) to March, 1938; Series III, from March, 1938 (*Anschluss*) to September 3, 1939.[41]

Thirteen volumes have appeared to date, all of primary importance not only for the quantity of material included, but because this is at present the most significant documentary source for research in the diplomacy of this

---

[41] *Documents on British Foreign Policy 1919–1939* (London: His Majesty's Stationery Office, 1947 *et seq.*).

period. The volumes of the American collection for the same period, in contrast, are not nearly as important owing to their largely legal character and to the special position of the United States with respect to many European problems of the immediate postwar period. Likewise, the recently initiated publication of the Soviet documents does not for the moment offer anything of particular importance. Until such time as the Italian documents, which are now in the process of publication, appear, one must refer to the British collection, especially for a reconstruction of inter-Allied relations after the termination of the Paris peace conference.

In a certain sense, an exception to what has been said above may be made for the first two volumes of the first series, which contain the minutes of the meetings of the Council of the Heads of Delegations, the organ which, during the six months that elapsed between the signing of the Treaty of Versailles (June 28, 1919) and the date it entered into effect (January 10, 1920), continued the work toward world reorganization initiated by the Big Four. Obviously, this material is of the greatest importance, but it had been made available earlier, in a supplement to the Paris peace conference published in the American collection.[42] In this case, the State Department collection is to be preferred because it contains the complete minutes of the sessions along with the documents; in the interest of brevity, the British collection summarizes the issues of secondary importance. However, the latter offers the double advantage of a more accurate edition accompanied by useful reference notes and the opportunity to examine (in the second part of Volume II) the unpublished minutes of the meetings of the prime ministers and foreign ministers held in London in December, 1919, and January, 1920. These discussions, which were at the highest level, considered relations with Russia, the Fiume and Adriatic questions, extradition of German citizens accused of war crimes, the preliminaries of the peace treaty with Turkey, etc.

The third volume of the first series contains hitherto unpublished material, mainly designed to provide a clear picture of British policy toward eastern Europe for the second half of 1919 and the early months of 1920. Obviously, the most significant material deals with Allied activities in Russia, activities that, while they did not achieve the declared objectives, sowed the seeds of long-lasting suspicion and distrust in the minds of Soviet leaders. On the other hand, the Allies, after the collapse of the Czarist government, had succeeded in organizing some resistance on the eastern front, thanks to the existence of anti-Bolshevik forces intended to prevent the Germans from taking over the economic resources on both sides of the

[42] See below, pp. 220–21.

Urals. They were not disposed to abandon either General Denikin or Admiral Kolchak to the mercies of the Communist government. The documents in this volume deal with the last phase of these events—down to the final defeat of the anti-Bolshevik forces and the armistices signed with the governments of Latvia and Estonia—and include both the consular correspondence and that of special missions to Russia and the inter-Allied negotiations to arrive at a common course of action in the Russian question. Such material invites reflection on the obvious inability of Allied statesmen to comprehend fully the Soviet phenomenon. Many errors were committed at the time, and numerous opportunities for an honorable settlement were lost.

The documents in the fourth volume may be divided into two distinct parts. The first deals with the negotiations entered into during the second half of 1919 to settle the problems of the Adriatic that were left unresolved by the Paris peace conference and that had suddenly been aggravated by D'Annunzio's occupation of Fiume. It should be noted that the material contained in the British archives does not always contribute to a clarification of the key issues in the negotiations because at this point the negotiations were largely Italian-American affairs. The second half of the volume treats British policy in the Middle East for the same period. Foremost among the principal issues are the Anglo-French negotiations on Palestine and Syria, which took a decisive turn as a result of the exchange of letters of September 15, 1919, between Clemenceau and Lloyd George. The decline of the influence of the United States after the return to Washington of President Wilson, the champion of self-determination, and the growing conviction in both Paris and London that neither could agree to total acceptance of the other's original proposals were the two principal elements inducing the governments of France and England to review their respective rigid positions and to reach an agreement. While the result appeared to favor British interests (France surrendered all claims to the Mosul oil fields), it allowed France a greater freedom of action vis-à-vis Emir Faisal, who lost the support of Britain.

Of equal interest is the section devoted to relations with Turkey, not simply insofar as it concerns the negotiations for the future treaty of peace, but first and foremost for the inter-Allied discussions on policy toward Asia Minor in the face of the growing power of Kemal Atatürk's nationalist movement and the first skirmishes stemming from the Greek occupation of Smyrna. Other chapters refer to the development of the Long-Beranger Accord on oil and to British activities in Persia after the agreement of August, 1919, which assured Britain of absolute primacy in that country. It should be pointed out that the editors introduced each chapter with a number of documents serving to explain the antecedents of the questions covered. Thus in Volume IV appear documents relative to the Sykes-Picot Agreement of 1916 for the divison of the Middle East into Anglo-French spheres of interest, the Anglo-French-Russian accords for the partition of the Ottoman Empire, and the agreements of St. Jean-de-Maurienne concluded between Italy and France, and Italy and Britain.

The fifth volume at first glance appears to have a more organic character. It is divided into only two chapters: the first deals with Britain's policy for western Europe between June, 1919, and January, 1920, and the second considers relations with the United States for about the same period. However, the area covered by the first chapter is so large and complex that this arrangement does not meet the criteria of organization according to subject laid down by the editors. The principal subject here is the revision of the treaties of 1839 relative to Belgian neutrality, whose efficacy proved to be nonexistent in the light of the German invasion. These negotiations, handled primarily by a special commission (Committee of Fourteen) which was charged with preparing agreements to facilitate a joint defense of Belgium and Holland and a new collective treaty, were without positive results, and the question was referred to the League of Nations. The Belgian request for a provisional Franco-British guarantee failed in its purpose because the British government insisted upon Belgium's temporary retention of the international agreement established by the treaties of 1839.

The central theme of the second chapter is Lord Grey's journey to Washington with the aim of inducing President Wilson to reach a compromise with his political adversaries in order to guarantee American ratification of the peace treaty. Despite the esteem with which Lord Grey was regarded in American political circles, his mission proved to be a failure. Furthermore, because of Wilson's serious infirmity, Lord Grey was unable to confer with him personally. On the other hand, the American President, isolated from the mainstream of American politics by illness and in no position to evaluate correctly the political situation in his country, refused to accept the modifications to the treaty requested by the Republicans, changes which the French and the British were willing to concede. He directed the Democratic senators to vote against the amended text of the treaty in the November 19, 1919, session of Congress. Wilson was confident he could win approval for the original text at a later date, but he was mistaken. In March, 1920, the Senate refused to ratify the treaty, the vote being seven short of the two-thirds majority required to win approval, and in the subsequent November elections the Democratic candidate for President was defeated by the Republican, Warren G.

Harding. And so the United States returned to its isolationist position (in August, 1921, the United States signed separate treaties of peace with Germany, Austria, and Hungary), abandoning the European scene and turning its attention to the Pacific basin.

The sixth volume of the first series also concerns the period between the signing of the Treaty of Versailles and January 10, 1920, the date it became effective, and completes the panorama of British policy in two specific areas, central Europe and the Far East. The documents in the first chapter should be consulted in relation to the work of the Council of the Heads of Mission charged with the task of arranging peace treaties with Austria, Hungary, and Bulgaria. These permit a wider perspective and clarify, on the basis of a detailed documentation, the origins of the position assumed within the Council by the British representatives, but the importance of the documents often transcends the problems under consideration, and they are indispensable for the comprehension of the position later taken by London on many problems such as those of the German minority in Czechoslovakia and the Austro-German *Anschluss*. If, on the one hand, one is struck by the remarkable brilliance of many of the evaluations made by British diplomats, one has the impression, on the other, that the policies of the Foreign Office were somewhat fragmentary in character, almost as if London often lost the thread that linked the various problems. It should be emphasized that this material is also basic to an understanding of events in central eastern Europe at the end of the war, especially in the Balkans. Several references are made to Italy's support of the Bela Kun regime in Hungary and to the attempts made by the Italian government to arrange a Bulgarian-Rumanian *rapprochement* in order to build an anti-Yugoslav bloc.

Chapter II concerns British relations with China and Japan, based on two principal themes: British policy confronted by evidence of Japanese expansion in China and in southeast Asia, and negotiations for renewal of the Anglo-Japanese Alliance. Obviously, these documents deal with problems that are closely interlocked, and, consequently, they are of a uniform character. This material is of fundamental importance, not only for a study of the specific questions to which it refers, but also for a clearer comprehension of Anglo-American relations and for the background of the Washington Naval Conference.

The two successive volumes (VII and VIII of the series) concern documentary materials relevant to 1920. They are devoted solely to the minutes of the inter-Allied conferences which, following World War I, constituted the normal means of diplomatic action between the victorious powers. In many countries the exigencies of war had led to the establishment of special organs (for example, the British War Cabinet) which handled the most important decisions—special bodies born of the necessity to make quick decisions, to maintain the highest secrecy, and to better co-ordinate, through frequent contact, the actions of those charged with the highest responsibilities.

Their existence was not inconsequential even in the normal course of international relations. Diplomats, particularly those of the Anglo-Saxon countries, had become suspect in the eyes of a large segment of public opinion, which accused them of being among those responsible for the conflict. Diplomats saw their influence diminish, and the Ministry of Foreign Affairs to some degree lost control of the policies of its government. During the war, and later, during the course of the peace negotiations, contacts between the most important exponents of Allied policies became increasingly frequent: personal emissaries were often used as substitutes for normal diplomatic channels. This explains why, in the immediate postwar period, the victorious governments preferred to operate by the technique of the conference, attended by Prime Ministers or Ministers of Foreign Affairs of the various countries. This system, it was believed, would permit a more rapid solution of the multitude of problems that faced the victors, and would also facilitate a reciprocal understanding of diverse points of view.

As a matter of fact, these optimistic expectations were not realized in practice, an observation confirmed by the minutes of the conferences published in the seventh and eighth volumes of the British collection. The progress of the conversations was often made more difficult by the lack of knowledge of international problems of the majority of the politicians, by disorder in the discussions, which were not infrequently conducted without any form of prearranged agenda, and, above all, by the absence of preliminary meetings in which it might have been possible to arrive at a compromise among the various positions. The negotiations for the treaty of peace with Turkey, the principal topic of the first conference of London, were brought to a close only with difficulty. In the discussions about the position to be taken with regard to Kemal Atatürk's national movement (whose strength Lloyd George appeared to underestimate), the British representatives assumed positions that were much more intransigent than those of either the French or the Italians, and a similar situation developed on the question of whether or not to recognize the Soviet government. Nitti was favorable, but Berthelot was opposed, convinced as he was that the Soviet regime would collapse within a short time. As to the Polish question, France and Great Britain held distinct and divergent views: Lloyd George wanted to advise the Poles to reach a compromise with the Soviets, while Millerand favored supporting Polish resistance by every available means. A similar situation developed with regard to Germany. French intransigence was highlighted by the more moderate approaches of Great Britain and Italy.

In any event, the minutes of these conferences are essential to an understanding of the relations between the Allies during this period and a comprehension of how certain decisions, which would be of fundamental importance to subsequent developments in European politics, were reached. Of course, these minutes do not explain the origins of the positions taken by the individual countries on the various issues. Insofar as Great Britain is concerned, such documents are to be found in the later volumes of the first series.

Of these, the ninth and the tenth deal with relations with Germany from the Treaty of Versailles to the end of 1920, a most difficult period in postwar German history and one which emphasized again the profound differences between the Allies. While London was seeking to avoid complete collapse of the German state, whether for economic reasons (the impossibility of obtaining total reparations) or for political considerations (the fundamental change that had taken place in the Continental balance of power), France, supported by Belgium, insisted on the rigid application of the Versailles clauses: the Paris government held that if Germany were allowed to re-establish itself on a sound basis and to reorganize its industries efficiently it would then embark on a policy of revenge, with France as primary target.

These fundamental differences were clearly exposed in the spring of 1920, when the German government was obliged to send military forces into the Ruhr to quash a movement by the extreme left which had developed as a reaction to the abortive Kapp *Putsch* in Berlin. Following the entrance of German troops into the demilitarized zones of the Rhineland, the French and the Belgians decided, in spite of British opposition, to extend Allied occupation to several Rhineland cities, among them Frankfurt and Darmstadt. The incident was not without consequences. For example, the government of Brussels was told, when it proposed to the British that the latter initiate negotiations for a three-power pact with France designed to guarantee the neutrality of Belgium, that after what had happened, Great Britain did not believe it was propitious to assume serious military obligations toward a country that had ignored British interests in a question of such magnitude.

The documents taken from the archives of the Foreign Office permit a precise reconstruction of these events. This volume not only contains material relative to the Franco-Belgian action in the Rhineland, but also a number of documents on the German internal situation and particularly on the Kapp *Putsch*, on the fruitless negotiations with the Dutch government to obtain extradition of the ex-Emperor of Germany, and on the preparations of the trials against the German war criminals before the Supreme Court of Leipzig, a precedent that had to be given most serious consideration at the close of World War II, when it was decided to try the Nazi leaders.

Numerous documents, the majority assembled in Volume IX, refer to the twin problems of reparations and German disarmament, two questions that led to the closing of the ranks among the victorious powers, brought about by the resistance of the Berlin government to fulfilling the obligations it assumed in the Treaty of Versailles. As noted, even in this case the alignment between London and Paris was far from perfect, and the British documents are of great value in determining the points of agreement and disagreement between the two governments and the reactions of the London government to certain independent initiatives taken by France.

The eleventh volume of the first series is also divided into two parts. The first concerns the plebiscite in Upper Silesia which, on March 20, 1921, affirmed the victory of pro-German elements over the Poles. The documentation ends with the plebiscite, and no reference is made to subsequent developments: the insurrection of the Polish minority, the Allied intervention, and the extremely questionable decision to divide Upper Silesia between Germany and Poland, problems which will most certainly be included in other volumes of this series.

The much more detailed second section refers to British policy in the Baltic area and Poland from the beginning of 1920 to the Peace of Riga, which brought the Russo-Polish conflict to a close on March 18, 1921. While the British attitude regarding the Baltic states was one of steady support (see also the documentation contained in the third volume of this series), the government and public opinion were certainly much less sympathetic toward the Poles, who were accused, not without reason, of being in the throes of an extreme nationalism which had brought them into conflict with the Germans of the western lands, with Czechoslovakia for Teschen, with the Ruthenians for eastern Galicia, and with the Lithuanians for Vilna. In practice, with all of their neighbors the Poles followed a policy of *fait accompli,* proceeding to occupy contested zones without paying too much attention to the warnings or to the decisions of the Great Powers. A similar policy was the basis of the conflict with the Soviets. In December, 1919, the Allied powers had drawn the eastern frontier of Poland along ethnic lines (the Curzon Line, as it was subsequently called), but the Poles refused to accept the new boundary, and after having rejected the Soviet peace offer, returned to the attack in the east.

The most interesting part of the British material concerns the last phase of this conflict, when the Poles, after several initial successes, found themselves unable to resist Soviet pressure, which had brought Red Army forces to the gates of Warsaw during the summer of 1920. At this point, it is apparent that Soviet objectives had changed. Contrary to their previous policy, they now pursued expansionist aims with the intention of creating in Poland a satellite state, a base of operations for the extension of communism into nearby countries, particularly into Germany. Notwithstanding the apparent danger and the opposition of the French government, which favored providing maximum support to the Poles, the Foreign Office documents reveal that the British Cabinet continued to insist that the Poles accept the terms of peace proposed by the Soviets until the latter's defeat in the battle of Warsaw (August, 1920), which paved the way for peace negotiations on a new basis and culminated in the Treaty of Riga in March, 1921.

This documentation is striking for two basic reasons. In the first place, the Polish policy of aggression toward neighboring states and the direction taken by Poland in the face of repeated warnings by the major powers was indicative of the attitude of Polish leaders in Warsaw toward a solution of the problems facing their country. In practice, they laid the groundwork for their isolation and alienated those who might have been allies and whose assistance they would need in order to face the dangers represented by Germany and by Russia.

In the second place, one has the impression that during the summer of 1920 the British government had lost control of the course of events in eastern Europe. The British refusal to provide maximum assistance to the Poles stemmed not only from fear of strengthening French hegemony on the Continent, but also from the increasing opposition of the British public. In August, this opposition had been increased to the point where a general strike was threatened in the event that the government decided to send Poland aid on a large scale. On the other hand, on August 4 Lloyd George had to inform the Soviet representatives that if the Red Army continued its advance into Poland a break between the Soviets and the Allies would become inevitable. The unexpected Polish victory on August 16, therefore, resolved a situation which, so far as the British government was concerned, appeared to be without solution.

The twelfth volume of this first series is presented in the form of a miscellanea for the purpose of rounding out events in Europe for the year 1920, despite the fact that the final chapter, concerning relations with the Soviets, extends the closing date of the volume to March, 1921, in order to include material on the negotiations for a commercial accord signed March 16, 1921.

The disadvantages of the system of organizing documentary material according to subject matter have been emphasized repeatedly, but they are nowhere more evident than in this volume. The documentary material is—as always throughout this collection—particularly rich and, for many subjects, exhaustive as well. Nevertheless, it is regrettable that an all-inclusive picture of British diplomatic action, perhaps because of the method of presentation, gives an extremely fragmentary impression. In fact, an examination of this volume leads to the conclusion that during 1920 British policy weakened somewhat everywhere, in a sense reflecting the weariness of the country after wartime sacrifices and the emotional support of the peace conference. British policy is characterized by disengagement wherever vital British interests are not directly involved. This evaluation is confirmed here, whether in the British refusal to assume new obligations toward Belgium to replace those in the treaties of 1839, in a policy of abstention in the Adriatic question, or in the token support given to Venizelos in his struggle with King Constantine.

Even the British attitude toward the Soviet government appears to be anything but straightforward, not to say openly contradictory. On the one hand, London sought a *rapprochement* through a commercial accord; on the other, Britain maintained troops in Batum, sent arms to General Denikin, and recognized counterrevolutionary governments in Georgia, Azerbaijan, and Armenia. It should be pointed out that this dual policy did not have a strategic intent; that is, it did not seek to exert pressure on the Soviet government by the threat of counterrevolution, but it was rather an expression of two contradictory policies, one of which was doomed to failure at its inception because of the inadequacy of the economic and military means employed. It was inevitable that such a procedure would lead to the result which actually took place: on the one hand, it produced a defeat that the Bolsheviks were able to exploit internally as well as externally as a basis for their ideological propaganda against the capitalistic world; on the other—and this was certainly more serious—it left a wake of suspicion and distrust that was to dominate relations between the U.S.S.R. and the western world for a long time.

Despite the fact that these documents do not reveal anything startlingly new, this phase of Anglo-Soviet relations is, in the main, the most interesting chapter of this volume. Consequently, it is a bit surprising to note that the compilers list twenty-seven documents whose texts are not included because they had already been made public in the press of the period. To be sure, it is true that the primary purpose of a collection is to issue unpublished materials, but such a procedure—even if partially justified by the tremendous scope of the British collection—presents certain practical inconveniences which are readily discernible.

Volume XIII contains materials on the problems of the Near and Middle East from the beginning of 1920 to March, 1921, documents relating to the problems posed in Volume IV.

The first of the three chapters of the volume concerns Turkey. The most important aspect of this material is that it confirms the grave doubts, already weighing heavily on the negotiators during the course of the talks, regarding the possibility of implementing the Peace of Sèvres—doubts aroused by the growing nationalist movement whose strength was beginning to be felt and by the extremely passive attitude assumed by the authorities at Constantinople regarding every problem and position they were to take with reference to the ratification of the treaty. The fall of Greek Prime Minister Venizelos in November, 1920, eliminated the last strong force capable of convincing the Great Powers to ignore the new situation unfolding in Turkey.

The documents contained in the second chapter provide a detailed exposition of British policy regarding the Arab territories wrested from the Ottoman Empire, particularly concerning Syria in relation to the definitive French takeover in Damascus and the successful British attempt to establish a solid position in the remaining Arab lands so as to guarantee imperial and oil interests. The same degree of success was not attained by British diplomacy in Persia. The documents included in Chapter 3 make it possible to trace developments from the failure to apply the Anglo-Iranian accord of August 9, 1919, to the agreement reached by the Persian government with the Soviets in March, 1921. The latter re-established in Persia that condominium of political influence which had been abrogated, to Great Britain's advantage, with the collapse of the Czarist regime. At the close of 1920 the substantially unfavorable balance sheet of British policy included even the Near and Middle East, the sole exception being oil interests, due in great part to the location of these fields in an area where British presence posed little, if any, threat.

To date, eight volumes of the second series have been published. The first four volumes deal primarily with two issues, disarmament and reparations. Concerning the former, we find here ample material that can even today be the subject of serious study because it demonstrates how disarmament—in the area of conventional weapons—is possible only in special and particular circumstances and is limited to certain areas.

The events of the years between the two world wars have underlined, first, that there will be enormous difficulties encountered by the victors in controlling the arms programs of ex-enemies even when large areas of ex-enemy territory are occupied; and second, that it is hopeless to think in terms of general disarmament when there is no practical possibility of control. To date, such control has been possible only in the area of naval construction, and it is in this field only that concrete results have been obtained. Furthermore, it should not be forgotten that the success of the Washington Conference of 1921–22 was primarily due to the weakness of the Japanese: Tokyo acquiesced to American demands in order to gain time to consolidate its position.

But if the experiences of those years have demonstrated the practical difficulties of achieving true disarmament in the area of conventional arms, the attempts made today to execute an agreement on atomic disarmament, which requires minute control over the entire territory of a country, appear even more arduous.

While the chapters concerning the Anglo-American and the Anglo-French negotiations, in addition to those concerning the Geneva disarmament conference, are extremely important for an exact understanding of certain aspects of a psychological situation that decisively influenced all of diplomatic history between the two world wars, it is particularly interesting for us to note the position of the Foreign Office on the Italo-French debates on naval parity and on Mussolini's proposal for a four-power pact. In effect, the British Cabinet of that day demonstrated a singular comprehension of the needs of the Italian government, and several comments inserted in notes by Craigie further reveal the importance attributed by British diplomats of that day to collaboration with Italy. This attitude is even more noteworthy in that it was the last manifestation of a concrete policy that, after the Ethiopian crisis, was no longer possible.

Evidently, every power concerned with the thorny reparations problems in the period between the two world wars profited from past experience, for at the end of World War II those errors were not repeated. The victors simply took what could be taken from the vanquished, and reparations provisions were realistic.

Of the documents worthy of special note in the second volume, the most important are those on the projected Austro-German Customs Union of 1931, in which the British position is revealed to have been much less rigid than that of either France or Italy. Equally significant is the documentation concerning the crisis period leading to Hitler's rise to power; through the dispatches of the British Embassy in Berlin, the crisis may be followed as it unfolded day by day.

The fifth volume emerges as a primary source for the reconstruction of the negotiations that preceded the signing of the Four-Power Pact and, in addition, includes a wealth of material on the British attitude in the matter of the *Anschluss*. It becomes apparent that, on the whole, the MacDonald government did not properly evaluate the threat posed by Nazi Germany and continued to press for a general arms limitation agreement and partial German rearmament despite the warnings of the British representatives in Berlin (Sir Horace Rumbold and his successor, Sir Eric Phipps) and various Foreign Office officials (see, for example, Vansittart's Memorial of August 28, 1933), who immediately recognized the peril and considered Nazi pressure on Austria simply the first phase of a new German expansionist policy.

In the sixth volume, covering the period November, 1933–February, 1934, the British collection returns to a consideration of the disarmament question in its final phase, that is, after Germany's withdrawal from the Geneva Conference and from the League of Nations in October, 1933. There were no noticeable changes in the attitude of the Great Powers during these negotiations. German rearmament was a reality, confirmed by the appearance of a German military air force, and the British government was inclined to try to reach a compromise with the Germans which, in legalizing the new state of affairs, would permit the establishment of a system of control, thus avoiding a total failure of the negotiations. The French position on these points was one of absolute intransigence: Paris would not entertain the thought of concessions to Germany and gave notice that France would not reduce her armaments until Britain would assume such obligations as would guarantee French security. The gulf existing between the British and French points of view could not be bridged during the long and involved negotiations between the two powers during the winter of 1933–34, and their failure was inevitable. However, it should be noted that, while the British government was opposed to assuming any new obligations on the Continent, the Foreign Office was much more receptive to the French requests; so much so that a memorandum of March 21, 1934, concludes that French security must be considered a part of the security of Britain.

The origins of the proposal for an eastern Locarno, advanced by Louis Barthou in the spring of 1934 (this fact is confirmed by the British documents), are to be found in the failure of these negotiations and in the increased tempo of German rearmament. London offered only qualified support to Barthou's proposal, fearing that, in the event that Barthou's project fell short of success, France would seek an alliance with the Soviet Union and thus return to a policy of power blocs which had been held to be one of the causes for World War I. At the same time, Britain urged that the French proposal be made fully reciprocal so as to be acceptable to the Germans. The results of this policy were not very encouraging. It aroused the suspicion of every power concerned and led the French to accuse the British of torpedoing any effective defense against German rearmament and the Germans to conclude that the British were embarking on a new policy detrimental to Germany.

The same volume contains the documentation relative to the Austrian crisis of 1934. This evidence confirms that the dispatch of Italian troops to the Brenner Pass, ordered by Mussolini at the time of Dollfuss' assassination, was received with some relief, although it aroused grave concern in Czechoslovakia and in Yugoslavia. In order to avoid any further unilateral actions, the French government, probably at the insistence of Prague and Belgrade, proposed early in August, 1934, the creation of an Italo-French-British committee through which the three powers could remain in constant consultation on the Austrian question.

The seventh volume contains materials relevant to Anglo-Soviet relations between 1929 (the date of the reopening of regular diplomatic relations between the two powers) and 1934 (the date of the entrance of the U.S.S.R. into the League of Nations). The data contained herein are of relatively minor importance because they deal largely with economic problems or with issues that concerned directly only the two countries and are of no particular importance to the general course of diplomacy.

The last volume of the series published to date concerns British policy in the Far East for the period 1929–31. Part I, dealing with the negotiations for the abolition of extraterritorial rights in China and in the leased concession of Wei-Hai-Wei, is primarily of technical interest as an example of the negotiating process with an Asiatic power. The documentation on the first phase of the Manchurian crisis is much more important. However, the details of the evolution of this crisis are sufficiently familiar as a result of the investigation conducted by the League of Nations' Lytton Committee, the documents published by the State Department, and the revelations emerging from the postwar Tokyo trials.

The third series is the only one presently completed. Its nine volumes were completed in six years, from 1949 to 1955, and in 1961 a tenth volume was added, consisting of a general index.

The first two volumes are limited almost exclusively to the Czech crisis of 1938—with the exception of the initial portion of the first volume, dedicated to the *Anschluss*—and remain an essential source, together with the corresponding volume in the German collection, for the study of the subject. As a result, too, of the debates in progress on the Munich Agreements, the commission included an extremely wide and detailed collection of pertinent materials, which suggests that all of the truly important materials on the subject contained in the Foreign Office archives have been published.

Regarding the questions that historians have posed in reference to the Czech crisis and to the actions of the Great Powers in that situation, it must be pointed out that, from the documents published thus far, not one single fact has emerged to give serious support to the hypothesis that Chamberlain was seeking an agreement with Germany in order to channel German dynamism towards the east. In all likelihood, the exclusion of the U.S.S.R. from the Munich conversations was not due to any preconceived plan, but simply to the need to move with great haste and to the desire to avoid raising issues which might have made the conclusion of an agreement more difficult, if not impossible. In substance, it can be concluded that Chamberlain and his collaborators conducted the negotiations in absolute good faith, as well as with a generous dose of naïveté, deluding themselves into thinking that an equitable compromise was possible without clearly understanding that the objectives of Hitler's foreign policy went much beyond a simple revision of the frontiers established by the Treaty of Versailles. Therefore, there is little evidence to support the idea—rather widely held among British conservatives—that the basis for Chamberlain's actions during the Czech crisis was to point German expansionist tendencies eastward. Instead, several instances of British foreign policy activity in the period immediately following the conclusion of the Munich Pact demonstrate the illusion, which had become more widespread, that peaceful coexistence with Nazi Germany was possible.

No less interesting is the third volume, which concerns the period from the Munich Conference to the first half of January, 1939. It contains detailed documentation on the Polish and Hungarian demands for Czechoslovak territory, as well as pertinent data on the implementation of the Munich Agreement. Of much greater importance is the material concerning the relations between the Axis powers on the *vexata quaestio* of a "free hand in the east." The material directly concerning Italo-British relations is of major importance: it includes the negotiations for implementing the Easter Pacts and the Chamberlain-Lord Halifax journey to Rome.

German violation of the Munich Pact and the end of Czechoslovak independence form the central theme of the fourth volume, which closes with the announcement of the British guarantees to Poland. This volume is of fundamental interest because of the importance of the events to which it refers, since the German occupation of Czechoslovakia, in effect, precipitated the crisis that led to World War II.

Up to that moment, Hitler's violation of the terms of the Treaty of Versailles (German rearmament, remilitarization of the Rhineland, the annexation of Austria and the Sudetenland) aroused anti-German feeling in the western world principally because the Nazis had taken unilateral action based on the use of military force, instead of seeking the same ends through revision of the Treaty of Versailles, in accord with the other Great Powers. In substance, however, it was recognized that the aims pursued by the German Chancellor were legitimate enough: it could hardly be expected that Germany would remain eternally disarmed or that her sovereignty could be forever limited by prohibiting German fortification of the Rhineland, while, in general, the incorporation of Austria and the Sudetes into the Third Reich appeared to be justified in that these actions concerned German peoples who had manifested in various ways their desire to be brought into the fatherland.

The dismemberment of Czechoslovakia, on the other hand, was considered an entirely new development of the gravest concern. Above all, it was the first time that Hitler had used military force to occupy a territory inhabited by non-Germans. It was also a blatant violation of the very agreements he had sworn to keep at Munich; that is, not to annex territory populated by Czechs. All of this led to a twofold conclusion: that the Nazi government was pursuing expansionist ends that went far beyond the declared intention of uniting all Germans to one fatherland and—much more alarming in the eyes of the British government and public—that there was not the remotest possibility of arriving at a *modus vivendi* with the Germans because Hitler did not keep his word. Thus Britain's decision to meet any further German violation of existing treaties with force definitely crystallized with the German occupation of Prague. Furthermore, British lack of faith in a Hitlerian promise would pave the way for the British government's refusal, once war broke out, to consider any Hitlerian overture for a compromise peace, even when, after the fall of France, Great Britain was alone in the struggle against him.

In the fifth, sixth, and seventh volumes the items of major interest are the Anglo-French-Soviet negotiations that were the last attempts to build a united anti-German front and whose failure opened the way to war. The material published in the British collection is extremely rich (the documents relating to the military mission to Moscow are published in the seventh volume), and its importance is even more critical in that it appears destined to remain the principal source for the study of those events; most of the archives of the Quai d'Orsay were destroyed in 1940, and it is not known whether the Soviets intend to publish a collection of documents of equal magnitude on the same subject.

During the postwar period a great debate arose on the causes for the failure of these negotiations, and it is still impossible to render a definitive judgment on the matter. However, it should be recalled that after the British guarantees to Poland the Soviet government had no further interest in assuming obligations to the western powers of a political and military nature. Polish-German collaboration had become highly improbable, and, furthermore, if Germany sought to force a passage through Poland to reach the Ukraine, British and French intervention would have occurred automatically. Given this situation, the U.S.S.R. had no motivation for surrendering its freedom of action and risking involvement in a conflict precipitated by a German attack in the west.

In the same volumes, the material relative to the Danzig crisis, negotiations with Berlin, relations with Warsaw, the information garnered in Rome, and the difficulties encountered in creating an identity of interests beween Paris and London is all of interest. The reports from the British Ambassador in Rome, Sir Percy Loraine, are singularly knowledgeable, and with these at hand the Foreign Office knew every detail of Mussolini's policies. This circumstance raises still another question—which leaves one greatly perplexed—as to what were the origins and the nature of the information so assembled. Were the data based on information authorized by Ciano, or were they gathered from conversations that took place without his knowledge? If the latter hypothesis is correct, are we faced with evidence of disapproval of Fascist policies on the part of high officials in the Palazzo Chigi, or with something much less commendable? The last weeks of peace in Europe, as they emerge from this material, produce the sensation that effective control of the situation had now been wrested from the hands of men of reason and good will.

The eighth and ninth volumes complete the series. These are entirely devoted to the activities of the British government in the Far East in the period from August, 1938, to the outbreak of the war with Germany. The documentation included herein is important not only for this part of the world but also for a reconstruction of British policy on the Continent of Europe. For example, the role played in the Anglo-French-Soviet negotiations by fear of the Japanese reaction to evidence of an Anglo-Soviet *rapprochement,* which might lead the Kremlin to embark on a much more active policy in China, cannot be ignored. Equally noteworthy are the documents which illustrate the activities of the British Ambassador to Tokyo, Craigie, in seeking to prevent the Anti-Comintern Pact from being converted into a Triple Alliance. Moreover, these documents provide vivid testimony of the startling accuracy of the information available to the Foreign Office on the Italo-Japanese-German negotiations. Insofar as this information is concerned, one can exclude the possibility that it reached the British with Ciano's approval.

In 1961 a tenth volume was added, containing a general index to the third series. In addition to the summary Tables of Contents of each volume, Volume X provides lists of the members of governments and of the diplomatic representatives of the various countries, a subject matter index, and an index of persons.

Without doubt, this collection is one of the most reliable instruments available for the study of diplomatic events in the period between the two world wars. Despite the fact that publication plans for the first two series are not known in full, the character of the volumes that have appeared to date indicates that they will be unusual in scope and detail. In this context it should be noted that, contrary to what normally occurs in other collections, the British editors appear to have been much more selective in the preparation of the last volumes, a decision that may have been caused by their desire to publish as soon as possible material of the greatest political interest and which, above all, was of major interest to historians. The importance of the British collection is emphasized and increased by the absence of an analogous French publication. Therefore, frequently it is only through the documents of the Foreign Office that it is possible to reconstruct the activities of the Paris government.

Given the very generous limits normally observed by compilers in choosing materials for a collection, the British editors received some criticism for not including notes and memoranda from within the Foreign Office, through which it would have been possible to reconstruct the evolution of British policy—not only from within the Foreign Office but also, albeit partially, from outside of it because the various offices often reflect the position of other organs of government (Admiralty, Economic Ministries, etc.) with whom they are in contact. To a certain degree this lacuna is filled by the inclusion of some personal letters, but the existing gap does not seem to be justified, particularly since the preceding British collection on the origins of World War I included a number of notes from within the Ministry, which proved to be of great value.

From the technical point of view, while the richness of the collection, along with the exactness of the notes, must be emphasized, it must be repeated that inconveniences do exist in consulting materials organized according to subject, although a chronological organization admittedly would have been very difficult in some cases. The indexes incorporated at the beginning of each volume are insufficient, but it can be assumed that the commission intends to publish a general index for each of the series, as it has for the third one.

It must also be emphasized that during the period covered by the collection the Foreign Office lost its exclusive control of British foreign policy,[43] so that, while the publication of the diplomatic documents at the close of World War I was exhaustive in nature, the same cannot be said for the collection published after World War II. However, this is a phenomenon common to all countries, certainly to Nazi Germany and Fascist Italy. It creates new problems for scholars and complicates every research project that seeks to be as complete as possible.

3. THE STATE DEPARTMENT COLLECTION AND OTHER AMERICAN DOCUMENTARY COLLECTIONS.

The American diplomatic document collection[44] has some unique characteristics. It is the oldest of its kind: it first appeared in 1861, as a documentary on the nation's foreign affairs accompanying the first annual message to Congress by President Lincoln. The fundamental purpose of the publication was to provide a working tool for the administration, for it assembled in book form the more important papers concerning foreign relations, especially those pertinent to the evolution of international law. For this reason, the collection has been of limited interest to the historian.

A legal tone continued to characterize the successive American publications until the appearance of the volume for 1917. Prior to the turn of the century, there was an average time lapse of one year in the publication of the documents for any given year. After the turn of the century, for a number of reasons it was no longer feasible to continue this rhythm of uninterrupted publication. The United States was now playing a much larger role in world affairs, which made it much more difficult to divulge immediately even a part of the diplomatic correspondence exchanged with other countries. Accordingly, in the Preface of the volume on 1914, it was explicitly announced that the material dealing with wartime diplomacy would be published later, in separate volumes.

[43] See also Craig, "The British Foreign Office from Grey to Austen Chamberlain," *The Diplomats*; John Connell, *The Office. A Study of British Foreign Policy and Its Makers 1919–1951* (London: Wingate, 1958).

[44] The original title of the collection was *Papers relating to Foreign Affairs accompanying the Annual Message of the President*. Beginning in 1870 the title was changed to *Papers relating to the Foreign Relations of the United States, Diplomatic Papers*. Beginning with the volumes published in 1948, the title was again changed to *Foreign Relations of the United States, Diplomatic Papers*. The first volume bearing this title refers to 1932. The volumes for 1942 have recently appeared.

This announcement made it perfectly clear that the State Department was committed to a policy of making its archives public in an even more concrete and substantial way than heretofore. The movement to make public the nation's diplomatic documents reached its apex in the immediate postwar period, when the United States took the lead in the drive against "secret diplomacy," diplomacy conducted behind the closed doors of the various chancelleries and beyond the direct control of either a parliament or public opinion and considered by that opinion to have been one of the primary causes for World War I. Against the concept of secrecy in diplomacy, Wilson launched the first of his Fourteen Points, "open covenants openly arrived at," which was the essence of "open diplomacy." Wilson envisioned public treaties concluded publicly as the process whereby all private and secret agreements between states would be eliminated and would be replaced by frank and open diplomacy conducted with the widest publicity.

In carrying out the Wilsonian mandate, Secretary of State Kellogg in 1925 established a new set of criteria that was to guide the editors in assembling the collection. Kellogg's goals for the collection were realized in the publication of nearly all of the State Department's diplomatic correspondence immediately after the negotiations on any given subject were brought to a conclusion, thereby presenting the documents for the history of American foreign policy in an easily accessible form. Thus much more material concerning American relations with other countries found its way into the collection, at the same time that special attention continued to be devoted to State Department decisions affecting the development of international law.

Under this new general line, the American collection assumed the nature of a true historical source, even though traces of its earlier legal character remained. For example, the volume concerning the year 1923 devotes almost thirty pages to the Tangier and Morocco question, essentially a legal one, while compressing the entire reparations problem into sixty pages, thus demonstrating an obvious imbalance from the historical point of view, even when allowance is made for the particular perspective from which Washington viewed certain questions.

It should also be noted that in this second phase, which, in effect, includes the period 1918–31, the documentation deals almost exclusively with the issues that had been the subject of negotiations between the government of the United States and foreign governments, while it does not include a single report from a head of mission on the internal affairs of the specific country to which he was accredited. In the volumes for the year 1922, the advent of Fascism to power is completely ignored, and Mussolini's name appears only in reference to his request for an increase in the Italian immigration quota of the United States.

The American collection assumed its present format after World War II on the basis of the regulation of October, 1947, defining its objectives as follows: "The publication, *Foreign Relations of the United States,* constitutes the official public record of United States foreign policy. These volumes include all papers relating to major policies and decisions of the Department in the matter of foreign relations, together with appropriate materials concerning the events and facts which contributed to the formulation of such decisions and policies."

In effect, this regulation introduced two principal innovations in the criteria governing the publication of American diplomatic documents. First, the collection had officially abandoned one of its two original objectives, that of serving as a collection of precedents and as a manual to be consulted on the legal aspects of international relations (although some trace of this still remains); second, it had adopted the criteria of almost all other official collections, that of publishing the material that may be pertinent to the study of international relations.

The new character of the collection is immediately revealed in the volumes beginning with 1932, in content and particularly in the scope and detail of the dispatches that refer to the internal situation of other states, such as those reporting the advent of National Socialism in Germany, which is abundantly documented in Volume II for 1933.

Despite the fact that this second change in the character of the American collection may have been brought about by a need to have the collection conform to those of other countries, the primary cause for the change appears to have been the fact that after the victorious conclusion of the war in 1945 the debate on the foreign policy of the Roosevelt administration reached such serious proportions as to make it advisable to publish as much of the material in the State Department archives as possible.

From an over-all point of view, the State Department collection has always differed (and continues to do so) from all other collections in that its publication was never interrupted by an international crisis or by America's involvement in a war.[45] Thus, for World War I, the American collection remains the only documentary source embracing the entire war period (the documents published by the Soviets terminate with March, 1916). And even for World War II the American collection continues to be the only one that is systematically publishing all of the wartime material. It will remain unique until such time as the Bonn government decides to

---

[45] However, the volume for 1869 was not published.

publish the German documents beyond the terminal date, December 7, 1941, set by the Anglo-French-American commission. The Italian collection will terminate with the proclamation of the Armistice of Cassibile, September 8, 1943.

This publishing practice has also given the collection another unique characteristic. The systematic and continuous publication of the documents means that scholars do not have to rely on a major international crisis to prompt the publication of documentary collections, as has been the case in other countries.

On the other hand, this practice creates its own serious inconveniences, which often make one lament the fact that the United States has not adopted the practice prevalent in other countries. For the very reason that no major crisis has destroyed the political value of the documents in the American collection, only those documents which could be published under these conditions are included in the collection. Consequently, one frequently discovers that there are many gaps in the material published and that what appears is far from exhaustive.

As to the technical aspects of the collection, it is organized by years, and the number of volumes for each year have gradually increased as a result of that general phenomenon in which the number of documents that find their way into the archives grows in every country in the world by leaps and bounds, and also because of the spread of American interests abroad. As a result of the change in the character of the collection decreed by the new regulation, beginning with 1932 the State Department has normally issued five volumes for each year. The first is limited to multilateral relations, problems of a general nature (such as disarmament and international organizations), conferences, international legislation, and so on. The second concerns relations with Europe and the British Commonwealth; Volume III and IV, the Far East; and Volume V, Latin America. Within the five-volume structure frequent shifts are made, depending on the exigencies. For example, there may be two volumes concerning Latin America, while the Far Eastern material may be concentrated in one volume, or an entire volume may be devoted to Near Eastern affairs if the events in that area warrant the increase. Beginning with 1941, the number of annual volumes has increased; generally, an additional volume of documents has been published for each of two areas, Latin America and the Far East.

Within each volume the documents are arranged according to the countries concerned, and within each country the documents are arranged by subject matter. The organization of the materials in this systematic manner gives rise to the inconveniences already mentioned. To these must be added the fact that, beginning with the volumes for 1937, in order to speed up the publication process the Tables of Contents in each volume were eliminated—temporarily, it is hoped. Despite the fact that they were compiled in the same manner as the documents, they were of some value to the reader. Now the volumes contain only a brief subject matter index. From this point of view, the American collection is the most difficult to consult. The difficulty is further aggravated by the fact that not all the periodic general indexes are available. One is available for the years 1861–99[46] and a second for the period 1900–18; however, the supplemental volumes relative to World War I are excluded from the second index.[47]

Another peculiar characteristic of the American collection, and for many reasons one of positive rather than of negative value, is that a number of supplementary volumes containing materials which, for a variety of reasons, had been omitted from earlier volumes are published periodically. This practice has been followed from the inception of the collection. Occasionally, it was decided to publish a supplement immediately after the selection of the material for inclusion in the regular volumes had been made. In these cases the supplementary material was appended to the regular volume. However, when a considerable period of time had elapsed since the publication of the regular volume or when a conspicuous number of documents had been assembled, a separate supplemental volume was published.

Among the oldest supplements is the one concerning Lincoln's assassination, in which hundreds of messages of sympathy from all over the world are gathered.[48] The two supplemental volumes for 1894 have something more than episodic value. The first contains, among a number of other matters, the correspondence of 1893–94 relative to the origins and course of the Sino-Japanese War, while the second contains material pertinent to the situation in the Hawaiian Islands, beginning with January, 1893, and includes an introductory comment by the State Department giving the history of American interest in Hawaii dating from the appointment of the first American consular representative to the Islands in 1820.[49] Of greater

---

[46] General Index to the Published Volumes of the Diplomatic Correspondence and Foreign Relations of the United States, 1861–1899 (Washington: U.S. Government Printing Office, 1902).

[47] Papers relating to the Foreign Relations of the United States, General Index 1900–1918 (Washington: U.S. Government Printing Office, 1941).

[48] Papers relating to Foreign Affairs accompanying the Annual Message of the President, 1865, p. iv.: Appendix to Diplomatic Correspondence of 1865 (Washington: U.S. Government Printing Office, 1866).

[49] Papers relating to the Foreign Relations of the United States, 1894, Appendix I; 1894, Appendix II: Affairs in Hawaii (Washington: U.S. Government Printing Office, 1895).

direct interest to European diplomacy and events is the supplement to the volumes for 1901, which contains the American documentation on the Boxer Rebellion.[50]

While these supplements are of some interest, their importance from the historical point of view is much less than that of the supplements published after 1925 according to the criteria established for them by Secretary of State Kellogg.

The first to appear after the Kellogg reforms were the supplements concerning World War I.[51] The value of the material incorporated in these volumes varies greatly, as far as it concerns the study of the diplomatic aspects of the conflict, because of the prolonged period of American neutrality. Until the end of 1916 the majority of the documents are largely legal in character (dealing with relations between neutrals and belligerents, the protection of Americans and their property in Europe and in the Far East, neutral commerce, territorial limits, and so forth). Materials concerning America's political and diplomatic activity in a more precise sense are to be found in the supplement volumes for the last two years of the war.

In the supplementary volumes for 1917, for example, there are some interesting data on the separate peace proposals formulated by Austria-Hungary in February, 1917, and in Volume I of the 1918 supplement there are a number of documents concerning the negotiations for the proposed armistices and relations with the Czechoslovak and Yugoslav independence movements.

In any event, the most important volumes, from the point of view of the history of international relations, are those concerning Russia. Despite the fact that these do not offer any especially startling revelations, they are, nevertheless, important tools for such studies as that of the relations between the western powers and the revolutionary governments that assumed control in Russia in March, 1917, the Allied intervention in Siberia and Manchuria, and the steps leading to the recognition of the independence of Finland and the Baltic states.

Concerning the American attitude toward the Bolshevik Revolution, it is necessary to recall that President Wilson was opposed to any Allied

[50] *Papers relating to the Foreign Relations of the United States, 1901, Appendix, Affairs in China* (Washington: U.S. Government Printing Office).

[51] *Papers relating to the Foreign Relations of the United States, 1914, Supplement, The World War; 1915, Supplement, The World War; 1916, Supplement, The World War; 1917, Supplement I, The World War; 1917, Supplement II, The World War* (2 vols.); *1918, Supplement I, The World War* (2 vols.); *1918, Supplement II, The World War; 1918, Russia* (3 vols.); *1919, Russia* (1 vol.) (Washington: U.S. Government Printing Office, 1928–37).

intervention in Russia and that furthermore, in the sixth of his Fourteen Points he had emphasized the need to assure the Russian people of complete freedom in the choice of political organization, without foreign influence and pressure. According to Wilson, a policy of tolerance and understanding would permit immediate, effective co-operation between the West and the new Russian government, as well as the inclusion of Russia in the League of Nations. Consequently, the subsequent Siberian intervention was due largely to the joint pressure applied to Wilson by the governments of Tokyo, London, and Paris and to the need to offset Japanese penetration in an area where the Americans opposed any change in the existing balance.[52]

Important materials are to be found in the two supplemental volumes containing Secretary of State Robert Lansing's papers.[53] The documents included herein concern the years 1914–20 and are especially significant for the later period (Lansing became Secretary of State in June, 1915). They contribute much toward clarifying several aspects of American policy in the Far East and toward the Entente. Among the most important of these documents are the minutes of the Ishii-Wilson and Ishii-Lansing conversations leading to that exchange of notes on November 2, 1917, whereby the American government recognized the "special interests" of the Japanese in China on condition that in no case would these circumscribe China's sovereignty or lead to discrimination against the trade of other countries with China.[54] There are also some interesting data concerning Italy, and the documents make it clear that, after the proclamation of Wilson's Fourteen Points, Italy's Adriatic claims had not yet encountered Lansing's strong opposition; on January 25, 1918, Lansing addressed a long letter to the American President in which he maintained that, in certain cases such

[52] On the Allied intervention in Siberia, see particularly John Albert White, *The Siberian Intervention* (Princeton: Princeton University Press, 1950). On American policy, see William S. Graves, *America's Siberian Adventure, 1917–1920* (New York: Cape, 1931); Betty Miller Unterberger, *America's Siberian Expedition, 1918–1920* (Durham, N.C.: Duke University Press, 1956); George F. Kennan, *Soviet-American Relations 1917–1920*, Vol. II: *The Decision To Intervene* (Princeton: Princeton University Press, 1961). On Japanese policy, see James William Morley, *The Japanese Thrust in Siberia, 1918* (New York: Columbia University Press, 1957). For the British attitude, see Richard H. Ullmann, *Anglo-Soviet Relations, 1917–1921*, Vol. I: *Intervention and the War* (Princeton: Princeton University Press, 1961).

[53] *Papers relating to the Foreign Relations of the United States, the Lansing Papers, 1914–1920* (2 vols.; Washington: U.S. Government Printing Office, 1939–40).

[54] On the question, see Mario Toscano, *Guerra diplomatica in Estremo Oriente (1914–1931)* (Turin: Einaudi, 1950), II, 190–204.

as the Italian, "geographic and strategic frontiers were to be taken into consideration in modifying the frontiers drawn on the basis of nationality."[55]

The thirteen-volume supplement on the Peace of Paris, published between 1942 and 1947, is of even greater importance.[56] This publication was designed to furnish the future American delegation to the peace conference, scheduled to convene at the close of World War II, with detailed background material. These volumes contain the materials relative to the preparation of the peace conference, the minutes of the plenary sessions, the minutes of the meetings of the Supreme Council in its various forms (Council of Ten, Council of Four, Council of Foreign Ministers), minutes of the American delegation to the peace conference, and, finally, the material concerning the Treaty of Versailles.

The historical importance of this supplement is truly exceptional and worthy of long and detailed comment. In the interest of brevity, reference here is only made (because they concern Italy specifically) to the minutes of the meetings of the Big Four, at which Orlando was not present, minutes which, according to agreements reached between the other allies, were kept secret up to that moment. In these it is possible to see how Wilson, during a meeting of the Council of Four that had been secretly assembled during Orlando's absence (he had left Paris following Wilson's famous message to the Italian people) justified the cession of the Shantung peninsula to Japan on the basis of the need to respect treaty rights even if their content was obviously contrary to the spirit and the letter of the Fourteen Points and even if they were concluded without American participation. These statements were in direct conflict with the affirmations made by Wilson when, in Orlando's presence, the Adriatic clauses of the Treaty of London were discussed.

The publication of the minutes of the meetings of the Big Four (included in Volumes V and VI of this supplement) voided the obligation not to divulge the contents of the daily discussions that took place between Wilson, Lloyd George, Clemenceau, and Orlando, not only on the most controversial problems of peacemaking, but also on the existing political situation in the spring of 1919. This lifting of the veil of secrecy has permitted the official interpreter at those meetings, Paul Mantoux, to

[55] Mario Toscano, "Un documento di eccezionale valore. I diritti adriatici dell'Italia, ufficialmente riconosciuti dagli Stati Uniti," *Rassegna Italiana*, 1942, August–September fasc.

[56] *Papers relating to the Foreign Relations of the United States, Paris Peace Conference, 1919* (13 vols.; Washington: U.S. Government Printing Office, 1942–47).

publish the day-by-day notes made by him during the course of the Big Four conversations.[57] The importance of these notes is twofold. First, they fill a gap in the American publication created by the very nature of the Four-Power Council: specifically, it was not an official organ of the conference but emerged from a proposal advanced by Wilson to discuss informally with the heads of the British, French, and Italian delegations the most vexious problems (German reparations, French security, Italy's eastern frontier), whose solution was vital to the success of the conference. These restricted meetings began on March 25 and, because of their informal character, no provisions were made for keeping minutes or for the participation of others, with the exception of the interpreter, Mantoux. After several sessions it was realized that minutes would have to be kept in order to facilitate the work of the committee, charged with drawing up the text of the treaty, by recording the discussions and the decisions taken. Sir Maurice Hankey, Secretary-General of the British delegation, assumed the task of keeping the minutes of the meetings of the Big Four beginning on April 19. Thus, for the period March 25–April 18, Mantoux's notes are the only direct testimony of what occurred in the meetings of the Big Four.

The notes taken by Mantoux were written in a style designed to facilitate his work as interpreter. The language he employed is alive and faithfully reports the atmosphere in which the discussions took place. In contrast, the minutes prepared by Sir Maurice for the use of the Big Four took into account the minute detail, but recorded it in dull, correct, official language. Consequently, Mantoux's notes are an extremely useful addendum to the minutes kept by Sir Maurice, and these two records make it possible to comprehend more clearly the discussions of the Big Four.

The supplemental volumes for the period between the wars are less numerous because the regular volumes are much more complete. This change was made possible by modifications introduced by the 1947 regulations governing the publication of these volumes (applied to those beginning with 1932) and to the greater time lapse between the dates of the documents and their publication. If, in a certain sense, these changes have made the supplements somewhat superfluous as devices for integrating certain documents with those published in the regular volumes, the growing time lag between the dates of the documents and their publication has made it necessary to print in supplements, when their immediate publication serves a specific governmental purpose, some documents that

[57] Paul Mantoux, *Les délibérations du Conseil des Quarte (24 mars–28 juin 1919)* (2 vols.; Paris: Editions du Centre National de la Recherche Scientifique, 1955).

would normally be included in the regular volumes. In effect, for this period the supplements have lost their integrative nature and have assumed the function of anticipating a part of the material issued in the regular volumes.

The criticisms advanced against the American government's attitude throughout the course of negotiations with the Japanese during 1941, prominent during the actual negotiations, became decidedly more pronounced after the Japanese attack on Pearl Harbor brought the United States into the war. The isolationist elements in the country attacked the President for having conducted the negotiations with the Japanese in a manner that precluded any possibility of compromise, an attack that gave rise to the accusation that the President had deliberately planned to drag the United States into the war.

The need to counter this accusation prompted the State Department to proceed with the immediate publication of two volumes devoted to Japanese-American relations during the prewar decade,[58] designed to demonstrate that no compromise was possible in the face of Japanese rigidity. This thesis is partly sustained by the documentation appearing in the two volumes, but, though copious, it is far from complete. It is particularly sketchy for the last phase of the negotiations with the Japanese, as was demonstrated after the publication of the regular volumes for 1941.

If the new and abundant material on the Far East appearing recently has not appreciably modified the impressions created by the documents published in the supplements, at least the documentation relative to other areas of American diplomatic activity offers a much wider basis for judgment. It has taken the problem of American intervention out of the restricted limits imposed by Japanese-American relations and incorporated it in the framework of the entire complex of American foreign policy during the period of neutrality. When the entire panorama of American foreign policy is at hand, it becomes readily apparent that in that period the United States had two objectives: in the Far East, America was endeavoring to contain Japanese aggressive tendencies; in Europe, she was co-operating with the British to bring about the defeat of Germany. While it cannot be denied that entrance of the United States into the war was a direct consequence of the Far Eastern situation, the precise influence of the elimination of Hitler on the final decisions taken by the White House in this matter still remains to be established.

[58] *Papers relating to the Foreign Relations of the United States, Japan, 1931–1941* (2 vols.; Washington: U.S. Government Printing Office, 1943).

The supplementary volume concerning the Soviet Union has the same anticipatory character as those mentioned above.[59] It incorporates the documents on the relations between Moscow and Washington from the American recognition of the Soviet Union (November 6, 1933) to the end of 1939. The volume is enriched by the inclusion of a large number of reports on the Russian internal situation, an emphasis that is usually absent in the regular volumes, while the monographic character of the publication (Soviet-American relations) has led to the exclusion of materials concerning the Anglo-French-Soviet negotiations and the Soviet-German negotiations of the summer of 1939, which are to be found in Volume I for 1939 of the regular series. On the other hand, because of the importance of the subject in eventually shaping the American attitude toward the U.S.S.R., the volume does include rich documentation on Soviet policy toward the Baltic states for the period September–October, 1939, and still remains the most important source for the study of this question.

Of an anticipatory nature and of even greater importance than the preceding ones—since the regular volumes for 1942 were the last to appear—are the supplemental volumes concerning the most controversial political questions of World War II. The criticism of the results obtained by American policy in the Far East during and after World War II has been much more violent than the criticism of Roosevelt for involving the United States in the conflict. It is noted that the failure of the negotiations with the Japanese during the second half of 1941 was due to the impossibility of reaching a compromise between the Tokyo government's demands for a free hand in China and Washington's decision to eliminate Japanese influence in China in order to maintain its own political and economic position in that area.

The proclamation of the Chinese People's Republic on October 1, 1949, demonstrated that the hard-won victory over Japan in 1945 had barred the road to China only for the Japanese. The repercussions of this diplomatic defeat, which was unprecedented in American history, were extremely violent on the part of the American public. The criticism, launched in a famous article by William C. Bullitt[60] even before the Chinese Civil War was over, consisted of an attack on all of the wartime diplomacy, with particular emphasis on the decisions taken by the United States regarding the Far East, whether unilateral or in concert with the Allies in wartime conferences. The criticism assumed even greater proportions because

[59] *Foreign Relations of the United States. The Soviet Union, 1933–1939* (Washington: U.S. Government Printing Office, 1952).

[60] William Bullitt, "How We Won the War and Lost the Peace," *Life*, XXV, Nos. 9 and 10 (August 30 and September 6, 1948).

during this very period the degeneration of Soviet-Allied relations paved the way to the Cold War, and the Democratic administration was forced to present Soviet policy in its proper light (see *Nazi-Soviet Relations*), provoking a revision of American public opinion on the U.S.S.R. to the opposite of what Roosevelt had created in the autumn and winter of 1941.

The first government publication to appear on this issue was a volume published outside and apart from regular *Foreign Relations* collections. It contains a long summary of United States-Chinese relations from 1844–1949,[61] was compiled by the State Department, and includes an Appendix of 186 documents, the most interesting of which deal with the missions of Generals Hurley and Marshall, who were sent to China in the period 1944–47. The volume casts limited light on Chinese developments and emphasizes, in the main, the errors of the Kuomintang.

It was only in 1954, after the Korean War and MacArthur's dismissal brought the criticism of government policy to a head, that the State Department, under pressure from the Senate, decided to publish two special series, one on China for the years 1942–49 and the other on the major wartime inter-Allied conferences, in order to provide the public and scholars with source materials concerning the subjects of the great debate.

Thus far, two volumes, for 1942 and 1943, have appeared in the series on China.[62] The first demonstrates clearly the position in which America found itself in relation to China after the United States entered the war. Chiang Kai-shek's government took advantage of this development in the most obvious manner, insisting on the recognition of its status as a belligerent and upon its rights within the United Nations coalition at the very time that Chinese armed resistance to the Japanese was growing progressively weaker. The Chinese constantly pointed out that the alternative left to them, in the event that their demands were not met, was to abandon all resistance to the Japanese. Washington accepted the conditions imposed by Chiang, concluding that the collapse of China would greatly aid the Japanese on a practical as well as on a moral plane, enabling them to acquire new sources of war matériel as well as freeing large contingents of their armed forces for service elsewhere. Therefore, the United States judged it to be absolutely necessary to keep China in the war.

[61] *United States Relations with China (1844–1949)* (Washington: Department of State, 1949).
[62] *Foreign Relations of the United States, 1942, China; 1943, China* (Washington: U.S. Government Printing Office, 1956, 1962).

All of the aspects of this situation are clearly reflected in the documents on these negotiations, which continued throughout the whole of 1942. A loan was granted, almost without hope of repayment, of half a billion dollars, which was requested by Chiang for the purpose of keeping the Chinese forces in the field. Despite the reservations of a number of State Department officials regarding the effectiveness of such a huge sum to sustain the Chinese war effort, at the year's end an agreement was reached whereby the United States accepted all of the conditions laid down by Chiang.

The soundness of the judgment of those State Department officials who voiced their reservations, which were ignored by key American policy-makers, is borne out by the documents in the volume for 1943. The lack of desire to fight the Japanese, the chaos existing within the Kuomintang, and the extremely limited sense of responsibility on the part of the Kuomintang leaders, as contrasted with the remarkable organizing talent of the Chinese Communists and the great ability of their leaders, are clearly noted and reported by an American official attached to the Embassy in Chunking. This same official was later forced to resign from the State Department because of his lack of discernment and credibility. The analysis provided in his reports is so clear as to render superfluous any further effort to reconstruct, in the light of later developments, the internal causes for the collapse of the Kuomintang.

Particularly interesting, too, are the repeated insinuations made by Chiang to the State Department that in his judgment the British were dragging their feet in the war against Japan. He attributed this lack of enthusiasm to a British decision to use the Japanese as a counterbalance against a resurgent China after the war. Churchill's intransigence toward Japan when he became aware of the fact that Secretary Hull was being swayed by Chinese propaganda can thus be explained.

The conclusion that may be drawn from the evidence presented in these volumes on the Chinese question is that the Communist victory was made possible, in large measure, by the internal disintegration of the Kuomintang, a development largely ignored by the United States.

The first volume on China had been preceded, a short time earlier, by the publication of another special series devoted to the wartime conferences of the Great Powers. The first to appear was a sizable volume[63] in which the material concerning the Yalta Conference, February 4–11, 1945, was included, the results of which formed a major part of the criticism of

[63] *Foreign Relations of the United States. The Conferences at Malta and Yalta, 1945* (Washington: U.S. Government Printing Office, 1955).

American foreign policy. This material, destined to arouse strong reactions in Europe as well as in America, integrates the already rich collection of source material provided by memoirs and makes it possible to reconstruct with reasonable accuracy the general lines of the Yalta meeting and the basis of several important decisions made on that occasion by the American delegation.

It seems almost certain that the generous concessions made to Stalin by Roosevelt during the Conference were dictated by a desire to draw the Soviet Union into the war against Japan at whatever cost, an intervention that was erroneously believed to be indispensable to a rapid conclusion of the conflict in the Far East. Subordinating every other consideration to this immediate requirement, Roosevelt was led to compromise on many points and to abandon to the Russians many positions of primary importance, both in eastern Europe and in the Far East.

From this point of view, the criticisms later directed against Roosevelt and his advisers appear to be justified. Somewhat less justified, however, is the belief of some American scholars that the Yalta accords produced totally negative results for the United States.

In order to offer an objective judgment on these agreements, it is necessary to distinguish, first of all, between the situation at the time of the signature of the treaty and the situation existing at the time that it went into effect.

Concerning the first, it is inaccurate to state that Stalin achieved all of his objectives at Yalta without making concessions to the West. As a matter of fact, Stalin made many concessions, enough to provoke strong reactions in the Communist parties of the countries affected. Thus, the collaboration between King Peter and Subasic, imposed on the Yugoslav Communists by Stalin in fulfillment of his Yalta obligations, aroused a great deal of discontent among the adherents of the movement headed by Tito. The same situation occurred in China, where the aid, which took the form of a new Russo-Chinese treaty, that the Soviet government continued to give to Chiang-Kai-shek prevented the Chinese Communists from taking over the state.

These limits imposed on an extension of the Soviet spheres of influence were precisely established during the course of the Yalta negotiations, and as is obvious, they concerned two areas of the greatest importance in the Far East and in eastern Europe. To be sure, during the period when the terms of the Yalta treaty were being applied, events took a different turn, but this is not sufficient ground for the assertion that Stalin purposely tricked the West by assuming obligations that he had no intention of keeping. The fact that he had noted, at the time, certain statements by Roosevelt concerning the difficulties he faced in keeping American troops in Europe was not vital to Stalin's decision, in that the demobilization of the American armies moved much more rapidly and extensively than the American President had anticipated. Initially, Stalin fulfilled his obligations and, as has been pointed out, did so even at the cost of numerous difficulties with some of his collaborators. It was the West, in the final analysis, that abandoned those positions adherence to which guaranteed the validity of the decisions taken at Yalta and assured the application of the terms of the treaty.

Great Britain, severely tried by the war, returned to power a Labour government whose only thought was to withdraw from every binding position in order to devote its complete attention to the realization of its internal program. At the same time the United States was swept by a clamorous and insistent public demand for an immediate return to normalcy, involving the rapid restoration to civilian life of members of the armed forces and the dismantling, in every phase of national life, of the whole wartime apparatus.

What could Stalin's policy be in this situation? On seeing before him a vacuum brought on by the war weariness of others, by indifference, or by incapacity, Stalin could do nothing else but what he did, given the principles that govern the Soviet Union's international activity: he exploited every situation to the utmost and continued to advance until such time as someone stopped him or, at least, until he encountered effective resistance.

Even that part of the Yalta agreement dealing with eastern Europe may be considered to be satisfactory, to the point where the "rollback" policy enunciated by Dulles when he assumed direction of the State Department was, in effect, nothing more than the acceptance of analogous principles, except that in this area too it was the implementation of Yalta that was to be found wanting.

In conclusion, in evaluating the results of Yalta, it is necessary to keep well in mind that the subsequent development of the situation cannot be considered the fruit of the accords subscribed to at the Black Sea resort, but rather the consequence of a massive retreat undertaken immediately after the end of hostilities by the two major western powers. This retreat altered the balance of power on which the Yalta agreements were based and permitted Stalin to ignore them. Furthermore, the measure of the formal success attained at Yalta appears in just proportion when one stops to think that today no one would dare hope for a reconfirmation on the part of the Kremlin of the clauses of Yalta relating to eastern Europe.

This special series was followed by the two volumes in the regular official collection regarding the Potsdam Conference (July 17–August 1, 1945).[64] This documentation is extremely rich and important and goes well beyond the chronological limits of the Conference. The first volume includes material regarding the preparatory phase of the Conference, together with the correspondence and the minutes of the Davies mission to London and the Hopkins mission to Moscow (May–June, 1945), rounding out what was already partly known.

The second volume is naturally much more important in that it contains the minutes of all of the meetings, plenary or private, in addition to the documents which were under discussion, making it possible to follow the developments in their smallest detail.

It should be noted at the outset that the extraordinary length of the Conference was caused not so much by the delay brought about by the change in the British representation (defeated at the polls, the Conservatives, Churchill and Eden, were replaced by Attlee and Bevin on July 28 after a suspension of the Conference's business for two days) as by the substantial differences that emerged over the two principal problems under discussion: the amount of reparations to impose on Germany and the question of the Polish frontier. At the time of the departure of the British delegation, for all practical purposes the negotiations had reached an impasse. The signs of the imminent collapse of the Anglo-Soviet-American coalition, which first appeared immediately after Yalta and President Roosevelt's death and became even more noticeable after Germany's surrender on May 8, 1945, were already clear: the common danger that welded it together had disappeared. In this connection, the reader is struck by the evidence of the re-emergence of the old basic motive for discord between the Anglo-Saxon nations and the Soviet Union: among the documents assembled for the President's study prior to the Conference, there is a long and detailed report on communism's expansionist character and the probable direction it would take in the immediate future.

Despite this, the idea that the Conference might end in failure was considered to be prejudicial to American interests. America was still at war with Japan, and Soviet intervention was strongly desired. Therefore, Secretary of State Byrnes convinced President Truman of the usefulness of proposing a package deal involving compromises on a world-wide scale, in which each of the three powers would have its way on a problem of pre-eminent interest to it and, in compensation, would withdraw its

[64] *Foreign Relations of the United States. The Conference of Berlin (Potsdam),* 1945 (2 vols.; Washington: U.S. Government Printing Office, 1960).

opposition on another problem of pre-eminent interest to one of the other powers.

In effect, the Byrnes proposal anticipated the recognition of the Oder-Western Neisse line as the frontier between Germany and the lands entrusted to Polish administration until a German peace treaty was signed, the establishment of the portion of German reparations due the Soviets, and the obligation to conclude a treaty of peace with Italy as soon as possible and to support its admission to the United Nations. In this way the Soviets would have had approval, at least *de facto,* of the line proposed by them as the German-Polish frontier. Great Britain, in view of its domestic needs, would not object to the proposed division of the reparations to be extracted from Germany, and the United States would have gained a degree of satisfaction by winning support for her Italian policy.

On this point, the Potsdam documents give an exact idea of the price the United States was willing to pay in order to help Italy regain her full rights and her place in the international life of nations. As a matter of fact, in order to overcome Soviet opposition to its proposals on Italy, the United States agreed to a shift in Poland's provisional frontiers almost one hundred miles further west, along the upper reaches of the Oder—the distance that lay between the Eastern Neisse, the line proposed by the Americans during the early days of the Conference, and the Western Neisse line demanded by the Soviets.

What the Americans obtained in the package deal did not completely correspond to what they had requested for Italy. The proposal advanced by President Truman in the first session contemplated the immediate acceptance by Italy of a provisional accord, which, until a definitive peace treaty was signed, would replace all of the clauses of the short armistice agreement of Cassibile and those of the longer armistice agreement of September 29, 1943. Such an accord was to be based on Italy's assumption of an obligation to abstain from committing any hostile act against the United Nations and to maintain only the armed forces authorized by the Allies. The latter would exercise control over Italian affairs only to the extent necessary for military purposes and to guarantee an equitable solution of territorial disputes. In addition to this agreement, in order to recognize tangibly Italy's contribution to the defeat of Germany and also in consideration of Italy's declaration of war against Japan on the preceding July 15, the American delegation proposed that the three Great Powers agree to Italy's entrance into the United Nations.

The special series on the major conferences of the war period ends, for the moment, with the volume concerning the Cairo Conference (November 22–26 and December 2–7, 1943) and the Teheran Meeting

(November 27–December 1, 1943),[65] which brought Roosevelt, Churchill, and Stalin together for the first time.

As noted, the overriding subject of discussion was the question of the Anglo-American landing in France (Operation OVERLORD), an operation that the Soviets had been urging repeatedly for many months. The Anglo-Americans had already come to an over-all agreement on the projected date for the invasion of France (early May, 1944) but agreed that it would be a mistake to allow the forces assembled throughout the Mediterranean theater to remain inactive. Churchill proposed that in the meantime these troops be employed either in stepping up the advance in Italy, or in an operation in the Aegean (which, if it served to draw Turkey into the war, would have opened the way to an attack against the Germans in the Balkans) or in a landing in the northern Adriatic aimed at reaching Austria through the Ljubljana region. Roosevelt also agreed to the latter plan but recommended, however, that it be joined by the Yugoslav Partisans and that it be directed eastward toward Rumania, where Anglo-American forces would link up with Soviet troops advancing from Odessa.

Churchill strongly supported this plan, and the western proposals led Stalin to conclude that the Anglo-Americans did not really intend to carry through with OVERLORD and that they were seeking Soviet acceptance of one of these projects as their major military effort for the immediate future. The misunderstanding was soon resolved when Churchill and Roosevelt, succumbing to Stalin's insistence, informed him that an Allied landing would be made on the northeastern coast of France the following May. Stalin agreed to launch a Soviet offensive to coincide with the Allied landing.

The Anglo-American decision denies the validity of the thesis, supported by some, that Churchill in reality sought to substitute a Balkan operation for OVERLORD. On the other hand, the documents printed in this volume do not justify, at least for this period, the political ends, later attributed to Churchill, of seeking to prevent Soviet occupation of as much of south central Europe as possible, including Greece, Yugoslavia, Austria, Hungary, and Czechoslovakia.

Furthermore, at Teheran Churchill did not hide the fact that a landing in the Balkans would have raised political as well as military problems. However, he made it very clear that he had no Balkan "ambitions" and added that if Stalin had any objections of a political nature to advance, these could be studied and an agreement reached. Moreover, it should be noted

[65] *Foreign Relations of the United States. The Conferences at Cairo and Teheran, 1943* (Washington: U.S. Government Printing Office, 1961).

that Stalin himself had told Churchill in September, 1941, that the Balkans was one of two areas, the other being France, where a second front might be successfully opened.

There were several exchanges of viewpoints on the future world order, but no definite agreement was ever reached. The Soviets also took advantage of the opportunity to repeat their demand that the Soviet frontier established in the summer of 1940 be recognized. Also worthy of note are Stalin's several proposals designed to prevent any future resurgence of German military might.

Stalin stated that this danger could be averted if (1) at least fifty thousand and perhaps one hundred thousand German senior officers were "physically liquidated"; and if (2) the victorious powers retained strategic bases throughout the world in order to crush Germany promptly at the first sign of a threat from that country. While there was reason to believe that Stalin's first condition was made with tongue in cheek, and Roosevelt recognized it as such, both Stalin and Molotov repeatedly referred to the second condition during the course of the conversations.

The latter was not a new idea: the same view had been expressed by Stalin two years earlier, in December, 1941, during the Moscow Conference with Eden. At Teheran the idea was further clarified and was the subject of specific conversations during which Stalin and Molotov suggested that the Americans might establish military bases in the west, in the Azores, at Dakar, and at Bizerte (since the French, Molotov stated, could not be relied upon), and in the Far East, in the Philippines, on Formosa, and on some archipelago under Japanese mandate. Great Britain might establish bases on the Iberian peninsula and in North Africa, adding to those she already held in those areas, and perhaps take over Dakar in place of the Americans.

From the documents contained in this volume it can be confirmed that at the close of the Moscow Conference of October, 1943, Stalin promised Hull that the Soviet Union would join the Allies in the war on Japan as soon as the war against Germany was concluded. This promise is noted in Hull's memoirs,[66] but, perhaps because Roosevelt assured himself of Soviet intervention in the war in the Far East through generous territorial concessions to the Soviets at Yalta, it was more or less ignored in the historiography of World War II. Furthermore, at Teheran Stalin reiterated the promise in the same terms to Roosevelt and Churchill without imposing any further conditions or reservations.

It should be further noted that at Teheran the discussion begun in

[66] *The Memoirs of Cordell Hull* (New York: Macmillan, 1948), II, 1309–10.

Moscow during the Conference of Foreign Ministers concerning the Soviet request for a quota of the Italian fleet was reopened, and terms were agreed upon. The material in this collection reveals the details of an episode that, in its day, stirred the emotions of the Italians. And since the documents go beyond the limits of the Conference, it is now possible to understand why Roosevelt and Churchill agreed to modify the execution of their obligations by substituting American and British warcraft, equal in number to the Italian units, to be transferred to the Soviets. Also included are several important messages exchanged at the time between Washington and London concerning the President's remarks at the press conference of March 3, 1944. Only hypotheses may be advanced regarding Roosevelt's strange conduct during this press conference episode, but the one that links his statements with the re-establishment of Italo-Soviet relations appears to be the most logical.[67] Among other facts, it appears that the Americans were aware of the shift in Italian policy from conversations picked up by a microphone installed in Marshal Badoglio's office.

The volumes mentioned thus far are all part of the official collection of the State Department, with the exception of the one on Chinese-American relations, 1844–1949. In addition, other volumes published by the State Department, although they are not part of the *Foreign Relations* collection, frequently include significant material contributing to a better understanding of the events of World War II.

The most important of these are a volume published immediately after America's entrance into the war that clarified the directives issued and the action taken by the American government in the period just prior to American intervention;[68] two volumes published to illustrate the diplomatic preparations undertaken to create a new world order;[69] two volumes devoted to peace negotiations;[70] and two volumes concerning relations with the defeated powers.[71]

[67] For other details on the episode, see Mario Toscano, "La ripresa delle relazioni diplomatiche tra l'Italia e l'Unione Sovietica nel corso della seconda guerra mondiale," *Comunità Internazionale*, 1962, fasc. I.

[68] *Peace and War. United States Foreign Policy, 1931–1941* (Washington: U.S. Government Printing Office, 1942).

[69] *Postwar Foreign Policy Preparation, 1939–1945* (Washington: U.S. Government Printing Office, 1950). *A Decade of American Foreign Policy. Basic Documents, 1941–1949* (Washington: U.S. Government Printing Office, 1950).

[70] *Making the Peace Treaties* (Washington: U.S. Government Printing Office, 1948). *Paris Peace Conference, 1946. Selected Documents* (Washington: U.S. Government Printing Office, 1948).

[71] *United States and Italy, 1936–1946* (Washington: U.S. Government Printing Office, 1946). *The Axis in Defeat. A Collection of Documents on American Policy toward Germany and Japan* (Washington: U.S. Government Printing Office, 1946).

In order to complete the reference to American documentary sources, mention must also be made of the rich material of a military nature that was brought to light during the acrimonious debates on the foreign policy of the Roosevelt administration. While these may not be classified as documents published by the State Department, they are nevertheless important to the study of World War II.

The first source of this type was the reports of the committee investigating the Pearl Harbor attack, which was appointed in 1946 to determine the responsibilities connected with that event.[72]

The importance of this material lies in the fact that the committee sought to study the specific question within the framework of the events that led to the war between Japan and the United States. To this end, the committee assembled a vast documentation from American as well as Japanese archives, in addition to the Japanese material deciphered by the very efficient American interceptors.

This investigation brought to light numerous minutes of meetings; diplomatic dispatches; unpublished and extraordinarily important *promemoria* from civil and military officials, such as the documents concerning the Roosevelt-Churchill meeting of August 9–12, 1941, during which the Atlantic Charter was born and important decisions were taken on policy regarding the Far East; the formulation of Japan's definitive program for negotiations with the United States; the steps taken by China and by Great Britain to induce the United States to abandon the project for a temporary *modus vivendi* with Japan, which was being contemplated by the State Department on the eve of the attack, and so on.

This material makes singularly exciting reading, particularly the final report of the investigating committee, in which attention is focused on the essential documents placed in their proper historical perspective, creating a profoundly impressive dramatic sequence. It is difficult to resist the temptation to evaluate the individual fragments of information on the Japanese plans in the perspective of the final event as it occurred. It is a deceptive impression, analogous to the one gained by reading the conclusion of a mystery novel whose preceding pages contain the entire story. Rarely does the reader uncover the exact solution before reaching the concluding pages. A similar situation appears to have existed in the Pearl Harbor affair. As a matter of fact, the Americans were aware of everything

[72] The proceedings are published in a final report: *Investigation of the Pearl Harbor Attack, Report of the Joint Committee on Investigation of the Pearl Harbor Attack* (Washington: U.S. Government Printing Office, 1946). The documents are in *Hearings before the Joint Committee on the Investigation of the Pearl Harbor Attack* (40 vols.; Washington: U.S. Government Printing Office, 1946–47).

in advance: the place of attack, the hour, the day of the week, etc., but these were fragmentary pieces of information among a multitude of others, and it was extremely difficult to distinguish between what was fact and what was fiction. Of course, Washington lacked intuition, but there is a world of difference between this deficiency and malicious intent. Perhaps the idea of a Japanese attack was not too displeasing to Roosevelt, but certainly not an attack with the results that Pearl Harbor in fact had. Apparently, imaginations were given free rein in the attacks on the Roosevelt administration in connection with the Pearl Harbor episode. Historians are not permitted this freedom. Often the truth is more closely approached by a simple hypothesis such as that of an error of judgment, rather than by a complicated structure made even more complex by vivid imagination.[73] The former is the kind of a situation that occurs frequently and is intensely human. Once this has been said, the exceptional psychological attraction of the documents in question is worthy of comment.

After MacArthur's dismissal and the violent reaction it provoked among masses of Americans, the United States Senate launched another investigation. This one, too, was broad and all-encompassing; in the course of it the investigators probed for antecedents as far back as Yalta and called a number of key civilian and military personnel to testify, including Secretary of State Acheson and Defense Secretary Marshall. The investigation was brought to a close without reaching any definite conclusions, but its reports[74] provide another interesting source, both for the documents they contain and for the depositions given.

However, even after this investigation the debate between Republicans and Democrats continued unabated, and in March, 1955, the Eisenhower administration published the material on the Malta and Yalta Conferences, to which reference was made previously—material that was received by Roosevelt's critics as conclusive proof of the validity of the accusations hurled against him. In reality, the publication did not end the controversy; it simply postponed it. The Democrats pointed out that in the decisions taken at Yalta military opinion carried great weight and that, consequently, primary responsibility lay with Eisenhower and MacArthur for having repeatedly insisted on Soviet intervention in the war against Japan and for

[73] On the issue, see Roberta Wohlstetter, *Pearl Harbor: Warning and Decision* (Stanford, Calif.: Stanford University Press, 1962).

[74] *Military Situation in the Far East: Hearings before the Committee on Armed Services and the Committee on Foreign Relations, United States Senate, 82nd Congress, First Session, To Conduct an Inquiry into the Military Situation in the Far East and the Facts surrounding the Relief of General of the Army Douglas MacArthur from His Assignment in That Area* (Washington: U.S. Government Printing Office, 1951), 5 parts.

having forced Roosevelt to accept all of the Soviet conditions in order to assure Soviet participation in the war in Asia.

These discussions prompted the Defense Department to publish, in October, 1955, a detailed report supported by documents drawn from its own archives on the events connected with the Soviet entry into the Japanese war.[75] The scholar may find in this volume a great deal of material for the study of the influence of the military on political decisions in time of war.

Separate note should be made of the collection of the private papers of Roosevelt's personal adviser, Harry L. Hopkins, assembled and published in two volumes by the dramatist Robert E. Sherwood.[76] These volumes are one of the most important sources available for the diplomatic history of the period 1939–45. In his role as adviser to the President, Hopkins not only participated in many of the major diplomatic conferences that took place during the war (Atlantic, Casablanca, Cairo, Teheran, Yalta), but he also frequently exerted a decisive influence on Roosevelt, to such an extent that he was accused of substituting his own views for those of the President on more than one occasion. The material contained in this volume is of the greatest value for the study of American policy throughout the course of the war; it makes possible the tracing of many decisions to their origins and reveals the behind-the-scenes activity of policymaking, especially in regard to the often-mentioned theme of relations with the Soviet Union. Despite the fact that many years have passed since the book was published and that a great many volumes on the same general subject have since appeared, this book has not lessened in value. Whoever seeks to reconstruct the evolution of American foreign policy during the war and after the surrender of Germany (Hopkins also collaborated with Truman in the latter's first adventure into the field of international relations) down to the present role of the United States in foreign affairs can in no way ignore it.

4. THE SOVIET COLLECTIONS.

After the hurried disclosures made during the first years of the revolution, referred to in the preceding chapter, the Soviet government maintained absolute secrecy on the contents of its archives. Meanwhile, the western powers were releasing enormous quantities of documents for study

[75] *The Entry of the Soviet Union into the War against Japan: Military Plans, 1941–1945* (Washington: Department of Defense Printing Office, 1955).

[76] Robert E. Sherwood, *Roosevelt and Hopkins. An Intimate History* (New York: Harper, 1948).

through the publication of the collections on the origins of both world wars and were opening their archives to scholars, at least for nineteenth-century materials.

This situation, which deprived students of an essential research tool with which to complete the picture of the recent history of international relations,[77] led to a lively dispute at the Tenth International Congress of the Historical Sciences, convened in Rome in 1955. During a discussion on the diplomatic origins of World War II, the Soviet delegation presented a paper on the Soviet interpretation of the events leading to the conflict, citing the Soviet archives as the source of documentary support. The reception given to the paper was an extremely cool one, and it was repeatedly pointed out to the Soviet scholars present that the allegations advanced in their presentation could be accepted as scientifically valid only if they were based on documents available to all.

This criticism probably had a certain reverberation in the U.S.S.R. The government and scientific circles were already aware that, particularly for the post-1939 period, the technique of replying to the revelations contained in the documents of the western powers by issuing brief commentaries in pamphlet form was proving to be absolutely inadequate on a scholarly level, although it had certain propaganda value. The absence of Soviet documentation resulted in the reconstruction of events solely on the basis of western materials.

Consequently, in 1957 a commission was created within the Soviet Ministry of Foreign Affairs for the publication of the diplomatic documents, under the chairmanship of Andrei Gromyko and composed of a qualified group of historians and writers. The chief of the historical division of the Foreign Ministry was named secretary-general of the commission. This body quickly developed a vast program that includes the publication of two large collections which will contain the Czarist and the Soviet diplomatic documents for the entire modern period, as well as of other minor collections (several of which have already been published) on specific questions relative to World War II or to Soviet diplomatic activity in specific geographical areas.

[77] Some material concerning the foreign policy of the Soviet Union may be found in A. Rothstein (ed.), *Soviet Foreign Policy during the Patriotic War. Documents and Materials* (2 vols.; London: Hutchinson, n.d.); and in Jane Degras (ed.), *Soviet Documents on Foreign Policy, 1917–1941* (3 vols.; London: Oxford University Press, 1951–53). The first of these works terminates with December 31, 1944, and includes Stalin's announcements and orders of the day, a number of documents released by the Soviet government, such as letters exchanged between heads of state, official speeches, and Tass releases, and the texts of a number of agreements concluded by the U.S.S.R. during the war. The second work is largely composed of press releases and official speeches.

The first of the two major collections is devoted to the foreign policy of Imperial Russia from March, 1801, to the Bolshevik Revolution of November, 1917.[78] On the basis of the criteria established for the collection and the extensive period it covers, the publication promises to be of primary importance and may focus the attention of scholars of international affairs on the problems of the first half of the nineteenth century, a period that recent historiography has all but ignored. As illustrated by the volumes published to date, this collection consists mainly of archival materials of the Ministry of Foreign Affairs in Moscow, where the entire existing Czarist archives were transferred from the Czarist capital, St. Petersburg, but also includes papers from other Russian archives and, in special cases, documents from foreign archives.

The standards of selection satisfy scholarly requirements in that the collections contain the most significant documents from which the general lines of Czarist foreign policy are derived, along with those documents which enable the reader to follow the details of the negotiations conducted by Russian diplomats on questions of major importance. In consequence, the collection includes a large number of instructions, rescripts, reports to the Czar from the Ministry of Foreign Affairs, diplomatic representatives, and consular officers abroad, the minutes of governmental meetings on problems of foreign policy, and also the texts of the treaties with other states signed by the Czars. The latter were largely known through the Feodor Fedorovic Martens collection,[79] but the editors saw fit to include them in order to complete the collection and to provide scholars with texts based on the originals preserved in the archives.

With the exception of the treaties published by F. F. Martens and of a number of documents appearing previously in other publications but republished here, the collection consists of unpublished materials. The documents of minor importance which were already known are not included in the collection, but precise reference to the volumes where they may be found, along with copious notes concerning them, are included in the accurate bibliographies appended to each volume. Detailed reference is also made to the publications in which the documents reprinted here first appeared. In the Preface to the first volume the commission states that the documents are reproduced in their entirety, with the exception of those sections devoid of political content. Where an omission exists, appropriate notes so inform the reader.

[78] Ministry of Foreign Affairs of the U.S.S.R., *Russian Foreign Policy in the XIX and Early XX Centuries. Documents of the Russian Ministry of Foreign Affairs* (in Russian) (Moscow: State Publishing House for Political Literature, 1960 *et seq.*).
[79] See p. 81.

The documents are assembled chronologically, and each volume contains, in addition to the bibliography and explanatory notes described above, an index of names, a very detailed table of organization, and a documentary index similar to that used in the Italian collection. From the technical viewpoint, the Soviet collection leaves little to be desired.

Given its dimensions, it is clear that the collections will not be completed soon. Nevertheless, in order to issue the volumes as quickly as possible, the collections have been divided into six series: I, 1801–15; II, 1815–30; III, 1830–56; IV, 1856–78; V, 1878–95; and VI, 1895–1917. The last series will also include the documents previously published by the Soviet government for the periods 1911–12 and 1914–16,[80] according to the criteria followed for the incomplete collections that are available for the more remote periods.

Publication of the collection began in 1960 with the appearance of the first volume of the first series (which will consist of seven volumes). This was followed by the second volume and then by the sixth, concerning 1812, the latter published to commemorate the hundred and fiftieth anniversary of the victory over Napoleon.

The motives for beginning the collection with March, 1801, are explained in the Introduction to the first volume of the first series. The commission had considered beginning the series on Czarist foreign policy with the date of the creation of the Ministry of Foreign Affairs, September 20, 1802. However, this date, though important in the internal history of Russia because it marked the introduction of ministries in place of the old "collegia" established a century earlier by Peter the Great, had little significance as a point of departure for the study of Russian foreign policy. It would have meant ignoring the documentation on the new course of Russian diplomacy instituted by Alexander I from the moment he ascended the throne, which was marked by a renewal of relations with England and Austria and the conclusion of the peace treaty with France on October 8, 1801, a treaty which removed Russia from the second coalition against France organized by Paul I. For these reasons, the commission decided to begin the collection with Alexander I's assumption of the throne, March, 1801, even if the documentation becomes more complete and systematic only after September 20, 1802.

Volume I terminates with the decision taken by the Russian government in April, 1804, to break diplomatic relations with France. The material of greatest interest is that dealing with Russia's role as mediator between France and Great Britain in seeking a solution to the problems that remained unresolved between those two powers after the conclusion of the

[80] See pp. 121–24.

Peace of Amiens on March 27, 1802. These hitherto unpublished documents provide a point of departure for an evaluation of Russia's attitude toward the creation of the third coalition.

Equally new is the material concerning relations with the Ottoman Empire. The documents relating to the negotiations between the Russians and the Turks in 1802 over Moldavia and Wallachia, in addition to the papers concerning Russo-Serb and Russo-Montenegrin relations, are published here for the first time. There are a number of interesting documents, too, concerning those questions that Alexander held to be most important from the point of view of Russian foreign policy: the trans-Caucasus, central Asia, the Far East, and Russo-Swedish relations. Less plentiful is the documentation relative to Russia's relations with France, for the reason that this was already well known. Nevertheless, detailed references to publications containing this material are included.

The most significant documents found in the second volume, which covers the period April, 1804–December, 1805, are those on the negotiations for the third coalition. The Novosiltzov papers covering his mission to London are published for the first time and bring to light the principles that inspired, and the objectives sought by the alliance of the third coalition, in addition to the little-known attempt of Czarist diplomacy to draw Spain and Portugal into the third coalition. This volume, like the previous one, is also rich in material on Russian policy in the Balkans and in Asia, and terminates with the instructions sent to Russian emissaries in European capitals at the end of 1805 defining the position of the Czarist government following the battle of Austerlitz and the Treaty of Pressburg between Austria and France.

The sixth volume refers to the years 1811–12, and the bulk of the material deals with the sixth coalition against France. The documents reveal how Russian diplomacy sought to achieve two aims simultaneously, i.e., win the firm support of England and prevent Austria and Prussia from allying with France. New material is presented relative to Russia's attitude toward the newly-formed Latin American states, and this volume continues to devote a great deal of space to Russian policy toward the Ottoman Empire and to the Balkan and Caucasus questions.

Scholars of the modern period await the publication of the second collection with keen anticipation.[81] This major collection will deal with the foreign policy of the Soviets beginning with the Bolshevik assumption of

[81] Ministry of Foreign Affairs of the U.S.S.R., *Foreign Policy Documents of the U.S.S.R.* (in Russian) (Moscow: State Publishing House for Political Literature, 1957 *et seq.*).

power on November 7, 1917, and will apparently terminate with the outbreak of World War II.

Technically, this collection has the same characteristics as the preceding one, but its historical interest, for the moment, is considerably less because it brings less new information to light—at least insofar as it is possible to judge from the volumes published to date.

This collection is not divided into series, and the first volume, covering the period November 7, 1917–December 31, 1918, appeared in November, 1957, as a contribution to the commemoration of the fortieth anniversary of the Bolshevik Revolution; it has now reached Volume IX, which brings the documentary account to December 31, 1926.[82] This is the period in which the Soviet government had few contacts abroad, and the functions of diplomatic representatives were often entrusted to commercial missions or carried out by Soviet delegates to the International Red Cross. The editors have taken this fact into account in publishing the material relating to the activities of these missions. The documentation contained in the collection comes mainly, however, from the archives of the Ministry of Foreign Affairs, and although it is natural that, given the structure of the Soviet state, the effective direction of foreign policy and at least a part of diplomatic activity was entrusted to the central and peripheral organs of the Communist party, there are only sporadic references to this material in the collection. Instead, the collection includes numerous texts of official speeches before the party congress, appeals to revolutionary committees in other states, and interviews with party leaders—documents that are generally well known and whose inclusion in the collection appears to serve the purpose of demonstrating the coherence, and, consequently, the nonsecret character, of Soviet foreign policy. On the other hand, keeping in mind that Soviet diplomatic activity—in this and later periods—has always had a markedly propagandistic character, it must be recognized that the publication of this material assumes far greater significance than is the case in the foreign policy of the western democracies.

However, because of the scarcity of new documents, the origins of the major decisions taken by the Kremlin in foreign policy are not further clarified—a circumstance that, as has been noted in preceding paragraphs, is characteristic of other collections as well, although for different reasons. But in the case of this particular collection, the fact assumes extraordinary

[82] The chronological limits of the other volumes are as follows: Vol. II, January 1, 1919–June 30, 1920; Vol. III, July 1, 1920–March 18, 1921; Vol. IV, March 19, 1921—December 31, 1921; Vol. V, January 1, 1922–November 19, 1922; Vol. VI, November 20, 1922–December 31, 1923.

proportions. For example, in the volumes issued to date there is no reference to Soviet-German military collaboration, which is one of the most intriguing areas of speculation of the post-World War I period. The documents on the Treaty of Rapallo of April 16, 1922, are another case in point. Aside from the text of the treaty, cited in Volume V, only one document appears in connection with it, a report in which Chicherin refers to his visit to Berlin on his way to the Genoa meeting. In this report Chicherin affirms, in essence, that the Soviet-German negotiations for a commercial treaty present certain difficulties and that these cannot be easily overcome. He concludes his exposition by noting that he left Berlin without achieving any concrete results. Nevertheless, he adds, the conversations received wide coverage in the press and the latter "in a favorable or unfavorable sense, exploits our talks with Rathenau to draw different conclusions."

Insofar as the minor collections are concerned—those relevant to the period following that covered by the two great collections or to specific problems—the major contribution made by the Soviet archives is the publication of the correspondence between Stalin, Churchill, and Roosevelt during World War II.[83] At first glance it would seem that, since reference is made to the correspondence of the Big Three for the years 1941–45, this publication would be of such fundamental importance as to overshadow the much larger production that has appeared in the West. In effect, it adds very little to our knowledge of the events of the war, for two reasons: first, because no light is shed on the origins of the decisions or of the positions taken by Stalin in his letters; and second, because the bulk of the correspondence published was to a great extent already known from western sources.

It seems that it was just these reasons that induced the commission to publish this correspondence: as one reads in the Preface, from what was published of Stalin's correspondence "outside of the U.S.S.R. there emerged a distorted picture of the Soviet attitude during the war years." Yet such an accusation is not supported by a comparison of the text of the correspondence previously published in the West with what appears in this collection. Rather, it is the similarity between the texts that leads one to the conclusion that on this occasion the Soviets observed the most rigid scientific criteria, publishing, as is affirmed in the Preface, all of the texts contained in the archives in their complete and original form.

[83] Ministry of Foreign Affairs of the U.S.S.R., *Correspondence between the Chairman of the Council of Ministers of the U.S.S.R. and the Presidents of the U.S.A. and the Prime Ministers of Great Britain during the Great Patriotic War of 1941–1945* (2 vols.; Moscow: Foreign Languages Publishing House, 1957).

However, in a certain sense the polemical assertions contained in the Preface approach the truth—in the sense that from this collection the Soviet Union emerges as the power that bore the brunt of the war for a long time, while the United States and Great Britain, despite the repeated messages from Roosevelt and Churchill recognizing Russia's position, appear on several occasions to have reneged on their promises of concrete support to the Soviet effort and, on other occasions, to have failed to consult with Stalin on their decisions.

This situation is illustrated by the correspondence exchanged between the Big Three in June, 1943, which includes some hitherto unpublished dispatches. Roosevelt and Churchill had met during the second part of May and had arrived at the conclusion that for the moment it was opportune to concentrate their efforts against Italy, since there was not adequate time to prepare for a landing in France. Stalin's reaction was extremely violent. He made it clear that the Soviet government could not agree to a decision that, in addition to being made without its participation, was in direct opposition to the obligations that London and Washington had earlier assumed. The creation of a second front in the west had already been postponed from 1942 to 1943, and a further postponement, he concluded, could have very grave consequences for the course of the war.

Roosevelt left to Churchill the task of replying, and the British Prime Minister did so in a firm but measured tone, reminding Stalin that not even the U.S.S.R. would be interested in seeing operations undertaken that were destined to fail. Churchill added that Stalin had been invited to meet with him and Roosevelt but that he, Stalin, had replied negatively and that insofar as the contribution of the West was concerned, the enormous quantities of supplies received by the Red Army from the western powers should not be forgotten. Stalin replied with a long bill of indictment, citing parts of documents from which (according to Stalin) it was crystal clear that the Allies had promised the second front in France in 1943 and that now Soviet faith in western promises was being severely tried. Churchill maintained his calm but could not avoid reminding Stalin that for a year Britain had fought alone against Hitler and that, after June 22, 1941, she had promptly made available to the Soviet Union all possible help.

Despite his courteous tone, Churchill's allusion to the period of Soviet-German friendship was clear, and apparently Stalin concluded that it was inopportune to continue an argument that would produce no positive results, while under certain conditions it might prove embarrassing. On the other hand, it might easily be inferred (in an effort not to underestimate Stalin's ability) that he did not interpret Anglo-American expressions of the intent to open a second front in France as soon as possible as an obligation to do so. Stalin himself must have understood the difficulties of such an operation, and, therefore, it is logically possible to develop the hypothesis that he was taking advantage of the opportunity to accuse his western allies of failing to meet their obligations, in order to exploit this gambit at a later date.

Two observations may be made on this point. First, the Allies played no such game in connection with the Soviet refusal to declare war on Japan, against whom the bulk of the American forces were engaged. The second observation is characteristic of Soviet policy. In 1938–39, German expansionist tendencies worried the western democracies as much as they did the Soviet Union. In the great diplomatic battle that preceded the outbreak of the war, Stalin won out with the Soviet-German Pact of August 23, 1939, which directed German energies toward the West. When this victory backfired, Stalin did not hesitate to insist that the West owed the Soviet Union its complete support. The West granted this support because it was in their interest to do so, but it could hardly be expected that the Anglo-Americans, for the sole purpose of reducing for a brief period the pressure on the Red Army, would launch a campaign that was predestined to fail.

The events leading to the Italian armistice are another point on which this collection offers some enlightenment. Apprised of the decisions reached by the Anglo-Americans relative to the surrender offered by the Badoglio government, Stalin stated that the Soviet Union "could no longer tolerate" remaining on the sidelines as a passive observer of events that concerned her directly. He proposed that a three-power politico-military commission be formed, with the authority to deal with Italy and with all other countries breaking their ties with Germany. Churchill and Roosevelt opposed granting the Soviets a determining influence in Italian affairs but accepted the proposal on condition that the three-power commission would be limited to a consultative role only, with final decisions left to the competence of the respective governments. Thus, Soviet participation was bereft of substance, but it did provide Stalin with an excellent precedent for restricting, in precisely the same way, Anglo-American participation on commissions dealing with eastern European states under Soviet occupation.

One should not jump to the conclusion that without this precedent the destinies of the eastern European countries would have been substantially different, but perhaps something more might have been done to prevent their communization. However, it is reasonably clear—and is confirmed by the correspondence in this collection—that in the absence of precise agreements, eastern Europe was destined inevitably to fall under Soviet influence. The American government underestimated this possibility and banked on the prospect of a postwar policy of co-operation with the Soviet Union; Churchill, much more realistically, insisted, as will be seen later,[84] on an accord by which he sought to keep as much territory as possible out of Soviet control.

This error in judgment by Roosevelt and Hull (even more serious when it is recalled that these very same Washington statesmen were the first to know that at the very moment that they chose to conclude the political agreements they would find themselves unable to keep their armed forces mobilized) is even clearer when seen from the Far East, the area entrusted to American troops. If the lack of realism in American policy had not led them to overestimate the positive results of close relations with the Soviet Union and the real strength of Chiang Kai-shek's China, the situation in the Far East would have provided the United States with fewer surprises than those they had to face in the postwar period.

While the collection is carefully edited and well equipped with clear and effective explanatory notes, several comments must be made on its organization. The two-volume division, one containing the correspondence with Churchill (and later Attlee) and the other the correspondence with Roosevelt (and later Truman), has certain obvious inconveniences. First, since the correspondence is between two parties, Stalin on the one hand and Churchill and Roosevelt on the other, the reader is obliged to study both volumes simultaneously; second, the need to reproduce in each volume those letters signed jointly by Roosevelt and Churchill and those directed to both of them results in a waste of space.

These two volumes were followed, in 1958, by a short collection, published jointly by the Czechoslovakian and the Soviet Ministries of Foreign Affairs on the Munich crisis of 1938,[85] in which sixty-one documents are included, drawn for the most part from the archives of Prague and Moscow (not all are unpublished and some are not diplomatic documents but rather official declarations, speeches by political leaders, etc.). The twofold aim of this collection and the unusual form of publication—by two governments jointly—are explained in the Preface of the volume. First of all, the volume was designed to demonstrate that, while the western democracies had abandoned Czechoslovakia to her fate, the Soviet Union was the only great power standing ready to fulfill the obligations undertaken on behalf of the Prague government. Further, the

[84] See pp. 532–34.
[85] The Ministry for Foreign Affairs of the Czechoslovak Republic-The Ministry for Foreign Affairs of the Union of Soviet Socialist Republics, *New Documents on the History of Munich* (Prague: Orbis, 1958).

Soviet government was ready to extend aid beyond what was specified in the terms of the alliance of May 16, 1935. According to the terms of the treaty, Soviet assistance was contingent on French intervention in defense of Czechoslovakia. However, the Soviets maintain that they would have gone to the aid of Prague on their own, on condition that the Prague government decided to defend its territory at all costs and requested Soviet assistance directly. Second, the collection was designed to demonstrate that the Czechoslovak bourgeoisie did not know how to protect the nation's interests and preferred to sacrifice Czechoslovak liberty rather than surrender its position of privilege.

Insofar as the first point is concerned, the Soviet Union's policy was fully consistent with its obligations, and, during the development of the crisis, on more than one occasion it declared itself ready to fulfill those obligations. Of course, it is possible that the Soviet attitude was conditioned by the fact that Moscow had concluded that the prospects of being called upon to implement the treaty were exceedingly remote, since all signs pointed to a French acceptance of Nazi demands. Furthermore, it appeared highly improbable that either the Polish or the Rumanian government would consent to transit rights across their territories for Soviet troops going to the aid of Czechoslovakia. Nevertheless, while the evidence is insufficient to support this hypothesis fully, the fact remains that, on a formal diplomatic plane, the Soviet attitude was much more precise and correct than that of the western powers. In this context it should also be noted that—in contrast to the assertions made by Bonnet in his memoirs—the Soviet documents reveal that early in September, 1938, Moscow proposed to Paris that the two governments immediately begin military consultations with the Czechoslovaks in order to plan joint military action in the event of a Nazi attack. On the other hand, the Soviet documents cited in support of the thesis that the Soviet Union was ready to come to the assistance of Czechoslovakia even without French intervention are not completely convincing. In fact, no Soviet document in the collection proves this contention beyond reasonable doubt. The only evidence supporting the contention that the proposal was *discussed* at the Kremlin is found in several communications of the Czechoslovak Minister to Moscow, where he refers to information reaching him indirectly.

Definite conclusions on the attitude of responsible Czechoslovak statesmen cannot be reached on the basis of this material. A comparison of these documents with copies of several of the originals, which were consulted by a western scholar in the Prague archives, reveals that the compilers of the collection were careful to omit the parts of the documents that referred to the steps taken by the "bourgeois" diplomats on behalf of their respective countries.[86] This observation raises some questions as to the validity of the documentation contained in this collection and as to the criteria of selection employed by the compilers.

A further contribution was made by the publication of a volume of documents on Franco-Soviet relations for the period 1941–45,[87] several of which were first published in a Soviet review and then translated into French.[88] This publication also had clearly defined political aims. Above all, it sought to demonstrate that, while the Gaullist movement had encountered serious difficulties in its relations with the western Allies, it had enjoyed the constant and disinterested support of the Soviet Union.

To this end, several documents are included concerning the attempts made by the government in Algiers to seek admission to the European Advisory Commission charged with arranging the terms of the German surrender and formulating the principles governing Allied policy in Germany. The documents prove that, on that occasion, the Soviet government was favorable to the French request, while the Americans and British were opposed. However, it should be noted that this episode, of no great significance because in practice the EAC's function was extremely limited (France joined the commission in November, 1944), is insufficient to support the view that the Gaullist movement enjoyed constant Soviet support. Before the German attack on the Soviet Union, the latter had not demonstrated the slightest sympathy for De Gaulle and his followers. At that time, the Soviet and Nazi propaganda lines were similar in their denouncement of the Gaullists as mercenaries in the service of the British; among other things, in the fall of 1940 the Soviet Union established diplomatic relations with Vichy. Of course things changed after June 22, 1941, but even so it is rather difficult to speak of "constant support." It is sufficient to recall that Stalin for some time was opposed to France's sharing in the occupation of Germany and that it was only after strong western pressure, and the intervention of Churchill in particular, that Stalin agreed to the transfer of part of the British occupation zone to French control. Furthermore, the Soviets then categorically refused to cede a part of their

[86] On the subject, see William W. Wallace, "New Documents on the History of Munich. A Selection from the Soviet and Czechoslovak Archives," *International Affairs*, October, 1959, pp. 447–54.

[87] Ministry of Foreign Affairs of the U.S.S.R., *Franco-Soviet Relations during the Great Patriotic War, 1941–1945* (in Russian) (Moscow: State Publishing House for Political Literature, 1959).

[88] "The German Question in Franco-Soviet Relations during the Great Patriotic War 1941–1945" (in Russian), *Mejdounarodnaia Jizn*, Supplement No. 4, April, 1959. A French translation may be found in *Recherches internationales à la lumière du marxisme*, No. 12, March–April, 1959, pp. 3–84.

Berlin zone of occupation to the French, and the French sector of Berlin was ultimately created out of portions of the British and American zones.

In the second place, now that Bonn and Paris were apparently effecting a *rapprochement,* the Soviet collection sought to call attention to the fact that during the course of World War II De Gaulle had advocated the most drastic solutions to the German problem, solutions which the Soviet Union refused to accept. This fact emerges from the minutes of the Stalin-De Gaulle conversations of December, 1944, that preceded the conclusion of the Franco-Soviet treaty of alliance. The content of these conversations was not known at the time of publication of the Soviet documents—the third volume of De Gaulle's memoirs appeared in October, 1959—and therefore the documents in the collection were entirely new.

It is now possible to compare the French and Soviet minutes of the conversations, and such a comparison is of interest because the two versions are not always in agreement. Thus, while the Soviet minutes indicate that it was De Gaulle himself who proposed the Oder-Western Neisse line as Poland's western frontier, the De Gaulle version clearly indicates that he abstained from expressing his approval of Stalin's precise references to the Oder-Western Neisse line. There is an analogous situation in regard to De Gaulle's request to annex the Rhineland. According to the French minutes, Stalin quickly agreed to the proposal; according to the Soviet minutes, Stalin simply emphasized that before any decision could be taken it would be necessary to consult the British and the Americans.

Excluding this and other significant differences, the general course of these conversations reflects an obvious desire on the part of De Gaulle to find in Moscow a counterweight to the influence exerted by the western Allies by exploiting the common desire of the two countries to arrive at a final solution of the German problem. On the other hand, Stalin's refusal to support the French general's proposals beyond certain well-defined limits reveals his desire to avoid damaging Moscow's relations with London and Washington.

The publication of these minor collections was followed by a volume on the relations between the Soviet Union and the Czechoslovak government in exile in London during the period 1941–45.[89] An integrated Soviet-Czechoslovak commission determined the selection of the material to be included in this collection, employing criteria somewhat like those adopted for the collection on the Munich crisis. In this case, too, it is obvious that the collection was designed to serve practical ends, that is, to demonstrate

[89] *Czecho-Soviet Relations during the Great Patriotic War, 1941–1945* (in Russian) (Moscow: State Publishing House for Political Literature, 1960).

that, while Beneš' pressures on the British government to denounce the Munich Pact were fruitless, Czechoslovakia's restoration was largely due to Soviet support. However, the volume does not contain material of any great importance and adds little to what was already known from Beneš' memoirs and, from the Communist viewpoint, what had been revealed by Fierlinger's diary.[90] Nor do the documents regarding the Czecho-Soviet agreement of June 29, 1945, by which the U.S.S.R. annexed sub-Carpathian Ruthenia, fully explain Beneš' and Stalin's initial positions on this point. The subject remains controversial.

Nothing new emerges from the volume concerning Soviet policy toward the Arab world from 1917 to 1960.[91] It is little more than a compendium of declarations and documents previously published, for the most part, in *Pravda* or in *Izvestia*.

The publication of documents from Soviet sources has not been limited to the above-mentioned official collections. Much has been published in connection with questions of contemporary political importance. However, this tactic has led to serious controversy and to differences of opinion not necessarily of scientific or scholarly origin. These documents have appeared in such specialized journals as *Mejdounarodnaia Jizn* ("International Life") or in other reviews such as *International Affairs* and *Temps Nouveaux*, which are also published in German.

In this unofficial way, for example, the U.S.S.R. published the Soviet version of the minutes of the Anglo-French-Soviet military conversations of August, 1939.[92] The nature of these conversations was already known, particularly through the disclosures of the British Foreign Office. The Soviet version, even though more detailed, adds nothing sufficiently important to persuade scholars to alter their previous conclusions. In substance, it is reasonably clear that, while the French expected a broad general agreement quickly, the British and the Soviets wanted to proceed with the negotiations more cautiously. The British were not ready to assume any military obligations until certain political problems had been resolved, and the Soviets were anxious to postpone any final agreement until the Berlin negotiations, which were then under way, gave some

---

[90] See pp. 586–91 and p. 596.

[91] Ministry of Foreign Affairs of the U.S.S.R., *The U.S.S.R. and the Arab World, 1917–1960* (in Russian) (Moscow: State Publishing House for Political Literature, 1961).

[92] "The military negotiations between the U.S.S.R., Great Britain, and France in August, 1939" (in Russian), *Mejdounarodnaia Jizn*, II (1959), 140–58; III, 139–58. A French translation may be found in *Recherches internationales à la lumière du marxisme*, No. 12, March–April, 1955, pp. 130–220.

indication of success or failure. It may be added that on the very day the military conversations were begun the Berlin talks entered their final and conclusive phase.

These factors aside, it is fairly evident that these conversations, rendered difficult by the atmosphere of reciprocal suspicion, took place under unusual circumstances. It was most extraordinary for negotiations between General Staffs to take place before the conclusion of a definite political agreement. Lacking such an agreement, it was hardly to be expected that the westerners would reveal the details of their strategic plans—Voroshilov, too, while he insisted on giving the negotiations a more precise character, avoided giving details of the Soviet military plans—or that the French and British delegations would be authorized to conclude a military agreement without referring the matter to their respective governments. The criticism on this point cannot be given serious consideration, and, therefore, it does not provide a basis from which it is possible to reach an objective evaluation of the Anglo-French position in the over-all negotiations with the U.S.S.R.

In the same way, one month after the appearance of the American volume on the Teheran Conference the Soviets published their principal documents on the same question in the Soviet journal *International Affairs*.[93] Similarly, while a desire is expressed to refute "the inventions regarding the Soviet attitude" contained in the American volume, the material published (i.e., the minutes of the four plenary sessions, of the meetings of the General Staffs, and of several bilateral conversations with Roosevelt and Churchill) is substantially the same as that contained in the American documents. The two most obvious differences noted are first, that the Soviet documents, as the editors state, are not cited in their entirety; and second, that the Soviet documents lack the minutes of several informal meetings, such as the one that took place after the tripartite dinner on the night of November 29, at which Stalin spoke at length on the precautions to be taken to prevent a postwar resurgence of Germany.

Also missing are the minutes of the November 30 meeting between Eden, Hopkins, and Molotov, at which the principal topic was the question of military bases for the control of postwar Germany and Japan. Therefore, what appears in the Soviet documents on this subject is only what Stalin stated in the bilateral conference with Roosevelt held on November 29. The American and Soviet minutes are in substantial agreement on this meeting, although the language used in the Soviet version is somewhat less

[93] "Documents: Teheran Conference of the Leaders of the Three Great Powers," *International Affairs* (Moscow), No. 7, July, 1961, pp. 133–45; No. 8, August, 1961, pp. 110–22.

explicit and there is no mention made of the location of the bases (the American minutes refer to Dakar). In effect, because of the circumspection and the absence of the above-mentioned minutes in the Soviet collection, the Soviet version of what was said at Teheran on these points assumes a considerably different significance and relevance than does the account found in the American collection.

Nevertheless, the fact remains that, apart from the polemical nature of these documentary reports, the publication of the Soviet sources, even in this unofficial way, is of real value to the scholar. Therefore, it is to be hoped that the Soviet government will fulfill the obligation it has assumed and will promptly publish the documents on the other international wartime conferences.[94]

5. THE ITALIAN COLLECTION AND OTHER ITALIAN DOCUMENTARY SOURCES.

We have seen how almost every Great Power in the years after World War I undertook, in varying degrees and with differing selection criteria, the publication of its diplomatic documents for the period prior to the outbreak of the war. Nothing comparable occurred in Italy, where the archives remained closed from the time the Kingdom was created. The simple reason is that Italy was not burdened with the problem of "war guilt," having entered the conflict only in May, 1915, on the side of the Allies. Consequently, Italy was not directly involved in the violent debates that gripped the public the world over, and the Italian government saw no reason to follow the lead of the other major powers in publishing its diplomatic documents.

It soon became evident, however, that this policy of abstention was having a singularly detrimental effect. In treating Italy's role in the arena of international politics, world historiographers were necessarily limited to the evidence obtainable from non-Italian sources—sources that were not particularly well designed for the presentation of a precise and impartial analysis of Italian policy, at least so it seemed from the Italian point of view. This fact explains the "bad press" Italy received in the postwar period and accounts for the persistent epithet of "Machiavellianism" applied to Italian policy; it was the result of an ignorance of the facts for which the Italians themselves were responsible, since they had not made them public. To be

[94] It should be noted that Soviet publications of the documents taken from the German archives are not cited here. Reference has been made to them in the section dealing with the Wilhelmstrasse documents.

sure, a commission was established in 1932, presided over by Senator Salata, charged with publishing the material concerning the 1861–1915 period, but a combination of circumstances prevented the realization of the project, and in time the proposal was pigeonholed.

At the end of World War II, therefore, conditions seemed propitious for making up for lost time by bringing to the attention of scholars not only the documents pertinent to the period between the two world wars, as nearly every other power was doing, but all those materials that had been under lock and key in the archives since 1861. After the removal of the few remaining obstacles, a commission was finally created in 1946 authorized to publish all of the material relative to the period from the founding of the Kingdom in 1860 to the proclamation of the armistice of Cassibile on September 8, 1943.[95]

During the initial phase, the commission faced several difficult problems, the most important being that of reorganizing and assembling the archival materials that had suffered as a consequence of the war.

After the fall of the Fascist regime the new Foreign Minister, Raffaello Guariglia, decided to ship a portion of the archival materials to a point outside the national territory, the Italian legation in Lisbon, in view of the predictable German reaction and of the peculiar situation in which Italy would find herself after an armistice with the Allies.

This material consisted of a number of typewritten volumes containing data assembled during Ciano's tenure at the Palazzo Chigi and was divided as follows:

> Four volumes containing the Hitler-Mussolini correspondence from March, 1938, to May, 1943, and the exchanges between Ciano and the British Ambassador, Sir Percy Loraine, during the crisis of July–August, 1939.
>
> Five volumes containing the minutes of Ciano's meetings between 1936 and 1942.
>
> Six volumes regarding special problems, that is, the Alto Adige question, Eden's resignation, the first and second arbitration treaties of Vienna, the Albanian question of 1938–39, and the Munich crisis.
>
> A large file labeled "Germany," containing material referring to Italo-German relations from the Salzburg meeting to the outbreak of the war. In addition, the file contained separate folders with important documents regarding relations with other states and particularly with Great Britain during the final phase of the crisis.

[95] *The Italian Diplomatic Documents* (Rome: La Libreria dello Stato, 1952 *et seq.*).

Naturally, the transfer of this material to Lisbon was to remain secret, but the news was leaked to the Americans, who, on the basis of a clause in the armistice agreement, demanded and obtained the material in question. At the time a tumultuous debate was in progress over the admission of Argentina to the United Nations, and the American government, by a thorough examination of these documents, hoped to determine whether or not the rumor was true that Argentina had concluded a secret pact with the Axis powers committing herself to their support. In truth, there was no trace of such an accord in these documents. The documents were carefully studied and microfilmed, and after the peace treaty was signed, they were returned to the Italian government.

A second series of files, much larger and comprising the most important sources, was the archive of the Office of Coordination, an office in the Ministry of Foreign Affairs. All the documents of a secret nature were included in this archive after 1927, when the office of Secretary-General of the Foreign Office was allowed to remain vacant.

Immediately after the armistice of September 8, 1943, this material was secretly transferred to the cellars of the Palazzo Lancellotti in Rome. The files were put into leather cases, the cases put into suitcases, and the suitcases put into wooden boxes to prevent water damage. In this way they eluded first a German and later an Allied search and were brought to light only in September, 1947, after the peace treaty was signed. However, despite all of the precautions, dampness had penetrated the cases and had caused the greatest damage to the thickest papers, i.e., the "diplomatic papers," fusing them together into completely useless great blobs.

The gaps resulting from this damage are undoubtedly great but not completely irreparable, since the copies of the telegrams, which were typed on onionskin paper, were not especially damaged.

A second source placed in safekeeping at the time of the armistice consisted of materials that were not directly pertinent to diplomatic activity, such as the papers of the Intelligence Service, the documents belonging to the office charged with formulating the conditions for the armistice and the peace terms (Armistice-Peace Cabinet), and the papers of several other special agencies (for example, the files relative to the transfer of the Grand Mufti and to the activities of the center created in Rome during the war for action in the Arab world). This material, too, was kept from German and Allied hands, but it was partially destroyed in the process. However, such material will not appear in the diplomatic document publication, since it is the practice in all countries to withhold it from publication.

What remained at the Palazzo Chigi on September 9, 1943, after the materials noted above were removed and successfully hidden, consisted of the "General Archive," that is, the archives of the various divisions of the Foreign Office in which, especially during the last days of the Fascist regime, only the least confidential papers were filed. This material suffered by far the heaviest damage, principally because those documents which referred in specific terms to Italo-German relations or which appeared to be the most compromising were deliberately destroyed in order to prevent their falling into German hands immediately after the armistice. Among the files destroyed at that time were those concerning the activities of the Italian government to block the expansion of Germany in various areas (in Austria, for example) and concerning the anti-German activities of foreign statesmen (to the extent that these were known and encouraged by the Italian government). Naturally, as always happens in such circumstances, many personal papers were also destroyed.

Immediately after the armistice of September 8, 1943, the Germans appeared at Palazzo Chigi to take over that part of the archive that was of special interest to them. Not finding the material they were looking for, they removed and shipped to Germany only part of the general archive.

Recently, through the study of one of the files of documents taken from the Wilhelmstrasse by the English and American forces at the end of the war, it has been possible to learn something about the disposition of the Italian documents taken by the Germans and to determine their nature far more precisely than had been possible through a study of the archives at the Palazzo Chigi.

The order to confiscate the archives of the Italian Ministry of Foreign Affairs was issued by Von Ribbentrop on September 12, 1943. The operation was completed in six days and on September 18, 1943, forty-one wooden cases of documents were shipped to Berlin, where they arrived a few days later. There is no information concerning the ultimate fate of these files, but it is presumed that they were destroyed during one of the many Berlin bombings. It is absolutely certain that they were not returned to the government at Salò, nor were they found among the Wilhelmstrasse papers captured by the British and Americans. There is the possibility that they are in the possession of the Soviets or that they fell into private hands.

Von Ribbentrop's primary reason for issuing the order was to learn the details of the negotiations leading up to the Italian armistice, but Berlin was also interested in knowing the present tenor of Italo-German relations, the Japanese view of Hitlerian policy, and finally, the attitude of the other Tripartite members and of Spain, Portugal, and Turkey.

Despite the lacunae discovered by the Germans in the Palazzo Chigi archives, Von Ribbentrop's primary goal was the only one not achieved by the detailed examination of the Italian documents in Berlin, since the confiscated Italian material, while it fell short of German expectations, was of no minor importance and represented a substantially greater prize than that taken by the S.S. earlier in Warsaw, Paris, Belgrade, and Athens. Its contents were as follows:

1. Documents from the archive of the Cabinet of the Foreign Ministry from 1932 to August, 1943. While there were serious gaps in the documentation for the later period, the material dealt with the major events of the period in which Fulvio Suvich served as Undersecretary for Foreign Affairs (including the first contacts with National Socialist Germany, the Hitler-Mussolini meeting at Venice, the Four-Power Pact, the Stresa meeting, and the *Anschluss*). Suvich's notes on the various political meetings were especially numerous for the period 1933–35.

2. Numerous files from the central division of the Foreign Office for the European and Mediterranean areas, dealing with the normal affairs of its competence.

3. A complete file of the telegrams sent and received during the period 1940–43.

4. The originals of Hitler's letters to Mussolini (with the exception of those of March 11, 1938, and February 5, 1941), the copies of which, in Italian translation, had been preserved in the Cabinet safes and, as has been noted, transferred to Lisbon). For the Germans the recovery of these letters was particularly important because there was the danger that they might fall into Anglo-American hands, there to be exploited for the politico-military information they contained or for their propaganda value.[96]

What remained of the general archives after the German confiscations was transferred to Salò, and when that area was liberated, the archives fell into the hands of the partisans and the Allied troops, with the exception of that portion of the archives that the employees of the Salò government were able to destroy. The archives were returned to the Ministry of Foreign Affairs in Rome, enlarged, on the one hand, by the diplomatic documents of the Republic of Salò and reduced, on the other, by the above-mentioned destruction and by other losses occurring at the time of their recovery.

Following the example set by many other collections, the Italian one has been divided into various series.

The first series covers the period January 8, 1861, to September 20, 1870

---

[96] A more detailed list of the captured documents may be found in Mario Toscano, "Le vicende degli Archivi segreti di Palazzo Chigi," *Nuova Antologia*, 96th year, Vol. 481 (March, 1961), fasc. 1923, 299–326. The reports on the investigations on this material conducted by officials of the Wilhelmstrasse are also included here.

(the occupation of Rome), and to date the first two volumes and the last volume of the series have been published. Volume I was originally planned to begin with the proclamation of the Kingdom of Italy, but in the interest of contributing to a greater comprehension of the individual events leading up to the proclamation, it was decided to include the material for the entire year.

Obviously, many aspects of Italian foreign policy for this period were already well known through the published Cavour papers,[97] but this volume of the collection considerably enlarges the documentary base because in addition to the documents found in the archives of the Ministry of Foreign Affairs, material from many private archives was also included, especially Victor Emanuel II's correspondence with Ricasoli and Vimercati, taken from the archives of the House of Savoy at Cascais, and the Baron Ricasoli papers, preserved in the Brolio Palace. The addition of these supplementary materials makes possible a more exact reconstruction of the diplomatic action undertaken than is usual when only a single source, such as the archives of the Ministry of Foreign Affairs, is drawn upon.

These enlarged sources throw new light on Italian diplomatic activity during a singularly difficult period in Italian history, when it fell upon the Turin government to insert the new kingdom into the European state system and to induce the other powers to accept the dramatic changes of the past two years in the map of Italy.

The issue that seemed to incorporate something of all of the problems facing the new kingdom—which, it should be noted, achieved its unity largely through revolutionary actions, internal forces being mainly responsible for toppling the legitimate sovereigns of Parma, Modena, Tuscany, and Naples and for absorbing almost all the territory of the Holy See—was that of gaining recognition. Albeit in diverse ways, almost all of the European powers opposed these changes and the methods by which they were accomplished, and even Great Britain was not entirely satisfied with the developments, despite the fact that in the recent past she had been the most favorable to the cause of Italian unity. Thus the question of recognition had to be posed in such a manner as to avoid provoking a crisis, by resorting to a series of subtle compromises that occasionally might wound national pride but that, for the moment, offered an acceptable

[97] *Carteggi di Camillo Cavour: Il carteggio Cavour-Nigra dal 1858 al 1861* (4 vols.); *La questione Romana negli anni 1860–1861* (2 vols.); *Cavour e l'Inghilterra, carteggio con V. E. D'Azeglio* (2 vols. in 3 tomes); *Carteggio Cavour-Salmour* (1 vol.); *La liberazione del mezzogiorno e la formazione del Regno d'Italia* (5 vols.) (Bologna: Zanichelli, 1926–54). Indexes for the first fifteen volumes were published by Zanichelli, Bologna, 1961.

solution. By bridging the immediate dangers, the way was open for a definitive solution of the problem in the future.

A study of the diplomatic skirmishes of the first half of 1861 once again reveals Cavour's admirable qualities as a negotiator and as a statesman: his ability, on every occasion, to come up with an adequate solution to the most pressing problem of the moment, or, when this was impossible, to work around it or postpone it, and especially his remarkable sense of the limitations governing his actions are all demonstrated here. Of course, Cavour's greatest efforts were directed toward winning French recognition, which was singularly important for the connection it had with the Roman question and with the problem of the removal of French troops from Papal territory. On this point, the diplomatic documents do, in effect, cast new light, not on the negotiations with the Holy See, since these are well known through other sources, but on the negotiations undertaken with Paris, which, if they had not been abruptly terminated by Cavour's death, might very well have anticipated by a year or more the solution reached in September, 1864.

The second volume of the first series starts with the end of 1861 and terminates with July 31, 1862, that is, the eve of the Aspromonte crisis. Among the problems of greatest significance in this volume are the negotiations conducted by Ricasoli for Prussian recognition of the Kingdom of Italy. These negotiations were rather difficult because the Prussian government, as a condition for recognition, insisted on a guarantee that under no circumstances would Italy attack Venetia, directly or indirectly. However, at that very time relations between Vienna and Berlin were becoming increasingly strained over the German question, and Prussia abandoned her demand for the Venetian guarantee and asked instead for a similar guarantee with regard to the German Confederation, a promise that caused the Italians no particular difficulty. Negotiations had produced positive results and were on the verge of being concluded when Ricasoli fell from office and was replaced by Rattazzi. The Prussians insisted in reopening the negotiations from the beginning and made it very clear that they had no faith in Rattazzi, whom they considered to be too friendly to the French and incapable of restraining the more extreme elements of the Action party. Thus Prussian recognition was preceded by Russian recognition, the latter relying on this action to please the French and to win Louis Napoleon's support for Russia's Balkan policy.

On the other hand, the negotiations conducted by Ricasoli with Berlin were part of a much larger design tending toward a loosening of the alliance ties with France so as to establish greater freedom of action for Italy and to enable Italy to emphasize this autonomy by moving closer to Great

Britain and to Prussia. These tendencies in Ricasoli's policy served to aggravate the already existing dissension between the Prime Minister and Victor Emanuel II, whose personal actions did not always appear to be compatible with the constitutional regime in Italy. Among other things, the King apparently favored a popular rising in the Balkans designed to put the Austrian Empire in difficulty and to make an intervention in Venetia possible; this undertaking Ricasoli judged to be "childish and foolhardy," but it was abandoned only because of the open opposition manifested by Napoleon III. By the beginning of 1862 the differences between Ricasoli and his sovereign had become irreconcilable, and the Prime Minister asked his friends in the British Cabinet for advice on how to bring an unbearable situation to an end. The latter advised against precipitating a constitutional crisis which, given the fragility of the new kingdom, might have unpredictable repercussions. Ricasoli's resignation in March brought the issue to a momentary close.

It is apparent, then, that the documentation included in this volume is of great interest, not only for the reconstruction of Italian diplomatic actions, but also for the comprehension of various aspects of the relations between the Crown and the government, as well as for descriptions of many "unofficial," behind-the-scenes activities, knowledge of which is necessary for an understanding of the historical realities of this period.

The second series covers the period from the day following the occupation of Rome (September 21, 1870) to the fall of the Crispi government on March 5, 1896, after the defeat at Adowa. Only the first volume of this series, covering the period to the end of 1870, has been published.

The key issue at this time, as far as Italy is concerned, was the Roman question. However, there is little here that is new. A portion of the material was known through the publication of Green Book No. 17,[98] from Giovanni Lanza's papers,[99] and from Raffaelle Cadorna's volumes on the liberation of Rome.[100] Professor Federico Chabod, in the introduction to his history of Italian foreign policy,[101] had made use of the most important

[98] Italian Ministry of Foreign Affairs, *Libro Verde 17. Documenti relativi alla questione romana presentati alla Camera il 29 dicembre 1870.*
[99] C. De Vecchi di Val Cismon (ed.), *Le Carte di Giovanni Lanza* (Turin: Regia Deputazione Subalpina di Storia Patria, 1938), Vol. VI (September–December, 1870).
[100] R. Cadorna, *La liberazione di Roma nell'anno 1870 ed il Plebiscito* (Turin, 1898).
[101] Federico Chabod, *Storia della politica estera italiana dal 1870 al 1896, Le premesse* (Bari: Laterza, 1951), Vol. I.

documents in the archives on the subject. Only a few special elements emerge as truly new.

A number of documents refer to the problem of whether or not to leave the Leonine city to the Pope, a question that left Visconti Venosta perplexed, aroused the opposition of Minghetti, and attracted the support of the Ministry's Secretary-General, Blanc, who once again demonstrated a concept of the Roman problem considerably different from that of Visconti Venosta.

The documentation concerning the Catholic missions in the East is also of some interest. After the occupation of Rome and the defeat of France in 1870, these Catholic missions tended to seek the protection of the Italian government. Visconti Venosta indicated a certain interest in the development, which was strongly supported by the Minister of Public Instruction, Correnti, but his interest was circumscribed by an overriding desire not to strain relations with France and to avoid any action that would lead to the accusation that he sought to profit from the French disaster by replacing French with Italian influence over the eastern Roman Catholics.

Insofar as the Italian attitude toward the Franco-Prussian War—a situation of fundamental importance during this period—is concerned, the documents confirm Visconti Venosta's desire, which was seconded by Nigra, to aid France by supporting a move to offer either the collective mediation services of the Great Powers or that of the British government. Among the various episodes of some consequence is the near-incident provoked by Bismarck's refusal to allow De Launay, Italy's Minister to Berlin, to confer with William I at Prussian headquarters at the front. De Launay had been commissioned by Visconti Venosta to ask, in Victor Emanuel II's name, for the King of Prussia's opinion on the Roman question, on the possibility of reaching some agreement with the French to end the conflict, and on the Duke of Aosta's candidacy for the Spanish throne. However, Bismarck, who evidently had no desire to give Italy any guarantees on these points and who certainly was not ready to commit himself in the matter of the Hohenzollern candidacy to the Spanish throne, refused to allow De Launay to see William I. This refusal aroused grave political concern in Florence, as well as some anti-Prussian sentiment because of the lack of courtesy displayed toward the Italian sovereign.

In the same period, Italian diplomacy was drawn into the struggle between the Great Powers over the Straits question, negotiations which, at that very time, were entering a delicate phase because of the Russian denunciation of the Black Sea clauses of the Treaty of Paris of 1856. While the Czarist government was insisting that Italy maintain a neutral position on the issue, the British government was applying heavy pressure to bring Italy into the anti-Russian camp. In this attempt the British were actively supported by the Austrians, who made veiled threats to reopen the Roman question if Italy refused to go along with the western powers in this matter. For a time it appeared that Visconti Venosta, influenced by Nigra, might support Russia in the hope that such a stand would bring Russia around to taking a more favorable attitude toward France. However, on November 20, fearing that the Roman question might be reopened by the very powers that had previously supported the Italian position vis-à-vis the Church, the Italian Foreign Minister decided to align himself with Vienna and London on the Straits question.

The third series covers the period March 6, 1896–December 31, 1907. The first volume opens with the creation of the Rudinì government and closes with April 30, 1897. It offers valuable details that enable one to see the emergence of the first symptoms of Italy's abandonment of her policy of intimate alignment with the other powers of the Triplice. The evidence brought to light by the new documents indicates that the shift in Italian policy, instead of being the product of a precise plan evolved by Rudinì, was due to an evolution in the relationship between the Great Powers and, specifically, to the anti-British tendencies appearing in German foreign policy. This shift became very clear during the course of the negotiations for the renewal of the Triple Alliance, negotiations that were complicated by Italian insistence on the insertion into the treaty of the so-called "Mancini Clause," which guaranteed Italy that under no circumstances would the Triple Alliance assume an anti-British significance. At the time of the two previous renewals (1887 and 1891) the Mancini Clause had been considered superfluous in the light of the cordial relations existing between Great Britain and the Central Powers. But in 1896 the symptoms of the nascent Anglo-German rivalry were already clear, and the rivalry reached new heights in the aftermath of the famous telegram sent by William II to Krüger.

At this same time, British friendship had become increasingly important to Italy in view of the situation developing in East Africa, where a British position favorable to Italy was deemed absolutely vital. With the benefit of hindsight, one may conclude that the breach between Rome and Berlin at this point became fundamental, a breach that because of its very gravity was not handled with the necessary understanding and that, as a result, led to the first crack in the armor of the Triple Alliance.

On the other hand, Italy's Mediterranean policy was a matter of indifference to its allies, and this lack of support forced Italy to resolve many Mediterranean problems of common interest directly with the

French and pretty much on French terms, particularly in the case of Italian interests in Tunisia. The new material available in this volume clarifies the details of the Paris negotiations that led to the accord of September 28, 1896, and reconfirms the difficulties encountered by Italian diplomacy in seeking to negotiate with a government that could assume with impunity a position of rigid intransigence, taking advantage of a favorable situation and of a moment when Italy was particularly weak. However, on a more general plane, the Italo-French accord assumed a far greater importance than might be implied from the text of the agreement. In resolving one of the most serious problems coloring Franco-Italian relations, the door was opened to that *rapprochement* between the two countries which, in the brief span of a few years, was to lead to the Mediterranean ententes of 1900 and 1902 and which, in turn, led to a special position for Italy within the framework of the Triple Alliance.

The problem of Franco-Italian relations is further treated in great detail in the second volume of this series, which begins with May 1, 1897, and concludes with the fall of the Rudinì ministry in June, 1898. On the whole, these documents add little to what had already been known about the negotiations for the commercial treaty with France. The major obstacle to the treaty was the French insistence on prefacing the commercial agreement with a clarification of the relations between the two countries which, according to the ideas advanced by Hanotaux, would lead, if not to Italy's outright exit from the Triple Alliance, at least to its foregoing any anti-French obligation assumed in the Triple Alliance. When Visconti Venosta's adamant refusal blocked French attempts to neutralize Italy, the negotiations for the commercial treaty and for a joint declaration of support of the status quo in Tripoli were abandoned.

Considerable space is devoted to the question of Crete, a problem covered in a Green Book published in 1898. The most interesting part of this documentation is the revelation of the repercussions felt in Vienna and Berlin from the clearly pro-Russian and pro-French attitude assumed by Rome in this crisis, which can be considered to have brought about the first real fissure in the solid front of the Triple Alliance.

The third volume covers the period June 29, 1898 (the date of the creation of the first Pelloux Ministry), to July 29, 1900 (the date of the assassination of King Humbert), a period in which the Ministry of Foreign Affairs was directed first by Canevaro (to May 14, 1899) and then by Visconti Venosta.

The documentation on the Italian attempt to obtain a concession in China is of some significance. This problem was handled by Canevaro with very little skill. He obtained the purely formal support of France and

Germany in the venture but encountered strong resistance from the Russians and, to a minor extent, also from the United States. As for the British—whose attitude was of vital importance—it was clear that Salisbury did not look favorably on the Italian initiative, although, in order not to disturb the cordial relations existing with Rome at a time when the European situation was deemed to be very critical, he made no effort to oppose the venture formally. Thus, Salisbury settled for an ambiguous position. He was convinced that a China concession would not be forthcoming without the dispatch of a naval squadron to Chinese waters, and so he offered British support of the Italian project on the condition that no coercive measures be employed.

Apparently, Canevaro did not fully comprehend the real value of Salisbury's promise, and, furthermore, the Italian Minister to China, De Martino, acted too hastily. The result was a major diplomatic *gaffe* by De Martino. He presented the Chinese government with an ultimatum without having taken into account the countermanding instructions sent to him by Canevaro, who, in the meantime, had given London certain guarantees against precipitate Italian action. The immediate difficulties provoked by the incident were overcome, but the issue dragged on until Visconti Venosta, who succeeded Canevaro, modified the original Italian requests and set about, under pressure from the Parliament, to remove the causes for the controversy.

Insofar as the problems of the Mediterranean and relations with France and Great Britain are concerned, these documents add little that is new. In 1899, the traditional Anglo-Italian friendship was under severe strain as a result of the Anglo-French accord of March 21, 1899, which delineated the spheres of influence of the two nations in Africa. The accord seemed to indicate that the Tripolitan hinterland had been assigned to France without regard for the extensive Italian interests in the region. The spirited reaction in Italian governmental circles is not surprising. Further-more, Canevaro, at the time of the Fashoda crisis of October, 1898, with the express purpose of preventing any possible Anglo-French compromise from weakening Italy's position in that region, had made it clear to London that Italy regarded control of Tripoli as vitally important to her interests. Apart from its specific content, the March 21 accord aroused serious doubts in Italian minds concerning the value London placed on Italian friendship and the extent to which Italy could count on Great Britain to champion Italian interests in the Mediterranean.

This conclusion emphasized the urgency of a direct understanding with France, and the prospects for such an agreement appeared to be much more favorable after Delcassé, seconded by the new Ambassador to Rome,

Barrère, pursued the same objective as his predecessors, that is, the weaning away of Italy from the Triple Alliance or, at least, the neutralizing of the Triple Alliance insofar as it affected France. However, Delcassé was much more realistic and believed that the ultimate goal should be approached gradually, without the imposition of manifestly unacceptable conditions beforehand. The first important step toward this end was taken on November 21, 1898, with the signing of an Italo-French commercial agreement that brought the ruinous tariff war between the two countries to an end. At approximately the same time, negotiations for an accord based on a reciprocal pledge of nonaggressive intent in Morocco and in Tripolitania were reopened and pressed vigorously by Visconti Venosta when he returned to the Ministry of Foreign Affairs.

As has been noted, the contents of the volume do not suggest any substantial revision in the accounts that historians have written on the basis of documentation published in other countries. Nevertheless, it does make it possible to fill in the details of many episodes influencing the decisions of the Italian government.

Thus far, only the last volume of the fourth series, designed to embrace the period January 1, 1908–August 2, 1914, has been published and concerns the final days of the crisis, June 28–August 2, 1914, the day on which Italy declared her neutrality. As we have seen, the quantity of documentary material on this period is enormous; nevertheless, the Italian collection (which is particularly large, exceeded in number of documents only by the Austrian collection) is of major significance not only for an understanding of Italian diplomatic activity, but also for the positions of the other protagonists during the crisis.

In fact, the Italian Minister of Foreign Affairs, San Giuliano, facing a situation fraught with dangerous possibilities, immediately sought to assemble as much information as possible on the attitudes of the various governments involved in the crisis. The Italian representatives in Vienna, Berlin, Paris, London, St. Petersburg, Belgrade, Bucharest, and Cetinje responded fully to his appeal, to such an extent that, in the light of the documentary materials published, it is evident that the clearest picture of the developing situation was to be found in Rome. The volume makes public for the first time the text of Prince Alexander of Serbia's appeal to Victor Emanuel III, and the latter's reply. Moreover, the correspondence of San Giuliano, Bollati, and Avarna early in July, 1914, on the position of Italy in the Triple Alliance is of great importance for an understanding of San Giuliano's thinking on such a fundamental question. The importance of several other documents should also be emphasized in that they clarify San Giuliano's current views on the prospects of terminating Italian occupation of the Dodecanese Islands in return for economic concessions in Asia Minor. Negotiations with Turkey leading to this end were not concluded, and the outbreak of the war led San Giuliano to reverse his stand on the question.

The information sent by the Italian Chargé d'Affaires in Belgrade, Cora, is particularly useful. Thanks to his personal contacts, he was able to follow closely the development of the Austro-Serbian crisis. The information transmitted to Rome by Cora regarding the arrogant attitude of the Austrian representatives, Serbian intransigence, and the Belgrade government's 'absolute certainty of Russian aid (among other things, Cora immediately was in possession of the text of the Austrian ultimatum and the tenor of the Serbian reply) gave San Giuliano a clear and up-to-the-minute concept of the seriousness of the crisis and led him to realize—apparently somewhat earlier than his counterparts in other governments—that Russian intervention on the side of Serbia was a foregone conclusion.

In this situation, San Giuliano's policy was influenced, above all, by the fear that an Austro-Serbian war would be prejudicial to Italian interests in the Adriatic. He was primarily concerned about the fate of the new state of Albania and the possibility of Austria's acquiring, by force or through negotiations with Montenegro, Mount Lovchen, whose possession was considered decisive for the control of the Adriatic by the military experts of every country. In reality, the importance of the control of this point had been vastly exaggerated. During the war, Austria-Hungary took Mount Lovchen without, however, being able to dominate the Adriatic. Nevertheless, especially during the early phase of the conflict, this belief exerted considerable influence on the Italian government, inducing it to assume an attitude of more or less open opposition to Vienna.

In this context it should also be noted that the documents contained in this volume tend to modify the negative evaluation of many scholars, and of Albertini in particular, of San Giuliano's policy during the crisis of 1914. The latter was accused of not having made sufficiently clear the fact that Italy would not enter the war on the side of the Central Powers in a general conflict provoked by an Austrian attack on Serbia, and of not having co-operated in attempts to avert war, in the hope that the eventual expansion of Austria in the Balkans would open the way to compensations for Italy on the basis of provisions in Article VII of the Triple Alliance. As a matter of fact, from the documents contained in this volume, it appears that the position taken by San Giuliano was much more explicit than had heretofore been believed. In full accord with the Rumanian government, he did not fail to make it clear to Vienna that Italy considered the crushing of Serbia as contrary to Italian interests and, as the crisis deepened, he repeated his warnings, although in anything but blunt language, so that in the minds of the ruling groups in Berlin and Vienna there should have been little doubt that in the event of a general war Italy would remain neutral.

However, despite the clarification provided by these new documents, a complete revision of the judgments expressed earlier on San Giuliano's activities is not necessarily in order. For whatever reasons—belief in the military superiority of the Central Powers, fear that in alienating the Central Powers Italy would find herself completely isolated, and, finally, in order not to close the door to the possibility of compensations—the Italian Foreign Minister initially preferred to avoid taking a clear-cut position. As he himself stated in a letter to Salandra on July 26, 1914, his feeling was that it was not only useless but extremely dangerous to make precipitate decisions and that it was important to leave everyone uncertain as to Italy's course of action in order to obtain "some positive advantage." San Giuliano's position, so expressed, lends credence to the belief (the head of the Foreign Office had immediately noted the possibility of gaining compensations in the Italian-speaking areas of the Hapsburg Empire) that, for a time, he did not exclude the possibility of Italian intervention on the side of the Central Powers in order to force Vienna and Berlin to accept the Italian interpretation of Article VII of the treaty. This hypothesis must be considered independently of the fact that San Giuliano did not hesitate to criticize Vienna's policy immediately and to point out clearly that such a policy was in violation of the terms of the treaty.[102]

The fifth series concerns the war years, beginning with August 3, 1914, and terminating with November 4, 1918. To date, only the first volume has been published, and it covers the weeks from August 3 to the death of San Giuliano on October 16, 1914. This series is fundamentally important because, as noted, the majority of the collections published in other countries prior to 1939 do not include the war period, and the Italian collection, together with the American Department of State collection and the documents published by the Soviets, seems to be destined to become the primary source for the study of diplomatic developments during the war years.

The first volume of the fifth series deals with the early period of Italy's neutrality and may be considered one of the most valuable sources published thus far in the Italian collection. The most important revelation in this volume is the fact that Rome apparently was veering toward war

[102] On this entire question, see also Mario Toscano, *L'Italia e la crisi europea del luglio 1914* (Milan: Giuffrè, 1940).

with Austria-Hungary from the very first days of the conflict, far earlier, that is, than had previously been believed. This trend was due primarily to the influence of the Prime Minister, Salandra, whose role in the formulation of foreign policy appears to have been particularly striking in this period; on occasion he was not above undertaking an action in foreign affairs that was totally unknown to his Foreign Minister. On the other hand, the shift toward a pro-Allied point of view was anything but smooth, in part because San Giuliano was prudently awaiting a clarification of events, in part because of the influence of military operations (the fall of Liege, the battle of the Marne), and in part because of the fear that a French victory would have serious repercussions on the balance of power in the Mediterranean even in the event that Italy intervened on the Entente side. This last factor appears repeatedly in the Salandra-San Giuliano correspondence and was to be decisive in inducing the Italian government to remain neutral until such time as it was able to gain from the Allies acceptance of the precise Italian demands for compensation. The inevitable result was the negotiations that culminated in the Pact of London, setting forth the conditions for Italy's entrance into the war.

The sixth series begins with November 5, 1918, and ends with October 30, 1922 (the creation of the Mussolini government). The first volume of this series, covering the period to January 17, 1919, that is, to the eve of the official opening of the Paris peace conference, has appeared.

In general, documentary material for this period is extremely limited. Consequently, this volume is particularly significant and can be used profitably for the study of the foreign policies of other countries as well. It contains the documents relating to the diplomatic preparation undertaken by the Italian commission prior to the peace conference (in effect, it deals with all of the major problems affecting Italy). The documentation makes it possible to examine the different attitudes and positions taken by the principal Italian statesmen, and, specifically, to comprehend clearly the differences existing between Sonnino and Orlando, the former insisting on a rigid adherence to the terms of the Pact of London, the latter somewhat more receptive to compromise, especially as far as Italian relations with the Slavic peoples were concerned.

Those documents referring to the first quarrels between Italy and her allies, which developed immediately after the close of the conflict, are of major importance. Admiral Thaon de Revel's opposition to the sending of French warships into the upper Adriatic, for example, sparked a violent debate which Orlando conducted with great vigor although personally he was not convinced of the merits of the case that he was forced to defend. Much more significant are the Italian reactions to the news of French penetration in Ethiopia, and these contributed to increasing the bitterness of the debate with London and Paris over the Adriatic question. Within this framework, it should also be noted that the attempt made by the Italian government to get the Allies to honor the obligations assumed at St. Jean-de-Maurienne foundered on the shoals of Great Britain's adamant opposition.

The seventh series covers the period October 31, 1922–April 14, 1935 (the end of the Stresa conference), and four volumes of this series have appeared.

The first volume (November 1, 1922–April 26, 1923) is devoted to the first steps taken by the Fascist government in the field of foreign affairs and in substance confirms what was already known of Mussolini's attitudes as revealed during the short period that he held the Ministry of Foreign Affairs portfolio immediately after coming to power. Somewhat out of his element as Minister of Foreign Affairs, in practice Mussolini allowed himself to be guided by the Secretary-General, Contarini, and by the upper echelons of the Ministry, without imposing that vigorous and adventurous policy he had advocated prior to assuming control of the government. It was only on the occasion of the meetings in Territet and in Lausanne that he sought to reopen the mandate question, but the attempt was fruitless. After those conversations, Mussolini informed the Consulta that Lord Curzon had declared that he was ready to discuss the problem. However, when Ambassador Della Torretta appeared at the Foreign Office to take up the negotiations, he was informed that the Italian Prime Minister had misinterpreted Lord Curzon's words completely and that issues of this nature were not subject to discussion.

However, even in this early period, the first symptoms of what was to characterize Mussolini's future policy appeared, and a typical example of his characteristic method of approach—abrupt departures and equally abrupt returns to his original positions—was offered during the Franco-Belgian occupation of the Ruhr. After having supported the French action, Mussolini proposed a "continental bloc" whose anti-British character was so clear that it provoked an immediate and violent reaction in Great Britain. This unexpected move, causing consternation among the functionaries of the Consulta, did not foreshadow a dramatic shift in Italian foreign policy. Frightened by the turn events were taking, Mussolini executed an abrupt about-face: going from one extreme to the other, he identified Italy's position with Britain's and called on the latter for support in urging a policy of moderation on the Paris government.

These events, which for the moment appeared to be of passing importance, were indications of the incipient conflict between the new

Minister and the Consulta. This was revealed even more clearly during the Italo-Greek crisis stemming from the murders at Janina and the occupation of Corfu, an episode that exposed many typical aspects of Mussolini's character and contributed in no small measure to altering the substantially favorable opinion of him held by Europe and the United States up to that time.

On this important episode, which forms the central theme of the second volume of the seventh series, the recently published documents provide new elements on which to base a judgment; they reveal a number of particularly significant behind-the-scenes activities that contribute to an understanding of the true objectives pursued by Mussolini on that occasion.

The most controversial question of the entire episode was that of establishing precisely what Mussolini's real intentions were in ordering the landing on Corfu; that is, whether he intended to obtain a better bargaining position in negotiating a solution with the Greek government or whether it was his intention to take advantage of the critical state of European affairs to acquire a strategic base that would convert the Adriatic into an Italian lake.

While the documents do not provide a definite answer to this question, they do make it possible to arrive at certain important conclusions, particularly through the examination of the dispatches exchanged between Mussolini and the Italian Ambassador at Paris, Romano Avezzana, and between Mussolini and Salandra, first Italian delegate to the League of Nations.

Mussolini's insistence that the evacuation of the island be effected only after those guilty of the murders were discovered and punished (a condition that was manifestly impossible to fulfill); his obstinacy in maintaining a position that threatened to enlarge the Italo-Greek incident into a conflict with Great Britain; his dissatisfaction with a solution which, in effect, satisfied every Italian demand, but, of course, included the evacuation of the island—all of these, together with other facts already known (the nomination of an Italian governor, the projected construction of military barracks, etc.), seem to confirm the belief that Mussolini really intended to hold Corfu, adopting a tactic very similar to that employed by his predecessors with success in the occupation of the Dodecanese Islands.

On the other hand, undoubtedly the diplomatic developments stemming from the crisis had a significant effect on the manner in which the island was occupied. Admiral Solari's squadron had received orders to attempt a peaceful occupation of the island and was to provide two hours' advance notice of the landings to the foreign consulates in order that their personnel could seek safety in the event force had to be employed. Instead, the squadron arrived at Corfu five and one-half hours behind schedule. The result was that the advance notice to the foreign consulates was reduced to thirty minutes, and, in the face of purely verbal resistance on the part of the Greek authorities, it was decided to use force: the precipitate action by the Italians was taken in order to effect a landing before nightfall, which would have further delayed the operation. Moreover, medium-caliber guns were employed, and the shells killed a number of civilians who had sought protection in the fort. As might have been predicted, these events aroused a vehement public reaction and certainly contributed toward making the diplomatic negotiations for a solution much more difficult.

Another revelation in this volume worthy of note is Mussolini's idea of winning German support in the event of an Italo-Yugoslav conflict in which France would intervene. The idea stemmed from several statements made by Stresemann to the Italian Ambassador in Berlin, De Bosardi, which Mussolini considered to be so important that he asked the Ambassador to seek further clarification. However, successive contacts with the German Chancellor made it clear that it was impossible for Germany to take a strong stand in the event of an Italo-French conflict, an opinion shared by De Bosardi because of Germany's political weakness and low morale.

The third volume of this series begins with the annexation of Fiume (February 22, 1924) and ends with the appointment of Dino Grandi as Undersecretary for Foreign Affairs (May 14, 1925), a period characterized by no events of major importance but from which it is possible to study the evolution of Fascist foreign policy and to note its characteristic aspects.

After the tension provoked by the Corfu crisis, Mussolini's diplomatic actions were distinctly unprovocative. Insofar as the League of Nations was concerned, he abandoned almost entirely his previous strongly critical position. At the same time, he moved rapidly toward a *rapprochement* with the British, which, after the designation of Austen Chamberlain to the Foreign Office, was to lead to very cordial relations between London and Rome.

This fluctuation from one extreme to another, this alternation of adventurous and nonadventurous policies, was, as has been noted, a characteristic of Mussolini's actions that was already apparent during the Ruhr crisis and subsequently revealed many times. Even in this "relaxed" phase, however, there were uncertainties and second thoughts indicating that a nonaggressive foreign policy was not particularly suited to the mentality of the Italian Prime Minister and Minister of Foreign Affairs. On the one hand, Mussolini was impelled to support a revision of the Treaty of

Versailles—which was the only really new element in his policies when compared to those of his predecessors—but, on the other hand, he hesitated to break with Italy's ex-allies, and it is from these uncertainties, rather than from a well-thought-out political design, that Italy's "equidistant position" emerged, a position that Italy assumed in the face of more and more obvious differences between the *status quo* and the revisionist powers. Even the implementation of the "Pacts of Rome" signed between Italy and Yugoslavia on January 27, 1924, revealed analogous oscillations. These accords were to have established the necessary premises for the reduction of tension in the Adriatic and, at the same time, to pave the way for a definite solution of the Fiume question. However, relations with Belgrade were relaxed and cordial only for a very brief period and deteriorated rapidly shortly afterwards over the Albanian problem. Thus, the impression was given that in signing the Italo-Yugoslav accords Mussolini, instead of paving the way for a good-neighbor policy, intended to eliminate French influence from Yugoslavia and to weaken the Little Entente in order to set the stage for a dynamic Italian policy in the Balkans, a hypothesis that successive developments of Fascist policy were to confirm in full.

To this should be added the perennially restless character of Italian diplomacy in almost every area: in the eastern Mediterranean relations between Italy and Turkey had become so strained as to lend credence to the rumors that war between the two was imminent; in Morocco Mussolini, in the hope of acquiring submarine bases, thought of intervening as mediator in the conflict between Abd-el-Krim and Spain. In the majority of cases, these adventures bordered on the ridiculous and were usually abandoned under the pressure of frantic objections by various high officials in the Foreign Office. Yet, despite these controlling influences, these proposals had a certain importance, if only because they contributed toward alarming others and alienating understanding and friendships.

The next volume, the fourth of the seventh series, covers the period to February 6, 1927, that is, the date on which the Ambassadors to London and Paris, della Torretta and Romano Avezzana, were replaced and the office of Secretary-General of the Foreign Office, hitherto occupied by Chiaramonte Bordonaro, was left vacant. These changes mark an important turning point in Fascist foreign policy. First, with the removal of diplomats of the old school from two key posts, it marks the Fascistization of the Foreign Service. Second, it marks the strengthening of the power of the Undersecretary for Foreign Affairs, Dino Grandi. The period covered—almost two years—is greater than that of previous volumes, a factor that imposed a more restrictive selection, especially with regard to certain negotiations, but, nevertheless, the picture that emerges is useful for an over-all evaluation of this phase of Fascist foreign policy.

Mussolini's attitude regarding the Locarno Pacts confirms his coolness toward a system which, by guaranteeing only Germany's western frontiers, might direct German revisionism toward Austria and reopen discussions on the Brenner frontier. His preoccupation with this problem appeared to be justified by the British government's attitude during the negotiations, when it refused to guarantee the German frontiers other than those with Belgium and France, and by the information repeatedly confirmed, despite the denials of the British Foreign Office, that the British Ambassador to Berlin, D'Abernon, was urging the German leaders to effect the *Anschluss*.

This situation led the French government to propose to Rome a two-power pact ensuring the *status quo* in the matter of Germany's southern frontier, an offer which, despite Romano Avezzana's support, Mussolini preferred to refuse, principally for reasons of prestige. Nevertheless, it is interesting to note that on June 8, 1925, Mussolini did not exclude the possibility that at some future date Italy might accept the *Anschluss* on condition that special safeguards would be forthcoming in the matter of the Brenner Pass frontier. Yet at the time the prospects for such an agreement were exceedingly remote since the rapport between Rome and Berlin was not particularly close. The episode serves to confirm once again the facility with which the Fascist dictator would shift from one position to a diametrically opposite one. As a matter of fact, a few months earlier Mussolini had wired Romano Avezzana affirming that an Austro-German *Anschluss* would make Italy the only Entente power to emerge from the war a defeated nation in that she would find on her northern frontier a powerful, ethnically homogenous state instead of a decadent empire—words of wisdom that were to be completely forgotten fourteen years later. It is lamentable that this extremely significant document was not included in the volume in question, which also omits the minutes of the Italian delegation to the Locarno Conference, published by the Soviet government in a collection mentioned elsewhere.[103] In summary, it may be concluded that Italian participation in formulating the Locarno agreements was determined by two basic considerations: first, the desire not to be excluded from any action affecting the fundamental organization of Europe, and second, the desire to maintain close ties with Great Britain.

In this period also, Anglo-Italian collaboration was a cardinal rule in Fascist foreign policy. In view of this, it would have been interesting to

[103] See p. 173.

locate some evidence of the content of the Chamberlain-Mussolini conversations at Rapallo on December 29, 1925, during which it was believed that accords of major importance were reached (such as Italian support for the British position in the Anglo-Turkish quarrel over Mosul and British support for Italian aspirations in Ethiopia), but the documents here do not cast any light on this question. Although Mussolini's notes on these conversations cannot be located, it would have been useful to refer to some other pertinent document, or at least to mention in a footnote the fact that documentary material on this meeting is not to be found.

Instead, Mussolini's notes on his conversations with Chamberlain at Leghorn on September 30, 1926, have been published. This event had a profound effect on European diplomatic circles and was generally considered to be a counterpoint to the Briand-Stresemann encounter at Thoiry. It evidenced the concern, perhaps greater in Rome than in London, with which the growing Franco-German friendship was viewed. According to the notes prepared by Mussolini and approved by Chamberlain several days later, it becomes apparent that the Leghorn meeting, despite its outward significance, was in fact of much less importance than was thought at the time. The question of Franco-German relations, as discussed by Chamberlain and above all by Mussolini, revealed the concern of the two leaders for the consequences an eventual Franco-German alliance would have on the European balance of power. However, the major points of interest may be reduced to two: Mussolini's declaration concerning Albanian independence, and Chamberlain's implied support of Italian aspirations in Asia Minor in the event of a Turkish collapse, an event considered not impossible at that time. And also, on the basis of these notes, it should be mentioned that insofar as Albania was concerned, and contrary to what was believed at the time, Mussolini did not inform Chamberlain of the status of the negotiations for a treaty then under way with Zog, nor did he mention the content that the treaty might eventually have; thus the possibility of British pre-agreement to the treaty of November 27, 1926, is excluded.

An important part of the material included in this volume concerns the Balkans, where the Italian government was exceedingly active in seeking to extend its influence in competition with France. The plan, proposed by Beneš in May, 1925, for a Danubian confederation which, in effect, would have reconstructed the Hapsburg system under the guidance of Prague and Vienna and fostered by the French was successfully blocked by Palazzo Chigi. This was followed by a discussion of the feasibility of a four-power pact between Italy, Yugoslavia, Czechoslovakia, and Austria, but Mussolini failed to pursue the proposal further because such an arrangement would have implied a guarantee of the Yugoslav frontiers against

Hungarian revisionism and would have severly restricted Italy's freedom of action. In reality, here as elsewhere the Fascist government's actions lacked the consistency necessary for the attainment of its objectives. On the one hand, Italy evinced constant preoccupation with the prospect of *Anschluss* and sought support for maintaining Austria's independence, to this end concluding a pact with Rumania—antirevisionist power par excellence—in the hope of weakening the French position in Bucharest; on the other hand, Rome pursued a policy of building a ring around Yugoslavia by extending Italian control in Albania and by encouraging Hungarian revisionism at the expense of Yugoslavia. There is much on these questions that is new in these documents. For example, it bears noting that, contrary to what has been generally believed, the Italo-Rumanian treaty of September 26, 1926, did not contain any secret clauses other than an exchange of letters concerning the question of recognition of the Rumanian acquisition of Bessarabia, recognition that had been repeatedly postponed by Rome, despite constant Rumanian pressure, in order not to aggravate Moscow. Now, the fact that Baron Aloisi in his dairy[104] (he was Italian Minister to Bucharest at the time when negotiations began) refers to a secret portion of the treaty indicates certain incongruities. It would have been of real value if, in a footnote, Aloisi had clarified the question of whether a gap existed in the Italian documentation or his comment was to be understood as a reference to the above-mentioned letter on Bessarabia. That letter, at the moment of the renewal of the Italo-Rumanian treaty (the period when Aloisi's diary was written), no longer had any factual validity, since the Italian government had long since recognized Rumania's acquisition of Bessarabia. In substance, at the beginning of the negotiations the Rumanian government had proposed an out-and-out military alliance, but the idea was soon abandoned, and during the course of the negotiations the outline of the treaty became more and more generalized, especially when Rome realized that a treaty would not be sufficient to wean Bucharest from a strong pro-French policy.

The eighth series of the Italian diplomatic documents deals with the period from the Stresa conference to the outbreak of the war. Its final two volumes have been published, that is, Volumes XII and XIII. The commission sought in this way to meet the requirements of scholars whose attention was focused, as it was immediately after the end of World War I, on the developments occurring during the final crisis before the outbreak of war, even though in the case of World War II the search for war responsibility presents problems that are far less complex.

[104] Baron Aloisi, *Journal* (Paris: Plon, 1957), p. 41.

The twelfth volume opens with the day after the signing of the Pact of Steel and closes on the eve of the Salzburg meeting, August 11–13, 1939. One characteristic of the material is the obvious imbalance between the number of dispatches sent by the missions abroad and the number dispatched by the Ministry of Foreign Affairs. This imbalance is not due to the existence of specific lacunae in the archives, much less to the adoption of restrictive criteria of selection, but is the result of a phenomenon which, beginning with World War I, continued to develop during the Fascist period.

In substance, during those years the concept of the "colloquy" between the Ministry and the missions abroad all but disappeared, and in practice the missions were forced to act without being adequately informed as to the general lines of the nation's foreign policy. The instructions sent by Palazzo Chigi were often limited to a statement of the steps to be taken, without their incorporation into a more complete framework of policy and without explanation of the nature of the aims to be achieved.

This phenomenon, emerging as the result of Sonnino's insistence on secrecy during the negotiations leading to the Pact of London of 1915, was observable during the Paris peace conference, when the Foreign Minister and the Secretary-General were in the French capital. It crystallized during the Secretary-Generalship of Contarini, who was completely averse to recording his thoughts in writing; after six years in office he left very few papers of his own.[105] By 1939 the practice was fully established and would later be carried to even further extremes. Undoubtedly, this accounts for the imbalance noted above. Nevertheless, it should also be emphasized that in specific cases it was accentuated by the lack of activity at the center.

The limited activity at Palazzo Chigi during this period originated not only in Ciano's frequent absences from Rome (at first, from June 26–July 2, because of the death of his father, and then from July 9–19, during his visit to Spain), but also in the conviction that for the moment the prospect of imminent conflict was remote. It was precisely this assumption that lay at the roots of the repeated manifestations of solidarity with Germany, and, in effect, it was the premise that justified subscribing to the Pact of Steel in those encompassing and absolute terms demanded by the Germans and accepted by the Italians without any particular reservations.

Undoubtedly, this optimistic view was strengthened by the fact that the German government had not met its obligations toward its ally by keeping the latter informed of German plans for the immediate future. In Milan,

---

[105] See Raffaele Guariglia, *Ricordi* (Naples: E.S.I., 1950), pp. 19–20.

during the meeting of the previous May 5–6, Ciano and Von Ribbentrop had re-emphasized the need to postpone any conflict with the western democracies for a four- to five-year period; and immediately following the signing of the Pact of Steel, Mussolini had reopened the question in the famous "Memoriale Cavallero," to which Von Ribbentrop replied that Hitler was "in general, in complete agreement." In reality, it is well known that the German assurances contained a mental reservation; that is, the Nazis distinguished between a general war and a localized war with Poland. Von Ribbentrop believed the latter to be highly likely, despite the precise warnings of the possibility of a general war given by Chamberlain and Daladier.

This misunderstanding, due in part to German insincerity and in part to Italian superficiality, was destined to continue for some time, despite the desperate appeals of Attolico, who, especially after the end of June, never ceased insisting that steps be taken to clarify the situation.

It is interesting to observe the reactions provoked by these warnings through the pages of Ciano's diary: Attolico is seen as something of a visionary in the throes of an "endemic crisis of fear," a man "who has lost his head"; "he is frightened by his own shadow." It was only toward the end of July that Ciano began to entertain his first doubts: "Either this ambassador has completely lost his head," he writes on August 2, "or he is aware of something that completely escapes us." Finally, a meeting was arranged to clarify the situation.

At the Salzburg meeting (the thirteenth volume of the eighth series opens with this encounter) Ciano was suddenly brought face to face with reality. Hitler and Von Ribbentrop were now determined to attack Poland, convinced that the war would be localized because neither Great Britain nor France would do anything more than offer formal protests.

The Salzburg conversations, to be examined again when we look at the content of the collection of *Ciano's Diplomatic Papers,* were to end on a note of misunderstanding. After having tried to convince Hitler and Von Ribbentrop—unsuccessfully—that a localized war with Poland was pure fantasy, Ciano, toward the end of the meeting, adopted an attitude of uncertainty. He did not accept the German view but did not make clear his objections. The result was that the Germans were convinced that they had Italy's complete support while, on the Italian side, the objections to a policy that would inevitably lead to a general war remained.

In any event, the Salzburg meeting had the immediate effect of clarifying the realities of the situation for Ciano and thus impelled him to move as quickly as possible to avoid plunging Italy into war. However, the undertaking was not an easy one. First of all, it was necessary to convince

Mussolini to take the necessary steps, a task that involved overcoming *il Duce*'s continued vacillations: at one moment he was determined to lend his complete support to Germany "in order not to re-enact the about-face of 1914"; at another moment he was inclined to declare Italy's nonbelligerency in view of the country's unpreparedness; at still another, he was ready to side with Hitler in order to take advantage of the situation to "liquidate" Yugoslavia.

Mussolini's vacillations made Ciano's task extremely difficult and made the latter's momentary successes always precarious. However, without these inconstancies Ciano's efforts would not have been possible. It must be remembered that even in the field of foreign affairs final decisions were always made only by Mussolini, and his collaborators were limited to acting only in those areas where *il Duce*'s will had not yet been determined.

At this point (August, 1939) Mussolini had not yet made a final decision on what course of action to take, and Ciano's endeavors did produce some positive results, thanks also to the concomitance of other factors. There was the uncertainty of the outcome of the struggle between Germany and the western powers and the hope, extremely appealing to Mussolini, that he might be able, for the second time, to play the role of mediator and repeat on a much larger scale the success he had achieved at Munich.

On the other hand, any effort to break the ties to Germany was fraught with difficulties. The Italian government's desperate attempts, which were designed to rectify once and for all existing misunderstandings, to reopen conversations with the Germans were ignored by Hitler and Von Ribbentrop, who believed that they had brought the consultation to a successful conclusion and saw no need for further talks.

The misunderstanding was abruptly clarified on August 25, when Hitler received a letter from Mussolini in which *il Duce* made known the Italian decision not to intervene in a general war provoked by a German attack on Poland. This decision caught the Germans completely by surprise, but it is unlikely that it was the sole reason for Hitler's decision to postpone the attack on Poland, which had previously been set for August 26. Instead, the postponement was primarily due to the news of the signing of the Anglo-Polish alliance, an event that obviously made the prediction of a localization of the conflict somewhat problematical. In order to understand the situation prevalent in Rome during those decisive days and the state of mind of the Italian dictator, it must be recalled that Mussolini, in writing to Hitler, took his cue from a letter the German Chancellor had written to him on August 25 informing him of the conclusion of the negotiations with the Soviet Union. The Nazi-Soviet Pact served to dispel the last remaining doubts in Mussolini's mind, although prior to this steps had been taken to prepare letters and notes designed to bring the Germans up to date on the realities of the situation. However, none of these notes was ever sent to Berlin.[106]

Most of these events were already known through disclosures in other sources (*Ciano's Diplomatic Papers* and the Hitler-Mussolini correspondence), but the material included in the Italian collection serves to complete the picture. For example, the steps taken by the British Embassy in Rome to inform the Italian government of the negotiations under way between London and Berlin can be put in their proper perspective. In the beginning, at least, the information divulged by the British Embassy was designed to facilitate Mussolini's intervention in the crisis as a moderator, but very soon the British government widened the perspective, to all intents with the aim of the creation of an atmosphere of trust between Rome and London which would lead to a collaboration between the two governments that was particularly desirable in view of the circumstances at the time. This explains the care the British took to keep the Italian government continually informed concerning the progress of the negotiations with Berlin and its emphasis on the extremely secret nature of the information transmitted. For example, on August 23 the British Ambassador, Sir Percy Loraine, transmitted the text of Chamberlain's message to Hitler, the text of which, according to the Ambassador's letter, had not been given to the French.

This British action had one particularly important result. It provided Rome once again with a clear demonstration that the Germans kept their ally in the dark in matters concerning German diplomatic activity. A truly paradoxical situation was created; Palazzo Chigi was kept informed on the course of Anglo-German negotiations by its potential adversary, not by its ally. This fact contributed immeasurably toward orienting Mussolini to nonbelligerence.

The material assembled in the first two volumes of the ninth series has substantially different characteristics. Together, these volumes cover the period from the outbreak of the war to December 31, 1939.

The generous selection of documents for these volumes indicates that practically all of the material of any interest preserved in the ministerial archives is included. These volumes offer an exceptionally wide panorama, which, in addition to clarifying the action of Italian diplomacy during the period of nonbelligerency, furnishes information of great interest for the reconstruction of the atmosphere prevalent during the first months of the

[106] On the crisis in Italo-German relations during the summer of 1939 and on the events leading to Italy's declaration of nonbelligerence, see Ettore Anchieri, "Dal convegno di Salisburgo alla non belligeranza italiana," *Il Politico*, I (1954), 23–43.

war. The inactivity on the western front kept alive virtually everywhere the hope that the conflict could be resolved without further bloodshed.

The various peace initiatives, the reactions aroused by the events in Poland and by the further concrete manifestations of Soviet-German collaboration, the evolution of government positions and of public opinion in the direction of increasing rigidity—all pointed to all-out war. These developments may be traced with consummate clarity in the dispatches sent by Attolico, Rosso, Guariglia, and other heads of mission; even if they do not reveal anything new, they contribute a great deal toward a comprehension of the events and of their psychological background.

Perhaps the most important documents are those that serve to illustrate Italo-German relations beginning with Italy's declaration of nonbelligerence. The reaction of the German public to this unexpected decision was undoubtedly intense, since the German people, of course, were not aware of the differences that had developed between the two countries during the last phase of the crisis. There were many signs of dissatisfaction following the outbreak of hostilities. German official circles displayed either an attitude of complete comprehension of the Italian action or one of absolute reticence. However, the actual state of mind of the Nazi leaders on this issue emerges with great clarity from the minutes of the meetings between Goering and Magistrati and those with the Air Attaché, Teucci. In the conversations with Teucci in particular, Goering did not hide his disappointment with the Italian position, which, even if under certain conditions it could be useful to Germany, did not fail to arouse extremely negative psychological reactions in the Germans.

Toward the middle of October, when the possibilities of a compromise peace, a project in which Italy could have played a major role and amply satisfied Mussolini's personal ambitions, had all but vanished, Italian diplomatic activity entered a less crucial phase. Simultaneously, Italo-German relations worsened. Practical evidence of this was the deterioration of the situation in Alto Adige and the negative turn of the trade negotiations between the two countries. These differences were exploited by Ciano in seeking to give Italian foreign policy a more independent character. Two of these issues are worth recording: the increased tension between the Soviet Union and Italy, in obvious contrast to the policy of close collaboration with the Soviets launched by Von Ribbentrop, and the attempt to create a neutral Balkan bloc under Italian aegis.

While for the first of the two issues the pertinent documents were already known prior to the publication of these volumes,[107] the material on

[107] See Mario Toscano, *Una mancata intesa italo-sovietica nel 1940 e 1941* (Florence: Sansoni, 1953).

the Balkan bloc project is very interesting. Because of its detail, this documentation permits not only the reconstruction of the position assumed by Italy but also the essential elements of the negotiations of the Balkan states with each other, negotiations in which Italy played virtually no role. In fact, Rome only very briefly considered participating in a neutral bloc. The concept of a neutral bloc including Italy appealed to Ciano, who visualized it as a means of strengthening Italian neutrality and of turning his father-in-law away from perilous decisions. However, the idea of a neutral Italy aroused absolutely no enthusiasm in Mussolini, who considered the label "neutral" as something only just short of an insult. In this case, too, the complete lack of agreement existing between the head of the Fascist state and his Foreign Minister on the real meaning of nonbelligerence is brought to light. Mussolini understood nonbelligerence to be a temporary expedient made necessary by Italy's military unpreparedness, which was to end as soon as possible, with Italy taking her place alongside her German ally. Ciano, instead, saw nonbelligerence, for the moment at least, as the first step toward neutrality and, in any event, a position that should be strengthened until such time as events permitted more opportune decisions to be made.

Volume III of the ninth series covers the period January 1–April 8, 1940 (the date of the German attack against Denmark and Norway), which was a period of fundamental importance for the story of Italy's nonbelligerence. It was during these months that Mussolini decided to enter the war against the western democracies on the side of Germany.

The volume begins with Mussolini's letter to Hitler of January 5, 1940, a letter that seemed to indicate almost totally divergent views between the German Chancellor and the Italian head of state. However, the letter should actually be interpreted as a last attempt by Mussolini to convince Hitler not to attack in the west (Rome had recently been informed of an imminent attack on Belgium) but rather to seek a negotiated solution to the conflict.

Undoubtedly this message aroused deep emotion, but there is no evidence that Berlin ever gave any serious thought to postponing the operations planned for the western front and accepting Mussolini's advice. The procrastination in replying to the Italian letter despite the repeated inquiries by the Italian delegation deepened the already existing concern in Rome. The numerous attempts made by the Italian Embassy in Berlin to ascertain German reaction to the letter of January 5, and later, to find out the causes for the procrastination, provide a valuable indication of the atmosphere prevailing in Germany prior to the attack on the West.

In substance, the reason for ignoring the Italian letter was that all of the Nazi leaders, including Goering—who could be considered representative of the moderates within the Nazi hierarchy—were convinced that the situation would never be more auspicious for an armed resolution of the conflict with Germany's western opponents than it was at that moment. According to them, it was imperative to exploit the situation at all costs in order either to crush Franco-British opposition or, at the least, to achieve such successes as to ensure that negotiations would be conducted on a basis advantageous to Germany. Insofar as Mussolini's attitude was concerned, it is clear that Hitler and his collaborators were convinced, and not without reason, that overwhelming German military victories would be sufficient to change Mussolini's mind.

It is likely that Hitler's reply might have been delayed even longer had it not been for Sumner Welles's visit to Rome in February, 1940. The accomplishments of this visit were, in fact, rather modest, but they led Berlin to fear that Italy might slip into an even more strongly neutralist position. Therefore, on March 8, Hitler decided to dispatch the long-awaited reply and sent Von Ribbentrop to Rome with it. Apparently, the Germans did not expect to reap a rich harvest from this journey, despite the fact that in recent days several of Mussolini's personal actions demonstrated him to be somewhat more favorably inclined toward Germany than he had been in the immediate past. Actually, according to what can be deduced from a note probably prepared during the morning of March 10, prior to Mussolini's colloquy with Von Ribbentrop, it does not appear that the Italian head of state intended to abandon his erstwhile critical attitude, much less to assume any precise commitments. The first meeting took place the same day at Palazzo Venezia, at which time Mussolini maintained an attitude of cold reserve. However, on the following day things changed dramatically and in a manner that even now cannot be clearly understood. Nothing in the course of the conversations justified such action, but Mussolini at one point abruptly declared that Italy could not remain outside of the conflict and that at the appropriate time it would enter the war on the side of her ally. Despite the fact that no date was set for Italian intervention, a factor that gave the commitment considerable elasticity, it is indisputable that Mussolini had not only completely abandoned his previous position and categorically confirmed Italy's solidarity with Germany, but had also heavily compromised Italy's future freedom of action. The Brenner Pass meeting of March 18, often referred to as the occasion that brought about this abrupt shift in the Italian position, simply confirmed the result achieved by the Mussolini-Von Ribbentrop meeting of March 10. At the Brenner Pass, it should be noted, Mussolini parried Hitler's repeated attempts to ascertain the precise date of

Italy's intervention. Mussolini repeated that time was required in order to complete Italy's military preparations and that, in any event, Italy did not have the means to sustain a long war.

Just how deep the change was in Mussolini's position is clearly established by the documents contained in the fourth volume of this series, which carries the story to Italy's entrance into the war on June 10, 1940. *Il Duce*'s replies to the numerous messages sent by President Roosevelt, the British and French Prime Ministers, and the Pope are very revealing. The fact is that Mussolini sidestepped every opportunity to reopen a dialogue with the western democracies. Furthermore, the negotiations under way with the British to resolve the difficulties created by the blockade were abruptly broken off despite the conciliatory offers made by London. What was even more serious, the blockade question was used from that moment on as an instrument of internal propaganda in order to prepare public opinion for the conflict.

The German military victories had a decisive effect on Mussolini's attitude toward the democracies and on Italo-German relations. At the time of the conversations with Von Ribbentrop and the Brenner Pass meeting, Mussolini, despite the fact that he was now determined to enter the war as Germany's ally, held that the Italian declaration of war could not come before the spring of 1941. After the Norway campaign had revealed once again the startling efficiency of the German military machine, in contrast to the hesitations and uncertainties of the western powers, the Fascist leader advanced the date for Italy's intervention to early September, 1940. Germany's overwhelming victories in the French campaign brought about further changes in Mussolini's plans. The fear of arriving too late to participate in the war against France induced Mussolini to reduce the time schedule even further and to thrust his country into a war that he—like so many others—believed would not last more than a week or two. The documents in this volume prove once again that the affirmation that Mussolini was not sufficiently informed on the true state of Italy's military and economic unpreparedness for war is totally without foundation. The Fascist leader knew very well that Italy could not undertake a long war, but he was convinced that immediately after the fall of France—now a foregone conclusion—Great Britain would also be forced to sue for peace. Consequently, the idea of a long war was not a factor to be considered.

Therefore, the Italian intervention occurred under conditions which, from a military point of view, did not allow any serious prospects of success if the conflict should last longer than a month or two. Nevertheless, in this case Italy found herself again in a difficult position because the unpreparedness of the Italian armed forces was so great as to make it impossible to achieve victories of the magnitude necessary to justify Mussolini's claims against Great Britain and France and to counterbalance in part the grandiose German victories.

These disadvantages were to influence, in large measure, Mussolini's subsequent actions and the relations between the Axis powers during the second half of 1940. The fifth volume, whose publication is imminent, throws considerable light on these matters, particularly on Mussolini's French policy and his activities in the Danubian-Balkan area.

While the German victories on the western front had constituted the premise for Italy's intervention, they also aroused justifiable concern over the prospect of the Europe of tomorrow under the complete domination of Germany. It is characteristic that at the very moment of Italy's entrance into the war Mussolini's actions reflected this concern. In seeking a counterweight to German hegemony, the Fascist leader made preliminary moves toward a *rapprochement* with the Soviet Union (normal diplomatic relations were reopened and the possibility of a political agreement was also probed[108]), and he avoided humiliating France by demanding armistice terms that would have been too onerous, in order to leave the door open for possible future collaboration with Paris. Typical was the decision, made spontaneously by Mussolini, not to insist on the armistice demands, approved by Hitler at Munich, for Italian occupation of Corsica, Tunisia, Djibuti, and the left bank of the Rhone. However, this moderate attitude toward France underwent a rapid change when it became evident that Franco-German collaboration was not beyond the realm of possibility and that it could lead to the reopening of discussions on the Italian claims, as well as threaten Italy's position as Germany's principal ally.

Again, fear of German hegemony must be considered basic in Mussolini's Balkan projects during this period. The certainty that, once the war was brought to a victorious end, Hitler would treat the Balkans as an exclusively German sphere of influence, at best with recognition of certain Soviet interests but with Italian ones ignored, induced Mussolini to conceive the idea of immediately extending control over those zones of greatest interest to Italy. Italian projects for attacks on Yugoslavia and Greece were twice vetoed by Hitler, who desired to maintain peace in the Balkans in order not to endanger the important sources of supply for the German war machine (Rumanian oil). However, the German occupation of Rumania induced the Fascist head of state to prepare the attack against Greece as a means of re-establishing the equilibrium upset by Hitler's Rumanian venture. As is well known, the attack against Greece was a total

[108] *Ibid.*

failure, the reason being (as is confirmed by the documents) the conviction that the enterprise would be resolved on a political plane rather than on a military one. The consequences of this blunder were enormous and ended with the complete subordination of Italy to Germany in the military and political conduct of the war.

The publication of the volume of German documents for the same period has reduced the news value of a part of the material contained in this volume (which terminates with the Hitler-Mussolini encounter of January 19–20, 1941), particularly as it concerns the second arbitrage of Vienna and the negotiations for Spanish intervention. Regarding the arbitrage, it should be noted that in the Italian volume a number of documents have been included that have considerable interest for the study of the Bulgarian-Rumanian negotiations undertaken to resolve the Dobrudja controversy and the Hungarian-Rumanian conversations on the Transylvanian question. On the issue of Spanish intervention the documents reveal that Mussolini was not especially interested in pressing for Spain's entry into the war, an intervention which would have compromised Italy's position as Germany's only Mediterranean ally.

Several factors contribute toward making the Italian collection of diplomatic documents the one which perhaps best meets scholarly requirements. In the first place, it should be noted that the objectives of the publication are essentially historical: the present Italian governments have no particular ax to grind, nor do they have to deny any particular accusations of "responsibility," as did most of the other collections dealing with the origins of World War I. Insofar as Fascist foreign policy is concerned, the present Italian governments require simply that as much light as possible be cast on the period in order that a completely objective historical evaluation may be drawn—the political evaluation has long since been made.

These conditions have made it possible for the commission charged with the publication to carry out its obligations completely free of any real or implied restrictions; in other countries, despite protests to the contrary, certain political considerations had to be taken into account. As a case in point, it should be noted that the first volume of the seventh series contains a letter from Count Sforza to the Secretary-General of the Ministry of Foreign Affairs, Contarini, in which Sforza refers to the possibility of joining the Mussolini government as Minister of Foreign Affairs. This letter was selected for inclusion in the collection at the very time that Count Sforza was Minister of Foreign Affairs in the postwar government.

A second element that enhances the value of the collection is the exceptionally broad criteria adopted in the selection of material. Thus, documents referring to specific problems, as well as general documents, are included. Only those documents dealing with matters of a purely episodic character, which did not have the slightest effect on the over-all conduct of foreign policy, are excluded. It should also be mentioned that the material contained in the ministerial files has been integrated with that found in the other archives when it was decided that the added material would be useful in reconstructing the story. This procedure has been followed to an extent that has no precedent in the collections published by other countries. The following examples illustrate the variety of sources, in addition to the normal sources for diplomatic documents, from which materials for the Italian collection were drawn: the Avarna-Bollati and the San Giuliano-Salandra correspondence, the Orlando papers, the archives of the House of Savoy, the Caetani papers, the Visconti Venosta archives, and the Blanc archive. To a varying degree, depending on the period under consideration, documentary material from such archives as those of the military ministries and the office of the Prime Minister has also been included.

Equally broad criteria were used to determine whether the collection should be based on telegrams or on reports. Naturally, the texts of telegrams are more cryptic, but they offer the advantage of establishing the precise moment and the method in which the information first reached the ministry, a factor that is of singular importance during a crisis period, when decisions must be made rapidly. On the other hand, the reports contain the same information in greater detail. Since both types of communication present advantages and disadvantages, the commission decided to publish both the telegrams and the reports when they refer to problems of major importance or when the reports add new data.

A study of the other collections made it possible to avoid a number of weaknesses and to benefit from the experiences of others in choosing the best of the available solutions. Accordingly, the commission chose to organize the material chronologically, by the transmission date of the communication, in order to avoid the inconveniences and the negative features of compilations by subject matter. In addition, very special care was taken in preparing the tables of contents, indexes, and appendixes. There is a summary table of contents, where reference is made to each document, the date sent, the names of the sender and the addressee, and a brief summary of its contents; a subject matter table, wherein the documents are grouped according to the problem to which they refer; an index of persons, including the office they held during the period covered by the volume; an appendix listing the embassies and legations of the Kingdom of Italy abroad and the personnel attached to each; a second appendix listing the personnel attached to the various offices of the Ministry of Foreign Affairs; and, finally, a third appendix listing the embassies and legations accredited to Rome and the personnel of each of these.

In addition to the collection of Italian diplomatic documents, the Ministry of Foreign Affairs has also published a series of volumes documenting Italian undertakings in Africa. A special committee is in charge of this project.

Given the nature of this publication, which is designed to illustrate Italian activities in several areas, not all of the volumes are of interest to diplomatic history. However, those that include the material from the historical section[109] serve as a supplement to the collection of Italian diplomatic documents and are of great value for the study of the colonial aspect of Italian foreign policy. Furthermore, this integrative character provided the guideline for the selection of the material. In cases where the document specifically refers to colonial affairs but concerns Italian foreign policy in general, only the essential elements of the problem are cited in the Africa series and reference is made to the complete text in the collection of Italian diplomatic documents. Conversely, in those cases where it is convenient and justified, the documents are included in the volumes of the historical section of *Italia in Africa* and omitted from the diplomatic document collection.

The archives providing the bulk of the documents included in these volumes are those of the ex-Ministry for Italian Africa, created in 1937 to replace the old Ministry for the Colonies instituted in 1912. Prior to 1912, African affairs were handled by special offices within the Ministry of Foreign Affairs, whose papers formed the original nucleus of the archives of the Colonial Ministry. After the suppression of the Ministry for Italian Africa the historico-political portion of its archives was returned to the historical archive of the Ministry of Foreign Affairs, together with the archive of the Government for Colonial Eritrea, which is the only archive of the former Italian colonies that did not suffer war damage.

Two volumes of documents of the historical section have been published to date and cover the period 1859–85. The new material here is found in the volume prepared by Carlo Giglio, who drew from these documents, as well as from all other available sources in Italy; Giglio's volume precedes the two volumes of documents in the historical section of *Italia in Africa*. Among the many interesting questions discussed, reference

[109] *L'Italia in Africa*, Serie storica, Vol. I: *Etiopia-Mar Rosso;* Vols. II and III, *documenti, 1859–1882 and 1882–1885* (Rome: Istituto Poligrafico dello Stato, 1959–60).

is made here only to two, in order to illustrate the nature of the contribution these documents made to the exact reconstruction of Italian colonial history.

The first question is that of the occupation of Assab (December, 1879) and the ensuing diplomatic conflict with Egypt (which claimed jurisdiction over the area) and with Great Britain, until the conclusion of the Anglo-Italian *modus vivendi* of February, 1882, which provided British recognition for Italy's first African possession. The documents pertinent to this question had been the subject of the Green Book *Assab,* which emphasized the elements of accord, rather than those of discord, with the British government. Now, the newly published material suggests a correction in the judgment rendered on the basis of the Green Book. London was strongly opposed to Italy's African projects, and the Italian Minister, Benedetto Cairoli, was able to overcome this opposition by a diplomatic coup, which guaranteed that Italy would not convert Assab into a military base but would allow it to remain the commercial port it had been ever since the day it was acquired by the Rubattino Company. Nor was Cairoli's achievement any the less impressive because he had to deal with Gladstone's Liberal government after April, 1880, since the Liberals maintained the same position on the question as had the preceding Disraeli government. Even if the Anglo-Italian *modus vivendi* was perfected by Pasquale Stanislao Mancini, Cairoli's efforts should not be forgotten, even more because his name in Italian colonial history is usually linked only to the renunciatory position taken by his government on the Tunisian question.

The second question is that of the next step taken by Italy in Africa, the occupation of Massaua in February, 1885. It has been generally accepted by Italian historians that Great Britain urged Italy to occupy Massaua, while the Green Book *Massaua,* published at the time, makes no reference to the Anglo-Italian-Egyptian understandings that had laid the diplomatic groundwork for this occupation. The rich documentation available in these two recently published volumes now makes it possible to trace the development of the events in detail. It is correct to conclude that in 1884, when the Egyptian garrisons evacuated the southern coast of the Red Sea and the Somali coast, British and Italian interests coincided in their desire to prevent the French from extending their control in the region. Despite the fact that the British government preferred an Italian occupation of the region to a French one, it showed no inclination to accept the view advanced by the Minister of Foreign Affairs, Mancini, to consider the occupation of Massaua as a service for which London should pay a price in other areas. For a time the British parried every invitation to discuss the issue by inviting the Italians to discuss the matter with the Turks, although the sovereignty of the latter in the area was contested. Only after tedious diplomatic negotiations were the Italians able to obtain a commitment from the British that they would not oppose the enterprise. In this case, too, it was impossible to reach a real agreement because, according to London, the Italian occupation of Massaua was to be considered as temporary, comparable to the British occupation of Egypt, while Rome was determined to make the occupation permanent.

In order to complete the references to the Italian documentary sources for this period, attention must be called to several collections published privately, some of intrinsic value. This unusual method of publication was made possible by the unique situation in which Italy found itself after the war.

A volume of letters exchanged between Mussolini and Hitler during the period 1939–43 is of particular interest.[110] The exchange of personal notes had been initiated by Hitler in March, 1938, on the eve of the *Anschluss*. The German Chancellor wrote directly to Mussolini to explain the reasons for his decision, in order to avoid any surprises of the 1934 variety. From this time on, the two dictators corresponded with increasing frequency, occasionally breaking off during times of stress, such as the period at the beginning of World War II when Italo-German relations had entered a critical phase.

Hitler resorted to the personal letter whenever he wanted to communicate his most important decisions to Rome (for example, the occupation of Czechoslovakia, the attack on Poland, the invasion of Denmark and Norway, the attack on France, the attack on the Soviet Union). These communications were usually delivered on the eve of the event, occasionally only a few hours before it, a practice that infuriated Mussolini, who, faced with a *fait accompli,* was obliged to approve publicly the actions of his German counterpart in order not to weaken the Axis. This fact must be kept in mind in order to understand Mussolini's psychological attitude toward Hitler and the reasons for a number of his undertakings, such as the attack on Greece, which was also conceived as an imitation of German practice. On the other hand, the public statements of support that the *Duce* was forced to give to Hitler's acts of force led London and Paris to conclude that the two dictators acted in full accord. This conclusion prevented the western democracies from exploiting the right psychological moment to weaken the Axis. A typical case in point was when the German government, in violation of the obligations it had assumed at the Munich conference, occupied Czechoslovakia. Once again Mussolini was taken by

[110] *Hitler e Mussolini, Letture e documenti* (Milan: Rizzoli, 1946).

surprise and reacted violently. He particularly feared that Hitler was also planning a coup against Croatia. However, the British and the French became aware of the situation only after several days had elapsed and when the acute crisis had been dissipated by assurances given to Rome by Hitler.

The collection of letters referred to here was obviously taken from the files in Mussolini's office, files which went astray in April, 1945. When the letters were compared with the copies preserved in the ministerial archives, they proved to be authentic. However, the privately published collection is incomplete. First, it does not include the correspondence prior to August, 1939. Second, there are a number of rather wide gaps of considerable historical interest.[111] For example, the two letters exchanged on June 22, 1940, are missing; as has been noted, it was in these letters, contrary to what was generally believed, that the decision was made not to include in the Italo-French armistice clauses giving the Italians the right to occupy the left bank of the Rhone, Corsica, Tunisia, and Djibuti. This decision was made by Mussolini, and not under pressure from Hitler, who received the news with obvious dissatisfaction. A truly impressive letter (it too is missing from this collection) is the one sent by Hitler to Mussolini on April 5, 1941, on the eve of the attack on Yugoslavia. In it the German Chancellor assumed the direction of operations in very explicit terms and proposed a plan whereby he would send to Mussolini, in the form of recommendations and requests, the necessary orders, which Mussolini, in turn, would transmit to the Italian High Command as his own directives. The fact that this humiliating ploy was readily accepted by Mussolini revealed the extent of Italy's subordination to Germany after the Italian military failures of the winter of 1940–41.

[111] The correspondence not included in this collection has been published by Mario Toscano in *Epoca*, Nos. 188–95, May 8–June 27, 1954. Using the letter "H" to indicate Hitler and the letter "M" to indicate Mussolini, the following letters are those appearing in *Epoca*:
   March 11, 1938 (H), only those extracts which had been suppressed in the published version; March 25, 1939 (H); August 21, 1939 (M), not sent; March 8, 1940 (H); April 9, 1940 (H); April 10, 1940 (H); April 18, 1940 (H); May 3, 1940 (H); May 9, 1940 (H); May 13, 1940 (H), partial text; May 18, 1940 (M); May 25, 1940 (H); May 31, 1940 (H); June 9, 1940 (H); June 22, 1940 (M); June 22, 1940 (H); July 13, 1940 (H); September 17, 1940 (H); October 19, 1940 (M); February 5, 1941 (H); February 22, 1941 (M); April 5, 1941 (H); April 6, 1941 (M); July 2, 1941 (M); July 20, 1941 (H); July 24, 1941 (M); October 29, 1941 (H); November 6, 1941 (M); December 29, 1941 (H); June 23, 1942 (H); July 22, 1942 (M); August 4, 1942 (H); October 21, 1942 (H), partial text; November 20, 1942 (H); November 26, 1942 (H); May 19, 1943 (H).
These letters have now been published in both the Italian and German diplomatic document collections covering this period.

Notwithstanding these and other important gaps, at the time of publication the collection of the Hitler-Mussolini letters presented material of extraordinary interest. The volume is enriched by the addition of a number of important documents, such as Mussolini's reports on his meetings with Hitler in Munich (June 18, 1940) and Salzburg (April 29–30, May 3, 1942); the minutes of the Feltre meeting (July 19, 1943) and of the Tarvisio conference (August 6, 1943); various intercepted Rome-Berlin telephone conversations of August 26–27, 1939; the minutes of the meetings at Palazzo Venezia of May 29 and October 15, 1940; and several letters from Mussolini to Victor Emanuel III.

Another similar publication of major importance for the reconstruction of Fascist foreign policy for the period 1936–42 is the collection of Ciano's conversations, published in 1948.[112]

After September 8, 1943, the Germans were able to acquire a copy of the collection containing Ciano's minutes, and they took it to Germany to be copied and translated. Perhaps the publication referred to here is based on one of these copies which went astray during the last days of the war. When compared with the dossier in the ministerial archives, this collection proves to be perfectly authentic but, like the preceding one, incomplete. However, this volume includes considerable material that was not a part of the Ciano file but that is, nevertheless, of major importance. The significance of these minutes increases markedly when it is noted that they go back to 1936, a period that is not covered in the Ciano diary, and, for the moment, no other source is comparable to this one in size and interest. Unfortunately, it is the minutes for the period prior to 1939 that are sketchy and contain obvious gaps. Following the occupation of Prague, the minutes become more complete and detailed. However, they should be used carefully, since Ciano tended to use them to influence his father-in-law's thinking. They were prepared in such a way as to give the reader a specific and biased impression by their judicious selection, their emphasis on specific developments, and even, on occasion, by the omission of essential facts.

A typical example is the report on the Salzburg meeting, which was edited in such a way as to prevent Mussolini, in the light of the probable Moscow-Berlin *rapprochement,* from giving his unconditional support to a German attack against Poland, which would have involved Italy in a war with the western democracies. In effect, the minutes on the state of Nazi-Soviet relations are so sketchy that there is little relation between them and what Ciano was told by Hitler and Von Ribbentrop. Further-

[112] *L'Europa verso la catastrofe.*

more, there is no mention of the Soviet telegram announcing Moscow's acceptance of the German proposals, which was delivered, apparently, at the very time when Hitler was talking to Ciano. To be sure, Ciano tended to underrate the importance of the episode[113] and was not convinced that the negotiations were serious. Rather, he feared that the Germans were using the negotiations as a device to win Rome's complete support for Germany's Polish policy. Nevertheless, there is little doubt that the minutes as written did not honestly reflect the true status of the situation and that they were designed primarily to influence Mussolini along lines pre-determined by the Minister of Foreign Affairs.

Two brief printed memoirs presented to the Council of State by two important officials of Palazzo Chigi belong in the category of private collections. The first, the work of Ambassador Aloisi,[114] at one time Mussolini's Chief of Cabinet, is a small collection of reports and telegrams concerning several important episodes that occurred during the initial phases of the Italo-Ethopian conflict.

The second, prepared by Minister Lanza d'Ajeta,[115] at one time Ciano's Chief of Cabinet, includes, among other things, the final report prepared by the Guariglia mission to Lisbon in August, 1943, which was charged with negotiating Italy's withdrawal from the war. The failure of this mission and of the parallel action taken by Minister Berio at Tangier transferred the negotiations from the diplomatic to the military sphere and led to the conclusion of the armistice of Cassibile.

Worth noting as a source for the study of the last days of the neo-Fascist regime in northern Italy and for a reconstruction of the events that led to the armistice of Caserta on April 29, 1945, is Cardinal Schuster's so-called White Book,[116] in the sense that it is a source *sui generis*. It is a collection of ninety-three documents from the archives of the Arch-bishopric of Milan, published in response to many requests for information on the role played by the Milanese *curia* and for data on those collaborating with the *curia* in seeking to save the population from the most serious privations during the last phase of the war and in bringing about the cessation of hostilities in northern Italy without serious damage to the industrial structure of the area.

The negotiations with the German authorities in Italy to achieve these objectives may be traced with reasonable precision through this material. In

[113] See Mario Toscano, *L'Italia e gli accordi tedesco-sovietici dell'agosto, 1939* (Florence: Sansoni, 1955).

[114] Pompeo Aloisi, *La mia attività al servizio della pace* (Rome: Tipografia del Senato, 1946).

[115] Blasco Lanza D'Ajeta, *Documenti prodotti a corredo della memoria presentata al Consiglio di Stato* (Rome: Tipografia Ferraiolo, 1946).

[116] Ildefonso Schuster, *Gil ultimi tempi di un regime* ("La Via"; Milan, 1946).

addition, it contributes to an understanding of the atmosphere existing in northern Italy during the spring of 1945.

6. THE HUNGARIAN AND YUGOSLAV COLLECTIONS.

The history of the Hungarian collection of diplomatic documents has been an especially troubled one.[117] It was started in 1939 by the Budapest government, and the first volume covered the period August, 1919–December, 1920, that is, from the fall of Bela Kun's Communist government to the ratification of the Treaty of Trianon by the Hungarian parliament.

Ever since 1920 there had been a pressing need to demonstrate that the Hungarian delegation to the peace conference had attempted everything possible to effect a modification of the harsh terms of the treaty, and this need induced the Magyar government to assemble, in appropriate volumes, all of the delegation's official correspondence for the period during which it remained in Paris (January–June, 1920), together with a number of notes exchanged between the conference organs and the Budapest government during the preceding period.[118] However, nothing was known either of the activities of the delegation in Paris and of the Hungarian government, beyond the official contacts, or of the diplomatic negotiations leading to the signing of the treaty with the victorious powers and with the neighboring states on Hungarian political and territorial matters. All of the pertinent documents are included in the first volume of this collection, which begins with the diary kept by the Hungarian delegation at Paris.

The importance of this material far transcends the sphere of Hungarian foreign policy. It has made possible a re-examination of a number of contemporary opinions concerning the origins of the Little Entente and French Balkan policy in the immediate postwar period.

In substance, this source proves that in 1920 French policy had assumed definite revisionist characteristics during the negotiations of the Trianon treaty, which led to the Franco-Hungarian accord of June 21, 1920,[119] wherein France promised to act as mediator between Hungary and her

[117] *Papers and Documents relating to the Foreign Relations of Hungary* (Budapest: Royal Hungarian University Press [later Budapest University Press], 1939–46), Vol. I, 1919–20; Vol. II, January–August, 1921; the third volume, September–December, 1921, has not been officially released.

[118] *Les Négociations de la Paix Hongroise (Compte rendu sur les travaux de la Délégation de Paix de Hongrie a Neuilly sur Seine de janvier à mars 1920)* (3 vols.; Budapest: Imprimerie Victor Hornyánszky, 1920–21).

[119] On the question, see Mario Toscano, "L'accordo revisionista franco-ungherese del 1920," *Pagine di storia diplomatica contemporanea* (Milan: Giuffrè, 1963), Vol. I.

neighbors in seeking to eliminate the especially onerous territorial clauses of the Treaty of Trianon. The strongest proponents of the program, which, in addition to keeping Hungary economically and politically subservient to France, would make Budapest the fulcrum of French policy in the Danube, were the Prime Minister and Minister of Foreign Affairs, Millerand, and the Secretary-General of the Quai d'Orsay, Paléologue. For the reason given above, they initially blocked the creation of the antirevisionist entente proposed by Beneš, which would have included Yugoslavia, Czechoslovakia, and Rumania.

Their efforts were doomed to failure when, unknown to Paris, Beneš concluded an accord with Yugoslavia on August 14, 1920. At the same time, Beneš was plotting within the Bourbon Palace for Paléologue's dismissal from the post of Secretary-General, and, by cleverly exploiting the existing political factions in France, he succeeded in his maneuver. To be sure, he was aided by the election of Millerand to the presidency of the French Republic, which thus removed him from his key post in the Quai d'Orsay. With the appointment of Berthelot to the post vacated by Paléologue, French Balkan policy underwent a complete reversal. France abandoned her support of Hungary and became the champion of Beneš' antirevisionism, and, taking advantage of the waning Bolshevik peril following the Treaty of Riga (March, 1921) ending the Russo-Polish war, France encouraged Rumania to join Czechoslovakia and Yugoslavia, thereby fostering the creation of the Little Entente.

In conclusion, it may be stated that, contrary to what has been generally believed, the Little Entente was not willed into being by the French but, on the contrary, was initially projected in defiance of France and to offset French support of Hungarian revisionism. Only later did the Quai d'Orsay reverse its position to the extent of making the Little Entente the touchstone of its Balkan policy.[120] During Sforza's tenure as Minister of Foreign Affairs, Italy supported the creation of the Little Entente, but with the advent of Mussolini as the new paladin of Hungarian revisionism, Italian policy was completely reversed.

The second volume of the collection was ready for the press when, in March, 1944, German troops occupied Hungary, and the new Sztójay government ordered the publication suspended. Fortunately, the commission's director was able to save the galley proofs, and the volume was finally published in 1946. The contents proved to be an excellent source not only for Magyar policy but also for an understanding of Balkan affairs in general. The volume makes it possible to trace the evolution of a number

[120] On this entire question, see Mario Toscano, "Le origini della Piccola Intesa secondo i document diplomatici ungheresi," *ibid.*, Vol. II.

of problems, among them, the negotiations with Austria on the question of the Hungarian western lands; the conclusion of the Franco-Polish, Rumeno-Czechoslovak, and Czechoslovak-Yugoslav alliances; the Polish-Rumanian, Czechoslovak-Rumanian, and the Czechoslovak-Yugoslav military conventions; the Russo-Polish peace negotiations; and the first attempt to restore Charles to the Hapsburg throne.

It is now possible to reconstruct these chapters in the history of Danubian Europe from a primary source, the existence of which reveals how careful and accurate the Budapest observers were in collecting and classifying the essential factors of the policies of the Great Powers and those of the Little Entente.

The third volume concerns the period September 1–December 31, 1921, and includes 654 documents. This volume was also ready for the press in 1948, when the Magyar government decided to destroy it and to cease publication of the collection. Only a few copies of the galley proofs were saved and taken out of the country.

Of the important questions treated in this volume, special attention should be called to that of the implementation of the peace treaty and the resolution of the problem of the Hungarian western lands by means of the Venice accord of October 13, 1921. The documents reveal the peacemaking role played by the Italian *Consulta*, without whose efforts the Austro-Magyar understanding would have been much more difficult to achieve. In this instance, Italian diplomacy not only made its weight felt in the Danube basin but also was able to establish the groundwork for a lasting *rapprochement* between Vienna and Budapest, on which Mussolini was later to base his policy as outlined in the Protocols of Rome.

The publication of this collection was suspended because it no longer satisfied either the scientific criteria introduced by the new regime or the political objectives pursued by that regime. Eleven years elapsed before any other documents from the Budapest archives were published.

The task was given to the Historical Institute of the Hungarian Academy of Sciences, which began its work with the publication of a brief collection on Hungary's position with respect to the origins and the course of the war.[121] This volume was issued on the twentieth anniversary of the outbreak of World War II. Despite the fact that it does contain some elements of interest (although many of the documents had already been published, either in *Nazi Conspiracy and Aggression*, in the journal

---

[121] *Magyarország és a második világháború. Tiktos diplomáciai okmányok a háború előzményeihez és történetéhez* [Hungary and the Second World War. Secret Diplomatic Documents on the Origins and Course of the War] (Budapest: Kossuth Köny-Kiadó, 1959).

Külügyi Szemle, or in memoirs), this collection strongly reflects, in its premise and in the criteria for the selection of materials, the political aims it was designed to satisfy. The compilers had to demonstrate the reasons why "reactionary Hungary and its antiproletarian ruling class" had made the country one of the first to recognize the Hitler regime in Germany and one of the last to abandon the Reich. Consequently, the documents selected were those that would prove the "irrepressible Hungarian drive toward the Nazi-Fascist camp and show how Magyar government policy was dictated by the party of the swastika under pressure from Hitler."

In reality, the documentation, particularly that drawn from the archives of the Ministry of Foreign Affairs, did not present adequate proof that the Budapest government was a docile instrument in Hitler's hands. However, the publishers included an essay at the beginning of each of the nine chapters, designed either to orient the reader toward a predetermined interpretation of the documents or, in some cases, to present conclusions that find no bases of support in the documents published in the chapter itself. For example, it is asserted that prior to the *Anschluss* Premier Gömbös discussed with Von Papen "the most secret details of Austro-German relations," an assertion that would seem to indicate obvious Hungarian connivance in Germany's expansionist program. However, no document is published in support of the statement. Instead, a letter written by the Minister of Foreign Affairs, Kánya, on March 2, 1938, is included, in which he expresses all of the Hungarian preoccupations regarding the projected German *Anschluss.* A long Preface completes these introductory studies, in which the collection's co-ordinator presents a picture of the history of Europe between the two world wars, modeled on Marxist historiography.

The useful portion of the volume is reduced to those hitherto unpublished documents that appear among the collection of 178 included in the work. Not all are diplomatic documents because the collection also includes various types of materials (minutes of the meeting of the Council of Ministers, extracts from diaries, summaries of daily developments) pertinent to Hungarian foreign policy from 1933 to 1945.

The documents are most numerous for the period 1938–39, when the Budapest government's revisionist policy, culminating in an open appeal for Axis support, was easy to emphasize. However, it is not explained to what extent this policy found support among the Hungarian public, and the erroneous impression is given that the action of the government was inspired only by the expansionist aims of a small ruling class. Material pertinent to the second arbitrage of Vienna is much more restricted, perhaps because, even today, the Magyars continue to be extremely sensitive to the Transylvanian question, notwithstanding the fact that Rumania (which was given the region once again by the 1947 treaty) has also become a people's democracy.

The minutes of the meetings of the Council of Ministers are of general interest in that they confirm what was already known rather than reveal anything startlingly new. In reference to the Hungarian declaration of war against the U.S.S.R., it is now shown by one of these sets of minutes that the Hungarian government was opposed to and rejected the suggestion of the Chief of the General Staff that Hungary volunteer its assistance to the Reich. No further light is cast on the circumstances that led to a reversal of this decision on June 26.[122]

Furthermore, there is nothing new concerning the negotiations conducted by the Kállay government with the Allies to effect Hungary's surrender. However, this comes as no surprise because in the introductory essay to the chapter in question Kállay's actions are severely criticized because they tended to ensure the "permanence of the capitalistic regime." This assertion is correct only in the sense that Kállay undertook the negotiations with the intent of preventing the occupation of the country by the Red Army.

The collection of Hungarian diplomatic documents for the period 1936–45 is much more scientific in character, and its publication has been taken over by the same institute.[123] The first volume has been published, dealing with the formation of the Axis and the annexation of Austria. Recently, the fourth volume appeared. The remaining volumes have been arranged as follows: II, the birth of the Munich pact and Hungarian foreign policy, 1937–38; III, Hungary's role in the dismemberment of Czechoslovakia, 1938–39; IV, Hungarian foreign policy during the period of the outbreak of the war, 1939–40; V, Hungary and the preparation of the war against the U.S.S.R., 1940–41; VI, Hungary's role in World War II, 1941–45.

The Yugoslav archives have made an especially rich contribution to the history of World War II. In 1949 the army's Institute for Military History,

[122] On the events leading to Hungary's entrance into the war against the Soviet Union, see Carlile A. Macartney, "Hungary's Declaration of War on the U.S.S.R. in 1941," in *Studies in Diplomatic History and Historiography in Honour of G. P. Gooch* (London: Longmans, 1961).

[123] *Diplomáciai iratok Magyaroszág Külpolitikájához 1936–1945* [Hungarian Foreign Policy Documents, 1936–1945] (Budapest: Akadémia Kiadó, 1962 *et seq.*). The volumes are accompanied by an Appendix containing a German translation of the *regesti* (records).

in co-operation with the Historical Section of the Central Committee of the Communist Party, launched the publication of a very large collection (eighty volumes have appeared in ten years) including all types of material relative to Yugoslavia's war of liberation, 1941–45.[124]

Evidently, the editors chose to gather and preserve all of the available documentation having any bearing on the birth of the new Yugoslav state, rather than to offer scholars a selection of the more important papers. In effect, the principal criteria of selection appear to have been the deletion only of material considered to be damaging to the political prestige of the present governing forces. Communist Yugoslavia's break with Soviet communism in 1948 and her exit from the Cominform also eliminated the impediments that people's democracies inherit from their general alignment with Soviet positions. Moreover, the Yugoslav editors have become increasingly interested in making known the real nature of their politico-diplomatic relations with the Soviet Union during the war and the real attitude of the Moscow government toward the Yugoslav liberation movement.

Naturally, this argument has led Yugoslav historiography to defend some rather questionable theses: for example, one that seeks to identify the date of the beginning of the Communist resistance in Yugoslavia with the date of the surrender of Yugoslavia to the Axis in April, 1941, and not with the order issued by the Comintern some two months later (that is, after the German attack against the U.S.S.R. of June 22, 1941, had brought Nazi-Soviet co-operation to an abrupt halt) to all European Communist parties to take the field to assist the Soviet peoples in their struggle.

However, the existence of a number of such interpretations does not materially affect the publication. Furthermore, there were no particular restrictions on the use of materials referring to the activities in the Partisan movement of such individuals as Djilas, who have subsequently fallen into disgrace. The bulk of the Italian, German, and Croatian material relative to Pavelic's government has also been included, along with the Serbian papers of the Nedic government that were captured by the Communist Partisans during the conflict. The material from Mihajlovic's archives is extremely limited, despite the fact that Tito's Partisans captured them when they overran his headquarters in September, 1944.

The collection is divided into seven series, not necessarily in order to meet publication requirements but rather to reproduce faithfully the plan

[124] *Zbornik dokumenata i podataka o Narodnooslobodilackom ratu Jugoslovenskih naroda* [Information and Documentary Collection relative to the Yugoslav Peoples' War of Liberation] (Belgrade: Vojnoiskoriski Institut Jugoslovenske Narodne Armije, 1949 *et seq.*).

by which the Yugoslav Communist Partisans carried on their struggle. In addition to the politico-military leadership provided by Tito and by his headquarters, it had a guiding force located in each of six regions, centers which ultimately contributed to the creation of the new Yugoslav federation. The series are as follows: Series I, Serbia and Voivodina; II, Supreme General Staff; III, Montenegro; IV, Bosnia and Herzegovina; V, Croatia; VI, Slovenia; VII, Macedonia.

With the exception of the second series, which, because of the general nature of its documentation, should have been the first, the organization follows the order in which the individual regions joined the Partisan struggle. Within each series the material is organized chronologically. However, this division is only indicative because not all of the documentation of major interest is included in the second series. For example, Tito's correspondence with the six regional headquarters, from which many important elements may be drawn, is often found in the regional series.

Though not exhaustive, this collection offers data of great value on many problems. Notwithstanding the aforementioned scarcity of material from the Mihajlovic archive, what does exist makes it possible to reconstruct the rapport between Tito and Mihajlovic with greater precision. Tito's summary account of the first of the two meetings with Mihajlovic (which took place during the second half of 1941), which he prepared immediately after the encounter and gave to one of his collaborators, is included in the collection. The data available on the second meeting are of minor importance. On the whole, it is possible to grasp the principal points at issue between the two resistance groups that led, early in November, 1941, to open conflict between them.

The break with Mihajlovic was the beginning of an extremely critical period for Tito's movement. While internally he faced the problem of survival against the offensive launched by the Axis forces, he found himself in conflict with the Kremlin, which had issued a directive censoring him for his failure to collaborate with Mihajlovic and for permitting his military units to assume openly too strong a communistic character. It is reasonably clear from the documents that Tito, overcoming the doubts of his lieutenants, did not hesitate to ignore Moscow's orders in order to maintain his policy of rigid opposition to Mihajlovic and to other Yugoslav forces.

Tito's attitude toward the Croatian Peasant party is particularly illustrative. When the Croatian Peasant party leader, Macek, was arrested for refusing to support the Pavelic government, Tito, because the strongly anti-Communist character of the Macek party prevented complete collaboration between the two forces, launched an open attack against his followers, accusing them of supporting the occupation forces. However, thanks to this policy, it was possible for Tito to establish Communist control of Yugoslavia without the assistance of the Red Army.

This collection is also useful for the history of Italy. A number of Italian documents are included relative to the Italian attack against Yugoslavia, directives issued for the territories occupied by the Italian armed forces, and other materials illustrating the Italian relations with the Chetniks and with the Croatian Ustaschi. A number of strikingly signifi- cant documents testify to the Italian command's strong disapproval of the excesses committed by the Ustaschi against the Serbian population. And, finally, attention is called to the documents revealing the links existing between the Slovene and the Italian Communist parties for mutual support of the inclusion of Trieste within Yugoslavia's borders.

Recent indications are that Yugoslavia will publish a part of her archival materials for the earlier period. In fact, in 1960 the Institute for the Social Sciences published a volume containing the minutes of the meetings of the delegation of the Kingdom of the Serbs, Croats, and Slovenes at the Paris conference of 1919–20.[125] Material on the preparatory work of the Yugoslav delegation for the plenary sessions, the commission meetings, and unofficial contacts is here made available to scholars. The references in the documents to the latter are the most useful because, as often happens in international conferences, it is precisely these personal and unofficial contacts that are the most productive, and, normally, they are not recorded in detail in the documents.

The minutes for the period January 10, 1919–June 30, 1920, touch upon all of the problems affecting the new Yugoslavia, including the difficulties in delimiting its frontiers, relations with the succession states, the settlement of the Adriatic question with Italy, the Albanian and Montenegrin issues, and the Greek and Bulgarian frontier problems. In addition to the minutes as such, a number of important documents for the study of Yugoslavia's foreign policy in the years immediately following World War I have been published. Among them are several of General Pesic's memoranda of Yugoslav frontiers, a memorandum of the delegation to the peace conference dated March 3, 1919, referring to the Fiume question, and, finally, a memorandum presented to the peace conference on Yugoslav claims in various contested areas.

The Adriatic question is amply treated, and the material includes a number of interesting items. Particular attention is called to the conversa-

[125] *Zapisnici sa sednica delegacije Kraljevine S H S na mirovnoj Konferenciji u Parizu 1919–1920* [Minutes of the Meeting of the Delegation of the Kingdom of the Serbs, Croats, and Slovenes at the Paris Conference] (Belgrade, 1960).

tions of April 5, 1919, between Pasic, Trumbic, Vesnic, and Smodlaka to explore the possibility of a direct secret agreement with Italy based on an acceptable compromise of the existing differences. Also included is an important summary by Pasic to the Yugoslav delegation of his colloquy with President Wilson on April 17, in which the American President asked to be brought up to date on the Yugoslav point of view on the Fiume, Dalmatian, and all other aspects of the Adriatic question.

On the whole, however, the disclosures are neither numerous nor of fundamental importance to the issues at hand. Furthermore, the minutes reporting the individual contacts of the delegates are exceedingly brief and succinct.

7. THE PORTUGUESE AND POLISH COLLECTIONS.

In 1961 the Portuguese government undertook the publication of a collection that will ultimately cover the period November 6, 1936–February 5, 1947,[126] the years when the Foreign Ministry portfolio was held by Prime Minister Antonio de Oliveira Salazar. To date, only two volumes have appeared, containing more than nine hundred documents relative to the years 1936–39, with the exception of the material concerning the Spanish Civil War, which will be published at a later date.

The principal theme of the first volume is relations with Great Britain, the traditional pivot of Portuguese foreign policy, which in 1936–37 were severely strained by the contrasting attitudes of London and Lisbon toward the Spanish Civil War. The Portuguese government took London to task for improperly evaluating the inherent dangers of a Communist victory in Spain. This difference of opinion and conflict in policy on a question that the Portuguese rightly defined as being vital to their country led to conflicts on issues that, while of purely secondary importance in themselves, reveal the crisis in the old alliance relationship. Thus the negotiations for arms

[126] Ministério Dos Negócios Estrangeiros, *Dez anos de política externa (1936–1947). A nação portuguesa e a segunda guerra mundial* (Lisbon: Imprensa Nacional, 1961 *et seq.*). According to the announced plan, the collection is to be organized as follows:

Part I: *O rearmamento do Exército no quadro político da Aliança Luso-Britânica (1936–1939)*.
Part II: *Portugal e a Guerra de libertação de Espanha (1936–1939)*.
Part III: *A campanha da neutralidade na segunda guerra mundial (1939–1943)*.
Part IV: *Em busca da decisão da guerra (1943–1945)*.
Part V: *A guerra no Extremo Oriente (1941–1945)*.
Part VI: *Portugal na guerra económica (1939–1945)*.
Part VII: *Portugal e os Estados Unidos da América (1945–1947)*.

purchases in Great Britain and for the sending of a military mission to Portugal—subjects to which a great deal of space is devoted—were conducted in an atmosphere of mutual distrust. The British refusal to guarantee delivery under all conditions triggered the failure of the first round of negotiations. The second round of talks came within a step of foundering as a result of a news leak which the Lisbon government interpreted as an attempt to make it known that Portugal was on the verge of abandoning its favorable attitude toward the Falangist movement.

It is within this framework and atmosphere that Lord Halifax's visit to Berlin, toward the close of 1937, produced great alarm in Lisbon. The Portuguese were aware that Halifax had explored the possibility of reaching an accord with Berlin on the basis of a redistribution of colonial territories. The mere fact that negotiations were under way on this problem put the Portuguese in a difficult position, because Lisbon's opposition to such a plan would have established Portugal as the major stumbling block in attempts to alleviate the crisis between the Great Powers. Portugal would antagonize Germany and simultaneously alienate British public opinion.

This fact aside, Lisbon's concern for the fate of the colonies seemed to be fully justified. To be sure, it is true—confirmed by the German documents now available—that during the Hitler-Halifax conversations of November 19, 1937, the colonial question was discussed only in a general way, without either side's advancing any concrete proposals. Nevertheless, the Portuguese could not forget that on two occasions, in 1898 and in 1912–13, London and Berlin had considered the possibility of a redistribution of colonial holdings, at the expense of Portugal, as a basis for an Anglo-German accord. Furthermore, it is probable that Lisbon was aware that immediately following the signing of the Locarno Pacts, when the outlines of the Franco-German *rapprochement* seemed to be clear, Paris and London had considered the possibility of reviewing the entire problem of the assignment of mandates for the old German colonial territories. In this event, consideration would have been given to a plan for rearranging the Portuguese colonies if Portugal had been amenable to the idea. On the other hand, it is now known that in March, 1938, Ambassador Henderson suggested to Hitler the possibility of creating an international regime for the African territories lying between the Zambesi and the fifth parallel north. The project was vague, but it did not appear to exclude organization of the colonies in this area along new lines, and the failure to develop the project further was due, in addition to questions of general policy which made the accord impossible, to the German refusal to accept anything less than the full restitution of the colonies lost in 1919.

These problems notwithstanding, Anglo-Portuguese relations—as is demonstrated by these documents—improved markedly, beginning in 1938. The deepening of the crisis in Europe, while it dissipated the prospect, among others, of an Anglo-German accord at the expense of Portugal, served to stimulate a mutual interest in strengthening the ties of the old alliance. For the British, Portuguese friendship assumed a new importance in view of the fact that a Falangist victory was now assured, and with it, the extension of Axis influence in Spain. On the other hand, Lisbon was becoming increasingly preoccupied with the possible course of Spanish foreign policy, considering the presence of ultranationalist elements among the Falangist leaders known to be favorable to the idea of Pan-Iberianism. Therefore, at the time of the Czech crisis Anglo-Portuguese relations appeared to be much improved, although they still had not regained all of their traditional cordiality.

It is worth recalling that in this period the British government, in reply to specific Portuguese requests, repeatedly stated that the obligations assumed in the alliance also applied to Portuguese colonial territories, which were being threatened at the time by German penetration of (for the moment) an essentially economic character. Many documents referring to this problem are included in the collection, for the obvious purpose of calling attention to recent events. The same is true for the material revealing the extent of the collaboration between the Hong Kong and Macao governments in the face of the Japanese threat.

The second volume is a chronological continuation of the first (as is the numbering system); it opens with the ending of the Czech crisis and closes with the outbreak of World War II.

With the relaxation of international tension following the Munich accord, Portuguese concern again focused on the possibility that a definite amelioration of the rapport between the Great Powers might be based on the redistribution of colonial territories. In the light of what is known today, this fear was not without foundation; at the time, it was justified by the position taken by the British press and, albeit unofficially, by the British government itself.

In November the visit by South African Minister Pirow to various European capitals, including Berlin, increased Portuguese fears. In his conversations with Salazar, Pirow declared that he favored the idea of restitution of the ex-German colonies but that his government had no intention of surrendering South-West Africa and was considering instead the payment of an indemnity to Germany. The South African Minister avoided discussing the problem of a common defense of South African territories (which the two governments had discussed previously, with some positive results), and this silence was interpreted in Lisbon to be the result of pressure by the British government, which was anxious to maintain complete freedom of action in view of the possibility of a colonial agreement with Berlin.

The March, 1939, crisis revealed the practical impossibility of an accord between Germany and the western democracies and reduced Portuguese fears for the future of their colonial empire. Lisbon was kept abreast of the radical shift in British policy by the reports of Ambassador Monteiro, who, in commenting on the reactions of the Chamberlain Cabinet and the British public to the latest German aggression, underlined the decisive importance of the shift in the British position. Despite its peripheral status with regard to the crisis, Portugal, too, had to face the problems created by the prospect of a conflict that was now believed unavoidable. It could become involved either through her alliance ties with Great Britain or as the result of a Spanish intervention on the side of the Axis.

In this situation Portugal's recent disagreements with London, the result of Britain's inconsistent position on the colonial problem, assumed particular importance. If the problem had lost its momentary urgency, these precedents had left a wake of suspicion and doubt. It is also evident that Salazar was struck by the hesitancy and uncertainty that seemed to paralyze the western democracies in the face of Hitler's aggressions, a situation that led him to criticize Great Britain's political institutions as well as its military unpreparedness, particularly for the influence they had on the British government's international activity.

The news that Great Britain and France were hurrying to negotiate an alliance with the Soviet Union introduced a new motive for friction between the two countries. In April and May Salazar repeatedly emphasized the dissatisfaction of his government and of the Portuguese public with the prospect of the reintroduction of the U.S.S.R. into European affairs and made clear his doubts of the effectiveness of Soviet aid, which, if it was significant on a military plane, could not help but weaken the moral bases of the anti-German front.

The friction between London and Lisbon was particularly serious because of the differences in attitude toward the Spanish Falangist government. Everyone was aware that in the coming conflict Portugal's position would be decisively influenced by the decisions taken by Franco. Now that the Civil War was over, there were a number of indications that Spain intended to re-establish an independent position in international affairs in order to escape undue Axis influence. In Lisbon it was believed that a first step toward this end might be the prompt application of the Berard-Jordana accords of the preceding February. But the difficulties raised by Franco over implementation of the accords and the suspicious, if not downright hostile, attitude of Britain toward Spain, especially after the latter's adherence to the Tripartite Pact, left little hope for a favorable outcome. Salazar complained that, while Britain insisted on emphasizing the old alliance ties with Portugal, London did nothing to improve relations with Franco and, moreover, acted in such a way as to make a Spanish intervention on the side of the Axis very probable, with the result that Portugal would be drawn into a conflict foreign to her interests and provoked by a policy that she had constantly opposed.

Salazar's criticism of British policy gave rise to a serious controversy with Ambassador Monteiro, the advocate of very close ties with London. The episode was an indication of the differences existing in Lisbon between the supporters of the traditional policy and those advocating greater independence of action. At the time these differences were reflected in the dilemma facing the Portuguese—neutrality or immediate intervention on the side of the democracies—and Salazar (whose actions, such as arms purchases in Axis countries, could not be ignored) was clearly in favor of neutrality.

The alertness with which Portugal now followed the developments on the European scene is reflected in the documents contained in this volume, which, beginning with the March, 1939, crisis, exceed the limits of problems directly of interest to the Portuguese and extend to the vast panorama of European politics. In this sense, after the disclosures of other postwar publications, the Portuguese collection could add little that was new. A number of revelations, however, have a certain importance: the persistence of faith in Mussolini's moderating influence on Germany, which was believed to be even more effective after the signing of the Pact of Steel; the information gathered by Ambassador Monteiro on British reactions to the occupation of Albania; and the estimates made in British political and military circles of the value of the contribution Italian intervention might make in the event of a war. This collection makes a significant contribution on Spanish policy and the complex diplomatic game played by the major powers to influence the Spanish government on the eve of the conflict. This point is barely touched by the other collections but is one of considerable importance in understanding Madrid's subsequent conduct with respect to the two groups of belligerents.

As planned, the collection is organized according to subject matter, and within each volume the documents are assembled chronologically. The system suffers from the usual inconveniences. For example, a number of documents concerning Portugal's attitude toward the Spanish Civil War are included in the first volume, although that subject, as has been noted, will be treated in a later volume. Neither a subject matter index nor an index of persons is provided, but at the end of the volume there is a list of the documents included, together with place and date of origin, sender, addressee, and location of the document.

A collection of Polish documents has been published by the General Sikorski Historical Institute which enriches the published sources on World War II.[127] Despite the fact that this collection is not a product of the Ministry of Foreign Affairs in Warsaw and is, consequently, an unofficial collection, nonetheless it contains the documentation collected and preserved in the archives of the Institute concerning the activities of the Polish government in exile, recognized by all of the major powers including (beginning in the summer of 1941) the Soviet Union.

To date, only the first volume has appeared; it covers the period September, 1939–April, 1943. One of the most interesting points documented is precisely those negotiations conducted in London in July, 1941, for Soviet recognition of the Sikorski government.

As is known, World War II formally began with Great Britain's and France's declaration of war against Germany on September 3, 1939, in support of Poland (which had been attacked two days previously by the German army) and in fulfillment of the guarantees given to the Poles. This aid did not save Poland; also attacked from the east by the Red Army, it was quickly overwhelmed and its territory divided between the Reich and the U.S.S.R., according to the terms stipulated in the Nazi-Soviet Pact of August 23, 1939. The Polish government in exile was established toward the end of September, 1939, under the presidency of General Sikorski. The Soviet Union refused to recognize its legitimacy, just as the United States and Great Britain refused to recognize the partition of Poland and the incorporation into the U.S.S.R. of Polish regions assigned to Russia by the agreement with Germany.

When the German attack on the U.S.S.R. on June 22, 1941, made the Soviet Union a *de facto* ally of Great Britain, the Polish question became one of the most controversial problems that beset the anti-Nazi coalition.

The Kremlin quickly demonstrated itself to be in favor of the reestablishment of an "independent Polish national state," whose boundaries would conform to Polish ethnographic frontiers. With this formula, the Soviet Union clearly indicated that it had no objection to a reconstituted Poland or to the Sikorski government, on the condition that no demands be

[127] General Sikorski Historical Institute, *Documents on Polish-Soviet Relations, 1939–1945* (London: Heinemann, 1961), Vol. I.

raised in conjunction with former Polish territories, inhabited largely by Byelo-Russians and Ukrainians, that had been acquired by the Soviet Union in the partition.

General Sikorski realized the need to normalize relations with the Soviet Union at the earliest possible moment. However, he could see no justice in the Soviets' repudiation of the agreement with Germany while at the same time insisting on the permanent possession of the territories acquired as a result of that agreement—possession of which, in any event, hardly served to improve the Soviet position vis-à-vis the United States and Great Britain.

In principle, the London government shared the Polish point of view but was extremely anxious to find a solution, albeit a temporary one, in order to prevent the Polish question from causing a rift in Anglo-Soviet relations in the militarily critical summer of 1941. Thus, the British government assumed the role of mediator in the Soviet-Polish negotiations and applied the strongest pressure to the Poles to agree to re-establish relations with Moscow on the basis of the Soviet denunciation of the 1939 agreement with Germany, while remanding the solution of the frontier problem to a later date. The acceptance of these conditions made possible the Polish-Soviet accord of July 30, 1941.

The documentation contained in this volume permits a detailed study of these negotiations, in addition to providing ample information on the principal sessions of the Polish Council of Ministers during the course of these exchanges. The documents reveal how the compromise, favored by the British government, in fact implied British acceptance of the conditions imposed by the Soviets. The only advantage to the British-Polish position was the fact that British agreement to the Soviet conditions was not a formal one, and this fact could serve as the wedge for reopening the discussions on the boundary issue at a later date. However, if this was London's intention, it is difficult to explain the motives prompting the Minister of Foreign Affairs, Anthony Eden, to declare in Parliament early in August that the exchange of notes through which Britain had assured the Sikorski government that Great Britain did not recognize the changes in the territorial status of Poland after August, 1939, did not at the same time imply any guarantee of Poland's prewar frontiers. This clarification was offered by Eden coincidentally with *Pravda's* official announcement that "the Soviet-Polish frontiers established by the Treaty of Riga of 1921 were not unchangeable."

Nevertheless, the sense of realism demonstrated by the British government served to direct the question toward a compromise more advantageous for the Poles than would have later been acceptable to the Soviets. It would

PUBLICATION OF THE SOURCES

have been asking too much of the leaders of the Polish government in exile, in view of their political acumen and state of mind, to expect that they would renounce their frontier claims in exchange for a Soviet assurance to recognize an independent and democratic but truncated Poland when it was not even certain that the Soviet Union would be able to defeat Germany. But the accord of July 30, 1941, left the way open for the Poles to act on the question at a time when they were able to evaluate objectively not only the weakness of their own position but also the weakness of the position of their allies vis-à-vis the U.S.S.R. on the Soviet-Polish frontier issue.

This occasion, favored by British diplomacy, presented itself early in December, 1941, when General Sikorski met with Stalin. The military situation had changed markedly. It now appeared unlikely that the Wehrmacht would annihilate the Red Army. If, on the one hand, this fact suggested greater reflection on the part of the Poles, on the other, they could profit by the fact that on the diplomatic plane it was to the Kremlin's interest to reach an agreement with the Poles on the matter of frontier revision in order to eliminate an obstacle that could have complicated the imminent conversations with Eden for the conclusion of the Anglo-Soviet treaty of alliance.

In his first meeting with Sikorski Stalin had clearly pointed out that the Byelo-Russians and Ukrainians living in ex-Polish territories had, to all intents and purposes, become Soviet citizens. During the second meeting Stalin asserted that, if the Poles would recognize the eastern ethnic frontier with the Soviet Union, the U.S.S.R. would work for the restoration of a Poland greater in size and stronger than before, in the sense that Poland would be allowed to absorb East Prussia and to extend her western frontier to the Oder. Sikorski's reply was completely in the negative. An examination of the Polish documents now reveals that at that moment, despite Anglo-American diplomatic efforts to modify the decision, the U.S.S.R. closed the door on further negotiations with the Sikorski government and sought new solutions.

The volume terminates with the rupture in the relations between the Soviet Union and the Polish government in exile in April, 1943, resulting from the discovery, announced by the Germans, of the slaughtered bodies of eleven thousand Polish officers in the Katyn Forest, near Smolensk. The Germans requested that a commission of the International Red Cross conduct an investigation, as they were certain that the commission's report would prove Soviet responsibility and support the denunciations of the German propaganda machine. The Polish government in exile seconded the German request for an investigation, claiming that documents in its possession supported the German accusation. The International Red Cross could not conduct the inquiry in the absence of a similar request from the other interested party, the Soviet Union, which vehemently denied all responsibility. Consequently, the Sikorski government found itself supporting the Germans in an issue that was never clarified.

These documents offer no new information that would clarify the question of responsibility in the Katyn Forest affair, one of the most heinous crimes of World War II. Nothing more is known about the massacre than what was provided by the German and Soviet investigations, which, obviously, arrived at diametrically opposed conclusions.

It should be added, however, that Goering and other Nazi leaders were accused of the crime by the Allied tribunal at Nuremberg. After the White Book prepared by the German Katyn Investigation Commission was offered in evidence by the defense, the tribunal acquitted the accused of the crime and thus of responsibility for the massacre.[128] The Soviet government failed to take advantage of the occasion to demonstrate that it was in fact not guilty of the crime for which it had been denounced by the German propagandists during the war.

8. THE FRENCH DOCUMENTARY SOURCES.

Of all the archives of the Great Powers involved in World War II, the French suffered the greatest damage. In May, 1940, when the entrance of German troops into Paris was deemed imminent, it was decided at the Quai d'Orsay to transfer to the western part of the country the documents of immediate interest and to burn those referring to the recent period. It is not known who gave this order, or whether it was in fact given, since no one has come forward to assume responsibility for it and no document concerning it has been uncovered. However, in the tension of the period, every rumor became fact, so that it would not be surprising if a rumor had led to the destruction of the archives. In the confusion of the moment a quantity of the material destined to be destroyed mysteriously disappeared, in all probability removed by members of the Communist party, and its fate remains unknown. Included among the missing material are a number of files referring to Italo-French relations in such cases as the Stresa conference,

[128] The decision of the court led to the conclusion that responsibility for the crime devolved on the Soviet Union, and in 1951 a special committee of Congress opened a new inquest on the matter. See *Hearings before the Select Committee To Conduct an Investigation of the Facts, Evidences and Circumstances of the Katyn Forest Massacre* (7 vols.; Washington: U.S. Government Printing Office, 1952).

the Mussolini-Laval conversations, and the Ethiopian war—questions of particular interest to an Italian exile in France who held an important post in the French Communist party and who recently died.

Nor was the material transferred to the west saved in its entirety; part fell into German hands, and after the war it was possible to salvage only a portion of the material taken by the Germans. Other portions of the archive were loaded onto a ship at Bordeaux to be transferred to the United States, but these papers were burned by the ship's commander when German aircraft forced him to reverse his course and return to Bordeaux. Other losses were sustained on August 25, 1944, at the moment of the liberation, when a fire at the Quai d'Orsay wreaked heavy damage, particularly among the materials of recent date.

In May, 1961, a commission was created, under the chairmanship of Professor Pierre Renouvin, which included historians and diplomats, charged with the publication of a general collection for the period 1919–39.

The commission directed its first efforts toward a reorganization of the material, which had already been begun by archive employees. The reorganization is not yet completed. This is understandable in view of the condition in which the archives were found at the end of the war, as well as their scope and breadth. From the inventory completed thus far, a rough estimate indicates that the losses for the period 1919–29 are not quantitatively great. However, some of the files suffering the greatest damage were of considerable importance, such as those concerning the Franco-Belgian military alliance, Franco-Italian relations for the period 1928–29, and, above all, the German problem. The gaps for the period 1929–39 are much more extensive; there are lacunae in the sources pertaining to relations with all of the major powers. Fortunately, the files containing the telegrams escaped with only slight damage, with the exception of those for 1938–39. They are of vital importance, since most of the correspondence was effected by wire.

The commission has sought to fill these gaps by careful research into the ambassadorial archives—where, among other documents, copies or "retransmissions" of the most important communications are preserved—and by using material furnished by private archives. On the whole, this imposing task of reorganization and recovery appears to have produced good results, so that, despite the inevitable gaps, the French collection will be an extremely valuable instrument in the study of international relations for the period between the two world wars.

In this context, the French commission should be lauded for its decision not to limit its work to the publication of the documents contained in the archives of the Ministry of Foreign Affairs but to include materials from various other sources that contribute to a better understanding of the course of French foreign policy. Thus, the collection will contain documents from the Supreme War Council, the Supreme Defense Council, General Headquarters, and from military and other ministerial offices such as the Treasury, where useful material may be found concerning the reparations problem and the question of inter-Allied war debts.

Despite the fact that the reorganization of the archives for the period 1919–29 is not yet complete, the commission has decided to begin publication of the material beginning with the final act of the Lausanne conference (July 9, 1932) to the outbreak of World War II. The publication of the materials for the earlier period will be undertaken later. Two series are planned for the years 1932–39. The first, referred to above, will begin with July 9, 1932, and will terminate with January 31, 1935. The second will continue the account to September 3, 1939. To date, one volume of the second series has been published, covering a three-month period, January 1–March 31, 1936.[129]

The key episode treated by the documents in this volume is the Rhineland question. Notwithstanding the fact that an abundance of material, including memoirs, exists on this problem, this volume contains new information of considerable significance, in addition to a number of confirmations of what was already known. Above all, attention should be called to the speed and precision with which information was transmitted to Paris from the Embassy in Berlin—information which not only revealed the German coup in the Rhineland to be imminent, but also made clear the doubts entertained in German military circles concerning the feasibility of a military operation in the Rhineland, as well as Germany's difficult economic situation. The Paris government was, therefore, in the fortunate position of being able to carry out promptly all military and political measures required by the specific circumstances.

In fact, discussions between the French military and political leaders were conducted in advance on this issue. From the beginning, French military leaders excluded the possibility that France could act alone and never budged from this position. Again, on March 8, 1936, Gamelin repeated that the entrance of French troops into the Rhineland would have meant war and that, therefore, it was not only imperative that general mobilization be decreed but that all the signatories of the Locarno Pact, including Italy, give their assistance. The documents contained in this volume reveal the grave responsibility assumed by the French military in

[129] *Documents diplomatiques français, 1932–1939,* Second Series (1936–39), Tome I: *January 1–March 31, 1936* (Paris: Imprimerie Nationale, 1963).

those circumstances. But they do not exclude the fact that French political leaders never seriously considered taking action without, at the very least, the aid of the British. Furthermore, Flandin's attitude, in the light of these documents, appears to have been much less firm than hitherto supposed.

Therefore, all things considered, it may be asserted that French reaction to the German act of force remained, by common consent, subordinated to a condition manifestly impossible to achieve. It was common knowledge that neither the British government nor the British public were ready to risk war in order to prevent the remilitarization of the Rhineland. All of this tends to confirm the suspicion that responsible French statesmen intended to use British opposition as a convenient pretext for their own reluctance to act. This suspicion is further strengthened by the fact—revealed in these documents—that Paris made no serious official effort to clarify Britain's position on the issue or to influence London toward the desired goal.

It must also be noted that, if the responsibility of French statesmen was a grave one, the same responsibility must be borne by the entire French nation, which clearly demonstrated that it had no desire whatsoever to face the perils and sacrifices that French interests demanded at that time.

For the moment, French documentary sources are extremely limited. However, important data have been furnished by acts of the Commission of Inquiry, created by the French Senate in 1946 to inquire "into the entire scope of political, economic, diplomatic, and military events that from 1933 to 1945 preceded, accompanied, and followed the armistice for the purpose of determining responsibility and to propose political and judicial sanctions if required."[130]

The commission began its labors in February, 1947, and terminated them in May, 1951, when its parliamentary mandate expired, without having entirely completed its task. Despite the length of the inquiry and the quantity of data gathered, the acts of the Commission of Inquiry contribute considerably less to the study of diplomatic history than had originally been expected. In effect, the commission, according to the law by which it was created, was charged with ascertaining individual responsibilities. Therefore, its attention was focused primarily on the internal aspects of French policy and particularly on the causes of military unpreparedness and on the positions taken on various occasions by the High Command, whose influence on the conduct of foreign policy was considered to be decisive.

The data collected have made it possible, for example, to ascertain that,

[130] *Assemblée Nationale, Première Législature, Session de 1947, Les événéments survenus en France de 1933 à 1945* (11 vols.; Paris: Presses Universitaires de France, n.d.); report, 2 vols., depositions and documents, 9 vols.

at the time of the remilitarization of the Rhineland, the French High Command was completely unprepared to act rapidly and effectively. It proposed to "exact a pledge" by occupying the left bank of the Sarre or by occupying Luxemburg in order to establish the necessary bases for a later advance toward undetermined objectives. Furthermore, it made very clear that such action would require general mobilization, the realization of which, in practice, was made impossible by political and economic considerations.

The emphasis given by the commission to the influence exerted by the French High Command may, in this case, be considered justifiable even if the failure of the French to react to the Nazi act of force was not due solely to the obstacles raised by the French military. But this same premise, applied in other circumstances, can lead to wholly or partially erroneous conclusions. In any event, the work of the commission has brought to light a complex of elements important to the study of French diplomatic activities on the international scene, particularly in those cases where the investigation was especially thorough, such as the Munich crisis, the declaration of war on Germany, and the origins of the armistice of June, 1940.

It would have been advantageous if the commission had used its discretionary powers to demand the inclusion of the documentary material known to be in the hands of many responsible French leaders, material that became extremely precious after the destruction of the ministerial archives in May, 1940. Unfortunately, it did not do so. The work of the commission was essentially based on the depositions made by French political leaders and diplomats, who were called first to give their accounts of the events and later recalled to answer questions on specific subjects. Although many of these men had already testified before the High Court of Justice or had written their memoirs, their testimonies are unquestionably interesting, whether for their number or for their detail (Daladier's testimony alone amounts to over one hundred pages of text). However, it is not always possible to determine the accuracy of certain assertions or to select between two contrasting points of view supported with equal vigor by persons worthy of trust, since in such cases the commission did not find it opportune to press for a direct confrontation of the opponents.

As has been noted, the documentation of a purely diplomatic nature is extremely limited. However, reference should be made to the several documents concerning the negotiations of March, 1940, between Paris and London to plan joint action in Norway and those concerning Franco-British relations at the time of the 1940 armistice.

Franco-German relations between June, 1940, and the end of 1941 are amply described in a collection devoted to the work of the French delegation with the German Armistice Commission.[131] This material has very special characteristics, as does the material concerning the relations between the German government and the Vichy regime during the armistice period. An important part of the documents refer to military or administrative problems, while the bulk of the material concerns economic questions, a subject of major interest to the Germans.

Nevertheless, this source is of extraordinary interest, particularly for the period beginning with the armistice and ending at the close of 1940. However, beginning in November, the importance of the Armistice Commission steadily declined because the weightiest problems were gradually taken over by the German Embassy in Paris, which, despite the fact that it was not an officially accredited agency, had assumed the role of maintaining regular contacts with the French government and of supervising French relations with other countries.

This fact is also borne out by the organization of the collection. While three volumes are devoted to the last six months of 1940, all of the material for 1941 is incorporated in the fourth and fifth volumes. The fifth volume is of special interest in that it devotes more space to the political aspects of Franco-German relations and limits that devoted to economic questions, in contrast to the other volumes. Furthermore, the chronological limits of the collection are extended, thanks to several appendixes incorporating a great deal of important data concerning the German request of July 15, 1940, to use Moroccan airports and the minutes of the Franco-German meetings of December, 1940, in which, under pressure from Laval, techniques were developed to implement Franco-German collaboration as outlined in the Montoire meeting between Hitler and Pétain. In addition, a long summary paper has been published (the Vignol dossier) which provides an over-all view of the work of the Armistice Commission throughout all of 1942. Finally, it should be noted that much more space is devoted in this volume to the negotiations with Italy. The documents disclose that in July, 1940, the Vichy government, while it rejected the German demand for bases in Morocco, immediately agreed to the Italian request for a base in Algeria, and that toward the end of 1941, under very different circumstances, it

[131] *La Délégation Française auprès de la Commission Allemande d'Armistice: Recueil de Documents publiés par le Gouvernement Français* (Paris: Imprimerie Nationale, 1947–59): Vol. I, June 29–September 29, 1940; Vol. II, September 30–November 23, 1940; Vol. III, November 24, 1940–January 19, 1941; Vol. IV, January 19–July 21, 1941; Vol. V, July 21–December 21, 1941.

consented to the transit of Italian trucks and goods across Tunisia, while earlier it had refused the same privilege to the Germans.

Certain cautions to the user of this material are necessary. In the first place, it should be noted that the collection is based exclusively on French materials which are unilateral accounts, not minutes agreed upon by the participating parties. The discussions taking place during the various meetings are thus viewed from only one vantage point and should, therefore, be examined with the necessary caution. In the second place, the material is incomplete because very often the most delicate questions were handled outside of the official sessions. The main lines of French policy were laid out in Vichy by Marshal Pétain and his collaborators, and for this purpose almost daily top secret meetings were held, the minutes of which have not been published.

A source of prime importance for the study of recent French history is provided by the trials, held at the close of World War II, of statesmen, military personalities, functionaries, and journalists accused of having collaborated with the Germans during the Vichy period or of having contributed by their action to the 1940 disaster. A source of this nature is not peculiar to France—similar trials occurred during the same period in many other countries—but the French trials assume major importance for their number, for the personalities involved, and for the significance of their revelations.

An early example of this kind of trial is found in the Vichy period, when Daladier, Leon Blum, Gamelin, and several minor personalities were tried before the court of Riom during the early months of 1942.[132] With this trial, the political aims of which were obvious, the Vichy government sought to reveal to the French public that the defeat of 1940 had been the inevitable consequence of the corruption in the government of the Third Republic. The Germans encouraged the trial for other reasons. They sought to obtain confirmation by a French court of French responsibility for the war.

At the trial the debate centered almost exclusively on the issue of French military unpreparedness—a condition for which Daladier could readily be blamed because he had been Minister of Defense from the end of 1932 to the beginning of 1934 and from June, 1936, to May, 1940—and on several aspects of the social policies of the Blum Cabinet which, according to the prosecution, had contributed to slowing down the French rearmament

---

[132] On the Riom trials, see Maurice Ribet, Le procès de Riom (Paris: Flammarion, 1945) (Ribet was Daladier's defense counsel); Coquet, Le procès de Riom (Paris: Fayard, 1945); Mazé, Les grandes journèes du procès de Riom (Paris: La jeune Parque, 1945).

program. It is clear that these minutes contribute little to the study of diplomatic history. The hearings, begun on February 19, 1942, were abruptly terminated on April 11 at German request, when it had become clear that the accused were turning the tables on the prosecution and were themselves becoming efficient accusers.

Conversely, there were many revelations in the course of the trial of Marshal Pétain, held in July–August, 1945.[133] The role played by the Marshal between 1940 and 1944 and the nature of the accusations against him (an attempt against the security of the state, communication with the enemy) demanded a more extensive debate on the events of the period. The restrictions imposed by trial practices were circumvented from the beginning, and the proceedings often developed into a minute examination of the events leading to the 1940 armistice and of the internal and foreign policies of the Vichy government. In these circumstances, all of the major French personalities were called to testify, and despite the atmosphere created by the trial, which induced the majority of the witnesses to assume an attitude of self-defense (a number of them were later tried before the High Court), their testimonies revealed an important complex of hitherto unknown elements.

Among the more important depositions, the often circumstantial ones of Reynaud and Weygand deserve special attention. These were often in conflict, which resulted in violent encounters between the two men, but they were productive in the sense that they revealed the differences existing within the French government in 1940 on the armistice issue. No less important is the testimony of Ambassador Charles-Roux, who, in his capacity as Secretary-General of the Ministry of Foreign Affairs from May to October, 1940, was able to provide precise data on the first phrase of Pétain's foreign policy; the testimony of the former Secretary-General of the Ministry of Public Instruction, Chevalier, regarding his contact in December, 1940, with Lord Halifax through the good offices of Dupuy, the Canadian Minister to Vichy; and Laval's deposition, in which he offered the details of the Montoire meetings, the particulars of the crisis of December 13, 1940, and the position of the French government at the time of the Allied landing in North Africa on November 8, 1942.

Thus, the Pétain trial revealed important facts about events in France between 1940 and 1944, and was rendered more enlightening by the direct confrontation of many of the witnesses with each other. Later on, many of

[133] The stenographic summary of the trial is published in the *Journal Officiel* of the period and in *Le procès Pétain. Compte rendu sténographique* (2 vols.; Paris: Albin Michel, 1945). The latter is incomplete. Other important aspects of the trial taken from the dossier of the High Court are in Nogueres, *Le véritable procès du maréchal Pétain* (Paris: Fayard, 1955).

these witnesses were to publish their memoirs, in which they often treated in even greater detail the same subjects, a fact that tended to lessen the actual import of the revelations at the trial. However, these memoirs serve as a basis for comparison with the testimony, and, frequently, the differences between the two versions are extremely important.

The disclosures produced by the trial of Pierre Laval,[134] October 4–9, 1945, resulting in the death sentence for the accused, have a very limited importance for the study of diplomatic history. Laval, who had defended himself with great energy during the first three hearings against the accusation of plotting against the security of the state, left the courtroom when the second crime of which he was accused, that of communicating with the enemy, was brought up for discussion. Laval's decision to leave the courtroom, which was motivated by the attitude of the presiding judge and by the obvious hostility of the jurors, reduced the significance of the proceedings at the very moment when discussion was about to begin on a phase of his activities from which it could be reasonably assumed that some new information would be added to the story of Vichy's relations with Germany. Of all the succeeding testimonies, only that of General Doyen, who had been the head of the French armistice delegation, contained anything of value. Ambassador Noël refused to testify in the absence of the accused, and the ex-President of the Third Republic, Lebrun, limited his testimony to his relations with Laval in June and July of 1940, without going beyond what he had said during the Pétain trial.

Of all the other trials held in France at the end of World War II (a total of 108 individuals were tried between 1945 and 1949), only a few are worthy of mention here: Flandin's[135] trial was important for the details on his activities as Vichy's Minister of Foreign Affairs, December, 1940–February, 1941, and for his role in the Rhineland crisis of 1936; the Benoist-Méchin trial[136] and the Brinon and Luchaire trials[137] reveal numerous details concerning relations between the Vichy government and the German occupation forces.[138]

---

[134] Le Procès Laval. Compte rendu sténographique (Paris: Albin Michel, 1945). The summary is incomplete.

[135] See Le procès Flandin devant la Haute Cour de Justice, 23–26 juillet, 1946 (Paris: Librairie de Médicis, n.d.).

[136] Le procès Benoist-Méchin (29 mai–6 juin 1947) (Paris: Albin Michel, 1947). The stenographic text is incomplete.

[137] Le procès de la collaboration. Ferdinand de Brinon, Jean Luchaire, Joseph Darnaud. Compte rendu sténographique (Paris: Albin Michel, 1948).

[138] The revelations during many other trials before the High Court are of major historical value as sources. Among the more important is the trial of the former Minister of Foreign Affairs of the Vichy government, Baudouin. However, the stenographic summary of this trial has not been published.

9. THE SCANDINAVIAN, DUTCH, AND BELGIAN DOCUMENTARY SOURCES.

At the end of World War II Swedish wartime policies were the subject of vigorous criticism. Many policies, which the Swedish government had adopted under heavy German pressure, had not been in keeping with the obligations assumed by a neutral power. The debate that followed, especially violent in Sweden, induced the Swedish government to publish, the year after the war ended, a series of White Books which, because of their special characteristics,[139] may, within certain limits, be included in a historical collection.

The first to be published, in February, 1947, were two volumes on the question of the transit of German troops and matériel across Swedish territory to Norway.[140] There are approximately five hundred documents dealing with this subject, providing a detailed account of the negotiations and clarifying broader aspects of Swedish policy during 1940.

The data show that immediately after the start of the Norwegian campaign German pressure on Sweden was not especially strong. Berlin was primarily afraid of a Franco-British expeditionary force's landing in Norway and then advancing across the peninsula to occupy the Swedish mining area, from which Germany received its supplies of iron ore, which was vital to the German war economy. Therefore, the Germans were anxious for the Swedes to guarantee that they would defend their territory against any invasion attempt. In return, the Germans offered to reassure Sweden that the latter's neutrality would be strictly observed. On this basis, it was not difficult to reach agreement, and toward the middle of April, at Goering's invitation, a Swedish delegation arrived in Berlin and quickly arrived at a *modus vivendi*, confirmed a few days later by an exchange of letters between Hitler and King Gustav.

In less than a month the situation changed abruptly. The Swedish industrialist Dahlerus, a close friend of Goering's, who had been entrusted on several occasions with unofficial missions,[141] was once again contacted by

---

[139] See p. 98.

[140] *Handlingar rörande Sveriges politik under andra världskriget. Transiteringsfragor och darmed sammanhangande spörsmal, april–juni 1940* [Proceedings relative to Swedish Policy during the Second World War. The Transit Problem and Related Questions for the Period, April–June, 1940]; *Handlingar rörande Sveriges politik under andra världskriget. Transiteringsfragan, juni–december 1940* [The Transit Problems, June–December, 1940] (Stockholm: Norstedt, 1947).

[141] See pp. 633–35.

the German Air Marshal. Goering informed him that Hitler was ready to make every sacrifice in order to prevent the German garrison at Narvik from being overwhelmed. The reasons were more psychological than strategic, since Hitler deemed it vitally important to avoid a German military failure at this juncture. Therefore, the Berlin government requested Swedish permission to ship several trainloads of military equipment across Swedish territory into northern Norway and warned that a refusal would have the most serious consequences because, if the Narvik garrison was forced to surrender for lack of supplies, Sweden would be held directly responsible.

Similar requests had been advanced several days before, but in those instances it was simply a question of allowing medicines and foodstuffs to be transported across Swedish territory, and the Swedish government had given its consent, justifying the decision on the basis of Swedish desire to assist the Norwegian civil population in the occupied zone. Goering's new request was an entirely different matter: it could not be honored without flagrantly violating the fundamental obligations of neutrality, nor could a convenient justification be found for granting such a request. The critical issue involved was that the arms shipped across Swedish territory would not only be used against the Franco-British expeditionary corps but also against the Norwegian army, which was fighting the German invader. On May 11 a special delegation arrived in Berlin from Stockholm for the express purpose of delivering Sweden's refusal to accede to the German request, and despite Goering's strong protests and his undisguised threats the Swedes remained adamant. Five days later, when Von Ribbentrop formally raised the question again, they refused to budge from their position.

Undoubtedly, the strong stand of the Swedish government had been taken in the knowledge that the Swedish people would never tolerate a policy supporting German aggression against Norway. However, it can be assumed that the decision was facilitated by the opening of the attack on the western front, which committed the bulk of the German armed forces and thus made a German attack on Sweden highly improbable. To resolve the difficulties of the situation, during the succeeding days an attempt was made to neutralize northern Norway. The Swedish Foreign Minister, Günther, proposed that northern Norway be occupied by Swedish forces for the duration of the war. The plan was accepted in principle by the London and Paris governments only when it became evident that the Allied expeditionary force could not long resist German pressure. The proposal was rejected forthwith by Berlin, and shortly thereafter it was abandoned.

Sweden's position was radically altered during the first weeks of June, after the Franco-British forces were withdrawn from Norway and the Norwegian army ceased its resistance (June 9, 1940). The Germans then requested that troops, as well as war matériel, be allowed transit across Swedish territory. Negotiations leading to the accord of July 8, 1940, were rapidly concluded, with Sweden agreeing to the transit "of materials for the German defensive forces in Norway," including the transit from and to Norway of German troops on leave. As is clearly demonstrated by the documents in the second volume of the White Book, the limits of this accord were to prove extremely elastic, while Swedish resistance to the constant requests from Berlin was, in most cases, a mere formality.

This clear violation of a neutral's obligations was justified by the conclusion that, since Norway had ceased its resistance, the war matériel shipped across Swedish territory could not be used against the Norwegian people. Undoubtedly, the changed situation in Norway was a decisive factor in the Swedish decision: the principal reason for Sweden's resistance to German demands had been, to a great extent, eliminated. It should also be noted that after the fall of France and the retreat of the Allied expeditionary corps from the Scandinavian peninsula German pressure on Sweden was greatly increased. There is still some question as to whether the weakening of Swedish resistance to German demands might not also have been dictated by the desire to rectify the position taken previously with regard to Germany; that is, after the great German victories, many responsible Swedes may have believed a total German victory imminent and acted accordingly.

A third White Book, published in Stockholm in September, 1947, contains material of greater general interest.[142] It consists of approximately two hundred and fifty documents concerning the period December, 1939–April 1940, and is an important source for the study of the origins of German aggression against Denmark and Norway and for the Allied projection of an invasion of the Scandinavian peninsula. These documents show that Hitler's and the western Allies' plans of action in the Scandinavian peninsula were developed almost simultaneously and that from the beginning of April both Oslo and Stockholm were more concerned with the prospects of an Anglo-French invasion than they were with a German attack. This situation had developed out of the pressures applied during the course of the Russo-Finnish Winter War by the western

---

[142] *Handlingar rörande Sveriges politik under andra världskriget. Förspelet till det tyska angreppet pa Danmark och Norge den 9 april 1940* [Proceedings relative to Swedish Policy during the Second World War. Prelude to the German Attack on Denmark and Norway of April 9, 1940] (Stockholm: Norstedt, 1947).

powers to obtain transit rights for an expeditionary corps destined for Finland and out of the steps taken to induce the Swedes to stop the shipment of iron ore to Germany. The precedents led the Scandinavians, not without reason, to conclude that the Anglo-French combine was seeking to involve Scandinavia in the war. Not until a few days before the German attack did the news of German preparations in the Baltic reveal the most immediate danger, but, on the basis of the evidence provided by these documents, it appears that the Stockholm government knew from the very beginning that Swedish neutrality would not be violated by Germany. Only on this basis is it possible to explain logically the complete absence of military preparations in Sweden. According to a *promemoria* issued by the General Staff, at the beginning of April, 1940, Sweden had only eighteen hundred soldiers in the southern provinces most directly threatened by a German attack.

A fourth White Book of the same series is devoted to relations with Norway for the period April, 1940–1943.[143] In this case, too, the documentation concerns a limited aspect of Swedish policy, but, like the others, it contributes to an over-all evaluation of the Swedish position during World War II.

It is worth noting, for example, that a few days after the beginning of the German attack on Norway, King Haakon and the Nygaardsvold government asked the Swedish government to permit them to establish themselves in Sweden with the guarantee that they would not be interned and that they would be free to leave when they so desired. Stockholm replied that of course the King and his ministers were authorized to reside in Sweden but that international law prohibited their exercising governing functions from an alien base and that no guarantee could be given for an eventual return to Norway. This reply was equivalent to a refusal, and King Haakon and the Norwegian government interpreted it as such.

Obviously, Sweden was doing everything possible to avoid being drawn into the conflict, and in this context the Swedish attitude, even if it can be criticized in the light of the cordial relations existing between the two Scandinavian countries, was amply justified. It is much more difficult to justify, however, the position taken somewhat later by the Swedish government on the institutional question raised in Norway by the departure of King Haakon for haven in Great Britain. On June 17 the

---

[143] *Handlingar rörande Sveriges politik under andra världskriget. Fragor i samband med Norska regeringens vistelse utanför Norge 1940–1943* [Proceedings relative to Swedish Policy during the Second World War. Problems surrounding the Norwegian King's Sojourn outside of Norway, 1940–1943] (Stockholm: Norstedt, 1948).

Swedish Minister of Foreign Affairs agreed to transmit an appeal by the President of the Storting to King Haakon to renounce his claim to the thone of Norway and that of his descendents. Several days later the same Foreign Minister refused to transmit King Haakon's message to the Storting, in which the Norwegian ruler declared that he could not accept a government established under the auspices of German occupying forces. Even more revealing was the position taken by Stockholm on the proposal to place Prince Harald (who with his mother had taken refuge in Sweden) on the Norwegian throne. On July 24, when it became known that the Prince was about to depart for the United States, the Swedish King dispatched a cable to King Haakon advising him that the departure of the Prince, according to opinion in Stockholm, would gravely compromise the future of the Norwegian royal house. Implicit in the advice was the suggestion that King Haakon abdicate, a revelation of what was obviously the Swedish evaluation of the future prospects of Norway and the outcome of the conflict. This episode confirms the impression that during the summer of 1940 the Swedish government tended to ally itself with Germany to an extent that cannot be explained simply by its preoccupation with its neutral status.

At the same time as the action taken by the Swedish government, the Norwegian government also published three White Books on Norwegian-Swedish relations during World War II.[144] Mention has already been made of the close connection between these two publications[145] and of the negative aspects of the situation, which almost certainly exerted a strong influence on the two commissions assigned to the task in the selection of the material to be included. A desire to avoid disturbing the good relations existing between the two countries induced the compilers of both collections, by common consent, to exclude material which would prove embarrassing to either government. Even if it is impossible to determine the nature of these omissions, their existence has undoubtedly reduced the usefulness of a comparison of the materials in the two collections.

Nevertheless, the Norwegian collection serves to clarify several interesting questions. For example, it is revealed that the Norwegian government never pressed the Swedish government to abandon its neutrality. Furthermore, on May 19, 1940, the Norwegian Foreign Minister, Koht, appealed to London and Paris to refrain from taking steps to involve Sweden in the

---

[144] *Norges forhold til Sverige under krigen 1940–1945. Aktstykker utgitt av Det Kgl. Utenriksdepartment* [The Norwegian Position vis-à-vis Sweden during the War, 1940–1945. Documents Edited by the Royal Ministry of Foreign Affairs] (3 vols.; Oslo: Gyldendal Norsk Forlag, 1947–50).

[145] See p. 98.

war. If, six months earlier (Koht noted in his *promemoria*), Sweden had been obliged to enter the war, it would have sided with the Allies, but now the situation had changed. The economic and military ties between Sweden and Germany were very strong, and Stockholm was fully aware of the fact that it would not be able to count on effective Allied support. If the Allies attempted to use force to block the shipment of Swedish ore to Germany, it was likely that Sweden would align herself with Germany.

On the other hand, strenuous efforts were made by Norway to win Swedish support of the kind that had been given by the Scandinavian countries to Finland during the Winter War, when volunteers were allowed to enroll for service in Finland and war materials were sent to the Finns. These requests were promptly denied by the Swedish government, which had reached a *modus vivendi* with Germany in mid-April. The reply given to the Norwegian government left no doubt as to the firm intention of Sweden to avoid any action that could serve as a pretext for German intervention or that could be interpreted by Germany as an unfriendly act.

Another point on which the Norwegian documents cast new light, in contrast to what appears in the Swedish White Books, is the projected neutralization of northern Norway. This material shows that the strongest opposition to the project came from the Norwegian government, which at the end of May was still opposing the plan, especially because it envisaged the occupation of Narvik by Swedish troops. Only in the first days of June did the Norwegian position undergo a change, which was undoubtedly brought about by the news that the Allies were about to remove their expeditionary corps from Norway. In this situation, the Swedish plan offered the advantage of permitting King Haakon and his government to remain on Norwegian soil and—it might be added—of avoiding a link between Norway's cause and that of the Allies, which at that moment appeared to be desperate. The recent military developments made it highly unlikely that Germany would accept the Swedish proposal, and when, in fact, the proposal was made to Berlin early in June, the German government flatly refused to consider it.

In summary, this Swedish and Norwegian documentation is not very enlightening. The concept of Nordic solidarity, cast aside for the first time in favor of egotistical national considerations by Oslo and by Stockholm when the Soviets attacked Finland, could not be restored when military fortune favored Hitler. Once Sweden had decided to resolve the grave questions of the time as they came along, primarily on an individual basis, logic dictated that it would inevitably be necessary to adopt a policy that was morally questionable but that would probably ensure its survival.

Despite the fact that fortuitous circumstances, largely beyond Sweden's control, made it possible for that policy to spare the country the horrors of an invasion, the lesson that can be learned from the experience should provide much food for thought for the future.

Adequate documentation on Danish policy during World War II is provided by the proceedings of the Parliamentary Commission of Inquiry,[146] created in June, 1945, to investigate the roles of certain statesmen and officials in internal and external policies which had provoked turbulent debate in Denmark. The commission promptly published reports, documents, and stenographic summaries of the interrogations as soon as it completed the inquiry on each individual issue.

The volumes of greatest interest are those containing the documentation annexed to the first, second, fourth, and fifth reports, in which the commission was primarily concerned with the reaction of the Danish government to the German ultimatum of April 9, 1940, and with problems of foreign policy during the German occupation.

New data on the first question contribute to a better understanding of the Danish position even though the facts are not substantially different from what was already known.

The Minister of Foreign Affairs, Peter Munch, has pointed out that Denmark was fully aware of the fact that it could expect no aid from the western powers in the event of a German attack. Eden had made this very clear to Munch in March, 1937. There remained the possibility of signing a mutual assistance pact with the other Scandinavian countries, but the Copenhagen government rejected such a proposal when it was advanced by Sweden in 1937, believing it to be inopportune to demonstrate that Denmark felt it was in some way being menaced. However, in May, 1939, Denmark accepted the German offer (also made to Sweden, Norway, and Finland) to conclude a nonaggression pact. After the outbreak of war, Churchill confirmed the fact that Great Britain could offer no guarantees to Denmark, adding that, personally, he was convinced that Hitler would not hesitate to violate the German-Danish pact when it was convenient for him to do so.

In regard to the country's military preparedness, Munch stated that the armed forces were equal to the task of protecting Danish neutrality and that an increase in their number would not noticeably increase their effective-

[146] *Betaenkning til Folketinget, I* [Summary Presented to Parliament]; *Bilag til Betaenkning til Folketinget, I* [Addendum to the Summary Presented to Parliament]; *Beretning til Folketinget, II* [Report to Parliament]; *Bilag til Beretning til Folketinget, II* [Addendum to the Report to Parliament] (Copenhagen: Schultz, 1945 *et seq.*). Successive reports under the same titles and addenda followed.

ness in the event of a direct attack. In fact, during the period of the "phoney war" the government rejected every plan proposed by the General Staff to improve the defensive posture of the country.

On the question of the information received by the Danish government about the German menace, the documents produced by the Danish Admiralty reveal that the Danish Naval Attaché in Berlin had reported in January, 1940, on the possibility of a German demand for permission to install air bases in northern Jutland. However, neither this nor the dispatch from the same source in February were interpreted by the Admiralty as presaging an attack, and so the government was not informed of the communications. It was only early in April that reports reached Copenhagen from the Danish Legation in Berlin on the German naval and military concentrations near the Danish frontiers. At the meeting of the Danish Cabinet on April 5, Minister Zahle's report contained nothing sufficiently alarming to prompt the adoption of the several defensive measures suggested by Munch, nor did the government receive significantly more concrete information from other sources.

On the morning of April 8, the German Minister to Copenhagen led Munch to understand that Denmark "should show comprehension" if, as a result of British minelaying in the North Sea, Denmark "were affected." Munch refrained from assuming any precise obligations at the time, but on the evening of April 8, when Munch was approached again in the same vein by the German Minister, he replied that if difficulties were to arise, "every effort would be made to resolve them in the same friendly spirit with which delicate problems arising between the two countries in the past had been resolved." As is known, when the German ultimatum was presented, the Danish government agreed not to offer resistance to the entrance of German troops into Denmark, declaring that it was doing so "under compulsion."

In effect, at that time Denmark was not only isolated but was also psychologically as well as militarily unprepared to offer any real resistance to Germany. The evidence reveals that the defensive potential of Denmark had remained at the low level of April, 1939. Nevertheless, it should be noted that this fact does not contradict, as it may appear at first glance, Munch's statement that Denmark had adequate forces to protect its neutrality. In order to understand the real meaning of Munch's words, it is necessary to have a clear concept of public and governmental attitudes at the time. For decades the Danes had been accustomed to consider a neutral policy sufficient in itself to guarantee Danish liberty. The creation of a military force larger than was necessary to effect normal frontier protection was viewed as a useless and costly luxury, serving only to divert precious resources from the economic and social development of the state. This had been the policy of the Liberal government during the first two decades of the century, and the results appeared to be excellent. Danish neutrality during World War I had resulted in the acquisition of northern Schleswig. Despite this success, the Liberals believed that the entire policy should be reviewed. This approach was one of the fundamental reasons for the breaking away of the left wing of the Liberal party to form the Radical party. Control of the government was taken over by a coalition of Social Democrats and Radicals, who continued the foreign policy of the preceding Liberal governments throughout the score of years between the two world wars.

The conclusion drawn from the proceedings of the Commission of Inquiry is that the Danish government could not have acted in any way other than it did in the face of the German ultimatum. On the political plane, the result has offered the Danish public ample food for thought and has led to important revisions in the programs of the several parties.

The two major foreign policy problems faced by the Danish government during the German occupation, those of relations with Germany and relations with the western powers as represented by the United States, are the subjects of the fifth report, which deals with several specific questions such as Denmark's adherence to the Anti-Comintern Pact and the position taken by the Danish Minister to Washington, De Kauffman, after April 9, 1940.

The investigation into the first question was designed to ascertain whether the government had been in substantial agreement on the need to accede to the request for a declaration of solidarity with Germany in the war against the U.S.S.R. It was maintained that several Ministers had opposed the declaration and that the Foreign Minister, Scavenius, had forced his Cabinet colleagues to accept it. The documentation emerging from the interrogation of Scavenius has revealed that there was a natural reluctance on the part of all members of the government to subscribe to the declaration, but that not even the most reluctant were ready to assume responsibility for the eventual consequences of a refusal. Insofar as the pressures reportedly exerted by Scavenius are concerned, the facts are that he limited himself to a request that his colleagues take a clear position on the issue, with a warning, however, that it would not be in Denmark's interest to break with Germany over a question of no decisive importance.

On the other hand, adhesion to the Anti-Comintern Pact did not lead to debate because of the German threat to revoke the obligations assumed on April 9, 1940 (regarding Danish independence and territorial integrity). Only the reference (made by Scavenius in a report on the results of his journey to Berlin) to the possibility that at some future date Denmark might be forced to join the Tripartite Pact encountered any opposition from the Ministers.

The inquiry produced no noteworthy clarification on the consequences of the autonomous position assumed by De Kauffman and other Danish representatives abroad after the German occupation. Members of the government have continued to insist that the failure to follow the instructions to harmonize their activities with the new status of the country was reprehensible because it not only exposed the government to German pressure for De Kauffman's dismissal, along with that of other dissident diplomats, but it also forced the government to take a position that accentuated its weakness in German eyes. The Danish Cabinet was in agreement in regarding as intolerable the assumption by some officials of the right to make decisions that conflicted with government directives and that, furthermore, made relations with Germany more difficult while they did not especially simplify those with the western democracies. De Kauffman defended himself by saying that his actions served Denmark well and insisted that had he acted differently, he would not have been invited to sign the United Nations Declaration of January 1, 1942, and that, if this had not occurred, there would have been no formal basis for the inclusion of Denmark in the United Nations Charter Conference at San Francisco.

The American diplomatic documents have demonstrated that De Kauffman was not immediately invited to sign the declaration because his country was not at war with Germany and also because of the opposition of the Norwegian representative. As for the situation that prompted King Christian X to write a letter recalling De Kauffman in April, 1941 (the establishment of American bases in Greenland), President Roosevelt indicated that he could comprehend the Danish King's decision and offered to maintain diplomatic relations with Denmark only through the American Minister in Copenhagen.

The proceedings of the Parliamentary Commission of Inquiry created by the Estates General in 1947 are also the primary source for Dutch history during World War II.[147] The task awaiting this commission was much more delicate and serious than that of the Danish investigators, since wartime developments in Holland were much more dramatic.

After long months of nerve-wracking anticipation of a probable German attack, the swift invasion and the rapid capitulation after only five days of

[147] *Enquêtecommissie Regeringsbeleid 1940–1945* (8 vols.; The Hague: Staatsdrukkerijen Uitgeberijbedrijf, 1949–56).

combat, during which the Queen and her government found refuge in Great Britain, stunned the Dutch public. The Dutch had been well aware of the German threat, but they were convinced that their army would be able to blunt the German attack until such time as Anglo-French aid could reach them. This they believed they could do by destroying the bridges and breaking the dikes, measures which in the past had successfully blocked would-be invaders.

However, events took an unforeseen turn when the Germans parachuted troops behind the Dutch lines and quickly gained control of the key bridges. The defensive possibilities of the Dutch army were thus largely undermined, and in those dramatic hours the flight of the Queen and the government left the impression that they were more concerned with saving their own lives than with defending the country. Rumors and accusations ran rife: the army High Command was accused of incapacity and the government of weakness, and, at the same time, a rumor that a fifth column had made possible the German capture intact of key bridges gained credence. In effect, all of the politico-military organs of the state were blamed for the disaster of May, 1940, and not even the Queen was exempted from responsibility.

Therefore, the Commission of Inquiry was granted wide investigative powers, subject to only one limitation provided by the Constitution; it was to abstain from evaluating the role of Queen Wilhelmina, either directly or indirectly—by ignoring, for example, any reference to the influence exerted by the Sovereign on the decisions taken by the executive which might emerge from the interrogations or from the documentary material presented in evidence. This limitation did not seriously affect the historical importance of the material gathered for the period preceding the invasion, since the constitutional organs of the state functioned normally during these months. The same cannot be said for the succeeding period, when the forced suspension of Parliament and the extraordinary conditions under which the Dutch government in exile in London had to operate naturally increased the Sovereign's powers. Therefore, the motives for the many decisions made by the government in exile, in which the Queen played a dominant role, are destined to remain only partially explained.

The material brought to light by the commission and the number of depositions gathered largely confirm the accusations made against the government, particularly as to the inadequacy of the military preparations. On the other hand, it has also been pointed out that the use in strength of parachute units by the Germans presented the Dutch military with a substantially new and unexpected situation. As had always been the case until World War II, defensive systems were based on the experiences furnished by previous conflicts, and no serious attention was paid to the possibility that the potential enemy would base his attack on new techniques and new arms.

The proceedings of the inquiry make it reasonably clear that a Nazi fifth column as such did not, in effect, exist, even though there were individual cases of Dutch Nazis utilizing Dutch military uniforms to create confusion. On the basis of the evidence, the logical conclusion is that the surprise landings of the parachute troops gave rise to the impression that a fifth column was largely responsible for the ineffective Dutch resistance. Naturally, this is not to deny that the Germans made great use of the information on the Dutch defenses gathered by secret agents, a common practice among the General Staffs of all powers.

The material reveals little that is new on the contrasting views existing within the Dutch government in exile in London during the first months of its existence, when the decision was made to risk the hope for Holland's future on the prospect of a British victory. In fact, Prime Minister Geer defended the need for opening secret negotiations with the Germans without the knowledge of the British. Unfortunately, this is one of those cases where the absence of references to the Queen's action in the matter makes it impossible to reach any exact conclusions on the influence she exerted, as well as on the other behind-the-scenes activities that led to the victory of the group advocating all-out resistance, headed by the Minister of Foreign Affairs, Van Kleffens.

Much more precise data are available on the attempt made in the summer of 1940 to negotiate the entire Dutch question with the Germans, an attempt that, in the final analysis, never quite reached the governmental level. A well-known Dutch businessman was able to contact Goering through the Dutch Embassy in Stockholm and to discuss with him a plan for a compromise that would serve as a basis for further negotiations. This plan envisaged the restitution of the ex-German colonies and the recognition of German protectorates over Poland and Bohemia-Moravia, while the political independence of Norway, Denmark, Holland, Belgium, and France, all areas which the Germans would evacuate, was to be completely restored. Future territorial controversies would be resolved by the United States in the two Americas, by Great Britain throughout her empire, and by Germany in Europe.

The commission had the task of extending its investigations to the close of the conflict. However, for the period following 1940, the problem of major interest is the policy adopted for the Dutch East Indies (Indonesia).

The Belgian internal crisis during and immediately following the war was the deepest and most serious of all of those besetting the small

European states as a result of the war. Perhaps because of the extreme violence of the debate, or perhaps because of an opportunistic gamble taken by one side in accusing the other of the gravest crimes, the publication of the ample source material available, material which in similar circumstances was published in other countries, was blocked.

The crisis stemmed from the surrender of the Belgian army on May 28, 1940, and from the decision taken by King Leopold not to follow the Pierlot government into exile in France. A speech by Pierlot on the afternoon of the same day, in which he accused Leopold of treason because he was negotiating with the enemy in defiance of the unanimous decision taken by the government, opened the polemics. This was followed by accusations that the King planned to establish a new government to collaborate with the Germans and that Leopold III had asked for a meeting with Hitler in order to receive assurances that he would be allowed to keep his throne in the new order to be established by the Reich.

The only materials available to date that cast any light on these events are the report of an Information Commission created by the King to explain his actions,[148] Pierlot's version of the facts as revealed in twelve articles published in the newspaper *Soir,* and the Information Commission's reply to these articles.[149]

This complex of sources, in part documentary and in part memoir, furnishes some reasonably accurate information on the key points of the debate, although definite conclusions are not possible on all of the issues. The differences of opinion and, perhaps, misunderstandings between Leopold and his Ministers during the dramatic days preceding the capitulation still remain a question of point of view and cannot be studied further without the assistance of much more documentary material and a detailed understanding of the general situation immediately preceding and during the development of the crisis. The conduct of the government and of the Sovereign after May 28 is reasonably well clarified by these sources.

The evidence makes it clear that while the government was exerting every effort to call to the attention of the parliamentary deputies who had taken refuge in France "the legal and moral impossibility" of the Sovereign to govern (the Limoges meeting of May 31, 1940), the latter made the first friendly overture to Pierlot and the other Ministers, informing them that he "recognized the legal status of the government and that he was morally at

[148] *Rapport de la Commission d'Information instituée par S. M. le Roi Léopold III le 14 juillet 1946* (Luxemburg: Imprimerie St.-Paul, 1947).

[149] *Note complémentaire publiée le 8 octobre 1947 par la Commission d'Information instituée par S. M. le Roi Léopold III le 14 juillet 1946* (Luxemburg: Imprimerie St.-Paul, 1948). Pierlot's twelve articles published in *Soir* between July 5 and July 19, 1947, are reproduced in their entirety at the beginning of this volume.

their side against the invader." Secondly, it was the government that had left the country to continue the struggle on the side of the Anglo-French and that at the news of the French surrender, instead of fleeing to London to continue the struggle from there, repeatedly appealed to the King to conclude an armistice with the Germans, offering its resignation if this would facilitate negotiations.

Insofar as Leopold's visit to Berchtesgaden on November 19, 1940, is concerned, the minutes of this meeting and the minutes of the meeting at which the Princess of Piedmont obtained the invitation for Leopold, published by the commission, show the accusations leveled against the King to be in this instance without factual foundation.

As confirmed by the recently published German documents,[150] Leopold had sought the meeting with Hitler in order to obtain some relief for the serious food shortage in Belgium, and to arrange for the total repatriation of Belgian prisoners of war (the Germans were releasing only the Flemings). Hitler limited the talks largely to political issues, and in these Leopold fought to obtain a guarantee that Belgium would not lose its independence. If it had been possible to subject all of the controversial questions to this kind of examination, it would have been easy to reduce to its bare essentials the controversy that has divided Belgium in the postwar period.

10. THE JAPANESE DOCUMENTARY COLLECTION.

The year 1868, which marked the beginning of the modern era for Japan, is also the opening date for the official Japanese diplomatic document collection. The first volumes of this collection appeared in 1936, although this did not represent a new undertaking by the Empire of the Rising Sun. From time to time a portion of the diplomatic documents for the preceding period had been published, as part of a vast cultural program promoted by the Japanese government.

During the early years of the nineteenth century, the Japanese Cabinet decided to proceed with the compilation of an official history of the country, beginning with the Tokugawa era (1603–1868). To this end, it created a special section within the office of the Prime Minister which immediately set about to collect all of the available material from public and private archives throughout the country. In 1910 it was decided that the task could be accomplished by the University of Tokyo, and the University created a special institute for this purpose, to which all of the material collected was transferred.

---

[150] See *Documents on German Foreign Policy, 1918–1945*, Series D, XI, 356.

In organizing the project Professor Katsumaru Nakamura, Director of the Institute, chose to provide scholars with all of the sources for the later period of the Tokugawa era when the modernization process of Japan was begun, rather than to publish a limited official text. The reasons for this choice are not known, but a number of Japanese historians believe that because Professor Nakamura was born on the feudal holdings of Nautsuke Ji, who was one of the persons largely responsible for the opening of Japan to the outside world, he decided to testify to the work of his "Lord" through the publication of the documents of that era.

In 1911 publication of the vast collection began. It included all of the significant historical material relative to the years 1853–68, that is, from the arrival of Commodore Perry in Japan to the time of the official replacement of the Shogunate by a constitutional government, which, with the transfer of the capital from Kyoto to Tokyo, paved the way for the enlightened Meiji era.

Because of the great variety of material incorporated, this collection has been divided into series, each of which contains the documentation pertinent to a single problem. A series devoted to foreign affairs[151] not only includes diplomatic documents as such but also diaries, personal correspondence of officials and private citizens, and anything else that could contribute to a better understanding of the development of Japanese foreign policy and of the first contacts of the Tokyo government with Europe and with the United States.

The documentation contained in this series is rich, varied, and extremely important. To date, thirty-two volumes and four supplements have been published, covering the years 1853–59. The negotiations conducted by Commodore Perry in behalf of the United States for the opening of Japanese ports to American ships forms the central theme of these volumes. Yet undoubtedly the most interesting part of the documentation concerns the discussions conducted within the government and the Japanese ruling class on the new course to be given to Japanese policy.

An equally large number of volumes will be required to cover the years up to 1868, and the waiting period will be quite long: no less than one hundred and eighty volumes are planned for the entire collection, and the rhythm of publication is set at one volume per year.[152]

---

[151] *Dai Nihon Komonjo: Bakumatsu Gaikoku Kankei Monjo* [Ancient Japanese Documents: Foreign Policy Documents of the Late Tokugawa Era] (Tokyo, 1911 *et seq.*).

[152] A part of the material for this period that remained in the archives of the Gaimusho was published during World War II in a special series (incomplete): *Bakumatsu Ishin Gaiko Shiryo Shusei* [A Documentary Collection for the Diplomatic

In 1934 the Japanese Foreign Minister, Hirota, decided to contribute to the foreign policy series by publishing the collection of diplomatic documents for the Meiji era (1868–1912).[153]

This new collection aimed to satisfy scholarly needs, and it was designed primarily to demonstrate the characteristics of Japanese foreign policy during Japan's first forty years of active participation in international affairs. But given the date of Hirota's decision (Japan was faced with difficult choices for the future of the Empire), the question arises as to whether the idea for this publication did not emerge from a desire to focus attention on the fundamental lines of Japanese foreign policy in order to show that a centuries-old Japanese national spirit had always conditioned Japan's actions in the international sphere. The emphasis on the traditional guidelines of Japanese foreign policy could be useful in clarifying the position that Japan should assume in the future, leading the ruling class toward the choice that would be in keeping with the traditional principles that guided the nation's policy.

The publication of the collection was controlled directly by the study branch of the Gaimusho, which, however, sought the collaboration of scholars and other experts. Progress was rapid, and by the time that publication was interrupted by the military defeat, nine volumes in twelve tomes had been published. These contained the documents for the period 1868–76.

The Gaimusho archives were, in part, casualties of war. The Ministry of Foreign Affairs transferred a portion of its files to the provinces, but because the aerial offensive against Japan reached almost every corner of the Empire, the transfer did not entirely negate the destructive effects of the bombings, bombings which proved to be catastrophic in a land where most of the buildings were still of wood.

Almost all of the documents remaining in the Gaimusho headquarters were destroyed when the buildings were razed by the bombardments. Those in the small archives building were damaged by fire on January 8, 1942, and others were destroyed by Japanese officials during the last days of the war.

History of the Late Tokugawa Era and the Restoration] (6 vols.; Tokyo, 1942–44). This documentation primarily concerns commercial matters and the Japanese mission sent abroad between 1859 and 1867.

For a selection of the principal documents contained in this and the preceding collection, and for other pertinent material on the same period, see W. G. Beasley, *Select Documents on Japanese Foreign Policy 1853–1868* (London: Oxford University Press, 1955).

[153] *Dai Nihon Gaiko Bunsho* [Japanese Diplomatic Documents] (Tokyo: Nihon Kokusai Kyokai, 1936–63), 45 vols. in 89 tomes.

Other gaps were created by the forces of occupation, which, on February 9, 1946, removed approximately five hundred files, to which must be added those taken during the preliminary phase of the Tokyo war crimes trials. A portion of this material was restored to Japan. A portion still remains in the United States, where it awaits classification and microfilming before being returned to the Japanese.

The Japanese faced not a few obstacles at the end of the war in attempting to continue the publication of the collection. Patient efforts at co-ordination and examination revealed that, while the gaps were many, they were not especially serious, at least as they concerned the Meiji era. In 1951 publication was begun again at the same high level of technical and scholarly effort that characterized the prewar publications.

Continuing the same intense rhythm of production, the foreign policy collection was completed with the forty-fifth volume, which deals with 1912. The forty-five volumes are divided into eighty-eight tomes because, in adhering to the rule that each volume should contain only the material of a given year, allowance for years in which the material was particularly extensive dictated that the volume be divided into two or more books. For example, multiple tomes were published for the years 1894–95 (Sino-Japanese War); for 1900, where three are published on the North China incident (the Boxer Rebellion); and numerous ones on the Russo-Japanese War.

Within each volume or tome the documents are organized by subject. In the first pages of the volume precise references with detailed subdivisions are located. At the end of each volume or, in the case of the multiple-tomed volumes, at the end of the last tome, there is a table listing the contents chronologically, to which is appended a brief outline of the contents.

Insofar as the technical characteristics are concerned, it should be noted that the documents are published in their original languages. Therefore, much of the correspondence exchanged between the Gaimusho and the foreign legations in Japan or between the Japanese legations abroad and the governments to which they were accredited is in western languages. This is of no great practical utility because the most interesting material, that is, the internal documentation of the Ministry of Foreign Affairs and of the government, the instructions to Japanese representatives abroad, and the reports of the latter to the Gaimusho, are in Japanese. It should be added that during the early years of the Meiji era telegrams—even those in code—were edited in English, but in the collection they have almost all been translated into Japanese.

The importance of the collection as an instrument for the study of Japanese foreign policy during the Meiji era, while not to be underrated, is in no way comparable to that of the preceding one, whose series on foreign policy, in addition to containing a very rich documentation that is not all diplomatic in a strict sense, incorporates data contained in the various series concerning the other organs and centers of national power. The Meiji collection, instead, was derived exclusively from documents taken from the archives of the Foreign Ministry, and this selection imposes a much greater limitation on the scholar's comprehension of Japanese foreign policy than is normally present in the diplomatic collections of other countries for the same period. It should be remembered not only that foreign policy in the Japanese Empire, more than anywhere else, was the result of a complex power stuggle between various Japanese factions, but also that diplomatic activity was often conducted through unofficial channels by these elements. Nonetheless, the results were binding on the country.

The existence of these limitations do not prevent the collection from being extremely useful in that it makes possible direct knowledge of the part played by Japan in the development of international affairs during the last years of the nineteenth and the first years of the twentieth century—an aspect of international relations that has not been properly weighed in the rich historiography of the period.

For example, concerning the Japanese position during the Boxer Rebellion, this collection furnishes important data on differences existing within the Tokyo government between those supporting a program of expansion in South China, that is, toward Fukien, in order to aid Formosa commercially and those pressing for the consolidation of the Japanese position in Korea. The striking contrast between these two forces, through which the Prime Minister, Yamagata, tried to steer a middle course, explains the vacillating Japanese position during the crisis; the Tokyo government first contemplated the occupation of Amoy and then retreated from this position, and later indicated a preference for an agreement with Russia on Korea.

The overtures made to St. Petersburg on this subject during July and August, 1900, which were based on a reciprocal recognition of Japan's pre-eminent interests in Korea and Russia's in Manchuria, were not previously known. Yet, their importance was hardly minor in the development of Russo-Japanese relations: Russia's rejection of the overtures revealed Czarist intransigence toward concessions which the Japanese were able to take by force. Russia's irreconcilable attitude contributed to the evolution of the Japanese concept of "now or never," which was to bear fruit in Korea in 1901.

From the soundings that were made simultaneously in Berlin to learn what the German reaction would be to a Russo-Japanese understanding (there is no reference to these in *Die Grosse Politik*), it is learned that

Germany was cognizant of Tokyo's "Korean Program" in August, 1900, and also knew that this situation could lead to a conflict between Russia and Japan. Perhaps this factor had considerable influence on the German decision to reach an agreement with the British on China. It is a fact that the German proposal to Lord Salisbury for the so-called Treaty of Yangtze Kiang of October 16, 1900, was sent immediately after the conclusion of the German-Japanese conversations. From these conversations, the Japanese received the assurance that Germany would not interfere in any complications arising between Japan and other powers over the Korean question. Tokyo interpreted this to mean that the danger of another Far Eastern Triplice such as was formed in 1895 was extremely remote. This clear definition of position by the Germans eliminates the questions that were raised concerning subsequent German policy in the Manchurian and Korean questions.

When the Meiji era is completed, the Japanese Foreign Ministry is planning the publication of its papers for the Taisho era (1912–26) and for the Showa era, to 1945. Upon completion, scholars will have available all of the Japanese diplomatic documents for virtually the entire century of modern Japan's participation in international affairs.

Meanwhile, it is already possible to consult the Gaimusho papers for the years 1868–1945, thanks to the work of the Library of Congress of the United States, which, in collaboration with the Japanese government, has microfilmed the most important holdings of the Tokyo archives. A precise inventory of the documents filmed has been published,[154] permitting the scholar to identify those which interest him and to obtain them on microfilm. The same procedure was used for the archives of the military ministries, which were transferred to Washington after the war.[155]

An examination of the inventory reveals that, in fact, the gaps caused by

[154] Cecil H. Uyehara and Edwin G. Beal (eds.), *Checklist of Archives in the Japanese Ministry of Foreign Affairs* (Washington: Library of Congress-Photoduplication Service, 1954). The Appendix to this inventory includes the lists published by the Gaimusho of the materials destroyed by war action.

For an application of this material to an account of the origins of the last war in the Far East, see David J. Lu, *From the Marco Polo Bridge to Pearl Harbor, A Study of Japan's Entry into World War II* (Washington: Public Affairs Press, 1961).

A rich and up-to-date bibliography of studies in Japanese and occidental languages on international relations in the Far East may be found in Hanabusa Nagamichi (ed.), *Nihon Gaikoshi Kankei Bunken Mokuroku* [Studies relative to the History of Japanese Diplomacy] (Keio University: Research Association Editions, 1961).

[155] John Young (ed.), *Checklist of Microfilm Reproductions of Selected Archives of the Japanese Army, Navy, and Other Government Agencies, 1868–1945* (Washington: Georgetown University Press, 1959). Several Gaimusho files are to be found among these papers.

military action during the war are not as serious as was supposed immediately after the conflict.

In addition to the work of reassembling the records done in Tokyo, a remarkable contribution toward filling the existing gaps was made by the American decoding service, whose perfect organization permitted the United States, prior to and during the conflict, to decipher a large number of telegrams exchanged between the Tokyo government and several of its major embassies abroad. This material has proved to be of great value on the occasions where doubt existed on the correctness of the translations and the exactness of the decoding. It was also extensively used by the Senate committee investigating the attack on Pearl Harbor[156] and in the Tokyo war crimes trials (April, 1946–April, 1948).

The proceedings of these trials[157] have brought to light documents of exceptional importance to the study of Japanese foreign policy beginning with the Manchurian crisis of 1931. Their value as a historical source is as great as that of the proceedings of the Nuremberg trials. However, it should be added that the documentation presented during the trials in Tokyo appears to be even richer in disclosures and of greater utility to the scholar, given the limited number of other sources available that illustrate the various aspects of the history of international relations in this area.

Unfortunately, this material has not produced organic publications such as those that appeared as a result of the Nuremberg trials. Consequently, the material must still be consulted on the sheets multigraphed for daily distribution during the course of the trials, on which the minutes of the sessions were transcribed, along with the texts of the interrogations, the documents presented by the prosecution and the defense, etc.

Until recently, consulting this source (consisting of approximately sixty thousand pages) was rendered extremely difficult by the absence of a systematic table of contents, but in 1957 this inconvenience was eliminated by two scholars, who published a subject matter table of contents in the style that was developed for the proceedings of the Nuremberg trials.[158]

Notwithstanding the fact that the proceedings are replete with data of little interest to the study of international relations, they are of exceptional importance to the study of Japanese relations with the Axis powers and to the history of the Far East. Among the many documents in the collection concerning the Axis are the following: the text of the clauses annexed to

[156] See pp. 234–36.

[157] *Records of Proceedings of the International Military Tribunal for the Far East* (Tokyo, 1946–48).

[158] Paul S. Dull and Michael Takaaki Umemura (eds.), *The Tokyo Trials: A Functional Index to the Proceedings of the International Military Tribunal for the Far East* (Ann Arbor: The University of Michigan Press, 1957).

the Anti-Comintern Pact, which were so secret that even Goering was unaware of them; and the very strong protest lodged by Japan with Berlin for the unlawful signing of the Nazi-Soviet Pact of August 23, 1939, which, in fact, violated the terms contained in the secret clauses of the Anti-Comintern Pact.

The Japanese government has also published an official version of the events of the last days of the war in the Pacific.[159] This account, amplified by the addition of numerous documents, casts new light on many episodes that were known only in part or totally unknown. Particular reference is made to the several Japanese attempts to open peace talks through the offices of unofficial intermediaries. Almost all of these approaches were made in 1945, and a chapter is devoted to each of them. Thus, there is "Operation Byo Ping," which refers to the attempt made to induce Byo Ping, an authoritative figure in the Nanking government, to act as mediator between Japan and the United States, Great Britain and the Chungking government; "Operation Bagge," the key figure here being the Swedish Minister to Tokyo, Bagge, which failed because of Japan's indicated preference for dealing with the Soviet Union; and "Operation Dulles," which refers to the conversations of May, 1945, between Allen Dulles, Chief of the O. S. S. in Europe, and the Japanese attaché in Berne, Fujimura, during which the possibility of peace between the United States and Japan was discussed. However, these latter conversations also accomplished nothing because the Japanese government considered them to be merely exploratory gestures, since there was no indication that the Americans were seriously interested in pressing the talks further.

11. THE CHINESE DOCUMENTARY SOURCES.[160]

China has a centuries-old archival tradition. Each new imperial dynasty wrote the history of the preceding one, basing the account largely on the material collected by the former. The documentation consisted primarily of the Shih-lu ("True Notes"), compilations for imperial court use, containing in chronological order annotations of the imperial government's proceedings. While the dynastic histories have been preserved because they were published and constitute a unique corpus of national histories, the

[159] Japanese Ministry of Foreign Affairs, Shusen Shiroku [Report on the End of the War] (Tokyo: Shimbun Gekkan Sha, 1952).
[160] This section was written by Giuliano Bertuccioli.

Shih-lu have been lost over the course of centuries, with the exception of those of the last dynasties.[161]

Other sources were historical writings of a private character; local histories incorporating the documentation pertinent to a particular locality, province, region, or city; and the *opera omnia* of writers who, as was frequently the case, had held public office and included in their works a variety of documents such as letters, government decrees, memorials to the throne, and diaries.

The publication of the original and integral documentary texts referring almost exclusively to China's relations with foreign powers was an innovation of the last century. Pressure from the western powers finally convinced the Court at Peking that its relations with them were something entirely new in the history of China. During the second half of the reign of the Emperor Tao-kuang (1820–50), the Imperial Court decided to establish an appropriate office for the purpose of recording, assembling, and transcribing edicts, memorials, rescripts, diplomatic correspondence, and all other documents referring to foreign countries and to China's relations with them. The office was called I-wu-chu (Office for Barbarian Affairs),[162] and it was put under the control of the Kuo-shih-kuan (State Historical Service). However, the latter was charged with the task of gathering historical and biographical material for future inclusion in the official dynastic history, while the former was to assemble all of the documentation relative to relations with foreign powers, even if they were not recorded in the *Shih-lu,* copy it, and present it to the Emperor and the Grand Council for study for the purpose of formulating Chinese foreign policy.

In 1856 the Director of the Office, Wen-ch'ing, presented to Tao-

[161] The texts of the *Shih-lu* of the last Chinese imperial dynasty, the Ch'ing, (1644–1912) were published by the photolithograph process in 4,485 chapters in the years 1937–38 by the Tokyo firm of Okura Shuppan Kabushiki Kaisha, under the title of *Ta-Ch'ing li-ch'ao shih-lu* [True Records of the Successive Reigns of the Ch'ing Dynasty]. Publication of a new edition, employing the same process but reduced in size, was begun by the publishing firm of Hua-lien in 1964 in Taipeh. Instead, the history of the Ch'ing dynasty was compiled by a committee of scholars and published in Peking in 1928 in 536 *chüan* (chapters). However, it was not officially recognized by the republican government. The title remained unchanged, *Ch'ing-shih-kao* [Projected History of the Ch'ing Dynasty], because it is not included in the corpus of the twenty-four dynastic histories. However, a new committee of scholars has published a revised and corrected edition, entitled *Ch'ing-shih* [History of the Ch'ing Dynasty] (2d ed., 8 vols.; Taipeh: Kuo-fang, 1963).

[162] There is a detailed study of the I-wu-chu and its work in assembling and compiling the documents: E. Swisher, *China's Management of the American Barbarians: A Study of Sino-American Relations, 1841–1861 with Documents* (New Haven, Conn: Far Eastern Publications, 1953).

kuang's successor, Emperor Hsien-feng (1850–61), the manuscript copy of all of the documents collected by that office for the period 1836–50, the last fifteen years of the reign of Emperor Tao-kuang. It was explained in the Preface that, in the interest of historical accuracy, the compilers had been charged with transcribing the documents in their entirety, a practice differing from that of the compilers of the *Shih-lu,* who did not hesitate to summarize or omit portions of the documents.

In 1867 Chia Chen, then Director of the Office, presented to Emperor T'ung-chih (1861–75) the manuscript copy of the documents of the reign of Emperor Hsien-feng. The documents for the reign of Emperor T'ung-chih were copied and presented to Emperor Kuang-hsu (1875–1908) in 1880 by the Office Director, Pao-yun.

The manuscripts of the three series of historical documents lay in the Court archives until they were discovered by republican officials in 1925. In 1928 the decision was made to publish them, and the task was entrusted to the Imperial Court Museum of Peking. The three series were published in 1930 by the photolithographic process and consist of forty volumes for the reign of Tao-kuang, forty volumes for the reign of Hsien-feng, and fifty volumes for the reign of T'ung-chih. The original title was retained: *Ch'ing-tai ch'ou-pan i-wu shih-mo* ("The Treatment of Barbarian Affairs by the Ch'ing Dynasty from Its Inception to Its End"). A new photolithographic edition in seven volumes was published in Hong Kong by the Chinese Ancient Book Service in 1964.

Differences in the character of the documents may be noted between those of the first two series (1836–50 and 1851–61) and those of the last series (1861–75). These differences stem from China's unfortunate wars with the western powers, which led to the creation of the Tsung-li ko-kuo shih-wu ya-men (abbreviated to Tsung-li ya-men), which served as a Ministry of Foreign Affairs.[163] From that time on, the diplomatic correspondence between China and the Occident assumed a character that formally recognized the position of parity between the two powers, something that cannot be said to have occurred during the preceding period.

In 1875 the I-wu-chu was abolished, and with this act the copying service, as well as the official collection of documents destined for publication, was also terminated. For the period from 1875 to the fall of the Empire in 1912, a collection of documents was edited privately by an

---

[163] See S. M. Meng, *The Tsungli Yamen: Its Organization and Functions* (Cambridge, Mass.: Harvard University Press, 1962); Masataka Banno, *China and the West, 1858–1891: The Origins of the Tsungli Yamen* (Cambridge, Mass.: Harvard University Press, 1964).

official of the State Grand Council, Wang Tao-fu (Yen-wei) and by his son, Wang Hsi-yün (Liang). This collection, titled *Ch'ing-chi wai-chiao shih-liao* ("Historical Materials concerning the Diplomatic Relations of the Last Period of the Ch'ing Dynasty"), was published in 1932 by the Imperial Palace Museum of Peking and is divided into two series: the first, for the reign of Emperor Kuang-hsü (1875–1908) is in 218 chapters; the second, for the reign of Emperor Hsuan-t'ung (1908–12) is in 24 chapters. This series differs from the *Ch'ing-tai ch'ou-pan i-wu shih-mo* collection in that it includes an index in 12 chapters (six volumes) in addition to illustrations, maps, etc.[164]

In addition to these two major collections, there are others supplementing them:

1. *Ch'ing-tai wai-chiao shih-liao* ("Historical Materials concerning the Diplomatic Relations during the Period of the Ch'ing Dynasty"), in two series: the first, for the reign of Emperor Chia-ch'ing (1796–1820), in six volumes; the second, for the reign of Tao-kuang (1820–36), in four volumes. These were published by the Museum of the Imperial Palace in Peking between 1931 and 1933.

2. *Ch'ing-chi ko-kuo chao-hui mu-lu* ("Index to the 'Notes' Sent by the Various Countries during the Last Period of the Ch'ing Dynasty"), published by the Museum of the Imperial Palace in Peking in 1936 in four volumes, listing no less than thirty-eight hundred "communications" received by the Chinese authorities after 1839.

3. Chiang T'ing-fu (T. F. Tsiang), *Chin-tai Chung-kuo wai-chiao-shih tzu-liao chi-yao* ("Compendium of Important Materials referring to the Diplomatic History of Modern China"), published in Shanghai by The Commercial Press between 1931 and 1934.

4. The historical documents (not necessarily diplomatic documents) published periodically by the Museum of the Imperial Palace in Peking, first under the title *Chang-ku ts'ung-pien* ("Collection of Historical Documents") in 1928–29 in ten volumes (a new edition was published in one volume by Kuo-feng in Taipeh in 1964); subsequently under the title *Wen-hsien ts'ung-pien* ("Collection of Documents Drawn from the Office of the Historical Section"), in 1930–36 in thirty-six volumes with seven volumes in 1937; and finally, under the title *Shih-liao hsün-k'an* ("Historical Materials Published Every Ten Days"), in forty volumes between 1930 and 1931. The first collection contains the text of the haughty reply

---

[164] For a description of the collection, see J. F. Fairbank and K. C. Liu, *Modern China: a Bibliographical Guide to Chinese Works, 1898–1937* (Cambridge, Mass.: Harvard University Press, 1950). A new edition of the collection of documents in ten volumes was published by the Wen-hai firm of Taipeh in 1963.

sent by Emperor Ch'ien-lung (1735–95) to George III of Great Britain, who had indicated the British desire to enter into commercial and diplomatic relations with China.

5. Historical documents (not necessarily diplomatic documents) published by Lo Chen-yü, who had the documents of the state archives in his private possession from 1924 to 1933, under the title *Shih-liao ts'ung-k'an ch'u-pien* ("Historical Materials of Various Kinds, First Series"), in ten volumes, and *Shih-liao ts'ung-pien* ("Historical Materials of Various Kinds"), in twelve volumes.

Numerous documentary collections have been published to illustrate various periods or episodes of the history of the last century of the Empire. By strict definition these are not true collections of diplomatic documents, since they include material on a variety of subjects: unpublished and published diplomatic documents, translations of foreign books, articles, treaty texts, etc. The most important collections are those concerning relations with Japan: *Ch'ing Kuang-hsü-ch'ao Chung-Jih chiao-she shih-liao* ("Historical Materials concerning Sino-Japanese Relations during the Reign of Emperor Kuang-hsü, 1875–1908"), in eighty-eight chapters, published by the Museum of the Imperial Palace in Peking in 1932 (a new photolithographed edition in two volumes was published by Wen-hai Press of Taipeh in 1963); *Ch'ing Hsüan-t'ung-ch'ao Chung-Jih chiao-she shih-liao* ("Historical Materials concerning Sino-Japanese Relations during the Reign of Emperor Hsüan-t'ung, 1908–1911"), in six chapters, published by the Museum of the Imperial Palace in Peking, in 1933 (a new edition in one volume was published by Wen-hai Press of Taipeh in 1963); *Chung-Jih chan-cheng* ("The Sino-Japanese War"), published in Shanghai by Hsin-chih-shih ch'u-pan-she in 1956, in seven volumes. The documents concerning relations with France are published in *Ch'ing Kuang-hsü-ch'ao Chung-Fa chiao-she shih-liao* ("Materials concerning Relations with France during the Reign of Emperor Kuang-hsü, 1875–1908"), published by the Museum of the Imperial Palace in Peking, from 1932–1933, in twenty-two chapters; *Chung-Fa chan-cheng* ("The Sino-French War"), published in Shanghai by Hsin-chih-shih ch'u-pan-she in 1955, in seven volumes. There is a collection of documents on the Boxer affair, titled *I-ho t'uan* ("The Boxers"), published in Shanghai by Shen-chou kuo-kuang she, in 1951.[165]

It is expected that in the near future many more documentary

---

[165] For greater bibliographical detail, see J. F. Fairbank, *Ch'ing Documents. An Introductory Syllabus* (2 vols.; Cambridge, Mass.: Harvard University Press, 1959).

collections concerning the history of the last imperial dynasty will be published. According to the journal *Li-shih yen-chiu*[166] the work of classifying nearly six hundred thousand memorials preserved in the archives of the Grand Council, two million memorials preserved in the archives of the office of the Secretary-General, and four hundred thousand documents preserved in the Imperial Palace was completed early in 1959. In turn, the Nationalist government has decided to publish collections of documents pertinent to relations with other countries which are preserved in the archives on Taiwan and come from the archives of the Tsung-li ya-men and from its successor, the Ministry of Foreign Affairs, with headquarters in Peking until 1927. The documentary material to 1927 will be subdivided and published in twenty-six collections. To date, the following have appeared: *Hai-fang tang* ("Archives of Maritime Defense") in nine volumes, published in 1957;[167] *K'uang-wu tang* ("Archives of Mines"), in eight volumes, published in 1960;[168] and *Chung-wo kuang-hsi shih-liao* (Historical Material on Sino-Russian Relations"), in eight volumes, published between 1959 and 1962. These collections appear under the editorship of the Institute of Research in Modern History of the Chinese Academy at Taipeh. Publication of another large collection of documents on the first years of the republic was begun in 1961 by the publishing firm of Cheng-chung of Taipeh, under the title *Chung-hua-min-kuo k'ai-kuo wu-shih-nien hsien*.

Insofar as Sino-Italian relations are concerned, the most interesting documents are published in the *Ch'ing-chi wai-chiao shih-liao* collection cited above. Specifically, these concern the San-mun Bay episode in Chekiang province, the area the Italians demanded to lease in the spring of 1899.

There are a total of eleven documents on this event, and they contain the imperial directives to the governors in view of the threatened Italian landing and the reports of the governors on defense preparations. These are preserved in the following *chüan* (chapters): 138, 139, 140, 141 of the first series, referring to the reign of Emperor Kuang-hsü, plus Chapters 8 and 173 of the Addenda and in Chapter 11 of the second series referring to the

---

[166] *Li-shih yen-chiu* [Historical Researches], 1959, No. 1, p. 95.
[167] The published documents cover the period 1860–1911.
[168] The documents cover the period 1861–1912. Of particular interest to Italy is Vol. III, *Che-kiang k'uang-wu* [Mines of Chekiang], Chapter 8, devoted to the Italian request for a mineral concession in the province of Chekiang presented after the Italian failure to obtain San-mun Bay. There are eleven documents covering the period August 9, 1899 (Doc. No. 1118, p. 1963) to February 2, 1902 (Doc. No. 1128, p. 1975).

reign of Emperor Hsüan-t'ung. These documents have not yet been translated into a western language.[169] Other documents concerning Italian policy in China appear in the work *Ti-kuo-chu-i yü chung-kuo hai*, published in Shanghai by Chung-hua in 1962, in ten volumes. In Volume X, pp. 154–57 there are three documents dating from May 15, 1934, to April 20, 1935, on the question of Italian renunciation of the Boxer indemnity.

---

[169] For a more complete study of the episode, note should be taken of the documents published in Vol. XXXVIII of the *Nihon Gaiko Bunsho* [Japanese Diplomatic Documents] (Tokyo: Nihon Kokusai Kyokai, 1955). Pp. 360 to 459, in Chapter XV, concern the correspondence exchanged between the Japanese foreign ministry and its legations abroad in reference to the Italian request. There are a total of twelve documents written in the period February 20–November 16, 1899.

Chapter V

MEMOIR SOURCES FOR WORLD WAR I
AND ITS ORIGINS *

⟨⟩ SUMMARY: 1. The Italian Memorialists. 2. The French Memorialists. 3. The British Memorialists. 4. The Russian Memorialists. 5. The German Memorialists. 6. The Austrian Memorialists. 7. The American Memorialists. 8. The Memorialists in Other Countries: a. The Belgians; b. The Serbs; c. The Rumanians; d. The Greeks; e. The Japanese; f. The Turks; g. The Bulgarians; h. The Spaniards; i. The Chinese

1. THE ITALIAN MEMORIALISTS.

The list of Italian memoirs is not very long, partly because Italy was not directly involved in the great debate on the question of war responsibility and partly because a tradition of memoir-writing comparable to that of France or Great Britain does not exist in Italy. For example, neither

---

* As in the case of the documents, this section devoted to memoirs is also divided into two chapters, whose common denominators are the origins and diplomatic development of World Wars I and II.

The brief review of the works listed in this chapter is designed only to introduce the student to the memoir material available on the subject. A much more accurate and detailed study of memoir sources for the period may be found in G. P. Gooch, *Recent Revelations of European Diplomacy* (4th ed. revised and enlarged; London: Longmans, 1940), which in many cases has been followed very closely here.

Greater space is allotted to Chapter VI, wherein the author's earlier study ("Fonti documentarie e memorialistiche per la storia diplomatica della seconda guerra mondiale," in *Questioni di storia contemporanea* [Milan: Marzorati, 1952], I, 531–92; III, 1457–65) on the sources for the study of the international relations of World War II and its origins has been further developed.

Victor Emanuel II[1] nor Humbert I[2] nor Victor Emanuel III[3] left memoirs.

The papers from Giovanni Lanza's archive[4] have been published, but only a minor part of these have any bearing on problems of foreign policy. For this same reason the two volumes by Alessandro Guiccioli on Quintino Sella[5] are important only for the events of 1870, while Visconti Venosta[6] left nothing in the way of memoirs.

Some documents pertinent to Benedetto Cairoli's foreign policy are to be found in the study by Michele Rosi,[7] who had access to the Cairoli family archive. These papers are particularly important for the Tunisian question,[8] but insofar as the action taken at the Congress of Berlin is concerned,

[1] Among the many biographies, see Giuseppe Massari, *La vita e il regno di Vittorio Emanuele II di Savoia, primo Re d'Italia* (Milan: Treves, 1901); Vittorio Bersezio, *Il regno di Vittorio Emanuele II* (8 vols.; Turin: Roux, 1878–95); Francesco Ruffini, *Vittorio Emanuele II* (Milan, 1918); Michele Rosi, *Vittorio Emanuel II* (2 vols.; Bologna: Cappelli, 1930); Antonio Monti, *Vittorio Emanuele II* (Milan: Garzanti, 1941); Francesco Cognasso, *Vittorio Emanuele II* (Turin: U.T.E.T., 1942).
The King's archives, presently located at Cascais, Portugal (for an inventory of the holdings, see L. C. Bollea, "L'archivio personale di Vittorio Emanuele II," *Il Risorgimento*, 1917, pp. 449–85), was exploited in part by Antonio Monti and by Alessandro Luzio. A number of letters from this archive have been published in the collection of Italian diplomatic documents of the Italian Ministry of Foreign Affairs. Pietro Pirri (*Pio IX e Vittorio Emanuele II dal loro carteggio privato* [Rome: Pontificia Università Gregoriana, 1944–61, 3 vols. in 5 tomes) carries the story down to 1870. A documentary appendix extends the account to the death of Victor Emanuel II in 1878.
[2] Costanzo Rinaudo, *Umberto I, Re d'Italia* (Turin, 1900); E. E. Ximenes (ed.), *Lettere di Umberto I, Re d'Italia* (Cremona: Fezzi, 1904); Luigi Luzzati, "Re Umberto I," in *Grandi italiani, grandi sacrifici per l'Italia* (Bologna: Zanichelli, 1924).
[3] See the biographies by Gioacchino Volpe, *Vittorio Emanuele III* (Milan: I.S.P.I., 1939), and Domenico Bartoli, *Vittorio Emanuele III* (Milan: Mondadori, 1946).
[4] Cesare De Vecchi di Val Cismon (ed.), *Le carte di Giovanni Lanza* (10 vols.; Regia deputazione di storia patria, 1935–41), including materials from other archives (Vols. VI–VIII concern the period January, 1870–July, 1873). In addition, see Enrico Tavallini, *La vita e i tempi di Giovanni Lanza* (2 vols.; Turin: Roux, 1887), based on the Lanza archive, a part of which has since been lost.
[5] *Quintino Sella* (2 vols.; Rovigo: Tipografia Minelliana, 1887–88). See also Silvio Spaventa, *La politica della Destra* (Bari: Laterza, 1910).
[6] Nevertheless, see Gaetano Salvemini, "La politica estera della destra," *Rivista d'Italia*, 1924–25; Francesco Cataluccio, *La politica estera di Visconti Venosta* (Florence: Marzocco, 1940); Federico Chabod, "Il pensiero europeo della Destra di fronte alla guerra franco-prussiana," *La Comunità Internazionale*, 1946, No. 1; Francesco Cataluccio, "Alleanze e principio di equilibrio nella politica di Visconti Venosta," in *Questioni di Storia del Risorgimento e dell'Unità d'Italia* (Milan: Marzorati, 1951).
[7] *I Cairoli* (2 vols.; Turin: Bocca, 1908), 1st ed.; 2d ed., Rome, 1929; "Il Congresso di Berlino e Benedetto Cairoli," *Bollettino dell'Ufficio Storico Corpo di Stato Maggiore*, May 1, 1927.
[8] Important material is contained in Luigi Chiala, *Pagine di storia contemporanea* (2d ed., 3 vols.; Turin: Roux, 1898), which, despite its defects, remains fundamental for the study of the period. On the same question see, in addition to the French diplomatic documents, Alberto Giaccardi, *La conquista di Tunisi. Storia diplomatica*

reference should also be made to the articles on Count Corti,[9] Minister of
Foreign Affairs in the first Cairoli Cabinet, March–October, 1878.

Agostino Depretis, ad interim Minister of Foreign Affairs on several
occasions, left no memoirs, nor did the ministers of foreign affairs who
served in his cabinets: Melegari (March, 1876–December, 1877), Mancini
(May, 1881–June, 1885), and Di Robilant (October, 1885–February,
1887). As for the diplomats of the period, mention can be made only of
the brief recollections of Count Bonin Longare,[10] an attaché in the Embassy
at Vienna. In this case, one must also refer to Chiala's writings. However
numerous critical studies appeared later, especially on the origins of the
Triple Alliance,[11] Pasquale Stanislao Mancini's African policy,[12] the first

---

dal Congresso di Berlino al trattato di Bardo (Milan: I.S.P.I., 1940); Francesco
Cataluccio, Italia e Francia in Tunisia, 1878–1939 (Rome: Istituto Nazionale di
Cultura Fascista, 1939); Enrico De Leone, La colonizzazione dell'Africa del Nord
(Algeria, Tunisia, Marocco, Libia) (2 vols.; Padua: Cedam, 1957–60); Maurice
Reclus, Jules Ferry, 1832–1893 (Paris: Flammarion, 1947); Thomas F. Power, Jules
Ferry and the Renaissance of French Imperialism (New York: King's Crown Press,
1944); Francis Waddington, "Le rôle de la diplomatie française dans la question
tunisienne," Revue politique et parlamentaire (April, 1934), based on the
Waddington papers; William L. Langer, "The European Powers and the French
Occupation of Tunis," American Historical Review, XXXI (October, 1925–January,
1926), and, by the same author, the pages on the question in European Alliances and
Alignments (2d ed.; New York: Knopf, 1950). Jean Ganiage, Les origines du Pro-
tectorat français en Tunisie (1861–1881) (Paris: Presses Universitaries de France,
1959), contains the best bibliography on the problem.

[9] E. C. Corti Delle Catene, "Il conte Corti al Congresso di Berlino," Nuova Anto-
logia, April 16, 1925; Egon Corti, "Bismarck und Italien am Berliner Kongres,"
Historische Vierteljahrschrift, May 1, 1927; on this phase of Italian policy see also
Ruggero Bonghi, Il congresso di Berlino e la crisi d'oriente (Milan: Treves, 1878);
Alberto Giaccardi, "La prima offensiva francese in Tunisia," Storia e Politica
Internazionale, 1939, pp. 757–80, 1940, pp. 50–67; Carlo Giglio, "Il secondo
gabinetto Depretis e la crisi balcanica (dicembre 1877–marzo 1878)," Rivista Storica
Italiana, II (1955).

[10] Lelio Bonin Longare, "Ricordi di Vienna nei primi anni della Triplice Alleanza,"
Nuova Antologia, November 16, 1932.

[11] See Luigi Salvatorelli, La Triplice Alleanza. Storia diplomatica, 1877–1912
(Milan: I.S.P.I., 1939), the most complete Italian study on the problem; Pribram,
Die politischen Geheimverträge Osterreich-Ungarns, 1879–1914; Archibald Cary Coo-
lidge, The Origins of the Triple Alliance (2d ed.; New York: Scribner, 1926); Eugenio Passamonti, "La questione tunisina. II domani del trattato del Bardo e la politica
europea contemporanea," Rivista Storica Italiana, 1933, pp. 373–21, and 1935,
pp. 49–126.

On the influence of the Roman question, see Francesco Salata, Per la storia
diplomatica della questione romana (Milan: Treves, 1929), drawn from the Austrian
archives; Emile Bourgeois, "Les origines de la Triple Alliance et la question romaine,"
Revue de Paris, January 1, 1926, based on Austrian and German sources; H. L.
Hartdegen, Die Vatikanische Frage und die Enstehung des Dreibundes (Bonn:
Röhrscheid, 1938), based on unpublished materials in the archives of Vienna and
Munich.

[12] Lucien E. Roberts, "Italy and the Egyptian Question 1878–1882," Journal of
Modern History, December, 1946; Carlo Giglio, L'impresa di Massaua (1884–1885)

renewal of the Triple Alliance,[13] and the Mediterranean Agreements of 1887.[14]

Francesco Crispi's writings[15] span a much longer period than that of his tenure as Prime Minister and Minister of Foreign Affairs (1887–91 and 1893–96). These are the first memoir contributions of considerable dimensions on foreign policy after the unification. They are of primary importance despite the fact that one must maintain certain reservations regarding their credibility, since the omissions and inaccuracies of the editor, T. Palamenghi-Crispi, must be added to Crispi's changes and readaptations. It should also be added that this memoir material has been distributed among unrelated works, making it difficult at times to grasp as an organic whole all of the aspects of Crispi's policy along with the pertinent documents for a given period.

Despite these defects, Crispi's writings retain their basic importance. The detailed summary of his missions to Paris, Berlin, Wildbad, London and Budapest, September–October, 1877, does not deny the modesty of their results. Only in the instance of his talks with Andrassy does it appear that he may have found it necessary, some years later, to correct his diary; in speaking of Irredentism, he states that Fiume was excluded in his definition of *Italia irredenta,* while, in all probability, he had referred to Trieste.[16] However, there is no need to subject Crispi's intentions to a

---

(Rome: Istituto Italiano per l'Africa, 1955), based on extensive archival research; Carlo Zaghi and Pasquale Stanislao Mancini, *L'Africa e il problema del Mediterraneo 1884–1885* (Rome: Casini, 1955).

[13] In addition to the works of Pribram, Langer, and Salvatorelli cited above, see Raffaele Cappelli, "La politica estera del conte di Robilant," *Nuova Antologia,* November 1, 1897; Gaetano Salvemini, "Di Robilant e la trasformazione della Triplice," *L'azione,* January 6, 1924.

[14] Pribram's and Chiala's studies contribute important data on this problem, while the best over-all presentation remains Langer's *European Alliances and Alignments.* In addition, see Dwight E. Lee, "The Proposed Mediterranean League of 1887," *Journal of Modern History,* I (1931); and William Norton Medlicott, "The Mediterranean Agreements of 1887," *Slavonic Review,* June, 1926, based on Austrian sources. For the accord with Spain, see Federico Curato, *La questione marocchina e gli accordi italo-spagnoli del 1887 e del 1891* (Milan: Edizioni di Comunità, 1961), based on Italian and Spanish archival materials.

[15] Among Crispi's writings—diaries, letters, notes—published by T. Palamenghi-Crispi, those pertinent to foreign affairs are: *Politica estera. Memorie e documenti* (Milan: Treves, 1912); *Questioni internazionali. Diario e documenti* (Milan: Treves, 1913); *La prima guerra d'Africa. Documenti e memorie dell'archivio Crispi* (Milan: Treves, 1914); *Carteggi politici inediti (1860–1900)* (Rome: Tiber, 1912); see also T. Palamenghi-Crispi, *L'Italia coloniale e Francesco Crispi* (Milan: Treves, 1928), with documents from the Crispi archives.

[16] On this question, see Gaetano Salvemini, "Alla vigilia del Congresso di Berlino. Il colloquio Crispi-Andrassy, 21 ottobre 1877 e la genuinità dei 'diari' crispini," *Nuova Rivista Storica,* I (1925).

detailed examination or to accuse him of retreating on the issue of Italian aims: a short time before, Bismarck had refused to promise him German support against Austria, and Crispi must have had a clear idea of the untimeliness of irritating Vienna by pressing long-range Irredentist projects.

Crispi's writings offer abundant information on the foreign policy of his government, from the meeting with Bismarck at Friederichsruhe in October, 1887, to the events of the war in Africa. However, the violent political debates surrounding the personality and actions of the Sicilian statesman too often directly influenced the evaluation and utilization of this material, and polemics divided scholars into camps on the basis of their political leanings rather than on the basis of an objective evaluation of Crispi's policies.[17] Of course, Crispi's writings added fuel to the fire of these debates, particularly because of certain allegations in his diaries. On the other hand, the diaries must be considered for what they are, memoir sources that possess the characteristics common to that type of source.

Crispi's successors (Pelloux, Saracco, Zanardelli) have left no memoirs.

---

[17] Among the biographies to be noted are: Gualtiero Castellini, *Crispi* (Florence: Barbera, 1915), 2d ed., 1924, on which most of the rest are based; Carlo Arturo Jemolo, *Crispi* (Florence, 1922), probably the best-balanced treatment; Mario Viana, *Crispi, l'eroe tragico* (Milan: Imperia, 1923), is particularly useful for the documents it contains; Gioacchino Volpe, *Francesco Crispi* (Venice: La Nuova Italia, 1928); and Franco Ercole, "La personalità storica di Francesco Crispi e il suo pensiero politico," in the volume *Pensatori ed uomini d'azione* (Milan: Mondadori, 1935). Both of these are apologiae. The negative results of Crispi's foreign policy are emphasized by Gaetano Salvemini, *La politica estera di Francesco Crispi* (Rome: La Voce, 1919), while Luigi Ambrosini's "Crispi" in the volume *Cronache del Risorgimento*, edited by "La Cultura," 1931, focuses on the totalitarian nature of Crispi's foreign policy in its various manifestations; Benedetto Croce, *Storia d'Italia dal 1871 al 1915* (1st ed.; Bari: Laterza, 1927), reprinted many times, emphasizes the antiliberal nature of Crispi's personality and actions. Equally negative is the judgment offered by Ivanoe Bonomi, *La politica italiana da Porta Pia a Vittorio Veneto (1870–1918)* (Turin: Einaudi, 1944), which expresses the Socialist point of view.

For the most recent studies, see Paolo Ettore Santangelo, *Francesco Crispi* (Milan: Tip. Tenconi, 1946), and "Esiste un problema Crispi?," in *Questioni di Storia del Risorgimento e dell'unità d'Italia* (Milan: Marzorati, 1951). See also Georges Bourgin, "Francesco Crispi," in *Les politiques d'expansion impérialiste* (Paris: Presses Universitaires de France, 1949), the most objective study done by a foreigner; on colonial policy, see Augusto Donaudy, *Da Cavour a Francesco Crispi* (Milan: Tempo, 1937); Carlo Conti Rossini, *Italia ed Etiopia dal Trattato di Uccialli ad Adua* (Rome: Istituto per l'Oriente, 1935), an important contribution; Raffaele Ciasca, *Storia coloniale dell'Italia contemporanea* (2d ed.; Milan: Hoepli, 1940); and the recent study by Roberto Battaglia, *La prima guerra d'Africa* (Turin: Einaudi, 1958). For Mediterranean policy, see Pietro Silva, *Il Mediterraneo dall'unità di Roma all'impero italiano* (7th ed.; Milan: I.S.P.I., 1942), which emphasizes the imbalance in Crispi's policy between goals sought and means available.

Domenico Farini's diary[18] is devoted exclusively to internal affairs. Moreover, it appears that responsible Italians considered foreign policy problems to be of extremely limited significance.

Some useful references to the foreign policy of the Di Rudinì government are found in Luzzatti's memoirs,[19] particularly concerning the economic aspects of the Franco-Italian *rapprochement*. However, the evaluation of the new direction taken by Italian foreign policy at the close of the nineteenth century and during the early years of the twentieth century has been repeatedly based on the materials found in private archives, many of which—the Visconti Venosta, Pansa, and Stucchi-Prinetti archives—are sources of prime importance.[20]

Tommaso Tittoni, Minister of Foreign Affairs from 1903 to 1909 almost without interruption, Ambassador to Paris from 1910 to 1916, and member of the *Consulta* from June to November, 1919, in the Nitti Cabinet, left numerous personal records.[21] However, while they clarify certain specific points at issue, because of their fragmentary nature they contribute very little to an over-all view of his actions as minister and diplomat. On the other hand, the work of Tittoni's secretary, Francesco Tommasini,[22] reconstructs in five large volumes not only the period during which Tittoni was Foreign Minister but also Italian policy beginning with the formation of the Triple Alliance. Despite the fact that Tommasini's work is apologetic in nature and his conclusions not always objective, it has the merit of being

---

[18] *Diario di fine secolo* (*1891–1899*), published under the editorship of Emilia Morelli (2 vols.; Rome: Bardi, 1961).

[19] Luigi Luzzatti, *Memorie* (2 vols.; Bologna: Zanichelli, 1931–35).

[20] See especially Enrico Serra, "Visconti Venosta ed 'il colpo di timone' alla base della politica estera italiana," *Nuova Antologia*, January, 1949, which includes a number of documents from the Visconti Venosta archives; *Camille Barrère e la intesa italo-francese* (Milan: Giuffrè, 1950), based on the materials in the Visconti Venosta and in the Stucchi Prinetti archives, among others; *L'intesa mediterranea del 1902. Una fase risolutiva dei rapporti italo-inglesi* (Milan: Giuffrè, 1957), based on the British documents and on the materials included in the Visconti Venosta and in the Stucchi Prinetti archives and on the Pansa diary and papers. See also Serra, "L'accordo italo-francese del 1896 sulla Tunisia," *Rivista Storica Italiana*, III (1961); Pietro Pastorelli, "Albania e Tripoli nella politica estera italiana durante la crisi d'Oriente del 1897," *Rivista di Studi Politici Internazionali*, III (1961). On Prinetti, see P. Ledi, "L'on. Prinetti ministro degli esteri," *Rivista Moderna*, 1903; " 'Semper,' Prinetti e l'Austria-Ungheria," *Nuova Antologia*, June 16, 1909; Francesco Cognasso, "Osservazioni su la politica estera del ministro Prinetti," *Atti della Regia Accademia delle Scienze di Torino*, LXXI (1936); Cognasso, "Per un giudizio sulla politica estera del ministro Prinetti," *ibid.*, LXXVII (1941–42).

[21] *Il giudizio della storia su le responsabilità della guerra* (Milan: Treves, 1916); *Questioni del giorno* (*Tunisia, Abissinia, Bessarabia, Libia, Jugoslavia, Albania*) (Milan: Treves, 1928); *Nuovi scritti di politica interna ed estera* (Milan: Treves, 1930).

[22] *L'Italia alla vigilia della guerra. La politica estera di Tommaso Tittoni* (5 vols.; Bologna: Zanichelli, 1934–41).

based on the still unpublished documents of the Italian Ministry of Foreign
Affairs and of presenting a number of interesting disclosures. For example,
Tommasini reveals the details surrounding the Italo-Russian negotiations
preceding the Racconigi Agreement. These negotiations were begun in
December, 1908, and interrupted shortly thereafter when Izvolski indicated
his lack of interest in this project for an understanding, which had been
developed by Tittoni and Ambassador Muraviev. The talks were not
reopened until September, 1909, when Muraviev divulged that Italy was
considering abandoning the project. The change in Izvolski's position and
Aerhenthal's inconstancy during the Italo-Austrian talks, which were going
on simultaneously, serve to explain more clearly Tittoni's uncertainty. In
attempting to gain recognition by the two empires of Italian interests in the
Balkans, Tittoni appeared to vacillate from time to time between a single
three-power pact and two separate bilateral agreements. At the same time,
this material proves Tittoni's good faith in connection with the origins of
the simultaneous negotiations with Vienna and St. Petersburg, and it serves
as a partial denial of the validity of the accusations leveled by a number of
historians such as Fay[23] against the conduct of the Italian government.

Despite the richness of detail and much new information, Tommasini's
work, of itself, is insufficient for a complete evaluation of Tittoni. Tittoni's
activity as Ambassador to Paris and as head of the Italian delegation to the
peace conference[24] is not yet entirely clear. Moreover, his actions during
these periods lend themselves to criticism: for example, his initiatives
against Sonnino (substantially the same as those of the neutralist Giolitti),
referred to in the Russian documents and in Barrère's dispatches, and his
role in liquidating certain Italian positions taken at the Paris peace
conference which, during the Orlando period, had been considered to be
only partially compromised.

Memoir material concerning various aspects of Italian foreign policy
during the first decade of this century is extremely limited. The memoirs of
the Italian Ambassador to St. Petersburg, Melegari,[25] are of little value
except for the few pages devoted to the background of the Racconigi
Agreement. Some data on Visconti Venosta's activities at the Algeciras
Conference is provided by Carlo Sforza,[26] who was the secretary to the

[23] Sidney Bradshaw Fay, *The Origins of the World War* (2d ed.; New York: Macmillan, 1930).

[24] On this issue see Amedeo Giannini (ed.), *Tommaso Tittoni e Vittorio Scialoja, L'Italia alla conferenza della pace. Discorsi e documenti* (Rome: Libreria di Scienze e Lettere, 1921).

[25] Giulio Melegari, "L'Imperatore Nicolò II e la sua politica. Ricordi ed impressioni," *Nuova Antologia*, August 1, 1923.

[26] "Autour d'Algeciras: Souvenirs diplomatiques," *Revue de Paris*, January 15, 1933.

Italian delegation. The memoirs of Francesco Guicciardini,[27] Minister of Foreign Affairs in the two Sonnino governments, 1906 and 1909–10, are of greater significance. His diary concerns the second of the two ministries (December, 1909–March, 1910) and, despite its brevity, contains useful information on the signing of the Italo-Austrian accord of December 19, 1909, which was negotiated by Tittoni, and on his conversations with Bethmann-Hollweg in March, 1910.

The memoirs of the Italian Chargé d'Affairs at Constantinople, De Martino,[28] offer substantive elements on the immediate origins of the Libyan war. Some details are also furnished by the diary of Carlo Galli,[29] Italian Consul in Tripoli, July–December, 1911. By far the most important memoir contribution on the background of the Italo-Turkish war, the diplomatic aspects of the conflict, and the conclusion of the Treaty of Lausanne[30] is made by Giovanni Giolitti.[31] His memoirs for the preceding period contain only generic references to foreign policy matters[32]—a

[27] *Cento giorni alla Consulta. Diario e ricordi* (Florence: L'arte della stampa, 1943), previously published in *Nuova Antologia*, December 1, 1942.

[28] Giacomo De Martino, "La mia missione a Costantinopoli per la guerra in Libia," *Rassegna di politica internazionale*, IV (1937). See also Alberto Theodoli, "La preparazione dell'impresa di Tripoli. Ricordi di una missione in Turchia," *Nuova Antologia*, July 16, 1934. The author was the Italian delegate on the board of the Ottoman *Caisse de la dette*.

[29] *Diarii e lettere. Tripoli, 1911, Trieste, 1918* (Florence: Sansoni, 1951).

[30] For the diplomatic events surrounding the Libyan war and its origins, see Arrigo Solmi, "La guerra di Libia e il Dodecanneso nei documenti segreti della diplomazia russa," *Politica*, VI (1923); Augusto Torre, "La preparazione diplomatica dell'impressa libica," *Rassegna di politica internazionale*, X (1936), and I and VI (1937); Torre, "L'impresa libica e un mancato accordo mediterraneo," *Storia e Politica internazionale*, June, 1939; Luigi Peteani, *La questione libica nella diplomazia europea* (Florence: Cya, 1939); Renzo Sertoli Salis, *Le isole italiane nell'Egeo dall'occupazione alla sovranità* (Rome: Regio Istituto per la Storia del Risorgimento, 1939); William C. Askew, *Europe and Italy's Acquisition of Libya, 1911–1912* (Durham, N.C.: Duke University Press, 1942); Angelo Piccioli, *La pace di Ouchy* (Rome: Regio Istituto per la Storia del Risorgimento, 1935); Gioacchino Volpe, *L'impresa di Tripoli 1911–1912* (Rome: Leonardo, 1946).

[31] An ample selected bibliography on Giolitti is to be found in A. William Salomone, *L'età giolittiana* (Turin: De Silva, 1949), and in the article by the same author, "Ritorno all'età giolittiana: Salvemini e Giolitti tra la politica e la storia," *Rassegna storica del Risorgimento*, II–III (1959). A second edition of the first study appeared in 1960 as *Italy in the Giolittian Era* (Philadelphia: University of Pennsylvania Press, 1960). Reference is also made to the successive publications, rich in documentary material, *Quaranta anni di politica italiana (dalle carte di Giovanni Giolitti)*, Vol. I: *L'Italia di fine secolo 1885–1900*; Vol. II: *Dieci anni di potere 1901–1909*; Vol. III: *Dai prodromi della grande guerra al fascismo 1910–1928* (Milan: Feltrinelli, 1962). However, scholars have generally ignored Giolitti's activities in foreign affairs. On this point, see Luigi Salvatorelli, "Giolitti und seine Auswärtige Politik," *Europäische Gespräche*, 1928.

[32] *Memorie della mia vita* (2 vols.; Milan: Treves, 1922); 3d ed. in one volume (Milan: Garzanti, 1945).

reflection of the limited importance Giolitti ascribed to such problems. However, his memoirs become a source of major importance with the creation of his fourth ministry in March, 1911. As Giolitti asserts, one of the key points in the program of the new ministry was the solution of the Libyan question, a solution believed by both Giolitti and San Giuliano to be attainable only by war. It was illusory, Giolitti continued, to hope, in the spring of 1911, to resolve the problem by negotiation. The Young Turk revolution prevented the realization of the policy of peaceful penetration begun by the previous ministry, and the new government in Constantinople appeared to be bent on blocking the Italian plans. On the local level, the Turkish government imposed a series of very restrictive measures limiting the activity of the Bank of Rome. On the international level, the Turks resorted to a series of delaying tactics; such as offering the Italians a sphere of influence in Mesopotamia, a region where Italian interests were almost nil and where the appearance of Italy would most certainly have aroused the opposition of both Great Britain and Germany. Since a peaceful solution was deemed to be impossible, only the question of the timeliness of a military action remained to be resolved. As Giolitti states, the decision was prompted by reasons of a general political nature. In the agreements that recognized British rights in Egypt and the dominant French interests in Morocco, Italy won the recognition of her pre-eminent position in Libya. With the arrival of French troops in Fez, Italy found herself faced with the alternative of exercising her rights in Libya without delay or surrendering them. If, Giolitti continues, Italy had not moved into Libya, another power would surely have done so, but, in that event, Italian public opinion would not have tolerated a repetition of the Tunis affair of 1881 and "we would have run the risk of war with another European power," undoubtedly a far more serious thing than a conflict with the Turks. And finally, another reason for the decision was to be found in the Turkophile policy of Austria and Germany, the latter vying with Constantinople in opposing Italian interests in Libya. Giolitti concludes with the apparently paradoxical statement that the only way to restore harmony in the policy of the Triple Alliance toward Turkey was to remove the obstacle by proceeding with the occupation of Libya.

Giolitti refused to give Parliament or his Cabinet the details of the evolution of the Libyan crisis or of the steps planned by the government to resolve the question, insisting that secrecy was essential to success. Only San Giuliano, Minister of Foreign Affairs, was kept fully informed, and he was in full accord with Giolitti on the need to act. However, San Giuliano proposed that Italy proceed with the occupation of Libya before the Moroccan question was resolved, insisting that the Italian undertaking would be treated lightly while the attention of public opinion and of the European governments was focused on the Franco-German rift. Giolitti, on the other hand, was of the opinion that Italy should not move until it was clear that the Moroccan issue would be resolved by negotiation because, in the event of a European war, it was to Italy's interest not to be embroiled in an undertaking that would seriously compromise her position. However, Giolitti's reconstruction of the events is not very convincing, particularly his assertion that as early as March, 1911, he had planned to resolve the Libyan problem. It is more likely that he arrived at this decision some time later, as a result of the developments in the Moroccan crisis and in response to public pressure. Furthermore, all of the evidence points to the fact that the differences existing between Giolitti and San Giuliano were much greater than Giolitti indicates in his memoirs.

Giolitti's opposition to Italy's intervention in World War I has long attracted the attention of historians. His reasoning on the situation is undoubtedly important, but there is some question about his adherence to the realities of the moment; his memoirs seem to reflect, instead, an *ex post facto* evaluation of the situation. It is very difficult to believe that Giolitti had such clear insight into the future developments of the conflict; that he could so accurately foresee that the war would last three years and not three months, as so many unduly optimistic interventionists were claiming; that he could know there was no danger of Austria-Hungary's concluding a separate peace in order to preserve her territorial integrity but, on the contrary, that the Empire would collapse and thus permit Italy to realize her territorial aspirations without the risks and sacrifices of a war. Nor was there a danger, according to Giolitti, of increased Slavic pressures on Italy's eastern frontiers and on the Adriatic coasts after the fall of the Hapsburg monarchy because the most powerful Slavic state, Russia, could not survive the strain of a long war.[33]

Giolitti's memoirs contain numerous errors of fact concerning the last renewal of the Triple Alliance in December, 1912. The first of these is his assertion that the negotiations were initiated by the Central Powers after the Manouba and Carthage incidents, when in fact the initiative came from Italy and occurred more than six months earlier. Important details may be found in the little volume by Carlo Avarna di Gualtieri, based on notes taken from the correspondence of his father, Italian Ambassador to

[33] On Giolitti's position during the period of neutrality, see, on a particularly important point, Gaetano Salvemini, "Giolitti e il Patto di Londra," *Quaderni di cultura e di storia sociale*, VII and VIII–IX (1953); and, based on the recently published Salandra papers (see n. 42, p. 355), Luigi Salvatorelli, "Del nuovo su Giolitti e il Patto di Londra," *La Nuova Stampa*, December 12, 1957.

Vienna.[34] According to this source, the first steps toward an early renewal of the alliance were taken by Avarna in a colloquy with his German colleague, Tschirschky, in April, 1911. This action had been authorized by San Giuliano, and immediately after these talks the negotiations assumed a more official tone and reached the final phase of high-level negotiation in mid-September, when Aerhenthal raised the question of an immediate renewal of the Triple Alliance on the basis of the preceding text. On the other hand, the Avarna summary shows that, if the initiative came from Italy, the Central Powers from the beginning demonstrated their agreement with the procedure suggested by Rome and that, in the face of the hesitation manifested subsequently by San Giuliano because of Italy's situation as a result of the war with Turkey, they exerted great pressure to speed up the negotiations.

Vittorio Cerruti, First Secretary to the Italian Legation in Vienna at the time, commented briefly on the immediate origins of the war,[35] referring only to the first reactions of the news of the assassination at Sarajevo. The observations of Giuliano Cora,[36] then secretary to the Italian Legation in Belgrade, are much more significant. Cora's precise reporting to his government—he was the first western diplomat to transmit to his government the news of the Austrian ultimatum to Serbia—enabled the *Consulta* to grasp immediately the seriousness of the crisis. Luciano Magrini's volume[37] contains important information on the assassination plot and on the position of the Serbian government. Magrini was attached to the Serbian army as a war correspondent in 1915 and was able to interview a number of important witnesses. According to his reports, the Serbian government was aware of the assassination plot, and early in June Pasic directed the Serbian Minister to Vienna, Jovanovic, to warn Berchtold of the plot. However, Jovanovic, at odds with Berchtold, limited himself to informing only Bilinski, Austrian Minister for Boznia and Herzegovina, in a general way.

Antonio di San Giuliano left no memoirs, nor are there many critical studies of the man available.[38] However, Prime Minister Antonio Salan-

[34] Carlo Avarna di Gualtieri, *L'ultimo rinnovamento della Triplice* (5 dicembre 1912) (Milan: Alpes, 1924). On the same question, see W. Kalbskopf, *Die Aussenpolitik der Mittelmächte in Tripoliskriege und die letze Dreibundserneuerung 1911–1912* (Erlangen: Dores, 1932).

[35] "Vent'anni dopo Serajevo," *Nuova Antologia*, July 1, 1934.

[36] "Belgrado 1914," *Rivista di Studi politici internazionali*, IV (1941).

[37] *Il dramma di Serajevo. Origini e responsabilità della guerra europea* (Milan: Athena, 1929).

[38] Francesco Cataluccio, *Antonio di San Giuliano e la politica estera italiana dal 1900 al 1914* (Florence: Le Monnier, 1935); Francesco Salata, "Il marchese di San Giuliano," *Rassegna di Storia e di politica internazionale*, I (1940), based on

dra's two volumes[39] are a basic source for the period of Italian neutrality. The outbreak of the European war in August, 1914, had not involved Italy in the debate on the immediate origins of the war, but the two decisions made, the neutrality declaration and the intervention in 1915, were historic turning points in Italian policy and remain subjects for debate. Salandra's testimony, written in a sober and restrained style (although not without emotion), presents a number of important details on why and how these decisions were made. Salandra affirms that Italy decided to remain neutral as soon as Rome became aware of the Austrian ultimatum to Serbia. If the Italian decision was formally justified by the aggressive nature of Austrian policy—and the German Ambassador, Flotow, was immediately so informed by San Giuliano and Salandra—the reasons for the decision go far beyond the mere legal aspects of the problem. Salandra added that "Italian public sentiment would have been anti-Austrian at any time, and more than ever at that particular moment," but that this sentiment also coincided with Italian interests in the Adriatic and the Balkan peninsula, which would have been overwhelmed by further German expansion in the area. It mattered little whether or not the destructive forces at work within the Hapsburg Empire achieved their ultimate aims, since Germany was ready to take over the Hapsburg positions. The essential problem, from the Italian point of view, was that of determining whether the war potential of the Central Powers was superior to that of the Franco-Russian duplice in the event that Great Britain remained neutral. In that case, any solution would have worked to Italy's disadvantage. Salandra wrote that, notwithstanding the uncertainty prevailing in those days regarding London's position, his decision was prompted by the belief that British intervention was inevitable. This conclusion excluded a priori the possibility of Italian intervention on the side of the Central Powers, and it appeared to weight the military balance in favor of the Entente. Furthermore, the Prime Minister, familiar with a characteristic Anglo-Saxon trait, was certain that the war would be fought to its logical end, that is, until every threat of German hegemony on the Continent had been eliminated.

The germ of the subsequent idea of Italy's intervention in the conflict may be found in the reasons given for the decision on neutrality in 1914.

———
unpublished documents; Guido Tadini, Il marchese di San Giuliano nella tragica estate 1914 (Bergamo: Istituto d'Arti Grafiche, 1945); Augusto Torre, "Il marchese di San Giuliano tra la neutralità e l'intervento," Nova Historia, Nos. 22, 23, 24, 25, 1954; Torre, "Ricordo di A. di San Giuliano," Nuova Antologia, January 1, 1955; Rino Longhitano, Antonino di San Giuliano (Rome-Milan: Bocca, 1954); Luigi Salvatorelli, "Agosto 1914," La Nuova Stampa, January 7, 1955.

[39] La neutralità italiana (1914) (Milan: Mondadori, 1928); L'intervento (1915) (Milan: Mondadori, 1930).

Salandra admits that, after having made the decision on neutrality, he was not immediately able to arrive at a precise course of action. However, he did not believe that the accusation of indecisiveness on the part of his government was justified. The responsibilities were grave, and the situation was anything but clear at the time. It was only after the Battle of the Marne, Salandra writes, that he arrived at a decision on the course of action to take. He added, "once it was evident that the German plan for a short war had failed, it seemed to me that the historic moment had arrived to achieve the complete unification of the state and to extend Italy's frontiers to the limits consecrated by nature and by tradition." This was the concept held by Salandra and like-minded men, who saw the war as the last of the Risorgimento struggles. It was this idea that guided the negotiations that, between pauses and hesitations due to internal and external pressures amply described by Salandra, led to the conclusion of the Treaty of London.[40]

Salandra's work terminates with Italy's intervention in the war. However, some reference to his activities during the first year of the war and to his resignation in June, 1916, may be found in a little volume published posthumously by his sons,[41] which includes a number of important notes and excerpts taken from the correspondence files. These also cover the period from his mission to the League of Nations as an Italian delegate to his retirement from public life in January, 1925. Further information may be obtained on Salandra's position in the period of neutrality and in the struggle between neutralists and interventionists from his recently published papers.[42]

Special note should be taken of the Ernesto Artom correspondence[43] for the period March–April, 1915, on several aspects of the struggle for

[40] On these negotiations, see Toscano, *Il Patto di Londra* (Bologna: Zanichelli, 1934); *Le convenzioni militari concluse fra l'Italia e l'Intesa alla vigilia dell'intervento* (Milan: Giuffrè, 1936).

[41] Antonio Salandra, *Memorie politiche 1916–1925* (Milan: Garzanti, 1951).

[42] See, in addition to Arrigo Solmi, "Carteggio tra Salandra e Sonnino nella prima fase della neutralità italiana (agosto–dicembre 1914)," *Nuova Antologia*, February 16, 1934; Corrado de Biase, "Da un carteggio inedito Salandra-di San Giuliano. La neutralità italiana (luglio–ottobre 1914)," *Quaderni di cultura e storia sociale*, III (1954); Alberto Monticone, "Salandra e Sonnino verso la decisione dell'intervento," *Rivista di Studi politici internazionali*, I (1957); Giambattista Gifuni, "Le memorabili giornate del maggio 1915 nel diario inedito di Antonio Salandra," *Il Mattino*, August 25, 29, and September 1, 1957 (the pages of the diary are reproduced in their entirety by Sinibaldo Tino, in *La politica parlamentare*, September–October, 1957); Bruno Vigezzi, "I problemi della neutralità e della guerra nel carteggio Salandra-Sonnino (1914–1917)," *Nuova Rivista Storica*, III (1961).

[43] Isacco and Ernesto Artom, *Iniziative neuralistiche della diplomazia italiana nel 1870 e nel 1915. Documenti inediti a cura di Angelo Artom* (Turin: Einaudi, 1954).

neutrality fostered by the Giolittian forces, in which Artom played a role in the unofficial contacts between the Italian government and the embassies of the Central Powers. Other references on the actions of the neutralists may be found in Bertolini's diary.[44] Bertolini supported the Giolittian maneuvers, but for very different reasons.

The documentation in the Avarna-Bollati correspondence[45] is more closely restricted to diplomatic activity. The ambassadors to Vienna and Berlin were clearly opposed to Italian intervention on the side of the Entente. They argued that Italy, allied for so long to the Central Powers, could not now stand against them and that, furthermore, there was the danger that the weakening—if not the complete disappearance—of the Austro-Hungarian Empire would eliminate the base of European equilibrium and the bulwark against the Slavic world. Both of these envoys faced the personal decision whether to support, as representatives of their government, a policy they considered to be disastrous or to tender their resignations before relations were broken. The problem was discussed by the two diplomats beginning in August, 1914, and was resolved, in the sense that both men considered it their duty to remain at their posts. However, the quantity of correspondence that resulted from this similarity of views goes far beyond the personal aspects of the problem. The letters become a significant source of data, complementing on many points the official documents of the *Consulta,* which have been published for this period up to the death of San Giuliano on October 18, 1914, and giving an account of the various personal initiatives taken by the two ambassadors. The breadth of view and the frankness of the language used in these letters regarding the Austrian and German situation and the attitude of the two governments toward an accord with Italy contribute to a more exact interpretation of the meaning of the dispatches sent to Rome by Avarna and Bollati.

The memoirs of the former Commercial Attaché in Paris, Sabini,[46] provide a view from the interventionist plane. Immediately after the outbreak of the war, Sabini had a series of conversations with Clemenceau and other French statesmen on a possible Italian intervention on the side of the Entente. The negotiations, conducted by Sabini on a purely personal

[44] Pietro Bertolini, "Diario (agosto 1914–maggio 1915)," *Nuova Antologia,* February 1, 1923.

[45] Carlo Avarna di Gualtieri (ed.), *Il carteggio Avarna-Bollati, Luglio 1914–maggio 1915* (Naples: Edizioni Scientifiche Italiane, 1953). On Bollati, see also Rodolfo Rogora, "Il neutralismo dell'ambasciatore novarese Riccardo Bollati (Da lettere inedite)," *Bollettino storico della Provincia di Novara,* 1953, pp. 202–15.

[46] C. Sabini, *Le fond d'une querelle. Documents inédits sur les relations franco-italiennes 1914–1921* (Paris: Grasset, 1921).

basis and without official sanction, produced no concrete results and were broken off in October, 1914, at the request of Ambassador Tittoni. However, these notes provide further clarification of the attitudes of responsible Frenchmen toward Italy and of Paris toward Italian territorial claims at a time when the question of Italian intervention had not yet been posed officially.

Olindo Malagodi's "conversations"[47] are among the most important sources for the period of neutrality, the war years, and for the peace conference. These volumes are not a memoir but rather a series of notes made during conversations between the former editor of the *Tribuna* and the most important Italian political leaders between 1914 and 1919, from which numerous facts important for a study of Italian policy of that period may be gathered.

Leaving aside those memoirs primarily devoted to internal affairs, reference should also be made to Leonida Bissolati's diary.[48] Bissolati was Minister without Portfolio in the Boselli ministry and held views opposed to those of Sonnino on matters of foreign policy. Within the government Bissolati represented left-wing sentiment favoring intervention. He was the first Entente government official to advocate publicly, in a speech at Cremona on October 29, 1916, the dismemberment of the Hapsburg Empire as a war aim—a policy that was in open contradiction to that of Sonnino—and, developing his ideas cogently, he later opposed the extension of Italian frontiers to include German and Slavic ethnic minorities.

The contribution by Count de Bosdari[49] is significant for the purely diplomatic aspects of the conflict. His memoirs cover the period from the Bosnian crisis to the spring of 1918 (he was Minister to Sofia from September, 1910, to January, 1913, and from this date to May, 1918, he was Minister to Athens). Of particular significance are his observations on Italian and Allied policy in Greece, observations that are rich in detail, although not always objective because of his strong anti-Venizelos and equally strong anti-French bias. The same approach is to be found in the memoirs of the Military Attaché to Greece, Colonel Caracciolo,[50] which complement Bosdari's exposition.

[47] Brunelli Vigezzi (ed.), *Olindo Malagodi. Conversazioni della guerra 1914–1919*, Tome I. *Da Serajevo a Caporetto*; Tome II: *Dal Piave a Versailles* (Milan: Ricciardi, 1960).

[48] *Diario di guerra. Ricordi e documenti di guerra* (Turin: Einaudi, 1935). For Bissolati's views, see also *La politica estera dell'Italia dal 1897 al 1920. Scritti e discorsi di Leonida Bissolati* (Milan: Treves, 1923).

[49] Alessandro de Bosdari, *Delle guerre balcaniche, della grande guerra e di alcuni fatti precedenti ad esse. (Appunti diplomatici)* (Milan: Mondadori, 1928).

[50] Mario Caracciolo, *L'intervento della Grecia nella guerra mondiale e la diplomazia alleata* (Rome: Magione, 1925).

Ambassador Macchi di Cellere's volume on his mission to Washington[51] is apologetic and defensive in character. It appeared anonymously (edited by his wife) not long after the end of the war and shortly after his death. The publication of the volume was prompted by debates arising from the accusation that Macchi di Cellere had irritated President Wilson and, in so doing, had prejudiced the Italian case on psychological grounds and that he had not kept his government fully and correctly informed on President Wilson's views prior to the latter's departure for Paris. The book is particularly valuable for the documents it contains and for the diary Macchi di Cellere kept during the Paris peace conference, which he attended at President Wilson's request.

With the publication of Orlando's memoirs, or, rather, that portion of his recollections that he was able to write during the period of his enforced inactivity from 1922 to 1945, another significant source has been added to the study of the war and the peace conference.[52] Taking a position that most memorialists studiously avoid, Orlando prefaces his observations by stating that he desired to assume personally the defense of his policies, policies which neutralists and interventionists alike were delighted to criticize. The first of the many points on which his testimony casts new light is the meeting of the Council of Ministers of May 13, 1915, at which the resignation of the Salandra government was debated. Orlando recalls that he opposed the resignation, pointing out to his colleagues in the Cabinet that the Pact of London was an agreement between states and not between governments and, as such, could not be modified—as Salandra and Sonnino were insisting it could be—by a new government so charged by Parliament as a result of the crisis. Orlando's argument did not prevail, but this observation leads to the conclusion that both Salandra and Sonnino underestimated the legal implications of the accord with the Entente powers. Consequently, the resignation of the Salandra government would not have been a simple maneuver to sway public support against Giolitti, and the latter, in turn, could not have learned from Salandra more about the legal status of the pact than the Prime Minister himself knew.

As for the politico-military situation in Italy when Orlando assumed control of the government, the most important revelation in his memoirs is the complete text of the letter to him from General Cadorna dated November 3, 1917. The last sentence in the long exposition by the General on the gravity of the situation clearly indicates that he was inviting

[51] V. Justus, *Macchi di Cellere all'ambasciata di Washington. Memorie e testimonianze* (Florence: Bemporad, 1920).

[52] Rodolfo Mosca (ed.), *Vittorio Emanuele Orlando. Memorie (1915–1919)* (Milan: Rizzoli, 1960).

the government to seek an armistice, even if this invitation was only an expedient by which Cadorna sought to escape responsibility at the gravest point of the crisis. The second half of the book is devoted to the peace conference, on which Orlando furnishes numerous details. While the over-all picture is not necessarily altered, it is interesting to note that Orlando reiterates his conviction that the attitude of the protagonists at the conference was strongly conditioned by the development of Italian problems, particularly concerning the Adriatic. According to Orlando, this conditioning often had an important bearing on the work of the conference, so much so that the Italian problems can be considered the key to an insight into developments at Paris.

If Sonnino, faithful to his retiring personality, left no memoirs of his service in the *Consulta* during the war (November, 1914–June, 1919), the gap has been rather amply filled by the writings of his Chief of Cabinet, Luigi Aldrovandi Marescotti.[53] The latter has published the portions of his diary concerning the most important questions Sonnino dealt with as Minister of Foreign Affairs during the war years and those periods at the peace conference when Italian problems were under discussion. Therefore, these volumes remain an important source for the study of Italian diplomatic activity during this period. The notes and recollections gathered in Aldrovandi Marescotti's diary supplement and complete Salandra's memoirs regarding the negotiations leading to the Pact of London, the Italo-Rumanian accord of February 6, 1915, the successive contacts between Rome and Bucharest, the steps taken by Von Jagow for a secret meeting with Sonnino in April, 1915, and the Italian intervention the following month. The volumes are replete with material relevant to the inter-Allied mission to Russia of January–February, 1917, in which Aldrovandi Marescotti participated as a member of the Italian delegation headed by Scialoja. Equally significant is the material regarding the meeting at St. Jean-de-Maurienne in April and the meetings at Rapallo and Peschiera in November. His notes on the last two enrich the succinct report of these meetings found in Orlando's memoirs; however, the portion of greatest interest remains that on the peace conference. At Paris, Aldrovandi functioned as secretary to the Italian delegation, and his position enabled him to attend the sessions of the Big Four beginning on April 19. Thus, the notes taken by Aldrovandi with reference only to Italian questions, together with those of the interpreter, Mantoux, and those of the "official" secretary, Sir Maurice Hankey, serve as a primary source for a close study of the

[53] *Guerra diplomatica. Ricordi e frammenti di diario (1914–1919)* (Milan: Mondadori, 1937); *Nuovi ricordi e frammenti di diario per far seguito a Guerra Diplomatica (1914–1919)* (Milan: Mondadori, 1938).

discussions of the Big Four. While Sir Maurice Hankey, because of his official role, preferred to use the indirect form in writing and occasionally tempered his comments for reasons of necessity, Aldrovandi employed the direct form, when necessary emphasizing tone of voice or significant gestures accompanying specific statements. Thus a comparison of the Italian diplomat's notes with Hankey's—the latter's have been published in their entirety in the American collection of diplomatic documents—serves a useful purpose, although no differences exist between the two versions except, perhaps, in matters of detail.

Aldrovandi's memoirs on the conference are complemented by Silvio Crespi's diary.[54] Crespi was Minister of Supply in the Orlando Cabinet and an expert with the Italian delegation to Paris. His notations begin in November, 1917, and, despite the fact that the first part of his diary mainly concerns internal affairs, it is possible to extract important data on the debates between those advocating and those opposing the dismemberment of the Hapsburg Empire. But it is with the armistice that this diary becomes significant. The detailed comments on the position of the Italian delegation at the peace conference and on the unofficial contacts between the various delegations contribute immeasurably to an understanding of the attitudes of the delegates in the official sessions.

Among military memoirs or sources that deal principally with military matters, the work of General Alberti[55] on the contacts between the general staffs of the Triple Alliance should be noted, along with the volumes by General Cadorna,[56] which contain frequent interesting references to political issues[57] and to relations between Italy and her allies. The latter question has also been the subject of the works of General Caracciolo[58] and Nicola Brancaccio.[59] Brancaccio headed the Italian section of the inter-Allied office of information, but he also had duties that went beyond the

[54] *Alla difesa d'Italia in guerra e a Versailles* (Milan: Mondadori, 1937).

[55] Adriano Alberti, *Il generale Falkenhayn. Le relazioni tra i Capi di Stato Maggiore della Triplice* (Rome: Libreria dello Stato, 1924).

[56] Luigi Cadorna, *La guerra alla fronte italiana fino all'arresto sulla linea del Piave e del Grappa 1915–1917* (2 vols.; Milan: Treves, 1921); *Altre pagine sulla Grande Guerra* (Milan: Mondadori, 1925), important for data on the expeditions to Albania and Salonika; *Pagine polemiche* (Milan: Garzanti, 1950).

[57] The pages Cadorna devotes to the state of Italian military unpreparedness in the summer of 1914 should be considered in relation to the influence the military weakness may have had on the decision of the Salandra government to declare Italian neutrality. On this point, see also Giorgio Rochat, "L'esercito italiano nell'estate 1914," *Nuova Rivista Storica*, II (1961).

[58] Mario Caracciolo, *L'Italia e i suoi alleati nella grande guerra* (Milan: Mondadori, 1932).

[59] *La Francia durante la guerra* (Milan: Mondadori, 1926).

purely military character of the information office. Angelo Gatti was sent to Versailles in December, 1917, as part of the Cadorna delegation to the Allied Supreme War Council and has left an interesting record of that experience.[60] General Segre, chief of the Italian armistice delegation, has discussed that particular subject.[61]

The work of Luigi Albertini[62] presents some unique characteristics. It is a detailed reconstruction of Italian internal and foreign policies for the period 1908–18, based on a wide collection of sources and on his personal recollections.[63] As publisher of the *Corriere della Sera* he played an important role in the events of the period and was aware of many behind-the-scenes incidents. His numerous autobiographical references serve to trace the history of his newspaper rather than his personal activity.

2. THE FRENCH MEMORIALISTS.

The disputes that raged in postwar France on the role of statesmen and parties in the events that led to the world war, disagreement over the results of the Peace of Paris, and the need to justify individual and governmental action on the whole question of war responsibility prompted French statesmen, diplomats, and military men who had held responsible positions before and during the war to publish their versions of the facts. This phenomenon, common to all countries in the postwar era, was most obvious in France, not so much as a consequence of a centuries-old tradition of memoir-writing—the bitterness expressed in these writings and the proximity of the events discussed bear little resemblance to such traditional French practices—but as a result of a political situation and a psychological attitude that were entirely unique.

[60] *Un italiano a Versailles (dicembre 1917–febbraio 1918)* (Milan: Ceschina, 1958).

[61] General Roberto Segre, *La missione militare italiana per l'armistizio (dicembre 1918–gennaio 1919)* (Bologna: Zanichelli, 1928). From among this author's many volumes on military history, see *Vienna e Belgrado 1876–1914* (Milan: Corbaccio, 1935).

[62] *Venti anni di vita politica.* Part 1, *L'esperienza democratica italiana dal 1898 al 1914* (2 vols.); Part 2, *L'Italia nella guerra mondiale,* Vol. I: *La crisi del luglio 1914, la neutralità e l'intervento;* Vol. II: *Dalla dichiarazione di guerra alla vigilia di Caporetto (maggio 1915–ottobre 1917);* Vol. III: *Da Caporetto a Vittorio Veneto (ottobre 1917–novembre 1918)* (Bologna: Zanichelli, 1950–53).

[63] Albertini utilized these documents for a study on the origins of World War I which is among the most significant published to date: *Le origini della guerra mondiale del 1914* (3 vols.; Milan: Bocca, 1942–43).

The writings of Joseph Caillaux, member of the Cabinet on several occasions and Prime Minister in 1911, are especially voluminous.[64] Of greatest significance is his discussion of the Agadir crisis; he reports in great detail his role in the negotiations that led to the Franco-German accord of 1911. It should be noted that Caillaux, convinced of the urgency of arriving at a peaceful solution of the crisis, often acted entirely on his own initiative instead of through the official channels of the Quai d'Orsay. Consequently, on many points the official documents do not report the entire story, and they must be supplemented by the account provided by the former Prime Minister.

In January, 1912, Caillaux was succeeded by Raymond Poincaré, who, the following year, was elected to the presidency of the French Republic. Poincaré has left a detailed chronicle[65] of his political activities, which, however, does not cover his entire seven-year tenure of office as President, nor does it encompass his premiership, 1922–24, nor the period 1926–29, when he was Minister of Finance. He chose to end his report with 1918, concluding that it was not opportune to reveal what followed until a long period of time had elapsed. Despite the limitations imposed by Poincaré, these memoirs remain an imposing contribution. They go far beyond his recollections based on his daily notes to include a summary of events occurring elsewhere simultaneously. The diary form has been maintained, but the over-all picture has been enlarged considerably by this inclusion. Poincaré supplemented the original text with a large number of documents, in part dispatches relating to purely diplomatic affairs that were transmitted to him by the Quai d'Orsay for his review, and in part the documents published after the war, particularly the Russian documents. Because of the style and form of Poincaré's work, the customary fragmentary character or spontaneity of a diary does not appear.

Despite their defects, these memoirs remain an essential source, especially because (his comments to the contrary notwithstanding) there exists

---

[64] Agadir (Paris: Albin Michel, 1919). The second edition published in 1921 is enriched by the addition of a number of confidential letters from the German Minister of Foreign Affairs, Kiderlen-Wächter. Caillaux, Mes prisons (Paris: Flammarion, 1921); D'Agadir à la grande pénitence (Paris: Flammarion, 1933); Mes Mémoires, Vol. I: Ma jeunesse orgueilleuse, 1863–1909; Vol. II: Mes audaces. Agadir, 1909–1912; Vol. III: Clairvoyance et force d'âme dans les épreuves, 1912–1930 (Paris: Plon, 1942–47).

[65] Au service de la France. Neuf années de souvenirs, Vol. I: Le Lendemain d'Agadir (1912); Vol. II: Les Balkans en feu (1912); Vol. III: L'Europe sous les armes (1913); Vol. IV: L'Union sacrée (1914); Vol. V: L'Invasion (1914); Vol. VI: Les Tranchées (1915); Vol. VII: Guerre de siège (1915); Vol. VIII: Verdun (1916); Vol. IX: L'année trouble (1917); Vol. X: Victoire et armistice (1918) (Paris: Plon, 1926–33).

no doubt about the influence Poincaré exercised on the decisions of the French government. However, the work is weakened somewhat by the author's constant effort in the first four volumes to portray French policy as constantly motivated by a peaceful intent, in contrast to that of the Central Powers. Poincaré was also very critical of the Russians, especially in his examination of Czarist diplomacy in the Balkans and Izvolski's activities in Paris. As for his journey to St. Petersburg with Viviani in July, 1914, and the meeting with Sazonov, the author's version is that Sazonov gave him no inkling that the mobilization order was imminent and that, consequently, the Russian mobilization took him completely by surprise.

This defensive position is also reflected, albeit in a minor way, in the last five volumes of Poincaré's memoirs, covering the war period. Yet their importance is augmented by the fact that the collection of diplomatic documents published by the Quai d'Orsay terminates with the outbreak of the war. These volumes, therefore, along with Pingaud's work,[66] must be considered a primary source for the study of the diplomatic aspects of the war. (This statement is true primarily for the fifth and sixth volumes, since in the last three the author tended to focus his attention on internal affairs, which are too often evaluated within the framework of personal ambitions and petty intragovernmental intrigues; the shift in emphasis may have been due, in part, to the creation of the Clemenceau government because the differences existing between the new Prime Minister and the President prevented effective collaboration between the government and the Elysée Palace.)

An important contribution to the study of the war years is made by Alexandre Ribot's two volumes.[67] They are especially significant for the period in which the author was Prime Minister, March–September, 1917. From the diplomatic point of view, they are especially pertinent for an insight into the peace negotiations motivated by Prince Sixtus, for the projected Briand-Lancken meeting, and for the peace initiatives of the Holy See. There are also numerous references to the Anglo-French attitude toward Italy. For example, Ribot's account of his meeting with Lloyd George at Folkstone, April 11, 1917, casts further light on the connection that developed between the negotiations for a separate peace with Austria and the negotiations between Italy and the Entente for a solution of the eastern Mediterranean problems. It reveals, among other things, the cautious position taken by London and Paris on the question of Italian

[66] Albert Pingaud, *Histoire diplomatique de la France pendant la Grande Guerre* (3 vols.; Paris: Alsatia, 1938–40).
[67] *Lettres à un ami* (Paris: Bossard, 1924); *Journal de Alexandre Ribot et Correspondances inédites* (Paris: Plon, 1936).

claims in Asia Minor and, therefore, helps to explain the failure to implement the accords of St. Jean-de-Maurienne.

Georges Clemenceau's memoirs[68] are clearly polemical in character. They were published by the former Premier of France for the express purpose of replying to the particularly strong accusation made by Foch that Clemenceau had not fought with sufficient energy at the peace conference for the security of France's eastern frontier. Clemenceau devotes the first part of his volume to a description of his relations with Foch, the appointment of the latter to the supreme command of the Allied forces, and Foch's conduct in this post. The account goes far beyond the question of personalities and becomes an important contribution to an understanding of the politico-military developments during the last phase of the conflict and the dissensions that developed on these issues among the Allies. However, the central theme of the work is the preparations for the Paris conference and the peace negotiations. The key issue discussed is the matter of French security. It is demonstrated that Clemenceau fully agreed with Foch and Poincaré that only by establishing the French frontier at the Rhine could France feel fully secure. However, Clemenceau was very soon aware that he could not overcome the opposition of Lloyd George and Wilson, and while Foch continued to insist on his impossible demands, Clemenceau sought to achieve analogous results by other means. Lloyd George's proposal of an Anglo-American treaty of guarantee against German aggression in exchange for French abandonment of the demand for a Rhineland frontier or the creation of an autonomous republic in the Rhineland served to break the deadlock in the negotiations. This solution, opposed by Foch and Poincaré, was accepted by Clemenceau. The latter easily defended himself against the opposition by asking whether, in similar circumstances, it would have had the courage to assume the responsibility for an open break with London and Washington in order to obtain the Rhine frontier.

The diary of Clemenceau's Chief of Cabinet, General Mordacq,[69] serves as a useful supplement to the Premier's memoirs. The diary was ready for the press in 1923, but publication was delayed until 1930 because the author chose to allow the bitter period of debate on the work of the Tiger of France to pass before making his notes public. It is possible, of course, that during the lapse of time Mordacq may have modified the original text of his diary more or less extensively in order to avoid presenting anything which might damage the reputation of the former Premier, whom Mordacq

[68] *Grandeurs et misères d'une victoire* (Paris: Plon, 1930).

[69] General Mordacq, *Le Ministère Clemenceau. Journal d'un témoin* (4 vols.; Paris: Plon, 1930).

greatly admired, as is revealed in this and others of his publications.[70] Nevertheless, the historical value of this diary remains very great because of the details it offers on Clemenceau's activities from November, 1917, to January, 1920, and for the insight it provides on the mentality and ideas of the ex-Prime Minister.

Tardieu's volume on the negotiations leading to the Treaty of Versailles[71] is of even greater interest. The first two chapters, outlining the events between 1870 and 1914, are merely introductory. The bulk of the book deals with the peace conference, and here Tardieu contributes his extremely significant memoirs, along with an abundance of official documents.

Tardieu's book on the Schleswig question[72] at Versailles may be considered an appendix to the preceding volume, since he was president of the commission looking into the Danish claims. The question itself was of no major importance, but what is singular in Tardieu's observations is his vigorous criticism of the Danish government for requesting only a plebiscite in the northern and central zones of Schleswig instead of demanding the restitution of all of the territories lost in 1864.

Among the diplomats, Maurice Paléologue was the most prolific writer, and his highly readable literary style attracted a wide public. His recollections are presented in diary form, but a careful examination reveals that, if his daily notes were the basis for his writing, they were extensively modified before publication, a factor which reduces their value as sources.

Paléologue's diary on the Dreyfus affair was obviously edited before its publication posthumously in 1955.[73] The tendency to focus on the colorful anecdote and on the approach having the greatest popular appeal is clearly evident. Instead of clarifying those points which remained obscure, which he might have been able to do, given his official position at the time and his knowledge of a number of important behind-the-scenes activities, he

[70] In addition to the volumes on military affairs, Mordacq's studies of general interest include *Le commandement unique* (Paris: Tallandier, 1929); *La Vérité sur l'Armistice* (Paris: Tallandier, 1929); *La crise du commandement unique* (Paris: Bossard, 1931); *L'Armistice du 11 novembre 1918. Récit d'un témoin* (Paris: Plon, 1937). Mordacq has also written *Clemenceau au soir de sa vie 1920–1929* (2 vols.; Paris: Plon, 1933).

[71] André Tardieu, *La Paix* (Paris: Payot, 1922).

[72] *Le Slesvig et la paix, janvier 1919–janvier 1920* (Paris: Meynial, 1928). In addition, other Tardieu studies include the following: *Questions diplomatiques de l'année 1904* (Paris: Alcan, 1905); *La Conférence de Algeciras* (Paris: Calmann-Levy, 1909); *La France et ses alliances 1871–1910* (Paris: Alcan, 1910); *Le mystère de Agadir* (Paris: Calmann, n.d.).

[73] *Journal de l'affaire Dreyfus 1894–1899. L'affaire Dreyfus et le Quai d'Orsay* (Paris: Plon, 1955).

raised more questions, since many of his statements are not supported by convincing proof and others are strangely generic.

His volume devoted to the diplomatic aspects of French policy for the period 1904–6[74] is of greater interest here because he was vice-director for political affairs at the Quai d'Orsay at the time. The Russo-Japanese War and its effect in Europe (the French government, particularly after the Dogger Bank episode, was very nearly forced into a choice between its alliance with Russia and friendship with Britain), the Björkö treaty, and the Moroccan crisis all contributed to making these years decisive in the area of international relations and led to contrasting historical evaluations of the period, especially concerning Delcassé's policies. However, Paléologue offers little that is new, and here, too, it is clear that the original text of his diary underwent numerous modifications before publication. A comparison of the diary with the official French documents reveals that the author did not always cite the documents accurately and that often his paraphrasing alters, to a greater or lesser degree, the real meaning of the document.

Paléologue published another work on the same period[75] two years before the one cited above, in which he seeks to show that "Germany cold-bloodedly planned a general war which would be launched by a lightning-like invasion of Belgian territory by German troops." This study is based primarily on information on the German plans acquired by the French General Staff in 1904 and on the reaction that it provoked in Paris. Some data furnished by the author on Franco-British relations and on the circumstances surrounding the fall of Delcassé are interesting, but his tendency to dramatize the events and the discernible inaccuracies of detail suggest a certain caution in the use of this volume.

That portion of Paléologue's diary published posthumously in 1947[76] (three years after the author's death), which deals with the period January, 1913–June, 1914, reveals almost nothing previously unknown. However, despite the fact that the diary adds little to what was available from the official documents and other memoirs, it has a certain value in clarifying Paléologue's role during the period of his mission to St. Petersburg, February, 1914–May, 1917. The author had published three volumes on the subject years earlier,[77] but they treat the diplomatic aspects of the mission superficially and cast little light on Paléologue's role in the crisis of July, 1914. Many years later the author returned to this question in a

[74] *Un grand tournant de la politique mondiale* (Paris: Plon, 1934).

[75] *Un prelude à l'invasion de la Belgique. Le plan Schlieffen* (Paris: Plon, 1932).

[76] *Au Quai d'Orsay à la veille de la tourmente* (Paris: Plon, 1947).

[77] *La Russie des Tsars pendant la Grande Guerre* (3 vols.; Paris: Plon, 1921–22).

book[78] that, despite its presentation as an historical study, contains a number of clearly memorialistic pages. Here Paléologue sought to reply to his many critics, particularly Jules Isaac, who accused him of failing to keep Paris sufficiently informed of Russian intentions and initiatives.[79] In this instance, too, Paléologue fails to offer a satisfactory explanation for his actions; furthermore, he concludes by recognizing, more or less openly, that he did not resist Russian mobilization with sufficient vigor because he was aware that the French "General Staff and the government" feared a German lightning attack which only the threat of a Russian attack could prevent.

In addition to Paléologue, all of the French ambassadors accredited to St. Petersburg in the years prior to World War I have left their memoirs, with the exceptions of Admiral Touchard and Delcassé. However, the latter's mission was extremely brief.

On Franco-Russian relations from 1903–8, the memoirs of Ambassador Maurice Bompard[80] are valuable. The volume is particularly rich in details of the economic relations between the two countries, on the policies of Izvolski and Witte, and on Bompard's efforts to promote the Anglo-Russian *rapprochement*. Despite his cordial rapport with Witte, Bompard was not always in a position to know the most secret aspects of Russian policy. For example, he knew very little about the contacts that preceded the signing of the Björkö treaty and could give Paris only information of a general nature on the subject. Yet he was one of the best-informed diplomats on the Russian internal situation and the influences prevailing at the Czarist court, and on the internal repercussions provoked by the defeat in the Far East. However, it should be emphasized that apparently Bompard did not properly evaluate the consequences of that defeat. On the other hand, he was deeply impressed by the fragility of the Russian internal structure, to the extent that he agreed with Leon Bourgeois' belief that the matter should be discussed openly with the Czar's government and it should be advised to adopt a more liberal policy. He was accused of having contacts with members of the opposition and was recalled to Paris in March, 1908.[81]

The memoirs of Georges Louis,[82] Director of Political Affairs at the Quai

[78] *Guillaume II et Nicolas II* (Paris: Plon, 1935).

[79] Isaac, *Un débat historique, 1914. Le problème des origines de la guerre* (Paris: Rieder, 1933).

[80] *Mon ambassade en Russie (1903–1908)* (Paris: Plon, 1937).

[81] Concerning his subsequent mission to Constantinople, Bompard has published a brief account containing a number of details regarding French penetration in the Middle East and the attempts made to delay Turkey's entrance into the war on the side of the Central Powers. See Bompard, "L'entrée en guerre de la Turquie," *Revue de Paris*, July 1, 15, 1921.

[82] *Les Carnets de Georges Louis* (2 vols.; Paris: Rieder, 1926).

d'Orsay beginning in 1905 and envoy to St. Petersburg from 1909–13, are rather unusual. Instead of having the form of a diary, they consist of a series of notes on the conversations he had with diplomats, statesmen, and French and foreign journalists, similar to a collection of minutes for personal use in which the author rarely records his own views or refers to his own actions. The picture that emerges is naturally fragmentary, yet of some worth even though occasionally there is undue emphasis on personal intrigues and rivalries that are of minor historical interest. These pages read like a list of accusations against personalities of the Third French Republic and of Czarist Russia (Poincaré is accused of having encouraged the intransigence of the Russian government and Izvolski, of having received the news of the outbreak of war with enthusiasm, etc.), but the bitterness with which the author views men and events warrants close scrutiny of his conclusions.

Paléologue's successor, the former Minister of War and of Finance, Joseph Noulens, has left two volumes of memoirs on his mission to Russia, June, 1917–December, 1918.[83] He arrived in Russia knowing little of the internal complexities of the country, and consequently his memoirs are not always reliable even though they are interestingly written. However, his recollections are worthwhile when they refer to the relations between Russia and her former allies, his contacts with the Bolsheviks in 1918, and the attempts to effect a collaboration between the French military mission and the Red army. On the last point, Noulens' version usefully supplements Trotsky's memoirs (which will be discussed below) and General Niessel's[84] (the latter was chief of the French military mission).

An eminent figure in the diplomatic world of the Third French Republic, Paul Cambon, Ambassador to Spain from 1886–91, to Turkey from 1891–98, and to London from 1898 to 1920, has left neither diary nor memoir of the work of his long career. However, his son published a biography of the diplomat in 1937, based largely on Cambon's personal papers,[85] which was received with great interest by scholars. This was followed by the publication of three volumes of his correspondence with his family and colleagues,[86] material that is as useful as any diary because the

---

[83] *Mon ambassade en Russie soviétique (1917–1919)* (2 vols.; Paris: Plon, 1933).

[84] Henri Albert Niessel, *Le triomphe des Bolshéviks et la paix de Brest-Litovsk. Souvenirs 1917–1918* (Paris: Plon, 1940). The author has also written a volume concerning his mission to obtain the evacuation of the Baltic states by the German troops according to the terms established by the peace treaty. See Niessel, *L'evacuation des Pays Baltiques par les Allemands* (Paris: Lavauzelle, 1935).

[85] *Un Diplomate, Paul Cambon Ambassadeur de France* (Paris: Plon, 1937).

[86] *Correspondance 1870–1924* (3 vols.; Paris: Grasset, 1940–46).

French diplomat had some well-qualified correspondents in his family: his son, Henrì, who was also a diplomat and with whom he carried on a detailed correspondence from 1900 to 1909, and his brother Jules, who received the principal part of his correspondence between 1910 and 1919 and who was Ambassador to Berlin and, later, Secretary-General of the Quai d'Orsay. Furthermore, in his correspondence with his wife he discussed the political affairs that absorbed his immediate attention, as well as personal matters. It is easy to see how the private character of this correspondence often contributes extremely important references of an historical nature and can serve as a means of arriving at a more objective evaluation of the official documents.

Insofar as Franco-Italian relations are concerned, little can be found in the two volumes by Ambassador Billot,[87] envoy at Rome from 1890 to 1897. Despite their limitations, a contribution of some importance was made in a series of articles by his successor, Camille Barrère,[88] Ambassador to Italy from 1897–1924, whose long mission coincided with a decisive change in the relations between the two countries.[89] These articles do not contain any sensational disclosures. Yet they continue to have a certain value, even after the publication of the Quai d'Orsay's general collection of documents, particularly for the details surrounding the fall of Delcassé and the action taken by Barrère during the Moroccan crisis of 1905–6. There are other details concerning a period for which the French documents have not been published.

Barrère's statements in these articles should be integrated with his letters to Delcassé,[90] with the memoirs of Jules Laroche,[91] and with the recollections of François Charles-Roux,[92] all his colleagues at the Farnese Palace for a long while. Charles-Roux, who had already published a study on the activities of the French Embassy in Rome on the eve of the war,[93] has also

[87] Albert Billot, *La France et l'Italie. Histoire des années troubles 1881–1899* (2 vols.; Paris: Plon, 1906).

[88] "L'Italie et l'agonie de la paix en 1914," October 1, 1926; "La responsabilité du Prince de Bülow," May 1, 1931; "Le prélude de l'offensive allemande de 1905," February 1, 1932; "Souvenirs diplomatiques: La chute de Delcassé," August 1, 1932, January 1, 1933; "Souvenirs diplomatiques: La conférence de Saint Jean de Maurienne," April, 1938; "Souvenirs diplomatiques: La conférence de Rapallo," August, 1938; "Souvenirs diplomatiques: La conférence de San Remo," August, 1938 (all in *Revue des deux Mondes*).

[89] On this point, see Serra, *Camille Barrère e l'intesa italo-francese*.

[90] "Lettres à Delcassé," *Revue de Paris*, April 15, 1917.

[91] *Quinze ans à Rome avec Camille Barrère (1898–1913)* (Paris: Plon, 1948).

[92] *Souvenirs diplomatiques. Rome Quirinal 1916–1919* (Paris: Fayard, 1958).

[93] *Trois Ambassades françaises à la veille de la guerre* (Paris: Plon, 1928). The volume includes three studies concerning the missions to London, Rome, and Berlin. The first study is also based on the author's personal experiences, while for the sec-

published a volume of memoirs on the early years of his career, when he was in Russia, Morocco, and Egypt.[94]

3. THE BRITISH MEMORIALISTS.

The British memoir sources are nearly as numerous as the French, but they are less rich in new information.

Although Asquith was Prime Minister from April, 1908, to December, 1916, his memoirs[95] do not offer a great deal of information for the study of British foreign policy in those years. Ignoring the second of his works, which is devoted entirely to internal affairs, we find that neither *The Genesis of the War* nor his autobiography contain the information which might have been expected from a person of Asquith's political importance.

The central theme of the first volume is the problem of British military preparedness for the war, in which Asquith defends himself at length against the accusation that he opposed universal military conscription. Asquith maintains that military conscription was strongly opposed by the public and that it was a dangerous step to take because of the reaction it would have provoked in Germany. After all, he concludes, the British government did not intend to take steps which might worsen the already dangerous international situation because it was possible to provide for the defense of the country without resorting to extraordinary measures.

In his autobiography the focus shifts exclusively to international affairs with the beginning of the July, 1914, crisis. These pages, reconstructed from the notes in his diary, reflect the uncertainty and perplexity that conditioned the actions of the government. As Asquith notes, the situation was complex. The economic sector opposed the idea of war, and within the Cabinet a powerful group of ministers were opposed to intervention of any kind. However, he affirms that his course was clear. Although Britain had not assumed any military obligations toward France or Russia, an intimate relationship existed between London and Paris at that time, strengthened by the fact that it was in British interest that France survive as a great power. Furthermore, His Majesty's Government could not permit Germany to extend a war to the Channel coast, and Britain was committed to defend

---

ond, Charles-Roux was able to consult official documents and the memoirs of Camille Barrère.

[94] *Souvenirs diplomatiques d'un âge revolu* (Paris: Fayard, 1956).
[95] The Earl of Oxford and Asquith, *The Genesis of the War* (2 vols.; London: Cassell, 1926); *Fifty Years of Parliament* (2 vols.; London: Cassell, 1926); *Memories and Reflections* (2 vols.; London: Cassell, 1928).

the independence of Belgium. The news that Germany had invaded Belgium greatly simplified British decisions.

Useful data is also provided on the Dardanelles campaign, particularly on Lord Fisher's resignation from a key post in the Admiralty, which convinced the author of the need to form a coalition government. However, the most important chapter in the autobiography concerns the ministerial crisis of December, 1916. The publication of the memorandum presented in November by Lord Lansdowne, along with Lord Robert Cecil's reply, clarified the nature of the conflict and led to the resignation of the Cabinet. Asquith's official biography[96] serves as an excellent supplement to his writings. The biography reveals that the lack of emphasis on foreign affairs in Asquith's writings reflected the situation within the government, in the sense that Asquith was little interested in the conduct of foreign policy and preferred to leave this question almost entirely in Lord Grey's charge.

Lord Grey condensed his recollections of long years at the Foreign Office (Undersecretary from 1892 to 1895 and Foreign Minister from 1905 to 1916) into two volumes.[97] If, after the appearance of the British documents, these recollections lost the importance they had at the time of publication as a primary source for the study of British policy in the prewar era, they continue to be an excellent foundation for an insight into the author's personality and an aid in interpreting his policies. Grey's narrative reflects the same detachment and calm that characterized him during discussions within the party or the government, and despite the numerous accusations leveled at him, his writings seem to remain aloof from the debates on the origins and conduct of the war. Instead, they focus on the useful lessons for the future that can be derived from those experiences.

Grey sought to present the facts so that they might be carefully studied, in order that the same blunders might not be repeated and another world war might be avoided. It was Germany, he stated, which bore the responsibility for precipitating the war, but this did not explain its origins: the war was made inevitable by the enormous increase in armaments and by the sense of insecurity and fear developing therefrom. While this judgment offers only a partial explanation of the origins of the war, it clearly indicates the approach taken by Grey in writing his memoirs.

The author's early years as Undersecretary in the Foreign Office are best remembered for his statement to Parliament of March 28, 1895, in which

---

[96] J. A. Spender and Cyril Asquith, *Life of Herbert Henry Asquith, Lord Oxford and Asquith* (2 vols.; London: Hutchinson, 1932).

[97] Viscount Grey of Fallodon, *Twenty-Five Years 1892–1916* (2 vols.; London: Hodder and Stoughton, 1925). On Grey, see also G. P. Gooch, *Before the War. Studies in Diplomacy* (London: Longmans, 1938), Vol. II, and the studies referred to in the bibliography.

he warned France not to seek to expand in the direction of the upper Nile. Lord Grey's explanation for the surprisingly strong position taken by the British government is not very convincing. Yet, indirectly, it serves to throw some light on the Cabinet's attitude on the Egyptian question.

In these pages Lord Grey deals in some detail with all of the problems arising during his tenure as Foreign Secretary, but nothing is offered that would suggest the need for a general revision of the accepted view of British policy. In effect, he confirms the fact that he considered the entente with France and Russia as the most satisfactory system for guaranteeing the balance of power in Europe and the preservation of British interests because it avoided the perils of splendid isolation while preserving freedom of action for Great Britain. In this situation, the attempts to induce Britain to assume hard and fast, binding obligations were destined to fail. Grey emphasizes that, as far as the Czarist Empire was concerned, a further difficulty existed in that the British public disapproved of Russia's internal policies. But if this factor undoubtedly played its part in determining British policy, it can hardly be considered to have been decisive, since a similar prejudice did not exist toward France, with whom Grey did not intend to assume any binding obligations.

Regarding the July, 1914, crisis, Grey's memoirs supplement and clarify a number of issues appearing in the official documents. In this context, it is interesting to note that at the time Lord Grey did not consider the Russian mobilization the decisive step toward war: he explains that it could have been interpreted as a wise precaution in the face of the deepening crisis. However, the issuing of a precise warning to Russia would have also meant the assumption of precise obligations toward that country, obligations that could not be assumed in view of the uncertainty of the British government's final decisions.

Extremely significant evidence on this point comes from Lord John Morley,[98] member of Asquith's Cabinet. During the last days of the crisis of 1914 Morley was the most authoritative representative of the neutralist position within the government, and his summary of the Cabinet discussions on the eve of the British declaration of war is the most precise and detailed of all. He emphasizes that the question of Belgian neutrality was not the main point of the discussions. Rather, the crucial issue was the exact nature of the obligations toward France, and dissension developed over whether a Russian or a German victory presented the greatest danger to Britain. According to Morley, in the event of a Russian victory nothing could block her expansion toward the Straits and southern Asia. Grey,

[98] John Viscount Morley, *Memorandum on Resignation, August 1914* (London: Macmillan, 1928).

instead, supported the cause of intervention on the side of France primarily to prevent Germany from dominating the Continent and then seeking to dominate the world, a conquest that Great Britain, left alone, would have found extremely difficult to counteract successfully. The British ministers were more immediately preoccupied with the prospect of the German fleet's extending its operations into the North Sea and along France's Atlantic coast, "the equivalent of carrying the war to the shores of England." But, Morley repeats, the question of Belgian neutrality was not discussed in detail until August 2, nor was it considered to be a determining element in a decision. Morley adds, "the surprising and decisive enthusiasm for the Belgian cause was due less to the indignation over the violation of the treaty than to the fact that it provided a logical argument favoring intervention on the side of France, in dispatching an expeditionary corps. . . ."

Logically, Morley's *Memorandum* reflected the opinion of the neutral-ists, but this does not mean that it was partisan in character or violently polemical. Instead, Morley's testimony complements the views of the champions of intervention such as Grey and Churchill; and a comparison of the points of view reveals that, if the angles of vision were different, the two versions of the facts were the same.

A good supplement to the official British and German documents on the negotiations for an agreement between the two countries early in 1912 may be found in the memoirs of the British Minister of War, Lord Haldane,[99] who went to Berlin to handle the decisive phase of the negotiations. In this volume, Haldane goes beyond the limits of the mission and adds a summary of Anglo-German relations covering the entire period that he was in charge of the War Office. These memoirs are amplified and completed by the information contained in his autobiography,[100] providing a reasonably complete picture of his efforts in strengthening the British army and in preparing the expeditionary corps for service in France. Here he refutes the accusations of his critics, who, after the outbreak of the war, had attacked his tendency to maintain good relations with Germany as an expression of extreme pro-Germanism that had almost prevented him from making the necessary military preparations for a war against the Central Powers.

[99] Viscount Haldane, *Before the War* (London: Cassell, 1920). Prior to the publication of the British and German documentary collections this volume served as one of the primary sources on the problem. The diary kept by Haldane during his mission to Berlin is to be found in Sir Frederick Maurice, *Haldane, 1856–1915. The Life of Viscount Haldane of Cloan* (London: Faber and Faber, 1937), which adds little to the autobiography cited below.

[100] Richard Burton Haldane, *An Autobiography* (London: Hodder and Stoughton, 1929).

Churchill's memoirs in *The World Crisis*[101] are of major importance for those years that he was in the government: from 1911 to 1915 as First Lord of the Admiralty, in 1918 as Minister of Munitions, and from January, 1919, as Minister of War. His account of his nomination to the Admiralty explains the origin of the decision that was to make it possible for Britain to fight a war on the Continent three years later. In the summer of 1911, the imminent threat of war aroused excited debate within the government. While the immediate question in the controversy appeared to be the strategic plans of the navy, the real issue was the plan to send an expeditionary corps to the Continent in the event of war. The War Office prevailed, and Churchill was called to the Admiralty for the express purpose of co-ordinating the plans of the navy with the requirements of the army for its operations across the Channel. While Churchill approached the problem with his usual energy—and his account is long and detailed on the question—he continued to support the idea that it was necessary to reach a compromise with Germany, and his comments are useful in completing the picture of the preliminary steps leading to the Haldane mission to Berlin.

Churchill's resignation, prompted by the failure of the Dardanelles campaign which he had supported and planned, forms the nucleus, at least in part, of his vehement criticism of the military operations conducted by the chiefs of both services, which fills many pages of his volumes on the period 1915–18.[102] It is important to note, however, that these same pages reveal the evolution of the idea Churchill was to apply during the course of World War II: that the authority of the government must prevail over that of the military in the conduct of war.

The last volume begins with the armistice of November, 1918, and Churchill refers to a conversation with Lloyd George in which both were in full accord on the impossibility of lifting Europe out of the devastation of war without German participation, a view, he continues, for which the British government was unfortunately unable to win support at the time of the treaty negotiations. In establishing the responsibility of each of the Allies on this point, he notes that the British delegation gave Lloyd George a mandate to exercise the strongest pressure in the Big Four conferences to mitigate the terms of the treaty, urging, above all, that Germany's eastern frontiers in the mixed zones be determined by plebiscite, that Germany be

[101] Winston Churchill, *The World Crisis 1911–1918* (4 vols.; London: Thornton Butterworth, 1923–27); *The World Crisis. The Aftermath 1918–1922* (London: Thornton Butterworth, 1929).

[102] These criticisms provoked various replies from the interested parties and from military experts, which have been gathered in a volume edited by Lord Sydenham, *Winston Churchill: The World Crisis. A Criticism* (London: Hutchinson, 1927).

given the right to join the League of Nations as soon as possible, and that the reparations clauses be modified.

Lloyd George, Chancellor of the Exchequer at the time of the declaration of war, Minister of Munitions in May, 1915, and Prime Minister beginning in December, 1916, published his war memoirs in six volumes.[103] Although not always accurate, they are of considerable interest concerning British policy during the war.

The diplomatic aspect plays only a minor role in these pages, which reveal the author's concentration on Britain's war economy and on military events. Concerning the crisis of July, 1914, Lloyd George has nothing new to add because, he says, questions of foreign policy were little discussed in the Cabinet meetings and, with the exception of the Prime Minister and the Foreign Secretary, the members of the government were not usually given detailed information. Therefore, his observations on foreign policy are generic and were formulated a posteriori.

On the other hand, Lloyd George furnishes significant data on the psychological crisis besetting the British government during the closing months of 1916, when the failure of the Somme offensive and the unfavorable reports from all other military fronts dashed all hope for a quick victory. The Asquith memoirs had already publicized the Lansdowne memorandum in which the possibility of a compromise peace had been explored, along with Lord Robert Cecil's reply. Lloyd George further clarifies the position of the other members of the Cabinet and publishes Balfour's important *promemoria* in which the First Lord of the Admiralty (later Foreign Secretary in Lloyd George's government) detailed the goals necessary to the establishment of a durable peace in Europe. The British government concluded that a compromise peace was impossible, but the fact that this eventuality was discussed seriously affected the unity of the Cabinet and opened the way to the crisis of December, 1916, which led to the formation of the Lloyd George government.

From 1916 on, Lloyd George's references to diplomatic affairs increase noticeably, even though the emphasis remains largely on military events. Referring to inter-Allied relations, the British Prime Minister recalls that at the Conference of Rome of January, 1917—he includes a portion of the minutes of the meetings—he suggested a plan whereby a hundred and fifty thousand men, along with adequate artillery support, would be sent to Italy to deliver the knockout blow to the Austro-Hungarian Empire which, presumably, would also lead to the surrender of Bulgaria and Turkey. The proposal would have implemented the strategic concept advanced re-

[103] David Lloyd George, *War Memoirs* (6 vols.; London: Nicholson and Watson, 1933–36).

peatedly by Lloyd George after the Allied offensives in France had brought only modest results at an enormous cost in human life. Lloyd George asked that without excessively weakening the French front, since that would remain the main theater of war, the Allies take the initiative on other fronts in order to strike at Germany through her weaker allies and thus isolate her. The project was not only blocked by French and British generals, who believed that decisive results could be only obtained on the French front, but it was also met without enthusiasm by Cadorna. Lloyd George was then obliged to abandon the idea.

Lloyd George adds very little to what was already known about the Prince Sixtus and the Vatican peace proposals. However, he contributes important material on the less well-known peace overture of September–October, 1917, instigated by the Secretary of State of the German Foreign Office, Von Kuhlmann, through the Spanish Minister to Brussels, Villalobar, and the Madrid government. This overture was quickly abandoned when the British government made it very clear that it would not undertake negotiations without the knowledge of its allies. This supports the opinion held by Balfour and by Lloyd George that the only purpose of the overture was to create dissension in the ranks of the Entente powers.

Of greater value is the summary of the conversations which took place in December, 1917, between Marshal Smuts and the ex-Austrian Ambassador to London, Mensdorff. Smuts' summary, published here in its entirety, attests to the fact that a separate peace with Austria was not contemplated at this meeting, but only the possibility of a general peace conference of all of the belligerents. Mensdorff asked that the Allies clearly state their conditions for peace in order to determine whether or not a common basis for an understanding existed. At the same time, Mensdorff stated that as far as future territorial adjustments were concerned, Austria was not disposed to make any concessions to either Italy or Rumania because both were guilty of betraying their alliance obligations. Concerning Italian demands, Mensdorff added that Austria could not consider the surrender of Trieste to Italy, not only because it was the only efficient port in the Empire, but also because the city had always been Austrian and had always demonstrated its desire to remain so. His refusal to consider eventual territorial cessions in the Trentino appeared to be somewhat less categorical. As for the British position, according to the statements made by Smuts it did not appear that Great Britain contemplated a breakup of the Austro-Hungarian Empire at that time. At most, Britain was interested in a major Austrian constitutional reform which would create a complex of largely autonomous states within the Empire.

Lloyd George's war memoir volumes terminate with the conclusion of the armistice, but he continues his recollections in his two volumes on the peace conference,[104] which to some extent constitute a reply to the unofficial writings of Tardieu and Baker. This is the first detailed summary of the activities of the British delegation at Paris, based not only on the author's recollections but also on rather copious documentation concerning inter-Allied conversations and discussions within the British delegation. The first volume concerns the preparation of the peace treaty with Germany and is especially important for the pages on the colonial and the Rhineland problems. The second volume concerns the treaties of peace with Germany's allies: it contains a long chapter on the Fiume question, but the greatest space is given to the peace with Turkey and to the other aspects of Allied policy in the Middle East (Sykes-Picot Accords, Balfour Declaration, etc.). Despite the fact that the study was written a considerable period of time after the events in question, its vigorous polemical nature seems to reflect the heat and passion of the days of the Paris conference. For example, Lloyd George's bitter attack on Beneš and his comments on Poincaré's extremist policies invite serious analysis of these assertions.

Lloyd George's volume on reparations and war debts,[105] published in 1932, is equally controversial. While it refers to the post-Paris conference period, it includes frequent references to differences arising between the French and British delegations at Paris over the financial clauses of the treaty.

Lloyd George's testimony can be supplemented by Lord Riddell's recollections.[106] As liaison officer between the British press and the government during the war and the peace conference and because of his personal friendship with the Welsh statesman, Riddell is in a position to provide numerous details—even if they are not always significant—on the activities of the Prime Minister. Among the many biographies of Lloyd George, Frank Owen's[107] is especially noteworthy because he had access to the private archives of the statesman.

Sir Harold Nicolson, a career diplomat and, later, a political writer and essayist of considerable fame, contributed three volumes[108] of particular

[104] *The Truth about the Peace Treaties* (2 vols.; London: Gollancz, 1938),
[105] *The Truth about Reparations and War-Debts* (London: Heinemann, 1932).
[106] *Lord Riddell's Intimate Diary of the Peace Conference and After, 1918–1923* (London: Gollancz, 1933); *Lord Riddell's War Diary, 1914–1918* (London: Nicholson and Watson, 1933); Lord Riddell, *More Pages from My Diary, 1908–1914* (London: Country Life, 1934).
[107] *Tempestuous Journey. Lloyd George, His Life and Times* (London: Hutchinson, 1954).
[108] *Lord Carnock. A Study in the Old Diplomacy* (London: Constable, 1930); *Peacemaking 1919* (London: Constable, 1933), 2d ed. revised, 1945; *Curzon: The Last Phase, 1919–1925. A Study in Post-War Diplomacy* (London: Constable, 1934).

importance for a study of the period, centered around World War I, although his approach to the issues is somewhat different in form.

The first volume is a biography of Sir Arthur Nicolson,[109] which Sir Harold prepared with the idea of offering a study on the "old diplomacy." In fact, Lord Carnock emerges as a reasonably good example of the typical British diplomat of the prewar period, but the study is particularly noteworthy for the new material it includes on his activities. In the winter of 1916–17, immediately after leaving the diplomatic service, Lord Carnock collected and organized his notes and diary fragments and from them developed a narrative based on his recollections. This manuscript—Sir Harold drew heavily from it and frequently reproduced entire passages in the biography of his father—presents an excellent synopsis of Lord Carnock's activities. His mission to Morocco, 1895–1905, to the extent that it refers to the work of the Algeciras Conference, is especially valuable. The same may be said for the pages on his mission to St. Petersburg, 1906–10, at the time of the development of the Anglo-Russian *rapprochement*. On this question, Lord Carnock recalls that, in the face of the apparent lack of solidarity demonstrated by the Anglo-French-Russian front during the Bosnian crisis, he was convinced of the necessity to conclude a hard and fast alliance with Russia in order to oppose effectively the evident hegemony of the Central Powers but that he ran up against the strong opposition of Lord Grey, who had no intention of taking such a clear-cut position.

The volume on the peace conference more closely resembles a true memoir than any of the others. The second half of the volume contains Sir Harold's diary for the period of his Paris sojourn as a member of the British delegation. As a young diplomat he did not enjoy a position of first importance, but his annotations (from January 1 to June 28, 1919) are nonetheless significant. It is apparent that the author included this diary in the volume not so much to contribute material information on the events already known and reported in more authoritative sources as to emphasize a factor which, in his estimation, had not yet been put into its proper perspective or which was not recalled when evaluating the work of the conference: the psychological influence of an atmosphere charged with bitterness and passion, which reigned throughout the many months of the meeting and made moderation and justice an impossibility. However, in writing this volume Sir Harold does not appear to have overcome entirely the electrical atmosphere of 1919 because his conclusions are far from being inspired by the objectivity that the passage of time should provide. This is especially true in his references to Italy, where he makes several assertions that are not only unjust but, occasionally, factually incorrect.

[109] Sir Arthur Nicolson, later Lord Carnock, was the author's father.

Sir Harold completes his trilogy with a third volume on postwar diplomacy, centered on the person of Lord Curzon, British Foreign Secretary from 1919 to 1924. Unlike the first volume, which was essentially a biography (and one on Lord Curzon had already been written[110]), this is, rather, a reconstruction of international politics for those years. Sir Harold's contribution is appreciable, as he served as Lord Curzon's secretary during the period when Curzon was Foreign Secretary.

The two-volume collection of the correspondence of Sir Cecil Spring-Rice[111] is a remarkable source. All of the author's extensive correspondence could not be included, so the editor selected not only those letters that best illustrated his diplomatic work but also a number from his most important correspondents, among them Theodore Roosevelt. Therefore, the panorama is often much broader than the one in which Spring-Rice personally participated.

The correspondence relative to his years as secretary to the British Embassy in Berlin, 1895–98, reveals little strikingly new even though it should be underlined that at this early date Spring-Rice was already of the opinion that a war between the Great Powers was inevitable.

After several tours in minor posts, Spring-Rice was assigned to St. Petersburg in 1903 as Counsellor to the Legation, and for a time he was also the Chargé d'Affaires. He remained at this post until 1906. It is for this period that Spring-Rice's correspondence becomes very valuable for the study of Anglo-Russian relations prior to the accords of 1907 and even more so for his detailed knowledge of United States efforts in mediating the Russo-Japanese War. Spring-Rice's close friendship with Theodore Roosevelt and with the Secretary of State, John Hay, found expression in a frequent exchange of letters and eventually became in fact the channel through which passed the communications between Washington and London. Therefore, this correspondence is decidedly important in evaluating the role played by the United States in the negotiations leading to the Treaty of Portsmouth.

Although Spring-Rice was transferred from St. Petersburg to Teheran before the negotiations for the accords of 1907 were begun, be contributed to their success. In Teheran, Spring-Rice conducted the negotiations with the Russian envoy which led to a delimitation of the spheres of influence in Persia. His last mission took him to Washington as British Ambassador, a post he had long coveted and for which he was well suited because of his wide circle of friends among American statesmen. However, when Spring-

---

[110] Earl of Ronaldshay, *The Life of Lord Curzon* (3 vols.; London: Benn, 1928).

[111] Stephen Gwyn (ed.), *The Letters and Friendships of Sir Cecil Spring-Rice* (2 vols.; London: Constable, 1929).

Rice arrived in Washington, he found that the elections of 1912 had put Wilson in the White House. Spring-Rice was never able to establish with him the rapport which he had developed from abroad with the preceding Republican administrations. This change in administrations had a certain influence on the information and suggestions that he transmitted to London and, in turn, rendered less effective British efforts to promote American intervention in the war. While the evidence was clear that pro-British feeling was not very strong among American political leaders, Spring-Rice recognized that, regardless of the thinking in Washington, the country's internal situation was such that intervention could not have come about any earlier than it did. With the American declaration of war, Spring-Rice's mission to Washington came to a close. As a result, for the last year of the war the rich information provided by his copious correspondence is lacking, and in the absence of the British official documents, this void is keenly felt.

Sir George Buchanan, British Ambassador to St. Petersburg from 1910 to 1917, published two volumes of his memoirs relating to his mission to Russia,[112] which continue to be an important source of information on Allied relations with the Czarist government during the war. They are even more important in reference to the Allied attempts to keep Russia in the war after the revolution eliminated the old regime. For the period before the war, Buchanan's memoirs retain their significance despite the publication of the Foreign Office collection. While they contain little not already known through the official documents on the crisis of 1914, his references to relations between St. Petersburg and London for the years preceding the war continue to merit the attention of scholars, especially on Anglo-Russian rivalry in Persia. Buchanan confirms that despite the 1907 agreements the status of the two powers in Persia was never completely clarified. If the Czar and Sazonov were motivated by the best of intentions in the Persian situation, there were powerful forces at work in Russia that had no intention of abandoning Russia's traditional objectives in the area. Buchanan's prosaic writing cannot be compared with Paléologue's linguistically brilliant exposition, but, in most cases, Buchanan's is the more convincing. However, it must also be acknowledged that the British Ambassador was obviously better informed on the realities of the Russian situation than his French colleague and, therefore, better equipped to comprehend the growing revolutionary threat—see, for example, his conversation with the Czar of January, 1917—and, later, to predict accurately the course to be taken by the post-Czarist governments on the war issue.

[112] *My Mission to Russia and Other Diplomatic Memories* (2 vols.; London: Cassell, 1923).

The attitudes reflected in the diary, limited to the war years, of the ex-British Ambassador to Paris, Francis Bertie,[113] are a surprising contrast. During the July, 1914, crisis, Bertie's notes are unsparing in their denunciation of Russian policy and, specifically, of Izvolski's action. According to Bertie, the latter was the principal instigator of French *revanchisme*. However, after the declaration of war, he launched into a continuous diatribe against the Germans and against all those who were ready to consider a compromise peace with the Central Powers. Yet despite these flaws, Bertie's diary is valuable for a study of Franco-British relations and for the evidence he presents on the French political situation during the war.

Among the most interesting passages from the memoirs of Sir James Rennell Rodd[114] are those on his mission to Rome, 1908–19. The most important references are to the Italian internal situation because on matters of diplomatic activity he maintained almost total reserve or refers to them in such general terms that they reveal little of interest to the historian. Yet his observations on men and events on the Italian scene are worthy of consideration, since this information was transmitted to London and had its influence in determining the British position toward Italy. As a case in point, Rodd considered the appeal for peace launched by the Holy See in August, 1917, to have been wholly negative in its effect, and he also regarded it as one of the morale factors that led to Caporetto.

The memoirs of Sir Arthur Hardinge[115] have somewhat similar characteristics; they contain several pages of worth-while observations on his mission to Madrid during World War I. Here, too, the author prefers to pass over his diplomatic activity and to emphasize the Spanish internal situation and the diverse attitudes concerning the war reflected in the various political circles and at the court. Hardinge notes that while public opinion largely favored an Entente victory a number of political leaders, some in the government, were wishing for a victory by the Central Powers, in the hope of obtaining a free hand in Morocco and reacquiring Gibraltar. This observation suggests a similar tug of war between the views of the Spanish government and public during World War II.

The memoirs of Lord Hardinge of Penshurst[116] are rather disappointing. Not only does he limit himself to recording generalities, but his recollec-

---

[113] Francis Leverson Bertie of Thame, *Diary 1914–1918* (2 vols.; London: Hodder & Stoughton, 1924).

[114] *Social and Diplomatic Memories 1884–1919* (3 vols.; London: Arnold, 1922–25).

[115] *A Diplomatist in Europe* (London: Cape, 1927).

[116] *Old Diplomacy. The Reminiscences of Lord Hardinge of Penshurst Covering the Years 1880–1924* (London: Murray, 1947); *My Indian Years* (London: Murray, 1948).

tions are often superficial and incorrect. For example, according to the author, the Italian delegation was withdrawn from Paris because Orlando could not tolerate being ignored in the conversations conducted in English, a language he did not understand.

Sir Horace Rumbold's volume on the crisis of 1914,[117] published over a quarter of a century after the event, is a memoir only in part. While the author refers to his experience as Counsellor in the British Embassy in Berlin, he also makes use of documents which were published later. It was printed shortly after the start of World War II and is openly biased. Through a detailed narration of the events of July, 1914, he arrives at the conclusion that German policy, as conducted by Bismarck, Bethmann-Hollweg, or Hitler, was undeviating and always aggressive, as it was based on two premises: certainty of a quick victory and belief in German ability to localize the conflict.

The volume by the former Undersecretary of the Foreign Office, John Duncan Gregory,[118] is only a modest contribution; its best chapters deal with Gregory's mission to the Vatican in 1914 and the unofficial mission to the Balkans entrusted to the journalist Valentine Chirol in June, 1915. The latter mission was aimed at preventing Bulgaria from joining the Central Powers, and on this episode Chirol has published his own interesting observations.[119] He emphasizes that Serbia's attitude toward Bulgaria was strongly influenced by the rumors circulating on the content of the Treaty of London. Once the Serbian government had learned that the Adriatic was to become an "Italian lake," it refused to budge from its demand for an outlet on the Aegean unless it was guaranteed compensation in Albania.

The work of another journalist, Henry Wickham Steed,[120] *The* (London) *Times*'s Rome correspondent from 1897 to 1902 and Vienna correspondent from 1902 to 1912, is noteworthy especially for his analysis of Italo-Austrian relations within the framework of the Triple Alliance, despite the fact that the author's objectivity is often questionable. As editor in charge of the foreign policy section of *The Times* during the war, Steed exercised considerable influence in shaping public opinion in favor of the dismemberment of the Hapsburg Empire.

Along with the memoir sources as such, the many "authorized biographies," which are part of the English publishing tradition, should also be

[117] *The War Crisis in Berlin July–August 1914* (London: Constable, 1940).

[118] *On the Edge of Diplomacy. Rambles and Reflections, 1902–1928* (London: Hutchinson, 1929).

[119] Sir Valentine Chirol, *Fifty Years in a Changing World* (London: Cape, 1927).

[120] *Through Thirty Years (1892–1922). A Personal Narrative* (2 vols.; London: Heinemann, 1924).

mentioned. These are usually based on the materials found in private archives and often make major contributions, either serving as or supplementing the volumes of memoirs of the leading British political and diplomatic personalities. Thus they often retain their value even after the official documents have been published for the period.

In addition to the volumes cited—Spender and Cyril Asquith on Asquith, Owen on Lloyd George, Maurice on Haldane, Nicolson on Lord Carnock, and Lord Ronaldshay on Curzon—one should mention the biography of Queen Victoria by Lytton Strachey,[121] who, however, was not able to utilize the Sovereign's very important correspondence,[122] and the biography of Edward VII by Sir Sidney Lee.[123] The latter is based on material in the Windsor and the Foreign Office archives and contains much useful information on the influence exercised by the Sovereign over the conduct of foreign policy and particularly on his meetings with William II, but the volume reflects the strongly anti-German bias of the author. Equally important is the more recent biography of George V by Harold Nicolson,[124] containing considerable unpublished material. The two volumes by Lord Edmond Fitzmaurice on Granville[125] are also well documented, and these can now be supplemented by the correspondence published by Ramm for the period 1868–86.[126] A comparable study on Gladstone is lacking, even though a great deal of pertinent material has been published from time to time by biographers and other scholars.[127]

[121] *Queen Victoria* (London, 1921).

[122] Arthur Christopher Benson and Viscount Esher (eds.), *Letters of Queen Victoria*, 1st Series (1837–61) (3 vols.; London: Murray, 1908); Benson (ed.), *Letters of Queen Victoria*, 2d Series (1862–85) (3 vols.; London: Murray, 1926); George Earl Buckle (ed.), *Letters of Queen Victoria*, 3d Series (1886–1901) (3 vols.; London: Murray, 1930–32). This collection is to be considered a primary source, especially for the last years of the reign. Not only do the letters permit an examination of the role played by Queen Victoria, but they help clarify the positions taken by prime ministers and ministers of foreign affairs on many of the major problems of foreign policy. For example, see Lord Salisbury's letters in reference to the agreement with Italy of 1887, in which he reveals the concepts that guided him in the negotiations and the significance he attached to the accord itself.

[123] *King Edward VII. A Biography* (2 vols.; London: Macmillan, 1925–27).

[124] *King George the Fifth, His Life and Reign* (London: Constable, 1952).

[125] *The Life of Granville George Leverson Gower, Second Earl of Granville, 1815–1891* (2 vols.; London: Longmans, 1905).

[126] Agatha Ramm, *The Political Correspondence of Mr. Gladstone and Lord Granville, 1868–1875* (2 vols.; London: Historical Society, 1952); *ibid., 1876–1886* (2 vols.; Oxford: Clarendon Press, 1962).

[127] See Sir John Morley, *Life of Gladstone* (3 vols.; London: Macmillan, 1903); Philip Guedalla, *Gladstone and Palmerston* (London: Hodder and Stoughton, 1928); Guedalla, *The Queen and Mr. Gladstone* (2 vols.; London: Hodder and Stoughton, 1933); Paul Knaplund, *Gladstone and British Imperial Policy* (London: Allen and Unwin, 1927); Knaplund, *Gladstone's Foreign Policy* (New York: Harper, 1935);

The biography of Disraeli published by Moneypenny and Buckle is particularly valuable,[128] the last volumes containing an especially rich documentation. Equally significant is the biography of Salisbury published by his daughter, Lady Gwendolyn Cecil,[129] which terminates with 1892, however, and thus does not include Salisbury's activities during his last tenure as Foreign Secretary, 1895–1900. Very little new material appears in the biography of Lord Rosebery written by his brother-in-law, Lord Crewe.[130] Rosebery was Foreign Secretary in 1886 and 1892–94 and Prime Minister, 1894–95.

The four volumes by Garvin and Amery on Joseph Chamberlain[131] are largely based on the latter's correspondence and personal papers, which, however, are directly pertinent to British foreign policy only for the period when Chamberlain was Colonial Minister, 1895–1903. In the area of foreign policy, the central theme is the Anglo-German conversations of 1898 and 1901, a period in which Chamberlain championed the attempt to reach a stable agreement with the Germans.[132] The volumes also contain valuable source material in the chapters concerning the Boer War and its origins.

The two volumes on Lord Balfour published by his niece, Blanche Dugdale,[133] are also of considerable consequence. The first volume, terminating in 1906, appears to be the most interesting and the best documented and should be considered an important source on British policy from 1898 to 1904. In addition to the pages on the attempted Anglo-German *rapprochement* of 1898, Balfour's views on the Russo-Japanese War are also significant. From one of his *promemoriae* of December, 1903, and from his letter to Edward VII a few days later, it can be concluded that Balfour did not share the opinion of the British military

---

Robert William Seton-Watson, *Disraeli, Gladstone, and the Eastern Question. A Study in Diplomacy and Party Politics* (London: Macmillan, 1935).

[128] William Flavelle Moneypenny and George Earl Buckle, *Life of Disraeli* (6 vols.; London: Murray, 1910–20).

[129] *Life of Robert Marquess of Salisbury* (4 vols.; London: Hodder and Stoughton, 1921–31).

[130] *Lord Rosebery* (London: Murray, 1931).

[131] J. L. Garvin and Julian Amery, *The Life of Joseph Chamberlain* (4 vols.; London: Macmillan, 1932–51). The first three volumes are the work of Garvin. Amery is responsible for the last volume.

[132] On this widely debated point in the postwar historiography, see (in addition to the memoirs of the German ex-Chargé d'Affaires in London, Baron Eckardstein) the critical studies of Eugen Fischer, *Holsteins grosses Nein: Die deutschen-englischen Bündnisverhandlungen von 1898–1901* (Berlin: Deutsche Verlagsgesellschafte Politik, 1925); Friedrich Meinecke, *Geshichte der deutsch-englischen Bündnisproblems, 1890–1901* (Munich: Oldenburg, 1927). See also William L. Langer, *Diplomacy of Imperialism (1890–1902)* (2d ed., 2 vols.; New York: Knopf, 1950).

[133] Blanche E. C. Dugdale, *Arthur James Balfour, First Earl of Balfour* (2 vols.; London: Hutchinson, 1936).

experts who believed that the Japanese would be overwhelmed in the event of a Russo-Japanese war. Balfour held that, in the event that the Russians were involved in a war in the Far East, it would be easier to reach agreement with the Czarist government on the questions that continued to block an understanding between London and St. Petersburg. Thus he made it clear that he did not intend to advise moderation in Tokyo, all the more because this would tend to wound the sensibilities of the Japanese and weaken the alliance concluded only the year before. The material published here on the *Entente Cordiale* is also extremely pertinent, especially its revelation that Balfour, despite the fact that he was informed by Landsdowne on the nature and course of the negotiations, did not grasp their full importance. This fact is borne out by Balfour himself, who later marveled at the results of the accords of 1904. The portions concerning the war years and the Paris conference are, as has been noted, less worth while, although on these matters reference may be made to the biography written by Balfour's secretary,[134] and for his mission to the United States in 1917, to the last chapter of his unfinished autobiography.[135]

The biography of Lord Lansdowne written by Newton[136] is especially useful for the period 1900–5, when Lansdowne was Foreign Secretary and had a direct hand in taking Great Britain out of her splendid isolation, first with the conclusion of the alliance with Japan in 1902 and later with the signing of the *Entente Cordiale*. The author re-evaluates the role played by Lansdowne and points out that the role attributed to Edward VII in bringing about the Anglo-French *rapprochement* has little, if any, basis in fact. Considerable space is devoted to Lord Lansdowne's activities in the coalition government formed by Asquith in 1915 and especially to the circumstances leading to the publication of his famous "Peace Letter" in the *Daily Telegraph*.

4. THE RUSSIAN MEMORIALISTS.

On the personality of Nicholas II, little can be determined from his diary,[137] published for the period 1898–1918, and it is almost completely

---

[134] Sir Ian Malcolm, *Lord Balfour* (London: Macmillan, 1930).

[135] Arthur James Balfour, *Chapters of Autobiography* (London: Cassell, 1930).

[136] Lord Newton, *Lord Lansdowne. A Biography* (London: Macmillan, 1929).

[137] *Dnevnik Imperatora Nikolaja II* [The Diary of Nicholas II] (Berlin: Slova, 1923). German translation, *Das Tagebuch des letzen Zaren von 1890 bis zum Fall* (Berlin: Ullstein, 1923); French translation, *Journal intime de Nicolas II* (Paris: Payot, 1925). This diary ends in December, 1917, but a later French edition concludes in July, 1918: *Journal intime de Nicholas II (Juillet 1914–Juillet 1918)* (Paris: Payot, 1934).

devoid of interest except for the pages relative to the Björkö meeting with William II. More important references are to be found in the correspondence between the Czar and the Czarina[138] and in the "archives" of Nicholas II.[139] Over one-half of the latter consists of letters exchanged between the Czar and his mother.[140] Although the letters are largely personal in character, they do contain various references to political questions (the correspondence is limited to the years 1905–6 and the references are almost entirely to the Russo-Japanese War and to relations with Count Witte). The "archives" also contain other more pertinent data of historical interest on the war years. The most notable are those on relations with Rumania during the first phase of the conflict, relations with Serbia, and the inter-Allied conference of February, 1917. It is a heterogeneous collection, but not without some import. For example, a letter from Prince Alexander of Serbia to Grand Duke Nicholas of April, 1915, reveals that the Italian request to intervene in the war on the side of the Allies encountered resistance in certain Russian circles and aroused the fear that a victorious Italy might play the same role in relation to the Slavic world as that played heretofore by Austria-Hungary. Other documents refer to British protests on the dismissal of Sazonov in 1916 or reveal that during the inter-Allied conference of February, 1917, the head of the French delegation, Doumergue, proposed that the Japanese send an expedition to the Persian Gulf area. Data of varying degrees of importance may be found in the letters of the grand dukes to the Czar[141] during the last decade of the

[138] *Pisma Imperatricy Alexandry Feodorovny K Imperatoru Nikolaju II* [The Letters of Czarina Alexandra Feodorovna to Czar Nicholas II] (2 vols.; Berlin: Slova, 1922). German translation, *Die letze Zarin. Ihre Briefe an Nicolaus II und ihre Tagebuchblätter von 1914 bis zur Ermordung* (Berlin: Ullstein, 1922); English translation, *Letters of the Tsaritsa to the Tsar, 1914–1916* (London: Duckworth, 1923) (the texts of the letters in English were retranslated from the Russian); French translation, *Lettres de l'Imperatrice à l'Empereur Nicolas II* (Paris: Payot, 1924). *Perepiska Nikolaja i Alexandry Romanovych* (3 vols.; Moscow: State Printing House, 1925–27); American translation, *Letters of the Tsar to the Tsaritsa, 1914–1917* (New York: Dodd, 1929); German translation, *Als deutsche Zarin im Weltenbrand. Intime Aufzeichnungen aus der Zeit Rasputins* (2 vols.; Dresden: Reissner, 1932).

[139] *Les archives secrètes de l'Empereur Nicolas II* (Paris: Payot, 1928).

[140] A French translation has been published: *Lettres de Nicolas II et de sa mère* (Paris: Les Documentaires, 1928). However, the best edition is *Der letze Zar. Briefwechsel Nikolaus II mit seiner Mutter.* [The Letters of Czar Nicholas and Empress Marie] (Berlin: Metzner, 1938).

[141] *Nikolaj II i velikie knjaz'ja* (Leningrad-Moscow: State Printing House, 1925); French translation, *Lettres des Grand-Ducs à Nicolas II* (Paris: Payot, 1926). The correspondence is reproduced in German translation in *Russland auf dem Wege zur Katastrophe Tagebücher des Grossfürsten Andres und des Kriegsministers Poliwanow. Briefe des Grossfürsten an der Zaren* (Berlin: Deutsche Verlagsgesellschaft für Politik und Geschichte, 1926).

Russian Empire. Of minor political interest but rich in commentary on the court are the memoirs of General Spiridovic.[142]

No direct account was left by Gorchakov,[143] Chancellor from 1867 to 1879. The memoirs of Giers were recently published,[144] but their interest is limited to the years 1873–75, when the author was Minister to Stockholm. Giers' work can be better understood through a study of Lamsdorff's diary[145] (before becoming Foreign Minister, a post he held from 1900 to 1906, Lamsdorff was the highly regarded adviser to his predecessors) and the important volume by Baron Nolde, legal adviser of the Ministry of Foreign Affairs, on the origins of the Franco-Russian Alliance.[146] Nolde based his study on the Giers papers and on the files of the Russian ambassadors to Constantinople and to London, Nelidov and De Staal. To these may be added the more recent publication of the diary of the Minister of War, Miliutin,[147] who, especially during the years 1878–81, exercised a major influence on the conduct of Russian foreign policy. His annotations are particularly important for the background to the Congress of Berlin and for the negotiations leading to the Three Emperors League.

Izvolski's memoirs[148] contain several chapters on the Russo-Japanese War

[142] Aleksandr Ivanovic Spiridovic, *Les dernières années de la cour de Tsarkoie-Sélo* (2 vols.; Paris: Payot, 1928–29).

[143] See also Charles-Roux, *Alexandre II, Gortchakov et Napoleon III* (Paris: Plon, 1913).

[144] Charles and Barbara Jelavich (eds.), *The Education of a Russian States-man: The Memoirs of Nicholas Karlovich Giers* (Berkeley: University of California Press, 1962). The editors had already published a portion of the Giers correspondence in "Russia and Bulgaria, 1879: The Letters of A. P. Davydov to N. K. Giers," *Südost-Forschungen*, 1956, pp. 427–58; "Bismarck's Proposal for the Revival of the Dreikaiserbund in October 1878," *Journal of Modern History*, June, 1957; "Jomini and the Revival of the Dreikaiserbund 1879–1880," *Slavonic and East European Review*, June, 1957; Charles Jelavich, *Tsarist Russia and Balkan Nationalism: Russian Influence in the Internal Affairs of Bulgaria and Serbia 1879–1886* (Berkeley: University of California Press, 1958); Jelavich and Jelavich, *Russia in the East 1876–1880. The Russo-Turkish War and the Kuldja Crisis as Seen through the Letters of A. G. Jomini to N. K. Giers* (Leyden: Brill, 1959).

[145] Vladimir Nikolaevic Lamsdorf, *Dnevnik* [Diary] *1886–1890* (Moscow-Leningrad: State Printing House, 1926); a selection of the most important excerpts referring to the failure to renew the Reinsurance treaty has been published in German translation in *Berliner Monatshefte*, February, 1931. Lamsdorf, *Dnevnik, 1891–1892* (Moscow-Leningrad: Akademia, 1934); excerpts relating to Russo-German affairs have been published in *Berliner Monatschefte*, May, 1936, Lamsdorf, "Dnevnik, 1894–1895," *Krasny Archiv*, XLVI (1931).

[146] Baron Borsi Nolde, *L'alliance franco-russe. Les origines du système diplomatique d'avant-guerre* (Paris: Droz, 1936).

[147] D. A. Miliutina, *Dnevnik* (4 vols.; Moscow: Gosudarstvennaia ordena Lenina biblioteka SSSR, 1947–50). The portion of the diary published is limited to the years 1873–82.

[148] Alexandre Iswolski, *Recollections of a Foreign Minister* (New York: Doubleday, 1921); French edition, *Mémoires* (Paris: Payot, 1923).

and on the Björkö treaty, but they end with his appointment as Minister of Foreign Affairs in 1906. For his activity as Foreign Minister and later as Ambassador to Paris, reference must be made to his correspondence published by his daughter and by Stieve and to the rich collection of official documents drawn from the archives of the Russian Embassy in Paris.[149]

Sazonov, Minister of Foreign Affairs from 1910 to 1916, completed his defense in exile, writing without the aid of the necessary documents.[150] He adds little not already known through the publication of the Russian collections and through the material published in other countries. However, the importance of his work lies in the interpretation the author gives to his actions and in the evaluations it contains. The most detailed exposition, of course, is devoted to the immediate origins of the conflict, and Sazonov develops the thesis of full Austro-Hungarian responsibility; he blames Germany for not having restrained Vienna, in part because Berlin lacked complete information on the situation and in part because it had not properly evaluated the seriousness of the circumstances. Here, too, the new elements he presents are few, but Sazonov's summary is worth noting for his observations on the last days of peace in St. Petersburg and for his dramatic meeting with the Czar when the decision for general mobilization was made.

The memoirs of Count Witte,[151] Minister of Communications in 1892, Minister of Finance from 1893 to 1905, President of the Council in 1905, and Prime Minister from the publication of the October Manifesto granting the Russians a constitution until his retirement to private life the following year, include a number of important passages, such as the pages devoted to the Hague Conference, in which he clearly outlines the objectives of Russian policy.[152] Equally important are the pages on the Russo-Japanese War[153] and the chapter on the Portsmouth Treaty,[154] Witte

---

[149] See pp. 124–25.

[150] Serge Sazonoff, *Fateful Years 1909–1916* (New York: Stokes, 1928).

[151] Sergej Jujievic Witte, *The Memoirs of Count Witte* (New York: Doubleday, 1921). The editions in translation are abridged from the original Russian-language edition, *Vospominanija Carstvovanie Nikolaja II* (2 vols.; Berlin: Slovo, 1922).

[152] On this issue, see also E. J. Dillon, *The Eclipse of Russia* (London: Dentand, 1918). The author was an intimate friend of Witte and treats this subject in greater detail. This volume also provides the first detailed summary of the Björkö meeting.

[153] See also "Perepiska Sergej Juljevic Witte i Aleksej Nikolaevic Kuropatkina v 1904–1905" [The Witte-Kuropatkin Correspondence, 1904–1905], *Krasny Archiv*, XIX (1926). On Kuropatkin, Minister of War, 1904–5, see also his diary: Aleksej Nikolaevic Kuropatkin, "Dnevnik" (Nizni Novgorod: Nizpoligraf, 1923); Kuropatkin, "Dnevnik," *Krasny Archiv*, 1922–27.

[154] On this issue, in addition to the volume by Rosen (see below), the Russian Ambassador to Washington, see the diary of Witte's secretary, Y. Y. Korostovetz,

being the principal Russian negotiator. The volume suffers from the author's animosity toward his political opponents and his frequent distortions of the truth.

Kokovstov's autobiography[155] is largely concerned with internal affairs (Kokovstov was Minister of Finance from 1905 to 1914 and President of the Council from 1911 to 1914). The structure of the Russian government, very different from that of a parliamentary regime, obliged Kokovstov on more than one occasion to concern himself with questions of foreign policy. In describing his activity, which was constantly aimed at avoiding a conflict for which Russia was not prepared, he reveals some important details: for example, the promise of the Czar to support the French position at the Algeciras Conference in exchange for the granting of a loan negotiated by Kokovstov with Rouvier; the steps taken by the author, in agreement with Sazonov, to block Russian mobilization in September, 1912, on the eve of the first Balkan war; his role as moderator during the Liman von Sanders crisis,[156] when Sazonov and, above all, the military did not exclude the possibility of a war to prevent German control of the Turkish army.

Baron de Taube's volume[157] lies somewhere between a memoir and a historical study. De Taube, former legal adviser to the Russian Ministry of Foreign Affairs, prepared his study on the basis of his personal experiences, documentary materials, and the memoirs of others published after the war. He was in a position to study the developments in the Ministry at close hand without having any direct responsibility for them, and, therefore, he had no personal role to defend. The objectivity of his work is unusual for a memoir, and the new data he presents retain their importance even after the publication of the official documents.

His narration begins with the Dogger Bank incident; as Russian representative on the commission of inquiry, he was in a position to supply

---

Pre-War Diplomacy. The Russo-Japanese Problem. Treaty Signed at Portsmouth, U.S.A. 1905. Diary (London: British Periodicals, 1920).

[155] Vladimir Nokolaevic Kokovstov, *Iz moego proslago Vospominanija 1903–1917* (Paris: Izd. Journala Illustrirovannaja Rossija, 1933); English translation, *Out of My Past* (Stanford, Calif.: Stanford University Press, 1935). The English translation is slightly abridged.

[156] On this question, see also Comte W. Kokovtzoff, "La mission Liman von Sanders. Les entretiens de Berlin en Novembre 1913," *Revue d'histoire de la guerre mondiale*, II (1935).

[157] Baron Michel de Taube, *La politique russe d'avant-guerre et la fin de l'Empire des Tsars (1904–1917)* (Paris: Leroux, 1928). The original edition is in French. The German translation is Freiherr von Taube, *Der grossen Katastrophe entgegen. Die russische Politik der Vorkriegszeit und das Ende des Zarenreiches (1904–1917). Erinnerungen* (Berlin: Neuner, 1929). The German edition was brought up to date with the help of documents appearing after the publication of the original edition in French.

lucid details. No less important is his reference to Delcassé's suggestion that the Anglo-French understanding be enlarged just as soon as the international situation warranted it, a suggestion that De Taube, at the request of the French Minister of Foreign Affairs, referred to Lamsdorff. However, Lamsdorff gave no indication that he was willing to abandon that "independent" policy which he considered, for the moment, to be the only one possible for Russia. De Taube observed that the soundness of this decision was indisputable but that after the resounding defeat in the war with Japan it was hardly likely that such a policy would be favored by St. Petersburg, now more than ever anxious to regain by a success in Europe the prestige lost in the Far East.

These aspirations found a fervent supporter in Izvolski, and it is on the latter that De Taube has written his best pages. De Taube's disclosures on this subject are of major significance. For example, attention is called to that portion of the study dealing with the Russo-German negotiations that preceded the "Baltic Accord" of October 28, 1907. Equally interesting for the historian is the picture he creates, through a series of episodes, of how the almost morbid ambition of the Foreign Minister became a significant factor in the foreign policy of Russia. In effect, De Taube observes, in Izvolski's mind national prestige often became confused with personal prestige, and this explains the radical change in Russian policy after the diplomatic defeat in the Bosnian crisis. This episode is described as a crucial turning point in European history because Izvolski swore revenge against Austria; from that moment on, any possibility of a Russo-German *rapprochement* had disappeared, and the Czarist Empire remained indissolubly bound to the two western powers and particularly to France.

Izvolski's successor, Sazonov, had neither the strength of character nor the necessary capacity to correct the errors made earlier. In practice, he permitted the military and Izvolski, now Ambassador to France, to have a free hand. Many European problems now became more acute, and what was even worse, in St. Petersburg the conviction was gradually strengthened that war was inevitable.

The part of De Taube's volume most open to question is the discussion of the immediate origins of the war and war responsibilities. He charges Serbia with the major responsibility, whether for the aggressive character of its policy or for the specific incident of the assassination at Sarajevo. Sazonov, instead, was responsible for having convinced the Czar to mobilize at a time when all diplomatic efforts toward a peaceful solution had not been exhausted, and Austria-Hungary was guilty of wanting a solution by force in the hope that the war could be localized, when this was manifestly impossible. De Taube considers German responsibility to be minor, although Berlin's declaration of war when Russia mobilized was unjustified, particularly since the Czar had given his word that Russian troops would not cross the frontier. Great Britain's responsibility is also classified as minor, although it did not clarify its position as promptly as it should have. France's conduct, according to De Taube, was irresponsible. Obviously, these conclusions are rather perplexing.

Two volumes of memoirs were published by Kerensky,[158] Minister of Justice and later of War in the First Provisional Government and President of the Second Provisional Government until the October Revolution. The first concerns internal affairs and attempts to answer the accusation against him of having facilitated the advent of the Bolsheviks by placing the blame on Kornilov, who, in his attempted *coup d'état,* opened the way for Lenin's assumption of power. In the second of his works Kerensky returns to the subject and discloses that the tragedy occurred when the policy of the Provisional Government was on the verge of bearing fruit. Kerensky states that a short time later, unbeknownst to Germany, Vienna offered to negotiate a separate peace with Russia. This step, he reveals, was of vital importance because the former Minister of Foreign Affairs, Tereschenko, with the collaboration of the American representatives in Sofia and Constantinople, had worked out a plan of negotiations whereby Bulgaria and Turkey would withdraw from the war. This information leads to the assumption that the Austrian request was followed by a similar request from Bulgaria and Turkey.[159]

Leon Trotsky's autobiography[160] is of interest primarily for the brief period in which the author managed Soviet foreign policy and for the negotiations at Brest Litovsk. Trotsky reveals that he intended to prolong these negotiations and that it was Lenin who insisted that peace be concluded as soon as possible. Trotsky adds a number of particulars on the negotiations and on the atmosphere surrounding the peace talks at Brest Litovsk.[161] An example is Trotsky's reference to General Hoffmann, who declared that he was not at Brest Litovsk as the representative of the German government but as the representative of the High Command of the

[158] Alexander Fedorovich Kerensky, *The Prelude to Bolshevism* (New York: Dodd, 1919); *The Crucifixion of Liberty* (New York: Day, 1934).

[159] A remarkable collection of material concerning the events in Russia between March and November, 1917, has been assembled by Kerensky in collaboration with Professor Browder. See Robert Paul Browder and Alexander F. Kerensky, *The Russian Provisional Government 1917* (3 vols.; Stanford, Calif.: Stanford University Press, 1961). The material pertinent to foreign affairs is extremely limited.

[160] Lev Davidovic Trotsky, *Mein Leben. Versuch einer Autobiographie* (Berlin: Fischer Verlag, 1930).

[161] On this question, see J. W. Wheeler-Bennet, *Brest-Litovsk. The Forgotten Peace. March, 1918* (London: Macmillan, 1956).

German army. While the Russian diplomatic memoirs are not numerous, generally they are replete with unusually significant data.

The memoirs which Ambassador Saburov had entrusted to the historian Simpson in May, 1917, for the purpose of eventually making them available to western scholars[162] are the primary source for the study of the negotiations leading to the creation of the Three Emperors League. Saburov was among those who believed that friendship with Germany was the best means by which Russia could re-establish her position after the events of the Congress of Berlin. With German support Russia would have obtained a guarantee against further Austro-Hungarian expansion in the Balkans and at the same time the danger of a new threat to the Straits in the event of war with Great Britain would have been eliminated, since Britain would be unable to find a Continental ally. Saburov began his talks with Bismarck in the summer of 1879, while he was on his way to his embassy post in Constantinople, and the positive results of these talks induced the Czarist government to send him to Berlin as Ambassador early in 1880. In Berlin he conducted the negotiations for the agreement concluded on June 18, 1881, and remained at that post until 1884. His detailed summary of the negotiations is still the most important source on the question.

The same value can be ascribed to the memoirs of Baron Rosen[163] for the reconstruction of Russian policy in the Far East from 1897 to the Treaty of Portsmouth. Rosen was Minister to Japan in 1897–98 and again from 1902–4 and then Ambassador to the United States to 1911. Rosen believed it to be damaging for Russia to oppose Japanese aims in Korea, but his suggestions for a policy that would be more in keeping with the military and economic resources of Russia were ignored by the Czarist government, and Rosen was transferred elsewhere. Four years later, at the conclusion of the Anglo-Japanese alliance, the Russian government found Rosen to be the perfect choice to send to Tokyo once again in an attempt, with a policy of friendship, to neutralize the effect created by this alliance on the Russian position in the Far East. Rosen ably seconded Lamsdorff's moderate approach, but, notwithstanding his efforts, Russo-Japanese tension exploded into open conflict, and he was able to continue his work only as a delegate to the peace conference at Portsmouth. If, from the point of view of diplomatic history, Rosen's memoirs decline in value after 1905—

[162] J. Y. Simpson, *The Saburov Memoirs or Bismarck and Russia* (Cambridge: Cambridge University Press, 1929). The volume also contains an article, "Russie, France, Allemagne (1870–1880)," originally published by Saburov in *Revue de Paris*, May 15, 1912.

[163] Roman Romanovic Rosen, *Forty Years of Diplomacy* (2 vols.; London: Allen and Unwin, 1922).

although his criticism of the policies of Izvolski and Sazonov are not to be ignored—from that date they become a major source for the study of the Russian internal situation up to the Bolshevik Revolution.

The contribution made by Charikov's autobiography[164] is limited to two issues: the Bosnian crisis and the brief account of his mission to Constantinople, 1909–12, with useful data on both. Charikov was a career diplomat and a friend of Izvolski's, and the latter recalled him to the Ministry of Foreign Affairs as political officer in charge of relations with the Duma in 1908. Thus he was able to follow the development of the Bosnian crisis personally in the absence of Izvolski from the Foreign Ministry. From his account it is learned that Stolypin and Kokovstov, hearing of the Buchlau talks, urged the Czar to send Izvolski new instructions for the negotiations with the Austrians. Several weeks later, in the face of the German ultimatum on recognition of the Austrian annexations, Charikov worked to convince the Czar to bow to German pressure, citing the example of Japan's acceding to Russo-German pressure in 1895 when she was not prepared to risk a war with Russia. However, at the same time he began preparations to seek revenge for this humiliation. In 1909 Charikov was sent to Constantinople to attempt to achieve a closer rapport with the Young Turks who had deposed Abdul Hamid. His mission, which was characteristic of a phase of Russian foreign policy aimed at reaching a direct agreement with the Ottoman Empire, culminated, in the fall of 1911, in his negotiations with the Porte to obtain the right of transit through the Straits for Russian warships.[165] As is known, these negotiations were publicly denounced by Sazonov, and Charikov was recalled to St. Petersburg in March, 1912, accused of negotiating without instructions from his government. This episode has never been completely clarified and has been the object of varying interpretations by scholars. At first it was considered to be a maneuver inspired by Izvolski to accomplish what had escaped him during the Bosnian crisis.[166] However, with the publication of the Soviet

---

[164] N. V. Tcharykow, *Glimpses of High Politics. Through War and Peace 1855–1929* (London: Allen and Unwin, 1931).

[165] The noted jurist Mandelstam, at that time First Secretary of the Embassy in Constantinople, has written two significant summaries of Russian policy toward the Ottoman Empire and Russian policy in general between the turn of the century and the revolution of 1917, which are also important contributions on the Turkish internal scene. See A. N. Mandelstam, *Le sort de l'Empire Ottoman* (Paris: Payot, 1917); "La politique russe d'accès à la Méditerranée au XXème siècle," in *Recueil des Cours de L'Académie de Droit International de La Haye*, Tome 47 (1934).

[166] On this point, see Sidney Bradshaw Fay, *The Origins of the World War* (New York: Macmillan, 1928), I, 413–26; William L. Langer, "Russia, the Straits Question and the Origins of the Balkan League, 1908–1912," *Political Science Quarterly*, September, 1928.

general collection, the new documents seem to indicate that Charikov's initiatives were mainly personal and that Izvolski's role in the affair, if any, was extremely limited.[167]

The solution to the Straits problem that had escaped Izvolski and Charikov in 1911 was sought through other means by the ministers to Belgrade and Sofia, Hartwig and Nekliudov. A part of their undertaking involved the attempt to create a Serbo-Bulgarian entente for the purpose of employing the armed forces of these two countries as a defensive bulwark in the most delicate sector of the Balkans. Nekliudov's memoirs[168] offer concrete details on the roles of the Russian representatives in the negotiations leading to the conclusion of the Serbo-Bulgarian Alliance of 1912 and to the formation of the Balkan League. Nekliudov's memoirs also provide details which make it possible to determine the extent to which the efforts of the ministers to the two Balkan states conformed to the directives of the Czar and Sazonov. Nekliudov's account covers the entire period of the Balkan wars, as he was transferred from Sofia to Stockholm only in 1914. His account of his mission to Sweden is of no particular interest, although his recollections, which begin with the events of 1917 and his collaboration with the Kerensky government, are worthy of note.

The memoirs of another diplomat, Savinsky,[169] Minister to Sofia, 1914–15, offer extremely significant data on Bulgaria's relations with Russia or, rather, with the Entente powers. They are a major source for the study of Russian policy toward Bulgaria in those years, supplementing on many points the documents published by the Soviet government.

Two factors characterized the Bulgarian situation after the outbreak of the war: first, King Ferdinand's desire to obtain that portion of Macedonia assigned to Serbia by the treaty of March 12, 1912, and the co-called contested zone, whose final disposition was to be determined by the Czar as arbiter (the area was assigned to Serbia at the Peace of Bucharest of August, 1913); and second, the strong Russophile character of Bulgarian public opinion. The prevalence of one of these factors over the other would have led to Bulgaria's siding with the Entente in the war against the Central Powers. Sazonov was absolutely opposed to negotiating with the Bulgars as long as the Radoslavov government was in power in Sofia, while

---

[167] Compare Edward C. Thaden, "Charykov and Russian Foreign Policy at Constantinople in 1911," *Journal of Central European Affairs*, April, 1956. This article is based largely on the Russian diplomatic documents, Series II, Vols. XVIII and XIX.

[168] A. V. Nekliudov, *Diplomatic Reminiscences* (London: Murray, 1920).

[169] A. Savinsky, *Recollections of a Russian Diplomat* (London: Hutchinson, 1927).

Savinsky advised a more flexible policy in consideration of the pressure Germany and Austria were exerting on King Ferdinand with their promise of all of Macedonia and offer of important financial aid. "If, in the end, Bulgaria joined our enemies, the fault was entirely ours," concludes Savinsky.

For ten years prior to his mission to Sofia, Savinsky had been Chief of Cabinet in the Ministry of Foreign Affairs and was Minister to Sweden from 1912 to 1914, but despite the fact that he was familiar with all of the secrets of Russian diplomacy (he was custodian of the secret Russian archives as well) and accompanied the Czar and his ministers on their long trips abroad, this portion of his volume contains little of importance, consisting only of a summary of the formal aspects of his activities.[170]

In contrast, Schebeko's recollections[171] are much more modest and less interesting. He had been Counsellor to the Embassy in Berlin from 1909 to 1912, Minister to Bucharest in 1912, and Ambassador to Vienna beginning in December, 1913. The author offers considerable detail on the development of the crisis of July, 1914, as seen from his vantage point in Vienna and through the information he transmitted to Sazonov. However, his revelations add little to what was already known. His thesis, that if neither side deliberately wanted the war only the Entente powers had done everything possible to avoid it, is not very convincing. Later, Schebeko restricts this assertion to mean only Russia: he insists—contrary to what is proved by the documents—that Russian mobilization occurred only after Austria mobilized, and he attributes to Asquith and Grey the error of not having made it clear, immediately after Serbia's reply to the Austrian ultimatum, that Great Britain would join the Franco-Russian block in case of a conflict. If this had occurred, Schebeko concludes, Germany would not have declared war.

The contribution of the two diplomats Schelking[172] and Nabokov[173] is even less important. Schelking had been Ambassador Osten-Sacken's secretary in Berlin, and Nabokov had been Russian Chargé d'Affaires in

---

[170] A more substantial contribution is made by the author in two articles on the events of the period: "Guillaume II et la Russie. Ses lettres et dépêches à Nicolas II, 1903–1905," *Revue des deux Mondes*, December 15, 1922; and "L'entrevue de Buchlau," *Monde slave*, February, 1931.

[171] N. Schebeko, *Souvenirs. Essai historique sur les origines de la guerre de 1914* (Paris: Bibliothèque diplomatique, 1936). The most important parts of this memoir were published earlier in Schebeko, "A Vienne en juillet 1914: souvenirs inédits de l'ambassadeur de Russie," *Revue de France*, May 15, 1933.

[172] J. N. Schelking, *The Game of Diplomacy* (London: Hutchinson, 1918).

[173] Constantin Nabokov, *The Ordeal of a Diplomat* (London: Duckworth, 1921).

London in 1917, after the death of Benckendorff. Schelking's memoirs are of little value because of the inaccuracies they contain, while Nabokov's contribute very little to the study of the dominant issues in 1917.

5. THE GERMAN MEMORIALISTS.

While William II's memoirs[174] are useful for a study of the Kaiser's personality, they make no serious contribution to the study of political and diplomatic events of the prewar period. In effect, William II seeks to explain his role as having been purely that of a constitutional monarch and affirms that he always acted in line with the policies established by his ministers, a thesis that may be tenable under certain circumstances (the Agadir crisis) but certainly not in others (the Boer crisis).

Much more important to the defense of the Kaiser than his not too convincing memoirs is the Willy-Nicky correspondence, published by the Soviet government after the end of World War I.[175] Only a portion of this correspondence was included in the German general collection of diplomatic documents, yet it remains a fundamental source even if it is not always possible to determine to what extent it reflects the Kaiser's personal views. According to William II, before any letter was sent, it was submitted to the Chancellor for approval. Moreover, the letters were usually written at the suggestion of the ministers or from notes prepared by the Ministry, indicating that the position taken in them was more likely to be that of the government than that of the Sovereign.

Concerning the relations between William II and Czar Nicholas, the memoirs of Count Lambsdorff[176] are especially worthy of attention. Lambsdorff was the Kaiser's personal representative to the Czar after the Björkö meeting. On that occasion, the two sovereigns agreed to exchange personal representatives who would report directly to their respective rulers. Lambsdorff was the first German officer entrusted with this mission, but his book also narrates the experiences of his successors and includes their reports. The most important are the reports of Baron von Hintze, German Foreign Minister from July to October, 1918.

[174] Wilhelm II, *Ereignisse und Gestalten aus den Jahren 1878–1918* (Leipzig and Berlin: Koehler, 1922).

[175] The best edition is the German one: Kaiser Wilhelm, *Briefe an den Zaren 1894–1914* (Berlin: Ullstein, 1920); French translation, *Correspondance entre Guillaume II et Nicolas II, 1894–1914* (Paris: Plon, 1924).

[176] Gustav Graf von Lambsdorff, *Die Militärbevollmächtingten Kaiser Wilhelms II am Zarenhofe 1904–1914* (Berlin: Schlieffen Verlag, 1937).

Bismarck's recollections are a splendid example of a memoir source,[177] entirely worthy of the author. Rarely does he deal with details (the dramatic pages on the editing of the Ems dispatch are an exception), and seeks, instead, to clarify the motives inspiring his policy by an examination of the events as they unfolded. Yet his testimony is never dissipated in generalities, and his memoirs are irreplaceable for understanding the real meaning of the documents included in the German general collection. It is in the field of foreign affairs that Bismarck's recollections make their greatest contribution. It is also evident that he considered himself to be primarily a diplomat and diplomacy his most important activity. Bismarck emphasizes Germany's need to preserve Russian friendship and demonstrates that he never lost sight of this necessity. To base German foreign policy exclusively on the Austrian alliance would be, he affirms, a tragic mistake because it would threaten to draw Germany into a conflict contrary to her specific interests.[178] What is most significant is the fact that the character he ascribes to his policies has never been denied by the evidence later brought to light. His was a policy of preserving the advantages gained by Prussia during the course of the last three wars. There is no indication in his memoirs of Pan-German tendencies or of any desire to expand in the colonial world or of the cult of *Weltpolitik,* a concept entirely foreign to him.

The third of the three volumes of his memoirs, devoted to the last period of his chancellorship, is clearly the least impressive. It lacks the detached sense of power found in the others. Moreover, the unquestionable bitterness in his account of altercations with William II leaves the soundness of his thesis open to question.

Bismarck's successor, General Caprivi, has left no record of his activities as Chancellor from 1890 to 1894.[179] However, Prince Hohenlohe, the third Imperial Chancellor, added a significant contribution.[180] His memoirs were published in two sections. In 1907 the first two volumes appeared; these terminate with the beginning of his term of office as Chancellor, and

[177] Otto von Bismarck, *Gedanken und Erinnerungen* (2 vols.; Stuttgart: Cotta, 1898); *Gedanken und Erinnerungen (1887–1890)* (Stuttgart: Cotta, 1921).

[178] Bismarck developed these same ideas in a personal letter to Crispi (unfortunately, the letter was eventually restored to the author by Crispi's secretary at the time, Senator Paratore, and the copy has disappeared), in which he added that the Triple Alliance, lacking the support of London and St. Petersburg, had been perverted in its defensive functions.

[179] Nevertheless, see J. Alden Nichols, *Germany after Bismarck, The Caprivi Era 1890–1894* (Cambridge, Mass.: Harvard University Press, 1958).

[180] Chlodwig Fürst zu Hohenlohe-Schillingsfurst, *Denkwürdigkeiten des Reichskanzlers* (2 vols.; Stuttgart: Deutsche Verlagsanstalt, 1907); *Denkwürdigkeiten der Reichskanzlerzeit* (Stuttgart: Deutsche Verlagsanstalt, 1931).

illuminate the workings of the Congress of Berlin, which Hohenlohe attended as Germany's third delegate. They created a sensation when they were published because of the judgments his diary and his correspondence contained on the political leaders of Germany and because of the exposé of the circumstances leading to Bismarck's dismissal. The third volume, published in 1931, is not a memoir at all but rather a collection of personal and official documents comprising part of his diary, his letters, notes, etc. This volume is of the greatest interest to scholars because it refers to the six years of his chancellorship, from 1894 to October, 1900.

It should be noted immediately that the portion of this collection devoted to international affairs and German foreign policy is extremely limited. However, the extraordinarily rich documentation is basic to an understanding of the thinking of the leaders of that period and to a comprehension of the complex psychology of the Kaiser. Hohenlohe, a distinguished gentleman with a family background almost as aristocratic as that of his sovereign, knew how to maintain a dignified control on the latter, nipping fantastic projects in the bud, circumventing his impatience, and preventing the Kaiser from committing rash acts. On this point, Hohenlohe states, by way of illustration, that in February, 1895, when the separation of Norway from Sweden appeared to be imminent, the Kaiser proposed that Germany annex a part of Norway as soon as the latter became independent. In his judgment, it was inevitable that Russia would take over the northern half of Norway and that Germany should do likewise with the rest of Norway in order to prevent another state—Denmark—from taking advantage of the opportunity. There are also interesting references to Italy. Cardinal Hohenlohe, the Chancellor's brother, working from Rome, had a hand in directing the Chancellor toward a more favorable policy toward Italy, insisting that Italy be given greater support by the other members of the Triple Alliance. The lukewarm attitude of the Central Powers toward their ally, the Cardinal noted, threatened to weaken the position of the pro-Triplice elements in Italy and to favor a French policy in the Mediterranean. These recommendations seem to have had the effect of inspiring, after Adowa, manifestations of friendship for Italy which culminated in the Kaiser's visit to Venice.

No other German statesman has left as detailed a memoir as the four volumes of recollections left by Prince Bernhard von Bülow,[181] Secretary of State for Foreign Affairs from 1897 to 1900, and Chancellor from 1900 to 1909. The last volume, containing the reminiscences of his youth and of his diplomatic activity, is of limited interest with the exception of a few

---

[181] *Denkwürdigkeiten* (4 vols.; Berlin: Ullstein, 1930–31).

references to his early work as a diplomat. The other three volumes need to be examined for the data they provide on the author's policies and for the vehement debate these triggered, especially in Germany.[182]

Their detail notwithstanding, these memoirs rarely contain information of real historical value. On the whole, the soundness of the premises advanced by the author as well as the bases for his judgment of men and events should be viewed with a great deal of skepticism. Bülow begins his narrative with his appointment as Secretary of State for Foreign Affairs in June, 1897, and in this first section the most important subject is the question of Anglo-German relations. Bülow confirms the fact that Chamberlain had made a clear offer for an understanding but that he (Bülow) allowed the matter to drop in order to avoid intensifying the danger of a war with Russia. Furthermore, he adds, the British did not seriously intend to pursue a policy of political understanding with Germany, and Chamberlain's overture was prompted by the embarrassing position in which Britain found herself after the Boer War and by Chamberlain's desire to increase the tension existing between St. Petersburg and Berlin in order to reduce Russian pressure on the areas of major interest to the British.

These assertions are open to question; in any event, they are not sufficient to diagnose the situation. That the British attitude was simply the consequence of the Boer War is denied by the fact that strong forces continued to work in Britain for an Anglo-German understanding and that initiatives were taken toward this end somewhat later. Certainly the fear of being dragged into a war with Russia profoundly influenced Bülow's decision to refuse the offer, but it was not the only reason. It is possible that the German Chancellor was convinced that Great Britain could never resolve her differences with France and Russia and that, therefore, he could continue to count on the benevolent support of London without assuming obligations in the colonial field or on the question of naval armament, which should have provided the logical grounds for an understanding between the two powers. If such was the case, Bülow committed a grave error in evaluation, to which he added others in succeeding years.

On the Moroccan crisis of 1905–6, one of the key issues discussed in the second volume, the German Chancellor affirms that he had no intention of provoking a war but that he threatened war for the express purpose of avoiding it. He maintains that Delcassé's position as head of the French

---

[182] On this issue, see Friedrich Thimme (ed.), *Front wider Bülow. Staatsmänner, Diplomaten und Forscher zu seinen Denkwürdigkeiten* (Munich: Bruckmann, 1931). Professor Thimme has assembled an important collection of testimonies challenging von Bülow's affirmations and the article by Jules Cambon, "Le prince de Bülow et ses Memoirs," *Revue des deux Mondes*, April 15, 1931.

government was the gravest threat to the peace of Europe and that after his resignation Franco-German relations immediately improved. In this, as in other circumstances, Bülow attests that his policy was conditioned by his preoccupation with the problem of preserving peace. This assertion is correct in the sense that Bülow had no desire to plunge Germany into war, but the fact remains that the role played by the German government during the crises that developed during his chancellorship was certainly one of the elements contributing to the outbreak of World War I.

One must be mindful of this in order to evaluate properly Bülow's accusations in the third volume of his memoirs against Bethmann-Hollweg, Kiderlen-Wächter, and Von Jagow. He recognizes that these men did not want the war but states that their weakness and uncertainty, particularly in allowing the Austrian government too great a freedom of action, plunged Germany and Europe into the crucible of war. These charges are basically true, but they must also be considered in the light of the circumstances these diplomats had inherited from Bülow himself when he resigned his office in 1909. The weakness demonstrated by his successor with respect to Austro-Hungarian policy was facilitated, if not determined, by the fact that now Austria-Hungary was the only ally Germany could count on. This isolation—strongly felt in Berlin—was in large measure the fruit of Bülow's labors. The same may be said of Russia's intransigence during the crisis of July, 1914, which stemmed in part from the psychological reaction to the humiliations experienced earlier (in which Bülow played a part), above all, the Bosnian crisis.

In the third volume Bülow included a long—and as usual, a very subjective—account of his mission to Rome from December, 1914, to May, 1915. In this summary he emphasizes that from the moment of his arrival in Rome he was aware of the intense gravity of the situation and of the need to apply strong pressure on Vienna to make a series of concessions to Italy in the Trentino. If the mission ended in failure, he adds, it was due to the influence of the Austrian Ambassador, Macchio, and the former German Ambassador, Flotow, who were both convinced that Italy would never dare to take a stand against the Central Powers, and to the blindness of the German leadership in refusing to talk to Vienna with the vigor that the situation made mandatory. Apart from the author's tendency to stress certain particular aspects and to blame others for every error, the facts he presents were already well known.

A word remains to be said concerning Bülow's evaluations of the many personalities he encountered and mentions in his memoirs. The bitterness of his judgments leave the reader stunned and incredulous. If the former

Chancellor is correct, the entire governing group of the German Empire consisted of individuals entirely devoid of the most elementary discernment and lacking even the most rudimentary training. Naturally, the most violent criticism, masked by a saccharine benevolence, is reserved for the Kaiser, who is described as erratic and superficial, possessed of a child-like vanity, bombastic, and of questionable sanity. This diatribe promptly raises the question of why, at the time of the famous *Daily Telegraph* interview in which Willian II expressed the thought of abdicating, Bülow did not encourage him to do so and thus free Germany and Europe of a public menace. If these ungenerous caricatures of the Kaiser can be ignored, Bülow does occasionally offer some elements of interest on the personalities of the era.

The memoirs of Bethmann-Hollweg,[183] Chancellor of Germany from 1909 to 1917, generally substantiate the judgment rendered on him by the most recent historiography. His policy was essentially peaceful, and he never thought of precipitating a general war, but his vacillations in making decisions and his weakness of character made him the man least suitable to direct the destinies of a great power in tempestuous times, and he succumbed to events that were more powerful than he. He himself admits this to be true, and this admission gives his memoirs a tone in strange contrast to that of the auto-apologetic character of Bülow's recollections.

The general lines of his policy are clearly summarized in the first volume of his memoirs. According to Bethmann-Hollweg, once it was impossible to reach an agreement with Russia, the objective was an accord with London: concessions had to be made by Germany, particularly in the area of naval armament, in return for a guarantee of British neutrality. The negotiations began in 1909, were interrupted by the Agadir crisis, and reopened with the Haldane mission in 1912. They had the effect of clarifying the relations between the two countries through joint diplomatic action during the Balkan wars, the accord reached on the question of the Portuguese colonies, and the agreement—realized only in June, 1914—on the Baghdad railway. But the anticipated entente with Great Britain did not materialize, nor did the situation that divided Europe into two blocks change substantially.

In truth, Bethmann-Hollweg observes, if William II was not inclined toward making a series of concessions and Von Tirpitz was unalterably opposed to reducing the naval armament program, neither did the British government appear to be disposed to conclude an entente in the sense desired. London restricted its statements to the fact that Great Britain

[183] Theobald Bethmann-Hollweg, *Betrachtungen zum Weltkriege* (2 vols.; Berlin: Hobbing, 1919–22).

would not take part in a war of aggression, but this declaration was insufficient to effect a substantial change in the provocative policy of the Franco-Russian combine.

As for the crisis of 1914, Bethmann-Hollweg defends a well-known thesis, i.e., that Germany found herself in a position of having to support Vienna in its conflict with Serbia because this was a question of survival for the Austro-Hungarian Empire. Naturally, he expected to be able to localize the conflict. However, if his honesty in making this statement can be believed in, it must be pointed out that it was illusory to deduce that Russian intervention in support of Serbia could be avoided. It should be noted here that the precedent set in March, 1909, when a German threat induced Izvolski to capitulate in the Bosnian question, weighed heavily on the minds of the German leaders in drawing up a German position. They failed to see the profound differences between the two situations or to understand that the precedent of 1909 made it impossible for Russia to accept another humiliation.

The compilation was interrupted midway in the second volume by Bethmann-Hollweg's death, which explains the confusion and the repetitions, as well as his failure to treat a number of important questions such as German relations with Italy and Rumania. However, there are several chapters that deserve the attention of scholars, those referring to the discussion with Vienna on the Polish question and on submarine warfare. The central theme remains, however, the problem of the internal conflict between the High Command and the civil government during the war. Bethmann-Hollweg concludes that real power in Germany was in the hands of the military. Before the war the opposition of Von Tirpitz had made it impossible for him to reach an agreement with the British; after the outbreak of the war, military influence increased appreciably, and in several situations the High Command forced its will on the government, as in the instance of unrestricted submarine warfare. In 1917, when there was the possibility of reaching a compromise peace, the military imposed its will and forced Bethmann-Hollweg to resign.[184]

The memoirs of Georg Michaelis,[185] Chancellor for a few months, from July 19 to November 1, 1917, are of limited importance. With the exception of the pages on the papal appeal for peace of August, 1917, and

[184] A number of Bethmann-Hollweg's assertions on German war aims must be re-evaluated in the light of the recent publication of the documentary collections. On this point, see Fritz Fischer, Griff nach der Weltmacht: Die Kriegszielpolitik des kaiserlichen Deutschland 1914–1918 (Düsseldorf: Droste Verlag, 1961), which includes a Bethmann-Hollweg promemoria of September 9, 1914, tracing an extensive plan for the expansion of Germany in Europe and elsewhere.

[185] Für Staat und Volk (Berlin: Furche Verlag, 1922).

the discussions on the future of Belgium, they contain little worth noting, although they do confirm Bethmann-Hollweg's comments on the preponderant influence of the military.

His successor, Georg Hertling, left no memoirs.[186] William II's last Chancellor, Prince Max of Baden, has published an amply documented volume of his personal recollections,[187] which continues to be a fundamental source for the study of the last days of the German Empire.

Prince Max was convinced of the necessity of reaching a compromise peace—he had emphasized this point during the preceding spring when the German offensive had reawakened German hopes for a quick victory—and believed that a change in government, followed by a basic reform in the democratic sense, would be a decisive step. The unity of the German people would have been strengthened by the support of the Socialists, and at the same time such a step would have aided the forces in the enemy countries who favored a compromise peace. However, the new Chancellor did not intend to launch a peace proposal. Instead, in his program Prince Max proposed to state Germany's war aims, which would include a number of important concessions to the enemy, and to fight to the end if the enemy imposed dishonorable conditions.

At the time when he assumed the chancellorship, events had made the realization of his program impossible. The High Command was convinced that now only an immediate suspension of hostilities could save the army, and the members of the government desired nothing else. Thus the first step that the new Chancellor was forced to take was to appeal to Wilson for peace terms, which was done on October 3, 1918. In his memoirs, Prince Max explains how he arrived at this decision. Had he refused to make the appeal, his refusal would not have prevented its being made. It would simply have been signed by Hindenburg or some other general, which would have given it the character of a capitulation and made negotiation extremely difficult. On the other hand, Prince Max was known to be a sincere advocate of peace, and an appeal signed by him might have strengthened the hand of pacifist elements in other countries. He adds that immediately after appealing to Wilson he considered delivering a speech to the *Reichstag* to soften the effect produced by his message to the American President and to give the Fourteen Points an interpretation that would be more favorable to Germany—for example, emphasizing that the future of

---

[186] See the biography written by his son, Karl Graf von Hertling, *Ein Jahr in der Reichkanzlei* (Freiburg: Herder, 1919), revealing new aspects of the power struggle between the civil government and the military.

[187] Prinz Max von Baden, *Erinnerungen und Dokumente* (Berlin-Leipzig: Deutsche Verlags-Anstalt, 1927).

Alsace-Lorraine should be determined by a plebiscite. However, this maneuver was blocked by the military and those ministers who feared that it would have an adverse effect on the attitude of President Wilson.

Prince Max of Baden also contributes important testimony on the events leading to the abdication of the Kaiser. He admits that only toward the end of October was he finally convinced that it was absolutely necessary that the Kaiser abdicate, not so much because it was requested by the Allies as a preliminary condition to negotiation, but rather because the continued presence of William II on the throne would have made it difficult to convince the German people to continue the struggle if the terms of peace offered by the enemy were considered dishonorable. Prince Max's attempts to induce the Kaiser to abdicate encountered tremendous resistance. In great detail, he describes the last dramatic days of the Empire, recalling the pressures he applied to force the Kaiser, who had taken refuge at Spa, close to High Command Headquarters, to resign. He speaks of the Emperor's dilatory tactics, the refusal of the military to allow themselves to be dragged into a civil war, and finally, his last attempt to save the monarchical principle by announcing the abdication of the Kaiser and the Crown Prince before he had received an official communication to that effect. When the Kaiser's official statement reached Berlin—William II abdicated as Emperor of Germany, not as King of Prussia, and nothing was said about the Crown Prince renouncing the throne—the republic had already been proclaimed.

In evaluating the contribution made by the memoirs of the secretaries of state of the German Foreign Office, it must be kept in mind that the creation of foreign policy in Germany was the prerogative of the Chancellor's office. Consequently, the role of the secretaries of state for foreign affairs in imperial Germany was not at all comparable in importance to that of the Minister of Foreign Affairs in a parliamentary regime.

The memoirs of Baron Schoen,[188] Ambassador to St. Petersburg from 1905 to 1907, Secretary of State for Foreign Affairs from 1907 to 1910, and Ambassador to Paris from 1910 to the outbreak of the war, are of no particular significance. His successor, Kiderlen-Wächter, did not leave his memoirs, but his diary and correspondence were edited in two volumes by Professor Jäckh,[189] and the latter was able to draw attention to a number of pertinent observations on foreign policy and to highlight Kiderlen-Wächter's

---

[188] Wilhelm Freiherr von Schoen, *Erlebtes. Beiträge zur politischen Geschichte der neuesten Zeit* (Stuttgart: Deutsche Verlagsanstalt, 1921); "Die deutsche Kriegserklärung an Frankreich am 3 August 1914," *Die deutsche Nation*, July, 1922.

[189] Ernst Jäckh (ed.), *Kiderlen-Wächter, der Staatsmann und Mensch. Briefwechsel und Nachlass* (2 vols.; Stuttgart: Deutsche Verlagsanstalt, 1924).

views. However, with respect to the documents published in the German collection, Kiderlen-Wächter adds little that is new, although his comments may serve to clarify several particular aspects of German foreign policy. From the diary it is apparent that he, like Bethmann-Hollweg, favored an agreement with Great Britain, although the official documents demonstrate that his policy contributed directly to the Agadir crisis and led Great Britain to seek closer ties with France and Russia.

Gottlieb von Jagow, Secretary of State for Foreign Affairs from 1913 to 1916, has focused on the last year of peace in order to give his version of the events leading to the war. His writings[190] leave the impression that he foresaw a general war, and his thesis is that Great Britain was largely responsible for its inevitability. Jagow insists that if Germany can be accused of not having restrained Austria in the Serbian question, the same may be said of Great Britain, which did nothing to restrain Russia. In protecting Serbia, Russia was pursuing imperialistic aims, but for Austria, the conflict was a matter of life or death. How could Germany have refused to support Austria? It would have meant the end of the alliance, the surrender of German interests in Turkey, and the complete isolation of Germany, which might have led to Austria's drawing closer to Paris and St. Petersburg.

Von Kühlmann's memoirs[191] cover the entire period of his diplomatic career, which included the years as Counsellor in the embassies at London and Constantinople, Minister to The Hague in 1915, Ambassador to Turkey in 1916, and Secretary of State for Foreign Affairs in 1917–18. Given the importance of the events in which Von Kühlmann often played a role, his contribution is rather modest. In his very general narrative, he adds little to what was already known about the key developments during his tenure of office as Secretary of State; that is, the negotiations for the treaty of Brest Litovsk and those for the Peace of Bucharest of May 7, 1918.

Before turning to the memoirs of the diplomats, special attention should be paid to the Friedrich von Holstein papers. The latter spent almost all of his long diplomatic career at the Ministry of Foreign Affairs, from 1876 to 1906, and became its most highly qualified expert and, particularly after the fall of Bismarck, the driving force of its political activity. This is the principal reason why Holstein was the target of such violent attacks and why he was referred to as "the gray eminence" of the Wilhelmstrasse. His

---

[190] *Ursachen und Ausbruch des Weltkrieges* (Berlin: Hobbing, 1919); *England und der Kriegsausbruch. Eine Auseinandersetzung mit Lord Grey* (Berlin: Verlag für Kulturpolitik, 1925); "Die deutsche Politik 1913–1914 vor dem Weltkriege," *Süddeutsche Monatschefte*, July, 1924; "Die deutsche politische Leitung und England bei Kriegausbruch," *Preussiche Jahrbücher*, July, 1928.

[191] Richard von Kühlmann. *Erinnerungen* (Heidelberg: Schneider, 1948).

power was attributed to shadowy intrigues and to the unscrupulous use of information reaching him through official channels or from his numerous correspondents. This notoriety was later crystallized by the memoirs of German statesmen and diplomats of the period to such an extent that judgments rendered on Holstein by historians in the immediate postwar period cannot be said to be particularly objective.

It is now possible to obtain a more objective image of Holstein's personality and of his political activity from his private papers, recently edited by Norman Rich and M. H. Fisher.[192] The Holstein papers can be divided into four categories: memoirs, diary, political memoranda, and correspondence. Holstein set about to write his memoirs on at least three occasions, in 1883, in 1898, and in 1906, but he never completed a systematic narrative of his career. The editors were forced to combine the portions of his memoirs that were available with excerpts from his other writings on German policy in order to reconstruct a picture that would include all of the fundamental aspects of his activities. Instead of being Holstein's memoirs, the compilation emerges as a complex of reminiscences and reflections on men and events of the era of Bismarck and of Kaiser William II.

Not even the diary, the second volume of the collection, is complete. Holstein began making occasional notes in 1882 but gave up the practice in 1888; thus in essence the diary is limited to Holstein's relations with Bismarck. However, it includes precise and significant data on the evolution of this rapport. These pages reveal, for example, that Holstein's role in the dismissal of Bismarck was something less than conspiratorial. On the contrary, it becomes apparent that for nearly a year prior to the "dropping of the pilot" the growing differences in point of view had been gradually alienating the two statesmen.

The third and fourth volumes, incorporating an ample selection of his correspondence, are the most important of the Holstein papers. They begin with 1880, the year in which Holstein began the systematic collection of his correspondence, which he was to continue throughout his life. Unfortunately, the procedure was interrupted on certain occasions when Holstein

[192] Norman Rich and M. H. Fisher (eds.), *The Holstein Papers*, Vol. I: *Memoirs*; Vol. II: *Diaries*; Vol. III: *Correspondence, 1861–1896*; Vol. IV: *Correspondence 1897–1909* (Cambridge: Cambridge University Press, 1955–63). On Holstein, see also Friedrich von Trotha, *Fritz von Holstein als Mensch und Politiker* (Berlin: Schröder, 1931); Helmuth Rogge (ed.), *Friedrich von Holstein: Lebensbekenntnis in Briefen an eine Frau* (Berlin: Ullstein, 1932); Helmut Krausnick, *Holsteins Geheimpolitik in der Aera Bismarck, 1886–1890* (Hamburg, 1942); Helmuth Rogge, *Holstein und Hohenlohe* (Stuttgart: Deutsche Verlagsanstalt, 1957); Rogge, *Holstein und Harden* (Munich: Beck, 1959).

destroyed a portion of his correspondence on his own initiative or at the request of his correspondents. A number of these gaps have been identified, such as the correspondence exchanged with Prince Eulenburg in 1890 and in 1894 relative to the fall of Bismarck and to the resignation of Caprivi. However, in this instance the editors were able to fill the gap from the files of the Eulenburg archives. The absence of files of correspondence with Von Waldersee and Von Schlieffen, with whom Holstein was known to have corresponded frequently, indicates the existence of other lacunae.

As the editors state, it may be surmised at this point that Holstein not only collected his correspondence but also personally edited it for publication and eliminated those documents which could reveal the "shadow area" of his personality and activity. Such a conclusion is rejected, for two reasons: first, as a case in point, it is proved by the correspondence taken from the Eulenburg archives that there was nothing compromising to Holstein in the correspondence he destroyed; second, it cannot be denied that there is a goodly amount of evidence on Holstein's participation in political maneuvers that can hardly be called unswervingly moral, as, for example, in the letters received by the journalist Harden, which do not exclude the possibility that Holstein inspired the press campaign against Prince Eulenburg.

It is evident that Holstein's private correspondence is of prime importance for a study of this singular personality and for his political activity—activity that, because of the unofficial way in which it was usually conducted, could not be adequately supported by documents in the German collections. Moreover, Holstein's correspondence reveals his lucidity and profound good judgment, and these facts explain why he was able to hold his position at the Ministry of Foreign Affairs for so long despite the changes in ministers and policies.

As Ambassador to St. Petersburg from 1875 to 1891, the post that Bismarck considered to be the most important for his policy, General von Schweinitz contributed significant testimony in his diary and correspondence.[193] The Eastern crisis from 1875 to the Congress of Berlin and the pattern of Russo-German relations from the Three Emperors League to the failure to renew the Reinsurance treaty are commented upon in detail in von Schweinitz's annotations and correspondence. These become an indispensable source because the German diplomatic documents published for this period are not very numerous. Nor is the author's contribution limited to these issues. His observations throw new light on the motives

[193] *Denkwürdigkeiten des Botschafters General von Schweinitz* (2 vols.; Berlin: Hobbing, 1927); *Briefwechsel des Botschafters General von Schweinitz* (3 vols.; Berlin: Hobbing, 1927–28).

prompting Bismarck to sign the Austro-German Alliance and, in addition, he furnishes a detailed summary on the meeting at Cowes during which Salisbury revealed to William II his plan for the partition of the Ottoman Empire.

Ludwig Raschdau's memoirs[194] offer useful data on the last years of the Bismarckian period and on the new course taken by Caprivi in foreign policy. Raschdau was one of the group in the Foreign Ministry who opposed the renewal of the Reinsurance treaty, on the grounds that the treaty had not succeeded in establishing a real friendship with Russia and did not prevent a Franco-Russian *rapprochement,* while there was the danger that Russia would reveal the existence of the treaty, thus provoking a serious crisis in Austro-German relations. In 1894, Raschdau moved from the Ministry to the post of Minister to Weimar. His recollections of this period and of his mission to Turkey are condensed in two estimable volumes of memoirs.[195]

During the height of the debate on the origins of World War I, Baron Eckardstein, First Secretary in the German Embassy in London and Chargé d'Affaires from 1899 to 1902 during Ambassador Hatzfeldt's illness, published his memoirs of those years.[196] The publication created a sensation because the author produced numerous documents that seemed to prove that the failure of the Anglo-German negotiations between 1898 and 1901 was entirely due to the incapacity of the German Ministry of Foreign Affairs and to Holstein's nefarious machinations. In refusing the British offer of alliance in 1901, Eckardstein concludes, Germany chose the road that was to lead to war and to the end of the German Empire. However, the publication of the German and British documents have proved Eckardstein's assertions to be completely inaccurate and show that Eckardstein was prone to modify the texts of dispatches and to create the wrong impression in reporting the results of his conversations with members of the British government held in the spring of 1901. His version was a substantial modification of events, in the sense that the British never actually proposed an Anglo-German alliance, as he affirms. From the German point of view, in addition to a fundamental reluctance to support British efforts in

[194] *Unter Bismarck und Caprivi. Erinnerungen eines deutschen Diplomaten aus den Jahren 1885–1894* (Berlin: Mittler, 1939).

[195] *Ein sinkendes Reich, Erlebnisse einer deutschen Diplomaten in Orient 1877–1878* (Berlin: Mittler, 1933); *In Weimar als preussischer Gesandter. Ein Buch der Erinnerung an deutsche Fürstenhöfe, 1894–97* (Berlin: Mittler, 1939).

[196] Hermann von Eckardstein, *Lebenserinnerungen und politische Denkwürdigkeiten* (3 vols.; Leipzig: List, 1919–21). Later, the author published another volume, *Persönaliche Erinnerungen an König Eduard* (Dresden: Reissner, 1927), adding some details to his account of Anglo-German relations, including some anecdotal material and some pages of interest on the Agadir crisis.

blocking Russian expansion in the Far East, all of the negotiations were conducted without exact knowledge of London's attitude, and this situation was the direct result of the misleading information provided by Eckardstein. However, the author's volumes are not cited here for their negative aspects alone. The important effect that these volumes had on more than a decade of German historiography is sufficient reason in itself for including Eckardstein's writings. Moreover, they offer a concrete example of the dominant role played by men, under specific circumstances, in the course of international relations.

Italo-German relations are the central theme of the memoirs of Baron Monts,[197] German Ambassador to Rome from 1903 to 1909, written primarily to indicate and to criticize the errors in Von Bülow's policy. Monts's disagreement with Von Bülow over what Italy's position should be in the Triple Alliance runs like a thread through his summary of the years spent in Rome.[198] Shortly after Monts's arrival in Rome, and despite the fact that he was not aware of the exact content of the recently signed Franco-Italian accords, he realized that Italian policy had taken a new turn and that it was necessary to obtain a complete clarification of this change in order to draw the proper conclusions. While the Chancellor recognized the correctness of Monts's observations, he chose not to follow his advice. The Italian position during the first Moroccan crisis and at the Algeciras Conference (Monts reveals important details on the pressure applied to the head of the Italian delegation, Visconti Venosta, by the German Chancellor) confirmed for Monts the shift in Italian foreign policy to a pro-British position—it will be found, Monts writes, where the Union Jack flies—and provided new motives for criticizing Von Bülow's policy. Monts, recognizing that the Central Powers could no longer count on the support of Italy in a crisis, believed that it was absolutely necessary for Germany to seek an understanding with Great Britain if it wished to maintain its present position. Monts left the Foreign Service early in 1909, but during Kaiser William II's visit to Venice in April, 1909, he took advantage of the occasion to present this idea to the Emperor. In reply, the Kaiser offered him the chancellorship, but considerations of internal policy forced the Kaiser to retract this offer in favor of Bethmann-Hollweg. The volume also includes a selection of the author's correspondence with key German foreign policy figures.

The two volumes of recollections assembled by Friedrich Rosen on his

[197] K. F. Nowak and F. Thimme (eds.), *Erinnerungen und Gedanken des botschafters Anton Graf Monts* (Berlin: Verlag für Kulturpolitik, 1932).

[198] On this issue, see Friedrich Thimme, "Fürst Bülow und Graf Monts. Ein vervollständigter Briefwechsel," *Preussische Jahrbücher*, March–June, 1933.

career[199] are of considerable value. The first volume is useful for the study of the Moroccan crisis of 1905 in that the author presents a summary of the negotiations he conducted in Paris from September 5 to 28, 1905, aimed at resolving the differences that had arisen between France and Germany over the Kaiser's visit to Tangier the preceding March. The mission did not achieve the results expected by Rosen and clearly reflected substantial difficulties that could not be overcome, even if these pages also reveal Rosen's preoccupation with the fact that he carried out his task with scrupulous exactness. He adds that Delcassé's fall had little effect on the rigid position taken by the Quai d'Orsay and that the Great Powers, with the exception of Austria, were aligned in a block against Germany. The second volume offers a significant exposition of the relations between Rumania and the Central Powers from 1910 to 1912, the years of Rosen's ministry to Bucharest. Rosen repeatedly warned his government that King Carol was entertaining a number of doubts about Rumania's position on the side of the Central Powers, which were the result of the increasing friction with Austria-Hungary over Vienna's sympathy for Bulgaria, its open hostility to the Serbs, and the mistreatment of the Rumanian minority in Hungary. Carol demanded that Germany guarantee that she would not surrender leadership in the Triple Alliance to Vienna because in that event the Alliance could no longer count on Rumanian support. At the same time Carol asked for German support in resolving his country's differences with Austria-Hungary. These requests were given little consideration by Kiderlen-Wächter, the stage was set for the alienation of Rumania from the Triple Alliance, and Rosen was transferred to Lisbon. The author provides ample and important detail on this mission, which came at the time that London and Berlin were discussing the question of the Portuguese colonies as a basis for an Anglo-German accord.

Lancken-Wakenitz, Counsellor in the German Embassy in Paris from 1907 to 1913 and chief of the political section of the German governorship in Belgium during the war, compiled a volume of his recollections,[200] but they do not provide a continuous record of his memoirs. Instead, he dwells on the numerous problems of major importance he was called upon to handle. In the first part of the volume there are characteristic pages on the reaction of Izvolski to the news of the Bosnian crisis (Izvolski told Lancken-Wakenitz that Russia was prepared to guarantee Germany against a French attack), the negotiations for a Franco-German accord on Morocco

[199] Aus einen diplomatischen Wanderleben (2 vols.; Berlin: Transmare-Verlag, 1931–32).

[200] Oscar von Lancken-Wakenitz, *Meine dreissig Dienstjahre 1888–1918, Potsdam, Paris, Brüssel* (Berlin: Verlag für Kulturpolitik, 1931).

in 1906 and the approval of this accord by Von Bülow, and, finally, the author's contacts with Caillaux after the Agadir coup. On this point, one of the two main issues treated in the volume, Lancken-Wakenitz is precise in his statements; he notes that he was recalled by Kiderlen-Wächter in order to present his views on the repercussions in France of Lloyd George's Mansion House speech of July 21, 1911. During these conversations, Lancken-Wakenitz states, he offered to enter into secret talks with Caillaux in order to resolve the crisis directly with the French Premier, and Kiderlen-Wächter accepted the proposal. Lancken-Wakenitz says that, in effect, the initiative for these talks came from Germany, as Caillaux often stated with little success. The second important question discussed in this volume is the Briand peace proposal. Lancken-Wakenitz states that he was informed in the spring of 1917 that several Allied circles desired a meeting between a French public figure and himself. Briand was agreed upon, and Lancken-Wakenitz was authorized by Bethmann-Hollweg, Hindenburg, and Ludendorff to show good faith in offering to cede part of Alsace-Lorraine to France. The meeting with Briand was set for the end of June, and at the last moment it was postponed until September 22, but Briand did not appear in Switzerland. Shortly afterwards the Ribot government fell, and the appearance of the Clemenceau government definitely closed the door to a negotiated peace.

Nothing very important appears in the little volume of memoirs by Prince Lichnowsky,[201] Ambassador to London from 1912 to 1914. In the summer of 1916 the author composed a brief memoir on his mission to London; the principal questions treated are Grey's mediation efforts during the Balkan wars and the conversations on the questions of the Baghdad railway and the Portuguese colonies. According to Lichnowsky, these negotiations would have led toward more cordial Anglo-German relations (a positive result which Lichnowsky ascribes largely to his own efforts), had the Berlin government not blocked the process by its ill-advised policy. The last error committed was the invasion of Belgium, Lichnowsky concludes, since it would have been possible to obtain almost anything from the London government through Grey, given the basic pacifist nature of his policy. The only impossibility was the preventing of British intervention after the violation of Belgian neutrality. This manuscript was published in a neutral country in 1917 without the author's permission (although contrary views on this point do exist) and unleashed violent debates in Germany, while the Entente powers used it effectively in their war propaganda. A number of years later Lichnowsky republished this me-

[201] Karl Max von Lichnowsky, *Meine Londoner Mission, 1912–1914* (Zurich: Füssli, 1918).

morial in a volume also containing discussions of other controversial topics and a selection of his dispatches.[202] The latter are all taken from *Die Grosse Politik*. Other important documents in the author's possession were turned over to one of the editors of the Kautsky documents, and they mysteriously disappeared from the latter's home.

The diary of the Ambassador to St. Petersburg, Count Pourtalès,[203] while not a source of particular importance, does vividly describe the last days of peace (July 24–August 1, 1914) in the Russian capital. Pourtalès was convinced from the beginning of the crisis that the greatest danger to peace lay in the military measures taken by the powers while the diplomatic talks under way indicated that a peaceful solution might be achieved. Germany had on several occasions warned St. Petersburg on this point, but notwithstanding these warnings, he writes, the Russians mobilized. From the author's talks with Sazonov, he gained the impression that during the last phase of the crisis the Ministry of Foreign Affairs had lost all control over the situation.

Count von Bernstorff, Counsellor in the London Embassy from 1902 to 1906, Ambassador to Washington from 1908 to 1917, and to Constantinople from 1917 to 1918, published his memoirs in two volumes, with fifteen years elapsing between the publication of the first and the second volume.[204] The most important observations are found in the first volume, wherein the author discusses his mission to Washington during the early years of the war and adds significant documents, especially on the American mediation efforts during the winter of 1916–17. Bernstorff expresses the opinion—which is supported by the dispatches he publishes—that Wilson was disposed to assure an acceptable peace to both sides. This was, as is known, also the opinion of Bethmann-Hollweg, who also shared Bernstorff's view that the renewal of unrestricted submarine warfare would make American intervention inevitable and assure victory to the Entente. Returning to Germany in the spring of 1917, Bernstorff was mentioned as Bethmann-Hollweg's successor, but this suggestion did not develop and he was sent to Constantinople as Ambassador. The second volume devotes little space to

[202] *Auf dem Wege zum Abgrund. Londoner Berichte. Erinnerungen und sostige Schriften* (2 vols.; Dresden: Reissner, 1927).
[203] Friedrich von Pourtalès, *Am Scheidewege zwischen Krieg und Frieden* (Charlottenburg: Deutsche Verlagsgesellschaft für Politik und Geschichte, 1919). In a second edition, entitled *Meine Verhandlugen in St. Petersburg Ende Juli 1914. Tagesaufzeichnungen und Dokumente* (Berlin: Deutsche Verlagsgesellschaft für Politik und Geschichte, 1927), he added his official correspondence copied from the German general collection.
[204] Johann Heinrich von Bernstorff, *Deutschland und Amerika, Erinnerungen aus dem fünfjähringen Kriege* (Berlin: Ullstein, 1920); *Erinnerungen und Briefe* (Zurich: Polygraphischer Verlag, 1936).

this last mission and focuses on Bernstorff's contacts with Germany's last Imperial Chancellor, Prince Max of Baden, and on the author's activities at the Foreign Ministry during the preparatory period for the Paris peace conference.

The influence exerted by the German General Staff on the conduct of foreign policy[205] was such as to give an extraordinary value to the memoirs of the military for students of international relations. The works of Waldersee,[206] Chief of the General Staff from 1886 to 1891, are worth noting in connection with the plans for a preventive war against Russia advocated by the military to crush the nascent *rapprochement* between Paris and St. Petersburg. They also contain important correspondence with the military attachés abroad—with those in Rome and Vienna in particular —which is useful in clarifying several aspects of the relations between the powers of the Triplice.

Moltke's memoirs,[207] published posthumously, are of minor interest even though they contain information of some importance on the crisis of 1914. Ludendorff's writings,[208] on the other hand, are extremely significant because of the vigor with which he entered the postwar debate in Germany on the problem of responsibility for the defeat. His thesis is not new and, in effect, is advanced in the memoirs of nearly all of the German military, from Colonel Bauer[209]—who sustains the thesis with the greatest vigor—to General von Wrisberg,[210] from General von Bernhardi[211] to Von Einem:[212] the German army was defeated without being conquered, and the cause for

[205] Among the many studies on the problem, see the most recent, Gerhard Ritter, *Staatskunst und Kriegshandwerk. Das Problem des "Militarismus," in Deutschland,* Vol. I: *Die altpreussische Tradition (1740–1890);* Vol. II: *Die Hauptmächte Europas und das wilhelmnische Reich (1890–1914)* (Munich: Oldenburg, 1954–60).

[206] Alfred von Waldersee, *Denkwürdigkeiten* (3 vols.; Stuttgart: Deutsche Verlagsanstalt, 1922–23); Otto Meisner (ed.), *Aus dem Briefwechsel dem General-feldmarschalls Alfred von Waldersee* (2 vols.; Stuttgart: Deutsche Verlagsanstalt, 1928).

[207] Helmuth von Moltke, *Erinnerungen. Briefe, Dokumente 1877–1916* (Stuttgart: Der kommende Tag, 1922).

[208] Erich Ludendorff, *Meine Kriegserinnerungen 1914–1918* (Berlin: Mittler, 1919); *Urkunden der obersten Heersleitung über ihre Tätigkeit 1916–1918* (Berlin: Mittler, 1919); *Französische Fälschung meiner Denkschrift von 1912 über den drohenden Krieg. Ein Beitrag zur "Schuld" am Kriege* (Berlin: Mittler, 1919); *Kriegführung und Politik* (2d ed.; Berlin: Mittler, 1922).

[209] Max Bauer, *Der grosse Krieg in Feld und Heimat. Erinnerungen und Betrachtungen* (Tübingen: Mohr, 1925).

[210] Ernst von Wrisberg, *Erinnerungen an die Kriegsjahre* (3 vols.; Leipzig: Koehler, 1921–22).

[211] Friedrich von Bernhardi, *Denkwürdigkeiten aus meinem Leben* (Berlin: Mittler, 1927).

[212] Karl von Einem, *Erinnerungen eines Soldaten 1853–1933* (Leipzig: Koehler, 1933).

the defeat is to be found in the political arena because German politicians, constantly interfering in military affairs, made defeat inevitable with their indecisions and their blunders. The failure to use the fleet offensively, the delay in reinstituting unrestricted submarine warfare, the peace proposal of 1916, but above all, the inability to maintain a united home front, according to Ludendorff, were the most serious errors committed by the civil government, which, in its attempt to reach a compromise peace, promoted the collapse of German morale at the moment that victory was within the German grasp. Ludendorff's testimony is of greater importance as a source for a reconstruction of the position taken by the General Staff on the major political issues that came to the surface during the last phase of the conflict, when Ludendorff and Hindenburg had a decisive influence on government decisions in the matter of negotiations for a compromise peace and, later, on the request for an armistice.

Hindenburg refers to the weakness of the home front as the German Achilles heel, but his memoirs[213] dwell particularly on Germany's relations with her allies, especially Austria-Hungary, whose rulers he accuses of contributing to the defeatist spirit by their lack of faith in the ability of the Central Powers to resist. Hindenburg also criticizes the Austrian plan for an independent Poland and Burian's repeated insistence on the need to seek a negotiated peace, affirming that the Austrian government had no conception of the country's real strength and that when the Austrian government advocated peace negotiations, toward the end of 1916, it was the only faction in Austria to desire them. Vienna's attitude lacked political understanding, as well as courage, and served only to strengthen the adversary's morale and to infect the Central Powers with the defeatist spirit, Hindenburg concluded.

Von Falkenhayn was Chief of the General Staff from 1914 to 1916, and his memoirs[214] contain only a few references of political interest and—on the basis of the recently published documents[215]—do not always reflect their author's real attitude. The writings of General Hoffmann[216] are a richer source. Among other roles, Hoffmann represented the General Staff at the

---

[213] Paul Hindenburg, *Aus meinem Leben* (Leipzig: Hirzel, 1920).

[214] Erich von Falkenhayn, *Die oberste Heeresleitung in ihren wichtigsten Entschliessungen 1914–1916* (Berlin: Mittler, 1920); *Der Feldzug der IX Armee gegen die Rumänen und Russen 1916–1917* (2 vols.; Berlin: Mittler, 1920–21). See also Adriano Alberti, *Il generale Falkenhayn. Le relazioni tra i Capi di Stato Maggiore della Triplice* (Rome: Libreria dello Stato, 1924).

[215] On Falkenhayn's position with reference to war aims, see the now published French documents referred to on pp. 138–39 of this volume.

[216] Karl Friedrich Nowak (ed.), *Die Aufzeichnungen des Generalmajors Max Hoffman* (2 vols.; Berlin: Verlag für Kultur-Politik, 1930). These volumes contain the previously published writings of the author.

Brest Litovsk negotiations. His diary reveals a number of interesting details of the discussions among the German leaders on the Belgian problem. Along with Hoffmann's diary, Prince Rupprecht of Bavaria's record[217] should be mentioned. In substance, he takes the opposite point of view of most of the military and accuses the latter of interfering with the civil government at a time when a favorable military solution to the conflict appeared to be no longer possible. Among the many passages of interest to the historian, there is his summary of his conversation with Czernin in August, 1917, in which the Austrian Minister of Foreign Affairs expressed his ideas on a method for arriving at a compromise peace—Czernin proposed to approach France as the most severely tried adversary—and the conditions to be offered to reach this goal.

A memoir and documentary contribution that in some respects has no substitute is offered by Admiral von Tirpitz,[218] whose importance goes far beyond the limits of the military sphere. His influence on German foreign policy and public opinion was far greater than that of the ordinary Chief of Naval Operations; his policy of strengthening the German fleet had a pronounced effect on international relations in the period prior to World War I.[219]

In denying the accusation that he had forged an instrument of war that had inevitably to lead to a conflict with Great Britain, Tirpitz observed that the construction of a high seas fleet had no aggressive purpose but was born of the desire to guarantee the German people the strength necessary to win respect for their interests from every power including Great Britain. Moreover, he said, a strong German navy was the best guarantee of peace because it created the equilibrium on the seas that already existed on the Continent between the armies of the various nations. At the same time, it was the only way to impress the British with the needs of Germany, an impression which was reflected in the increasingly conciliatory attitude of

[217] Rupprecht von Bayern, *Mein Kriegstagebuch* (3 vols.; Berlin: Mittler, 1929).

[218] Alfred von Tirpitz, *Erinnerungen* (Leipzig: Koehler, 1919); *Politische Dokumente*, Vol. I: *Der Aufbau der deutschen Weltmacht* (Berlin: Cotta, 1924); Vol. II: *Deutsche Ohnmachtspolitik im Weltkriege* (Hamburg: Hanseatische Verlagsanstalt, 1926). On Tirpitz see also the biography by Ulrich von Hassell, *Tirpitz. Seine Leben und Wirken mit Berücksichtigung seiner Beziehungen zu Albrecht von Stosch* (Stuttgart: Belsersche Verlagsbuchhandlung, 1920); and by Adolf von Trotha, *Grossadmiral von Tirpitz. Flottenbau und Reichsgedanke* (Breslau: Korn, 1933).

[219] On the Anglo-German naval rivalry, see E. L. Woodward, *England and the German Navy* (Oxford: Oxford University Press, 1935), in which the author draws from materials in the archives of the British Admiralty; Rudolf Stadelmann, "Die Epoche der deutsche-englischen Flottenrivalität," in *Deutschland und Westeuropa Schloss Laupheim* (Steiner, 1948); Walther Hubatsch, *Die Aera Tirpitz. Studien zur deutschen Marinepolitik, 1890–1918* (Goettingen: Musterschmidt, 1955).

London between 1912 and 1914. Furthermore, the conclusion should not be drawn, continues Tirpitz, that in 1914 the navy wanted war: it was to the navy's interest to complete its rearmament program before becoming involved in a conflict.

These are statements which permit a better evaluation of the mentality of the German Admiral and of the goals he sought, but they must be critically examined and placed in their proper historical perspective. It is possible that Tirpitz did not consider a war with Great Britain among his aims—the evidence available is conflicting, particularly if the question is considered from a long-range point of view—but it is indisputable that the increase in the size of the German navy constituted a major stumbling block to an Anglo-German *rapprochement,* repeatedly sought even after the failure of the negotiations of 1898 and 1901. Moreover, by his fleet policy Tirpitz aroused public opinion in both countries to the point where an understanding between the two countries was made extremely problematical. In Germany the press, controlled by the Admiral and the Navy League, carried on a decidedly Anglophobe campaign that had a strong effect on both Parliament and public opinion. In Great Britain the fears aroused by the growing German naval strength—reflected, too, in the growing commercial rivalry between the two countries—reached their highest point in 1908, when Tirpitz announced the *Reichstag*'s approval for starting the construction of two naval vessels one year ahead of schedule. In his memoirs, Tirpitz states that he acted in this case for purely administrative reasons, prompted by a desire to increase shipyard operations, but the reaction to the news in Great Britain was clamorous. The British Admiralty realized that it was no longer a question of the naval construction programs approved by the *Reichstag* but rather of German shipbuilding potential, and the British public, faced with the prospect of an accelerated naval race, looked upon Germany as the real enemy.

The fact is that the German naval program, as established in 1900 and enlarged repeatedly thereafter, was simultaneously the cause and the effect of Germany's *Weltpolitik.* For a variety of reasons the policy of extra-European expansion launched after the fall of Bismarck required acceleration and consolidation, with the result not only a threat to British security and economic warfare on a world-wide scale, but also an almost inevitable Anglo-German conflict, even if this was beyond Tirpitz's intentions. Logically, the changed situation required a change in German foreign policy, and Tirpitz is violently critical of the German leaders—especially von Bülow and Bethmann-Hollweg—for their inability to effect the changes demanded by the new situation. It was necessary, he observes, to abandon the traditional Wilhelmstrasse approaches in order to avoid facing

Russia and Great Britain as enemies simultaneously. Since the latter was the real obstacle to German expansion in the world, it was imperative to effect a *rapprochement* with St. Petersburg, to relegate the alliance with Austria to a secondary position or at least to avoid making it the pivotal point in German foreign policy, and to abandon the policy of expansion in the Near East, which was largely a question of prestige. These views were repeatedly presented to the German leaders, but they did not understand their significance, and this incapacity, concludes the Admiral, was the principal reason for Germany's defeat.

Tirpitz's writings must be considered a primary source for an understanding of the new course of German policy under William II. They add a number of new elements regarding relations with Great Britain and clarify many aspects of the internal struggle in the German government in the years preceding World War I. The second volume of the *Politische Dokumente* focuses on the military events of the war, and a great deal of space is devoted to the question of all-out war against Allied commerce on the high seas, which Tirpitz, despite the repercussions this would have had in the United States and in the other neutral countries, wanted to undertake as early as the spring of 1915.

6. THE AUSTRIAN MEMORIALISTS.

In contrast to the variety of information that we have about William II, there is little direct testimony on Francis Joseph, and it is difficult to determine the nature of the role played by the Hapsburg Emperor in foreign affairs and particularly in the formation of Austrian policy. However, on the basis of the data available,[220] the hypothesis that Francis Joseph was almost exclusively a figurehead is not completely convincing.

[220] See Otto Ernst, *Franz Joseph I in Seinen Briefen* (Vienna: Rikola, 1924), which ignores the political aspect almost entirely; Albert Margutti, *Kaiser Franz Joseph. Persönliche Erinnerungen* (Vienna: Manz, 1924). The author, ex-aide-de-camp to the Emperor, tends to emphasize the peaceful nature of Franz Joseph's policies and affirms that, even during the crisis of 1914, the Emperor opposed war as a solution to the problem. The work of Joseph Redlich, *Kaiser Franz Joseph von Österreich. Eine Biographie* (Berlin: Verlag für Kulturpolitik, 1928), is more of a study of the political system of the Dual Monarchy than it is a biography. Eduard Ritter von Steinitz, *Erinnerungen an Franz Joseph I, Kaiser von Österreich, apostolischer König von Ungarn* (Berlin: Verlag für Kulturpolitik, 1931), contains a number of interesting depositions. Karl Tschuppik, *Franz Joseph I. Der Untergang eines Reiches* (Hellerau bei Dresden: Avalunverlag, 1928), is an outstanding work on the reign of Franz Joseph. The biography by Eugene Szekeres Bagger, *Francis Joseph, Emperor of Austria and King of Hungary* (New York: Putnam, 1927), reflects the Hungarian point of view and is somewhat superficial.

Undoubtedly, the Hapsburg ruler, especially during the last phase of his reign, clearly understood the need for a conservative policy and considered war necessary only in defense of the Empire. At the time of the assassination at Sarajevo, Francis Joseph believed that the Empire was threatened by the Serbian menace—according to the majority of witnesses—and he did nothing to moderate the intransigence of the Ballplatz.

The controversial personality of Archduke Francis Ferdinand can be studied through a number of important eyewitness accounts, even though they are generally apologetic.[221] They conclude that the Archduke was not an extreme nationalist and hardly the head of a "war party," which in fact did not exist or, as best, consisted of a single individual, General Conrad.[222]

Moreover, Francis Ferdinand championed basic reforms in the internal structure of the Empire, and in foreign policy he advocated a *rapprochement* with Russia as a prelude to the re-creation of the Three Emperors League. These sources also confirm the Archduke's antipathy toward Italy. He was not in favor of a preventive war but at the same time disapproved of the weakness displayed by Aehrenthal and Francis Joseph toward a country whose comportment indicated that she would not be a faithful ally. Therefore, he urged that, once the *rapprochement* with Russia was effected, Italy be allowed to go her own way.

Polzer-Hoditz's volume on Emperor Charles[223] is much more than a personal memoir of the last Hapsburg ruler. Polzer-Hoditz had been political adviser to the Prince before he assumed the throne and in 1915 had become his Chief of Cabinet, which placed him in an excellent position to write authoritatively on many aspects of Austro-Hungarian policy. Though he dwells at length on internal affairs, there is much that is useful in his memoirs on Austro-German relations and on the Prince Sixtus affair. In substance, these are also the principal subjects treated in Baron Werkmann's volume,[224] the Baron having been Emperor Charles's secretary. Along with Polzer-Hoditz, he writes that Emperor Charles clearly

[221] See Paul Nikitsch-Boulles, *Vor dem Sturm. Erinnerungen an Erzherzog-Thronfolger Franz Ferdinand* (Berlin: Verlag für Kulturpolitik, 1925) (the author was the Archduke's private secretary); Theodor von Sosnoski, *Franz Ferdinand der Erzherzog-Thronfolger* (Munich: Oldenburg, 1929); Leopold von Chlumecky, *Erzherzog Franz Ferdinands Wirken und Wollen* (Berlin: Verlag für Kulturpolitik, 1929). Important testimony is presented by Von Chlumecky, who was a member of the Archduke's inner circle.

[222] On General Conrad, see Oskar Regele, *Feldmarschall Conrad. Auftrag und Erfüllung 1906–1918* (Vienna: Verlag Herold, 1955).

[223] Arthur von Polzer-Hoditz und Wolframitz, *Kaiser Karl. Aus der Geheimmappe seines Kabinettschefs* (Vienna: Amalthea, 1928).

[224] Karl Martin Werkmann von Hohensalzburg, *Deutschland als Verbundeter: Kaiser Karl Kampf um den Frieden* (Berlin: Verlag für Kulturpolitik, 1931).

perceived that the war could not be won and that it was therefore necessary to seek a compromise peace at any cost. Of particular interest is his assertion that the Hapsburg ruler believed this to be the best solution because a total German victory would have probably reduced the Austro-Hungarian Empire to a position similar to that of Bavaria, and this factor explains, in part, the basic lines of Charles's position at the peace negotiations of 1917.[225]

Significant testimony on Austro-Russian relations may be found in the volume edited by Eduard von Steinitz.[226] The observations made by Berchtold, his Head of Cabinet, Count Hoyos, and by the former ambassadors to Rome and St. Petersburg, Macchio and Szapary, all tend to demonstrate that Austro-Hungarian policy in the Balkans was defensive in nature, in contrast to Russian policy, which was definitely expansionist. According to Hoyos, after the annexation of Boznia-Herzegovina, Austria was no longer interested in acquiring further territory in the Balkans, least of all in annexing Serbia. If Vienna-Belgrade relations degenerated into war, this was due to Russia's intrigues, which forced Austria to act in self-defense. These accounts are significant for their interpretation of the facts, through which it becomes possible to understand the psychology of the Austrian leaders in the crisis, rather than for the disclosures they contain, which are much less important. However, Berchtold's comments are worth noting, especially as they concern the Buchlau conversations between Aerhenthal and Izvolski and the assertions of these two statesmen at the time of the meeting.

The publication of Berchtold's memoirs, repeatedly announced as imminent, has not taken place, but subsequent statements by the former Minister of Foreign Affairs contain some interesting ingredients.[227] In these, Berchtold affirms that the attitude of the Austro-Hungarian government at the time of the crisis of Sarajevo was strongly influenced by the prediction of the military that a modern war could only last a few months, a factor that seemed to reduce the dangers it might pose for the Empire. Concerning the negotiations with Italy in 1914–15, he adds that he was in favor of making concessions to Italy in order to prevent Italian intervention on the side of the Entente, for he considered this to be fatal from the military point of view and for the resultant political consequences of such a decision. However, his plans encountered the strong opposition of Tisza,

[225] In addition, on Emperor Karl, see Reinold Lorenz, *Kaiser Karl und der Untergang der Donaumonarchie* (Graz: Verlag Styria, 1959).

[226] *Rings um Sasonow. Neue dokumentarische Darstellungen zum Ausbruch des grossen Krieges durch Kronzeugen* (Berlin: Verlag für Kulturpolitik, 1928).

[227] Leopold Berchtold, "Habe ich den Weltkrieg gewollt," *Berliner Monatschefte,* June, 1929.

who rejected any compromise whatsoever, and the resistance of Burian and Merey, the latter recently appointed to the Embassy in Rome.

The memoirs of Count Burian,[228] successor to Berchtold, are especially important for the data they contain on Austro-German discussions on the subject of a compromise peace. The author had prepared such a plan as early as July, 1916, but the attempt to realize it was thwarted by Rumania's entrance in the war, and it was later blocked by the German refusal to publish the Central Powers' terms for a compromise peace. In December, 1916, Burian resigned in protest against the German decision to renew unrestricted submarine warfare, a policy he had always opposed.

Czernin replaced Burian at the Ballplatz at the close of 1916, and his memoirs[229] are a requisite to the study of Austrian foreign policy during the war, particularly for the peace attempts of 1917 and the peace negotiations at Brest Litovsk and Bucharest. Concerning the proposals for a compromise peace in 1917, the revelations of the former Austrian Minister of Foreign Affairs, along with the volume by Prince Sixtus of Bourbon,[230] Demblin's study,[231] and the memoirs of Erdödy[232] (which actually add very little), make it possible to reconstruct this affair, on which the historian's attention has been repeatedly focused because of its important political implications.[233] Not all of the aspects of these negotiations are entirely clear. While it is obvious that both the Emperor Charles and his Minister of Foreign Affairs understood the need to end the war insofar as Austria was concerned, it appears that the Emperor was not averse to a separate peace. On the other hand, Czernin believed that a negotiated peace was not possible without the inclusion of Germany. Because of this difference in method, if not in objective, two separate attempts for negotiation were initiated, the first by Prince Sixtus in London and Paris and the second by Czernin in Berlin. Although these two attempts at the bargaining table

---

[228] Stephan Burian von Rajecz, *Drei Jahre. Aus der Zeit meiner Amtsführung in Kriege* (Berlin: Ullstein, 1923).

[229] Ottokar Czernin, *Im Weltkriege* (Berlin: Ullstein, 1919).

[230] Prince Sixte de Bourbon, *L'offre de paix séparée de l'Autriche* (Paris: Plon, 1920).

[231] August Demblin, *Czernin und die Sixtus-Affäre* (Munich: Drei Masken, 1920).

[232] Pamas von Erdödy, *Memoiren* (Vienna: Amalthea, 1931).

[233] On this question, see Richard Fester, *Die Politik Kaiser Karls und der Wendepunkt des Weltkrieges* (Munich: Lehmann, 1925); "Die Friedenswermittlungsversuche 1917," *Berliner Monatshefte*, May, 1937; "Die Friedensoffensive Czernins," *ibid.*, July, 1937; "Die Sonder Friedensaktion des Prinzen Sixtus," *ibid.*, August, 1937; Charles Appuhn, "Le gouvernement allemand et la paix en 1917," *Revue d'histoire de la guerre mondiale*, April, 1923, and January, 1924; Les Négociations austro-allemandes de 1917 et la mission du prince Sixte," *ibid.*, July, 1935.

were separate and distinct, they must be studied together in order to understand the real position of the Central Powers on the question of a compromise peace.

The volume on Heinrich Lammasch, the last Chancellor of the Empire, edited by his daughter and his colleague, Hans Sperl,[234] primarily concerns the internal problems of the Dual Monarchy and, specifically, the reforms of a federative character. When Lammasch was entrusted by Emperor Charles in 1917 with the task of projecting these reforms, the plan had a direct bearing on the problem of a compromise peace. In fact, in February, 1918, Lammasch journeyed to Switzerland to discuss the question with President Wilson's unofficial representative, hopeful that by granting a large degree of autonomy to the peoples of the Empire, negotiations with the American President would be facilitated. However, Emperor Charles's hesitancy, the warnings from Berlin, and the strong pressure from certain circles within the Empire forced the abandonment of the proposal. When Lammasch became Chancellor in October, 1918, it was too late to reactivate the plan with any hope of success. The last pages of the work are noteworthy for their references to Lammasch's activities as a member of the Austrian delegation at St. Germain and to the discussions on the Tyrol frontier.

Constantine Dumba, Austrian Ambassador to Washington, gained wide notoriety during the war when he was arraigned and expelled from the United States for having a hand in sabotaging American war industries. The most interesting part of his memoirs[235] concern the years 1903–5, when he was Minister to Belgrade and from that post was able to follow closely the Serbian reaction to the Russian defeat in the Russo-Japanese War. Dumba records that Pasic offered to create an Austrophile party in Serbia if Vienna would guarantee to support Serbian claims to Macedonia, but Goluchowski preferred to ignore the proposal, which, had it been accepted, would have precipitated a crisis in Austro-Russian relations. This decision, continues Dumba, was a very serious error, but he adds that Pasic was completely untrustworthy and that his policy had only one aim—the realization of the Pan-Serb ideal even at the risk of a general war.

An interesting episode in Italo-Austrian relations in 1896 is also reported in Dumba's memoirs. During the period when negotiations between Rome and Paris were developing rapidly toward an agreement on Tunisia, Dumba, who was at the time an attaché in the Embassy at Paris, notes that

[234] Marga Lammasch and Hans Sperl (eds.), *Heinrich Lammasch: seine Aufzeichnungen, sein Wirken und seine Politik* (Vienna: Deuticke, 1922).

[235] Konstantin Dumba, *Dreibund-und Entente-Politik in der Alten und Neuen Welt* (Vienna: Amalthea, 1931).

the Austrian government, unknown to its ally, agreed to the French request on the matter of the capitulations in the Tunisian protectorate, thus prejudicing the Italian position at a particularly delicate moment in the negotiations. While the episode helps to explain the subsequent position of the *Consulta* in the negotiations with France, it also serves to explain why, in the face of the small consideration given by Austria to Italian interests in the Mediterranean, Rome was impelled to seek an understanding with Paris.

The central theme of Musulin's volume[236] is the Austro-Serbian crisis of July, 1914, which the author, whom the Ballplatz regarded as one of its more reliable experts on Balkan affairs, was able to observe in all of its phases. Musulin was responsible for writing the ultimatum delivered to Belgrade. He also insists that the ultimatum did not contain any completely unacceptable conditions and states that he received no instructions from Berchtold for such conditions. However, these assertions are incorrect. The Austrian demands could have been accepted only by a government that, finding itself with no other recourse, chose to capitulate. As to the second point, it is now known that the original text prepared by Musulin was modified by him on instructions from Berchtold, that to Point Six was added the demand that Austrian police authorities be allowed to participate in the search for the guilty parties in Serbian territory, and that this modification was made with the intent of ensuring Belgrade's rejection of the ultimatum.

A much wider area is covered by Count Hoyos' volume.[237] Hoyos, as Berchtold's Chief of Cabinet, played a key role in formulating Austrian policy during the crisis preceding the war. However, in his account he dwells on the long-range causes of the conflict rather than on the immediate ones. Hoyos asserts that the failure of Austria's Balkan policy and the subsequent Austrian collapse were due to the error of failing to cultivate British friendship in order to follow Germany's lead. British support gave renewed strength to the Russians in the Balkans, and, despite the good rapport existing between Vienna and Paris and Vienna and London, the two western members of the Entente supported the Russian maneuvers because in weakening the Hapsburg Empire they indirectly weakened Germany. Britain's alignment with the Franco-Russian Duplice, Hoyos continues, had the effect of rendering Italy's abandonment of the Triple Alliance inevitable because the Italian government had never made any

---

[236] Alexander Musulin, *Das Haus am Ballplatz. Erinnerungen eines österreichisch-ungarischen Diplomaten* (Munich: Verlag für Politik, 1924).

[237] Alexander Hoyos, *Der deutsch-englische Gegensatz und sein Einfluss auf die Balkanpolitik Österreich-Ungarns* (Berlin: de Gruyter, 1922).

secret of the impossibility of a conflict with the power that dominated the Mediterranean. The author concludes by giving the Austro-Serbian conflict an interesting interpretation. In effect, he does not deny that Vienna favored a preventive war, but he stresses that if Serbia had been reduced to a position no longer considered threatening to the Austrian Empire, European equilibrium would have been re-established and long-lasting peace secured.

The volume of memoirs of the former Austrian Ambassador to Rome, Macchio,[238] joins the collection of similar volumes designed as a reply to the accusations leveled by Bülow. Bülow, in referring to his mission to Rome during the period of Italy's neutrality, stressed the apparent blindness of his Austrian colleague in viewing an Italian intervention in the war as highly improbable and advising Vienna against making any concessions to the Italians. In his memoirs, Macchio denies many of Bülow's accusations on specific points, but nothing Macchio writes suggests the need to modify the earlier judgment on his actions. His disclosures, on the whole, are rather modest.

The testimony of other Austrian diplomats is of minor importance. The volume by the former Austrian Counsellor in the Embassy at St. Petersburg and later Minister to Athens, Szilassy,[239] is strongly critical of Berchtold. However, Szilassy presents no new evidence on the issue. On the other hand, the memoirs of the Austrian Military Attaché at Constantinople, Pomiankowski,[240] are of interest for the data contained on the Russian reaction to the Liman von Sanders mission. Much more important are the memoirs of Baron Giesl,[241] Minister to Cetinje from 1910 to 1913 and then to Belgrade until the outbreak of the war. His narrative of the Sarajevo crisis is a valuable supplement to the Austrian official documents.

The memoirs of the Austrian military leaders, from the point of view of political history, do not have an importance comparable to that of their German counterparts, largely because the influence exerted by the Austrian General Staff on the government was notably less.

An exception, of course, are the memoirs of General Conrad von Hötzendorf,[242] and these should be considered as a significant source for the

---

[238] Karl Macchio, *Wahrheit! Fürst Bülow und ich in Rom 1914–1915* (Vienna: Jung-Osterreich, 1931).

[239] Julius Szilassy, *Der Untergang der Donaumonarchie. Diplomatische Erinnerungen* (Berlin: Verlag Neues Vaterland, 1921).

[240] Joseph Pomiankowski, *Der Zusammenbruch des Ottomanischen Reiches. Erinnerungen an die Türkei aus der Zeit des Weltkrieges* (Vienna: Amalthea, 1928).

[241] Wladimir Giesl, *Zwei Jahrzehnte im Nahen Orient* (Berlin: Verlag für Kulturpolitik, 1927).

[242] *Aus meiner Dienstzeit* (5 vols.; Vienna: Rikola, 1922–25).

study of Austrian foreign policy during the years preceding the war (the five volumes cover the period 1906–14), along with the biography of General Beck written by Von Glaise-Horstenau.[243] General Beck was Chief of the Austrian General Staff from 1888 to 1906, and the documentation in his biography is very relevant to a study of the conflict between the Austrian and German general staffs and even more so to a study of a number of political questions such as the Austro-Russian accord of May, 1897.

Regarding the Hungarian statesmen and diplomats, Wertheimer's biography of Gyula Andrassy,[244] Prime Minister of Hungary from 1867 to 1871 and Foreign Minister of the Dual Monarchy from 1871 to 1879, is a significant contribution. It contains a number of worth-while pages on Austrian policy during the Franco-Prussian War—especially with reference to the pressure applied by Andrassy on Beust to avoid the danger of an intervention—but it becomes fundamentally important for the succeeding period and particularly for the eastern crisis of 1875–78.

Istvan Tisza, the dominant Hungarian political figure during the last years of the Dual Monarchy, did not leave his memoirs (he was assassinated in October, 1918), but this gap has been partially filled by the publication of his letters by the Budapest Academy of Science.[245] Tisza's position throughout the crisis of July, 1914, is well known from other sources,[246] and thus his letters serve to confirm what was already known and little else. However, they serve to emphasize the motives for his initial opposition to a war with Serbia, which does not appear to have been due solely to political considerations (a desire to avoid the inclusion of more Slavic elements within the Hapsburg Empire, a negative evaluation of the diplomatic situation at the moment, and a fear of a Russian intervention) but to his religious convictions as well, which prompted him to regard the prospect of war with horror. His later identification with the Berchtold position appears to have been primarily determined by the conviction that Austria-Hungary could count on the full support of Germany and by the

[243] Edmund von Glaise-Horstenau, *Franz Joseph Weggefährte. Das Leben des Generalstabschefs Grafen Beck* (Vienna: Amalthea, 1930).

[244] Egon Wertheimer, *Graf Julius Andrassy* (2 vols.; Stuttgart: Deutsche Verlagsanstalt, 1912–13).

[245] *Osszes munkai* [Unpublished Letters] (5 vols.; Budapest: Franklin-Tarsulat, 1923–33). French translation, Comte Etienne Tisza, *Lettres de guerre 1914–1916* (Paris: Les Oeuvres représentatives, 1931); German translation, Stefan Tisza, *Briefe (1914–1918)* (Berlin: Hobbing, 1928). The Tisza papers have been consulted by L. Lanyi, *Le comte Etienne Tisza et la guerre de 1914–1918* (Paris: Lagny, 1947).

[246] The role played by Tisza during the course of the crisis was revealed for the first time in a little volume by Bishop Wilhelm Franknoi, *Die ungarische Regierung und die Entsteung des Weltkrieges* (Vienna: Seidel, 1919).

fear—strongly felt in the political circles of Vienna and Budapest and particularly significant for Tisza, a strong supporter of friendship between the Central Powers—that without a trial of strength Austria-Hungary would lose its prestige in Berlin and that the Germans would perhaps be induced to seek an understanding with the Russians.

This material also provides new data on the period following the outbreak of war, especially concerning negotiations with Italy and relations with Rumania. The correspondence confirms the hypothesis that Tisza was frightened by the prospect of a simultaneous Italo-Rumanian attack on the Austro-Hungarian Empire, but despite this fear he remained one of the strongest opponents of the idea of making territorial concessions to Italy to ensure its neutrality.[247] Two factors were responsible for Tisza's position on this issue: first of all, his erroneous evaluation of Italy's position, which, early in January, 1915, led him to believe that an Italian intervention was impossible; and second, his desire to avoid establishing any precedents in this matter of territorial concessions, particularly with regard to Rumania. As has been noted, the Italian government demanded that the territories ceded to Italy be transferred to Italian control immediately, and this demand caused Tisza to fear that Rumania would advance similar claims for Transylvania. On the other hand, it is interesting to note that although beginning in March, 1915, Tisza was being converted to the idea of making territorial concesssions to Italy and indeed pressured Vienna in this regard, it seems that he considered the negotiations with Rome to be no more than a tactical maneuver. A number of phrases in his letters suggest that he proceeded toward carrying out an eventual accord with strong mental reservations.[248]

The other Hungarian memoir sources are of minor interest. The contributions of Prince Ludwig Windischgraetz[249] and of Prince Theodor Batthyany,[250] which differ at times in objectives, are both controversial—a warning that they must be used with great caution—but they are useful for an understanding of the position taken in Hungarian circles in relation to the alliance with Germany and to the politico-military events of the

[247] For Tisza's attitude toward Italy, see Arthur Weber, "Graf Tisza und der Eintritt Italiens in den Weltkrieg," *Berliner Monatschefte*, II (1927).

[248] In this context see also a letter from Tisza to Burian of May 7, 1914, published by the newspaper *As Ast* in February, 1929. In this note the Hungarian statesman declared that the promises of territorial concessions to Rumania and to Italy were to be considered legally null and void because they were extracted under duress and that, in any event, the outcome of the war would have determined the value of such concessions, which Austria-Hungary was forced to promise "at the point of a knife."

[249] *Vom Roten zum Schwarzen Prinzen* (Berlin: Ullstein, 1920).

[250] *Für Ungarn gegen Hohenzollern* (Vienna: Amalthea, 1930).

conflict. The memoirs of Gyula Andrassy,[251] second son of the former Prime Minister, the last Hapsburg Foreign Minister, and the initiator of armistice negotiations with Italy, contain little that is noteworthy. They aim, rather, at discrediting the policies of Andrassy's predecessors. Of interest for the last period of the reign of Emperor Charles is the volume by Mihaly Karolyi.[252] However, he makes no mention of the events in which he played a role after his appointment as President of the Council on October 30, 1918, and as Chief of State from November 16, 1918, until the revolution inspired by Béla Kun.[253] Albert Apponyi's brief recollections[254] include one chapter of real interest on the negotiation of the Treaty of Trianon, in which he participated as head of the Hungarian delegation.

Mention must also be made in this section on the Austrian memorialists to the contributions by Masaryk[255] and Beneš,[256] the two Czechs to whom this minority people in large measure owe their independence after the war. Beneš' memoirs complement Masaryk's, and the two should be studied together in order to understand the activities of these men, largely carried on abroad and particularly in France, for the establishment of the Czech state. Achievement of this objective was not a simple matter because for the Entente the principal enemy was Germany, while as far as the Dual Monarchy was concerned, there were no insurmountable obstacles to Vienna's indicating its willingness to abandon its ally. Masaryk and Beneš devoted all of their energies to altering this situation. Their activities began to take on definite shape in 1916, when Beneš created the Czech National Committee in Paris and became its Secretary-General, leaving the presidency to Masaryk, and the French became responsive to their appeals. However, it was only in 1918 that the Entente definitely included in its war aims the dismemberment of the Hapsburg Empire, and both Beneš and Masaryk in their memoirs stress the extent of their influence on this decision, which was destined to change completely the map of central eastern Europe.

[251] Julius Andrassy, *Diplomatie und Weltkrieg* (Berlin: Ullstein, 1920).

[252] *Egy egész világ ellen* (Munich, 1923). American translation, Michael Karolyi, *Fighting the World* (New York: Boni, 1925).

[253] On this point see the important study by the ex-Minister of Ethnic Minorities in the Karolyi Cabinet, Oszkar Jaszi, *Revolution and Counter-Revolution in Hungary* (London: King, 1924).

[254] *Erlebnisse und Ergebnisse* (Berlin: Keil, 1934).

[255] Tomas Garrigue Masaryk, *Světová Revoluce za války a ve válce 1914–1918* (Prague: Orbis, 1925). English translation, *The Making of a State. Memories and Observations, 1914–1918* (London: Allen and Unwin, 1927).

[256] Edward Beneš, *Světová Válka a Naše Revoluce* (3 vols.; Prague: Orbis, 1927–28). English translation, *My War Memoirs* (London: Allen and Unwin, 1928).

7. THE AMERICAN MEMORIALISTS.

The autobiography published by President Theodore Roosevelt several years after he had left the White House[257] contains very little new information on the conduct of American foreign policy during his administration, September, 1901–March, 1909. His role in mediating the Russo-Japanese conflict and his somewhat less well-known intervention in the first Moroccan crisis have been reasonably well covered in the biography by J. B. Bishop,[258] who made good use of the Roosevelt correspondence. However, the principal sources for the study of Theodore Roosevelt's foreign policy in all of its aspects are the volumes of his correspondence with Henry Cabot Lodge[259] and the collection of his letters recently published.[260]

President Wilson left no memoirs, but the man and his activities have been the object of numerous studies by his collaborators,[261] to which must be added various biographies.[262] For the wealth of information and the

[257] *An Autobiography* (New York: Macmillan, 1913).

[258] *Theodore Roosevelt and His Time. Shown in His Own Letters* (2 vols.; New York: Scribner, 1920). Concerning the Portsmouth treaty negotiations, see Tyler Dennett, *Roosevelt and the Russo-Japanese War* (New York: Doubleday, 1925).

[259] *Selections from the Correspondence of Theodore Roosevelt and Henry Cabot Lodge* (2 vols.; New York: Scribner, 1925).

[260] Eltin E. Morison (ed.), *The Letters of Theodore Roosevelt*, Vols. I–II: *The Years of Preparation, 1868–1900*; Vols. III–IV: *The Square Deal, 1901–1905*; Vols. V–VI: *The Big Stick, 1905–1909*; Vols. VII–VIII: *The Days of Armageddon, 1909–1919* (8 vols.; Cambridge, Mass.: Harvard University Press, 1951–54).

[261] In addition to the House papers and the memoirs of Bryan, Lansing, and Miller, to be examined later, attention is called to the volume by the Secretary of the Treasury, William Gibbs McAdoo, *Crowded Years. Reminiscences* (Boston: Houghton Mifflin, 1931), especially important for the insight it offers into the personality of the President; the volume by the Secretary of Agriculture, David Franklin Houston, *Eight Years with Wilson's Cabinet, 1913–1920* (2 vols.; New York: Doubleday, 1926), which, despite its emphasis on internal affairs, contains a number of interesting pages on international problems; and the correspondence of the Secretary of the Interior, Franklin K. Lane, edited by Anne Wintermute Lane and Louise Herrick Wall, *The Letters of Franklin K. Lane* (Boston: Houghton Mifflin, 1922), in which the author is critical of the President's actions. The volume written by the Secretary of War is, on the other hand, completely favorable to Wilson (Newton Diehl Baker, *Why We Went to War* [New York: Harpers, 1936]). Baker counters the claims of the President's critics by insisting that American intervention in the conflict was brought about by the German policy of unrestricted submarine warfare and not by the pressure of "bankers and munitions makers."

[262] See particularly David Lawrence, *The True Story of Woodrow Wilson* (New York: Doran, 1924); William Allen White, *Woodrow Wilson* (Boston: Houghton Mifflin, 1924); James Kerney, *The Political Education of Woodrow Wilson* (New York: Century, 1926); See also Thomas A. Bailey, *Wilson and the Peace Makers* (New York: Macmillan, 1947).

number of documents contained, the most important is the official biography by Ray Stennard Baker.[263] While the mass of information collected by Baker may not have the value of an autobiography by Wilson, it remains a significant report of the salient aspects of America's intervention in European and world affairs even though, at times, the author's judgment appears to be overshadowed by the apologetic intent of the work.

The best memoir on President Wilson's foreign policy is the four-volume collection of the papers of Colonel House,[264] Wilson's closest collaborator even though he held no official post.[265] Colonel House clearly emerges in the role of Wilson's personal representative, a role very similar to that of Harry Hopkins in relation to Franklin Roosevelt during World War II.

House did not write his memoirs, but he deposited the imposing documentation in his possession, along with his diary, in the Yale University library and invited Professor Charles Seymour to select and edit the material in such a way as to present a nearly continuous narrative: "My wish," declares House in the Preface, "has been to allow the documents to tell their own story." The author's goal was fully realized: there are few memoirs that can be compared to those of Colonel House from the point of view of faithful reproduction of their author's activities.

The data these contribute to the study of World War I are of major importance in that they make it possible to follow the formulation and execution of American foreign policy from the spring of 1914 to the summer of 1919.

The first two volumes focus on Colonel House's missions to Europe in 1914, 1915, and 1916, and serve as a connecting link between them; they illustrate the direction of American policy during the period of neutrality, that of intervention in European affairs to effect a mediation of the conflict. House believed that it was impossible for the United States to remain inactive in the face of European developments because in the Anglo-German rivalry there were elements that would assuredly affect American interests. In the spring of 1914 he obtained the approval of Wilson and the encouragement of Bernstorff, the German Ambassador to Washington, for a proposal to establish a co-operative effort on the part of the European

[263] *Woodrow Wilson: Life and Letters* (8 vols.; New York: Doubleday, 1927–39); *Woodrow Wilson and World Settlement* (3 vols.; New York: Doubleday, 1922); *What Wilson Did at Paris* (New York: Doubleday, 1919), a brief résumé of Wilson's activities at Paris. Also see Baker and Edward William Dodd (eds.), *Public Papers of Woodrow Wilson* (6 vols.; New York: Harper, 1925–27).

[264] Charles Seymour (ed.), *Edward Mandell House. The Intimate Papers of Colonel House* (4 vols.; Boston: Houghton Mifflin, 1926–28).

[265] For the relations between Wilson and Colonel House, see Alexander L. George and Juliette L. George, *Woodrow Wilson and Colonel House. A Personality Study* (New York: John Day, 1956).

powers, particularly Great Britain and Germany, whereby they would pool their resources to assist the "underdeveloped areas" of the world on the basis of an "open-door" policy and "equal opportunity for all." The plan envisioned a general arms limitation as well. House presented it to officials in Berlin and London, and it was favorably received by both William II and Lord Grey. However, the latter hesitated to press the proposal for fear of antagonizing the French and the Russians.

In the spring of 1915, after the first few months of the war had revealed that a rapid military solution to the conflict was not possible, House returned to Europe to attempt to end the conflict by a compromise peace. The proposal he submitted to the contesting powers envisaged a security system based on the limitation of armaments and a variety of reciprocal guarantees. Grey and Bethmann-Hollweg did not oppose House's plan, but House realized, even before the sinking of the "Lusitania" abruptly terminated the negotiations, that the German Chancellor, in particular, did not have the authority to make decisions in matters of this nature.

When events seemed definitely to point to an American intervention, the White House decided to take a decisive step. In January, 1916, House was again sent to Europe to force the belligerents to make peace; he declared that the United States would enter the war against those powers refusing to accept a solution by negotiation as suggested by the United States. House's declaration lacked the force of an ultimatum, a condition he had originally proposed as necessary to its acceptance, because Wilson believed that he could go no further than to define American intervention as "probable." As a result, Berlin did not interpret House's declaration as a threat, and the Entente saw no pressing reason for accepting the conditions imposed by Washington.

The last two volumes concern the period following the American intervention, the armistice, and the peace conference. The central theme is President Wilson's decision to establish the guidelines for the negotiations on the basis of his personal views, which differed markedly from the objectives sought by the Entente powers in the secret treaties. In order to distinguish clearly the American position from that of the Entente allies, President Wilson insisted that the United States was an "associated" and not an "allied" power and that in the declaration of war against Germany the United States felt no hostility toward the "German people."

The question of the secret treaties was discussed in April, 1917, when the Balfour mission arrived in the United States to co-ordinate the Allied political and military war effort. On April 28, 1917, during the course of a long conversation, House and Balfour carefully studied the new frontiers to be assigned to the victorious powers, and at the end of the discussion House bluntly asked him about the secret treaties and whether he was in a position to reveal their contents. The British Minister replied in the affirmative and on May 18, 1917, presented to Wilson the texts of the treaties by which Italy and Rumania entered the war, the Sykes-Picot Agreement, and the Anglo-French-Russian exchange of notes on Constantinople and the Straits question, along with the annex relative to the Turkish frontier in the Caucasus and the neutral zone in Persia. This fact, amply confirmed in Baker's work, definitely proves invalid the later assertions of President Wilson that he was unaware of the secret treaties. The conversations with Balfour indicated that there was a wide divergence of views between the British and the Americans on the future world order, but Wilson was not excessively preoccupied by them. In July, 1917, he wrote to House that for the moment it was impossible to force the issue but that after the victory the United States would be able to impose its point of view on the European allies, economically exhausted by their war efforts.

After Wilson's enunciation of the Fourteen Points and his successive declarations of the principles of the new international order on which the peace treaty should be based, the question of Allied acceptance of these principles became the crucial issue. The House papers provide a precise summary of this phase of American relations with the Allies, particularly in the matter of defining the armistice terms, in which House functioned as the President's personal representative.

House played the same role during the peace conference and served as chief of the American delegation during Wilson's brief absence from Paris. Baker accuses House of having taken advantage of Wilson's absence to join with the major European powers in sabotaging the application of the Wilsonian principles. However, the House papers prove the Baker accusations to be absolutely without foundation: they reveal that House informed the President daily on the developments at the conference and made no decision unless expressly authorized to do so. In addition, these papers contribute a great deal of information on the reasons why the treaties reflected little of the Wilsonian directives.

The revelations contained in the House papers on other major problems of the years 1917–19, such as the papal peace appeal and the position of the Entente vis-à-vis Russia after the revolution, make this collection one of the most detailed sources on the war years and on the establishment of the peace.

The biography of William Jennings Bryan,[266] Wilson's first Secretary of State, is of minor importance because the author did not develop his

[266] William Jennings Bryan and Mary Baird Bryan, *The Memoirs of William Jennings Bryan* (Chicago: Winston, 1925).

narrative beyond the elections of 1912, while the chapters covering the period of his tenure as Secretary of State were completed by his wife from his notes and papers. The important portion of the volume concerns the Bryan-Wilson correspondence on the sinking of the "Lusitania," in which Bryan expressed his disapproval of Wilson's strong second note to Germany on the incident and refused to endorse it. Bryan held that it was impossible to make a *casus belli* out of the "Lusitania" case because the ship was also carrying munitions. When Wilson refused to accept the Bryan thesis and ignored his recommendations for a new system of control of maritime traffic in the Atlantic, Bryan resigned.

The choice of Lansing as Bryan's successor was primarily determined by the former's knowledge of international law, a knowledge that was particularly useful to the President at that time in order to resolve the legal problems arising from America's neutrality. Lansing's tasks were of a technical and administrative character rather than political. In part, this was due to the very different personalities of the President and the Secretary of State, which prevented any close collaboration between the two men.

The continued conflict of opinion between the President and the Secretary of State finally led President Wilson to ask for Lansing's resignation in February, 1920. A few months after leaving the State Department, Lansing published a volume of his memoirs[267] on the period of the peace conference, in which he explains the reasons for his disagreement with the President and his own role in the peace negotiations. While this part of the memoir is of some interest, it contains nothing of great importance because, despite Lansing's participation in the meetings of the Council of Ten, his opinion carried little weight in the decisions of the American delegation, which was dominated by Wilson and Colonel House. House's role in the entire proceedings contributed to the difficulties in the Wilson-Lansing relations.

The most interesting pages of the volume concern Lansing's criticism of Wilson's actions and of the fundamental mistake Wilson made in attending the Paris conference in person. Lansing also emphasizes that Wilson subordinated his every decision to the single objective of creating the League of Nations, while he (Lansing) believed that once the principle of the League was accepted by the Great Powers it would be wiser to postpone all discussion on the subject. Moreover, there was no identity of view between the two men on the question of the authority to be given to the League and the position of each of the five major powers in the organization.

[267] Robert Lansing, *The Peace Negotiations. A Personal Narrative* (Boston: Houghton Mifflin, 1921).

However, Lansing reserved his strongest criticism for what he termed Wilson's loss of contact with American reality during the peace conference, which led to his making decisions which were not acceptable to the American public and which were later rejected by Congress. Lansing states that he foresaw this situation and that he had called it to the President's attention, but, he notes, Wilson considered an opinion differing from his to be a personal affront.

Lansing also published a little study on the principal personalities at the conference;[268] this is a useful evaluation, by an acute observer, of Wilson, Clemenceau, Lloyd George, Orlando, and other minor representatives.

During his last years Lansing devoted his energies to writing the memoirs of his entire political life, but he was unable to complete his narrative beyond 1917.[269] These memoirs primarily concern the problems emerging from America's neutrality: Lansing recognizes that, from the legal point of view alone, he would have been forced to oppose those countries who were sure to become America's allies. Thus, despite the fact that it was against his conscience as a jurist, he made every effort to give political considerations a decisive weight in arriving at decisions affecting the Entente powers. This exposé of the criteria he observed in carrying out his functions is the most significant part of the volume. The absence of chapters on the post-1917 period is not a great loss because the publication of the Lansing papers[270] offer excellent evidence on the activities of the former Secretary of State.

For nearly fifteen years the twenty volumes published in 1928 by David Hunter Miller,[271] legal expert of the American delegation to the Paris peace conference, were, perhaps, the most important single source for the study of the preparations leading to the Paris treaties. With the exception of the first volume, they contain a wealth of documentary material on the work of the conference which was superseded only by the publication of the supplemental volumes on the Paris conference in the official American collection.[272] The first volume, containing the diary Miller kept during his Paris stay, November 19, 1918–May 29, 1919, remains a valuable source. His annotations are especially important for an understanding of the behind-the-scenes activities of the American delegation and for the positions taken by Wilson and Colonel House.

[268] *The Big Four and Others of the Peace Conference* (Boston: Houghton Mifflin, 1921).

[269] *War Memoirs* (Indianapolis, Ind.: Bobbs-Merrill, 1935).

[270] See page 220.

[271] *My Diary at the Conference of Paris* (20 vols.; New York: Appeal Printing Co., 1928).

[272] See pp. 220–21.

In the two volumes by Miller on the drafting of the Covenant,[273] the author discusses in detail the work of the Commission for the League of Nations, examining the various proposals leading to the definitive text. In reviewing the work of the Commission, Miller praises President Wilson's decision to include the Covenant in the Treaty of Versailles at all costs, and expresses the opinion that if this had not been done, perhaps a generation would have passed before it would have been possible to realize the aspiration so strongly desired by world public opinion.

Useful information on the peace conference is also contained in the volume by Professor James T. Shotwell,[274] member of the Inquiry (the study committee created to prepare the materials for the American delegation and to assist it during the negotiations), which is essentially Shotwell's diary for the period of his stay in Paris, December 3, 1918–July 9, 1919. Equally useful is the collection of lectures given by a group of experts in the American delegation to Paris on topics of their competence, edited by Colonel House and Charles Seymour;[275] the volume by Bernard Baruch,[276] reparations expert, illustrating the work of that commission; and finally, the work of two consultants, the historians Haskins and Lord,[277] focusing on the controversial territorial questions considered by the conference, with special reference to the Polish and the Saar problems.

On the whole, the memoirs of the American diplomats are of minor importance in contrast to those of the European diplomats. This situation is explained by the fact that Europe was of marginal importance to American diplomacy; that the American diplomats were generally not career men and were therefore alien to the traditional environment of their European colleagues; and finally, that there was no great debate in America on the origins of the war.

Former Ambassador to Berlin David J. Hill is much better known for his historical writings[278] than he is for his volume of memoirs[279] on the personality of William II, while the volume by Ambassador James W.

[273] The Drafting of the Covenant (2 vols.; New York: Putnam, 1928).

[274] At the Paris Conference (New York: Macmillan, 1937).

[275] Edward M. House and Charles Seymour (eds.), What Really Happened at Paris (New York: Scribner, 1921).

[276] The Making of the Reparations and Economic Sections of the Treaty (New York: Harper, 1920).

[277] Charles Homer Haskins and Howard Robert Lord, Some Problems of the Peace Conference (Cambridge, Mass.: Harvard University Press, 1920).

[278] A History of Diplomacy in the International Development of Europe, Vol. I (1905): The Struggle for Universal Empire; Vol. II (1906): The Establishment of Territorial Sovereignty; Vol. III (1914): The Diplomacy of the Age of Absolutism (New York, Longmans, Green and Co.).

[279] "Impressions of the Kaiser: The Kaiser's Methods of Personal Control," The Century Magazine, 1918.

Gerard[280] on his mission to Berlin from 1913 to February, 1917, when diplomatic relations between Germany and the United States were broken, is much more useful.

Gerard narrates an interesting episode that occurred during the July, 1914, crisis. In discussing the latest developments with Ambassador Jules Cambon on July 30, 1914, the latter ventured the opinion that only an American mediation could prevent war. Gerard, without losing time in consulting Washington, decided to write to the German Chancellor asking whether there was anything he could do in his role as American Ambassador to prevent the outbreak of hostilities, assuring Bethmann-Hollweg that President Wilson would support any initiative he took to preserve the peace. Gerard received no reply. The failure to reply to Gerard's letter suggests that even if Wilson had sent his August 4–5 appeal for peace immediately after the American Ambassador to Paris had advised him to do so on July 28, the result would have been the same. Accordingly, it may be concluded that while the position taken by Ambassador Walter H. Page on the President's proposed peace appeal delayed its actual transmittal to the European governments, the delay had no practical effect. Gerard's account for the war period enables one to follow the developments in German-American relations in detail, particularly the growing tension between the two powers in the wake of the naval incidents.

The writings of the last two American ambassadors to St. Petersburg before the revolution, George T. Marye (1914–16)[281] and David R. Francis (April, 1916–November, 1918),[282] are only general accounts and provide little important data. Marye was not a very close observer of the Russian internal situation, and Francis' narrative on the revolution deals only with its esoteric aspects.

Brand Whitlock's account of his mission to Brussels from 1914 to 1917[283] is a vivid report of the sufferings of the Belgians during the war and a vigorous defense of King Albert. From the diplomatic point of view, these memoirs are not especially significant, but they complement his diaries and letters published by Nevins,[284] which are of greater interest, and the diary of his Secretary of Legation, Hugh Gibson,[285] providing some useful data on the beginning of the war.

[280] My Four Years in Germany (New York: Doran, 1917); Face to Face with Kaiserism (New York: Doran, 1918).

[281] Nearing the End in Imperial Russia (Philadelphia: Dorrance, 1929).

[282] Russia from the American Embassy (New York: Scribner, 1921).

[283] Belgium: A Personal Narrative (2 vols.; New York: Appleton, 1919).

[284] Allan Nevins (ed.), The Letters and Journal of Brand Whitlock (2 vols.; New York: Appleton, 1936).

[285] A Journal from Our Legation in Belgium (New York: Doubleday, 1917).

Completing the memoir accounts by American diplomats accredited to the wartime capitals are the volumes by the American Ambassador to Paris during the war, William Sharp,[286] revealing his efforts to maintain a high level of cordiality in Franco-American relations; that of Henry Morganthau, Ambassador to Constantinople from 1913 to 1916,[287] containing important observations on the Turkish internal situation; and the publication by Charles J. Vopicka, Minister to Bucharest, Belgrade, and Sofia between 1913 and 1920,[288] whose summary is rather superficial. The memoirs of two diplomats assigned to neutral countries, I. N. Morris, Minister to Sweden,[289] and Maurice F. Egan, Minister to Copenhagen from 1907 to 1918,[290] contain much more substantial information. The latter, in particular, provides an accurate description of the negotiations for the purchase of the Danish West Indies (the Virgin Islands) by the United States, a transaction which had been hanging fire since 1902 and which was finally concluded in August, 1916, because of the fear that Germany might occupy these islands and establish a base in the Caribbean.

As was noted in the numerous biographies of the presidents, the contribution of the American memoir accounts, while it does not always achieve the level of importance of the British "authorized biographies," is of significant value because they are usually based on primary sources, such as private correspondence and diaries, which would otherwise be virtually inaccessible.

Among others worthy of mention are the biographies of John Hay, American Ambassador to the Court of St. James in 1897 and Secretary of State from 1898 to 1905, by Thayer[291] and by Dennett.[292] Of value to the study of Hay and his activities in international affairs is the biography of his successor, Elihu Root, written by Philip C. Jessup,[293] particularly those

---

[286] *The War Memoirs of William Graves Sharp, American Ambassador to France, 1914–1919* (London: Constable, 1931). On the same question see also the diary of Sharp's colleague, Lee Meriwether, *The War Diary of a Diplomat* (New York: Dodd, 1919). For the military aspects, see John J. Pershing, *My Experiences in the World War* (2 vols.; New York: Stokes, 1931).

[287] *Ambassador Morgenthau's Story* (New York: Doubleday, 1918).

[288] *Secrets of the Balkans. Seven Years of a Diplomat's Life in the Storm Centre of Europe* (Chicago: Rand McNally, 1921).

[289] *From an American Legation* (New York: Knopf, 1923).

[290] *Ten Years near the German Frontier* (New York: Doran, 1919).

[291] William Roscoe Thayer, *The Life and Letters of John Hay* (2 vols.; Boston, 1915).

[292] Tyler Dennett, *John Hay* (New York: Dodd, 1933).

[293] *Elihu Root* (2 vols.; New York: Dodd, 1938). Reference should also be made to the biography of Root's undersecretary and for a brief period his successor, Robert Bacon, who later became American Ambassador to Paris, 1909–12. See James Scott, *Robert Bacon, Life and Letters* (New York: Doubleday, 1923).

sections referring to President Roosevelt's position on Moroccan affairs and Root's extraordinary mission to Russia in 1917.[294]

De Wolfe Howe's biography of George L. Meyer,[295] Ambassador to St. Petersburg from 1905 to 1907, contains valuable data on Russia at the turn of the century and on the Russo-Japanese War. Meyer's comments in his diary and his frequent personal correspondence with the President are fundamental sources for the reconstruction of the events that followed the American offer to mediate the Russo-Japanese conflict, which was presented to the Russian authorities by Meyer on June 6, 1905.

Among the biographies referring to the World War I period, that by Mott on Myron Herrick, American Ambassador to Paris at the outbreak of the war,[296] Hendrick's biography of Walter Hinds Page,[297] and Allan Nevins' work on Henry White[298] are the most important.

Walter Hinds Page, Ambassador to London from 1913 to the close of 1917, was convinced that Anglo-Saxon civilization could only survive with the defeat of Germany and became an active champion of American intervention. After the sinking of the "Lusitania," Page became very critical of the White House for its failure to enter the war. His letters to President Wilson are eloquent testimony of his views, and they are exceedingly important both for their content and their literary style. They also help us to understand the ideological motivation of those who were convinced that the peace of Europe could be achieved only through the defeat of Germany.

Nevins' volume is particularly important for the chapters on the Paris peace conference, attended by Henry White, who was chosen by President Wilson for this assignment because of the experience White had acquired during his long mission to London. Although White had also been the American Envoy to Rome from 1904–7, he was among the members of the American delegation least favorable to Italy's cause and bitterly assailed Colonel House for his moderation.

[294] For a compilation of generally excellent biographies of all of the American secretaries of state from Robert Livingston to Charles E. Hughes, see Samuel Flagg Bemis (ed.), *The American Secretaries of State and Their Diplomacy* (10 vols.; New York: Knopf, 1927–29). A new series bearing the same title has been initiated under the directorship of Robert H. Ferrell, and Samuel F. Bemis. To date, the following volumes have been published: Robert H. Ferrell, *Kellogg-Stimson* (New York: Cooper Square Publishers, 1963); Julius Pratt, *Cordell Hull* (2 vols.; New York: Cooper Square Publishers, 1964).

[295] M. A. De Wolfe Howe, *George von Lengerke Meyer* (New York, 1919).

[296] Thomas Bentley Mott, *Myron T. Herrick* (New York: Doubleday, 1929).

[297] Burton Jesse Hendrick, *The Life and Letters of Walter H. Page* (3 vols.; New York: Doubleday, 1922–25); *The Training of an American. The Earlier Life and Letters of Walter H. Page, 1855–1913* (Boston: Houghton Mifflin, 1928).

[298] Allan Nevins, *Henry White. Thirty Years of American Diplomacy* (New York: Harper, 1930).

8. THE MEMORIALISTS IN OTHER COUNTRIES.

a. The Belgians.

Belgian memoirs concentrate on the principal event of the war in which Belgium played a key role: the German invasion of the country at the initial stage of the war. A great deal may be learned of the actions of King Albert in these tragic circumstances from the volume by General Emile Galet,[299] Albert's military adviser, who comments on the personality and work of the King from the latter's accession to the throne in 1909 to the end of the conflict. This may be considered an official biography, since King Albert wrote the Preface to it and favored its publication. The biography of King Albert by the historian Cammaerts[300] is a solid and well-documented work and may also be considered as an official biography. Both books emphasize Albert's adamant rejection of the German ultimatum, the vigor he brought to Belgian resistance, and the reasons for these attitudes. From the beginning of his reign, King Albert was aware of the perils threatening the peace of Europe and concluded that Belgian neutrality should not only depend on treaties but also on an efficient defense system. He was able to realize the latter only partially, with the result that the German General Staff continued to consider Belgium an open door to the heart of France.

The preoccupation and anxiety caused by the events of the last week of July, 1914, and the sudden change in the course of events that Belgium faced during the early days of August are effectively narrated in the volume by Baron Beyens.[301] Beyens was Belgium's Ambassador to Berlin from the spring of 1912 to the outbreak of the war, and he draws heavily for his account on his contacts with officials of the German Foreign Ministry. It was only on August 1 that Beyens became cognizant of what was about to happen—by the embarrassed smile with which Zimmermann received the Belgian government's oral communication, in which the government noted that, in conforming to the strict requirements of neutrality, it desired to receive Germany's assurance regarding the inviolability of Belgian territory. Beyens also published a two-volume memoir of his entire mission to

[299] Emile Joseph Galet, *S. M. le Roi Albert, Commandant en Chef devant l'invasion allemande* (Paris: Plon, 1931). Replies to several affirmations made in this volume may be found in the study by the ex-Minister of France to Brussels, A. Klobukowski, "La résistance belge à l'invasion allemande," *Revue d'histoire de la guerre mondiale*, 1932, pp. 233–50; Galet's "La Belgique et l'invasion allemande. A propos du livre: S. M. le Roi Albert . . . ," *Revue d'histoire de la guerre mondiale*, 1933, pp. 46–54, is his reply to Klobukowski.

[300] Emile Cammaerts, *Albert of Belgium* (New York: Macmillan, 1935).

[301] Napoleon Eugène Louis Beyens, *L'Allemagne avant la guerre. Les causes et les responsabilités* (Brussels and Paris: Van Oest, 1915).

Berlin,[302] which is valuable for a study of the European picture in 1912–13 because of the author's close friendship with Kiderlen-Wächter. The reactions of the Belgian government and Parliament to the German ultimatum may be followed in detail in the volumes by Albert de Bassompierre[303] and by Count Lichtervelde.[304]

b. The Serbs.

Not many Serbian memoir sources are directly pertinent to diplomatic history. These are limited to the recollections of the former Minister to St. Petersburg, Spalajkovic,[305] referring to the reaction of Russian official circles to the news of the Austrian ultimatum to Serbia, and to the memoirs of the former Secretary-General of the Ministry of Foreign Affairs, Gruic,[306] vividly recalling the crisis of July, 1914, and focusing attention on the presentation of the Austrian ultimatum, the formulation of the Serbian reply, and the flight of the government to Nish. There is also the contribution of the former Minister of Finance, Protic,[307] describing the breakup of the Balkan Alliance in the spring of 1913 and the development of the crisis down to the opening battle between Serbian, Bulgarian, and Greek troops in Macedonia on June 29, 1913. This is more of a historical narrative than a memoir and is largely based on Bulgarian documents. It illustrates the influence of King Ferdinand on events and the active participation of the chief of the Bulgarian armed forces, Savov, in planning and ordering the attack.

Dusan Loncarevic's volume[308] covers a wider period. Loncarevic was a citizen of Austria but Serbian in origins and sentiment; he was the Belgrade correspondent of the Viennese Wire Service from 1903–14. He has written one of the best works on Serbian policy for this period, focusing primarily on relations with Austria-Hungary. Loncarevic's over-all evaluation of Serbian and Austro-Hungarian actions is somewhat distorted by the

---

[302] *Deux Années à Berlin 1912–1914*, Vol. I: *mai 1912–août 1913*; Vol. II: *septembre 1913–août 1914* (Paris: Plon, 1931).

[303] *La nuit du 2 au 3 août 1914 au Ministère des Affaires étrangères de Belgique* (Paris: Perrin, 1916).

[304] Comte Louis de Lichtervelde, *Le 4 août au parlement belge* (Brussels and Paris: Van Oest, 1918).

[305] Miroslav Spalajkovic, "Une journée du ministre de Serbie à Pétrograd. Le 24 juillet 1914," *Revue d'histoire diplomatique*, April–June, 1934.

[306] Slavko Gruic, "Persönliche Erinnerungen aus der Julikrisis 1914," *Berliner Monatschefte*, July, 1935. See also Hamilton Fish Armstrong, "Three Days in Belgrade, July 1914," *Foreign Affairs*, January, 1927.

[307] Balkanicus [pseud. for Stojan Protic], *La Bulgarie. Ses ambitions, sa trahison* (Paris: Colin, 1915).

[308] Dushan Loncharevic, *Jugoslawiens Entstehung* (Vienna: Amalthea, 1928).

author's obvious bias, which he carries to the point of ignoring almost completely the influence of Russia on Serbian attitudes. However, the volume is important for the numerous details presented on the economic struggle between the two powers, economic pressure being considered by the Austrians to be an effective means of curbing Serbian resistance to the Dual Monarchy. Loncarevic affirms that these attempts at control of Serbia by Aehrenthal and Berchtold not only failed to achieve their principal objective but created an unbridgeable abyss between the two countries, while it would not have been difficult to reach an understanding in this area that would have been advantageous to both parties. The annexation of Bosnia-Herzegovina by the Austrian government was its most serious blunder, the author asserts: first of all, because it transformed the Serbian problem into a European one; second, because it converted the Pan-Serb ideal into a program of action. While Loncarevic confirms the bellicose attitude of Pasic and the radical party at the time of the annexation of Bosnia-Herzegovina, as well as the decision of the Serbian leaders to seek revenge at the earliest opportune moment, he also provides numerous details on the action taken by Milanovic in the western capitals, by Pasic in St. Petersburg, and by Novakovic in Constantinople.

A detailed study of the events leading to the assassination of Archduke Francis Ferdinand is only indirectly important to diplomatic history. However, the memoirs on this episode are numerous, and the various phases of the plot can be reconstructed from the proceedings of the trial of the assassins which took place in October, 1914,[309] and from the volume by Jevtic[310] containing valuable data on the affair. The work of Professor Stanojevic[311] (of questionable value), the proceedings of the Salonika trial of the Union or Death society,[312] and the volume by Boghicevic on the

---

[309] The proceedings of the trial were published in French by Albert Mousset (ed.), *L'attentat de Serajévo. Documents inédits et texte intégral des stenogrammes du procès* (Paris: Payot, 1928). In addition, see "Dr. Pappenheim's Conversations with Princip," *Current History*, August, 1927. For a detailed study of the trial, see Luciano Magrini, *Il delitto di Serajevo. Processo e sentenza* (Bologna, 1930).

[310] Borivoje Jevtic, *Sarajevski Atentat. Secana i utisci* [The Assassination at Sarajevo. Memoirs and Impressions] (Sarajevo: Gakovic, 1924). Abridged German translation, "Weitere Ausschnitte zum Attentat von Serajevo," *Die Kriegschuldfrage*, October, 1925.

[311] Stanoje Stanojevic, *Die Ermordung des Erzherzogs Franz Ferdinand. Ein Betrag zur Enstehungsgeschichte des Weltkrieges* (Frankfurt: Frankfürter Societatsdruckerei, 1923).

[312] *Tajna Prevratna Organizatzia* [A Secret Revolutionary Society] (Salonika: Velika Srbija, 1918). The results of the trial have been examined by Boghicevic in *Le procès de Salonique* (Paris: Delpeuch, 1927), an interesting but partisan view. See also Cedomir Popovic, "Sarajevski Atentat i organizacija 'Ujedinjenje ili Smrt,' " *Nova Europa*, July 26, 1932 (the author was a member of the society). German translation, "Das Sarajevoer Attentat und die Organisation 'Vereinigung oder Tod,' " *Berliner Monatschefte*, November, 1932.

activities of Colonel Dimitrievic,[313] head of the Black Hand society, reveal that the Sarajevo tragedy was the logical result of the agitation engineered by the nationalistic Pan-Serb organizations, whose activities the Serbian government either knew nothing about or refused to control. On the issue of the responsibility of the Serbian government, important revelations have come from the former President of the Skupština, Ljuba Jovanovic, who, in an article published in 1924,[314] affirmed that Pasic was aware early in June that several young revolutionaries intended to assassinate the Austrian Archduke during his visit to Sarajevo and that Pasic had so informed his Cabinet colleagues. The Serbian government issued instructions that the plotters be arrested, but the frontier guards, who were part of the secret organization, pretended that they received the order too late. However, the Austrian government was warned by the Serbian Minister to Vienna, Jovan Jovanovic,[315] who "on his own initiative" advised the Austrian Minister, Bilinski, to persuade the Archduke not to take the trip.[316]

c. The Rumanians.

The autobiography of Queen Marie of Rumania,[317] King Ferdinand's consort, reveals the influence that she exerted on the conduct of Rumanian policy, especially during the years of World War I, when Rumanian ruling groups were seriously divided as to what course to take in the conflict. The Queen's character was stronger than Ferdinand's, and she firmly believed in Great Britain's ultimate victory even when news from the battle fronts seemed to favor the cause of the Central Powers. On more than one occasion she all but replaced her husband as ruler and prescribed the course of Rumanian policy; she contacted foreign diplomats or appealed directly to her cousins George V and Nicholas II in an effort to gain their support during particularly trying periods of the struggle. Her testimony is rich in

[313] Milos Boghitschewitsch, *Le Colonel Dragoutine Dimitrievich Apis* (Paris: Delpeuch, 1928). See also Alexander Szanto, *Apis der Führer der 'Schwarzen Hand.' Ein Beitrag zum Kriegschuldproblem* (Berlin: Verlag der Neuen Gesellschaft, 1928).

[314] Ljuba Jovanovic, "Posle Vidov-dana 1914 Godine" [About St. Vitus Day, 1914], *Krv slovenstva*, 1924. English translation, *The Murder of Serajevo* (London: British Institute of International Affairs, 1925). On the question, see also Carlo Sforza, *Makers of Modern Europe* (Indianapolis, Ind.: Bobbs-Merrill, 1930).

[315] On this question see Jovanovic's testimony in "Meine Warnung an den Erzherzog Franz Ferdinand," *Neues Wiener Tageblatt*, June 28, 1924.

[316] For a detailed study of the problem, see Robert William Seton-Watson, *Sarajevo. A Study of the Origins of the Great War* (London: Hutchinson, 1926). The author sees Jovanovic's testimony as a complete fabrication.

[317] *The Story of My Life* (New York: Scribner, 1934); *Ordeal, the Story of My Life* (New York: Scribner, 1935).

useful references on the period of Rumanian neutrality—for example, the summary of the conversations with the Austro-Hungarian Minister, Czernin, and the pages relative to the Crown Council of August 27, 1916, when the decision was made to intervene in the war—and on the period following Rumania's entry into the war, when she embodied the spirit of resistance.

Some data concerning the Rumanian neutrality declaration and relations with Austria-Hungary can be found in the works by Take Jonescu,[318] authoritative member of the Conservative party and member of the Crown Council, who shared in all of the major decisions of the moment. Much more revealing is the work of Alexandru Marghiloman,[319] head of the Conservative party and President of the Council at the time of the signing of the Treaty of Bucharest, May 7, 1918. His diary, consisting of five large volumes, contains valuable notes for the reconstruction of the most important phases of Rumanian policy during World War I, from the Crown Council of August 2, 1914, during the reign of King Carol, when the decision was taken to proclaim Rumanian neutrality, to the Crown Council of August 27, 1916.[320] Important data can be found in the diary on the negotiations for a separate peace with the Central Powers that was begun in February, 1918, by General Averescu,[321] and continued, after the preliminaries of Buftea of March 5, by Marghiloman, who assumed power as *persona grata* to the governments of Vienna and Berlin. The economic aspects of these negotiations are particularly important to historians[322] in that they reveal the German tendency to seek economic supremacy in all of east central Europe, occasionally at the expense of the Hapsburg monarchy. On the other hand, the territorial gains made by Bulgaria—gains which included the entire Dobrudja and comprised much more territory than was held by Bulgaria in 1913—raised the question of compensation to Turkey, whose troops had contributed to the victory over the Rumanians. The quarrel that developed between Sofia and Constantinople over territorial compensation and the subsequent intervention by the Central Powers as mediators (they imposed a four-power occupation of the Costanza area until such time as the controversy could be resolved) were responsible for

---

[318] *Les origines de la guerre. Déposition d'un témoin* (Paris: Didier, 1915); *Souvenirs* (Paris: Payot, 1919). American translation, *Some Personal Impressions* (New York: Stokes, 1920).

[319] *Note Politice, 1897–1924* [Political Notes, 1897–1924] (5 vols.; Bucharest: Eminescu, 1927).

[320] A French translation of passages from Marghiloman's diary concerning these two events is found in *Revue d'histoire de la guerre mondiale*, II (1928).

[321] Alexandru Averescu, *Notice zilnice din rasboiu* (Bucharest: Appolo, 1937).

[322] For this aspect of the negotiations, see Gustav Gratz and Richard Schuller, *The Economic Policy of Austria-Hungary during the War* (New Haven, Conn.: Yale University Press, 1928).

the change in Bulgarian public opinion and the new course taken by the
Molinov government. In effect, these developments created a situation that
undoubtedly facilitated Bulgaria's subsequent withdrawal from the war.

Among the memoirs of Rumanian diplomats, Trandafir Djuvara's[323] are
of no importance, while the articles by Diamandy,[324] Minister to Rome
from 1912 to 1914 and to St. Petersburg until 1917, are of considerable
value. Diamandy seeks to demonstrate in the first of his articles that the real
cause of the war can be found in the internal situation of the Dual
Monarchy. In defending this thesis, he cites the statements made by the
former German Ambassador to Rome, Von Jagow, and his Austrian
colleague, Merey, in which both recognized that the progressive strengthening of the centrifugal forces within Austria-Hungary made it impossible
for the Hapsburgs to continue a successful defense of the present positions.
Moreover, in November, 1912, Von Jagow supposedly suggested the
cession of Austrian Galicia to Russia, and shortly thereafter Merey is
reported to have been in favor of discussing the Transylvanian question
with Bucharest. However, the information Diamandy offers in his last two
articles on his mission to Russia is much more significant, particularly
concerning the negotiations leading to the accord of October 1, 1914, by
which the Czar's government recognized Rumania's right to annex those
Austro-Hungarian territories inhabited by Rumanians without, however,
setting a precise date for Rumania's intervention in the war. The course of
the negotiations for Rumania's entry into the war should be kept in mind in
order to understand the Rumanian position during the negotiations with
Italy, taking place at that time, for a simultaneous Rumanian-Italian
intervention on the side of the Entente.

d. The Greeks.

The dramatic developments during World War I stemming from the
conflict between Venizelos and the crown in Greece and the violation of
Greek neutrality by the Entente powers constitute the major themes of the
few Greek memoir sources available.

The point of view held by Venizelos and his supporters is expressed in a
volume based on his speeches before the Chamber in August, 1917,[325] but

[323] *Mes missions diplomatiques, Belgrade, Sofia, Athènes, 1887–1925* (Paris:
Alcan, 1930).

[324] Constantin Diamandy, "La Grande Guerre vue du versant oriental: un nouvel
homme malade en Europe," *Revue des deux Mondes*, December 15, 1927, and
January 1, 1928; "Ma mission en Russie," *ibid.*, February 15, 1929, and November
15, 1930.

[325] Eleutherio Venizelos, *The Vindication of Greek National Policy* (London: Allyn
and Unwin, 1918).

finds its strongest justification in two White Books published during the war.[326] The White Books reveal that, after the clash between Greek and Allied troops in Athens in December, 1916, King Constantine repeatedly asked William II to launch a strong offensive in the Balkans that would permit Greece to escape Allied control.

On the other hand, King Constantine is cast in a favorable light by the memoirs of Prince Nicola.[327] Notwithstanding the purely defensive character of these memoirs, they contribute a number of fundamental facts that are useful in seeking a more objective evaluation of the work of the Greek Sovereign.

The author denies that King Constantine was pro-German and that he intended to drag Greece into the war on the side of the Central Powers; in contradiction to Venizelos, he states that Constantine immediately perceived that the war would last many years and that, in this event, Greece could not be involved without the full consent of the Greek nation. Entente policy, continues Prince Nicola, could not be justified by the fear of a Greek attack especially since, in the summer of 1916, Prince Andrew gave London precise assurances on this point and Prince Nicola himself was sent to Russia to solemnly affirm to the Czar that King Constantine had no intention of abandoning Greek neutrality.

However controversial, Prince Nicola's memoirs reflect the actual state of affairs much more accurately than does the thesis defended by Venizelos. The assertion that King Constantine did not sympathize with the cause of the Central Powers is certainly excessive, but the accusations leveled against the Greek Sovereign by Venizelos' supporters and by the Entente propaganda is even more inaccurate. The fallacies in these accusations were clearly exposed in the richly documented works of the Greek diplomats A. F. Frangulis[328] and S. Cosmin,[329] and in the somewhat more balanced study reaching substantially the same conclusions contained in the fifth volume of the Greek diplomatic history by Driault and Lhéritier.[330] In effect, in refusing to intervene in the war on the side of the Allies, King

[326] Ministère des Affaires Étrangères de Grèce, *Documents diplomatiques 1913– 1917. Traité d'alliance gréco-bulgare; invasion germano-bulgare en Macedonie* (Athens, 1917); *Documents diplomatiques 1913–1917. Supplement* (Athens, 1917).

[327] Prince Nicholas of Greece, *My Fifty Years* (London: Hutchinson, 1926); *Political Memoirs, 1914–1917* (London: Hutchinson, 1928).

[328] *La Grèce et la crise mondiale* (2 vols.; Paris: Alcan, 1926).

[329] *L'Entente et la Grèce pendant la Grande Guerre* (2 vols.; Paris: Société mutuelle d'edition, 1925).

[330] Edouard Driault and Michel Lhéritier, *La Grèce et la Grande Guerre. De la Révolution turque au Traité de Lausanne, 1908–1923* (Paris: Presses Universitaires de France, 1926).

Constantine was doing no more than reflecting the will of the overwhelming majority of the Greek people. Nor is it possible to criticize him for not joining Serbia in August, 1914, or the following year at the time when Bulgaria entered the war on the side of the Central Powers, since the Serbian-Greek treaty of June 1, 1913, did not establish any such obligation for Serbia, while the Bulgarian intervention had to be considered an episode in the general conflict.

The legal aspects of the case aside, King Constantine's attitude, in the light of the published documents, was never clearly hostile to the Entente even though occasionally his pro-German sympathies were manifest. His refusal to make any territorial concessions to the Bulgars, as requested by the British and the French in the hope of winning the diplomatic battle in Sofia, was an act in defense of Greek interests, since the promised compensations in Asia Minor seemed to be hypothetical and, in any event, would not have served to preserve the equilibrium in the Balkans that had emerged from the Balkan wars. Nor is it possible to blame Constantine's policy for the German-Bulgarian intervention in eastern Macedonia, an intervention which, on the basis of the evidence, was a direct result of the violation of Greek neutrality (the occupation of Salonika) by the Entente powers with the consent of Venizelos. Elements are brought to light, particularly in the works of Frangulis and Cosmin, that clearly reflect unfavorably on Venizelos and on the policy pursued by the Entente. For example, the action taken by the French government was apparently inspired by ends that are very difficult to justify on strategic grounds and completely irreconcilable with the ethno-political principles repeatedly proclaimed by Allied propaganda.

e. The Japanese.

Japanese memoirs are not particularly plentiful, and what is available is not readily accessible, although the few works that are known and translated make a significant contribution. One of the major architects of the transformation of Japan into a modern state, Prince Ito, Prime Minister on repeated occasions (1892–96, 1898, 1900–1) and Resident General in Korea from 1905 to 1909, left his diary and personal papers.[331] They concern principally his mission to St. Petersburg in the fall of 1901 and the conclusion of the Anglo-Japanese Alliance of January 30, 1902. From this material it becomes clear that Prince Ito was not too favorably disposed toward binding his country to Great Britain in an alliance and that,

[331] Atsushi Hiratsuka, *Ito Hirobumi Hiroku* [The Hirobumi Ito Documents] (Tokyo: Shinjiusha, 1929).

moreover, he entertained some doubts as to Great Britain's motives in seeking a hard and fast agreement with Japan. He appears, instead, to have been convinced that his efforts toward reaching an accord with Russia which would assure Japanese domination in Korea could be successful if, in return, Japan would recognize Russia's pre-eminent role in Manchuria. However, it seems certain that the St. Petersburg government would have regarded such an agreement only as a temporary *modus vivendi* until such time as the completion of the Trans-Siberian railway opened the Far East to further Russian expansion. For a detailed study of Prince Ito and his activities, reference should be made to the well-documented biography by Kengi Hamada,[332] considered to be of fundamental importance for an understanding of Japanese policy at the turn of the century.

For this period, the volumes on Prince Ito find an important supplement in the memoirs of Count Tadasu Hayashi,[333] Minister and, later, Ambassador to London from 1899 to 1906 and Minister of Foreign Affairs from 1906 to 1908. Some doubts had been raised about the care exercised by the publisher to ensure the accuracy of the memoirs, but a comparison of these volumes with the documents appearing in the volumes on Prince Ito prove that these doubts are unfounded. The importance of these recollections lies in their reference to the negotiations for the Anglo-Japanese Alliance. Hayashi's contribution is of major significance, not only because it adds copious detail to Prince Ito's documents, but because it provides a clear picture of the forces in Japan favoring the agreement with London, of which Hayashi was one, and compares them with those elements favoring a close arrangement with Russia. After the author became Foreign Minister, despite the fact that he saw no need for an agreement with Russia, since Japan was allied to Great Britain, he did not oppose the French initiative to arrange a Russo-Japanese *rapprochement.* It is entirely possible that this attitude was prompted by questions of internal policy; that is, Hayashi may have wished to avoid placing himself in conflict with the very influential Prince Ito. Hayashi's memoirs emerge as a major source of information on this cycle of negotiations, concluded with the accord of July 30, 1907, which delimited Russian and Japanese spheres of influence in Manchuria, Mongolia, and Korea.

The two autobiographical volumes left by Shigenobu Okuma[334] are a

---

[332] *Prince Ito. A Biography of Japan's Greatest Statesman* (London: Allen and Unwin, 1937).

[333] A. M. Pooley (ed.), *The Secret Memoirs of Count Tadasu Hayashi, 1850–1913* (London: Nash, 1915).

[334] *Kaikoku gojunen shi* [Fifty Years of Modern Japan] (2 vols.; Tokyo: Waseda, 1908–9). English translation, *Fifty Years of New Japan* (2 vols.; London: Smith, 1910).

significant digest of the long and active public life, spanning almost the entire second half of the nineteenth century, of one of Japan's most eminent statesmen. From the point of view of foreign policy, the volumes containing the Okuma papers are infinitely more important,[335] and they also cover the years in which he returned to public service as Prime Minister, 1914 to 1916. The latter part of this work is probably the more significant because it refers to the debates in the government over the question of Japan's intervention in World War I and the issue of the Twenty-one Demands, particularly as they concerned the internal aspects of the treaty negotiations in Peking.

The diplomatic negotiations relative to this treaty are discussed in detail in the two-volume biography of Baron Takaaki Kato by Masanori Ito,[336] incorporating a number of Kato's papers. Baron Kato had been Minister of Foreign Affairs in the Okuma Cabinet of 1914–15 (the same post he had held in the Ito ministry of 1900–1 and again in 1906 and in 1913) and was responsible for the creation of Japan's expansionist program in China and for its implementation when the outbreak of World War I provided the ideal opportunity. In addition to the value of the data they provide on these negotiations,[337] Kato's papers are of prime importance for a study of Japanese policy during the last years of the nineteenth century, when it was faced with the problem of escaping the isolation that had forced it to accept the Peace of Shimonoseki after the Sino-Japanese War. During that period, 1894–99, Kato was Japan's Minister to London, and returned to that post as Ambassador from 1906 to 1913. From the beginning, he was among the strongest advocates of an Anglo-Japanese alliance, even to the point of offering his resignation after the negotiations of 1898 failed to produce an accord.

Kato's successor at the Foreign Ministry, Viscount Ishii,[338] Ambassador to Paris from 1912 to 1915 and Director of the Gaimusho until 1916, has left an important account of his public service. However, he is best remembered for the agreement that bears his name, along with that of the American Secretary of State, Lansing, signed at the conclusion of his negotiations in Washington in the fall of 1917. Ishii reports the details of his efforts in Washington, which were the climax of the intense Japanese diplomatic activity designed to facilitate the implementation of the Twenty-one

---

[335] Kenkichi Ichijima (ed.), *Okumako Hachijugonenshi* [The Marquess Okuma's Eighty-five Years] (3 vols.; Tokyo, 1926).

[336] *Kato Takaaki* (2 vols.; Tokyo: Kato Haku Denki Hensan Iin-Kai, 1929).

[337] On this question, see Toscano, *Guerra diplomatica in Estremo Oriente, 1914–1931. I trattati delle ventun domande* (2 vols.; Turin: Einaudi, 1950).

[338] Kikujiro Ishii, *Gaiko Yoroku* [Diplomatic Recollections] (Tokyo: Iwatami Shoten, 1930); American translation, *Diplomatic Commentaries* (Baltimore: The Johns Hopkins Press, 1936).

Demands agreement. This is perhaps the most significant part of his memoirs, which are also extremely useful for a study of their author's diplomatic activity.

f. The Turks.

Turkish memoirs are generally of only marginal interest, and the majority focus on the internal controversy over the policies of the various factions in power after 1908. General Moukhtar Pasha, Navy and War Minister between 1910 and 1912 and then Ambassador to Berlin until 1914, has written on Turkish policy from the Congress of Berlin to World War I,[339] basing his study on his memoirs and on modest documentation drawn from the Turkish archives. In this study, the author seeks to demonstrate that the dissolution of the Ottoman Empire was due to the excessive Germanophile tendencies among the extremist elements of the new movement. In his view, if the Young Turks had sought the friendship and help of the French and the British, from whose institutions they had drawn their inspiration, the catastrophe would have been avoided. Moreover, Moukhtar adds, siding with Germany brought no assurance of German support and friendship. The latter, according to the author, failed to inform the Sublime Porte of the Serbo-Bulgarian alliance, of which he was aware, and during his stay in Berlin he discovered that the German government was not averse to discussing with other countries the partition of Turkey into spheres of influence. Despite the fact that many of Moukhtar's observations are not readily acceptable, his contribution is worthy of attention.

Marshal Izzet Pasha, Chief of Staff of the Turkish armed forces from 1908 to 1912 and Minister and Grand Vizier on repeated occasions, is equally critical of the policies of the groups led by Talaat and Enver Pasha. Notwithstanding the fact that the subtitle of his memoirs[340] indicates that the volume is a critical examination of war responsibility, the author includes a detailed summary of his personal political and military experiences. He reveals that he was acutely aware of the military deficiencies of the Ottoman Empire and for this reason contributed to the decision of the government to accept the loss of Bosnia-Herzegovina, as well as to recognize the complete independence of Bulgaria during the crisis of 1908, without serious protest. On the other hand, Izzet Pasha adds, it was obvious that war in the Balkans was only a matter of time and therefore it was imperative that Turkey at least assure herself of Greek friendship. However,

[339] Moukhtar Pascha, La Turquie, l'Allemagne et l'Europe depuis le traité de Berlin jusqu'à la Guerre mondiale (Paris: Berger-Levrault, 1924).

[340] Denkwürdigkeiten des Marschalles Izzet Pascha. Ein Kritischen Bertrag zur Kriegschuldfrage (Leipzig: Koehler, 1927).

the Turkish government rejected his advice, nor did it accept his suggestion that Italy be allowed virtually a free hand to expand economically in Libya, in order to avoid a war. In the light of what Giolitti writes in his memoirs, Izzet Pasha's observations on this point are not without foundation. Concerning the Libyan war, Izzet Pasha states that an even more serious error was committed in continuing the conflict after it became obvious that territorial concessions could not be avoided. In so doing, the Balkan states were given time to prepare their attack against European Turkey. The final blow to the fortunes of the Ottoman Empire, he concludes, came with the decision to intervene in the European war, and this responsibility lies exclusively with Enver Pasha.

Turkish intervention in the European war is seen from an entirely different perspective by General Gemal Pasha, Navy Minister in 1914. In his memoirs,[341] Gemal Pasha views the alliance with Germany of August 2, 1914, as inevitable and adds that Germany was the only European power with no designs on Turkish territory. However, this was not the only condition that prompted Turkey to seek German friendship. Germany also had well-defined political and economic reasons for seeking to prevent the dismemberment of the Ottoman Empire desired by the Entente. If the Entente's ambition was realized, Germany stood to lose an area of great commercial importance to it, and the German world would be surrounded by Entente powers. If these observations are correct, it can also be added that the problems of the "Goeben" and the "Breslau" had no decisive influence in drawing the Ottoman Empire into the conflict, as so many have asserted. This memoir also contains pertinent data on the Arab revolt of 1915–16. For the war years, the volume by Ahmed Emin in the Carnegie Series should be mentioned,[342] although the author depended almost exclusively on the papers in the Turkish Embassy in Paris to reconstruct the events leading to Turkey's entrance in the war.

g. The Bulgarians.

King Ferdinand left no memoir on Bulgarian foreign policy from the Balkan wars to World War I. However, useful data may be found in the biographies of the Bulgarian ruler,[343] especially in the biography by Madol,

---

[341] Ahmed Djemal Pascha, *Erinnerungen eines türkischen Staatsmannes* (Munich: Drei-Masken-Verlag, 1922).

[342] *Turkey in the World War* (New Haven, Conn.: Yale University Press, 1930).

[343] Dimitri Jotzoff, *Zar Ferdinand von Bulgarien* (Berlin: Ostergaard, 1927); Paul Lindenberg, *Ferdinand I. Das Buch von Zaren der Bulgaren* (Berlin: Curt Hamels, 1928); Hans Roger Madol, *Ferdinand von Bulgarien* (Berlin: Universitas, 1931).

who was privileged to see some of the King's papers. Two important contributions are made by the prime ministers Gheschov (1911–13) and Radoslavov (1913–18). Especially in the first of his works,[344] Gheschov describes the motives that led him to press for the creation of the Balkan League and provides an accurate summary of the negotiations leading to the alliances with Serbia and Greece. Obviously, Gheschov is trying to defend his position by denial of responsibility for the aggressive policy begun by Bulgaria in 1911. This responsibility was rightfully his because he set in motion the events that were to be so disastrous for Bulgaria. Within certain limits, Gheschov succeeds in defending his actions and in shifting the responsibility for the second Balkan war to King Ferdinand. However, the fact remains that by the Treaty of London, which ended the first Balkan war, Bulgaria did not achieve the objectives Gheschov hoped to realize, and the country was placed in a difficult situation.

Radoslavov's volume[345] is also defensive in character, but this fact does not reduce its value, particularly since it is well documented and covers the period from 1913 to the end of the war. Despite the fact that he was writing during a period of Bulgarian defeat because of his pro-Austrian policy, he refuses to deny that such a policy was justified, asserting that in 1912 Russia demonstrated that it paid little attention to Bulgarian interests and that in 1913 Russia had aided Bulgaria's enemies by encouraging Greece and Rumania to attack Bulgaria. In contrast, Austria was the only European power to assume a revisionist position regarding the Treaty of Bucharest. In effect, Radoslavov insists that Bulgaria did not simply make a choice but followed the only course compatible with its interests. The author also furnishes a number of particulars on the negotiations with Russia in 1915, supplementing the data provided by Savinsky on Russian diplomatic activity in Sofia. One of the wartime episodes that the author discusses in some detail concerns Bethmann-Hollweg's attempts to open negotiations with Russia, both before and after the fall of the Czar, through Radoslavov's son-in-law, Rizov, who was Bulgarian Minister to Berlin.

The memoirs of the Bulgarian diplomats cover the same period and the same problems: the memoirs of Kalinkov,[346] Minister to Bucharest from 1911 to 1913, contain some new elements on the first Balkan war; the

[344] Ivan Estratieff Guechoff, *L'alliance balkanique* (Paris: Hachette, 1915); *La genèse de la guerre mondiale. Le débâcle de l'alliance balkanique* (Berne: Haupt, 1919) (the latter is a continuation of the former and, in part, a revision); *Spomeni i studii* [Studies and Recollections] (Sofia: Glushkov, 1928).

[345] Vasil Radoslawoff, *Bulgarien und die Weltkrise* (Berlin: Ullstein, 1923).

[346] Georgi Kalinkov, *Romanija i nejnata politika spremo Bulgarija prez 1911–1913. Dokumenti i spomeni* [Rumania and Her Bulgarian Policy, 1911–1913. Documents and Recollections] (Sofia: Balkan, 1917).

recollections of Magiarov,[347] Minister to London from 1912 to 1914 and then to St. Petersburg until 1915, are useful as supplements to Radoslavov's contribution. On the whole, however, they are much inferior to the writings of the two prime ministers.

Only general references to Bulgarian policy, but with some pertinent comment on the court circles in Sofia and on Bulgarian politicians, are to be found in the volume by Madame Pétroff,[348] wife of General Ratcho Pétroff, Prime Minister from 1903 to 1906. Somewhat more interesting are the comments by Anna Stanchoff,[349] the Queen's Lady-in-Waiting and the wife of Dimitri Stanchoff, Foreign Minister from 1906 to 1908 and Minister to Paris from 1908 to 1915.

h. The Spaniards.

The fact that Spain for a long time remained at the periphery of major European policy renders Spanish memoirs useful largely for the study of problems in which Spain had a direct interest.

The memoir covering the longest period is that of Count de Romanones,[350] President of the Council on several occasions (in November, 1912, from the end of 1915 until April, 1917, and from December, 1917, until April, 1918) and Foreign Minister from February to April, 1931. While his memoir reveals his considerable knowledge of European affairs, its major interest lies in Romanones' comments on the Moroccan question, which, particularly after the loss of Cuba and the Philippines, had become the key issue in Spanish policy.[351] He provides a detailed account of the negotiations of 1902 with Delcassé, which, despite the fact that they resulted in an accord on Morocco, were not effective. The Conservative government led by Silvela, who replaced the Liberal, Sagasta, did not consider it opportune to reach an agreement with France without British participation. Romanones also comments in detail on the Agadir crisis and on the negotiations leading to the Franco-Spanish treaty of 1912. His narrative is not limited to the purely diplomatic aspects of the situation but includes detailed commentary on the differences existing between the Conservatives and the

[347] Michail J. Madzarov, *Diplomaticeska Podgotovka na nasite vojni* [The Diplomatic Preparation of Our Wars] (Sofia: Mir, 1932).

[348] Sultane Petroff, *Trente ans à la cour de Bulgarie 1887–1918* (Paris: Berger-Levrault, 1927).

[349] *Recollections of a Bulgarian Diplomatist's Wife* (London: Hutchinson, 1932).

[350] Alvaro Figueroa Y Torres Conde de Romanones, *Las responsabilidades políticas del antiguo régimen, de 1875 a 1923* (Madrid: Renacimiento, 1924).

[351] For the Spanish point of view on this issue, see José María Areilza and Fernando María Castiella, *Reivindicaciones de España* (Madrid: Instituto de Estudios Políticos, 1941); José María Campoamor, *La actitúd de España ante la cuestión de Marruecos, 1900–1904* (Madrid: Instituto de Estudios Africanos, 1951).

Liberals on matters of foreign policy, differences which contributed to blocking Spain's entry into the war throughout the entire period of the conflict.

Among the memoirs of Spanish diplomats, reference should be made to those of the Marquis Leon y Castillo,[352] Ambassador to Paris for a long period and Spanish delegate to the 1898 conference to resolve the United States-Spanish conflict, who later negotiated the treaty of 1904 on Morocco. Equally important are the memoirs of the Count of Cartagena on his mission to Russia,[353] which provide new data in support of the thesis that major responsibility for the war lay with the Czarist government. The author notes that by mid-July, 1914, important concentrations of Russian troops were already at the frontier and that Poincaré's visit to St. Petersburg greatly strengthened the extremist elements in Russia. Note should also be made of the memoirs of the Spanish military attaché in Sofia, Lon,[354] for his recollections on Bulgaria during the war.

i. The Chinese.[355]

The "discovery" of the Occident by the Chinese occurred toward the end of the last century, after the opening of China to trade and the establishment of diplomatic relations between the Imperial Court at Peking and the major western powers, when the Chinese developed an interest in European culture. This interest was aroused primarily by the translation of the western classics into Chinese, especially those concerning political and economic thought, but also by the summaries, the diaries, and the books written by Chinese (in truth, not many) who, for reasons of trade or study, had occasion to visit Europe or America.

These writings are of no particular importance to the study of diplomatic relations between China and the Occident. In general, they are expository writings in which the authors sought to condense their impressions of foreign lands and focus on the strange, curious, and "esoteric" aspects of the lives of the foreigners.

The majority of these accounts were contained in an enormous collection published in three series between 1891 and 1897.[356] The last series contains

---

[352] Fernando Leon y Castillo, *Mis tiempos* (2 vols.; Madrid: Hernando, 1921).

[353] Anibal Morillo Conde de Cartagena, "En homenaje. Recuerdos de mi Embajada en Rusia," *Boletín de la Academia de la Historia*, October–December, 1931.

[354] Manuel M. Lon, *Bulgaria en la guerra europea* (Talleres del depósito da la guerra, 1920).

[355] This section has been written with the advice and direction of Giuliano Bertuccioli.

[356] *Hsiao-fang-hu chai yu-ti ts'ung-ch'ao* [Collection of Documents on the Geography of the Study of the Little Square Teapot] (Shanghai: Chuitang, 1891,

a summary account by Hung Hsün,[357] a Chinese official who made an official visit to Italy in 1887–88, perhaps for the purpose of purchasing arms. His is a detailed summary similar to the reports sent periodically by diplomats to their home governments to give a view of the situation existing in the countries to which they are accredited. In the same period the diplomat Hsieh Fu-ch'eng also published his memoirs of his stay in Italy during the spring of 1891, and these were later translated into Italian.[358]

The diary kept by K'ang Yu-wei of his journey in Italy,[359] a journey he undertook immediately after the failure of the experiment of the Hundred Days of Reform, is of greater interest to Italians. He proposed to describe to his fellow countrymen a country that he delighted in comparing with China. Like China, he noted, it possessed an ancient civilization, and, like China, it had been invaded and enslaved by foreigners. If Italy, infinitely smaller than China, had been able to rid herself of the foreign barbarians, why could not the Chinese do the same? K'ang Yu-wei also insisted on laboring the point of Italy's small size in order to invite his compatriots to resist the demand of the Italian government for a concession on San-mun Bay, which was being advanced in that period.

Important work was done in the general area of diplomatic relations by the principal figures on the Chinese political scene, and it has been collected in their complete works. Let it suffice here merely to list some of the most important authors: Li Hung-chang,[360] Chang Chih-tung,[361] and Yuan Shih-k'ai.[362] If it is recalled that Li Hung-chang conducted Chinese

---

1894, 1897). Reprinted by the photolithographic process in Taipeh by Kuang-ta, 1962.

[357] *Ibid.*, Vols. IX–XI, chih: *Yu-li I-ta-li wen-chien-lu* [Notes and Experiences during a Journey across Italy].

[358] Z. Volpicelli, *Le impressioni di un cinese in Italia (10 marzo–3 aprile, 1891)* (Naples: Pierro, 1902).

[359] *Ita-li yu-chi* [Memoirs of an Italian Journey] (Shanghai: Kuang-chih, 1905). The Italian translation of the most interesting pages was done by G. Bertuccioli, "Il viaggio in Italia di K'ang Yu-wei," in *Cina*, III (1958).

[360] *Li Wen-chung kung ch'üan-chi* [The Complete Works of Li Hung-chang] (100 vols.; no publisher, n.p., 1908). New edition published by the Shanghai Commercial Press, 1921. Reprinted by the photolithographic process in seven volumes in Taipeh by Wen-hai, 1962.

[361] *Chang Wen-hsiang kung ch'uan-chi* [The Complete Works of Chang Chih-tung] (no publisher, n.p., 1928), 229 chapters in 120 vols. New edition, 1937. Reprinted by the photolithographic process in six volumes in Taipeh by Wen-hai, 1964.

[362] Shen Tzu-hsien (ed.), *Yang-shou-yuan tsou-i chi-yao* [Selected Memoirs of Yuan Shih-k'ai] (no publisher, n.p., 1937), 44 chapters in 6 volumes; Hsü Yu-p'eng (ed.), *Yuan ta-tsung-t'ung shu-tu hui-pien* [The Collected Correspondence of President Yuan] (Shanghai: Kuang-i, 1920); reprinted in Taipeh by Wen-hsin, 1962.

foreign policy during the last decade of the nineteenth century, that Chang Chih-tung was one of the most "enlightened" of all of the Chinese statesmen of that period, a governor of provinces and an instigator of reforms, and that Yuan Shih-k'ai terminated his career as President of the Chinese Republic, it is possible to understand the significance of their works to the study of recent Chinese history.[363]

Insofar as Italy is concerned, reference should be made to the complete works of Liu K'un-i (posthumously called Chung-ch'eng),[364] a government official who, during his long career, held many important posts, among them the governorships of the two provinces of Kiangsu and Chekiang from 1891 to his death in 1902.[365] It was he who had to take defensive measures to protect the Chinese coasts against the threatened Italian landing when it appeared that Italy might insist on its demands for a concession on San-mun Bay by force. Yet Liu K'un-i was one of the high government officials who realized the need to reach agreements with the foreigners in order to avoid greater damage to China. During the crisis provoked by the Boxer Rebellion, he was clearly opposed to the Boxers, with the result that the foreigners living in the provinces under his control were spared and, in turn, his provinces were spared invasion by the international expeditionary force.

[363] On these memorials, see Chung-li Chang and Stanley Spector, *Guide to the Memorials of Seven Leading Officials of Nineteenth-Century China* (Seattle: University of Washington Press, 1959); J. K. Fairbank, *Ch'ing Documents* (Cambridge, Mass.: Harvard University Press, 1959); and the tables of contents prepared by the Seminar for Modern Chinese Studies of the Toyo Bunko of Tokyo, 1955 *et seq.*

[364] *Liu Chung-ch'eng Kung i-chi* [The Works of Liu Chung-ch'eng], in 66 books, 1921. A new edition has been published under the title *Liu k'ung-i i-chi* [The Works of Liu K'un-i] (6 vols.; Shanghai: Chung-hua, 1959). The writings of Liu K'un-i also include telegrams, dispatches, memorials to the throne, etc. The San-mun episode is of most direct concern.
    Letters:
    1) Vol. V, p. 2250, n. 27: To Li Shou-t'ing (14th day of the IV lunation of 1899)
    2) Vol. V, p. 2251, n. 30: To Li Shou-t'ing (V lunation of 1899)
    3) Vol. V, p. 2257, n. 40: To Yu Shou-shan (10th day of the X lunation of 1899)
    Memorials to the throne:
    1) Vol. III, pp. 1139–40 (23rd day of the VI lunation of 1899)
    2) Vol. III, pp. 1169–70 (20th day of the X lunation of 1899)
    3) Vol. III, pp. 1194–96 (16th day of the XII lunation of 1899)
    Telegrams:
    1) Vol. III, p. 1422, n. 87 (14th day of the IV lunation of 1899)
    2) Vol. III, p. 1423, n. 88 (16th day of the IV lunation of 1899)
    3) Vol. III, p. 1428, n. 94 (1st day of the X lunation of 1899)
    4) Vol. III, p. 1428, n. 95 (30th day of the X lunation of 1899)

[365] See the biography in A. W. Hummel, *Eminent Chinese of the Ch'ing Period* (Washington, 1943), Vol. I.

Chapter VI

MEMOIR SOURCES FOR WORLD WAR II
AND ITS ORIGINS

SUMMARY 1. The Italian Memorialists: a. Ciano; b. Aloisi; c. Guariglia; d. The Other Italian Memoir Sources. 2. The French Memorialists: a. Bonnet; b. Charles-Roux; c. De Gaulle; d. The Other French Memoir Sources. 3. The British Memorialists: a. Henderson; b. Churchill; c. Hoare; d. The Other British Memoir Sources. 4. The German Memorialists: a. Stresemann; b. Curtius; c. Kordt; d. The Other German Memoir Sources. 5. The American Memorialists: a. Hull; b. Welles; c. Leahy; d. The Other American Memoir Sources. 6. The Japanese Memorialists: a. Konoye; b. Shigemitsu; c. Togo; d. The Other Japanese Memoir Sources. 7. The Chinese Memorialists. 8. The Polish Memorialists: a. Beck; b. Ciechanowski; c. The Other Polish Memoir Sources. 9. The Czechoslovak Memorialists: a. Beneš; b. The Other Czechoslovak Memoir Sources. 10. The Austrian Memorialists: a. Schuschnigg; b. The Other Austrian Memoir Sources. 11. The Hungarian Memorialists: a. Kállay; b. The Other Hungarian Memoir Sources. 12. The Yugoslav Memorialists: a. Fotic; b. The Other Yugoslav Memoir Sources. 13. The Rumanian Memorialists: a. Gafencu; b. The Other Rumanian Memoir Sources. 14. The Finnish Memorialists: a. Tanner; b. The Other Finnish Memoir Sources. 15. The Swedish and Norwegian Memorialists: a. Dahlerus; b. The Other Swedish and Norwegian Memoir Sources. 16. The Belgian and Dutch Memorialists: a. Van Zuylen; b. The Other Belgain and Dutch Memoir Sources. 17. The Spanish Memorialists: a. Serrano Suñer; b. Doussinague. 18. The Memorialists of Other Countries: a. The Swiss; b. The Greeks; c. The Soviets; d. The Turks, the South Africans, and the Argentines

1. THE ITALIAN MEMORIALISTS.

a. Ciano.

The most important Italian memoir source is undoubtedly Ciano's diary. It consists of daily annotations made by the Foreign Minister in a Red

Cross notebook, a practice copied from Ambassador Aloisi, Mussolini's Head of Cabinet and Ciano's *de facto* predecessor. Seven of these notebooks make up the diary, and it was kept almost uninterruptedly for the entire time Ciano held his post at the Foreign Office; that is, from June, 1936, to February, 1943. After July 25, 1943, five of these notebooks, comprising the annotations beginning with January 1, 1939, were transferred to Switzerland and sold by Ciano's wife, Edda, in order that the public could be given a manuscript which, according to Ciano, would demonstrate to the world the steps taken by him to resist German policy and the efforts he made to keep Italy out of the war.

The American edition was the first to be published;[1] however, it was incomplete because of the omission of those topics that were considered to be of little interest to the American public. This was followed by a French edition, published in Switzerland,[2] which can be assumed to be the most accurate, since it was published directly from the original. The Italian edition,[3] which appeared before the French one, was assembled from photographic copies, and this method presented a number of disadvantages due to the fact that a few of the photographed pages were lost and several others were inserted in the volume incorrectly.

The diary itself is preceded by an introduction written by Ciano while he was in prison in Verona, in which he emphasizes his resistance to the course that events were taking during the Salzburg meeting of August 11–13, 1939, and the steps he took to prevent Mussolini from immediately supporting Hitler. These assertions should be clarified, since they coincide directly with the popular evaluation of Ciano's attitude during the period which, on the whole, is incorrect.

Concerning the Salzburg meeting, which now can also be reconstructed on the basis of the published Italian and German documents, there is no doubt that Ciano arrived on the scene determined to resist and that, in fact, he maintained an unyielding position during the first two meetings with Von Ribbentrop and Hitler. However, during the course of the third colloquy, when Hitler reaffirmed his point of view, Ciano's determination to stand fast clearly waned, and toward the end of that meeting, his attitude became, in effect, one of acquiescence. This act definitely weakened Italy's position and culminated in the misunderstanding referred to in the discussion on the Italian diplomatic documents.

The action taken by Ciano to block the Italian declaration of war also requires clarification. It is true that in the summer of 1939 he worked assiduously to eliminate the danger of Italian intervention on the side of

---

[1] *The Ciano Diaries (1939–1943)* (New York: Doubleday, 1945).

[2] *Journal Politique (1939–1943)* (Neuchâtel: La Baconnière, 1946), Vol. II.

[3] *Diario I (1939–1940); II (1941–1943)* (Milan: Rizzoli, 1946).

Germany, but it is equally true that, after the German occupation of Denmark and Norway, he did very little to prevent Mussolini from dragging Italy into the war. It may be noted, in this context, that the situation in 1940 was profoundly altered because Mussolini was now firmly determined to intervene and neither Ciano nor anyone else would have been able to force him to retreat from that position. Moreover, the limited opposition Ciano offered Mussolini was due less to the knowledge that he could do nothing to change the course of events than to a shift in his thinking which, in the light of the military developments on the western front, brought him around to Mussolini's point of view and led him to share the latter's objectives.

Consequently, when Ciano wrote the introduction to his diary, he altered the facts in the belief that it would thus show him in a more favorable light. He recorded that he fought against Italian intervention in 1939, but made no mention of his failure to oppose it in 1940. Moreover, he completely forgot to mention that he had been the master architect of the foreign policy leading to the creation of the Rome-Berlin Axis, the Pact of Steel, and the crisis with France. He neglected to mention that he displayed no particular haste in tackling current crucial problems in order to eliminate quickly the misunderstandings that had developed, nor did he mention that immediately after the conclusion of military operations against France he sought excessive territorial compensations. Finally, he overlooked the major role he played in reaching the decision to attack Greece, as well as his responsibility for the conduct of Italian foreign policy until the attack on the U.S.S.R.

What remained firmly in Ciano's memory, apparently, were those of his activities that were critical of what he himself had helped to fashion. However, if the historical value of Ciano's introduction is relatively limited, the contrary is true of the diary itself, which remains a source of prime importance.

His annotations were made when events had just crystallized or when they were in the development stage, and he faithfully reports not only episodes of major interest but also his impressions, state of mind, and the "atmosphere"—a complex of elements that cannot be found in official documents but that effectively re-create the environment and serve to place the "document" in its proper perspective.

Obviously, the diary, hurriedly written without any thought given to form or style, was not designed for publication but was to serve the author as primary material on which to base his memoirs at a later date. This explains its frequently irritating frankness, its crudity, its cynicism, and its inclusion of assertions that are not always complimentary to himself or to the point of view he defends. But the very fact that Ciano was unable to edit what he had written[4] makes this source exceptionally valuable, and it has a genuineness and immediacy that is extremely rare.

As has been noted, the first part of Ciano's diary, covering the years 1937–38, had been left in Rome by Countess Ciano. These two notebooks fell into German hands, were recovered only at the end of the war, and were published in an Italian edition.[5] They reveal a completely different Ciano, a great admirer of his father-in-law and completely under the latter's influence, and there is something to be gained from comparing Ciano's attitude as the faithful executor of orders with his strongly critical attitude in the later period.

b. Aloisi.

No other Italian memoir source for the period between the two world wars can be compared with Ciano's diary for historical interest. Nevertheless, there is no dearth of important memoirs, principally the work of diplomats or former diplomats, whose usefulness is very great because only a small part of the documentation contained in the archives of Palazzo Chigi has been published in the collection of Italian documents.

Among these, the diary of Baron Pompeo Aloisi[6] is of primary significance. Aloisi's career took him to Bucharest and Tirana as Minister and later to Tokyo and Ankara as Ambassador. In July, 1932, he became Chief of Cabinet in the Foreign Ministry and head of the Italian delegation to the League of Nations in September, 1932.

At the time when Aloisi assumed these posts, the Italian government seemed to be oriented toward a policy of international collaboration. In contradiction to this constructive bent, there was evidence of attitudes and initiatives that indicated a desire to make Italian policy more dynamic, capable of creating new situations from which Italy could profitably strengthen its position or weaken that of its probable adversaries. These largely contradictory platforms were to merge into a single aggressive policy during the course of the Ethiopian crisis.

The failure of the disarmament conference clearly forecast the renewal of international rivalries among European nations and had the effect of inducing Mussolini to step up the time schedule for a solution of the Ethiopian problem in order to avoid the obstacles that other rearmed nations might present to the execution of his plans.

[4] An exception to this concerns some points relative to the compaign in Greece that Ciano himself modified when, after February, 1943, he became Ambassador to the Holy See.

[5] *1937–1938 Diario* (Bologna: Cappelli, 1948).

[6] Aloisi's diary, to date, has been published only in French translation: Baron Aloisi, *Journal (25 juillet 1932–14 juin 1936)* (Paris: Plon, 1957).

There is no doubt that Mussolini, in pursuing his expansionist objectives in East Africa, was also attracted by a desire to strengthen the military prestige of the Fascist regime, a factor that made him extremely reluctant to accept a peaceful solution to the controversy with Ethiopia. On the other hand, at the Foreign Ministry, at least in the initial stages, an attempt was made to pursue a different course, that is, to seek a solution to the problem within the framework of the League of Nations and to do so without rupturing the European solidarity which was also to Italy's interest.

This course was characterized by the common action taken in defense of Austrian independence and in a policy of *rapprochement* with France culminating in the Mussolini-Laval accords of January, 1935. Evidently, Mussolini hoped to gain the good will of the western powers and French acquiescence primarily because of the concessions made in consular conventions for the Italians in Tunisia. However, considered as preliminary moves in preparation for the Ethiopian undertaking, the action of the Italian government was weak on two counts: first, on the diplomatic level, no agreement had been reached with London, which had a major interest in maintaining the *status quo* in East Africa; and second, from the psychological viewpoint, no consideration was given to the reactions he would arouse by openly defying convictions that were deeply-rooted in Anglo-Saxon public opinion.

These events marked a decisive turn in Fascist foreign policy, and since the documentation on the period is extremely limited, Aloisi's testimony assumes singular importance. Aloisi was in the position of viewing events from two vantage points, Rome and Geneva, and he recorded his day-by-day impressions of events, his personal activity, and the work of the entire ministry. These were hurried notes without regard for form or style, designed to serve as source material for a volume on foreign policy which Aloisi planned to write after his retirement from active service. These circumstances occasionally make it difficult to interpret his notes, but this difficulty is offset by a spontaneity and immediacy that would probably have been lost if the author had planned on the diary's publication from the start.

c. Guariglia.

The nearly eight hundred pages of Ambassador Guariglia's memoirs,[7] covering the period 1922–43, differ substantially from the Aloisi recollec-

[7] Raffaele Guariglia, *Ricordi* (Naples: E.S.I., 1950). Guariglia also wrote a brief article, "Primi passi in diplomazia," (*Nuova Antologia*, December, 1951), concerning the early years of his career down to 1922.

tions. In contrast to the Ciano and Aloisi diaries, this volume was written some years after the events to which the author refers, and, despite the fact that it includes documentary material from the author's private files, it is obviously the result of careful *post factum* reflection. Thus, the spontaneity evident in the two previous sources is lacking here. On the other hand, Guariglia's exposition is more detailed and better organized, and the author does not limit his memoir to his personal activity but seeks to illustrate the more important phases of Italian foreign policy for that period in order to make evaluations and draw conclusions that could serve as lessons for the future.

When these memoirs were published in 1950, they were received with widespread curiosity: Guariglia had been Foreign Minister in the Badoglio Cabinet, and it was assumed that his testimony would throw considerable light on the events leading to Italy's withdrawal from the war.

However, those who expected to find dramatic revelations were disappointed. To be sure, the memoirs undoubtedly contain important data and new facts of some importance, but these have led neither to a radical revision nor a modification of the general outline of the historical picture established earlier. This fact should not be surprising because once the attempts to negotiate with the Allies on the diplomatic level had failed (the missions of Pirelli to Switzerland, Lanza d'Ajeta to Lisbon, and Berio to Tangier), the work of Palazzo Chigi was terminated, and conduct of the negotiations to conclude an armistice was transferred to the military.

The Guariglia memoirs disappointed those who, forgetting the exact limits of the problem, hoped to find information that these documents could not possibly have contained. On the other hand, the memoirs are of major interest to historians, particularly the pages that escaped the attention of most readers, dealing with the period 1922–38.

What Guariglia writes concerning several of his missions—to Spain, October, 1932–August, 1934; to Argentina, December, 1936–September, 1938; to France, December, 1938–June, 1940; to the Holy See, February, 1942–February, 1943; and to Turkey, February–July, 1943—is of minor importance. However, the pages referring to the periods when he was at the ministry are much more significant; that is, from October, 1922, to the summer of 1932 as Director General of Political Affairs for Europe, the Levant, and the Mediterranean, and from April, 1935, to November, 1936, when he was put in charge of a special office for Ethiopian affairs. This is the part of the memoir which is the most revealing, and scholars should focus their attention on it also because of the critical comments with which the author accompanies his exposition. A specific example may be found in the complex negotiations conducted over many years between Rome and

Paris to settle the remaining war claims (which resulted from the failure to fulfill the terms of the Pact of London) and to reduce the rivalry between the two Latin countries in the Mediterranean. Guariglia's memoirs provide an adequate reconstruction of the events, as well as a remarkable exposition of the Italian view and position on the issues. These chapters clearly describe the nature of Italian interests in the Mediterranean and the interpretation Mussolini gave to them. No such discerning analysis had previously been attempted.

d. The Other Italian Memoir Sources.

Italian memoir sources for the years immediately following World War I are limited and usually deal with specific problems. Reference is made here to the writing of the former Prime Minister, Nitti,[8] who has recalled with vivid detail the events of the San Remo Conference of 1920; the recollections of the former Ambassador to London and Minister of Foreign Affairs, Della Torretta,[9] who has described the action taken by Italy to solve the Austro-Hungarian controversy over Burgenland; and Sforza's memoirs,[10] which deal in particular with the foreign policy of the last Giolitti Cabinet. To these must be added the important volume by Vittorio Emanuele Orlando[11] on Italian relations with the Holy See, especially the last chapters dealing with the period immediately following the war. On the Fiume question, the memoirs of General Caviglia[12] offer interesting judgments, and the same may be said for Badoglio's recollections,[13] along with the last chapters in the memoirs of Ambassador Carlo Galli.[14] Galli is also responsible for an excellent article[15] containing important data on the attempts made by King Alexander to arrive at an Italo-Yugoslav understanding. The previously cited posthumous memoirs of Antonio Salandra, despite the fact that they are largely centered on internal affairs, contain a number of interesting pages on his activities as Italian delegate to the League of Nations, especially the part concerning the Corfu crisis. For a clearer view of Italy's Albanian policy for the period 1925–30, particular

[8] Francesco Saverio Nitti, *Meditazioni dall'esilio* (Naples: E.S.I., 1947); *Rivelazioni* (Naples: E.S.I., 1948).
[9] Pietro Tomasi Della Torretta, "Ministero degli Affari Esteri 1921," *La Pace*, fasc. June, 1951.
[10] Carlo Sforza, *L'Italia dal 1914 al 1944 quale io la vidi* (Milan: Mondadori, 1946); *Jugoslavia* (Milan: Rizzoli, 1948).
[11] *Miei rapporti di governo con la S. Sede* (Milan: Garzanti, 1943).
[12] Enrico Caviglia, *Il conflitto di Fiume* (Milan: Garzanti, 1948).
[13] Pietro Badoglio, *Rivelazioni su Fiume* (Rome: De Luigi, 1946.)
[14] *Diari e lettere* (Florence: Sansoni, 1951).
[15] "La politica serba per un accordo con l'Italia," *Mondo Europeo*, fasc. January–February, 1946.

attention should be given to Ambassador Quaroni's penetrating study on the Albanian situation.[16]

Alberto Pirelli, the well-known Italian industrialist, has written a volume on the reparations question,[17] one of the problems of major concern to postwar diplomacy. Pirelli records his experiences as an economic expert at the peace conference and at all subsequent economic and financial conferences up to the Lausanne Conference of 1932. Though it is largely a synopsis, the account offers a clear and precise explanation of the main issues involved in the various questions and includes a number of useful particulars for a study of these problems.

On Fascist policy from the advent of Hitler to the outbreak of World War II, the memoirs of Ambassador Roberto Cantalupo[18] are especially noteworthy; their central theme is the activities of his mission to the Franco government, February–April, 1937. His contact with the realities of the Spanish situation led Cantalupo to conclude that a quick end to the civil war was unlikely and that therefore it was in Italy's interest to re-examine its position in order not to become involved in a long war that would be politically and militarily much too costly. He repeatedly warned Rome of the dangers involved, but unsuccessfully, and Ciano preferred to recall him rather than listen to his advice. The volume is limited to a very brief period, but it is nonetheless interesting for what can be learned about the relations between the Falangist government and the Italian authorities and for Franco's important declarations concerning the politico-military lines he intended to follow in prosecuting the war.

Several aspects of Fascist policy on the Austrian problem are illustrated by Dante Maria Tuninetti,[19] who, in February, 1937, was sent to Vienna in an attempt to stabilize relations between Schuschnigg's Patriotic Front and the Austrian Nazis so that Hitler might be prevented from using the Austrian internal situation as a pretext for a solution by force. An understanding in this direction was reached during the Venice meeting of April 22, 1937, between Mussolini and Schuschnigg, but a short time later a journalistic indiscretion by Gayda, designed to commit the Austrian Chancellor publicly, induced the latter to renege on his decision.

A longer period is covered by the memoirs of the former Minister-

[16] Pietro Quaroni, *Valigia diplomatica* (Milan: Garzanti, 1956); see also Quaroni, *Ricordi di un ambasciatore* (Milan: Garzanti, 1954), and "L'Italie et l'Europe," in *L'Europe du XIX et XX Siècle: Problèmes et interpretations historiques* (Milan: Marzorati, 1964), Vol. II.

[17] *Dopoguerra 1919–1932. Note e esperienze* (Milan: n.p., 1961).

[18] *Fu la Spagna. Ambasciata presso Franco (febbraio–aprile 1937)* (Milan: Mondadori, 1948).

[19] *La mia missione segreta in Austria (1937–1938)* (Milan: Bianchi and Sacchi, 1946).

Counsellor in Berlin, Magistrati,[20] who worked with Attolico from 1936 to 1940. Magistrati's recollections consist of a series of articles first published in the *Rivista di Studi Politici Internazionali* and then assembled in one volume.[21]

The chapters of greatest interest are those on the period leading to the signing of the Pact of Steel, on which the Italian diplomatic documents have not yet been published, and on the critical weeks of August, 1939. These pages may profitably be consulted, for they serve to supplement the official documentation with important particulars, including the prevailing atmosphere in Berlin which provided the setting. In general, the work is highly objective, even though the author goes to some length to point out that Italy's responsibilities in precipitating the war should not be allowed to obscure what it did to preserve the peace in 1938 and 1939. Magistrati's detailed exposition of the activities of the Italian Embassy in Berlin in the first of the two crises furnishes additional data and confirms the importance of Italy's role in the Sudeten problem. However, his observations on the events of the summer of 1939 are less satisfactory. It should be noted that Magistrati was not as acutely aware as was Attolico of the need to stress the gravity of the Polish-German crisis immediately, with the result that the impact of Attolico's warnings in Rome was reduced. However, once this difference in evaluation was resolved by the course of events, Magistrati supported Attolico's efforts to stem the drift toward war or, at least, to keep Italy from becoming involved. Other sections that should be mentioned, particularly for their contemporary interest, are those referring to the developments in the Alto Adige question after the *Anschluss* and to the negotiations Magistrati was empowered to conduct with the Wilhelmstrasse for the transfer of the alien South Tyrolese to Germany.

The former Minister to Athens, Emanuele Grazzi, has written a detailed account of the last phase of Italo-Greek relations before the Italian attack of October 28, 1940,[22] making use of an important collection of documents in his possession. The value of this volume as a source diminished considerably after the publication of the official Italian collection of diplomatic

[20] Massimo Magistrati, *L'Italia a Berlino (1937–1939)* (Milan: Mondadori, 1956).

[21] The following articles by Attolico appeared in the *Rivista di Studi Politici Internazionali*: "L'Anschluss austro-tedesca visto da Berlino" (1948, pp. 77–106); "Salisburgo" (1949, pp. 479–510); "La settimana decisiva (agosto 1939)" (1950, pp. 187–232); "Come andammo a Monaco (1938)" (1951, pp. 405–51); "Berlino 1939: da Praga al Patto d'Acciaio" (1952, pp. 597–652); "Berlino 1937: Campo di Maggio" (1953, pp. 525–46). Excluded because of the chronological limits of the volume (1937–September 3, 1939) is the article, "La Germania e l'impresa italiana in Etiopia" (1950, pp. 563–606).

[22] *Il principio della fine (L'impresa di Grecia)* (Rome: Lo Faro, 1945).

documents. However, it remains important for details on specific events, even if certain of Grazzi's interpretations are questionable in the light of the material subsequently published. The same subject is treated by Mondini,[23] while the volumes by Generals Visconti Prasca[24] and Pricolo[25] are concerned primarily, although not exclusively, with the military aspects of the question.

Alfieri's memoirs[26] are less interesting than they were expected to be. Alfieri replaced Attolico as Ambassador to Berlin in the spring of 1940 and remained at that post until the fall of the Fascist government. The volume was written several years after the events occurred, and its style often does not reflect the author's real thoughts at the time of his mission even though there is no reason to doubt the sincerity of his intentions. A case in point is the attempt made during the Salzburg meeting of April 29–30, 1942, to end the war on the Russian front by a compromise peace, exploiting the psychological effects the Germans hoped to obtain by their spring offensive against the U.S.S.R.

The volume by the then secretary of the Embassy in Berlin, Lanza, published under the pseudonym of Simoni,[27] covers approximately the same period. The value of this account, presented in the style of a diary, would have been far greater if it really contained the author's daily annotations. Instead, the publication of the Italian diplomatic documents suggests that the diary was composed after the events, based on material in the Embassy files. In fact, many of the annotations faithfully reproduce the entire text of the communications sent to the ministry or received by the Embassy, and often they are adapted to meet the needs of the account, either in the matter of the date or the content of the document. Meanwhile, the value of the volume has continually diminished as the volumes of the official Italian collection of diplomatic documents have appeared. Yet, the memoir retains some usefulness for the period following Italy's entrance in the war, of course, with the reservations noted above.

Passages of a certain importance are to be found in the memoirs of Anfuso,[28] a career diplomat and Ciano's Head of Cabinet from 1938–41,

[23] Luigi Mondini, *Prologo del conflitto italo-greco* (Rome: Treves, 1945).

[24] Sebastiano Visconti Prasca, *Io ho aggredito la Grecia* (Milan: Rizzoli, 1946).

[25] Francesco Pricolo, *Ignavia contro eroismo* (Rome: Ruffolo, 1946).

[26] Dino Alfieri, *Due dittatori di fronte* (Milan: Rizzoli, 1948).

[27] Leonardo Simoni, *Berlino: Ambasciata d'Italia 1939–1943* (Rome: Migliaresi, 1946). Lanza began his career with Attolico in Moscow and, under the pseudonym Mario da Baranca, has published a volume on his Russian experiences, *Russia e Germania. Vent'anni di storia diplomatica* (Milan: I.S.P.I., 1942), which was immediately withdrawn from circulation.

[28] Filippo Anfuso, *Du palais de Venise au lac de Garde* (Paris: Calmann-Levy, 1949). The following year the work was published in Italian as *Roma-*

later Minister to Budapest, and finally, in response to Mussolini's appeal in September, 1943, representative of the neo-Fascist Salò government in Berlin. Although the author did not set about to prepare an organized and precise account of the events to which he was witness during his tenure in the Palazzo Chigi (he did not have at his disposal any personal annotations or papers), these passages have a certain value in helping to understand the psychological aspects and the personal attitudes of the individual protagonists in the negotiations between Rome and Berlin during the critical days of the Sudeten question, in those leading to the Pact of Steel, the outbreak of the war, and the Italian intervention. The same may be said for what the author writes concerning his mission to Budapest. Anfuso clearly describes the Magyar leadership's preoccupation with suspicion of Germany at the time when Hungary was allied to the Axis in the war against the Soviet Union. Under these conditions the offer made to Ciano in August, 1942, during his visit to Budapest, of a personal union between the Crown of St. Stephen (vacant since 1918) and that of Savoy is not without significance. Ciano received the offer with enthusiam and noted that the proposal raised the prospect of the creation of a block of states, composed of Italy, Croatia, and Hungary, without strong ties to Germany—to the extent that this would be possible. The project was not pursued further because of Mussolini's opposition, which was based on his fear of German reaction to the proposal.

Italo-Rumanian relations during World War II constitute the principal theme of the memoirs of the former Minister to Bucharest, Bova Scoppa.[29] They are a primary source for the study of Rumania's relations with the Axis powers during the war and are of fundamental importance in explaining the changes in German-Rumanian relations after the reconquest of Bessarabia in September, 1941. In effect, at the very moment that Germany needed maximum military support from her allies, the Rumanians realized that further participation in the war against the U.S.S.R. would not produce any tangible advantages for them. Moreover, they saw no possibility of regaining that part of Transylvania assigned to Hungary

---

Berlino-Salò (Milan: Garzanti, 1950). A third and revised edition was subsequently published, Da Palazzo Venezia al lago di Garda (Bologna: Cappelli, 1957).

[29] Renato Bova Scoppa, Colloqui con due dittatori (Rome: Ruffolo, 1949). Recently, Bova Scoppa has summarized his recollections of his entire career in La pace impossibile (Turin: Rosenberg and Sellier, 1961), which is especially useful for the Ethiopian crisis. Bova Scoppa was the secretary of the Italian legation at the League of Nations for that period and consequently in a position to offer direct testimony on the Italian diplomatic activity at Geneva. Although not very detailed, the memoir offers interesting data even though these do not suggest a revision in earlier judgments. As far as other matters touched on in the previous volume are concerned, only a few details are added.

by the Second Arbitrage of Vienna.[30] In this climate, Italo-Rumanian relations improved markedly, with the Rumanians moving to seek Mussolini's support against German control of the Danubian state and, later, with repeated Rumanian attempts to reach an understanding with Italy for a simultaneous withdrawal from the conflict. The numerous contacts, aimed at achieving this goal, between the Vice-President of the Rumanian Council of Ministers, Mihai Antonescu, and Ambassador Bova Scoppa are amply documented in this volume. In the preceding pages, although less dramatically and in less detail, Bova Scoppa summarizes the work of his mission to Lisbon.

Giuseppe Bastianini, Ambassador to Warsaw from 1932 to 1936 and again from February to July, 1943, has recorded his memoirs as a statesman and diplomat in one volume.[31] While it is badly organized, it does contain some important notes. As a source, it is especially valuable for what the author has to say on the conduct of Italian foreign policy during the months preceding the fall of the government in July, 1943, the months in which Bastianini replaced Ciano in the Foreign Ministry, nominally as Undersecretary, but, in practice, as director of the Ministry. Realizing the gravity of the Italian situation, Bastianini aligned himself with those who believed that it was imperative to make it very clear to the Germans that Italy would abandon the alliance if Germany did not recognize the urgency of bringing the war with the Soviet Union to an end. On this issue, Bastianini broke with Mussolini. While pressing Hitler to negotiate a peace in the east, Mussolini was unable to draw the proper consequences from the German refusal.

A wealth of memoir material exists on the events leading to the 1943 armistice between Italy and the Allies. Regarding the initial phases of the negotiations on the purely diplomatic plane, in addition to the volumes by Guariglia and D'Ajeta, the summary by Minister Alberto Berio[32] is noteworthy. Berio engaged in negotiations with the British in Tangier that paralleled those promoted by Guariglia in Lisbon. As is known, these initiatives failed to produce any positive results, but their importance is not reduced because through these talks the Italian government was able to understand the realities of the situation and to learn that the Allies

[30] On this question and on the Rumanian decision to enter the war against the Soviet Union, see Aldus, "Il maresciallo Antonescu e la guerra contro l'U.R.S.S.," *Rivista di Studi Politici Internazionali*, 1948, Nos. 3–4, pp. 335–76.

[31] *Uomini, cose, fatti. Memorie di un ambasciatore* (Milan: Vitagliano, 1959).

[32] *Missione segreta (Tangeri, agosto 1943)* (Milan: Dall'Oglio, 1947). Berio has also published a volume of memoirs on his career, *Dalle Ande all'Himalaya* (Naples: E.S.I., 1961). However, nothing particularly new is revealed on the events leading to the armistice or on other important questions.

intended to conduct the negotiations on a purely military basis. The narratives by Generals Castellano[33] and Zanussi,[34] who were assigned the task of proceeding with the negotiations on the new basis, are, therefore, the starting point for every serious study of the issue. To these must be added the volumes by General Carboni[35] and General Francesco Rossi,[36] which contain other details useful in reconstructing the events.[37]

Memoir sources for the diplomacy of the Republic of Salò are extremely few in number, largely because the sphere of activity of the republic was practically nonexistent. The memoirs of Anfuso, Ambassador to Berlin of the Social Republic, cited above, contain several chapters on this period, but the personal element, rather than a narrative of the events of real historical value, predominates. Considerably more information may be obtained from the memoirs of Mellini Ponce de Leon,[38] Chief of Cabinet in the Ministry of Foreign Affairs of the Republic of Salò, who, after the death of Secretary-General Mazzolini, became liaison officer between Mussolini and the Ministry. The volume includes passages from Mazzolini's unpublished diary, several dispatches sent to Anfuso, and Mellini's diary for the period, February 15–April 23, 1945, a diary that focuses on the internal events related to the final crisis of the neo-Fascist regime.

Concerning the negotiations leading to the surrender at Caserta of April

[33] Giuseppe Castellano, *Come firmai l'armistizio di Cassibile* (Milan: Mondadori, 1945).

[34] Giacomo Zanussi, *Guerra e catastrofe dell'Italia* (2 vols.; Rome: Corso, 1945–46).

[35] Giacomo Carboni, *L'armistizio e la difesa di Roma. Verità e menzogne* (Rome: De Luigi, 1945). This little volume contains the account by General Carboni following the opening of the investigation into the reasons for the failure to defend Rome, prepared in his own defense and as a rebuttal to the account of events written by the journalist Paolo Monelli in 1943. In a second volume, *L'Italia tradita dall'armistizio alla pace* (2d ed.; Rome: Edizioni dell'Ateneo, 1947), the General assembled a series of his articles concerning the armistice and related problems that had appeared in Italian newspapers beginning in 1944 during the violent debate on the events of 1943. In a third volume, *Più che il dovere. Storia di una battaglia italiana (1937–1951)* (Rome: Danesi, 1952), essentially a memoir, Carboni narrates in detail his work with the Italian High Command and devotes particular attention to the position he assumed during the trying summer of 1943.

Some useful information on this subject may be found in "Il Processo Carboni-Roatta," *Rivista Penale*, May–June, 1949, fasc. 5–6. In this article only the motivation for the sentence is published.

[36] *Come arrivammo all'armistizio* (Milan: Garzanti, 1946); *Mussolini e lo Stato Maggiore* (Rome: Tipografia Regionale, 1951).

[37] For a particular aspect of the consequences of the armistice, see Pasquale Jannelli, "Italia e Giappone dopo l'armistizio dell' 8 settembre 1943," *Storia e Politica*, II (1963).

[38] Alberto Mellini Ponce de Leon, *Guerra diplomatica a Salò* (Bologna: Cappelli, 1950), which is primarily a history of the period; *L'Italia entra in guerra* (Bologna: Cappelli, 1963).

29, 1945, which terminated the hostilities between the German armed forces south-west (northern Italy and the Tyrol) and the Allies, the volume by the journalist Ferruccio Lanfranchi,[39] in which he reported the summary account of the event by Luigi Parrilli, is of some importance. As is known, these negotiations originated with Himmler's directive, in the fall of 1944, that an attempt was to be made, by an accord with the Anglo-Americans, to withdraw the German forces from Italy in order to deploy them on the eastern front to stem the Soviet drive toward the heart of Germany. The attempt failed because of the opposition of the Allies to any type of compromise with the Third Reich. Nevertheless, the fact that Berlin was considering an accord of this kind had a deleterious effect on the attitude of the German authorities in Italy. At first it was the Milanese *curia*, toward the end of 1944, that sought to arrange an accord by acting as mediator between the German High Command, the National Committee of Liberation of Northern Italy, and the head of the American Strategic Services, Allen Dulles. In substance, the project envisioned a German retreat from Italy without interference from the partisans of the CLNAI, which the Germans would effect without destroying property other than what was absolutely necessary to protect their retreat. This attempt failed and contact was resumed only toward the end of the winter of 1944-45. Again, the basis for compromise was the same as in the preceding project, and despite the fact that the negotiations were vigorously conducted, due largely to the able mediatory efforts of Baron Parrilli, who was supporting the efforts of the Milanese *curia*, the accord was reached only a few days before Germany's unconditional surrender. While the aim of reducing the period of hostilities in Italy was not fulfilled, these negotiations did, however, have the very important result of saving the Italian industrial complex from the destruction that would have been inevitable in a German retreat, for it was anticipated that they would adopt scorched-earth tactics.

The memoirs of the Italian military should not be ignored as sources, for although they relegate politico-diplomatic affairs to a secondary role, they frequently contain data of some significance. In addition to the military memoirs noted above, special note should be made of Badoglio's recollections.[40] However, these should be used with caution because of the numerous errors, distortions, and omissions they contain. Moreover, note

---

[39] *La resa degli ottocentomila* (Milan: Rizzoli, 1948).

[40] Pietro Badoglio, *L'Italia nella seconda guerra mondiale* (Milan: Mondadori, 1946). A biography of Badoglio has been written by Vanna Vailati, *Badoglio racconta* (Turin: ILTE, 1955). In a later volume, *Badoglio risponde* (Milan: Rizzoli, 1958), Vailati focuses on Badoglio's role in two crucial issues, Caporetto and the armistice of September 8, 1943, subjects which are still often debated.

should be taken of the memoirs of Roatta,[41] Cavallero,[42] Armellini,[43] Graziani,[44] and Favagrossa.[45]

The volume on Mussolini's foreign policy published immediately after the war by the present Ambassador, Mario Luciolli, under the pseudonym of Mario Donosti[46] is unique. By strict definition this work should not be included among memoir sources: it is rather more a piece of historical writing than an actual memoir. However, the distinction in this case is a purely formal one; the author has depended primarily on the material he had occasion to see during his tenure of office in Ciano's Cabinet and later as secretary in the Italian Embassy in Berlin, and integrated it with his personal experiences. Published in 1945, the volume was for a considerable time one of the most important sources for the study of the Fascist government's diplomatic activity, especially useful for the period following the Ethiopian war. In this sense, Donosti's work has lost a good portion of its importance with the publication of the Italian diplomatic documents and other Italian and foreign sources. But, contrary to what normally occurs in such cases, the volume has retained its significance for the correctness of Donosti's over-all judgments and for the often subtle, though fiercely polemical, interpretations that the author gives of Mussolini's diplomacy.

2. THE FRENCH MEMORIALISTS.

a. Bonnet.

Not long after the end of World War II, Georges Bonnet, Minister of Foreign Affairs from April, 1938, until September, 1939, published two volumes of memoirs[47] that immediately attracted the attention of scholars.

[41] Mario Roatta, *Otto milioni di baionette* (Milan: Mondadori, 1946).

[42] Ugo Cavallero, *Comando Supremo. Diario 1940–1943 del Capo di S.M.G.* (Bologna: Cappelli, 1948).

[43] Quirino Armellini, *Diario di guerra. Nove mesi al Comando Supremo* (Milan: Garzanti, 1946).

[44] Rodolfo Graziani, *Ho difeso la Patria* (Milan: Garzanti, 1948); *Africa Settentrionale (1940–1941)* (Rome: Danesi, 1948). Interesting data may be found in the summary of the trial of Marshal Graziani: *Processo Graziani* (3 vols.; Rome: Ruffolo, 1949–50).

[45] Carlo Favagrossa, *Perchè perdemmo la guerra* (Milan: Rizzoli, 1946).

[46] *Mussolini e l'Europa. La politica estera fascista* (Rome: Leonardo, 1945).

[47] *Défense de la paix*, Vol. I: *De Washington au Quai d'Orsay;* Vol. II: *Fin d'une Europe* (Geneva: Bourquin, 1946 and 1948). Recently, Bonnet published a historical survey of French foreign policy from 1919 to 1960, incorporating his personal experiences: *Le Quai d'Orsay sous trois Républiques* (Paris: Fayard, 1961).

It was not only an extremely important memoir—at least at first glance—but also an extremely valuable, if not irreplaceable, documentary source that was being made available, because in these volumes Bonnet included numerous documents for which the originals had been lost in the destruction of parts of the archives of the Quai d'Orsay.

A perfunctory comparison of the Bonnet volumes with the sources then available, in particular the French Yellow Book on the origins of the war,[48] was to modify greatly the favorable reception that had been given to Bonnet's work.[49] This substantially negative second evaluation was confirmed by the documentary and memoir publications published subsequently.

In effect, Bonnet's inaccurate reporting of specific events, when taken as a whole, culminated in distorting his portrayal of his policy and that of the other countries involved. Therefore, his testimony must be subjected to a minute and critical analysis. Despite these limitations, the memoirs continue to be among the most outstanding for this period because they cast considerable light (occasionally more than the author intended) on a number of questions that are still under discussion concerning the policies of the western powers from the time of the Sudeten crisis to the outbreak of the war.

One of these issues concerns the attitude of the French government during the winter of 1938–39, when a group believed that it was possible to direct German expansion toward the east. Postwar historiography has considered the problem primarily in the light of the action taken by the British government because, as early as 1948, the Soviets published important documentation on the question.[50] On the other hand, it was believed that London provided the real inspiration for such a policy. Whether this thesis is true or not, there is little doubt that Bonnet followed a similar course, a course that was in full agreement with the concepts that inspired his policy, which was designed to avoid war with Germany at all costs, and it is within this framework that the Franco-German declaration of December 6, 1938, must be considered. In referring to this declaration, Bonnet asserts that it was his intent to restore the equilibrium of the French position after the agreement initialed by Hitler and Chamberlain at Munich, September 30, 1938. His assertion is to be viewed with a certain amount of skepticism, for if it is possible that he momentarily overestimated

---

[48] On this, see pp. 96–97.

[49] For these criticisms, see the article by Lewis B. Namier in *The Times Literary Supplement*, January 1, 1949, republished in Namier, *Europe in Decay* (London: Macmillan, 1950). See also the polemic between Namier and Bonnet in *The Times Literary Supplement*, February 19 and 26, and April 9, 1949.

[50] See pp. 170–72.

the import of the Anglo-German accord—apprehension was also evident in Rome—it is difficult to believe that preoccupation with this accord was the basic reason for the negotiations initiated by Bonnet with Berlin. It should also be recalled that a real *rapprochement* between London and Berlin was extremely improbable. Furthermore, shortly after the Munich agreement Anglo-German relations deteriorated, partly because the Nazi persecution of the Jews was shocking to the Anglo-Saxon world.

Thus, the objectives pursued by Bonnet were substantially different. From the point of view of contingency, Bonnet sought to prevent Germany from supporting Italian claims to French territory. Bonnet's version of the talk with Von Ribbentrop—a version that differs markedly from that of the interpreter, Schmidt,[51] but that on this point is confirmed by Ambassador Phipps's telegram[52] and, indirectly, by Guariglia's memoirs[53]—is that he received some assurance in the desired direction because the German Foreign Minister supposedly noted that, if Germany solemnly renounced its claims to Alsace-Lorraine, it was surely not disposed to become involved in a conflict designed to give Djibuti or Corsica to Italy.

On the other hand, the attempted Franco-German *rapprochement* presupposed broader co-operation between the two interested powers, and, specifically, it aimed at a revision of their respective positions in eastern Europe. On this point, the assumption that a fundamental difference of opinion developed between Bonnet and Von Ribbentrop has been sustained. Von Ribbentrop, in asking for recognition of a German sphere of interest in eastern Europe, meant to refer to Poland and Czechoslovakia; Bonnet, implying the possibility of a revision of French policy in that area, meant to encourage German expansion toward the Ukraine. He also let the Germans know that in the event of an indirect aggression against the Soviet Union the Franco-Soviet alliance would not be in force.[54]

Despite the fact that this thesis has a sound factual basis, it is not completely convincing because it presupposes the existence of carefully developed designs in the minds of both statesmen that in all probability did not exist. Specifically, it should be pointed out that Berlin had not yet made a choice. This is confirmed by the fact that, the following January, the

[51] Compare *Documents on German Foreign Policy 1918–1945*, Series D, Vol. IV, Doc. 370. Bonnet affirms instead (*Fin d'une Europe*, p. 36) that Schmidt was not present at the colloquy and, despite Schmidt's denial in his memoirs (see p. 523) and the publication of the German minutes of the meeting, Bonnet repeats his version again in his volume, *Le Quai d'Orsay sous trois Républiques*, p. 243.

[52] Phipps telegram to Halifax, December 7, 1938, in *Documents on British Foreign Policy 1919–1939*, Series 3, Vol. III, Doc. 405.

[53] Compare Raffaele Guariglia, *Ricordi 1922–1946*, p. 372.

[54] In this sense, see André Scherer, "Le problème des 'Mains libres à l'est'," *Revue d'histoire de la deuxième guerre mondiale*, No. 32, October, 1958.

German government initiated other attempts to reach an understanding with Warsaw on the question of German expansion to the east. It is possible that Bonnet, in hinting at a revision of French policy in eastern Europe, was giving primary consideration to an eventual German expansion to the Ukraine. However, keeping in mind Bonnet's subsequent attitude and the direction of his policy, it is reasonable to conclude that he was not opposed to a change in the relations with Poland in order to allow Germany greater freedom of action in successfully resolving the problems of the Polish Corridor and of the German minorities in Poland.

The position subsequently taken by Bonnet supports these conclusions, particularly when the situation created by the German occupation of Czechoslovakia, March, 1939, made it necessary to clarify the relations between Warsaw and Paris.

With Chamberlain's declaration of March 31 and with the conclusion of the provisional agreement of April 6 during Beck's visit to London, the British government assumed greater obligations toward Poland than the French had in the Franco-Polish alliance. This action was due to the fact that these obligations were not connected with the decisions of the League of Nations but were based on the premise of direct aggression. Therefore, it was necessary to bring the Franco-Polish alliance into line with the more advanced position assumed by Great Britain.

In his memoirs Bonnet comments in detail on the negotiations with the Polish government on this issue and blames the Poles for the delays and for the difficulties encountered during the course of the talks. Notwithstanding Bonnet's allegations to the contrary, the evidence shows that it was he, instead of the Poles, who conducted the talks in a dilatory manner for the obvious purpose of avoiding specific obligations, particularly because on May 19, at Gamelin's insistence, a military convention between the two countries had been signed, to become effective only after the conclusion of the political agreement.

In fact, during the height of the crisis of the summer of 1939, Bonnet was clearly in favor of reaching a compromise with Germany, and under the prevailing circumstances there was no misunderstanding his course of action: it was the surrender of the French position in eastern Europe and the abandonment of Poland. Furthermore, this assumption was discussed explicitly by Bonnet in the meeting of the Council of Ministers of August 23, 1939, and the fact that it was not approved was due primarily to the opposition of Gamelin, who believed Polish military assistance to be essential in the event of a German attack against France. Yet, despite the position of the Council of Ministers, on the eve of the declaration of war Bonnet had not abandoned the idea of another "Munich," and this attitude is confirmed by the alacrity with which he accepted Mussolini's proposal of mediation of August 31, 1939.

To be sure, behind all of this there lay the desire to avoid an immediate conflict and to gain time to permit the French to complete their military preparations. However, the attitude of the French Foreign Minister was also influenced by the conduct of the Polish government during the Anglo-French-Soviet negotiations. The failure of these negotiations, according to Bonnet, was due entirely to Warsaw's refusal to permit Soviet troops to cross Polish territory.

His resentment over the Polish action induced Bonnet to give greater consideration to the idea of abandoning Poland even though it could be foreseen that, without the support of the western powers, Poland would be partitioned between Germany and the Soviet Union. In fact, such an eventuality was not particularly displeasing to the French Minister, a fact that he himself confirms in his memoirs. To be sure, he observes, France would lose an ally, but, with the disappearance of Poland, Germany would share a border with the Soviet Union, which would make a conflict between the two very probable. Furthermore, in the case of German aggression against France, the latter could invoke the alliance of 1935 (which, Bonnet emphasizes, Molotov and Voroschilov had declared to be in effect even after the conclusion of the Soviet-German nonaggression pact) and the Red army would be in a position to intervene immediately without having first to resolve the problem of transit across the territory of an independent state.[55]

Thus, in the light of his attitude during the entire period of his tenure as French Foreign Minister, Bonnet is revealed to be the strongest champion of the policy of appeasement toward Germany. In this sense he was far in advance of Chamberlain, Halifax, and other British statesmen. The latter were not motivated solely by the desire to gain time in what appeared to be an inevitable conflict with Germany but were attempting to arrive at a *modus vivendi* with Hitler; they were hopeful that once the problem of the German minorities had been resolved he would put an end to his policy of expansion in Europe. Apparently, Bonnet never entertained any such illusions, nor did he consider the Munich Pact the touchstone for a policy of peaceful co-existence with Germany. On the other hand, it should be noted that the so-called "policy of a free hand in the east" was conceived by the French Foreign Minister not only to encourage the Germans to expand

[55] On this, see also what Bonnet confided in 1944 to the former Rumanian Minister of Foreign Affairs, Gafencu, in Toscano, "Colloqui con Gafencu," *Rivista di Studi Politici Internazionali*, 1945, pp. 85–100.

in the Ukraine but also as a device for the relinquishment of the French position in eastern Europe. There may be some debate over whether or not, toward the end of 1938, Bonnet was already disposed to abandon Poland, but there is no doubt that he intended to reduce French obligations in eastern Europe and that, despite Hitler's assurances, Bonnet considered what was left of Czechoslovakia to be lost.

It is especially important to note the difference in the reaction of the British leaders and that of Bonnet to the news of the German occupation of Prague in March, 1939. This event was a decisive turning point for the London government: it marked the collapse of every illusion of reaching a lasting agreement with Hitler and was the conclusive demonstration that Hitler did not respect his obligations and that, therefore, any compromise with him was impossible.

Bonnet regarded the question from a substantially different point of view. He had never believed in the German Chancellor's good faith, and on the occasion of his meeting with Von Ribbentrop in Paris he had clearly led the latter to understand that he considered further German action against Czechoslovakia to be the logical development of the Munich policy and that France would offer no opposition.

While London, beginning in March, 1939, had reached the decision to reply forcefully in the event of further German aggression—a decision expressed in the Chamberlain declaration of March 31 and the agreement with Beck on April 6—Bonnet, as has been noted, sought to intensify his policy of *desistement* in eastern Europe to the extent of planning the abandonment of Poland. The differences between British and French policy now came to the surface, and they were to be repeatedly manifested throughout the summer of 1939—differences for which Bonnet was only partially responsible because, in actual fact, they also reflected the divergent positions of the French and British public, the consequences of which were to be strongly felt during the course of the war.

b. Charles-Roux.

François Charles-Roux, an enormously prolific writer, in addition to numerous historical works[56] has left two volumes of memoirs regarding the period between the two world wars: one concerns his mission to the Holy

[56] Especially pertinent to the study of diplomatic history are *Alexandre II, Gortchakov et Napoleon III* (Paris: Plon, 1917); *La paix des Empires Centraux* (Paris: SPID, 1947); and, in collaboration with Jacques Caillé, *Missions diplomatiques françaises à Fes* (Paris: Larose, 1955).

See from 1932 to 1940,[57] and the other deals with his activities as Secretary-General of the Quai d'Orsay in 1940.[58]

The second is by far the most important. While the memoirs published by French statesmen and military men on the armistice of 1940 and on Vichy France are extremely numerous, none of them focus on the purely diplomatic affairs of that period to the extent that Charles-Roux has done in his second volume. Of course, the fact that he was outside of the restricted circle of Pétain's collaborators prevented him from knowing the many behind-the-scenes activities, knowledge of which is a prerequisite for an understanding of the background of many of the Vichy government's most important decisions. Ample information on backstage operations is available from other sources, such as the memoirs of Baudouin or Bouthillier, but Charles-Roux's testimony cannot be replaced for an understanding of the various phases of execution of French foreign policy for this period. Moreover, he offers a much wider perspective than is usually the case; that is, he does not limit himself to relations with Germany or the Anglo-Saxon powers.

On May 18, 1940, Charles-Roux was called to the post of Secretary-General of the Quai d'Orsay, where he remained until the end of October, 1940, when the Montoire meetings and the nomination of Laval as Minister of Foreign Affairs induced him to resign. Essentially, he was the prototype of the government official who, despite the fact that he does not agree with his government's policy, considers it his duty to continue to serve his country, comforted by the hope of being able to exert a certain favorable influence on the course of events. This state of mind is clearly reflected in his book, which is a volume written by a career diplomat who is trying to confront problems with the instruments known to his profession, even though all too frequently these instruments prove to be inadequate.

Because of these unique characteristics, Charles-Roux's work, prepared from a sound documentary base, furnishes the historian with a significant number of new elements available nowhere else in the French memoir sources for this period. Insofar as the events pertaining to the conclusion of the armistices of June, 1940, are concerned, his version of a number of important episodes—the communication of the text of the German demands to Ambassador Campbell, the vicissitudes of the two British telegrams of June 16, etc.—is to be considered, on the whole, as the most accurate. For the period immediately following the armistices, he adds many precise details on the attempts to prevent a complete break with Great Britain after

[57] *Huit ans au Vatican 1932–1940* (Paris: Flammarion, 1947).

[58] *Cinq mois tragiques aux affaires étrangères (21 mai–1 novembre 1940)* (Paris: Plon, 1949).

the attack on Mers el Kebir and on the action taken during the summer of 1940 by the French and British embassies in Madrid to re-establish contact between the Vichy government and London.[59]

Charles-Roux's volume contains some interesting pages on Germany (see for example, what he writes regarding French reactions to the German note of July 15 on the use of Moroccan airports). However, it was precisely in this area that the Ministry of Foreign Affairs was least effective, largely because the more important problems were handled by the Wiesbaden commission and also because the atmosphere prevailing in Franco-German relations arose from the personal initiatives of French statesmen: not only Laval but also Pétain, Baudouin, and other major and minor Vichy figures. The new materials found in his memoirs (outside of the direct relations with Germany and Great Britain, which were already known through other sources) are the explanations of the action of the French government to block the dismemberment of the Empire, particularly in Morocco, Indo-China, and in the American colonies. Especially significant are the French negotiations with Spain for a modification of the respective protectorate zones of the two countries in Morocco. These sections are extremely interesting in that they make it possible to evaluate more objectively the changes in the Spanish position during the conflict and to learn the major characteristics of French policy during that period.

The request that France transfer to Spanish control portions of northern and eastern Morocco (Beni-Zeroual and Beni-Snassen) was made by the Spanish Foreign Minister, Beigbeder, on June 21, 1940, before the Franco-German negotiations for the armistice were concluded. Evidently, the Spanish government feared that Morocco would be used by the French as a bargaining instrument for the favor of either Germany or Italy and consequently sought to anticipate the action of the Axis powers while simultaneously stressing the fact that any eventual modification of the *status quo* in Morocco was within the exclusive province of the two protecting powers. The French government was able to ascertain, shortly afterwards, that neither Germany nor Italy intended to present their demands for North African territory immediately. Nevertheless, the French government considered it inopportune to close the door on these negotiations with Madrid. Undoubtedly, this decision was also prompted by fear of a Spanish coup in Morocco and by a desire to keep the question

[59] While Charles-Roux's memoirs on this question are the best French source available, note should be made of Hoare's memoirs of his mission to Madrid (see below) and particularly of the documents published by the British government in 1945: *Despatch to His Majesty's Ambassador in Paris regarding Relations between His Majesty's Government in the United Kingdom and the Vichy Government in the Autumn of 1940* (London: His Majesty's Stationery Office, 1945), Cmd. 6662.

476 PUBLICATION OF THE SOURCES

within the framework of Franco-Spanish relations, but, as Charles-Roux
observes, it was also symptomatic of the new direction Pétain intended to
give to French policy, based on the gradual insertion of France into the
"new order" of Europe. However, in this case, it is conceivable that
Baudouin was pursuing a different course and that, in eliminating the
major cause of friction between France and Spain, he hoped to take the first
step toward a "Latin Triplice" with which to resist, as much as possible,
German hegemony in Europe. This idea appears to have been given some
consideration in Rome also and seems to have influenced Mussolini's
decision to offer the French very moderate armistice terms. But, according
to references contained in the German documents, the idea met with no
response in Madrid.

As the negotiations developed, several surprises emerged. Without going
into detail—Charles-Roux deals with them at length—it should be mentioned that on October 15 the Spanish government declined the French
offer made at the end of September, an offer to examine the question of a
revision of the protectorate zones, taking as a basis for discussion the 1925
agreement providing for the cession of the territory of Beni-Zeroual.

What prompted this refusal? At the time, negotiations were under way to
bring Spain into the war on the side of the Axis, an intervention that the
Falangist leaders hoped would lead to the recognition of Spanish rights to
all of Morocco. On the basis of this premise, it is possible to advance the
hypothesis that Beigbeder replied negatively to the French offer because,
with a global solution to the Moroccan problem in sight, he considered any
eventual agreement with France insignificant. Furthermore, as a result of
Serrano Suñer's journey to Berlin the preceding September, the Spaniards
were aware of the extent of German pretensions to Morocco. Consequently,
the Spanish refusal to continue the negotiations with France appears to
have been due not so much to their desire to leave the door open for more
favorable concessions but, rather, to their conviction that a Franco-Spanish
accord would be vetoed by Hitler. Further, the refusal should be considered
within the framework of the decision to remain neutral, a decision which
was just then beginning to take shape, in view of the failure of Germany to
invade the British Isles.

In general, Charles-Roux's work must be considered one of the most
reliable sources available on the Vichy regime even though on some points
the author is reticent or inaccurate. Perhaps the most serious inaccuracy—
frequently repeated by the author without equivocation—is his assertion
that the Pétain government did not ask for a separate peace with the
Germans either during or after the armistice negotiations. This assertion is
contradicted by Noël's testimony (very exact on this point) and by the

recently published German documents, which definitely prove that the French plenipotentiaries at Rethondes inquired about the "conditions of peace and armistice." However, General Keitel, according to instructions received, limited the discussions to the terms of the armistice.

Charles-Roux is more cautious in his statements in the volume concerning his mission to the Holy See from 1932 to 1940. Notwithstanding the anecdotal character of several of the chapters in the volume, which serve to describe the Vatican setting, a scholar can find many points of interest on the attitude of the Holy See toward international affairs, as well as on Italian foreign policy. The memoir reveals that occasionally the French Embassy to the Holy See was better informed on Italian affairs than the Embassy accredited to the Quirinale, especially during the period when Italo-French relations were strained. For example, Charles-Roux reveals that he was aware of many behind-the-scenes activities concerning the Italo-Ethiopian conflict, activities that show that only at the last minute did Mussolini decide to annex the African state. Although the favorable results of the military operations made the fall of Addis Ababa only a matter of time, the Italian head of state, as late as the beginning of April, 1936, was disposed to conclude a compromise peace with the Negus, fearful that the latter might be able to prolong the conflict by guerrilla warfare now that the rainy season, which favored such activity, was imminent. Thus, according to Charles-Roux, Italian proposals for a direct agreement with Haile Selassie were communicated to the Vatican on April 9, 1936, with the request that they be brought to the attention of London and Paris. However, neither the French nor the British governments would have anything to do with a solution that was contrary to the principles of the League of Nations and in conflict with the position they had assumed during the war. Early in May, the news that the Emperor of Ethiopia and the Crown Prince had fled their country completely changed the picture. With the danger of guerrilla warfare against the Italian forces completely dissipated, Mussolini could safely ignore any compromise solution—in the absence of the second party—and proclaim the entire territory to be under Italian sovereignty.

c. De Gaulle.

In General de Gaulle's memoirs[60] we have a work that merits careful study, not only for the wealth of information it contains and the scope of

[60] Charles de Gaulle, *Mémoires de guerre*, Vol. I: *L'appel (1940–1942)*; Vol. II: *L'unité (1942–1944)*; Vol. III: *Le salut (1944–1946)* (Paris: Plon, 1954, 1956, 1959).

the subjects treated but also for an insight into the personality of the author, who, as champion of the principle "defeated are they who accept defeat," contributed decisively to the regeneration of France after the sudden collapse of 1940.

The memoirs are also important as source material for understanding a man who has maintained a unique position in French political life and symbolizes the attitudes of a significant section of the French public. To be sure, De Gaulle does not openly reveal his sentiments and character in these pages, but they can be ascertained from his political activity, from his attitudes, and from the way in which he poses the problems and narrates the events. Many of his critiques of the French internal situation in the immediate postwar period, of the efficiency of French parliamentary institutions, his oft-recurring theme of French "grandeur," and the obvious satisfaction he displays in telling of his struggles as a man destined to raise France to her former position as a great power are all indicative of his political concepts and his course of action after assuming power.

From the historical point of view, these memoirs are undoubtedly the most important source for a study of the relations between Free France and the Allies, and they are strengthened by an important appendix containing hitherto unpublished letters, notes, and reports exchanged with Free France's wartime allies or with the leaders of the liberation forces.

De Gaulle had signed an accord with the British government in August, 1940, but this document, despite Eden's pro-French views, did not prevent the development of frequent controversies between the British and the Free French. London did not intend to break relations with the Vichy government entirely, as De Gaulle requested, because it was fearful of what would happen to the French fleet. Moreover, General de Gaulle's exasperating nationalism, his intransigence, and his often puzzling maneuvers aroused open distrust of his intentions in many British circles and especially in the Foreign Office, where there was constant fear that a man so difficult to control might commit some inopportune and rash act.

The crisis in the relations between the British government and the De Gaulle movement became particularly serious after the failure of the attack on Dakar. The failure of this operation was attributed by the British military to indiscretions by one or more of De Gaulle's collaborators. On the other hand, the refusal of the French fleet to join the De Gaullist forces seemed to indicate that his magnetic power had been overestimated. From that moment on, therefore, the Foreign Office decided not to keep De Gaulle abreast of military and diplomatic plans, even when they were of direct concern to France or to her colonial empire. Naturally, the memoirs reflect this state of affairs, and for the period from September, 1940, on, they contain markedly less information on Allied policy. For example, they have very little data on the Rougier mission, the Halifax-Chevalier Accords, and generally, on the negotiations between London and Vichy during the winter of 1940–41—negotiations that marked an important phase in the relationship between the two governments.

De Gaulle's relations with the United States government were even worse. In Washington the Free French movement had aroused even greater distrust than in Great Britain, and many were convinced that it was nothing more than a "Fascist movement from the other side of the wall." The State Department was inclined to resolve French problems by a series of local *de facto* accords and was not at all disposed to accept De Gaulle's request that he be considered the sole intermediary between the Allied nations and the French Empire. A typical illustration of the American position can be seen in the Weygand-Murphy Agreements concerning North Africa, and Washington did not change its attitude until much later, that is, until Laval came to power in April, 1942, and it became clear that the Vichy government was well on the way toward losing whatever freedom of action independent of the Germans that it had thus far retained.

Particular attention should be given to the pages referring to the relations between the De Gaullists and the Soviet government. As long as the Nazi-Soviet Pact was in force, the Moscow radio poured out an unending torrent of abuse on the "De Gaullist mercenaries in the service of the pound sterling." However, after the German attack on the U.S.S.R., Soviet propaganda, with its usual aplomb, reversed itself and lauded the heroism of the Free French fighters and the genius of their leader. Relations between De Gaulle and the Soviet government took an immediate and decisive turn for the better, particularly after the Molotov-De Gaulle talks during the former's visit to London in June, 1942.

The warmth of the De Gaulle-Soviet rapport disillusioned some of the rightist elements among the Free French, but, in return, De Gaulle gained the active collaboration of the French Communists. Much more important, however, was the fact that after the Soviet entrance into the war De Gaulle could test the usefulness of a friendship which served as a counterweight to his relations with the western allies by reducing his dependence on Washington and London, a dependence that had wounded his pride.

This experience had an important effect on the General; it convinced him that an agreement with the Kremlin was an excellent diplomatic gambit that would contribute toward reinstating France as a great power on the international chessboard.

De Gaulle's memoirs provide new and significant source material on all these events, and, therefore, they cannot be ignored in any study of the

French position during the war or of the war in general. Yet once their importance has been emphasized, they should be examined with a critical eye. Putting aside the merits of the many debates these memoirs provoked in France because of the stinging political spirit that inspired them, the fact remains that on several points well-founded reservations may be entertained.

Insofar as Italy is concerned, these memoirs offer the opportunity to examine more carefully De Gaulle's position on the questions raised by Italian intervention in the conflict.[61] De Gaulle's first opportunity to advance his point of view came in October, 1943, at a meeting with Count Sforza, who was passing through Algiers on his way back to Italy. De Gaulle states that he told Sforza that he was anxious to re-establish friendly relations between the two countries but that such friendship had its price. It was time to liquidate the Tunisian question, and France also intended to acquire Briga and Tenda, along with other minor frontier rectifications, and to press for a plebiscite in the Aosta Valley to determine whether the population desired to become French citizens. Italy's frontiers with Yugoslavia should be altered, although De Gaulle promised to help Italy retain Trieste. Insofar as the colonies were concerned, it was De Gaulle's view that if Great Britain remained in Cyrenaica and France in the Fezzan, Italy should retain Somaliland and Tripolitania and should not lose its position in Eritrea, while recognizing Haile Selassie's sovereignty in the region.

De Gaulle had his second contact with Italian leaders during the summer of 1944 in Naples. He recalls receiving the Secretary-General of the Italian Foreign Ministry, Prunas, who conveyed the greetings of the Italian government and that he (De Gaulle) expressed his desire to reopen direct contact with the Italian government through his representative, Couve de Murville. Two documents in the appendix testify that he had also suggested the creation of an entente between the Latin states following the war. Moreover, a few days later Prunas told Couve de Murville that, according to Prime Minister Bonomi, there were no problems outstanding between France and Italy other than the Tunisian question on which the Italian government was ready to negotiate. Profiting from De Gaulle's suggestion of an understanding, Prunas added that Italy hoped it would be possible to find a general formula on which to base an agreement for reciprocal aid in the postwar period. Couve de Murville replied that he had no objections to discussing the Tunisian problem because the Italians had lost all of their privileges in Tunisia and that this would be the point of departure in any conversations. Couve de Murville made no mention of

[61] See Toscano, "La ripresa delle relazioni diplomatiche fra l'Italia e la Francia nel corso della seconda guerra mondiale," *Storia e politica*, 1962, fasc. IV, pp. 523–604.

Prunas' second suggestion. Moreover, the French representative did not specify any further reservations regarding other claims.

De Gaulle returns to the question of Italo-French relations in referring to the events of late spring, 1945. The first reference concerns the orders given to a detachment of French Alpine forces to occupy all of the areas he intended to claim for France. In the second, the General offers his version of the controversy between the French and the Anglo-Americans over the Italian territory occupied by French troops. He states that he agreed to the evacuation of the Aosta Valley and Ventimiglia because the annexation of these regions was not an essential part of the French claims but that he remained adamant regarding the other zones, to the cession of which, he continues, the Italian government had become resigned as an extremely moderate price to pay for Franco-Italian reconciliation. Bonomi, Sforza and, later, De Gasperi were to express themselves in the same terms.

In the light of the corresponding Italian sources, a number of doubts are raised concerning the accuracy of De Gaulle's account, and omissions and inaccuracies are revealed that alter on some points the substance of the facts.

It is somewhat perplexing to learn that as early as October, 1943, De Gaulle had a precise list of claims against Italy which corresponded in almost every detail to the acquisitions which France was later to make from Italy. Moreover, in outlining these claims to Sforza, who was believed to be the future Italian Foreign Minister, the impression is created that De Gaulle made his intentions known to Italian leaders with clarity and sincerity. This impression is erroneous because even if some such statements were actually made to Sforza, he was not then the Italian Foreign Minister; moreover, the French never referred again to the statements made in this colloquy.

Secondly, the manner in which De Gaulle refers to his conversation with Prunas in Naples leads the reader to conclude that the meeting was purely a courtesy visit and that little or nothing of importance was said. As a matter of fact, according to Prunas' account, De Gaulle during this meeting expressed himself clearly on several points of major political significance concerning the future course of Franco-Italian relations. The General not only referred to the Tunisian question at length but also emphasized that France had no territorial claims of any kind that would be damaging to Italy and stressed that the defense of Italian territorial integrity was an important factor in French policy and that he intended to see that it was continued. In conclusion, he saw no reason why Franco-Italian relations could not be normalized in the immediate future.

However, these statements were to create some difficulties in the early stages of the renewed Franco-Italian relations. The Italians interpreted De Gaulle's statements literally and concluded that once the Tunisian question was resolved there would be no further obstacles to a Franco-Italian *rapprochement*, but later negotiations revealed that De Gaulle's statements, if taken literally, did not precisely reflect the General's thoughts on the problem. It is presumable that his announced desire to respect Italian territorial integrity was to be interpreted in the sense that Italy was not to suffer major territorial losses and that the frontier rectifications that he had in mind were not in that category. But the Italian government could not so interpret his views because it had no knowledge of his plans. De Gaulle's failure to comment in his memoirs on this point, which is the basis of the controversy, makes it difficult to reconstruct the events in their exact detail.

De Gaulle's statement that Bonomi and de Gasperi (leaving aside Sforza, inaccurately referred to as the Italian Minister of Foreign Affairs, though he assumed that office only in March, 1947) had agreed, in the summer of 1945, to accept the French demands for frontier rectifications in the western Alps is totally incorrect. To disprove his assertion, it is only necessary to read the minutes of the two conferences he had with the Italian Ambassador to France, Saragat, on July 16 and on September 12, 1945, which are included in the appendix of the third volume of the memoirs. However, it should be added that the French Foreign Minister, Bidault, in announcing renunciation of France's claims to the Aosta Valley, informed Saragat that the French government desired to negotiate a bilateral agreement for the cession of Briga and Tenda and other minor border changes. The Italian reply to this request, delivered to the Quai d'Orsay by the Italian Ambassador upon instructions from his government, was entirely negative. Couve de Murville, in taking note of the Italian position, made it clear that France was left with no choice but to present the claim at the peace conference, and this was eventually done.[62]

d. The Other French Memoir Sources.

Among the numerous French memoir sources, attention is directed to the work of Paul-Boncour,[63] former Prime Minister and Minister in several

[62] See Aldus, "Le rettifiche apportate alla frontiera italo-francese con il trattato di pace del 1947 nelle Memorie di guerra del generale De Gaulle," *Rivista di Studi Politici Internazionali,* 1962, fasc. IV.

[63] Joseph Paul-Boncour, *Entre deux guerres. Souvenirs sur la III République,* Vol. I: *Les luttes républicaines (1877–1918)*; Vol. II: *Les lendemains de la victoire (1919–1934)*; Vol. III: *Sur le chemin de la défaite (1935–1940)* (Paris: Plon, 1945–46).

French cabinets. In three thick volumes, the author has attempted to reconstruct the history of the Third French Republic on the basis of his personal experience. In his narrative, Paul-Boncour has brought many details to light, especially concerning French policy vis-à-vis the Little Entente, the origins of the Four-Power Pact, the Franco-Soviet Alliance of May 2, 1935, and the *Anschluss* crisis. The pages devoted to the work of the Quai d'Orsay at Geneva are especially noteworthy because for many years Paul-Boncour was the French permanent delegate to the League of Nations.

The period covered by Flandin's memoirs[64] is equally long, although he writes in less detail and on a much more personal plane. Particular attention is given to the Franco-Italian Accords of January, 1935,[65] the Ethiopian crisis, and the Stresa Conference and the remilitarization of the Rhineland, events in which Flandin played a major role as Prime Minister of France (November, 1934–May, 1935), Minister of State (June, 1935–January, 1936), and Minister of Foreign Affairs (January–June, 1936). Perhaps most interesting is his discussion of the Rhineland crisis, during which he strongly urged that Hitler's violations of the Treaty of Versailles be met with force. His recommendation was successfully opposed by the British government and the French military. From that time on, Flandin reversed himself and championed a policy of European conciliation based on reaching agreements with the dictators. He was accused of being pro-Nazi, especially after the conclusion of the Munich Pact, which he enthusiastically approved, and this accusation blocked his return to power in the French government. For this reason, the last part of his memoirs contains no important new information and is significant only for his interpretation—often questionable—of the events leading to the war.

The memoirs of Jules Laroche,[66] French Ambassador to Warsaw from 1926 to 1935, refer to the middle period between the two world wars. His contribution to the study of the foreign policy of the Pilsudski regime, which coincided with his mission to Poland, is particularly noteworthy because Laroche does not limit himself to a general narrative of the events he observed but summarizes his activities in detail, making frequent reference to the reports and telegrams he sent to Paris. While limited to the

---

[64] Pierre-Etienne Flandin, *Politique française* (*1919–1940*) (Paris: Les Editions Nouvelles, 1947).

[65] On this question, see William C. Askew, "The Secret Agreement between France and Italy on Ethiopia," *Journal of Modern History*, March, 1953; D. C. Watt, "The Secret Laval-Mussolini Agreement of 1935 on Ethiopia," *The Middle East Journal*, Winter, 1961.

[66] *La Pologne de Pilsudski. Souvenirs d'une Ambassade* (*1926–1935*) (Paris: Flammarion, 1953).

diplomatic aspect of the problems facing Poland, Laroche's account is clear and of considerable value for a study of the Lithuanian problem, relations with the Soviet Union, Germany, and France. The author's synthesis of the motives leading to the cooling of Franco-Polish relations and Warsaw's *rapprochement* with Berlin, culminating in the nonaggression pact of January, 1934, are especially significant.

Further details on Franco-Italian relations between 1932 and 1936 are provided by Hubert Lagardelle,[67] who was charged with a mission to Rome which, despite its unofficial character, gave him the opportunity to observe the diplomatic events of that period from an important vantage point. His volume is rich in new data on the negotiations leading to the Four-Power Pact, to the Franco-Italian Accords of January, 1935, and on the diplomatic aspects of the Ethiopian war as seen from the point of view of Franco-Italian relations. Special note should be taken of the Mussolini-Laval colloquies as reconstructed by the author on the basis of the letters exchanged between Laval and Mussolini from December 1935 to February, 1936, published in the appendix.

Four French ambassadors holding key posts have written on the events preceding the outbreak of World War II. Ambassador Noël, Laroche's successor at Warsaw from 1935 to 1939, published a volume of his memoirs immediately after the war[68] in which he nicely balances his personal recollections with an analysis of the events as they developed. These recollections contain significant new material on the problems of the period, and the author is extremely frank in his criticism of Colonel Beck's policies. During the course of his mission to Warsaw, his judgment of Beck's policy had led him to urge Paris to loosen the alliance ties that bound France to Poland.

Interesting, too, are the two volumes of memoirs written by François-Poncet,[69] Ambassador to Berlin from 1931 to 1938 and to Rome from 1938 to the outbreak of the war. Among the most significant pages are those on the German internal crisis leading to Hitler's rise to power and those on the events of 1934: the collapse of the disarmament negotiations, the liquidation of the Roehm group, and the attempt at *Anschluss*. On the other hand, it is difficult to find important references to his activities as French

---

[67] *Mission à Rome. Mussolini* (Paris: Plon, 1955).

[68] Léon Noël, *L'agression Allemande contre la Pologne* (Paris: Flammarion, 1946).

[69] André François-Poncet, *Souvenirs d'une ambassade à Berlin, septembre 1931–octobre 1938* (Paris: Flammarion, 1946); *Au Palais Farnèse, souvenirs d'une ambassade à Rome 1938–1940* (Paris: Fayard, 1961); *De Versailles à Potsdam. La France et le problème allemand contemporain 1919–1945* (Paris: Flammarion, 1948).

Ambassador to Berlin in these recollections; according to the author, this lacuna is the result of scanty rapport between himself and the Quai d'Orsay. As a matter of fact, François-Poncet, who was not a career diplomat, wanted his mission to play a decisive role in determining the course of events, and when he recognized that it was impossible for him to influence German foreign policy seriously, after Munich he asked to be transferred to Rome, where he hoped to be able to work more effectively. In Rome he committed a serious psychological blunder in not immediately recognizing the profound differences between Italian and German mentalities and in continuing on a course that, while it may have been fairly effective in Germany, succeeded only in irritating the Italians. However, the situation he faced had already crystallized, and the failure of his mission, dramatically brought to a close by the declaration of war, was inevitable.

Ambassador Coulondre[70] has contributed interesting data on his mission to Moscow from November, 1936, to October, 1938, and to Berlin, where he succeeded François-Poncet, from 1938 to the outbreak of the war. While the scholar may find ample documentation on the second period in the French Yellow Book and in the German general collection, the Coulondre volume remains a primary source for the study of Franco-Soviet relations and is particularly useful for understanding the French attitude toward Franco-Soviet relations.

Recently, René Massigli published his significant volume[71] on his mission to Ankara, October, 1938–July, 1940. This narrative is both a memoir and a historical account because Massigli, while he based the work on his experiences, often widens the perspective by examining with the eyes of a historian the diplomatic events in which he was both spectator and actor.

His account is based on his apparently very extensive personal archive, on the Italian, German, and British documents published since the end of the war, and on the memoirs of other diplomats such as Von Papen and Knatchbull-Hugessen in addition to those of Bonnet, with whom he differs on repeated occasions. The result is a precise and detailed exposition of the events, but the fact that it is also history and not simply memoir-writing reduces its spontaneity and, as a consequence, its value.

Regardless of its limitations, Massigli's volume deserves the attention of scholars for its contribution concerning French and Turkish policy in the

[70] Robert Coulondre, *De Stalin à Hitler. Souvenirs de deux Ambassades* (1936–1939) (Paris: Hachette, 1950).

[71] *La Turquie devant la guerre. Mission à Ankara, 1939–1940* (Paris: Plon, 1964).

Near East and in the Balkans. Moreover, it is a primary source for the study of the negotiations leading to the Anglo-French-Turkish Accords of 1939, by far the most important account of this event available from French sources.

The violent debates on the origins of the French collapse in 1940 and on the circumstances surrounding the signing of the armistices with the Axis powers have given rise to an enormous number of memoirs of widely varying value. Paul Reynaud, former Prime Minister, published his memoirs in two separate editions,[72] one differing greatly from the other. The first of these, written while he was in prison, suffers from the absence of documentation but includes a number of significant observations which were omitted in the second edition. The second edition is more clearly polemical and reflects the author's preoccupation with the defense of his policies and with his replies to the accusations leveled at him by his opponents. In both editions Reynaud introduces his account with a historico-descriptive narrative of the major events from the Treaty of Versailles to March, 1940, when, after Daladier's resignation, he formed the new French government. From this point on, the narrative becomes singularly important and touches upon a number of the critical issues related to the military disaster: the attitude of the French ministers toward the problem of the armistice; the Reynaud-Weygand controversy, which stemmed from divergent evaluations of the nature of the war and led to a conflict between the civil and military authorities; relations with Great Britain; and the much-discussed Reynaud resignation of June 16, 1940, which paved the way for the creation of the Pétain government. The references to the efforts of the French government to prevent Italy's intervention in the war and the aims pursued by Reynaud in these negotiations are worthy of note. The former Prime Minister affirms that from the beginning he was certain that Italy would enter the war but that he continued the negotiations with Rome for the sole purpose of making it clear to everyone that the break in relations was due entirely to Mussolini.

Immediately after the war Ambassador Noël published anonymously an extremely important little volume[73] on the negotiations leading to the armistices with Germany and Italy. This is a highly detailed chronicle of the Rethondes and Villa Incisa negotiations, the nature of which was almost completely unknown prior to the publication of this book. The

[72] *La France a sauvé l'Europe* (2 vols.; Paris: Flammarion, 1947); *Au coeur de la mêlée (1930–1945)* (Paris: Flammarion, 1951).

[73] *Un témoignage. Le diktat de Rethondes et l'armistice franco-italien de juin 1940* (Paris: Flammarion, 1945).

successive publication of the Wilhelmstrasse's diplomatic documents has provided scholars with the German version of the meetings at Rethondes, but this does not detract from the value of Noël's volume. The existence of the latter permits a comparison between the two versions—the differences are limited to nonessential points—and it retains its importance for the author's comparison of the Franco-German armistice of 1940 and the armistice signed by Germany in November, 1918.

On the whole, the memoirs of the President of the French Republic, Lebrun,[74] and those of the President of the Chamber of Deputies, Herriot,[75] are of minor importance. Despite the high level of their offices, these statesmen played relatively unimportant roles in the events of May and June, 1940. However, in another book[76] Herriot has written an exciting account of the policies of the Third French Republic and of his role as Prime Minister and Foreign Minister.

Vastly more important is the testimony of Paul Baudouin,[77] Undersecretary in the Reynaud Cabinet and later Minister of Foreign Affairs in the Pétain government until November, 1940. His memoirs are one of the richest sources available for the details on the fall of France and on the first months of the Vichy regime. The recollections are in the form of a diary and appear to be based on daily annotations, which were apparently modified by additions and omissions prior to publication in order better to defend the author's actions. These alterations make it quite difficult to ascertain precisely what Baudouin's position really was and, therefore, to evaluate some of his statements, especially those on the significance of his conciliatory policy toward Great Britain when compared to an ill-defined prospect of collaboration—at least on an economic basis—with Germany. Nevertheless, Baudouin was an extremely well informed and acute observer, and his comments on the personalities and events of the restricted world of Vichy are very revealing, as are his observations on the rivalries existing between Pétain's followers and the effect these had on the foreign policy of the Vichy regime.

The importance of the economic factor in Vichy's relations with Great Britain and Germany makes the memoirs of the former Minister of Finance, Yves Bouthillier,[78] very valuable. The author treats the problem

[74] Albert Lebrun, *Témoignage* (Paris: Plon, 1945).

[75] Edouard Herriot, *Épisodes (1940–1944)* (Paris: Flammarion, 1950).

[76] *Jadis*, Vol. II: *D'une guerre à l'autre 1914–1936* (Paris: Flammarion, 1952).

[77] *Neuf mois au Gouvernement (Avril–Décembre 1940)* (Paris: La Table Ronde, 1948).

[78] *Le drame de Vichy*, Vol. I: *Face à l'ennemi. Face à l'allié*; Vol. II: *Finances sous la contrainte* (Paris: Plon, 1950–51).

with indisputable competence and precise data, commenting in detail on the direction of internal and external affairs and on the complex situation existing within the French government, where personal conflicts were as important as conflicts over policy. But by far the most interesting subject discussed is the economic one. The account is not at all restricted to the technical aspects of the problem but, on the contrary, touches all of the policies of the Vichy government and is of fundamental importance to an exact understanding of French foreign policy for this period, given the tendencies of both London and Berlin to use economic pressure as one of the most effective means of influencing the policies of the Pétain Cabinet.

On the *vexata quaestio* of the unofficial contacts during the summer and fall of 1940 between London and Vichy in an effort to arrive at a provisional *modus vivendi*, Louis Rougier, a participant at one of the meetings, in two studies, published a number of years apart,[79] gives his version of the facts. These contrast completely with the official British version. Rougier affirms that during his visit to London in October, 1940, an accord was reached, and later approved by Pétain, by which France agreed not to surrender the French fleet to the Germans and not to attempt to regain control of the colonies that had gone over to De Gaulle, while the British government agreed not to enforce rigidly the economic blockade of France and not to violate French sovereignty in the colonial sphere. This version, despite the abundant data provided in its support, is not wholly convincing. The most probable hypothesis is that Rougier, knowingly or not, overestimated the importance of his contacts with the British officials.

The memoirs of Prince Xavier de Bourbon[80] have a similar central theme and make it possible to reconstruct the Franco-British negotiations of November–December, 1940, that were arranged by Jacques Chevalier, Secretary-General of the Ministry of Public Instruction and personal friend of Halifax and the Canadian Minister to Vichy, Dupuy. While these negotiations did not produce any formal agreement they did lead to an oral and unofficial exchange of declarations which markedly lessened the tension in Franco-British relations after the events of the summer of 1940 and dissipated, at least in part, the impression created by the Hitler-Pétain meeting at Montoire.

Among the numerous memoir sources on Vichy France, reference should

[79] *Mission secrète à Londres. Les accords Pétain-Churchill* (Geneva: Bourquin, 1946); *Les accords secrets franco-britanniques. Histoire et imposture* (Paris: Grasset, 1954).
[80] *Les accordes secrets franco-anglais de décembre 1940* (Paris: Plon, 1949).

be made to the recollections of François Piétri,[81] Ambassador to Madrid from 1940 to 1944. These are useful for an insight into the Spanish internal situation rather than for what they offer on Franco-Spanish diplomatic relations. Of some importance are the memoirs of Admiral Fernet,[82] who, in his capacity as Secretary-General to the Prime Minister, refers to several personal initiatives by Pétain to renew contacts with Germany prior to Montoire and to the Marshal's attitude on the problem of Franco-German collaboration. Mention should also be made of the memoirs of Girard,[83] which, on the basis of his personal experience and the testimony of others, provide an over-all view of Vichy policy, and of Du Moulin de Labarthète,[84] who adds other details on crucial events such as the Montoire meeting, Laval's arrest in December, 1940, and the advent of Darlan. To these should be added, for their references to the overseas territories, the adventurous recollections of the Governor of Dahomey and Madagascar, Armand Annet;[85] those of Ambassador Puaux[86] on his mission to Syria and Lebanon in 1939–40; those of Admiral Robert,[87] who, as Governor of the Antilles, was faced with a difficult situation because of the presence of a French naval squadron in the waters of Martinique; the memoirs of the Governor-General of Indo-China, Decoux;[88] and of Ambassador Peyrouton,[89] former Minister of the Interior in the Vichy government, who, after the Allied landing in North Africa, transferred his allegiance to General Giraud and was named by the latter to the post of Governor of Algeria.

Turning to the memoirs of the exponents of *France Libre*, reference is made to the two volumes by General Catroux,[90] who was at De Gaulle's side from the summer of 1940 on. The first volume covers the period to 1943 and is particularly significant for its testimony on the events that took place in the Levant in the summer of 1941 after the *coup d'état* by Rashid

[81] *Mes années d'Espagne, 1940–1948* (Paris: Plon, 1954).
[82] *Au côté du Maréchal Pétain. Souvenirs (1940–1944)* (Paris: Plon, 1953).
[83] Louis-Dominique Girard, *Montoire, Verdun diplomatique* (Paris: Bonne, 1948).
[84] H. du Moulin de Labarthète, *Les temps des illusions. Souvenirs (Juillet 1940–Avril 1942)* (Geneva: Les Editions du Cheval Ailé, 1946).
[85] *Aux heures troublées de l'Afrique française (1939–1943)* (Paris: Conquistador, 1952).
[86] Gabriel Puaux, *Deux années au Levant. Souvenirs de Syrie et du Liban 1939–1940* (Paris: Hachette, 1952).
[87] Georges Robert, *La France aux Antilles de 1939 à 1943* (Paris: Plon, 1950).
[88] Admiral Decoux, *A la barre de l'Indochine, Histoire de mon Gouvernement Général (1940–1945)* (Paris: Plon, 1949).
[89] Marcel Peyrouton, *Du service public à la prison commune. Souvenirs* (Paris: Plon, 1950).
[90] *Dans la bataille de Méditerranée* (Paris: Julliard, 1949); *J'ai vu tomber le rideau de fer. Moscou 1945–1948* (Paris: Hachette, 1952).

Ali el-Gailani in Iraq. From this source, far more than from De Gaulle's memoirs, it is possible to determine the motives dictating the position taken by *France Libre* in the difficult situation emerging in Syria and in Lebanon. In fact, the leaders of the Free French movement were faced with the danger that, in wresting control of these two territories from Vichy, France would lose her strong position in the Near East. The different points of view on this question held by De Gaulle and by Catroux, which, under the circumstances, prompted their respective activities, are of vital importance in understanding the course of action later taken by Catroux in becoming the spokesman for the moderate wing of the De Gaullist movement while still remaining the General's loyal and faithful collaborator. No less important is the second volume, in which the author refers to his mission to Moscow, at the request of De Gaulle, in 1944, during which he participated in the negotiations leading to the Franco-Soviet Alliance and to the peace treaties.

Soustelle's memoirs[91] are entirely different. He too was one of De Gaulle's intimate collaborators and the latter's Vice-Chief of Cabinet in 1944, after a long period in the Free French propaganda and information service. Despite the fact that Soustelle did not hold key posts for any long period, he was fairly well informed on developments. However, he used his knowledge to glorify De Gaulle's work rather than to provide an objective account of the events and their background. If the first volume, which covers the years 1940–42, may still be regarded as a useful source for information concerning relations between the De Gaullist movement and the United States, particularly during the period of the St. Pierre and Miquelon incident, the second volume, which appeared three years later and concerns the years 1942–44, is no more than an indictment of General Henri Honoré Giraud and as such is of little interest to the historian.

To complete the picture of the events through which the unity of the French forces fighting side by side with the Allies was achieved, reference must be made, along with De Gaulle's and Catroux's writings, to General Giraud's memoirs.[92] By radically different methods, Giraud was also seeking to raise France from the ashes of defeat. After his daring escape from a German prison in April, 1942,[93] he had proposed a plan whereby the Vichy government's military forces would be used to establish a bridgehead to facilitate the Anglo-American landing in France. This project was abandoned, but, in any event, it was with Giraud that the Allies worked out the

[91] Jacques Soustelle, *Envers et contre tout*, Vol. I: *De Londres à Alger. Souvenirs et documents sur la France libre (1940–1942)*; Vol. II: *D'Alger à Paris* (Paris: Laffont, 1947–50).

[92] *Un seul but: La Victoire. Alger 1942–1944* (Paris: Julliard, 1949).

[93] See the account in Giraud, *Mes évasions* (Paris: Julliard, 1947).

agreements that made it possible for them to land in North Africa without encountering resistance. It is precisely on these negotiations that Giraud's recollections are invaluable (these should be studied, along with those of Lemaigre-Dubreuil,[94] who acted as intermediary between Giraud and the American Consul General in Algiers, Robert Murphy) because they also contain the documentation on the accords reached by Giraud by virtue of which the American government, for the first time, guaranteed the re-establishment of France as a great power and the restoration of her prewar possessions.

The influence exerted by the military on French foreign policy gives unusual importance to the memoirs of General Gamelin,[95] Army Chief of Staff from 1931, Vice-President of the Supreme War Council from 1935, and Chief of the General Staff from 1938. The content of his three volumes of memoirs is largely technical, but the student of international relations finds significant material, particularly concerning the attitude of the French leaders during the crisis of August, 1939, on relations between Belgium and the Allies during the period of the "phoney war," the plans for a Norwegian campaign, and the first phase of the German offensive in March, 1940.

Equally noteworthy are the memoirs of General Weygand,[96] who, in three thick volumes, has reconstructed his long military career from the events of World War I to his mission to North Africa as delegate-general of the Vichy government from October, 1940, to November, 1941. As Foch's principal collaborator, Weygand is in a position to provide firsthand information on the position taken by the French Supreme Command during the armistice negotiations of 1918 and their application, the peace conference negotiations, and the German problem in the period imme-diately after World War I. Weygand also offers valuable data on his mission to Warsaw in 1920 as military adviser to the Poles during the Russo-Polish war.

The part of his memoirs that attracts the scholar's attention deals with the period after May 19, 1940, when he was called to replace General Gamelin, who had been dismissed from his poisition as Chief of the General Staff following the defeats suffered by the French armies during the first phase of the French campaign. Weygand's memoirs are one of the best sources available for the study of the process by which the Frenchmen in authority arrived at the decision to request an armistice. Undoubtedly,

[94] J. Lemaigre-Dubreuil, "Giraud et De Gaulle à Alger," *Revue de Paris*, July, 1949.

[95] Maurice Gamelin, *Servir*, Vol. I: *Les Armées françaises de 1940*; Vol. II: *Le prologue du drame (1930–août 1939)*; Vol. III: *La guerre* (Paris: Plon, 1946–47).

[96] Maxime Weygand, *Mémoires*, Vol. I: *Idéal vécu*; Vol. II: *Mirages et réalité*; Vol. III: *Rappelé au service* (Paris: Flammarion, 1950–57).

Weygand's influence in this question was far from minor. The General held an entirely Continental view of the conflict then in progress and was certain that Great Britain would soon be obliged to surrender. On the basis of this premise, Weygand refused to end hostilities with the surrender of the armed forces of metropolitan France and then continue the struggle from the Empire. He was also afraid that the French populace, left to its own devices, would fall prey to Communist extremism.

If, in these crucial circumstances, General Weygand was guilty of serious errors of judgment, his conduct after the conclusion of the armistice was unquestionably straightforward. Among the Vichy ministers he represented most clearly those opposed to collaboration with Germany, insisting that it was only necessary to observe the armistice terms rigidly and to oppose any German violation of these terms or any British attempts to draw France into the war once again. He applied these principles when, in October, 1940, he was sent to North Africa as delegate-general of the Vichy government, and many details show that on more than one occasion Hitler was dissuaded from intervening forcibly in unoccupied France because he feared that such an action would impel Weygand to ally himself with the British. On the other hand, it should be emphasized that the faith that the Washington leadership had in Weygand formed the basis for the Weygand-Murphy Accords, which assured the maintenance of the *status quo* in North Africa for a time and permitted the American government to exercise an indirect control in this area—a development that was to prove exceedingly important some time later in planning the Allied landing of November, 1942.

Weygand's successor in North Africa, General Juin, has also left two volumes of memoirs.[97] The first describes events related to the Allied landing in North Africa in November, 1942, and the successive Tunisian and Italian campaigns that found him in command of the French troops. In spite of his eminent position among the Free French leaders, his contribution outside of the military field is extremely modest. The same may be said for the first part of the second volume, concerning the liberation of France.

3. THE BRITISH MEMORIALISTS.

a. Henderson.

The first British memoir contribution on the events immediately preceding the outbreak of World War II is the volume by Sir Nevile Henderson,[98]

[97] Maréchal Juin, *Mémoires* (2 vols.; Paris: Fayard, 1959–60).
[98] *Failure of a Mission* (London: Hodder and Stoughton, 1940).

Ambassador to Berlin from 1937 to 1939. Today, the Henderson image is that of a man who firmly believed in the possibility of reaching a *modus vivendi* with the Germans, provided that a policy of friendship toward Germany was followed in which concessions on those points that he believed were justifiable objectives of Hitlerian policy were made. When he arrived in Berlin, Henderson pursued this objective passionately, indicating his approval of the *Anschluss,* urging the acceptance of the Munich Pact, and to the very end working for a German-Polish understanding. The failure of his mission exposed him to widespread criticism. Yet today it may be said that Henderson's efforts, in effect, were extremely useful to the cause of the Allies. The attempts toward reaching an understanding made by a man who, in all honesty, believed in peaceful coexistence with Germany, demonstrated by their very failure that the only way to stop Hitler was by force of arms.

When in September, 1939, the French and the British decided on war against Germany, they did so with heavy hearts but with the conviction that it was no longer possible to avoid the conflict if they hoped to preserve the moral and material values of their societies. There are many who criticized and who still criticize the long series of efforts made to arrive at a peaceful adjustment with Hitler prior to the war and who point to Munich as the most ignominious of diplomatic defeats. Unquestionably, these were all defeats, but their failure was of fundamental importance: Hitler's bad faith was exposed in a way that left no room for doubt when, after solemnly declaring that he would not incorporate any non-Germans into the Third Reich, he destroyed the independence of Czechoslovakia in March, 1939, within only a few months of his promise to the contrary. With the occupation of Czechoslovakia, the democracies lost the support of the Czechoslovak divisions, but they gained something more: the conviction that they were fighting for a just cause. Those who insist that the western democracies were in a more favorable position to fight a war in 1938 forget that being well armed is not enough for victory, but that behind the arms there must be men willing to die for their beliefs.

Henderson wrote another important volume on his activities prior to his mission to Berlin, and it was published posthumously in 1945.[99] Among the most interesting chapters are those concerning his mission to Yugoslavia, where Henderson's personal friendship with Prince Paul made it possible for him to observe political developments there from a particularly favorable vantage point. Among other details, Henderson reveals that he was aware of the major effort made by King Alexander to resolve the many problems

---

[99] *Water under the Bridges* (London: Hodder and Stoughton, 1945).

existing between Belgrade and Rome and to reach an accord with Italy, an attempt which demonstrates, despite its failure and contrary to prevailing opinion, the tenacity with which the Yugoslav Sovereign sought to reach a compromise with Italy.

The Italo-Yugoslav negotiations were begun in February, 1931, and were conducted in complete secrecy by the Italian architect Malagola, who, having known King Alexander since childhood, had been called to Belgrade to modernize the royal palace. Despite the tensions existing between the two countries and the negative results of the frequent meetings between Grandi and Marinkovic, Alexander continued to believe that an agreement could be reached if only a meeting between himself and Mussolini could be arranged at a spot far from the Rome and Belgrade influences, which, by their very extremism, constantly blocked any attempt to reach a compromise acceptable to both sides.

On the other hand, the support given by the Italian government to Hungarian revisionist policy and the close contacts that the Italians maintained with Croatian organizations rendered it particularly advisable to reach an agreement with Italy. Among other things, it would put an end to the armament policy that was severely damaging both the Yugoslav economy and the country's finances.

From the beginning the negotiations appeared to be taking a favorable turn,[100] even though, because of their nature, they could move only very slowly. While there were no particular obstacles in reaching agreements on many points, it was extremely difficult to find acceptable grounds for compromise on the key issue of the negotiations, that is, Albania.

In the years following World War I the Italo-Yugoslav struggle for control of Albania adversely affected the relations between the two powers, and the Italo-Albanian treaty of November, 1927, was a principal factor in deepening the already existing tension between Italy and Yugoslavia. Two schools of thought on the issue developed in both capitals. One advocated a compromise on the order of the one realized in 1897 between Visconti Venosta and Goluchowski, which proved to have a beneficial effect on Italo-Austrian relations. The other advocated an integral solution, that is, the absorption of Albania into one nation's exclusive sphere of influence.

In this situation Mussolini proposed an accord obliging the two contracting powers to respect the independence and the integrity of Albania but also requested that Yugoslavia recognize the "predominance" of Italian interests in that country. King Alexander refused to recognize formally this Italian "predominance" but, in turn, proposed a formula whereby Yugosla-

[100] Further details on these negotiations may be found in the volume by J. F. Montgomery (see below).

via obligated herself not to interfere with Italian interests in Albania, which was the equivalent of a *de facto* recognition of the existing situation.

Agreement appeared to have been reached on the basis of this formula. However, just as the Mussolini-King Alexander meeting was about to take place, riots in a Bosnian village induced the Fascist dictator to break off negotiations until the Yugoslav internal situation was clarified.

b. Churchill.

No other memoir source on World War II can compete with Churchill's memoirs[101] in the amount of evidence and the wealth of documentation presented in his six volumes, which cover the political and military aspects of the entire conflict.

Because of the posts he held and his tremendous personal prestige, the British Prime Minister was truly the soul of the anti-Nazi coalition. The roles of such men as Roosevelt and Stalin must not be minimized, but he, more than anyone else, was in a position to provide an over-all picture of events, along with details on behind-the-scenes activities that permit an accurate reconstruction of the incidents as they occurred. On the other hand, the very nature of his character led Churchill to extend the sphere of his activities as far as possible and to play a determining role in decision-making in every instance where it might influence, even indirectly, the proper functioning of the whole. At this point it should be noted that the British Prime Minister's memoirs are also, although not exclusively, a source for diplomatic history and that, moreover, the portion of the memoirs devoted to military events is, on the whole, the most thoroughly detailed. This is explained partly by the author's tendency toward writing a complete history of World War II, incorporating the part he played, but it is also due to other factors.

In the first place, one should remember that the influence exerted by the civil authorities on military operations during World War II was unequaled in history, even during World War I. This is more easily understood in the Soviet situation, where Stalin held the highest post in the armed forces, or in the United States, where the Constitution confers on the President the role of Commander-in-Chief as well, but in Great Britain this situation was possible only because of Churchill's prestige and personal inclinations. The reader is surely surprised by the number and importance of the decisions made by Churchill in purely military matters. Not only did

[101] Winston Churchill, *The Second World War* (6 vols.; London: Cassell, 1948–53).

he bring his personal influence to bear on the general conduct of operations, but he also participated in the planning of operations, in the selection of objectives, in the distribution of forces, and so on. The detail with which Churchill treats the military aspects of the war stems, therefore, perhaps even more from the profound interest in military affairs which he manifested throughout his entire life than from the actual wartime situation in which absolute priority is given to military operations.

On the other hand, it is evident that problems of a military character can also have a precise political content. A typical case was the much-discussed Churchill proposal for an Allied operation in the Balkans, a project that was clearly dictated by the desire to protect British interests in that sector in the face of the Soviet advance.

The disagreements, on occasion rather serious, that developed between London and Washington concerning the political and military conduct of the war are discussed by Churchill in very moderate terms, and the same may be said of his objective account of relations with the Soviet Union.

In this context, it is interesting to note that the Prime Minister's memoirs reaffirm the extraordinary influence on the relations between the Soviet Union and the western allies exerted by the fear of each party that the other would sign a separate peace with Germany. Among the many episodes illustrating this point, especially indicative is Moscow's violent reaction to news of the contact between the German S. S. general, Wolff, and the head of the American Strategic Services in Europe, Allen Dulles, in Switzerland in March, 1945. In addition, Churchill's narration of the events leading to his decision not to oppose Stalin's claims regarding Poland and to the decision to support Tito instead of Mihailovic are particularly significant.

However, Churchill's moderate tone does not prevent the reader from noting the substantial difference in the attitudes of the British Prime Minister and the leadership in Washington on the matter of relations with the U.S.S.R. On this point, while Churchill's obvious preoccupation revealed his much more exact idea of the difficulties that would be encountered, they also brought to light the persistent optimism of Roosevelt and Hull, who, even though they had been alarmed by several independent actions by the Kremlin (a typical example was its unilateral action in establishing diplomatic relations with the Badoglio government in Italy[102]), continued to believe for a long time that it was possible to collaborate with

---

[102] For further details, see Toscano, "La ripresa delle relazioni diplomatiche tra l'Italia e l'Unione Sovietica nel corso della seconda guerra mondiale," *Comunità Internazionale*, 1962, fasc. I.

the Soviets effectively. As a matter of fact, it was only after disagreements emerged during the Dumbarton Oaks Conference of August–September, 1944, that Washington began to look at the problem realistically, without, however, completely abandoning all hope of being able to include the Soviet Union in the future world organization.

These differences in evaluation between London and Washington were to become more acute during the last phase of the conflict, when military operations assumed a greater political significance. Churchill did not overlook the enormous importance of extending the zone of occupation as far to the east as possible and of doing so by exploiting the very minor resistance in west Germany. Unfortunately, during this decisive phase of the war, President Roosevelt died, and Truman, despite his unquestioned capacity, was not yet sufficiently well informed to grasp fully the import of the new situation which was emerging in Europe following Germany's defeat.

The disappearance of the German peril, the only factor capable of guaranteeing the stability of the coalition, restored to Stalin a freedom of action that he intended to exploit to the limit that the western powers would permit. It is to Churchill's credit that he understood that the validity of the Yalta agreements and, in general, of all of the accords signed with the Soviet Union depended primarily on the capacity of the Anglo-Saxon powers to maintain sufficient armed forces in Europe to preserve the equilibrium. This was fundamental, for the different concept of the value of treaties held by Moscow made illusory any hope of reaching a satisfactory *modus vivendi* with the Soviets and reopened a number of questions that the western powers considered as resolved.

Finally, from a literary standpoint, it should be noted that passages from Churchill's volumes have outstanding merit and that, together with General de Gaulle's, these memoirs deserve the highest praise of all those that have appeared to date on World War II.

c. Hoare.

Another important British political personage, Sir Samuel Hoare (later Lord Templewood), has published two volumes of his memoirs. He was a member of government almost without interruption from 1931 to May, 1940. The fall of Chamberlain, whose policies Hoare had ardently supported, signaled the end of Hoare's career as well. He had been Secretary of State for India, First Lord of the Admiralty, Air Minister, Home Secretary, and Minister of Foreign Affairs. Having left the government, he accepted the post of Ambassador to Madrid, one of the neutral capitals of primary concern to all of the belligerents.

The first volume of Hoare's memoirs[103] concerns his mission to Spain and was written immediately upon his return to London, while the second volume[104] was completed later and covers the longer period of his tenure as Secretary of State. They are quite different in character because the second not only reflects the change in the author's viewpoint but also the changes in the international political climate that developed after the first volume was written.

In the first book Hoare, in effect, sought to demonstrate that although he was obliged to leave his ministerial post, he was able to make an important contribution to his country's victory. From a psychological standpoint, this attitude is entirely understandable in a man who has been removed from a responsible position in the government at the very moment of decisive action, but it hardly reflects the facts. While the action of the British Ambassador was undoubtedly of some importance, it was far from being decisive in blocking Spain's intervention in the war on the side of the Axis. Moreover, his evaluation of Spanish policy is colored by his crusading spirit against Nazism and by the conviction that collaboration between the victorious Great Powers would continue into the future. It should be noted, however, that his was a typical attitude in the first months following the war.

In the second volume it is possible to see clearly that time and the changing international scene have permitted the author to present a more objective account of events, even though the central theme of the book is a defense of British policy or, rather, an explanation of the circumstances that determined the policies of the MacDonald, Baldwin, and Chamberlain governments. Moreover, in addition to his notes and personal papers, Hoare made use of the material that had been published in the meantime, and these additions served to make his narrative more accurate.

Hoare provides numerous interesting details on his mission to Spain, particularly on the economic negotiations between Spain and Great Britain, on the activities of the German diplomats in Spain, and on the political atmosphere of Madrid during the war. It is precisely on the subject of the political situation in Spain that Hoare demonstrates his lack of understanding of Franco's game. During Hoare's sojourn there, he saw four different ministers assume control of the Spanish Foreign Ministry, Beig-

[103] Samuel Hoare Viscount Templewood, *Ambassador on Special Mission* (London: Collins, 1946).
[104] *Nine Troubled Years* (London: Collins, 1954).

beder, Serrano Suñer, Jordana, and Lequerica. Each of their tenures of office coincided with a particular phase of Spanish policy, always closely related to the military fortunes of the Axis, but the significance of this relationship almost completely escapes the author because he was unable to find the nucleus of the Spanish problem.

If, in the summer of 1940, German troops had landed on the British Isles, Franco would probably have imitated Mussolini's action in deciding to intervene at the last moment to partake of the victor's booty. The failure of the Germans to invade Britain exposed the Italian error to Franco, and he decided to play a waiting game. The onerous demands made by Franco during his meeting with Hitler at Hendaye in October, 1940, are reminiscent of Mussolini's demands to Hitler in his letter of August 25, 1939. In both cases (and keeping in mind the relativity of historical comparisons) the demands were such that they could not all be met. However, the presence of Serrano Suñer at the Foreign Ministry indicated that Franco was still banking on an Axis victory.

In September, 1942, Serrano Suñer was succeeded by Jordana. Hoare devotes his attention to describing the delicacy of his task in Spain on the eve of the Allied landing in North Africa. It cannot be denied that these were difficult days, but the presence in the Foreign Ministry of Jordana, a man far less sympathetic to the Axis cause than his predecessor, was an indication that Spain would continue to maintain its neutrality, perhaps with even more rigidity. It is interesting to recall in this context, the exchange of notes between Jordana and Hoare of February, 1943. Hoare insisted that the time was ripe for a shift in Spanish policy and urged that Spain openly embrace the cause of the Allies. He outlined the reasons why the latter would surely win the war and presented his views of what postwar Europe would be like in an effort to dissipate Spanish fears regarding the Soviet Union. Jordana's reply, read today, becomes singularly prophetic. He clearly predicted the situations that developed in Europe after 1948 and the difficulties that Europe finds itself in today. As for the substance of Hoare's request, he did not take into account that his suggestion could not have gained for Spain more than what that country's economic and political conditions permitted it to give.

Particular attention should be given to the pages in the second volume referring to the months when Hoare was the British Foreign Secretary, June–December, 1935. The Ethiopian crisis was reaching a climax in the shadow of resurgent German dynamism. Hoare immediately understood that it would be extremely difficult to continue to support the principles of the League of Nations without, at the same time, the willingness to back the consequences of such a policy by the force of arms. In order to avoid this eventuality he authorized Eden's mission to Rome, which, as is known, failed.[105] The Geneva discussions that followed did not force the Italian government to back down in its decision, and in October Italy invaded Ethiopia. France made it clear that it would not resort to military measures and that, therefore, the only road open to the British was that of negotiations. Therefore, the Committee of Five of the League of Nations re-examined and amplified their original proposals granting further concessions to Italy, and these became the bases of the Hoare-Laval project to resolve the controversy.

Hoare records the details of his meeting with Laval in Paris and emphasizes his astonishment at the publicity given his visit to the Quai d'Orsay. After the meeting, he journeyed to Switzerland, where he planned a few days' rest. A trifling incident made it impossible for him to return to London immediately after the French press had revealed the details of the Hoare-Laval plan, which provoked a violent reaction among the British public, and Prime Minister Baldwin was forced to face the first Parliamentary criticisms alone. Upon his return Hoare was invited to retract the commitments he had made in Paris, but, rather than do so, Hoare preferred to resign. His resignation weakened the prospects that existed for the compromise toward which Mussolini was favorably disposed.

In searching for the causes of this failure, Hoare blames himself for not having anticipated the reaction of the British public to the project. It seemed to be so obviously right, he states, to keep Italy on the British side that he did not think that it would be too difficult to explain to his colleagues in the government and to the country the exact nature of the controversy and the exact nature of the dangers that would accompany failure. On the other hand, Hoare insists that in the entire question the military weakness of Great Britain was not taken into account, and he blames Baldwin for not having spoken out clearly in Parliament instead of hiding behind useless reticence.

Many more subjects of interest are touched upon in this volume, among them the messages exchanged between Roosevelt and Chamberlain early in 1938; the meetings between the Italian Ambassador, Grandi, Chamberlain, and Eden during the discussions for the Italo-British *rapprochement* in the spring of 1938; and the last-minute hesitations of the French before deciding to fight in defense of Poland. These topics indicate the importance of the Hoare volumes to the study of international relations for the period 1935–39.

[105] For the details, see Toscano, "Eden a Roma alla vigilia del conflitto italo-etiopico," *Nuova Antologia*, fasc. January, 1960.

d. The Other British Memoir Sources.

In contrast to French memoir-writing, the British sources are less abundant and, on the whole, of minor interest. This is due to the almost universal tendency on the part of the British writers, a very wise one on the part of career diplomats especially, to maintain a distinct reserve in compiling their memoirs.

For the period preceding the advent of Hitler to power in Germany, the diary of Lord D'Abernon,[106] British Ambassador to Berlin from 1920 to 1926, is especially noteworthy. In his three volumes of annotations, Lord D'Abernon is revealed to be a champion of Anglo-German collaboration, a collaboration which he believed to be necessary in order to achieve a durable peace in Europe and to put the British Empire in a position to defend itself against the Bolshevik peril.

Recently, an important contribution on the immediate postwar years has been made by Lord Beaverbrook in his richly documented memoirs of that period.[107] These recollections now make it possible to examine in detail the whole question of Lloyd George's resignation, which was prompted by the debates on British foreign policy led by Bonar Law following the development of the Greco-Turkish crisis in the fall of 1922. On that occasion, the prevailing opinion was that Great Britain should not intervene in international crises without the support of France and the other Allies because she could not alone assume the burden of being keeper of the peace for the entire world. The comparison of the causes leading to Bonar Law's support of a nonintervention policy and those leading to Chamberlain's appeasement policy are important to an understanding of the British position on the eve of World War II.

Several significant references may be found in the volume by Randall,[108] who, as secretary of the British Legation accredited to the Holy See from its establishment in 1925 to 1930, is able to discuss several problems that were subjects of negotiations between London and the Vatican (the question of the Maltese Catholics) and the events leading to the Lateran Pacts. Considerably richer are the memoirs of Sir Walford Selby,[109] who was

---

[106] *Lord D'Abernon's Diary*, Vol. I: *From Spa (1920) to Rapallo (1922)*; Vol. II: *The Years of Crisis (June, 1922–December, 1923)*; Vol. III: *The Years of Recovery (January, 1924–October, 1926)* (London: Hodder and Stoughton, 1929–30).

[107] *The Decline and Fall of Lloyd George* (London: Collins, 1963). See also Lord Beaverbrook, *Politicians and the War, 1914–1916* (Vol. I; London: Butterworth, 1928. Vol. II; London: Lane, 1932.

[108] Alec Randall, *Vatican Assignment* (London: Heinemann, 1956).

[109] *Diplomatic Twilight 1930–1940* (London: John Murray, 1953).

British Minister to Vienna from 1932 to October, 1937, and to Lisbon from November, 1937, to December, 1940. The chapters on his Austrian mission contain important data, particularly in reference to the crisis of 1934. Somewhat more sketchy is the account of his mission to Portugal, where he faced a situation rendered difficult by the divergent positions of Britain and Portugal on the issue of the Spanish Civil War.

The scholar's expectations were not fulfilled by Simon's memoirs,[110] for it was hoped that he would contribute significant material on the events of 1934–35, when he was British Foreign Secretary. In fact, he adds little to what was already known on that period, while the pages in which he defends British action during the Sudeten crisis are much more interesting. Simon asserts that the critics of the Munich Pact attacked the work of the Chamberlain government without indicating what alternative action could have saved Czechoslovakia. It should be emphasized, Simon adds, that if Munich did not represent a brilliant page in the annals of British diplomacy, it prevented a similar situation from developing later, as demonstrated by the reaction of the British government when faced with Hitler's aggression against Czechoslovakia in March of the following year.

The same subject is examined in the memoirs of Lord Halifax,[111] who was Viceroy of India from 1926 to 1930, Minister of Foreign Affairs from February, 1938, to December, 1940, and then Ambassador to Washington until May, 1946. He affirms that criticisms of British policy during the Munich crisis may be explained by the public resentment felt in the democracies at having witnessed the demise of a small country at the hands of a dictator while French and British intervention never went beyond the level of diplomacy. Criticisms on this basis are not well founded, Lord Halifax adds. Instead, the critics should recall that not many months before neither the governments nor the public in the democracies had understood the necessity of rearming to face the German threat and that, therefore, no steps were taken to crush Hitler's aggressive tendencies when their cost would have been slight. The price for these blunders was paid during the Sudeten crisis, and the result could not have been otherwise because both France and Britain were unprepared to contest Germany on a military plane. If this portion of the memoirs contain some elements worthy of note, the same cannot be said for Lord Halifax's treatment of the later period. He has little to say about his activities as Foreign Secretary in the Churchill Cabinet, and this omission is serious because it is known that the differences in the points of view held by Churchill and Halifax played a role in the formulation of British policy during the summer of 1940, particularly

[110] Viscount Simon, Retrospect (London: Hutchinson, 1952).
[111] The Earl of Halifax, The Fullness of Days (London: Collins, 1957).

on such matters of significance as the question of relations with Vichy France. The references to his mission to Washington are largely general, so there is little to be learned from them.

Lord Strang's volume[112] is particularly interesting. Strang was head of the Central Department of the Foreign Office from 1937 to 1942, Undersecretary for Foreign Affairs in 1942, member of the European Consultative Commission (E. C. A.) in 1943, and Permanent Undersecretary in the Foreign Office from 1947 on. Writing shortly after the publication of the British diplomatic documents, he was able to refer more freely to the various events preceding the outbreak of the war, and on some he wrote in great detail, such as the Sudeten crisis and the Anglo-French-Soviet negotiations of the summer of 1939. On these he provides important summaries, adding many incidents drawn from his personal experiences. Concerning the Munich crisis, Strang adds that the agreement initialed by the democracies at that time was a tragic necessity because of previous blunders. He also provides information on the London and Paris positions vis-à-vis the Czechoslovak problem, the effect of Henlein's maneuvers on the attitude of the British government and public, and on the discussions leading to the joint Hitler-Chamberlain declaration of September 30. Strang was extremely skeptical of the possibility of Soviet intervention on behalf of Czechoslovakia, in the light of the difficulties that were underscored the following year when joint action was proposed in defense of Poland.

One of the most significant segments of the book is devoted to the Anglo-French-Soviet negotiations of 1939. The author is rather sparing in his disclosures and, in effect, rarely goes beyond a reconstruction of the events that is already possible through the documents published in the official collection of the Foreign Office. Yet his treatment is rich in observations and clarifications that are important for an understanding of the mental attitude of the British statesmen at the beginning of the negotiations, their reaction to the French position, and the difficulties they encountered in dealing with the Soviets. The portion of the memoir dealing with the work of the European Consultative Commission, a subject already known from the Hull memoirs and the Hopkins papers, is well worthy of mention, especially for the details furnished by Strang as British representative on that commission.

The most important part of the Kirkpatrik memoirs[113] deals with the period when he was the secretary of the British Embassy in Berlin, 1933–39. The author not only followed the developments of the Czechoslo-

[112] *Home and Abroad* (London: Deutsch, 1956).
[113] Ivone Kirkpatrik, *The Inner Circle. Memoirs* (London: Macmillan, 1959).

vak crisis from Berlin but also participated directly in the Anglo-German negotiations as Chamberlain's interpreter. His observations on British policy regarding Germany do not vary greatly from those of Halifax and Strang, although he had no personal position to defend as a policymaker. Other useful data are also provided by Kirkpatrik relative to the European Control Commission, of which he was a part in 1944 to 1945.

The Robert Vansittart memoirs[114] contain little new information, despite the fact that during his career he held several key posts, among them those of membership in the British peace delegation to Paris in 1919, secretary to Lord Curzon, and Permanent Undersecretary at the Foreign Office between 1930 and 1937. The author chose to interpret the events to which he was witness with the idea of drawing some useful conclusions for the present, rather than to describe his own role in the events. His temperament is reflected in the polemical nature of some of his conclusions, but at the same time his memoirs contain some very valuable observations. These are employed by the author to defend specific positions and are supported by details drawn from his personal experiences that are of real interest to historians.

The recently published Eden memoirs for the years 1931–38[115] are clearly superior to the usual British memoir published in the postwar period. The volume is distinguished not only by the personality of the writer but also by the fact that he was able to consult the official documents, which he cites at length, in addition to his personal papers. Consequently, his memoir is to be considered a primary source, particularly since the official documents for the period have not yet been published by the Foreign Office.

Eden's comments on his visit to Italy and his talks with Mussolini in June, 1935, support what was revealed in the Italian documents.[116] The conversations at the Palazzo Venezia were not conducted in an atmosphere of tension, as described by the press of the period, nor did Eden receive treatment inferior to what was due his ministerial rank. However, the proposals he was authorized to make to Mussolini for a compromise solution to the Ethiopian question were not satisfactory. On the other hand, Eden

---

[114] *The Mist Procession* (London: Hutchinson, 1958); *Lessons of My Life* (London: Hutchinson, 1943); *Bones of Contention* (London: Hutchinson, 1945); *Events and Shadows. A Policy for the Remnants of a Century* (London: Hutchinson, 1947); *Even Now* (London: Hutchinson, 1949); "The Decline of Diplomacy," *Foreign Affairs*, January, 1950.

[115] The Earl of Avon, *The Eden Memoirs. Facing the Dictators* (London: Cassell, 1962).

[116] See Toscano, "Eden a Roma alla vigilia del conflitto italo-etiopico," *Nuova Antologia*, January, 1960.

did not fully exploit the situation to discover what were the minimum demands that Italy was prepared to accept.

Moreover, Eden's first ventures as Foreign Secretary were not very auspicious. He had replaced Hoare in the Foreign Office when the Ethiopian crisis was well on its way toward being resolved in the manner that he had hoped to prevent, and shortly thereafter the remilitarization of the Rhineland was to create a fundamental problem for European stability. As a matter of fact, the new crisis was not entirely unexpected. The French government was perfectly well aware that the ratification of the Franco-Soviet Alliance would provoke extreme reactions in Berlin, the most probable of which was an action in the Rhineland. Flandin repeatedly consulted with Eden for the purpose of establishing a common course of action, but he was invariably told by Eden that Great Britain could not advise France on problems that were primarily of French concern. Eden's thesis was that Great Britain should not choose a position that offered the alternatives of either fighting to defend the Rhineland or accepting the remilitarization of the area but that it was necessary, instead, to initiate negotiations immediately to re-examine the pertinent clauses of the Treaty of Versailles.

One of the most important contributions made by Eden emerges from his notes and account of the Rhineland crisis. Until the publication of this volume, it was generally believed that France was largely responsible for the failure of the two western democracies to act forcefully in the Rhineland question. Instead, it appears that France was far more ready to act than had generally been supposed. Therefore, the thesis that the failure of the democracies to act was due primarily to the reluctance of the French government and of the French military to risk the consequences of war must be modified, in the sense that in addition to the effect of the pessimistic evaluation of the military situation by the French General Staff, the Paris government was profoundly influenced in its negative stand by the attitude of the British Foreign Office.

If we assume this conclusion to be valid, it becomes necessary to point out that Eden's criticisms of the policy of appeasement are greatly weakened because, in effect, it was Eden himself who took the first concrete step to implement that policy. Naturally, Eden insists that on the occasion of the remilitarization of the Rhineland he became convinced that Hitler would not keep his word, and, since an accord with him was impossible, Britain should rearm. However, in the first place, it should be noted that his convictions on this point were not effectively implemented during the two years that he remained in the government, while at the same time he continued his rigid opposition to Italian activities when it was obvious that

Italy did not pose the major threat to the peace of Europe. Second, the question of whether the Rhineland crisis was—as the defenders of the appeasement policy insist—the last favorable occasion to stop Hitler is still open to debate. However, this was not the first concrete illustration of Hitler's methods, and from this standpoint much of the criticism that Eden reserves for some of his colleagues can also be applied to him. Finally, once the mistake of allowing Hitler to succeed in his Rhineland venture was made, Chamberlain's attempt to re-establish close collaboration with Italy in order to circumscribe Germany's expansionist tendencies acquires great significance—an attempt that Eden consistently opposed during his tenure of office.

The volume with which Eden has recently completed his memoirs[117] has, in its organization, the merits of the preceding one. However, its value as a source is somewhat more limited. What he writes concerning the months of 1938–39 when he was not part of the government is of little interest. Essentially, it is simply a projection of the position that led to his resignation in February, 1938, with no such examination of the problems that threatened the peace of the world as is found in Churchill's attack on the Chamberlain Cabinet. For the war years, when Eden was in the government, first as Minister for the Dominions, then as Minister of War (May–December, 1940), and thenceforth as Foreign Secretary, his testimony would be invaluable if we did not have Churchill's memoirs. Consequently, Eden's memoirs simply reflect what, as a matter of fact, was his position in the government, that of a good administrator under the firm guidance of the Prime Minister, whose activities were conducted in Churchill's imposing shadow. Of course, Eden did not always passively accept the Prime Minister's directives, but the differences of opinion between the two men never reached the stage of a personal clash, as was the case between Roosevelt and Hull. While Eden's volume adds some details to Churchill's narrative (see, for example, the summary of his mission to Moscow in December, 1941, his journey to the United States in March, 1943, and the Yalta Conference), it adds little to the general picture of British policy during the war given in Churchill's volumes.

On the period preceding World War II, the Peterson memoirs[118] contain important information. Peterson held a high-level post in the Foreign Office from 1931 to 1936 and was head of mission in various European capitals and ultimately Ambassador to Moscow from 1946 to 1949. Especially pertinent are his observations on British policy during the Ethiopian crisis

[117] *The Eden Memoirs: The Reckoning* (London: Cassell, 1965).
[118] Maurice Peterson, *Both Sides of the Curtain. An Autobiography* (London: Constable, 1950).

and on the role he played in elaborating the Hoare-Laval compromise proposal.

Sir David Kelly has condensed, in a very valuable volume,[119] the essence of the lessons learned during his brilliant diplomatic career. This work should be examined carefully for its interesting disclosures, for example, on his Cairo mission of 1935–38, during which the Anglo-Egyptian treaty of August, 1936, was signed.

As has been noted, British memoir-writing on World War II is dominated by Churchill's work, not only because of its intrinsic value but also because of the obvious limitations of the other contributions. However, the memoirs of Hugh Dalton,[120] Minister of Economic Warfare from 1940 to 1942 and Minister of Trade until 1945, are somewhat above the average. As an authoritative representative of the Labour party, Dalton provides a significant contribution on the attitude of the party regarding the Spanish Civil War and in the period 1929–31, when he held the post of Undersecretary for Foreign Affairs in the MacDonald government. The part of the memoir referring to World War II is less satisfactory because, while he bases his recollections on the diary he kept during his entire political career, the omissions for the period after 1940 are so extensive as to reduce the value of his account. Thus, for example, he makes few references to Anglo-American economic relations that were of fundamental importance to the British war effort, nor does he discuss the question of the economic blockade of unoccupied France or the negotiations on this problem between London and Washington.

The little volume, containing interesting disclosures, written by Lonsdale Bryans[121] is of particular importance because of the author's frequent contacts with German anti-Nazis. During his prewar German sojourn, Bryans became aware of the deep-rooted opposition to Hitler that existed especially among the military, and immediately after the outbreak of the war Bryans went to Italy and, with the help of Von Hassell's son-in-law, was able to meet with the former German Ambassador to Rome on two occasions in Switzerland, in January and April, 1940. On these occasions Von Hassell declared that if Britain would assure reasonable treatment of an anti-Nazi Germany many German political and military leaders would rebel against Hitler. He and Bryans prepared a *promemoria* on the subject which was to have been approved by Lord Halifax. London's failure to

[119] *The Ruling Few, or the Human Background to Diplomacy* (London: Hollis and Carter, 1952).

[120] *Memoirs*, Vol. I: *Call Back Yesterday* (1887–1931); Vol. II: *The Fateful Years* (1931–1945) (London: Frederick Muller, 1953, 1957).

[121] J. Lonsdale Bryans, *Blind Victory* (*Secret Communications, Halifax-Hassell*) (London: Skeffington, 1951).

reply aborted the initiative, for after the German victories in France it had become meaningless; nor did Bryans have any greater success, after shifting his operations to Lisbon, in interesting the British government in contacting the leaders of the opposition in Germany and Italy.

The contributions of the diplomats are extremely modest. Among them are the memoirs of the former Ambassador to Ankara, Knatchbull-Hugessen;[122] those of Sir Gerald Campbell,[123] who held several posts including that of Minister-Counsellor to Washington; those of the former Minister to Sofia, Rendel;[124] and those of Sir Robert Craigie,[125] Ambassador to Japan from 1931 to 1937. On the other hand, the memoirs of the politicians are considerably more valuable. The former Minister of Information in the Churchill Cabinet, Duff Cooper, has published a volume of recollections[126] covering his entire political career, but from the point of view of diplomatic history the account of his mission to Morocco in June, 1940, is particularly pertinent. Duff Cooper was charged with contacting Mandel and other French political leaders opposed to the armistice with Germany who had left France aboard the "Massilia." Equally significant are the pages devoted to his embassy to the French Liberation Committee in Algiers. In this situation, Duff Cooper took a different position from that of his colleague, General Spears, in Lebanon and Syria, made every effort to arrange a conciliation between Churchill and De Gaulle, and accompanied the latter to London shortly before the Normandy landings. Later, in September, 1944, he followed De Gaulle to Paris, where he remained as British Ambassador until 1947.

An important exception to the observation made above concerning the memoirs of British diplomats is the work of Fitzroy MacLean,[127] who, from time to time, was entrusted with a diplomatic mission, was in the Intelligence Service, and was a member of the House of Commons. His volume is especially important for clarifying numerous aspects of British policy in the Balkans and, specifically, for an understanding of London's attitude toward Tito and his regime. During the war MacLean parachuted into Yugoslavia, and there he became convinced that it was necessary to relegate the forces led by King Peter to a secondary position and to support Marshal Tito instead. MacLean's memoirs outline the phases of the

[122] Hugh Knatchbull-Hugessen, *Diplomat in Peace and War* (London: John Murray, 1949).
[123] *Of True Experience* (London: Hutchinson, 1948).
[124] George Rendel, *The Sword and the Olive. Recollections of Diplomacy and the Foreign Service 1913–1954* (London: John Murray, 1957).
[125] *Behind the Japanese Mask* (London: Hutchinson, 1948).
[126] A. Duff Cooper, *Old Men Forget* (London: Rupert Hart-Davis, 1954).
[127] *Eastern Approaches* (London: Jonathan Cape, 1949).

evolution of British policy and describe many events through which it is possible to identify the forces at work in the British attempt to create, after the fall of France, a new Balkan structure based on the division of the peninsula into Soviet and British spheres of influence.

Among the memoirs of the British military containing data of interest to the diplomatic historian are the two volumes written by General Spears,[128] who was Churchill's personal representative to the French government down to the armistice of June, 1940. Spears was a well-informed and acute observer, and, consequently, the important details he presents in his work make it a fundamental source for the study of the events leading to the French disaster of 1940 and of Franco-British relations in the days just before the French withdrawal from the war. In addition, the testimony of Colonel Woodhouse[129] should not be ignored. He was chief of the British mission to the Greek resistance movement from 1942 to 1944 and describes the events leading to the restoration of Greece as a democratic state under the old monarchy. Some references to the political aspects of his missions may be found in the memoirs of General Wilson,[130] who devotes considerable space to his embassy to Iraq in 1941 and to his activities as Eisenhower's successor in command of the Mediterranean sector. The excellent volume by Admiral Cunningham[131] is limited almost exclusively to military affairs; he gives details of the naval operations in the Mediterranean and the preparations for the North African landing. For the student of diplomatic history, the memoirs of General Carton de Wiart,[132] who accompanied Castellano to Lisbon, those of the military attaché to Tokyo, Piggott,[133] and those of Marshal Montgomery[134] are of minor interest. The latter's work, aimed at self-glorification, is not always convincing, not even on the most important strategic question, that of pressing the advance in France north of the Seine, a question that revealed the profound differences of opinion existing between Eisenhower and Montgomery.

---

[128] Edward Spears, *Assignment to Catastrophe,* Vol. I: *Prelude to Dunkirk* (July, 1939–May, 1940); Vol. II: *The Fall of France* (June, 1940) (London: Heinemann, 1954).

[129] C. M. Woodhouse, *Apple of Discord. A Survey of Recent Greek Politics in Their International Setting* (London: Hutchinson, 1948).

[130] Lord Wilson of Libya, *Eight Years Overseas 1939–1947* (London: Hutchinson, 1950).

[131] Viscount Cunningham of Hyndhope, *A Sailor's Odyssey* (London: Hutchinson, 1951).

[132] Adrian Carton de Wiart, *Happy Odysseus* (London: Jonathan Cape, 1950).

[133] Stewart Gilderoy Piggott, *Broken Thread. An Autobiography* (Alderhot, Gale, and Polden, 1950).

[134] *The Memoirs of Field-Marshal the Viscount Montgomery of Alamein* (London: Collins, 1958).

4. THE GERMAN MEMORIALISTS.

a. Stresemann.

The papers of Gustav Stresemann[135] hold a position of absolute pre-eminence among the German memoir sources. As Chancellor of the Weimar Republic from August to November, 1923, and Foreign Minister from that date until his death on October 3, 1929, he was the principal architect of the policy that permitted Germany to emerge from the difficult burdens imposed by the Treaty of Versailles to become once again a major European power. His name is linked to the significant steps taken by the German Republic in this period, from the abandonment of the policy of passive resistance after the Franco-Belgian occupation of the Ruhr, to the Locarno Pacts, to the entrance of Germany into the League of Nations, to the Hague Conference of 1929, which anticipated the complete evacuation of the Rhineland.

As early as 1927 Stresemann had planned to publish his memoirs and contracted with a publishing firm for the first volume to appear the following year on the occasion of his fiftieth birthday. However, his failing health, which soon led to his death, did not permit him even to begin the preliminary work. After his death his heirs came into possession of the vast amount of material he had assembled for his memoirs (his diary, correspondence, notes on his meetings with various European political leaders, speeches, articles he had published in his role as leader of the German People's party since 1918). Rather than using the material to compile an official biography—as was eventually done for Briand[136]—they chose to turn the material over to Stresemann's secretary, Bernhard, in order that he, with two collaborators, might arrange for the publication of an ample selection of the most important papers, so organized as to provide a complete and detailed account of Stresemann's political activity from the beginning of his chancellorship to his death.

Bernhard executed his task with great care and within a short time published three ponderous volumes, in the preparation of which he observed only in part the directive to avoid creating a sensation but to serve truth and the interests of Germany—a directive given him by the German Minister of Foreign Affairs, who was acting also on behalf of Briand, who

[135] H. Bernhard, V. Goetz, and P. Wiegler (eds.), *Gustav Stresemann, Vermächtnis. Der Nachlass in drei Bänden* (Berlin: Ullstein, 1932–33).
[136] Georges Suarez, *Briand, sa vie, son oeuvre* (6 vols.; Paris: Plon, 1938–52).

was concerned lest too much be revealed about his confidential conversations with Stresemann.

If it is easy to understand the reasons for the posthumous publication of the Stresemann papers, the same cannot be said for Stresemann's decision to publish his memoirs before leaving government office. The most likely hypothesis is that, in the face of the bitter criticism of his actions in Germany and of the tendency at the time toward the radicalization of German political life, he intended to show, in a manner that he had never been able to do with his speeches and articles, that only through the policy which he had put into practice had Germany's conspicuous accomplishments been achieved.

If this was the political aim Stresemann sought to attain, his untimely death and the rapidly moving events in Germany prevented him from achieving it. Moreover, the publication of his papers did nothing to resolve the debate that had developed on the journalistic level as well as on the level of historical evaluation, in Germany and abroad, about the German political personality. The numerous opponents of Briand's policies, especially those in France, found new arguments in the Stresemann papers for asserting that Briand had been a puppet in the hands of the German statesman, who had used him to reach his goal of revising the Treaty of Versailles.

These accusations were substantiated by reference to the famous letter to the Crown Prince in which Stresemann, shortly before the Locarno Conference, stated that Germany's renunciation of war against France for the recovery of Alsace-Lorraine as an instrument of national policy (a key point of the accords) was purely a technical matter because Germany did not have the means to make war. Moreover, it was vital that the Weimar Republic acquire an instrument that would guarantee it against future French occupation of the western frontier zones. Once this security was achieved, the way was open to resolve the reparations problem, which was linked to the question of the complete evacuation of German soil by the occupation forces of the victorious powers. For this reason, he continued, Germany had to pursue a policy similar to that adopted by Metternich for Austria after the Treaty of Schönbrunn of 1809 regarding Napoleon, that is, *finassieren* (play the game with ability and finesse) and avoid critical debates. Once the evacuation of foreign troops from German soil was completed, he added, German foreign policy could then be directed toward the reacquisition of Danzig and the Polish Corridor and a rectification of the frontier of Upper Silesia, while the annexation of Austria could be considered at some future time. As to the requirement of German membership in the League of Nations that had been imposed by the signatories of the Locarno Pacts, Stresemann made it clear to the Crown Prince that this too was useful and would work to the advantage of still another objective, one of great concern to all Germans, that is, the protection of German minorities residing in the neighboring states. Within the League (entrusted with the protection of minorities) Germany, as a permanent member, could make her authoritative voice heard.

Aside from the statement of objectives, the word *finassieren,* in French translation *finasser* and bearing a most depreciatory meaning, added fuel to the flames of criticism.

In effect, the Locarno Pacts were a great victory for Stresemann's policy in that, while obligating Germany to maintain the *status quo* in the west, he had not assumed a similar obligation for the eastern borders, leaving the door open for a peaceful revision of the Polish frontier in line with the objectives indicated in the letter to the Crown Prince. However, the results were not "one hundred per cent" in Germany's favor, as Stresemann asserted, because Germany had agreed to recognize, definitively and of her own free will, French possession of Alsace-Lorraine and, in effect, had renounced her revisionist demands against France.

On the other hand, the degree of astonishment produced by the revelations of the objectives of German policy in this and other documents was not at all justified, since Stresemann had mentioned them rather explicitly in his speeches, for example, the speech of December 14, 1925.

The specification of these objectives, which, in effect, coincided with the aims of Hitler's foreign policy, in precise terms has given rise to the speculation that Stresemann pursued for purely tactical reasons the policy that led his admirers to proclaim him "the apostle of conciliation" and that contributed to his winning the Nobel Peace Prize in 1926. In practice, the speculations continue, in view of the fact that Germany was unarmed, he selected the only possible alternative, but he remained the extreme nationalist that he had been in his youth and until the end of the war, ready to return to methods more in keeping with this spirit as soon as circumstances permitted. Acceptance of this hypothesis would make necessary the elimination of the division of German history from 1919 to 1945 into two contrasting periods, hitherto believed to be a valid assumption.

However, it is reasonable to observe that Stresemann was playing the role of a statesman and not that of a moralist, and therefore his policies could aim at nothing less than the recovery of Germany's lost territories. This objective could not be achieved without a revision of the peace treaty, but this was also Hitler's aim. The heart of the situation is clear; the difference between the two men was in method. Stresemann sought revision by common consent with the idea of giving his successes a sense of permanence. Hitler chose to achieve the changes by force, which, in the long run, brought about the Franco-British reaction of meeting force with force. On the other hand, from the historical point of view, no further conjectures are possible because there is no way of knowing how Stresemann would have realized the rest of his program, the program ultimately achieved by Hitler.

Insofar as new evidence is concerned, it may be said that not only at the time of publication but today as well, in the absence of the French and German documents, these volumes remain the primary source for the study of the foreign policy of the Weimar Republic and, to a large extent, for French foreign policy as well for the period 1923–29.

In addition to the mass of material contained in these volumes, it is now possible to study the Stresemann papers in their original form. These papers, which Bernhard was obliged to turn over to the archives of the German Foreign Ministry, have been located among the Wilhelmstrasse documents captured by the Americans at the close of World War I, and they have been made available on microfilm to scholars by the American government.

A comparison between the originals and what was published by Bernhard has not brought to light any sensational new material. Nevertheless, it can be seen that, as the editor stated, the documents were edited somewhat but the substance was not altered. It has also been possible to establish that the most important political papers were included in the published collection, with the exception of those referring to Germany's eastern frontiers and to its secret rearmament.[137]

The latter, of interest to the historian in order properly to evaluate the relation between Stresemann's policy and that of the Third Reich, was the immediate object of the most detailed study.[138] In substance, this study has led to the conclusion that Stresemann was obviously aware of what was being done to rearm Germany in violation of the Versailles clauses and that he did nothing to oppose it. Moreover, he himself was convinced that Germany one day should have a strong army that would restore its military position as well as its status as a great power. This does not indicate that he desired to use the army in a war or that he wanted the immediate re-establishment of the army in violation of the Versailles Treaty, as was desired by the General Staff. Considerations of internal policy, however,

[137] See Hans W. Gatzke, "The Stresemann Papers," *Journal of Modern History*, XXVI, No. 1 (March, 1954), 49–59.

[138] Hans W. Gatzke, *Stresemann and the Rearmament of Germany* (Baltimore: The Johns Hopkins Press, 1954).

led Stresemann to follow the lead of the General Staff in this matter; but it should also be noted that the same considerations of internal policy condition many other aspects of policy.

In conclusion, whoever is interested in a detailed study of the subject must not ignore the original documents in arriving at a detailed and complete picture of the events. However, the opening of the Stresemann archives, half of which concern his political activity prior to 1923, does not reduce the value of the published volumes, nor does it substantially alter the judgment of the statesman that might be rendered on the basis of the material in these volumes.

b. Curtius.

For the period between the death of Stresemann and the coming of Hitler to power in Germany, the most important German memoir material is to be found in the recollections published by Julius Curtius, who, after having been Minister of Economics from 1926 to 1929, succeeded Stresemann at the Wilhelmstrasse until October, 1931, when the Volkspartei became an opposition party and Curtius was forced to resign.

Of the three volumes he published, the first[139] concerns the aborted economic *Anschluss* of 1931, the most widely discussed of the episodes in which Curtius played an important role during the years when he was in charge of the Wilhelmstrasse. Curtius returns to the same question in the second volume,[140] wherein he discusses his political activity for the period 1926–31. The third,[141] published posthumously, was written largely as a reply to his critics for the purpose of reconstructing with greater accuracy those facts that, according to the author, had been distorted by political passions and by the propaganda of the extreme right, which had labeled him as "Minister of the Young plan," an odious appellation in the eyes of the Germans of the early thirties.

Curtius states that he wrote the first draft of his political memoirs between 1934 and 1938, after his retirement to private life, supplementing them with a copious documentation, part of which, however, was lost during the war. The final draft was, therefore, completed many years after the events in question, a fact that should have given the author a better historical perspective but which he did not always exploit. For example, in regard to Curtius' criticism of the Dawes plan, if, on the one hand, it

---

[139] *Bemühungen um Österreich. Das Scheiten des Zollunionsplans von 1931* (Heidelberg: Winter, 1947).

[140] *Sechs Jahre Minister der deutschen Republik* (Heidelberg: Winter, 1948).

[141] *Der Young Plan. Enstellung und Wahrheit* (Stuttgart: Mittelbach, 1950).

clarifies the controversial points existing between the author and Stresemann concerning the objectives and methods of German foreign policy, it
seems, on the other, to lack a sense of history because it is indisputable that
apart from its economic effects—of unquestioned importance—the adoption
of the Dawes plan constituted the indispensable premise for the reintroduction of Germany into the pattern of European politics. But it is evident that
here Curtius found himself attempting his own defense. In emphasizing
the advantages accruing to the German economy under the Young plan, he
tends to counter the accusations of the German rightists of having accepted
a reparations plan that would keep the German economy shackled for many
more years to come. The truth is, he asserts, that the German rightists
considered the Young plan to be a provisional solution even if, in fact, it
was the best means to ensure the complete resurgence of German industry
and to guarantee the American loans.

However, the most important part of Curtius' testimony concerns the
attempted Austro-German customs union of 1931. In his first volume the
author has reconstructed in detail the negotiations conducted by Schober
beginning with the first exchange of views in the fall of 1930. He points
out that the opposition manifested in the various capitals to the projected
customs union came as something of a surprise. The German representatives in Paris, Rome, and Prague were in agreement in reporting that
an Austro-German economic tie would not have created any particular
difficulties among the former allied powers, and as for Great Britain, it had
never been opposed to such an arrangement even though it was anxious to
avoid antagonizing the French.

Curtius returns to this question in his second volume, primarily to reply
to the statements made by François-Poncet, according to whom the
attempted *Anschluss* was nothing more than a maneuver to test the
resistance of Europe and to ascertain just how much freedom of action
Germany had after the suspicions aroused by the demonstration of Nazi
strength at the polls in September, 1930. Was this a first test of the tactic
that Hitler was to use habitually a few years later? Curtius reacted violently
to this hypothesis by pointing out that the opinion of Von Hoesch, then
German Ambassador to Paris, was that, despite some hesitation, the French
government would not be completely opposed to the customs union. The
project had to be abandoned because Briand "sounded the alarm" against
the customs union and aroused European public opinion against it. But in
so doing, Curtius continues, Briand assumed a grave responsibility, to the
extent that he should be considered as one of those responsible for Hitler's
rise. The perennial French suspicion of Germany was certainly of no help
to the young German democracy in establishing itself on firm foundations.

In foreign policy the German democratic leaders had to cloak their activities in deception. They were forced to fight on two fronts, internally, against the accusation of surrender, and externally, against the suspicion that Germany was seeking revenge. In the end, the prestige of Germany's democratic institutions was severely damaged because the government, in an attempt to bolster its strength on the internal political scene, could not point to a single major success in foreign policy, and the widespread discontent in Germany explains the growing numbers of Nazi adherents.

These assertions are only partly true, and it is clear that in this case as well Curtius is supporting a defensive argument born of the need to justify not only the failure of, but also the method employed in seeking, the customs union. The fact that the negotiations between Vienna and Berlin were conducted in the utmost secrecy and the results suddenly announced without preparation of any kind was one of the reasons for the turbulent reaction of the European public; it was recalled that this was the very technique employed by the Wilhelmstrasse and the Ballplatz during the Agadir crisis and the annexation of Bosnia-Herzegovina.

On the question of reparations and the Young plan, Curtius, in his third volume, reacted violently to the statements made by Schacht in his volume published in 1931.[142] Curtius' principal theme is well known: at the beginning of the thirties it was clearly evident that the reparations problem had to be resolved along substantially different lines from those adopted in the immediate postwar period, since a lifeless German economy benefited no one. Therefore, it was necessary to restructure the amount of the reparations and the time in which they should be paid, and this was done through the Young plan.

Curtius writes at great length on the battle conducted by the government against the extreme right, whose economic expert was Hjalmar Schacht. The latter affirmed that any discussion of reparations should be kept entirely apart from the other crucial question which was then the subject of debate: the complete evacuation of the Rhineland by the French, who were indicating a reluctance to leave. Curtius also believed that the two issues should be kept separated because Germany was not obliged to offer the French any kind of compensation for what they were still holding without justification and in flagrant violation of the rights of the people. But, Curtius asserts, Schacht, in negotiating with Young during the conference of economic experts at Paris in the spring of 1929, acted in such a way as to place the blame for what had happened on the shoulders of the government then in power in Germany, while privately giving his approval and,

[142] Hjalmar Schacht, *Die Ende der Reparationen* (Oldenburg: Stalling, 1931).

moreover, declaring that he was convinced that only a general agreement on reparations would permit Germany to allay the suspicion with which she was surrounded and to carry out a foreign policy with greater freedom.

c. *Kordt.*

Not long after the end of World War II, Von Ribbentrop's former Head of Cabinet, Erich Kordt, gave the press a history of Nazi foreign policy,[143] in part drawn from his personal recollections and in part from the documentation published during the Nuremberg trials.

When his work appeared, it was greeted with some favor by scholars, particularly since it was one of the first German attempts to reconstruct the major lines of Hitlerian policy, but after the publication of the Wilhelmstrasse documents the work lost much of its interest, even though it still retains some usefulness for the over-all evaluations it contains.

Kordt's second volume, published in 1950,[144] is much more personal and much more important in illustrating the activities of the Wilhelmstrasse during the Nazi period.

In referring to the collection of German diplomatic documents relative to World War II, Kordt calls attention to the fact that a unique situation had developed in Germany after the rise of Hitler to power. The German Foreign Ministry had lost many of its prerogatives because all of the major foreign policy decisions were made, in the final analysis, by Hitler personally and not infrequently in opposition to, and often without the knowledge of, the Wilhelmstrasse.

The influence exercised by Hitler on the conduct of foreign policy was undoubtedly decisive, but Kordt increases the number of factors that contributed to limiting the authority and the autonomy of the Ministry of Foreign Affairs. In the Third Reich, he notes, there were other organs outside of the control of the Wilhelmstrasse that were involved in international activities, but they did not maintain the contacts necessary for the co-ordination of these activities.

The phenomenon, within certain limits also common to other countries, assumed extraordinary proportions in Germany to the point of becoming an expression of rivalry between the principal Nazi leaders, each one of whom

---

[143] *Wahn und Wirklichkeit. Die Aussenpolitik des Dritten Reiches Versuch einer Darstellung* (Stuttgart: Union Deutsche Verlagsgesellschaft, 1948).

[144] *Nicht aus den Akten. Die Wilhelmstrasse in Frieden und Krieg. Erlebnisse, Begegnungen und Eindrucke 1928–1945* (Stuttgart: Union Deutsche Verlagsgesellschaft, 1950).

sought to extend his own sphere of activity by increasing the authority of
the organizations under his control. Thus, Goebbels, at the Ministry of
Propaganda, insisted on a special autonomy, necessary, according to him, in
order to carry out his functions properly. This extension of authority
culminated in his usurpation of the press functions of the Foreign Ministry
and in his replacing the Foreign Office with his own ministry in all that
concerned cultural relations with other states. Other difficulties were
created by the independent initiatives of the Nazi party organization, the
Auslandorganisation, whose activities abroad were often conducted without
the consent of the Foreign Ministry, while the military, with Goering's
support, frequently operated independently of the Wilhelmstrasse.

However, the most serious interference with the work of the Foreign
Ministry came from the famous *Dienststelle Ribbentrop,* which functioned as a foreign ministry of the Nazi party. The original functions of this
organ were carefully restricted, but as fortune favored Von Ribbentrop its
area of operation increased, to the extent where it replaced the Foreign
Ministry on more than one occasion. At times the degree of independence
enjoyed by this agency became disconcerting. Suffice it to recall that,
according to Kordt, the Anglo-German Naval Agreement of June, 1935,
was negotiated without the participation of the Foreign Ministry or of the
German Embassy in London. To be sure, in Great Britain the Admiralty
also favored an understanding with Germany and carried out the first phase
of the negotiations without the participation of the Foreign Office. (The
latter saw the danger in abandoning the principles established at Stresa and
succeeded for a time in getting the Cabinet to accept its view.) Another
example of the practice may be cited in the note indicating German refusal
to participate in the work of the League of Nations after the remilitarization of the Rhineland, sent without the Wilhelmstrasse's having had a
hand in its preparation.

This situation, which Kordt describes with considerable clarity, put the
administration of the Foreign Ministry in an extremely delicate position
and forced it into almost daily conflict with those organs usurping its field
of activity. At the Foreign Ministry, many officials still hoped that in time
things would change and that Hitler would restore the traditional functions
to the Ministry, but these hopes were dashed when Von Neurath was
replaced by Von Ribbentrop as Foreign Minister.

On this point, Kordt notes that the appointment of Von Ribbentrop to the
Embassy post in London, generally believed to be a step toward the control
of the Foreign Ministry, was in fact, desired by Von Neurath, who
influenced Hitler in this instance with the intention of ending the career of
the "amateur diplomat" by assigning him to a mission that was destined to

certain failure. In fact, Von Neurath's predictions were realized in part because Von Ribbentrop's mission to London was a total failure. Meanwhile, however, Von Ribbentrop, who had kept his personal organization alive, ably changed his point of view, abandoning his pro-British tendencies and shifting over to a support of the new Axis policy; he successfully negotiated the Anti-Comintern Pact without the participation of the Wilhelmstrasse or the two embassies in Rome and Tokyo. With Italy's adherence to the pact, he became the fervid champion of the Berlin-Rome-Tokyo Tripartite. In effect, when he replaced Von Neurath in February, 1938, he was already the real Foreign Minister.

After these events, Kordt continues, the opposition of the Wilhelmstrasse became more active, largely due to the efforts of the Secretary of State, Von Weizsäcker, as well as of other high officials of the Foreign Ministry who were acutely aware of the dangers Germany was facing in pursuing the policy of force that Hitler and Von Ribbentrop intended to launch.

It is interesting to observe (and Kordt makes no mystery of it) that Von Weizsäcker and his collaborators did not object to the goals to be achieved: the *Anschluss* and the solution of the problem of German minorities in Cechoslovakia and Poland were considered to be absolutely necessary by the Wilhelmstrasse as well. What they hoped to alter was the method to be followed in reaching these goals, a method that, because of its brutal character, would inevitably lead to the isolation of Germany and a general war.

However, with Von Ribbentrop directing the Foreign Ministry, opposition to his policies from within the Ministry was limited. The course of events could not be changed without a change in regime or, at least, the elimination of intransigent and unqualified personnel. The origins and growth of the opposition to Hitler are amply described by Kordt in his memoirs, and on this point they are to be considered one of the better-informed sources, since the author appears to have served as liaison officer between officials of the Wilhelmstrasse and several officers of the Wehrmacht who were opposed to the regime.

d. The Other German Memoir Sources.

The apologetic character common to most memoir sources is especially evident in the work of the German memorialists. Those who held major posts during the Nazi period tend to emphasize those of their actions that best portray their opposition to the regime, exaggerating the importance of these to the point of altering the historical perspective and the roles they played. Minor functionaries, instead, are concerned with convincing the reader that the mechanism of the state was such that it was impossible to elude the directives from above and that therefore there was no way to escape participation in the events. Both types of memorialists, as a rule, seek to explain that if the German people were guilty of accepting the Nazi dictatorship, the democracies were also guilty—first of having saddled Germany with a punitive peace treaty, and second, of having failed to react in time to Hitler's policy of aggression.

The memoirs of Wipert von Blücher[145] are an important source for the first phase of the foreign policy of the Weimar Republic. Early in his career, from 1918 to 1922, Von Blücher held the post of secretary in the eastern European section, one of the most important offices of the Auswärtiges Amt, under the direction of Baron von Maltzan, who, as is known, was one of the principal architects of the policy of collaboration with the Soviets that was formalized in the Treaty of Rapallo. According to Von Blücher, insistent French pressure to force Germany to turn over the war criminals for trial led Von Maltzan to conceive the idea of a *rapprochement* with the Soviets. Negotiations were begun immediately by the two delegations charged with the task of protecting prisoners of war and bore fruit in an accord whereby Germany agreed to re-establish diplomatic relations with the new Russian regime and to reopen trade between the two countries, while the Soviets guaranteed to respect the German frontiers. The decisive step was taken in January, 1922, when the Germans learned that the French had offered the Soviet Union recognition *de jure*, credits, and an alliance in exchange for Soviet recognition of the Treaty of Versailles. It was under these circumstances that, during Chicherin's stopover in Berlin on his way to the Conference of Genoa, the *coup de théâtre* of the Rapallo treaty was prepared. By the terms of the agreement, diplomatic relations between the two countries were regularized and commercial relations were established on the basis of the "most favored nation" clause of the treaty. Notwithstanding the abundance of detail, there are obscure areas in Von Blücher's narrative of the events, giving rise to the suspicion that he may have overestimated the role of Von Maltzan in the affair. However, his account remains the best source on the subject despite the publication of the Soviet documents on this period.

Earlier, Von Blücher had published another volume of memoirs[146] on his

---

[145] *Deutschlands Weg nach Rapallo. Erinnerungen eines Mannes aus dem Zweiten Gliede* (Wiesbaden: Limes Verlag, 1951).

[146] *Gesandter zwischen Diktatur und Demokratie. Erinnerungen aus den Jahren 1935–1944* (Weisbaden: Limes Verlag, 1951). The first volume published by the author concerns his recollections of his mission to Teheran as German Minister: *Zeitenwende in Iran. Erlebnisse und Beobachtungen* (Biberach a.d. Riss: Koehler, 1949).

mission to Helsinki, where he was Minister Plenipotentiary from 1935 to 1944. This was the most important post of his career, and his account of it, although on occasion reticent and foggy, is nevertheless a primary source for the study of German-Finnish relations and Finnish foreign policy for this entire period. The volume acquires extraordinary significance beginning with the events of the summer of 1939, when the signing of the Nazi-Soviet Pact aroused the suspicion—in spite of Von Ribbentrop's denials—that the accord with Moscow had been reached at the expense of Finland. The clearly pro-Soviet attitude of the Nazi government during the Russo-Finnish War, while it confirmed the suspicions, gave rise to a serious controversy between Von Ribbentrop and Von Blücher, the latter believing that it was vital to German interests that Finland be kept out of the Soviet sphere of influence. On repeated occasions he sought to induce Von Ribbentrop to intervene in the Russo-Finnish conflict to mediate the differences, and when Von Ribbentrop refused to do so, he contemplated resigning his post. Von Blücher's account remains valid even after the publication of the German diplomatic documents, which confirm the author's opposition to the pro-Soviet policy then popular in Berlin. Equally interesting are the particulars he provides on the progressive *rapprochement* between Finland and Germany during the last months of 1940, reflecting the growing tension in Nazi-Soviet relations. He also points out—and this has been confirmed by the official documents—that the Nazi position began to change in the summer of 1940 and contributed to a progressive radicalization of the situation in Finland which eventually made it possible for Finland to join Germany in the war against the Soviet Union. But the most dramatic pages, and probably the most important in view of the scarcity of source material on the subject, concern the relations between Helsinki and Berlin during the war against the Soviets, particularly after the German defeats indicated to the Finns that victory against the Soviets was highly improbable. Von Blücher's significant contribution is the information he provides on the desperate German attempts to block Finnish defection in the war; he emphasizes, for example, the unexpected visit of Hitler to Finland in June, 1942, and the Ryti-Von Ribbentrop Accord of June, 1944, which guaranteed greater military aid to Finland and represented the Wilhelmstrasse's major effort to keep Finland in the war.

An extensive period is covered by the memoirs of Hjalmar Schacht,[147] President of the Reichsbank from 1923 to 1939. The chapters of the memoir vary greatly in importance because the author quite naturally accented those years in which his prestige as an economists and political

[147] *76 Jahre meines Lebens* (Munich: Kindler und Schiermeyer, 1953).

figure was at its highest level. Consequently, his recollections concerning the years 1923–25 are particularly important; he describes in detail his work in defense of the *Rentemark,* introduced during Stresemann's chancellorship to combat the economic crisis prevailing in Germany after the reparations payments and the passive resistance campaign supported by the German government. Special note should be taken of the negotiations of 1924 between Schacht and the governor of the Bank of England because of his appraisal of the influence exercised by the British bank on the diplomatic negotiations during the winter of 1923–24. The interest of the account increases—and this time in a political sense—with the emergence of the controversy between Hitler and Schacht, leading to Schacht's resignation of his post at the Reichsbank in 1939 and continuing until his arrest by the Gestapo in July, 1944. However, Schacht's narrative of these events is a repetition of what he had written in a previous volume[148]—one of the first to describe the internal opposition to Hitler that culminated in the Von Stauffenberg plot of July, 1944—outlining the defensive position he maintained during the Nuremberg trials.

Von Papen, who, along with Schacht and Von Fritsche, was absolved at the Nuremberg trials, has written a volume of memoirs[149] in which it is evident that he felt compelled to supplement his legal defense with an account that would also rehabilitate him on a moral plane. Von Papen's first concern is to clarify his role in the events that led to Hitler's assumption of power, but despite the fact that his narrative offers an abundance of detail, it is too personal and not always convincing, especially the explanation of the origins of Von Hindenburg's appointment of Hitler as Chancellor. Nor does he make sufficiently clear how he was able to survive what was perhaps the most critical moment of his career: after his resignation from the government in June, 1934, he was arrested and appeared destined to share Roehm's fate, yet immediately after Dollfuss' assassination he was appointed German Minister to Vienna. In any event, his account of his mission to Vienna contains very few vague points. It presents significant information on German activities in Austria and on Hitler's attitude on the *Anschluss* that is virtually impossible to extract from the documents. Even more important, perhaps, is the account of his activities as Ambassador to Ankara from April, 1939, to August, 1944. The need for apology is less evident in these pages, and, consequently, Von Papen's account gains strength as a source on German policy in Turkey, particularly for the data on the negotiations leading to the economic accord of June, 1941, and for the steps that he took to prevent Turkey's entrance into the war on the

[148] *Abrechnung mit Hitler* (Hamburg: Rowohlt, 1948).
[149] Franz von Papen, *Der Wahrheit eine Gasse* (Munich: List, 1952).

Allied side. Greater precaution should be exercised in accepting what he has to say concerning his efforts from 1941 to 1944 to arrive at a negotiated peace with the Anglo-Americans, efforts which, in any event, were of little significance.

Paul Schmidt's memoirs[150] are distinctive. In his capacity as interpreter for the Wilhelmstrasse, he participated in many of the major diplomatic events of the period after World War I and after the advent of Hitler was almost always present at the meetings between the German Chancellor and foreign leaders and diplomats. Schmidt's memoirs are those of an eyewitness rather than a protagonist, but the fact that German diplomacy was frequently effected through high-level talks placed him in a unique position to observe the course of events. Keeping this in mind, along with the fact that the author is an indisputable master in the technique of recording his observations—Schmidt's minutes can be considered a model of their kind—the volume is a bit disappointing to those who, while awaiting the completion of the official German collection of diplomatic documents, expect to find important data on the content of the talks he witnessed. All too often, Schmidt provides only a summary account (occasionally not completely accurate), but he almost always describes in great detail the personalities of the principals involved—Matsuoka, Franco, Antonescu—or the atmosphere in which the conversations were held. By referring, for example, to the pages concerning Hitler's journey to Rome and the Hendaye meeting, one finds that Schmidt frequently adds significant details on the preparatory phase of the meetings and on Hitler's and Von Ribbentrop's reactions after the sessions.

Von Dirksen's memoirs[151] contain little that is new. Although they cover a longer period, they are of interest primarily for the years 1933–39, when their author was the German Ambassador to Tokyo, and for May, 1939, to the outbreak of the war, when he was Ambassador to London. Von Dirksen's account of his first mission is inadequate as a foundation upon which to reconstruct the story of Japanese-German relations because the policy of *rapprochement* with Japan, culminating in the signing of the Anti-Comintern Pact, was conducted outside of the regular diplomatic channels, directly between Von Ribbentrop and the Japanese military attaché in Berlin. The chapters dealing with his London mission are somewhat richer, but, again, really new information is scant, especially since the Soviets had

[150] *Statist auf diplomatischer Bühne 1923–1945. Erlebnisse des Chefdolmetschers im auswärtigen Amt mit den Staatsmännern Europas* (Bonn: Athenäum Verlag, 1950).

[151] Herbert von Dirksen, *Moskau, Tokyo, London, Erinnerungen und Betrachtungen zu 20 Jahren deutscher Aussenpolitik 1919–1939* (Stuttgart: Kohlhammer, 1949).

already published the papers they had found in his villa at Groeditzberg.[152] Therefore, the author was able to add only some details on the unofficial negotiations, which had little bearing on the events but are of interest as typical expressions of the opposing factions and personal rivalries existing among the Nazi leaders.

Equally disappointing are the memoirs published by Ernst von Weizsäcker,[153] Secretary of State in the Foreign Ministry from 1938 to 1943. Von Weizsäcker's case is typical of those German government and military officials of the old ruling class who, when called upon by the Nazis to assume responsible posts, found themselves in the position of having to choose between two alternatives—either to express openly their hostility to National Socialism and face the consequences that such action would inevitably bring, or to collaborate in the hope of being able to influence the course of events. It was natural for the author to choose the second alternative because there were many at the Foreign Ministry who shared his point of view. But as an increasing number of Hitler's followers took over the key posts in the ministries, Von Weizsäcker realized the difficulty of his mission. He records a number of instances when he worked to prevent the situation from getting out of control, precipitating a war: his advice to the British government during the Czechoslovak crisis to take a strong stand against an act of force, his warnings to London of the imminent signing of the Nazi-Soviet Pact, and his colloquies with western diplomats to examine the possibilities of taking a strong position in favor of Poland are all episodes that demonstrate Von Weizsäcker's failure to influence Von Ribbentrop and his efforts to halt the Hitler machine from within. The author's comments on German foreign policy are limited to a discussion of the main lines of activity and rarely touch on particulars, but the accuracy of his historical interpretations is to be appreciated. Von Weizsäcker's work provided a surprise for the Italian diplomats who considered him to be a sincere friend of Italy. His obvious lack of sympathy for the German ally led him to blame the Italians for many mistakes which cannot be included in an objective list of errors committed in Italian policy during that period.

Von Ribbentrop's memoirs[154] can be dismissed with the observation that they are virtually useless because of their tendentiousness and the many

---

[152] See p. 171.

[153] *Erinnerungen* (Munich: List, 1950).

[154] Annalise von Ribbentrop (ed.), *Joachim von Ribbentrop. Zwischen London und Moskau. Erinnerungen und letze Aufzeichnungen aus dem Nachlass* (Leoni: Druffel, 1953).

inaccuracies they contain. In contrast, the Goebbels diary[155] is an extremely significant record by one of the principal figures of the Third Reich, who was also its Minister of Propaganda. He kept a diary from the beginning of his political career, but unfortunately part of it was destroyed. To date, only a portion of the numerous pages that remained have been published, and these cover the years 1925–26 and the period January, 1942–December, 1944. One of the best features of this record is that the author did not have time to edit it and thus its authenticity as a daily record is preserved. Goebbels made frequent references to international developments and to German foreign policy, either in the light of the need to change the focus of German propaganda or because of the tendency, which he shared with other Nazi leaders, toward extending his sphere of activity. Among the most interesting pages are those concerning the Italian crisis prior to July 25, 1943, and the attitude of German government circles toward the problems created by the fall of the Facist dictator. Goebbels saw no advantage to be gained in liberating Mussolini because the formation of a new Fascist government would make it difficult to punish Italy by incorporating not only the Alto Adige in the Third Reich—as the Austrian *gauleiters* had immediately requested—but also the territory "south of Venice."

An important contribution is made by Otto Abetz, a journalist, who after the Franco-German armistice of June, 1940, was sent to Paris as Von Ribbentrop's emissary and shortly afterwards was appointed to the post of Ambassador, charged with the task of handling all questions of a political nature with the Vichy government. As a champion of the plan to insert France into the new European order, Abetz actively worked for Franco-German collaboration, on which the continuation of his unexpected good fortune depended. On more than one occasion his action had an important influence on the course of Germany's relations with the Pétain government. By way of illustration, on December 13, 1940, Laval's arrest appeared to undermine the very bases of Franco-German collaboration. For a variety of reasons—the impossibility of taking a decisive action in the Mediterranean without Spanish co-operation, the Italian military failures in Greece and in Africa, and the fact that the Germans were concentrating their attention on plans for the attack against the Soviet Union—news of the event was received in Berlin with indifference, leading to the conclusion that the active co-operation of France could not be obtained. But Abetz saw the entire structure he had so patiently built in serious danger, and he reacted

[155] L. P. Lochner (ed.), *Goebbels' Tagebücher aus den Jahren 1942–1943* (Zurich: Atlantis, 1948).

quickly and sharply. In so doing, he led the Vichy leaders to the wrong conclusions. In the absence of other links with the Germans, they failed to grasp the significance of the differences developing between the Abetz and the German governmental position. The first of the three volumes published by Abetz[156] is a collection of documents which was extremely important at the time of publication but whose value declines as the volumes of the German general collection are issued. The second includes a portion of the proceedings of the Abetz trial in the French courts. Only the third volume is a true memoir, even though the author tends to trace the history of Franco-German relations outside of the framework of his personal experience. On the whole, however, the three volumes continue to be a primary source for the study of Germany's Vichy policy, and they show that the policy of collaboration, at least in the extreme form desired by Abetz and Laval, found little support on either side.

Rudolf Rahn, Abetz's Embassy Counsellor in Paris until the summer of 1943, writing on the same subject,[157] adds little of importance. Perhaps the most valuable pages deal with his mission to Syria in May, 1941, to organize the shipment of materials to the Iraqi rebels. On the relations with Vichy, he adds very little to what had already been written by Abetz. Rahn was assigned the post of Chargé d'Affaires in Rome for the deliberate purpose of preventing the Badoglio government from taking Italy out of the war. He arrived in Rome only a few days before the announcement of the armistice, too late to achieve his goal, and shortly thereafter he was transferred to the post of Ambassador to the Republic at Salò. Rahn narrates his activities there in detail, but only occasionally does he specifically discuss German relations with the neo-Fascist republican government. His comments on the negotiations during the winter of 1944–45 for the surrender of German troops in Italy are much more enlightening, not so much for the data he provides on the negotiations themselves—Rahn played no official role in them—but for what he has to say concerning the attitude of the German military and of Kesselring in particular. Note should also be taken of Rahn's observations on his mission to Budapest in October, 1944, where he was charged with the task of preventing the Hungarian government from signing an armistice with the Soviets. Here, too, Rahn arrived too late to be effective, for an armistice had already been

---

[156] *Pétain et les Allemands. Mémorandum d'Abetz sur les Rapports Franco-Allemands* (Paris: Gaucher, 1948); *D'une Prison* (Paris: Amyot-Dumont, 1949); *Das Offene Problem. Ein Rückblick auf zwei Jahrzehnte Frankreichpolitik* (Cologne: Greven Verlag, 1951).

[157] *Ruheloses Leben. Aufzeichnungen und Erinnerungen* (Düsseldorf: Diederichs Verlag, 1949).

arranged, but the crisis was resolved by a coup which led to Horthy's abdication and to the creation of the pro-Nazi Szállasy government.

Rahn's closest collaborator in France and in Italy, Eitel Moellhausen, has also written his memoirs, dividing them into two distinct volumes.[158] One concerns his mission to Paris during the fall and winter of 1940; to Syria in May, 1940; to French West Africa in October, 1942; and finally, to Tunisia from November, 1942, until the Axis was driven out of Africa. With the exception of the discussion of his mission to Dakar, the volume parallels Rahn's account. The second volume deals directly with Italian affairs and concerns the period of his counsellorship in the German Embassy in Italy after the fall of Mussolini, including the period in which he directed the Rome office of the German Embassy after Rahn was transferred to Salò. The numerous details in his account contribute to a better understanding of "Nazi Rome," but the most interesting pages are the final ones, dealing with the negotiations for the surrender of German troops in Italy, which were conducted by the German authorities through Allen Dulles of the Office of Strategic Services. Moellhausen states that he learned the details from the German delegates to these negotiations, since he himself was not a party to the attempt to bring the war to an end in Italy in March, 1945. From his account it can be learned that it would have been possible to terminate the war in Italian territory in March, 1945, if serious difficulties had not been created for General Wolff, who was conducting the negotiations, by the unexpected replacement of Marshal Kesselring with General Viettinghof, who was opposed to the project.

The volume on the war years by Peter von Kleist,[159] one of Von Ribbentrop's associates who was concerned with eastern European affairs, are of some importance. The first part of his memoirs concerns the period of Nazi-Soviet friendship and adds little to what has been revealed in the published Wilhelmstrasse documents. Of greater interest are the pages referring to the work of the Reichskommissariat for occupied Russia, while from the diplomatic point of view the significant pages concern the soundings apparently made by the Soviets between 1943 and 1945 through Kleist, on the occasion of his mission to Stockholm, for a separate peace with Germany. Kleist's testimony on this subject is one of the most important sources available.

[158] Eitel Friedrich Moellhausen, *Il giuoco è fatto!* (Florence: Sansoni, 1951); *La carta perdente. Memorie diplomatiche (25 luglio 1943–2 maggio 1945)* (Rome: Sestante, 1948). The two volumes were originally published in Italian.
[159] *Zwischen Hitler und Stalin. Aufzeichnungen* (Bonn: Athenäum-Verlag, 1950).

Worth noting among the memoirs of the German military are the writings of the former military attaché to Rome, Von Rintelen,[160] whose narrative, from the historico-diplomatic viewpoint, contains data that have proved to be accurate when compared with the official documents published to date; the recollections of the former military attaché to London, Schweppenburg,[161] who focuses his attention on the possibilities for collaboration existing between the German and British military before Hitler's violations of the Versailles Treaty in 1935–36; the memoirs of the former military attaché to Helsinki, Erfurth,[162] still one of the best sources for the study of German-Finnish relations between 1941 and 1944; the volume by Dollman,[163] who, in his position as interpreter with the German military forces in Italy, is able to supply information on the content of many Italo-German meetings and on the negotiations for the surrender of German troops in Italy; the recollections of Otto Skorzeny,[164] the S. S. officer especially remembered for having liberated Mussolini in September, 1943, but who was also the author of other, no less spectacular, undertakings; the memoirs of Admiral Doenitz and those of his adjutant, Lüdde-Neurath,[165] which furnish a detailed account of the events between Hitler's death on April 30, 1945, and the German capitulation on May 8, 1945; and the writings of Guderian,[166] Manstein,[167] Kesselring,[168] and Rommel,[169] which are limited almost exclusively to military matters.

The volume by Walter Hagen,[170] pseudonym of a member of the German Intelligence Service, deserves special mention. By strict definition this is not a memoir because the author not only discusses events in which he played a role but also describes the work of the Intelligence Service,

---

[160] Enno von Rintelen, *Mussolini als Bundesgenosse* (Tubingen: Wunderlich, 1951).

[161] Leo D. F. Geyr von Schweppenburg, *Erinnerungen eines Militäratachés: London, 1933–1937* (Stuttgart: Deutsche Verlags-Anstalt, 1949).

[162] Waldemar Erfurth, *Der Finnische Krieg, 1941–1944* (Wiesbaden: Limes Verlag, 1950).

[163] Eugenio Dollman, *Roma nazista* (Milan: Longanesi, 1949).

[164] *Geheimkommando Skorzeny* (Hamburg: Toth, 1950).

[165] Walter Lüdde-Neurath, *Regierung Dönitz* (Goettingen: Musterschmidt, 1950); Karl Doenitz, *Zehn Jahre und Zwanzig Tage* (Bonn, 1958).

[166] Heinz Guderian, *Erinnerungen eines Soldaten* (Heidelberg: Vowinchel, 1951).

[167] Erich von Manstein, *Verlorene Siege* (Bonn: Athenäum-Verlag, 1955).

[168] Albert Kesselring, *Soldat bis zum letzten Tag* (Bonn: Athenäum-Verlag, 1953).

[169] Erwin Rommel, *Krieg ohne Hass, Afrikanischen Memoiren* (Heidenheim: Heidenheimer Zeitung, 1950). The English translation was edited by H. Liddell Hart under the title *The Rommel Papers* (New York: Harcourt, 1953), with the addition of other Rommel papers.

[170] *Die Geheime Front* (Zurich: Europe, 1950).

reconstructed from his personal experience and from the documents he was able to examine. Given the peculiar nature of the subject, it will be extremely difficult, even in the future, to check the accuracy of most of the interesting statements made by Hagen. In any event, where it has been possible to check their accuracy, they have proved to be correct. Among the many major revelations in this volume, attention is called to Hagen's statement that Heydrich was responsible for transmitting the falsified documents to Stalin that were later used to support the accusations against Marshal Tuckachevsky. Supposedly, the reason for this maneuver was Hitler's desire to put an end to the close rapport between the German and Soviet military which had continued despite the ideological incompatibility between the two regimes. Heydrich's plan had the double advantage that it achieved this goal without the risk of antagonizing the German military caste and at the same time deprived Stalin of one of his best generals. On the events linked to the *coup d'état* in Yugoslavia of March, 1941, Hagen contributes interesting data. He states that initially the Soviet Union offered Belgrade a military alliance and later substituted a friendship pact containing obvious political implications but that was, on the whole, rather platonic, given the circumstances. The closing chapters of the book are no less significant. One concerns Hungary—Hagen's version of the Hungarian crisis of October, 1944, should be compared with the Rahn and Skorzeny versions—and the other, Italy in the period after the fall of the Fascist government; it contains numerous revelations that cannot be verified concerning several contacts between a representative of the Badoglio government and the Germans for the purpose of effecting Italy's neutrality, an original version of the plans prepared in Berlin for Mussolini's liberation, and the German plan for transfering Ciano to a neutral country in exchange for his diary.

The internal opposition to the Nazi regime is a subject of primary concern to students of the internal history of the Third Reich, but it also has a certain importance for the study of diplomatic history. The opponents of Nazism soon realized that their forces were too weak to overthrow the Hitler regime, and, in different ways, they sought external help, at least in the form of a major defeat for German foreign policy, a defeat that would be clamorous enough to justify a *coup d'état* in German public opinion and to attract to the anti-Nazi movement those persons, especially among the military, who were still hesitant to take a stand against the Nazis. This led to a series of secret contacts between the anti-Nazi leaders and foreigners that produced no positive results but had a certain influence on the course of events. For example, early in the war, when there was no military action on the western front (the period of the "phoney war"), it appears that the

British government was encouraged to refrain from taking any military initiatives by the hope that the Nazi regime could be overthrown by a *coup d'état*, a hope nurtured by British contacts with the German anti-Nazis, whose strength was certainly overestimated.

One of the most important sources on this subject may be found in the diary of the former Ambassador to Rome, Ulrich von Hassell.[171] The diary does not concern his diplomatic activity but the period following his mission, that is, from 1938 to 1944, when Von Hassell fought to overthrow the Nazis and to take Germany out of the war. Von Hassell recalls these struggles in detail, and from them it is possible to learn the contents of the various peace proposals projected by the anti-Nazis, their contacts with the Allies, and the various phases of the plot culminating in the attempt on Hitler's life on July 20, 1944, which led to Von Hassell's execution. On the same subject, one of the more pertinent sources is the Goerdeler papers. Goerdeler was one of the leaders of the German resistance, and the historian Gerhard Ritter has utilized these papers as the principal source for his volume on the anti-Nazi opposition.[172]

5. THE AMERICAN MEMORIALISTS.

a. Hull.

Cordell Hull was Secretary of State from March, 1933, to November, 1944, that is, from the years of Hitler's advent to power in Germany to the last phase of World War II.

His memoirs,[173] published in 1948, are an especially important source for the study of the dramatic evolution of American foreign policy during this period and, more generally, for the reconstruction of the diplomatic aspects of the war.

Hull's influence on Roosevelt, who in the final analysis had the task of formulating the aims of American foreign policy, was very considerable for many years, partially because of the friendship that existed between the two leaders. However, it should be remembered that the extent of Hull's influence depended on the particular issue involved and the period in question, although this fact is clearly evident from the memoirs.

Hull's writing is discursive in character, and wherever possible he avoids

[171] *Vom Andern Deutschland. Aus Nachgelassenen Tagebüchern 1938–1944* (Vienna: Humboldt-Verlag, 1948).

[172] *Carl Goerdeler und die deutsche Widerstandbewegung* (Stuttgart: Deutsche-Verlag Anstalt, 1954).

[173] *The Memoirs of Cordell Hull* (New York: Macmillan, 1948).

the inclusion of the documentary texts to which he refers in order not to burden his narrative excessively. From the historian's point of view, this method is not the most rewarding, but as the volumes of the official American collection of diplomatic documents become available this inconvenience is gradually diminishing. However, the memoirs, as is usually the case with sources of this kind, retain their value, especially for what they have to say concerning the background of various major decisions, the attitude of the responsible American leaders on them, the discussions that preceded and followed certain diplomatic moves by Washington, etc. When the State Department's collection of documents covering the war is completed, Cordell Hull's memoirs will continue to serve as a useful instrument for placing the documents in their proper perspective, providing data on their origins, and assisting in evaluating their significance. However, it should be noted that despite the absence of complete documentary texts, the entire narrative was based on guidelines provided by those texts.

From the moment that Hull's memoirs were published, they attracted the attention of scholars, not only for the information they contain but particularly for the insight they provide into the psychological attitudes of certain circles in Washington. Scholars also looked to the memoirs for an insight into Hull's political philosophy because his theoretical hypotheses frequently exerted a conspicuous, if not always a positive, influence on developments.

Accordingly, one must recall that the American Secretary of State's opposition was a determining factor on more than one occasion in the failure of the Anglo-Soviet negotiations for a political accord on eastern Europe.

In December, 1941, during Eden's visit to Moscow, Stalin proposed that an agreement be reached by which the British would recognize the Soviet western frontier as of June, 1941. This was tantamount to a recognition of the Soviet acquisitions during the war (eastern Poland, the Baltic states, Finnish territory, Bessarabia, and northern Bukowina). This request was immediately rejected as contrary to the principles of the Atlantic Charter and the obligations assumed by Great Britain toward the United States. But with the approach of spring and the inevitable reopening of military operations on the eastern front, London deemed it inopportune to continue to maintain a totally negative attitude toward the Soviet Union, which at that time was carrying the major burden of the war against the Nazis. Therefore, Churchill reopened the negotiations in March, 1942, prompted by the fear that eventual future German military victories might drive Stalin to seek a separate peace with Germany.

News of this initiative by the British government provoked extremely violent reactions in Washington. In December, 1941, when Eden had communicated to Washington the content of his conversations with Stalin, Hull had expressed his complete approval of the British refusal to subscribe to an accord containing territorial clauses. Confronted by a reversal in the positions of the British Prime Minister and his Foreign Secretary, Hull protested vigorously, making it clear that in the event that such an agreement was signed, the United States would immediately and publicly declare its complete opposition, even at the cost of provoking a split in the Allied ranks by making it common knowledge.

The reasons for Hull's stand may be found in his conviction that it was preferable to arrive at the end of the conflict without any agreements that would in any way compromise the principles for which the United States was fighting. Meanwhile, every effort should be concentrated on winning the war. This was a laudable theoretical concept, but in practice an extremely dangerous one, in that it underestimated the importance of pledges and *de facto* situations, while it presupposed an Anglo-American position of strength at the end of the war.

Consequently, when Molotov arrived in London on May 20, 1942, to discuss the question, the opposition of the United States had forced the British to re-examine their previous position on territorial changes in eastern Europe, with the result that Britain and the Soviet Union concluded an alliance in which no reference was made to the U.S.S.R.'s future frontiers.

Two years later, in May, 1944, the same question was raised, albeit in a somewhat different form but with much more serious implications. The victorious Red army had already occupied several Balkan areas, and it was apparent that the Soviet advance would continue without encountering strong resistance. The dangers created by the new situation prompted London to reopen negotiations with the Soviets to define the respective spheres of influence in the Balkans, in order to avoid the prospect of a series of *faits accomplis* that would make future negotiations on these issues extremely difficult.

The British government was particularly worried by developments in Greece, where the Communists had organized a resistance movement, the E. A. M., and in March, 1944, they created a committee for national liberation obviously designed to replace the Greek government in exile, whose headquarters were in Cairo.

In view of this state of affairs, Churchill and his collaborators favored an agreement with the U.S.S.R. that would guarantee British control of Greece in return for British recognition of a completely free hand for the

Soviets in Rumania. However, when Hull was informed of this project, he repeated his adamant opposition to accords that would run counter to the fundamental principles of Allied policy on the one hand, while, on the other, they would reduce the authority of the future international security organization.

This difference of opinion led to a bitter exchange of notes between the two western allies, and it was resolved only when Churchill, taking advantage of Hull's momentary absence from his post, was able to appeal directly to President Roosevelt and convince him of the necessity of this accord. The agreement was to remain in effect for three months and was not to be interpreted as a precedent for permanent settlements to be reached in the future peace conference. Nevertheless, the agreement was to have a significant effect on subsequent developments in Greece. Great Britain was able to send troops to Athens, the committee of national liberation was dissolved on the advice of the Soviets, and the Papandreu government was able to regain control of a situation that for a time had appeared to be seriously compromised.

Negotiations were once again reopened on this matter during Churchill's and Eden's visit to Moscow in October, 1944. The situation in the Balkans had taken a further turn for the worse, from the western point of view, during the summer of 1944, when Soviet occupation of Bulgaria put control of that country in Soviet hands, while Tito's visit to Moscow was interpreted as a confirmation of Yugoslavia's eastern orientation. These developments prompted the British to seek a clarification of previous accords and to arrive at an understanding with Moscow for the entire Balkan peninsula. When it became apparent that a proposed Big Three meeting could not be arranged because President Roosevelt would not leave the United States during the election campaign, Churchill reopened the discussions on the Balkan problems, à deux, during the Moscow meeting. The British Prime Minister advanced a proposal defining spheres of influence in terms of percentages. His plan assigned the Soviet Union a 90 per cent interest in Rumania, 75 per cent in Bulgaria, 50 per cent in Hungary and Yugoslavia, and 10 per cent in Greece. Such a plan, according to Churchill, was purely indicative and would serve to resolve the immediate emergency situations and to prevent disagreements that would be prejudicial to the prosecution of the war. In no way was it to have any influence on the decisions to be made at the peace conference.

During these negotiations, attended by the American Ambassador to Moscow, Harriman, with the status of an observer, Hull maintained a purely passive attitude even if it was obvious that he could not approve of an understanding that went beyond the accord of May, 1944. In his memoirs he affirms that Churchill's proposal had a negative effect on the future of the Balkans because, while it recognized Soviet interests in Yugoslavia, it gave Stalin the opportunity to demand later that the Soviet Union be assigned the paramount role in Rumanian and Bulgarian affairs.

From an historical point of view, Hull's purely negative evaluation of the event must be accepted with some reservations. His opinion was evidently conditioned by the mental attitude that was typical of him; he believed sincerely in the goodness of the ideals for which the western world was fighting and could not admit, on a political plane, any deviation from those ideals even when the realities of the situation dictated otherwise. In effect, Hull possessed a purely religious concept of foreign policy and could not be swayed in matters of principle, and he was utterly incapable of bowing to tactical exigencies. This characteristic had been revealed earlier on the occasion of the negotiations with the Japanese prior to the attack on Pearl Harbor, but it was also seen in all of his actions as Secretary of State. It was certainly not happenstance that led to his being relieved of office on the eve of the Yalta negotiations, accords that he assuredly would not have approved.

b. Welles.

The volumes written by Sumner Welles,[174] Undersecretary of State from 1937 to September, 1943, are clearly polemical in character. In addition to the data contained, which were of considerable interest at the time of their publication—particularly the first volume, published in 1944—these memoirs are useful scholarly tools both for illuminating the degree of collaboration that existed in the State Department between Hull and Welles and for an authoritative interpretation of the factors that motivated Roosevelt in defining American foreign policy in those years.

Welles was linked to Roosevelt by close bonds of personal friendship. During their frequent meetings, Welles took advantage of his opportunity to make suggestions and to advise the President freely, and Roosevelt often consulted Welles, even on matters outside the competence of the Undersecretary of State. Hull was fully aware of this situation, and, although naturally he was not especially pleased by it, he accepted it, although it was unusual for a Secretary of State to permit an Undersecretary to deal

[174] *The Time for Decision* (New York: Harper, 1944); *Where Are We Heading?* (New York: Harper, 1946); *We Need Not Fail* (Boston: Houghton Mifflin, 1948); *Seven Decisions That Shaped History* (New York: Harper, 1951).

directly with the White House on matters rightfully within the competence of the Secretary himself. On the other hand, if the friendship existing between Welles and Roosevelt originated in a common social background, a similar cultural training, and a close similarity of ideas and plans, the President highly esteemed Hull and approved his views on policy. Thus the good relations existing between Roosevelt, Hull, and Welles were governed by a delicate balance that could be broken at any time that the Undersecretary's initiatives ran counter to Hull's views. Such a development was soon to occur.

In the fall of 1937 the American President, recognizing the growing threats to world peace (the Spanish Civil War, the reopening of the Sino-Japanese conflict coming on the heels of the Italian occupation of Ethiopia, and the open repudiation of the Treaty of Versailles by Germany), took a strong position against those endangering the peace of the world in his famous quarantine speech, delivered in Chicago. After the address, Welles proposed to the President that the United States take even more concrete action to eliminate the threat to peace. The plan was based on two essential points: first, on the anniversary of the armistice ending World War I, the President would launch an appeal to all diplomatic legations in Washington to urge their respective governments to co-operate in preserving international order and to undertake consultations with each other aimed at reducing armaments; and second, an invitation would be extended to nine small powers to join with the United States in forming an executive committee to develop the above-mentioned proposals and to serve as a co-ordinating agency for the other states.

Apparently, the President did not object to the plan, but Hull's determined opposition induced Roosevelt to abandon it. In fact, it does not seem that Hull's opposition to the plan blocked the last fragile occasion to preserve world peace, as Churchill defined it. First of all, in the light of the extremely negative reaction of American public opinion to the quarantine speech, it was highly improbable that the President could obtain the necessary support for a policy so clearly in contrast to traditional American isolationism. Second, the plan offered no changes in the appeasement policy of the democracies, since the alternative of war was not even mentioned in the plan, while it was obvious that only the employment of force could arrest German expansionism.

The final break between Hull and Welles came in January, 1942, as a result of the position taken by the Undersecretary as head of the American delegation to the Rio de Janeiro Conference. The conference had been arranged after the Japanese attack on Pearl Harbor for the purpose of finding an effective way to implement the declaration, made earlier at the

Havana Conference in July, 1940, by the twenty-one American states, that a violation of the territorial integrity or of the political independence of one state would be considered a violation of the rights of all the contracting parties. The U.S. government sought to obtain a commitment from all of the American states to break relations with the Tripartite powers, a maneuver opposed by Chile and Argentina. Thus it became a question of whether or not it was preferable to restrict the obligation to the nineteen powers favoring the American plan or to seek to preserve the unity of the Americas by agreeing to a formula that would allow Chile and Argentina, in effect, to make the decisions they thought best.

Hull favored the first alternative, believing that the isolation to which the two dissenting powers were subjecting themselves would have internal consequences that would force them to alter their positions. Welles instead accepted the second alternative, which, as he states, he knew Roosevelt would not oppose in the event that it became impossible to reconcile the American and Argentine positions. Welles justified his action by his assertion that Brazil would not intervene in the war on the side of the United States if she had to contend with a hostile Argentina on her southern frontier. Hull's opposition was extremely sharp, but the President approved Welles's proposal, either because he believed it to have been the proper one or because the decision had already been made. Hull and Welles report different versions, so it is impossible to determine exactly what motivated the President's decision.

Further differences of opinion on the direction of American policy made co-operation between Hull and Welles increasingly difficult. The President was finally forced to choose between them, and in the summer of 1943 he asked for Welles's resignation. Hull's resignation followed in December, 1944.

Despite the fact that circumstances made this action necessary, Welles retained the President's friendship, and in his writings—especially in the second and fourth volumes—he ably defends Roosevelt's policies at a time when criticism of the administration was at its peak.

The second volume is in the nature of a critical review of American foreign policy from the Atlantic Charter to the peace conference, containing interesting data on the origins of that document and on the President's projects for an international organization, in which Welles seeks to prove that the United States could not have pursued a policy different from that of Roosevelt. In effect, according to Welles, Roosevelt sought to confer all the prestige and strength possible on the United Nations, which he considered to be the only instrument capable of preserving world peace, and to establish close co-operation with the Soviet Union, without whose support the U. N. would inevitably fail. As to the methods employed to achieve these goals, Welles states that Roosevelt demonstrated a conciliatory spirit and a willingness to compromise on secondary issues but was rigid and uncompromising on the major ones. In Welles's view, it was the abandonment of Roosevelt's position toward the U.S.S.R. and the unwillingness to compromise on the secondary issues that led to America's difficulties in international affairs immediately after the end of the war.

In the fourth volume, Welles focuses on what, in his judgment, were also the errors of Roosevelt's policy, with the obvious purpose of making Hull responsible for them. As the title indicates, the volume examines seven decisions that, according to Welles, determined the course of World War II.

The first decision, the failure to implement the plan suggested by the Undersecretary in the fall of 1937 to eliminate the threats to world peace, has already been discussed. The second decision, of a positive character, was the recognition of the Vichy government by the United States. This assertion seems to be excessive. If it is true that the decision to recognize Vichy favored the American landing in North Africa, it cannot be said that the successful outcome of the operation was largely determined by such recognition unless the attitude of the government officials loyal to Pétain and of the majority of the men of Vichy is completely ignored.

Welles attributes to Hull the failure to apply the "quarantine" measures and, as noted above, believed this to have been the error that eventually led to the war with Japan. The fourth historic decision, made by Welles at the Rio Conference, saved the unity of the American continent.

The fifth decision was to postpone until the end of the war all territorial arrangements for the future. While the assertion of the importance of this decision may have to be limited to the problems that remained unsolved during the wartime conferences (Cairo and Yalta in particular), it is difficult to deny its logic. However, Welles's opinion that the independence of the Baltic states could have been saved if in the winter of 1942–43 the United States had recognized the other conquests made by the U.S.S.R. with the assistance of Germany is to be seriously questioned, since even in the moments of greatest danger the Soviet Union refused to compromise on this issue. The other explanations offered by Welles in criticizing that decision are more convincing than the defense of the action given by Hull in his memoirs, but they should be further developed.

The validity of the American position at the time depended upon two conditions which clearly did not prevail: a military strategy designed to impose the peace and the ability to maintain American military strength intact at the termination of hostilities. While the American High Command was concerned only with the problem of winning the war as quickly as possible, President Roosevelt stated at Yalta that it would be difficult for him to keep American troops in Europe indefinitely, the maximum time that they could be expected to remain being two years after the end of the conflict. Apparently, this statement had a profound effect on Stalin. Under these conditions, the decision in question appears to have been not only unfortunate but downright negative in its effect, in that it contributed toward pointlessly arousing Soviet suspicions of the democracies.

Completing the volume are Welles's comments on the decisions made by Roosevelt at Yalta and those centering around the creation of the United Nations before the end of the war. The author's observations on these issues are worthy of attention.

The third volume is limited to a history of the Palestine question, which had been referred to in part in the preceding volume. Despite the fact that the volume contains no particularly significant disclosure (and Welles's memoirs would not be expected to be especially helpful on this point), the book is important for an understanding of the American attitude on the creation of the state of Israel.

c. Leahy.

Toward the end of 1940, President Roosevelt decided to send Admiral William Leahy,[175] then Governor of Puerto Rico, as Ambassador to the Vichy government. The choice was determined by two considerations: first, with the selection of a major public figure, the United States intended to emphasize the importance it ascribed to the French situation; and second, the appointment of a military man—at first, General Pershing, Commander-in-Chief of the American Expeditionary Forces in Europe during World War I, was considered for the post—was expected to facilitate contact with Marshal Pétain. Admiral Leahy was entrusted with the task of strengthening the spirit of resistance of responsible French leaders and of assuring them that, in return for a firmer stand against the Germans, they would receive the support of the United States, particularly in the form of economic assistance. Moreover, Leahy was to promise that America would seek to moderate Great Britain's position toward Vichy, a position that, despite the unofficial contacts between London and Vichy during the last months of 1940, remained fundamentally intransigent.

Leahy himself supported this conciliatory policy, not out of any sympathy toward the Vichy regime, but because he was convinced that Pétain, if

[175] William D. Leahy, I Was There. The Personal History of the Chief of Staff to Presidents Roosevelt and Truman, Based on His Notes and Diaries Made at the Time (New York: Whittlesey House, 1950).

left to himself, would not be in a position to resist for long the pressures of the Germans and of the extremists led by Laval. Leahy's limited contacts probably prevented him from fully grasping all of the complexities of the French situation, but it should not be forgotten that, at least for all of 1941 and early 1942, the policy followed by the United States was the most convincing and fruitful one. In the first place, apart from the fact that De Gaulle was not particularly well regarded by the leaders in Washington, he had not yet developed an effective force, while, during the same period, Pétain enjoyed the support of a large segment of the French public of both zones and a pre-eminent position in the Vichy regime, giving him the key role in all of the major decisions taken by that government. Moreover, the fact that the United States had taken a position differing from that of the British with regard to France gave both of the Anglo-Saxon powers greater freedom of action and permitted a policy of either greater conciliation or marked rigidity, depending upon the case. Finally, the presence of a diplomatic mission in Vichy and of consular representation in France and in North Africa put the United States in a position to receive a mass of information of a political and military nature that proved to be extremely useful in the preparations for the landing operations in North Africa of November 8, 1942.

The events related to this policy are discussed by Leahy at length, particularly as they concerned the Weygand-Murphy Accords of February, 1941, the long negotiations leading to the concession of economic aid to France, the reactions to Admiral Darlan's collaborationist policies, and the dismissal of Weygand from his post as delegate general for North Africa. Obviously, Leahy's testimony lost some of its importance with the publication of the official collection of the American diplomatic documents for the period in which he was Ambassador to Vichy, but his work can in no way be considered superseded. First of all, it is a well-known fact that the State Department's documentary collection has some serious limitations. Moreover, Leahy's personal views on French problems, although at times open to criticism, had a significant effect on the attitude of the American government and particularly on President Roosevelt, so that Leahy's judgments were of unquestioned importance. It should also be noted that after Leahy's recall in May, 1942, he continued to be questioned on almost all of the problems concerning relations with France, and his opinion, for example, played an important role in the decision to accept the accords concluded by the American military with Darlan immediately following the landings in North Africa.

Returning to the United States, Leahy was appointed Chief of Staff to the President and in this role participated in the formulation of the major Allied war plans. On this point, his memoirs increase in importance, not only for the many behind-the-scenes activities he describes, but also because his comments make it possible to "personalize" the origin of the inter-Allied disagreements concerning the conduct of the military operations, an aspect of the question that is rarely found in the official documents. Generally, these disagreements appeared in every combat area, but they were especially serious in the European theater of operations. In practice, once it was established that precedence was to be given to operations against Germany while a holding position was maintained in the Pacific, the concept was never seriously questioned, despite the fact that American naval circles continued to emphasize the dangers that could result from lessening the pressure on Japan. Nevertheless, during the first half of 1942, American and British leaders discussed at length the question of whether or not it was opportune to speed up preparations for a limited action in France the following year or whether, in the meantime, it was not advisable to proceed with the landing in Africa (Operation TORCH).

Even after Operation TORCH was finally decided upon, the disagreements between the British and the Americans were not terminated. The American military was very reluctant to effect a major landing in the Mediterranean for fear that the Germans might be able to block the passage of the convoys at the Straits of Gibraltar, and the Americans proposed to shift the center of action to the Moroccan Atlantic coast. On the other hand, the British pressed for landings at Oran and Algiers so that a German counteroffensive could be more easily resisted and, at the same time, to relieve the pressure on the Allied forces in Libya. The differences were finally resolved in a plan providing for three simultaneous landings: at Oran, Algiers, and at Casablanca, and this plan was put into effect in November, 1942. However, the disagreements continued. In fact, they became more serious: the British General Staff, seeing a favorable opportunity developing in the Mediterranean, was inclined to concentrate its efforts in that sector to drive Italy out of the war, while the Americans hesitated to commit major forces to a Mediterranean campaign for fear of prejudicing the operations against Japan and, above all, out of fear that the preparations for the landing in France might be seriously hampered. At the Casablanca Conference of January, 1943, it was finally agreed to give priority to the operations against Italy, but the agreement was only partial because these operations were not developed in the detail required by such a campaign, nor were the dates established for the landings in France. A more precise character was given to the Allied war plans only during Churchill's visit to Washington in May, 1943 (the so-called Trident Conference), when, among other things, it was determined that the opening of the second front in France should be effected no later than May, 1944.

Of course, the most detailed source for the study of the events remains Churchill's memoirs, but Leahy's testimony—which does not always coincide with the British Prime Minister's version—expresses the American point of view and makes it possible to trace more effectively the origins of certain disagreements influenced by the diverse orientation of the American armed forces or by the personal views of many of the political and military leaders in Washington. Moreover, Leahy participated in all of the major inter-Allied conferences of the period with the exception of the Casablanca meeting, from which he was absent because of illness. He was present at the Trident Conference in Washington; at the Quadrant Conference in Quebec of August, 1943, when the timetable for the second front and the landing in southern France was definitely established; at the subsequent Washington meetings during which the position to be taken regarding Italy was finally determined; at the Cairo and Teheran Conferences, November–December, 1943; at the second conference of Quebec in September, 1944, which was almost exclusively devoted to Far Eastern problems; at the Yalta Conference of February, 1945; and at the Potsdam meeting of July–August, 1945. As expected, this part of Leahy's memoirs became less important with the publication of the State Department documents on the conferences of Teheran, Cairo, Yalta, and Potsdam, but a comparison of the memoirs with the documents reveals that the former remain an exceptional source for understanding the process that led to the American decisions on many of the major military and political problems of the war.

d. The Other American Memoir Sources.

In evaluating the American memoir sources it is necessary to keep in mind that many of the American representatives abroad are not career diplomats but are individuals chosen from political or business circles. This fact has an important bearing on their evaluation of developments in international affairs, and it is inevitably reflected in the character of their memoirs.

Thus, the former Ambassador to London, Dawes, who was at the Court of St. James from April, 1929, to February, 1932, arrived at the post with a rich experience in politics stemming from his having been president of the commission of experts on reparations, and Vice-President of the United States. Dawes published a volume on his experiences as president of the reparations commission,[176] based largely on the notes of his diary. It

[176] Charles Gates Dawes, *A Journal of Reparations* (New York: Macmillan, 1939).

represents one of the most significant contributions for the study of that
question and for the reconstruction of the origins of the plan that bears his
name. On his mission to London, his published memoirs[177] are of particular
interest for the part concerning the Naval Conference of 1930, the fall of
the Labour government, and the beginning of the Manchurian crisis.

The contribution of John Gilbert Winant,[178] Ambassador to London
during World War II, is much more modest. Winant was in an excellent
position to be fully informed on the situation in Great Britain during the
war and on the problems facing the British government, but his summary,
limited to 1941, is singularly lacking in significant data and is limited
largely to minor aspects of Anglo-American relations.

The volume by William C. Bullitt,[179] Ambassador to Moscow from 1933
to 1936 and to Paris from 1936 to 1940, should not be considered as a
memoir but as a study of Soviet policy designed to emphasize the danger
inherent in the Soviet Union's world-wide expansionist policies. Bullitt's
work is particularly significant because of his personality. In his position
as Ambassador to Paris, he exerted an unusually strong influence on the
political leaders of France, who apparently regarded him as a respected
counsellor. He was also able to influence President Roosevelt, with whom
he was in direct contact outside of the regular State Department channels.
In effect, Bullitt had arrived in Moscow with the hope of creating a
workable program of collaboration with the Soviet Union, but once he
came in contact with the realities of Soviet life, he concluded that there was
not the slightest chance of an understanding with the U.S.S.R. and that,
furthermore, communism represented the gravest threat to Europe and the
entire western world. This explains his attitude during his first years in
Paris, when he favored the attempts being made by the democracies to
reach an accord with Germany. Only repeated manifestations of the Nazi
aggressive policy ultimately convinced Bullitt to reverse his position and
support, especially after 1938, a policy of resistance to Hitler.

The memoirs of Bullitt's successor in Moscow, Joseph E. Davies,[180] are
completely different in spirit. His recollections of his mission to Moscow
from early 1936 to June, 1937, were published in December, 1941, a few
days after America entered the war, for the express purpose of moderating
the suspicious attitude of the American public toward the Soviet Union.
The heroic action of the Red army in resisting the German onslaughts had

[177] *Journal as Ambassador to Great Britain* (New York: Macmillan, 1939).
[178] *Letters from Grosvenor Square. An Account of a Stewardship* (Boston: Houghton Mifflin, 1947).
[179] *The Great Globe Itself* (New York: Scribner, 1946).
[180] *Mission to Moscow* (New York: Simon and Schuster, 1941).

aroused strong admiration in the United States, but it did not erase from American memories the fact that, for a time, the Soviet Union had been Germany's closest collaborator and with Nazi connivance had extended its European frontiers at the expense of all of its European neighbors. Thus, the idea of fighting side by side with the Soviets against Germany was greeted with mixed emotions by an American public that was still somewhat disoriented by the violent debates between isolationists and interventionists.

In this climate, the appearance of Davies' volume (he being one of the strongest supporters of the program to send large-scale aid to the U.S.S.R.) mitigated much of the American concern because, once having described the lights and shadows of the Communist system, he took a stand that led the reader toward a pro-Soviet position. The volume does not end with the termination of his mission to Moscow but also contains his notes and observations concerning the U.S.S.R. down to October 28, 1941. The pages devoted to the period following the German attack on the Soviet Union were written to support the author's views on aid to Russia, but since the debate on that issue has long been examined from every conceivable angle, there is no point in evaluating again the assertions they contain. Aside from this portion of the volume, it has certain historical value. Davies' recollections were drawn from his diary, his agenda, the official reports prepared for the State Department, and his personal letters to friends and government officials, and he reconstructs a detailed account that is valuable not so much for a study of Soviet-American relations as for an understanding of the major internal developments in the U.S.S.R. and a comprehension of the psychological attitude of the Soviet leaders in their contacts with westerners. It is strangely significant that Davies' views on the public trials in the Soviet Union during the period appear much less critical than those of the present Soviet leadership in the de-Stalinization era.

The attitude of Admiral Standley toward the U.S.S.R. at the end of his mission as Ambassador from April, 1942, to October, 1943, is markedly different from that of his predecessor. Once he had gained firsthand knowledge of the Soviet world, albeit within the narrow limits normally permitted western diplomats, Standley arrived at conclusions similar to those of Bullitt, and in his book[181] he has left a vivid account of the disagreements arising between the Soviet government and the Allies during the period of his mission to Moscow. However, his contribution is rather modest because, as he repeatedly emphasizes, problems of major importance were handled outside of the Embassy through accords reached at the

[181] William H. Standley and Arthur A. Ageton, *Admiral Ambassador to Russia* (Chicago: Regnery, 1955).

summit level or by personal representatives, a technique that is characteristic of American diplomacy.

While Ambassador Dodd's diary[182] is less brilliant than the Davies
volume, it is a much more solid contribution. Dodd was American
Ambassador to Berlin from the summer of 1933 to 1938. Like Davies, he
was not a career diplomat, and their writings reveal their different
backgrounds, the one an academician and the other an industrialist. When
Dodd returned to Germany, where he had spent his university days, he was
struck by the fact that the Germany that he knew no longer existed, and he
devoted his time to finding out what had caused the dramatic transformation. This investigation absorbed his attention to the extent that he was not
able to give the same close scrutiny to the diplomatic events he witnessed.
Moreover, his instinctive revulsion for official Nazidom led him to frequent
nonofficial circles, in which it was much more difficult for him to obtain the
information necessary for an accurate evaluation of Hitler's foreign policy,
which, in his diary, is reported as an echo, if not almost a secondary aspect,
of German reality.

Hugh R. Wilson, Dodd's successor in Berlin, was the last American
Ambassador to Germany before the war. He was recalled in November,
1938, in protest against the Nazi persecution of the Jews, and from that
moment on the Embassy was directed by a Chargé d'Affaires. Recently, his
son has edited and published a small volume of his principal reports
concerning the German internal situation and the consequences of the
Anschluss on German-American relations.[183] Together with these documents, which are not included in the State Department collection, the book
contains pages from Wilson's diary for 1938, data that, although interesting, is not especially revealing. Earlier, Wilson, who had been one of the
first American career diplomats to hold a post of major responsibility in the
Foreign Service, had published two volumes of memoirs[184] on the early
years of his career, from which very little can be learned about the foreign
policy of the United States.

The memoirs of Claude G. Bowers,[185] Ambassador to Spain from June,
1933, to the end of the Civil War, aroused enormous interest. The book
appeared in 1954, not long after the signing of the Madrid accords in

[182] Martha Dodd and William Dodd, Jr. (eds.), *Ambassador Dodd's Diary* (New
York: Harcourt, 1941).

[183] Hugh R. Wilson, Jr. (ed.), *A Career Diplomat. The Third Chapter: The Third
Reich* (New York: Vanguard Press, 1960).

[184] *The Education of a Diplomat* (New York: Longmans, 1938); *Diplomat
between Wars* (New York: Longmans, 1941).

[185] *My Mission to Spain: Watching the Rehearsal for World War II* (New York:
Simon and Schuster, 1954).

September, 1953, which established military collaboration between Spain and the United States, and, keeping in mind the lively polemical nature of the book, the circumstance does not seem devoid of significance. In effect, Bowers emphasizes that if communism represents the gravest threat to democracy today, this is not a reason for underestimating the danger posed by a return of fascism, which yesterday had proclaimed itself to be the only valid alternative in the struggle against communist ideology. In supporting his thesis, the author observes that the dictatorial regimes supported the Falangist forces not against communism—which, in Spain, had few followers—but against the democracies. In reality, he affirms, the Spanish Popular Front in 1936 was a democratic regime with socialist tendencies which, presumably, would have undergone an evolution similar to that of socialism in France; nor, in that situation, was there the serious possibility of seeing the Communists increase their strength because the extreme individualism of the Spaniards made it very difficult for Communists to establish themselves firmly there. These assertions leave the reader somewhat perplexed. First of all, it is difficult to conceive of the Spanish political scene in 1936 as an example of an efficient democracy, nor does it seem possible to find real parallels between Spanish and French political realities in the light of their different traditions, development, and social structures. Regarding Bowers' contention that communism did not have then, nor could it have today, any reasonable prospect of penetration, it should be noted that this is a dangerous assertion from the historical point of view and an extremely questionable one on a prophetic plane, particularly when one is mindful of the situation existing in countries with a heritage and structure similar to that of Spain. In any event, Bowers' testimony, once the polemical aspects which are of purely marginal interest to the historian are eliminated, is valuable for the study of many of the diplomatic facets of the situation and the framework within which the events occurred.

The memoirs of Carlton J. H. Hayes,[186] Ambassador to Madrid from May, 1942, to January, 1945, are based on a substantially different premise. Hayes, an eminent professor of history at Columbia University, began his mission when the danger of a Spanish intervention on the side of the Axis powers had virtually disappeared and the threat of a German thrust across Spain was considered highly improbable because of the difficulties of the campaign in Russia. It seems that the State Department had not accurately evaluated the situation, perhaps because it overestimated the importance of the oral pronouncements of the Falangists and of Serrano Suñer, in particular. Thus, once Hayes had arrived in Madrid and had grasped the

[186] *Wartime Mission in Spain 1942–1945* (New York: Macmillan, 1945).

reality of the Spanish situation, he found himself in frequent conflict with
the directives emanating from Washington. These disagreements, which
principally concerned the question of the flow of supplies to Spain (the
most effective means by which the Anglo-Saxon powers could apply
pressure to Madrid), were reproduced in the dissension between Hayes and
his British colleague, Hoare, which often led to a breakdown in the co-
operation and common purpose of the two embassies. While Hoare did not
hide his antipathy for the Falangist regime and maintained rather close
rapport with Spanish monarchists, Hayes preferred to remain aloof from
the internal affairs of the country and search for a *modus vivendi* with the
government in power. Hayes hoped to avoid aggravating the crisis in the
relations between Madrid and Washington, fearing the effect that this
would have on the attitude of the Latin-American countries toward the
United States. Thus, a comparison between the memoirs of the Anglo-
Saxon ambassadors to Spain serves to clarify not only several aspects of the
policies of Washington and London toward Spain, but also the motives for
certain reactions of the Falangist government toward the occasionally
contrasting policies of the Anglo-Saxons.

The memoirs of William Phillips,[187] Ambassador to Italy from September, 1936, to December 11, 1941, when Italy declared war on the
United States, are only of limited interest. Much of the volume is devoted
to this mission, but it contains little pertinent information because Phillips
had little contact with the current ruling group in Italy and, therefore, was
not aware of the behind-the-scenes activities in Fascist foreign policy.

The recollections of Joseph Grew cover a wider period because he spent
most of his life in the diplomatic service. He began his career in 1904, and
from 1908 until 1917 he was secretary to the American legation, first in
Vienna and then in Berlin, where he was Chargé d'Affaires when the
United States entered the war. After participating in the work of the peace
conference and short periods as Minister to Denmark and to Switzerland,
he became Undersecretary of State from 1924 to 1927, Ambassador to
Turkey until 1932, and Ambassador to Japan until the Japanese attack on
Pearl Harbor. Returning to Washington, he again became Undersecretary
of State, from 1944 to 1945.

Grew's first volume[188] is not a memoir, as strictly defined, but rather a
collection of his speeches delivered in the United States in 1942, aimed at
dispelling any illusions the American people had concerning the military
abilities of the Japanese. Grew emphasized the threat that the Empire of

[187] *Ventures in Diplomacy* (Boston: Beacon Press, 1952).
[188] *Report from Tokyo. A Message to the American People* (New York: Simon and
Schuster, 1942).

the Rising Sun posed to the United States in the Pacific and continued to stress the fighting capabilities of the Japanese armed forces.

His book on his mission to Japan[189] is much more important. Now that the official documents have been published, the work has lost some of the importance it had when it appeared in 1944, but the conclusions reached by the author remain valid for an explanation of the American attitude toward postwar Japan. Rather than emphasize his activities as head of the American mission in Tokyo, Grew provides a detailed picture of the Japanese political scene before the war, pointing out the distinction between the extremists who had brought on the war and the many others who had tried to prevent the conflict and to whom the United States should turn for support in the moral reconstruction of Japan after the war. This concept had an important effect on Grew's attitude during his term as Undersecretary of State in 1944–45, as he explains in his third volume.[190] This is, perhaps, the most interesting of the three books, and, like the earlier ones, it is based on an ample documentation, which includes his diary, supplemented by his private correspondence and numerous documents that he had sent to the State Department. On the most important mission of his career, his ambassadorship to Tokyo, Grew stresses again in this volume that Japan, or at least the majority of the ruling class, was not wholly responsible for the war in the Far East. He notes that the growing American intransigence during the negotiations of the summer and fall of 1941 also played a role in the Japanese decision to attack the United States. A point of particular interest to Italy emerges from the pages concerning the dramatic days of the spring of 1945, when the occupation of Venezia Giulia by Tito's forces aroused the fear that Trieste and its surrounding territory were permanently lost. Grew's study contains the minutes of the Truman meetings to study the question and includes testimony of primary importance on the action taken by the Washington government during the crisis.

One of the fundamental sources for a study of American foreign policy is the Jay Pierrepont Moffat papers.[191] From 1932 to 1935 Moffat directed the western European division of the State Department, and from 1937 to May, 1940, he was in charge of its European section. Because of his personal rapport with Hull and Stimson, Moffat enjoyed a particularly influential

[189] *Ten Years in Japan* (New York: Simon and Schuster, 1944).

[190] *Turbulent Era. A Diplomatic Record of Forty Years (1904–1945)* (2 vols.; Boston: Houghton Mifflin, 1952).

[191] Nancy Harvison Hooker (ed.), *The Moffat Papers. Selection from the Diplomatic Journals of Jay Pierrepont Moffat* (Cambridge, Mass.: Harvard University Press, 1956).

position. He kept a day-by-day account of his activities and of the events he witnessed, and after his death in 1943 his diaries, consisting of twenty typewritten volumes, in addition to a quantity of other material, were turned over to the Harvard University library. It is impossible in this brief survey to list the major points of interest in these documents. Suffice it to say that this source is irreplaceable not only for reconstructing American diplomatic activity in specific circumstances but also for studying the internal process of policymaking and the function of the State Department.

John F. Montgomery, American Minister to Budapest from 1933 to 1941, has condensed his experiences in one volume,[192] of interest for several reasons. The book is something more than a memoir in that the author seeks to correct many American misconceptions regarding Hungary and to point out the errors committed by the State Department in dealing with Hungarian political problems during and after World War II.

The three elements of his thesis are: (1) in a war of coalition, it often happens that powers fighting in good faith and for a just cause do so side by side with powers pursuing a policy that can only be condemned; (2) the behaviour of Czechoslovakia, Poland, Yugoslavia, and Rumania was much more in line with Nazi theory and practice than that of the government of Budapest; (3) Hungary, caught in the German and Slavic vise, did not have a freedom of choice, especially after the *Anschluss,* and its entire policy was aimed at protecting the national interests while doing the least damage possible. One must admit that here the author frequently hits the target, and many of his observations are worthy of serious reflection and greater attention in that they are dictated by the laudable desire to search for the truth wherever it may be found. On the other hand, the entire volume reflects the tendency to justify Hungarian actions to the point of accepting as fact certain data that are possibly too favorable to Hungarian government policy and that are not historically accurate. Thus, according to Montgomery, the First Arbitrage of Vienna was imposed by Hitler, while, in reality, the initiative was taken by Budapest and supported by Italy. The occupation of Ruthenia was effected upon Von Ribbentrop's recommendation and without the knowledge of either Ciano or Mussolini, just as soon as Hitler decided to march on Prague. It was not a unilateral decision by Hungary for the purpose of restoring order in a chaotic local situation. Montgomery's version of the Second Arbitrage of Vienna is also not completely accurate. For example, his assertion that the Hungarians would have preferred to negotiate separately with Rumania is not true. The

---

[192] *Hungary: The Unwilling Satellite* (New York: Devin Adair, 1947).

negotiations of Turnu Severin, which Montgomery does not mention, were interrupted under strong pressure from Budapest, which was threatening aerial military activity.

Obviously, the author's arguments would have been more persuasive if the list of Hungarian errors had been more complete, but perhaps he was trying to correct an existing imbalance wherein all mistakes had been credited to Budapest. This raises the question of the effectiveness of an approach that goes to excessive lengths in praising certain aspects of Hungarian policy. It is possible that the results are counterproductive. Among the many significant disclosures, there is the interesting report of a meeting between Stalin and the Magyar Minister to Moscow during the summer of 1940, in which Stalin encouraged Hungary to attack Rumania, a suggestion that was rejected by Budapest; and the steps taken by King Alexander of Yugoslavia to reach an understanding with Mussolini, referred to in the discussion of the Henderson memoirs.

Robert Murphy has recently published a good descriptive account of his activities during World War II.[193] From his post as Embassy Counsellor in Vichy he suddenly found himself involved in high-level diplomacy when, in the winter of 1940–41, he was sent on a special mission to Algiers by President Roosevelt. Later, he became Diplomatic Counsellor to General Eisenhower's headquarters, a privileged position from which to observe the diplomatic developments of the war. Still later, he was entrusted with several important missions by the President. The publication of the American documents for the crucial years of World War II reduces the importance of much of Murphy's account and makes it possible to correct some of his assertions. Nonetheless, the volume is an important supplement to the documents and should be carefully studied, particularly for American policy toward the Vichy government in the period 1941–42 and for the preparation of Operation TORCH.

Turning to a consideration of the memoirs published by American statesmen,[194] attention is called to the diary of Henry L. Stimson,[195] Secretary of State under Hoover and Secretary of War under Roosevelt. His recollections as Secretary of State cover the period 1929–33 and are particularly important for the Far Eastern crisis, while the memoirs of his experiences in the War Department from 1940 to 1945 deal primarily with

---

[193] *Diplomat among Warriors* (New York: Doubleday, 1964).

[194] President Roosevelt left no memoirs. His son Elliott has published a large selection of his personal letters, half of which refer to the period after 1929 (*F. D. R.: His Personal Letters* [4 vols.; New York: Duell, 1947–50]).

[195] Henry Lewis Stimson and McGeorge Bundy, *On Active Service in Peace and War* (New York: Harper, 1948).

military problems, although there are numerous references to the diplomatic events of World War II.

Some useful material may be found in the diary of the Secretary of the Navy, Forrestal,[196] which begins with 1944 and covers the final episodes of the war. The most interesting pages concern the origins of the decision to demand unconditional surrender of the Japanese and the position that the United States should have adopted after the Yalta Conference and especially after the death of Roosevelt.

Edward Stettinius, Undersecretary of State from September, 1943, after the forced resignation of Welles, and Secretary of State after the retirement of Hull in December, 1944, has also left two useful volumes of memoirs.[197] The first concerns his activities as administrator of the lend-lease program for two years beginning in September, 1941. The second refers exclusively to the Yalta Conference. Stettinius had no intention of writing his memoirs of the period he spent in office as Secretary of State. However, in 1948 the flood of criticism of the Yalta Agreements,[198] for which he, after Roosevelt, was principally responsible, induced him to reveal what he knew concerning the developments at the conference in order to put the positive results of the meeting in their proper perspective and to explain why a number of the decisions made at Yalta had proved to have negative value. Notwithstanding the defensive position taken by Stettinius, the volume remained, for a time, an essential source for the study of this controversial historical event because the author was able to consult the official documents on the conference. The publication of a volume of documents on Yalta in the official collection of the State Department has largely confirmed Stettinius' summary and, moreover, has strengthened several of his theses. Without repeating the observations made earlier on the subject, it should be noted here that one of the questions raised by the memoir concerns the effect on Stalin of the Roosevelt statement at Yalta that American troops would be withdrawn from Europe within two years after the end of the war. As is known, Stalin also made concessions to the western powers at Yalta, concessions that were not implemented due to the abrupt change in the equilibrium of the armed forces in Europe as a result of the rapid Anglo-American demobilization, which allowed the Soviets to advance in several vital areas of Europe and Asia. At this point, the problem is a twofold one. First of all, it remains to be proved whether or not Stalin was in good faith

[196] Walter Millis (ed.), *The Forrestal Diaries* (New York: Viking Press, 1951).

[197] Edward R. Stettinius, Jr., *Lend Lease: Weapon for Victory* (New York: Macmillan, 1944); *Roosevelt and the Russians. The Yalta Conference* (Garden City, N.Y.: Doubleday, 1949).

[198] See pp. 224, 227, *et seq.*

when he assumed certain obligations during the conference or whether he negotiated with the foreknowledge of the void that would exist in Europe, to be filled by the Red Army. Second, it would have to be established that the reason why he maintained his obligations for a time was, in fact, his desire to facilitate the withdrawal of the Anglo-American forces in order to create a situation that would permit him to annul the concessions he had made at Yalta.

The memoirs of President Truman[199] are also useful for a reconstruction of the international events of the last months of the war, although his narrative, as he notes in his preface, is restricted by limits imposed by national security and by his regard for living persons who took part in the events. However, the recollections are noticeably lacking in significant revelations, in contrast to the accounts of the same period written by other Americans such as Leahy, Byrnes, Stettinius, or Forrestal. To these should be added the official documents published on the Potsdam Conference and on the Soviet Union's intervention in the war against Japan, which provide an exhaustive treatment of the way Truman handled these two major problems during his first months in office as President. Nevertheless, it was reasonable to expect something more from Truman's memoirs on the grave decision he was forced to make on the question of the use of the atomic bomb. Instead, he does not dwell on this point, and in assuming total responsibility for the decision he simply notes that he considered the atomic bomb an instrument of war and that he had no doubts about the fact that it should be used but that, in deciding to do so, he had insisted that it be employed as any other tool of war, in a manner prescribed by the rules of war. In effect, he required that it be dropped as closely as possible to the center of a war production area of major importance. The first volume concerns the events of 1945 and the second covers the period down to the close of his second term of office in 1952.

As soon as Truman succeeded to the presidency after the death of Roosevelt, he decided to replace Stettinius as Secretary of State with James F. Byrnes. Stettinius remained in office until the completion of his mission as American delegate to the San Francisco Conference, April 25–June 25, 1945. Byrnes was not a novice in government service. From October, 1942, to May, 1943, he had been Director of the Office of War Mobilization, involved in all of the internal problems connected with the war effort, and earned the title of "Assistant President." The great trust and intimate collaboration that tied him to Roosevelt, in addition to his long career as a

[199] Harry S. Truman, *Memoirs,* Vol. I: *Year of Decision;* Vol. II: *Years of Trial and Hope* (Garden City, N.Y.: Doubleday, 1955).

Democrat in both houses of Congress (he was a member of the House of Representatives from 1911 to 1925 and of the Senate from 1931 to 1941), put him among the ranking candidates for the office of Vice-President on the Democratic ticket prior to the nomination of Truman as Roosevelt's running mate in the election of 1944. A few months after his resignation as Secretary of State in January, 1947, Byrnes published an interesting volume of memoirs[200] on all of his activities in the international sphere. These had begun in February, 1945, when he accompanied Roosevelt to Yalta; he later attended the Potsdam meeting and the Moscow conference of foreign ministers in December, 1945, followed by the cycle of conferences of foreign ministers (London, September–October, 1945; Paris, April–May and June–July, 1946) in which the terms of the treaties were hammered out for Germany's former allies, completed in the Paris meeting of July–October, 1946, and in the New York conference of November–December, 1946. When the Byrnes volume was published, it aroused considerable curiosity because for the first time some light was cast on the activities of the inter-Allied conferences of the preceding two years and the major behind-the-scenes maneuvers were revealed. Now, after the publication of the American documents on the Yalta and Potsdam conferences, Byrnes's memoirs have been reduced to secondary importance, but they retain their original value in what concerns the elaboration of the peace treaties, including the treaty with Italy. Moreover, they provide valuable information on the Soviet and American attitudes on the German question. Specifically, Byrnes reveals the repeated offers made to Stalin of an Anglo-American-French treaty guaranteeing the demilitarization of Germany, which leads to the conclusion that today the Soviet Union is opposed to the reunification of Germany on grounds independent of the issue of Bonn's rearmament or West Germany's membership in N. A. T. O.

Byrnes has recently published a second volume of memoirs[201] on his activities as a statesman, but these add little to what is included in the first book on his role in international affairs, nor does he add anything to what is already known about the differences with Truman that led to his resignation in January, 1947. One might observe that these differences perhaps stemmed not so much from Byrnes's attitude as from the questionable psychology behind Truman's decision to entrust an extremely delicate post in his administration to a man who had been his opponent for the post of Vice-President and whom he recognized as being accustomed—because of the unrestricted power which Roosevelt had given him—to almost absolute autonomy in the fulfillment of his duties, while Truman intended to

[200] *Speaking Frankly* (New York: Harper, 1947).
[201] *All in One Lifetime* (New York: Harper, 1958).

assume personally all the powers that the United States Constitution delegated to the President. The negative effect of this choice, in the delicate period of transition between war and peace, especially beginning with the Moscow conference of December, 1945, was reflected in the marked contrast between the foreign policy aims of President Truman and those of Byrnes, particularly with respect to the Soviet Union.

Among the memoirs of the American military, worthy of particular attention are those of General Deane,[202] head of the American military mission to Moscow during the last phase of the conflict; Stilwell's diary,[203] which provided, until the publication of the official documents on Chinese-American relations, one of the most useful sources available on the relations between Washington, London, and Chungking from 1941 to 1944; and several chapters in the memoirs of Eisenhower,[204] Clark,[205] and Butcher.[206]

6. THE JAPANESE MEMORIALISTS.

a. Konoye.

Prince Konoye was the first of the Japanese statesmen to publish his memoirs. During the late summer of 1945, when the American authorities began assembling materials for the investigation into the attack on Pearl Harbor, Konoye consigned to the Commission of Inquiry the original copy of his memoirs, written between October, 1941, and the spring of 1942, immediately after he left the government post which he had occupied since July, 1940. Konoye had also been Prime Minister during 1937–38, but he limited his memoirs to the notes and documents in his possession covering only the period April–October, 1941, months during which he had conducted the negotiations with the United States for reaching a peaceful solution on the questions at issue between the two countries.

From the deposition made at the Tokyo trials by his private secretary, Ushiba, it was verified that this copy of the manuscript was translated into English by the Commission of Inquiry under Ushiba's supervision and that

---

[202] John R. Deane, *The Strange Alliance. The Story of Our Efforts at Wartime Cooperation with Russia* (New York: Viking Press, 1947).

[203] Theodore H. White (ed.), *The Stilwell Papers* (New York: Sloane, 1948).

[204] Dwight D. Eisenhower, *Crusade in Europe* (Garden City, N.Y.: Doubleday, 1948).

[205] Mark W. Clark, *Calculated Risk* (New York: Harper, 1950).

[206] Harry C. Butcher, *My Three Years with Eisenhower. Personal Diary 1942–1945* (New York: Simon and Schuster, 1946).

Konoye had had his private secretary's co-operation in writing his memoirs. Moreover, Ushiba revealed that early in 1944 Prince Konoye prepared a revised edition of his original manuscript in Japanese, which was mimeographed, and plans were made for early release. The revised edition differed from the original in that it contained many corrections and several omissions. A few days after the death of Prince Konoye on December 16, 1945, the revised edition was published serially in the Japanese newspaper *Asahi Shimbun*[207] and, later, in book form.[208]

Therefore, there are two official editions of the Konoye memoirs, an English edition included in the documents on the Pearl Harbor inquiry and a Japanese edition revised by the author. A careful comparison of the two texts reveals that the omissions and corrections in the Japanese text are found almost exclusively in the portions dealing with the delicate problem of the Emperor's influence on major decisions. While the omissions do not seriously affect the value of the memoir, it is regrettable that they do exist.

The motive prompting Konoye to keep a record of his actions during the last months that he was at the government's helm was his desire to demonstrate that he alone was not responsible for the failure of the negotiations which proved fatal for Japan. As is apparent from the explanatory letter he left just before he took his own life in order to avoid the humiliation of going before the War Crimes Tribunal, he intended to clarify the matter of responsibility for the outbreak of war because he was acutely aware that he personally bore the weight of the China incident of 1937, which had occurred during his premiership. Throughout 1941 he recognized the adverse effect that the Japanese military penetration of China was having on American-Japanese relations. During the American-Japanese negotiations of 1941, the United States repeatedly showed its intransigence on the Chinese question, provoking a similar reaction among the Japanese opposition. This impasse was the decisive factor in Konoye's failure to reach a compromise on the controversial issues with Washington, a settlement ardently sought by him in order to avoid war.

Konoye's efforts are clearly outlined in his memoir, but it is also apparent that they were part of an ill-starred maneuver: he was not able to impose his views on the military with sufficient vigor; on the contrary, the latter ably exploited his concern with avoiding war and converted him into an

---

[207] A limited edition of these installments was published in English translation: see Okuyama Service (ed.), *The Memoirs of Prince Fumimaro Konoye* [translated from the *Asahi Shimbun*, December 20–31, 1945] (Tokyo, n.d.).

[208] *Ushinawareshi Seiji, Konoye Fumimaro Ko no Shuki* [Defeated Government. The Memoirs of Prince Fumimaro Konoye] (Tokyo: Asahi Shinbunsha, 1946).

instrument of their war policy. During the entire course of the negotiations with Washington, the hostile tactics of the military, which insisted on certain reservations and delays and imposed a series of obstacles designed to prevent a solution of the problems, were a success. This forced the decision of September 6, 1941, whereby the military won its point, i.e., if negotiations did not succeed in resolving the differences by October 10, 1941, a solution would be sought by force of arms.

Notwithstanding the wealth of data contained in the documentary collections produced by the Tokyo trials, the Pearl Harbor inquest, and the numerous memoirs pertaining to events in the Far East, from the point of view of diplomatic history the little volume by the former Japanese Prime Minister retains its importance. This work cannot be ignored in any attempt to reconstruct the internal history of negotiations with Washington. The facts narrated by the author are based solidly on the documents. The differences, the debates, and the discussions between the supporters of a diplomatic solution and those advocating armed conflict with the United States are clearly and effectively reported by Konoye, and information on these subjects is largely dependent on this source.

An aspect of the Konoye memoirs deserving of particular attention for the light it casts on the relations between the Tripartite powers is the role played by the Axis or, more precisely, by Germany, in the negotiations between Tokyo and Washington. During the period of American neutrality, Japan's partnership in the Tripartite Agreement served to guarantee to the Axis powers that the United States, obliged to concentrate the bulk of its forces in the Pacific in order to counter the permanent threat to its interests posed by Japanese politico-territorial ambitions, could not make a decisive contribution to Great Britain's European defense. Any consideration of a probable American intervention in the European conflict aside, it was obvious that a Japanese-American *rapprochement* would have had a negative effect on the Axis powers because the United States would have been able to increase its aid to Great Britain greatly by concentrating its war potential on the European fronts.

When Tokyo was informed of the American proposal of April 18, 1941, in which Article 2 included the restriction on Japan's military obligations to the Axis—obligations based on the Tripartite Agreement—in the eventuality that the Axis was attacked by a power not yet involved in the conflict, the Japanese government was faced with the embarrassing alternative of having to choose between faithful adherence to the terms of the Tripartite Agreement and the practical possibility of keeping Japan out of the conflict by accepting the basic premises of the American proposal. After some hesitation the Japanese government deemed it advisable not to inform its allies of the negotiations, in view of the predictable German opposition, but at the same time to inform Washington that Japan had no intention of violating the Tripartite Agreement. To achieve this end, Tokyo proposed to insert a clause which would oblige the United States to use its good offices to help Japan resolve the conflict between Great Britain and the Axis powers. However, this proposal was developed in Tokyo during Foreign Minister Matsuoka's long European tour, and it was rejected by him upon his return to Japan.

After long discussions, it was agreed that the reply to Washington on this point would emphasize the fact that Japan intended to observe faithfully the obligations undertaken in the Tripartite Pact. At the same time, Matsuoka informed the Italian and German ambassadors in Tokyo of the negotiations with Washington and asked the latter to inquire whether Von Ribbentrop had any suggestions to make on the matter. As was to be expected, Berlin's reply pointed out that the armed protection of American convoys to Europe, recently ordered by President Roosevelt, was designed solely for the purpose of forcing Germany to commit an act of war against the United States so that America could enter the war after being attacked. Therefore, Von Ribbentrop added, any clause that would restrict Japan's obligations under the Tripartite Agreement would be unacceptable. Moreover, he added, in general any treaty concluded by a member country of the Tripartite Pact with a third party would necessarily weaken the diplomatic position of its allies.

Matsuoka's communication to the Axis ambassadors had a further negative effect on American-Japanese negotiations. By enlarging the circle of people aware of the negotiations with Washington, it was inevitable that the information would leak not only to the General Staff but also to the officer corps of the army. This group was one of several which was convinced that it was necessary to resolve the issues by war, and, through the power it wielded, it was able to exert tremendous influence on the government's decisions. This leak, combined with the strengthening of the Japanese war party's position by the promised support of a Germany at the crest of her military successes, seriously weakened Konoye's dwindling hopes for a peaceful settlement of the difficulties. What emerges from Konoye's memoirs makes it possible to place this factor in its proper perspective in the total evaluation of the American-Japanese negotiations prior to the attack on Pearl Harbor.

Undoubtedly, many errors were committed by Konoye during the period in which he governed Japan, and his two principal mistakes were the Chinese adventure and the Tripartite Pact. However, Konoye had the courage to stop when confronted with the prospect of plunging Japan into war with the United States. While he risked his life in making this decision in the face of pressure by the Japanese General Staff, which makes it possible to judge his policies less harshly, his incompetence as a statesman is revealed in his failure to anticipate the consequences of the weakness of his earlier policy toward the military. Moreover, his choice of Matsuoka as Foreign Minister proved to be disastrous.

b. Shigemitsu.

A completely different spirit from that of Prince Konoye has been displayed by other Japanese statesmen concerning their responsibilities for the war and the tragic effect it had on the Empire of the Rising Sun.

The defeat brought various social consequences to all the statesmen of the former member countries of the Tripartite Pact, such as purges, trials, and persecution. But their attitudes in the face of these adversities varied according to the country they represented. In Italy, the purges resulted in a "camouflaging" of the ex-gerarchs. In Germany, instead, they produced a guilt complex in the representatives of the old regime, typical of the German temperament, which has left traces visible down to the present. Japan, too, experienced a profound transformation in its social structure, but the attitude of those of its former leaders who survived the war and imprisonment has been very different. They have defended their actions without the slightest feeling of guilt, even to the point of blaming their adversaries for their own errors. This psychological attitude must be carefully considered when evaluating the memoirs they have written.

Furthermore, it should be noted that the position taken by the Japanese statesmen has produced a favorable reaction among many American historians, and much American historical writing tends to picture the Japanese situation at the outbreak of the war in a more favorable light than heretofore and shows remarkable comprehension of the needs of the Japanese Empire.

Great interest was aroused in Japan by the appearance of the volumes of memoirs of Ambassador Shigemitsu, who had been Minister of Foreign Affairs in the Tojo Cabinet (a term of office limited to the period April, 1943–July, 1944), the Koiso Cabinet (July, 1944–April, 1945), and the Higashikuni government (August 15–autumn, 1945). In the first volume[209] the author has assembled the recollections of his official life. The memoirs cover the entire period from his early career, when as a young secretary he joined the Japanese delegation to the Versailles Conference,

[209] Mamoru Shigemitsu, *Gaiko Kaisoruku* [Memoirs of a Diplomat] (Tokyo: Mainichi Shinbunsha, 1953).

through his years of service in China and as Vice-Minister of Foreign Affairs (1933–36). The volume concludes with the account of his missions to Moscow (1936–38) and to London (1938–41), where he served as Ambassador. The second volume[210] contains the notes he wrote during the four years he spent in Sugamo prison. In addition to providing an acute commentary on the Tokyo trials, it is also important for the summaries it contains of the conversations that the author had with other Japanese political and military leaders confined in the same prison.

Our discussion concerns only Shigemitsu's most important volume.[211] Rather than a true memoir, it is a general summary of Japanese policy from 1931 to 1945, written in order that the author's compatriots might learn from his meditations on the turbulent years something which might be of value to Japan's rebirth. When the volume appeared in 1952, only those portions concerning Japan's surrender which cast new light on the event were translated into English. However, a complete translation of the volume is now available.[212] The most important pages refer to the war years, during which the author's activity as Ambassador to the Nanking government (January, 1942–April, 1943) and, later, as Minister of Foreign Affairs, are carefully detailed because they form an integral part of the general policy of the Japanese government.

Shigemitsu, along with all the other Japanese political and diplomatic personnel, was in open conflict with the military, who were champions of a war that, in the judgment of the majority, appeared from the very beginning to be without hope of success. In Nanking he worked steadily to achieve a change in his country's foreign policy, taking as a point of departure a proposal for a revision of Japanese relations with China, which, in effect, had pushed Japan along a course leading inexorably to a break with the United States. This shift in policy, based on premises not very different from those of the United States, would have furnished an effective base from which to attempt a compromise with Washington on the conflict. In the spring of 1942, as a result of the Japanese military victories, the conditions seemed to be most propitious for the development of such an approach.

Shigemitsu proposed that his government terminate its interference in Chinese internal affairs and aid the Chinese to reacquire their complete sovereignty; logically, as soon as the military situation permitted, Japanese

---

[210] *Sugamo Nikki* [Sugamo Diary] (Tokyo: Bungei Shunju Sha, 1953).

[211] *Showa no Doran* [The Turbulent Years of the Showa Era] (2 vols.; Tokyo: Chuo Koronsha, 1952).

[212] *Japan and Her Destiny. My Struggle for Peace* (London: Hutchinson, 1958).

troops should be removed from China. This policy, said Shigemitsu, could not fail to produce beneficial results for the Japanese, for two reasons: (1) the supply of raw materials coming from China, which was causing serious concern in Tokyo because of the increasing shortage of resources for payment and the difficulties created by the extension of Chinese sabotage, would be assured in a new climate of co-operation; (2) if the spirit prompting this new course also permeated military and governmental circles, it would be possible to establish the life of the nation on an entirely new basis.

Shigemitsu's plan was not limited to China, but was extended to all of east Asia under foreign domination. Japan's virtual recognition of the sovereignty and independence of such nations, and the assistance that Japan could give them in achieving these objectives, would have given Japanese policy an entirely new character.

Prime Minister Tojo responded favorably to these ideas, but their realization was delayed by the opposition of the military and became possible only when the conditions favoring the change were disappearing. Therefore, the attempt was only partially successful. In June, 1942, the tide of the Pacific war turned in favor of the United States, although it was difficult for the Japanese government to get an exact evaluation of the situation from the Supreme Command, which was very reticent to release any information (throughout the war, Tojo was never able to learn the precise details of the Battle of Midway). Meanwhile, Chiang Kai-shek's growing diplomatic and military strength virtually eliminated any prospect of an accord with the Wang Ching-wei government that would restore Chinese unity. When Shigemitsu entered the Cabinet in April, 1943, as Foreign Minister, the pressure he was able to bring to bear produced positive results in only one aspect of his program, that of recognizing the independence of foreign possessions under Japanese occupation, which occurred at the Conference for Greater East Asia, which met in Tokyo in November, 1943, and was attended by delegates from the Philippines, Burma, India, Thailand, Manchukuo, and the Nanking government of China. The plan for China failed completely and thus the creation of conditions that would have made it possible to attempt to resolve the conflict with the United States by negotiation was blocked.

As is evident, from the moment Shigemitsu became Minister for Foreign Affairs he considered a negotiated peace as one of the principal goals of his office. General Tojo was aware of his objective and it appears that he personally shared this aim. However, to support the need for an armistice and to lay the groundwork for such an appeal would have deprived Tojo of the support of the military circles that had brought him to, and supported him in, power. The most violently bellicose elements were to be found among the middle-grade officer corps, which was drawn largely from the *petite bourgeoisie* and the agricultural classes—the exponents, that is, of that Japanese military tradition which was almost proletarian and which, because of its narrow outlook, remained most receptive to intransigence and rhetoric.

The major obstacle to a negotiated peace was the obligation assumed by Japan in the Tripartite Pact—and insisted upon by the Japanese—not to conclude a separate peace. Therefore, preliminary consultations with Japan's allies were necessary before any action could be taken. The soundings made by Shigemitsu in Berlin in the late spring of 1943 to induce Germany to accept Japanese mediation in the Nazi-Soviet conflict as an indispensable preface to Japan's suspension of the war in the Pacific met with the violent opposition of Hitler, who knew that he could count on the Japanese war party to support the German position effectively in Tokyo. In Japan there was no fear, as there was in Italy, that the Germans could prevent the suspension of hostilities by an invasion of the country, but there were equally grave risks in the probable rebellion of the armed forces against the decisions of the government. Nor did the German position change after the Italian armistice, which offered, on the basis of the alliance, a justification for seeking a solution to the conflict. Meanwhile, Shigemitsu was forced to await the moment when, in the light of the apparently forthcoming German defeat, the Emperor could have used his unquestioned authority to force the extremists to accept his decision to terminate the war.

In the meantime, however, other approaches were being considered. The concern resulting from the worsening military situation led many statesmen to the idea of contacting the Allies directly. In order to ensure the strictest secrecy of the operation, it was necessary to avoid contacts with the Japanese legations in neutral countries, and even the possibility of sending a mission to Europe via submarine was considered, a plan for which Yoshida and Prince Konoye volunteered their services.

By the spring of 1945, those urging peace negotiations were fully aware of the imminent collapse of Nazi Germany, and all indications suggested that it was imperative to take those steps that would facilitate the cessation of hostilities at the opportune moment. Shigemitsu conferred with the Swedish Ambassador to Japan, Jacob Bagge, just before Bagge returned to Stockholm, and Bagge agreed to use Sweden's good offices to seek an armistice in terms commensurate with Japanese honor. But at this point the Koiso government fell, and the new ministry, which did not include

Shigemitsu, approached Moscow instead of Stockholm for the same purpose.

Shigemitsu reappeared on the political scene after August 15, 1945, and he assumed the onerous task of signing, in the name of the Japanese government, the surrender terms aboard the battleship "Missouri," anchored in Tokyo Bay, on September 2, 1945.

Undoubtedly, the events referred to here, which reflect an experience analogous to that of Italy insofar as the armistice is concerned, deserve to be studied objectively, and they become singularly important for what they contribute to an understanding of the events in Italy in 1943. Shigemitsu's explanation of the facts invalidates whatever differences were believed to exist between the Italian and Japanese conduct vis-à-vis the Tripartite Pact. On the historical plane, there remained only a question of time for the outcome of the negotiations, negotiations that were contemplated even before the Italian ones, while the German veto on seeking an armistice has been documented.

c. Togo.

Shigenori Togo's volume[213] focuses on two hotly debated issues: the American-Japanese negotiations of 1941 and the Japanese attempts to conclude an armistice in the summer of 1945. That part of Togo's memoirs dealing with his missions as Ambassador to Berlin (1937) and to Moscow (1938–41) has, in fact, been omitted in the English translation. In the latter, the narrative begins with the formation of the Tojo ministry in October, 1941, the date Togo joined the new government as Foreign Minister, a post he held until September, 1942, when, as a result of a series of differences with the Prime Minister on the policy to be followed toward the other countries of east Asia, he resigned and returned to private life. He returned to the post of Foreign Minister in the Suzuki government (April 6–August 15, 1945), which was formed under the pressure of military defeats in order to find a way out of the country's tragic situation. He remained in office until the promulgation of the Imperial decree announcing Japan's surrender.

Togo wrote his memoirs in 1949–50, during the last months of his life, which were spent mostly in Tokyo hospitals, where he had been taken from Sugamo prison because of his failing health. Several chapters were hurriedly written in the fear that he would not have time to complete his work.

[213] *The Cause of Japan* (New York: Simon and Schuster, 1956).

However, the knowledge that the end was near did not induce him to modify the explanation of his activities, which he had already presented during the war crimes trials in Tokyo. Therefore, despite its interest, Togo's volume does not appear to be very objective but constitutes, instead, a tenacious defense of Japanese policy in general and of the author's role in particular. This fact can be determined by noting the differences in the accuracy of detail and in the force of the argument presented by the author in the two parts of the volume. The first part, dealing with the Japanese-American negotiations, whose tragic conclusion gave rise to the twofold accusation leveled against the Japanese statesmen—of premeditated aggression and of the violation of international norms for failing to declare war against the United States according to established practice—is highly detailed and the narrative is strongly polemical. The second part, instead, which does not have a specific aim (with the possible exception of making it appear completely logical that the Japanese should seek the use of the good offices of the Soviets to arrive at an armistice), is obviously less important to the author.

Given the general premise of the book, it is logical that the author should seek to show that at the moment Prince Konoye resigned (because of the impossibility of modifying the military's attitude toward negotiations with the United States) there still existed only a few but well-founded hopes of resolving the differences with Washington peacefully. It is interesting to note how Togo develops these possibilities. He states that he was convinced by a study of the documentation on the earlier phases of the negotiations that the United States was disposed to go to war in order to achieve all of its objectives and that, if peace were to be preserved, Japan would have to make substantial concessions to the Americans. Such concessions required a less rigid attitude from the military on the Chinese problem. Army leaders were convinced that it was impossible to accede to the American demand to withdraw Japanese troops from China because this withdrawal would have deprived the Japanese of the fruits of four years of hard campaigning, gravely humiliated the entire army, and created serious difficulties in the supply of raw materials.

In the joint session of the Foreign Ministry and the General Staff of November 1, 1941, called at Togo's insistence to establish a terminal date for the evacuation of China by the Japanese armed forces, a compromise between the two years proposed by him and the *ninety-nine* years proposed by the military was reached, establishing the terminal date at twenty-five years, a period of time long enough to destroy any sense of the reality of the promise to evacuate China. Nevertheless, Togo affirms that the agreement represented a positive accomplishment because until that time the army had consistently refused to admit that the stationing of troops in China could be regulated by anything other than the needs of Japanese policy. Therefore, Togo had not gained any significant advantage that would have allowed him even to approach the American demands, but the problem was not even considered, since Washington rejected the Japanese proposal in its entirety, including the above-mentioned clause, because of lack of faith in Tokyo's good intentions.

Togo criticizes Prince Konoye's tendency to bow to the demands of the military on several points, but he gives no indication of being aware that he was a prisoner of the very same military organs that circumscribed Konoye's activity. During the November 1 meeting, mentioned above, along with the decision to continue the negotiations with the Americans, it was also established that if they were not concluded satisfactorily by the end of the month, a solution would be sought by force of arms. Accordingly, Togo found himself in exactly the same situation that Konoye had faced after the decisions of September 6, 1941.

As far as the American position during the course of the negotiations is concerned, the author, logically, supports the revisionist thesis (the view that Roosevelt waited for the Japanese attack in order to have a motive for dragging the United States into the war) and frequently cites the work of Charles A. Beard,[214] one of the major exponents of this point of view. As a matter of fact, the position taken by the United States at that time seems to have been excessively rigid and entirely lacking in comprehension of Japan's real situation and of the true significance of the factors involved. On the question of whether this attitude was due to faulty judgment or to malicious intent, the arguments advanced in support of the latter, despite whatever appeal they may have, leave the dispassionate reader perplexed and without a real basis for accepting them. However, Roosevelt appears to have wanted terms which could have been acceptable only to an adversary determined to avoid an armed encounter with the United States at all costs. This view is also expressed by Togo in his comment on the Hull note of November 26, which, it cannot be denied, had the flavor of an ultimatum, given the war-like atmosphere dominating Tokyo, under the influence of the militarists.

Togo advances a unique argument to describe Washington's unfavorable attitude toward Japan. The American Intelligence Service had broken the Japanese codes and during the negotiations was able to decipher all of the dispatches from the Japanese Foreign Ministry to its Embassy in Washington. Togo emphasizes the "malicious distortion" by the Intelligence Service

[214] *President Roosevelt and the Coming of the War, 1941* (New Haven, Conn.: Yale University Press, 1948).

in translating the intercepted dispatches by a comparison of an English translation of an original document in his possession with the translation provided by the American Intelligence Service. It would be interesting to compare the most important documents intercepted by the American Intelligence Service, often accepted as proof during the inquiry on Pearl Harbor and in the Tokyo trials, as well as those intercepted Japanese documents missing in the Tokyo archives due to war action, with the copies of the originals still preserved in the personal files of the various Japanese statesmen.

Togo also defends himself against the accusation of not having delivered a formal declaration of war to the United States before the attack on the American fleet at Pearl Harbor on December 7, 1941, at 1:25 P.M. (Washington time). In effect, the Japanese army and navy high commands were unwilling to communicate to the government the exact moment at which the attack would begin in order to take maximum advantage of the element of surprise. On the other hand, the Emperor had expressly requested that the attack not take place until the United States had been presented with a formal declaration of war. However, Togo was finally able to learn that it would be possible to inform Washington of the Japanese decision at 1:00 P.M. on December 7, and it is confirmed that the Japanese Foreign Ministry sent instructions to this effect to the Japanese ambassadors in Washington. The telegrams arrived in Washington during the morning of December 7, but there was a delay in decoding and in copying the dispatches because it was Sunday and the typists were not at the Embassy and because the Embassy Counsellor decided to present a copy free of corrections. Thus the Japanese ambassadors were forced to postpone their mission to the State Department for almost an hour, arriving there only at 2:20 P.M., fifty-five minutes after the attack on Pearl Harbor had begun. As usual, these telegrams had been intercepted, and President Roosevelt saw them during the morning of December 7. Despite the fact that the telegrams simply announced that Japan was breaking off the negotiations in reply to the unacceptable American demands of November 26, it must be admitted that, on the basis of the known situation of the moment, there was little doubt as to the meaning of the Japanese note.

The second part of the Togo volume makes it possible to follow, in the usual climate of rivalry between the military and political leaders, the process by which Japan arrived at the armistice. The narrative is limited to the period of the Suzuki government, but is clearly significant.

In mid-May, 1945, the Japanese government decided to contact Moscow in order to achieve three objectives : (1) to prevent the U.S.S.R. from entering the war against Japan; (2) to induce the U.S.S.R. to adopt a favorable attitude toward Tokyo; and (3) to find a way to end the war. To attain these objectives, the Japanese government was disposed to make vast territorial concessions to the U.S.S.R. However, Ambassador Hirota, who was entrusted with the task of secretly negotiating with the Soviet Ambassador to Tokyo, Jacob Malik, was limited to discussing only the first two points during the preliminary contacts, and only on June 18, after the last military opposition was overcome, did he receive instructions to inform Malik of the Japanese intention to seek an armistice. The talks were prolonged by Malik because, at first, the Soviet government suspected that Tokyo had some hidden objective in mind. When Stalin was certain that the Japanese were intent on seeking an armistice, he decided to exploit the situation to the Soviet advantage. Meanwhile, the Japanese, realizing that the talks in Tokyo were fruitless, on July 12 requested that Prince Konoye be allowed to go to Moscow as Ambassador Plenipotentiary in the hope of bringing the negotiations to a quick and successful conclusion with the men of the Kremlin. This new request served only to strengthen the Soviet decision and received no reply. During the Potsdam Conference, which opened a few days later, Stalin limited himself to referring to Japanese intentions in generic and ambiguous terms. The failure to inform the Americans of the exact tenor of the Japanese peace proposal, along with the momentary refusal of the Japanese to accept the Potsdam Declaration as the formula for the Japanese surrender, led Washington to persist up to the last moment in its erroneous evaluation of the Japanese capacity to resist.

Unquestionably, the Japanese committed a major blunder in choosing the Soviet Union as the intermediary in the negotiations for its withdrawal from the war, and the choice undoubtedly delayed the termination of the conflict. Togo's account does not offer an adequate explanation of the motives for this choice. He limits himself to reporting the reasons advanced by the military, who believed that the Soviet Union, conscious of the fact that it would have to face the United States alone following the war, would not want to see Japan seriously weakened. This was a strange illusion and reveals how far Tokyo was from a real understanding of the game the Soviets were playing in the Far East and the strength at their disposal.

d. The Other Japanese Memoir Sources.

Even if the Japanese memoir-writing is equal in quantity to that of any other major power involved in World War II, objective difficulties limit this examination to those memoirs translated into western languages and to brief references to the others, knowledge of which is made possible through the work of the specialists in the area who have made use of the volumes in Japanese in their own excellent studies of Japanese events.[215]

Shortly after they were published in Japanese, the memoirs of the diplomat and statesman, Shigeru Yoshida,[216] were translated into English. The contribution made by the translation for the period under consideration is extremely limited because publication requirements reduced the four original volumes to one. This decision determined that the emphasis would be placed on the most important years of Yoshida's political life, those of the postwar period covering his long tenure as Prime Minister, 1946–47 and 1949–55.

Therefore, the references to his mission to London, from April, 1936–March, 1939, are limited to a few observations, while the war years are given somewhat more attention. During the war Yoshida held no public office, but he was active in political affairs, lending his support to the moderates and taking part in activities developed in these circles to bring the war to an end. However, he adds little to what was already known from the disclosures during the Tokyo trials and from other memoir sources. Nevertheless, it is interesting to observe that these activities were undertaken in collaboration with members of the government and not, as was the case in Europe, by the forces in opposition to the government in the form of a resistance movement. This explains the earlier observation concerning the attitude assumed by the Japanese ruling class toward their country's defeat and the continuity that has distinguished Japanese political life, in contrast to that of other defeated states, where the discriminations introduced by the victors were not only tolerated but accepted.

Toshikazu Kase wrote his memoirs in English for the American reading public.[217] Kase was a career diplomat who had held important posts in the Foreign Ministry during the war and accompanied Shigemitsu aboard the "Missouri" to sign the surrender terms.

The publication of this volume was greeted with considerable interest because it was the first Japanese account of the war years that was not linked to the needs of the defense at the Tokyo trials. The account

[215] See Robert Butow, *Japan's Decision To Surrender* (Stanford, Calif.: Stanford University Press, 1954); *Tojo and the Coming of the War* (Princeton, N.J.: Princeton University Press, 1961); and, with Yale Candee Maxon, *Control of Japanese Foreign Policy. A Study of Civil-Military Rivalry, 1930–1945* (Berkeley and Los Angeles: University of California Press, 1957).

[216] *Kaiso Junen* [Memoirs] (4 vols.; Tokyo: Shinchosha, 1957–58). English translation: *The Yoshida Memoirs, The Story of Japan in Crisis* (Boston: Houghton Mifflin, 1962).

[217] *Journey to the "Missouri"* (New Haven, Conn.: Yale University Press, 1950).

concentrates on the years 1942–45, particularly on the projects planned or considered by the Japanese to end the war in the Pacific and on the question of Japan's surrender, but the author also mentions what he knew of the negotiations in Washington in 1941, thereby offering a complete picture of the two major problems of historical interest on the question of Japanese participation in World War II.

Kase has little of importance to add regarding the Washington talks to what is already known from the Tokyo tirals and from the Pearl Harbor inquiry. It is worth noting, however, that the author, despite a sober presentation which is completely free of polemics, does not deviate from the views stated by the accused during the trials, which hold Roosevelt co-responsible for the failure of the negotiations and, therefore, for the war. This position, as has been noted, was also sustained by the other Japanese memorialists, and it also seems to find support in the Japanese documentary sources, while, on the American side, the gap that exists in the material available regarding the communications exchanged between Roosevelt and Churchill during the second half of 1941 is singularly perplexing.

Concerning the question of Japanese attempts to abandon the conflict, Kase, without seeking to draw an explicit correlation, emphasizes the gravity of the Cairo Declaration that spelled out the territorial losses Japan was to suffer after the defeat.

However, the most interesting part of these memoirs concerns the Japanese attempts to conclude an armistice before the dropping of the atomic bomb forced the acceptance of unconditional surrender, attempts that have already been mentioned in the references to the memoirs of Shigemitsu and Togo. On this problem, too, a definitive answer to the ponderous question of whether there was a real need to drop the bomb in order to bring about Japan's surrender has not yet been provided. It has long since been recognized that in the summer of 1945 the Anglo-Americans committed a mathematical error in arriving at an evaluation of the Japanese capacity to resist. Yet perhaps it is not unreasonable to exercise more caution in justifying that decision on the basis of the military experts' mistake. The documents regarding the Potsdam Conference have officially confirmed what was already known; that is, that if it was true that the Soviets did not inform the Anglo-Americans immediately, and with proper emphasis, of the formal surrender offer of the Japanese on the eve of the conference, the American Intelligence Service on its own had intercepted the telegrams between the Japanese Minister of Foreign Affairs, Togo, and the Japanese Ambassador to Moscow, Sato, containing the offer to surrender. Therefore, Washington should have been fully apprised of the situation. These facts, now indisputable, deserve to be carefully considered before an attempt is made to render an objective judgment on the decision. At the same time, however, there are circumstances that should not be forgotten. (1) The importance ascribed to information gathered by intelligence services can never be certain because the possibility always exists that, despite the fact that the deciphered documents are authentic, they were prepared expressly to deceive the adversary. It is common practice to send messages with the knowledge that they will be intercepted by enemy services, and, therefore, the content is designed to mask the real intent of the government sending the message. A coded portion of the communication, either at the beginning or the end of the message or sent separately, destroys the value of the instructions it contains. (2) It was also clear that, while there was no doubt in the minds of those who worked on the construction of the first atomic bomb of their opportunity to press forward in order to achieve a break-through and thus anticipate German efforts in the same field,[218] at the same time there was no real concept of the effects of radiation, since all attention was focused on the explosive potential of the bomb. (3) Washington at the time gave serious consideration to the intimidatory effect that the explosion would have on the men of the Kremlin. For those who were standing in Red Square in Moscow watching a military parade on the day that news arrived of the dropping of the bomb, the psychological effect must have been appalling. But there were to be no precise indications of this awareness in either the United States or the Soviet Union.

Turning to the memoirs that, to date, have not been translated into western languages, reference should be made to the wartime recollections of Naotake Sato,[219] who, after having been Minister of Foreign Affairs in the Hayashi Cabinet from March to June, 1937, and diplomatic adviser to Prime Minister Konoye, became Japan's envoy to Moscow from February, 1942, to the Soviet declaration of war against Japan on August 8, 1945. His volume concerns this last mission and is rich in interesting details. The fact that he had been a young legation secretary in St. Petersburg from 1906 to 1914 offered the author the opportunity to compare Czarist and Soviet Russia.

The memoirs of the prince of the Japanese royal family, Naruhiko Higashikuni,[220] are greater in detail, if not in usefulness. Higashikuni was a

[218] See especially Ronald W. Clark, *The Birth of the Bomb* (London: Phoenix House, 1961).

[219] *Futatsu no Roshia* [The Two Russias] (Tokyo: Sekai no Nihonsha, 1948).

[220] *Watakushi no Kiroku* [My Report] (Tokyo: Toho Shobo, 1947); *Ichi Kozoku no Senso Nikki* [The War Diary of a Member of the Imperial Family] (Tokyo: Nihon Shuhosha, 1957).

career army officer who, after having been Commandant of General Headquarters for Territorial Defense and military adviser to the Emperor from December, 1941, to July, 1944, was appointed Prime Minister on August 15, 1945, to give the government the authority and prestige necessary to promote acceptance by the armed forces and by the people of the Emperor's decision, made the same day, to bow to the unconditional surrender terms.

The only notes existing of this Imperial Cabinet meeting and of the others held during the Suzuki ministry were kept by Minister Hiroshi Shimomura, who assembled them in a volume[221] that also contains depositions obtained from the other participants present concerning these meetings. Shimomura's summaries were examined by Premier Suzuki, who found them to be accurate reports of the discussions that took place.

The articles by Kichisaburo Nomura[222] are, in effect, his memoirs of the Washington negotiations of 1941, as is the work of Saburo Kurusu,[223] who joined Nomura in Washington to aid him in the talks. Their writings add to an understanding of Tokyo's position, where the decision to resort to war was preceded by a period of uncertainty and of hope that a peaceful compromise might be reached. However, today it seems clear that sending Kurusu to the United States was in fact an expression of the desire to strengthen Nomura's diplomatic position and was not designed as a maneuver to gain time better to prepare the surprise attack on Pearl Harbor.

For the period between the two world wars there is no lack of important books by Japanese statesmen and diplomats. Mention should be made of the memoirs of Baron Kijuro Shidehara,[224] Ambassador to Washington from 1921 to 1922 and to Moscow from 1927 to 1929 and Minister of Foreign Affairs in the years 1924–27 and 1929–31. He retired to private life after the Manchurian incident and returned to the political scene in October, 1945, succeeding Higashikuni as Prime Minister. His memoirs cover his entire political career. Somewhat more limited but no less important are the memoirs of Baron Reijiro Wakatsuki,[225] Prime Minister

[221] *Shusen Hishi* [Secret History of the End of the War] (Tokyo: Kodansha, 1950).

[222] *Beikoku ni Shishite* [My Mission to America] (Tokyo: Iwanami Shoten, 1951); "Stepping Stones to War," in *United States Naval Institute Proceedings*, LXXVII, No. 9 (September, 1951), 927–31.

[223] *Nichi-Bei Gaiko Hiwa: Waga Gaiko-shi* [Secret History of Japanese-American Relations: A History of Our Diplomacy] (Tokyo: Sogensha, 1952).

[224] *Gaiko Gojunen* [Fifty Years of Diplomacy] (Tokyo: Yomiuri Shinbunsha, 1951).

[225] *Kofuan Kaiko-roku* [Memoirs] (Tokyo: Mainichi Shinbunsha, 1950).

from 1926 to 1927 and from April to December, 1931, during the period of the Manchurian incident and the subsequent crisis. He continued to play a role in Japanese politics as an elder statesman, that is, as an Imperial adviser in accordance with the provisions of the Japanese Constitution.

Admiral Keisuke Okada, Navy Minister from 1927 to 1929 and Prime Minister from July, 1934, to March, 1936, has written a very useful volume of memoirs,[226] and in 1954 the diary of General Kazushige Ugaki was published.[227] Ugaki had been Minister of War on various occasions and Foreign Minister in the first Konoye Cabinet from May to October, 1938.

Mention should be made, solely for the purpose of reference, to the principal Japanese memoirs, such as the diary of the Marquess Koichi Kido, covering the period 1930–45, during which he was secretary to the Keeper of the Emperor's Privy Seal, Minister in the Konoye and Hiranuma cabinets, and, from 1940 to 1945, Keeper of the Privy Seal, a post that in practice made him the Emperor's top adviser. Despite the fact that only a part of the diary was published,[228] it may be consulted in its entirety because it was microfilmed by the American occupation authorities and extensive excerpts were translated into English and incorporated in the proceedings of the Tokyo trials. In effect, it is one of the most important sources available for an objective reconstruction of the behind-the-scenes activities leading to the most significant Japanese political decisions of the entire war crisis.

7. THE CHINESE MEMORIALISTS.

A study of the Chinese memoir sources for the period from the fall of the Empire in 1911 to the end of World War II reveals numerous gaps created by the scarcity of publications by the Chinese diplomats. These lacunae are perhaps explained by the scrupulous observation of professional rules of secrecy; perhaps by the fact that memoir-writing requires a literary capacity that, at a time when the written language was undergoing major transformation and reforms, was not readily found among individuals who were selected for missions more on the basis of their knowledge of western languages and culture than on a knowledge of their own country (a conflict between culture and career did not exist under the Empire); or perhaps because diplomatic memoirs had no precedent in Chinese literary tradi-

---

[226] *Okada Keisuke Kaiko-roku* [Memoirs] (Tokyo: Mainichi Shinbunsha, 1950).
[227] *Ugaki Nikki* [Diary] (Tokyo: Asahi Shinbunsha, 1954).
[228] *Kido Nikki* [Diary] (Tokyo: Heiwa Shobo, 1947).

tion.[229] In any event, the major exponents of Chinese diplomacy have left precious few memoirs or diaries. This characteristic is not restricted to career diplomats such as Ku Wei-chün (Wellington Koo), dean of the Chinese diplomatic corps, who had been a very young minister to Washington in 1919 and to London in 1920; Prime Minister and Minister of Foreign Affairs in 1927, Ambassador to the United States from 1946 to 1956, a crucial period in Chinese-American relations, and, beginning in 1957, a judge on the International Court of Justice.[230] It also applies to noncareer personnel, such as the brilliant philosopher-writer Hu Shih (1891–1962), who represented his country in Washington from 1938 to 1942 during an important period of the war against Japan, and who left no personal record of his mission.[231]

Consequently, among the very few memoirs pertinent to our subject it is possible to cite those of Lu Chen-hsiang (Lou Tseng-tsiang) (1871–1949),[232] who represented his country in the Netherlands from 1905 to 1911, was Minister of Foreign Affairs in 1912 and 1915, and head of the Chinese delegation to the peace conference in 1919. He was a symbol of a former era, indecisive by nature, and was forced to make grave decisions at a time when Japan, with her Twenty-One Demands, was attempting to transform China into a quasi-colony of the Japanese and later, at Paris, was seeking to appropriate the province of Shantung. Because he did not display sufficient energy to resist the pressures on China, Lu was demoted and transferred to Bern, where he remained from 1922 to 1927. Tired and disillusioned, he resigned his post and took religious vows in an order of Belgian monks. Only one volume of speeches comprise the written record left by Shih Chao-chi (Alfred Sze Sao K'e) (1877–1958),[233] head of the Chinese mission to London from 1914 to 1920 and from 1929 to 1932 and

[229] The writings of the major figures on the Chinese political scene before the fall of the Empire such as Li Hung-chang, Chang Chih-tung, Yüan Shih-k'ai, and, of lesser importance, those of Liu K'un-i, referred to in Chapter V, are essentially documentary sources. In general, they are the posthumous collections of official documents edited by the authors during their tenures in specific posts.

[230] The memoranda presented to the League of Nations by the Chinese delegation led by Wellington Koo at the time of the Japanese aggression appear in *Memoranda Presented to the Lytton Commission* (2 vols.; New York: The Chinese Cultural Society, 1932). A Chinese edition (reprint) has also been published: *Memoranda Submitted by the Chinese Assessor to the Commission of Inquiry of the League of Nations, April–August, 1932* (Taipeh: Wen-hsin, 1962).

[231] It should be noted that one of the few articles on diplomatic history written by Hu Shih, "China in Stalin's Strategy" (*Foreign Affairs*, XXIX [1950–51], 11–40), in which the author presents a highly subjective account of the history of Sino-Soviet relations from 1924 to 1949, is not included in the *Collected Works of Hu Shih* (in Chinese) (4 vols.; Taipeh, 1954).

[232] Lou Tseng-tsiang, *Souvenirs et pensées* (Paris: Editions du Cerf, 1948).

[233] Alfred Sze Sao K'e, *Addresses* (Baltimore: The Johns Hopkins Press, 1926).

Minister to Washington from 1921 to 1928 and 1933 to 1938. From 1952 until his death he was Vice-Minister of Foreign Affairs in the Nationalist Chinese government.

Much more interesting are the memoirs of a minor diplomat, Ch'en Lu (1876–1939), who was Minister to France from 1920 to 1927 and who was executed in Shanghai as a collaborationist by Nationalist agents. He had been the principal Chinese negotiator at the Kiakhta Conference of 1915 and was appointed as Resident in Urga from 1915 to 1917. Ch'en left two diaries[234] recording his experiences at that post, and they are an important source for the history of Chinese-Russian relations and for the events leading to the creation of the People's Republic of Mongolia. During the negotiations culminating in the Treaty of Kiakhta of June 7, 1915, between Russia, China, and Mongolia, he sought to protect Chinese claims to the region but was forced to recognize its autonomy, the preliminary step toward conceding Mongolian independence.

The wives of two brilliant diplomats, the above-mentioned Wellington Koo and the present Nationalist Chinese Ambassador to Japan, Wei Tao-ming, have written two volumes of memoirs, designed, however, for western readers. Huang Hui-lan, wife of Ambassador Koo, wrote her autobiography in English,[235] while Cheng Yü-hsiu, wife of Wei Tao-ming, wrote hers first in French and it was later translated and published in English.[236] She had been a member of the Chinese delegation to the Paris conference in 1919, and in her memoirs she recalls the efforts she, along with Wellington Koo and Wang Shih-chieh, later to become Chinese Minister of Foreign Affairs, made to convince the timid Lu Cheng-hsiang not to sign the peace treaty, which virtually assured continued Japanese occupation of Shantung province. The orders from the Peking government, controlled by the Japanese, were to sign, but these young secretaries laid siege to the head of their delegation and prevented his active participation in the signing ceremony. The result was that Japan continued to occupy Shantung province but without Chinese approval, and in 1922, at the Washington Conference, Japan agreed to evacuate the province.

If the Chinese diplomats were miserly in leaving their memoirs, the same cannot be said for the Chinese political leaders. Sun Yat-sen left a little book which should be cited among the Chinese memoir sources for the

[234] Published under the title *Chih-shih pi-chi* (Shanghai: Commercial Press, 1917).
[235] Hui-lan Koo (Madame W. Koo), *An Autobiography as Told to Mary Van Rensselear Thayer* (New York: Dial Press, 1943).
[236] Tcheng Soumay, *Souvenirs d'enfance et de revolution*, trans. B. Van Vorst (Paris: Payot, 1921); *My Revolutionary Years—The Autobiography of Madame Wei Tao-ming* (New York: Scribner, 1943).

period prior to 1911, but, given the influence of Sun on the Republic, it also deserves mention here. On October 11, 1896, shortly after his arrival in London, already under suspicion of revolutionary activities, Sun was brought to the residence of the Chinese legation under a plausible pretext. There he was kept prisoner while Embassy officials waited for the opportune moment to ship him back to China in a trunk. Fortunately, he was liberated by some English friends, with whom he had succeeded in communicating under the most bizarre circumstances, and Sun published an amusing account of these experiences in English.[237]

If Sun Yat-sen's capture in London threatened the Chinese revolutionary movement with the loss of its leader, a similar situation served to precipitate the events that led to the outbreak of hostilities between China and Japan. Toward the end of 1936, menaced by the threat of Japanese aggression, China was torn by civil war between the Nationalist government, which controlled nearly all of China from Nanking, and the Communists operating from bases in far-off Shensi, where the "long march" had terminated in 1934.

The military superiority of the Nationalists was overwhelming, and their Generalissimo, Chiang Kai-shek, planned to destroy the Communists even at the cost of temporizing in the face of the Japanese threat. This policy did not take into account the growing anti-Japanese feeling of the Chinese masses, a feeling that was ably intensified by the Communist propaganda appeal for a united front against the foreigner. The Communist accusations against the government of weakness and submissiveness toward the enemy brought excellent results. This thesis convinced the "Young Marshal," Chang Hsüeh-liang, son of the old warlord in north China Chang Tso-lin, and after his father's death in 1928 he joined the Nationalist government, retaining for himself the command of all the troops arrayed against the Communist forces in northern China. On December 12, 1936, Chiang-Kai-shek visited the headquarters of the Young Marshal at Hsi-an and was taken prisoner by Chang Hsüeh-liang. On the same day Chang and the other leaders of the revolt publicly proclaimed their eight-point program, which included a reorganization of the government, the creation of a "national front" comprising all parties, an end to the civil war, the liberation of political prisoners, etc. A number of the rebels, including Chang Hsüeh-liang, still considered Chiang Kai-shek to be their leader,

[237] *Kidnapped in London, Being the Story of My Capture by, Detention at, and Release from the Chinese Legation, London* (Bristol: J. W. Arrowsmith, 1897). For a detailed account of Sun's revolutionary activity, see Sun Yat-sen, *Memoirs of a Chinese Revolutionary* (London: Hutchinson, 1927). These memoirs were reprinted by the China Cultural Service, Taipeh, 1953.

and they sought only to convince him of the justice of their cause. Others, instead, would have preferred executing him, and, for a time, the rumor was spread that they had already done so. The order was given by Nanking to all of the troops and air force that had remained loyal to attack the rebels. Apparently, this chaotic situation, which threatened to extend the civil war, was resolved by the Communists, who for some time had been seeking to effect an agreement with Nanking and who had no interest in extending the internecine strife. A Communist delegation led by Chou En-lai arrived in Hsi-an on invitation of the Young Marshal, and in the negotiations that followed it was decided to free Chiang Kai-shek. Meanwhile, in a gesture laden with romantic overtones, Soong Mei-ling, Chiang's wife, arrived in Hsi-an by plane accompanied by her brother. On December 26 Chiang Kai-shek returned to Nanking, accompanied by his wife, his brother-in-law, and by the man who had imprisoned him, Chang Hsüeh-liang. A few months later an accord between the Nationalists and the Communists was reached. A united China was now ready to resist Japanese threats, and the Japanese attack of July 7, 1937, gave cohesion to the policy of reconciliation.

On the Hsi-an episode, which proved to be a decisive event in the history of modern China, Chiang Kai-shek and his wife have written two accounts that are wise and enlightening on the subject of conjugal bliss but add little historical information.[238] According to his diary, Chiang refused to negotiate with the Young Marshal and invited him to shoot him or to set him free. Moreover, he refused to assume any obligation on the matter of the eight-point program; he had no meeting with the Communist delegates, to whom he never refers. Thus, according to this version of the episode, it appears that Chang Hsüeh-liang, frightened by the thought of the trouble he had created for himself, overwhelmed by the superior personality of his Generalissimo, worried by the attacks launched by the government troops, and realizing his mistake, not only decided to free the Generalissimo but also insisted on accompanying him back to Nanking in order to win the General's complete pardon for his actions.[239]

Hollington K. Tong, Vice-Minister of Information during the Sino-Japanese War and later Ambassador to Tokyo, in an official biography of

[238] Chiang Kai-shek, *Hsi-an pan yüeh chi* [Diary of a Fortnight in Hsi-an] (Nanking: Cheng-chung, 1937); and with Soong May-ling, *Hsi-an shih-pien hui-i-lu* [Recollections of the Hsi-an Coup *d'État*] (Nanking: Cheng-chung, 1937). An English edition was published almost simultaneously in which Soong May-ling appears as the only author: *Sian: A Coup d'État* (*A Fortnight in Sian, Extracts from a Diary by Chiang Kai-shek*) (Shanghai: China Publishing Company, 1937). The German, French, and other versions were based on this English edition.

[239] Chang Hsüeh-liang did not write his version of the episode. He was condemned to ten years in prison and to a loss of his civil rights for five years, but he never completely regained his freedom.

Chiang Kai-shek refers in passing to the role of the Communists at the Hsi-an meeting in these words:

> During the Generalissimo's detention in Sian, the Northwest Communists had shrewdly refrained from exploiting the situation to their advantage. Having laid the foundation for the coup by their propaganda among the Shensi troops, they stood aside and permitted Chang and Yang[240] to be the scapegoats when the plot collapsed. By these tactics, they won considerable good will for themselves among government supporters. . . . Chiang's attitude toward the Communists had not altered, after his experience in Sian. However, in the uncertainty of the Northwest situation, he saw little gain to the Government in exhausting its resources in further military action against them. With his usual resilience, he began to explore in his mind the advantage of reaching an agreement with Mao Tse-tung's forces, and assuring their cooperation in the inevitable showdown with Japan.[241]

This view reappears in a more recent work by Chiang Kai-shek,[242] which is of interest to the historian only because it is a highly personal assessment of modern Chinese history by one of its principal figures. However, an objective account of the episode still remains to be written.[243]

Hollington K. Tong has also written a volume of memoirs[244] of his activities as Vice-Minister of Information for Nationalist China from 1937 to 1945. As Chiang Kai-shek's former teacher, in 1907, he enjoyed the Generalissimo's confidence. Thus, his memoirs, while tending to be apologetic, are a useful source of information on Nationalist Chinese policy during the war. Of interest, too, is his reference to the attempt made in 1937 by Wang Chin-wei to induce Mussolini to mediate the Sino-Japanese conflict:

> During the autumn . . . Chen Kung-po,[245] Minister of the Fifth Board and Wang Ching-wei's right hand . . . secured authorization to visit

[240] General Yang Hu-cheng, another commander of the Nationalist forces in North China.

[241] *Chiang Kai-shek, Soldier and Statesman* (Shanghai, 1937). Reprinted by the China Publishing Company, Taipeh, 1953, p. 233.

[242] *Su-ou tsai Chung-kuo* [Soviet Russia in China] (Taipeh: Chung-yang, 1956). The English translation appeared under the title, *Soviet Russia in China: A Summing-up at Seventy* (New York: Farrar, Straus, 1957), pp. 74–82.

[243] See also Liu Pao-ch'uan, *Chiang wei-yüan-chang Hsi-an meng-nan chi* [Chronicle of President Chiang's Narrow Escape at Hsi-an] (Shanghai: Han-hsueh, 1937); J. Bertram, *First Act in China* (New York: Viking Press, 1938); and Edgar Snow, *Red Star over China* (London: Gollancz, 1937), pp. 397–437.

[244] *Dateline: China* (New York: Rockport Press, 1950).

[245] Ch'en Kung-po (1890–1946) joined the Nanking puppet government under Wang Ching-wei and became its Minister of Propaganda.

Italy to try to win sympathy and support for China from Mussolini's government. Chen was a friend of Count and Countess Ciano, and Wang Ching-wei believed that Chen might have some influence in Italy. Wang's motive was to strengthen his own position by getting Chen to bring about peace in the Far East through intervention by Mussolini. Wang hoped that such a coup might give him the desired opening to replace the Generalissimo as leader of China. This flirtation with a Fascist country was a forehint of the role Wang and Chen were to play later as arch-traitors. Just before his departure for Italy, Chen asked me to remit a large sum of money to Shanghai which would enable him to take with him a woman who was a friend of Count Ciano, and who might be able to influence Ciano. I told Chen that China, though hard pressed, would not stoop to what the Chinese called "the intrigue with women." I considered it base and unworthy of China. He was offended, and became ever more embittered in his attitude toward me. Shortly before Chen left for Italy I took over his work, by order of the Generalissimo, and served as acting Minister of the Fifth Board. . . . Chen returned to China unsuccessful in his efforts to bring about a Fascist-manipulated peace in the Far East, only to find his post as Minister of the Fifth Board abolished.

No memoirs of the members of the collaborationist government of Nanking are available for the simple reason that they all died violent deaths; some were assassinated and some were tried and executed at the end of the war.[246] Ch'en Kung-po has left his recollections of four years of service in the Generalissimo's government,[247] and a collection of his speeches[248] was published after his official visit to Japan in May, 1940. A collection of the speeches and statements of the Minister of Foreign Affairs of the collaborationist government of Nanking, Ch'u Min-i, has also been published.[249]

Among the various war lords sharing power in China before 1927, Feng Yü-hsiang, referred to as the "Christian General," wrote several volumes of memoirs: an autobiography covering the period to 1928;[250] a diary of the

[246] For the literature on this period, see F. W. Mote, *Japanese Sponsored Government in China, 1937–1945: An Annotated Bibliography* (Stanford, Calif.: Stanford University Press, 1954).

[247] *Ssu-nien ts'ung cheng lü* [Notes of Four Years in Government Service] (Shanghai: Commercial Press, 1937).

[248] *Ch'en Kung-po hsien-sheng yen-lun chi* [Collection of the Speeches of Mr. Ch'en Kung-po] (Nanking: Ministry of Propaganda, 1940).

[249] *Ch'u Min-i hsien-sheng tsui-chin yen-lun-chi* [Collection of the Most Recent Speeches of Mr. Ch'u Min-i] (Shanghai: Chien-she, 1939). The comments on this work and the one immediately preceding it are based on the references in Mote, *Japanese Sponsored Government in China*, because this writer was unable to see the actual volumes.

[250] *Wo-ti sheng-huo* [My Life] (4 vols.; Chungking: San-hu, 1944).

period 1920–1927,[251] and an account of the life of Chiang Kai-shek,[252] whom he knew intimately and of whom he was an unsparing critic. The seventy-seven chapters of the work cover the period 1927–47, the year in which Feng Yü-hsiang left China for a tour of inspection of the United States that was to end tragically with his death aboard a ship in a Black Sea port in 1948, during the leg of his return journey that, strangely enough, was to take him back to China via the Soviet Union. A Chinese political leader who was not a member of either of the two major political parties, Chang Chün-mai (Carsun Chang), head of the Social Democratic party, has written a history of China from 1911 to the Communist takeover,[253] in which he is extremely critical of the Nationalists, the Communists, and the Americans, who, for a time, had placed great faith in Chang's "third force" as a means to resolve the Chinese civil war. Journalists and political figures of minor importance have contributed memoirs of some interest, but these, in general, deal with Chinese internal policies and problems rather than with foreign affairs. By way of illustration, there is the volume by T'ao Chü-yin,[254] describing his journalistic experiences in Shanghai during the Japanese occupation of 1937–45, the puppet rule by Wang Ching-wei, the liberation of the city, and the trials of the principal collaborationists; the autobiography of Chiang Meng-lin, Minister of Education, written in English,[255] summarizing the history of the Kuomintang from the revolution to World War II from a pro-Nationalist point of view; the volume by T'ang Liang-li,[256] a "secret" history of the Chinese revolution, etc. These works are cited for their essential importance to an understanding of the period 1911–45,[257] even though they were written by individuals who played little or no part in the events or who reported on the roles of the "great" through their intimate association with them. This is also true for the major Communist

[251] *Feng Yü-hsiang jih-chi* [The Diary of Feng Yü-hsiang] (2 vols.; Peking, 1930).

[252] *Wo so jen-shih ti Chiang Chieh-shih* [Chiang Kai-shek as I Knew Him] (Shanghai: Wen-hua, 1949).

[253] Carsun Chang, *The Third Force in China* (New York: Bookman Associates, 1952).

[254] *T'ien-liang ch'ien ti ku-tao* [Shanghai before the Dawn] (Shanghai: Chung-hua, 1947); *Tsui-hou i nien* [The Last Year] (Shanghai: Chung-hua, 1947).

[255] Chiang Meng-lin, *Tides from the West* (New Haven, Conn.: Yale University Press, 1947). Reprinted in Taipeh, 1957.

[256] *The Inner History of the Chinese Revolution* (New York: Dutton, 1930).

[257] For detailed bibliographies, see E. Wu, *Leaders of Twentieth-Century China* (Stanford, Calif.: Stanford University Press, 1956); C. O. Hucker, *China, A Critical Bibliography* (Tucson: University of Arizona Press, 1962); J. F. Fairbank and K. C. Liu, *Modern China: A Bibliographical Guide to Chinese Works, 1898–1937* (Cambridge, Mass.: Harvard University Press, 1961); and the two bibliographies, *China in Western Literature* and *Index Sinicus*, by T. L. Yuan and J. Lust, respectively.

figures, who have been extremely careful not to reveal to the outside world episodes of their political lives which might conflict with the party lines. The Communist ruling elite has maintained its monolithic unity, and the few purges or cases of leaders falling into disgrace (Li Li-san, Kao Kang, Peng Teh-huai) have not been followed by "flights" abroad and the subsequent publication of sensational revelations regarding the foreign policy of the Chinese Soviet Republic, which was founded on November 7, 1931, at Juichin in Kiangsi province and whose capital was later transferred to Yenan.

The student of contemporary Chinese history can find useful information on the life and personality of Mao Tse-tung in the confidences he shared with the American journalist Edgar Snow, who included them in his report published under the title, *Red Star over China*.[258] In this volume, Snow provides a biographical sketch of Mao which may be considered autobiographical, since Snow quotes what Mao told him word for word. The work does not contain anything of great value on the foreign policy of the Chinese Communist movement prior to 1937, but the book had a significant impact abroad in that it created the image of a Chinese Communist movement with liberal tendencies, inspired only by the principles of sound agrarian reform and anxious to collaborate with the other nationalist forces in resisting the foreigner. This was exactly what the Communist leaders sought to accomplish when they invited the American reporter to Yenan. Other personal data on the Communist leaders, useful only for a reconstruction of their little-known biographies, are to be found in the work by Nym Wales.[259] Among the works written by personalities of the Peking government, reference may be made to those of Soong Ching Ling[260] and Chen Po-ta,[261] which, however, are of little importance to foreign policy.

8. THE POLISH MEMORIALISTS.

a. Beck.

Colonel Beck, Minister of Foreign Affairs of the Polish Republic from November, 1932, to September, 1939, wrote three separate studies during

---

[258] *Red Star over China* (London: Gollancz, 1937).
[259] *Red Dust, Autobiography of Chinese Communists* (Stanford, Calif.: Stanford University Press, 1952).
[260] *The Struggle for New China* (Peking: Foreign Language Press, 1953).
[261] *Notes on Ten Years of Civil War, 1927–1936* (Peking: Foreign Languages Press, 1954).

his internment in Rumania, and these were published in a single volume in 1951.[262] Beck wrote under particularly difficult conditions and without the opportunity of referring to the necessary documents. The resulting work suffers from inaccuracies and serious gaps, to such an extent that the reader is led to suspect that these were planned by the author in order to lend greater support to his defense.

The principal value of these memoirs does not lie in the revelations they contain, but rather in what they reveal concerning the psychology of Beck and the Polish ruling group in the period between the two world wars. This is a highly significant factor because, at a certain moment, Poland became the key to the destiny of Europe, and it was precisely because of the attitude of the Warsaw government that a number of initiatives failed that might have decisively changed the course of events.

It should be recalled that, in the winter of 1938–39, the European situation was still rather fluid. Specifically, the Munich Pact had given Germany the opportunity to expand in either of two directions: toward the west, which would have brought it into direct conflict with France and Great Britain, or toward the east, where the Ukraine was a rich prize for the German government but one which would mean war with the Soviet Union.

For a time at least, the second alternative appeared to have been adopted by Von Ribbentrop, especially because certain attitudes in Paris and London could be interpreted as encouraging this policy. Moreover, the exclusion of the Soviet Union from the Munich Conference, the declaration of September 30 signed by Hitler and Chamberlain, the Franco-German Accord of December 6 (which also contained the renunciation of German claims to Alsace-Lorraine), and the rather singular questions posed by Chamberlain to Mussolini during the British Prime Minister's visit to Rome in January, 1939, could be explained as indirect support of the anti-Soviet flavor that Von Ribbentrop seemed disposed to give to German foreign policy.

However, such a plan presupposed an understanding with Poland, without which German expansion toward the Ukraine could hardly be discussed. It was precisely for the purpose of establishing the basis for a German-Polish anti-Soviet policy that Von Ribbentrop advanced a relatively moderate plan for solving the Danzig and Polish Corridor problems. But this proposal was categorically rejected by the Polish government on the grounds that the territorial clauses were unacceptable and because

[262] Joseph Beck, *Dernier rapport. La politique polonaise 1926–1939* (Neuchâtel: La Baconnière, 1951).

Warsaw insisted on maintaining a position equidistant between the two great powers on her borders.

The German offers were repeated at Berchtesgaden during the Hitler-Beck talks of January 5, 1939, and in Warsaw during Von Ribbentrop's visit to the Polish capital at the end of January, but in both instances the Polish government refused to consider them and, by its attitude, was responsible for the failure of the entire project.

It should be noted that the German demands for Polish territory and the negotiations stemming from these demands were kept secret from Paris and London, leading the British and the French to draw a wrong conclusion, i.e., that Germany's next objective was Rumania. Thus, the British government guaranteed the independence and territorial integrity of Poland without being aware of these negotiations and, in so doing, irreparably compromised the success of the British negotiations with the Soviet Union, which was being given, indirectly and without conceding anything in return, a guarantee against a German attack through Polish territory.

The responsibility of the Polish government on this point is significant. It becomes even more important when Poland's attitude is examined in relation to the Anglo-French-Soviet negotiations to establish a united front against further German aggression. It should be kept in mind that these negotiations produced positive results so far as the political aspects of the question were concerned, but the political accords were not to become effective until the accompanying military convention was ratified.

From the start of the military conversations, the Soviets requested a clear statement of the Polish attitude and stated that they were ready to come to Poland's aid but that it was imperative to know whether Poland was disposed to permit the Red army to enter Poland in the event that this became necessary. Once again the decisive reply had to come from Warsaw. And once again the reply was negative. The Polish government made it clear that it did not intend to allow Soviet troops to enter Polish territory and, moreover, that it had no desire to assume a position that obviously favored one of its strong neighbors over the other.

The Polish refusal led the negotiations to a dead end, and this fact was undoubtedly to have an important effect in pointing the Soviets toward an understanding with Germany. The official Soviet view is precisely as follows: the government of Moscow had endeavored to conclude an alliance with the western powers but was unable to resolve the practical aspects of the accord because of the negative position taken by Warsaw; therefore, in this situation, the Soviets had no choice but to seek to guarantee their own security through direct negotiations with Hitler, leaving the Poles to follow their own destiny. Certainly, the Soviet thesis becomes rather provocative because the evidence indicates that their decision to conclude a nonaggression pact with Germany was made before the Polish refusal. However, the Soviet view is not illogical, and while it may not justify the accord of August 23, 1939, it tends to place it in a somewhat less unfavorable light.

In his memoirs, Beck looks upon these events from an extremely significant point of view. Beck wrote at a time when Poland had already been erased from the map of Europe, and yet his pages reveal that megalomania and that lack of sense of proportion which were so typical of Warsaw's policies and which must be considered among the principal causes of the Polish tragedy. For example, the refusal to admit Soviet troops to Polish territory in the event of war with Germany was considered by Beck to be doubly justified: first, on the formal level, because the Poles were not invited to participate in the negotiations that directly concerned Poland; and second, on the practical level, because the Poles completely distrusted the Soviet Union and, moreover, Poland sought to maintain a perfect balance in her relations with both of her more powerful neighbors.

Aside from the fact that such attempts at justification are entirely without foundation, since the Poles never asked to participate in the negotiations and never advised London and Paris to consider the Soviet Union as an enemy nation, Beck's statements show the habit, typical of Polish statesmen of that day, of constantly operating as though other countries did not exist or as though Polish forces were the strongest in Europe. In this context, it is not inopportune to recall the part played by Poland in sabotaging the Four-Power Pact, through which Rome and London were seeking to include Hitler in a new European system and to keep the Soviet Union distant from Continental affairs, nor should it be forgotten that as Europe was approaching the brink of war over a question of direct concern to Poland, the Warsaw government permitted the last months to pass without making any attempt to adjust its differences with Berlin. In spite of all of this, it must be recognized that the problems the Warsaw government was called upon to resolve were exceptionally grave, and it is always doubtful that they could have been peacefully resolved. But the course chosen by Beck does not seem to have been either the best or the most appropriate one.

b. Ciechanowski.

In March, 1941, the Polish government in exile appointed Jean Ciechanowski as its Ambassador to Washington; he was one of the ablest men they had available and had been Poland's Ambassador to the United States from 1925 to 1929. Ciechanowski remained at his Washington post until July, 1945. The mission began under auspicious circumstances, when hopes were still alive that a democratic Poland would emerge at the end of a victorious war. The mission came to a close when the United States recognized the Warsaw provisional government and Poland was absorbed into the Soviet sphere of influence.

Ciechanowski published his memoirs of this unfortunate mission,[263] and they must be regarded as one of the most important sources available for the study of the diplomatic aspects of World War II because the events to which he was witness completely superseded the Polish question to embody the more general one of the relations between the Soviet Union and the western Allies.

The volume is also a human document to which no reader can remain indifferent. The drama of the Polish exiles, of these men who, though responsible for grave errors in the past, now knew how to fight with desperate energy for their country's independence, is narrated without hate or recriminations but with a nobility of style that is moving.

As a source, Ciechanowski's volume has the value of having been written shortly after the events in question occurred, and it is based on documents and notes that enabled the author to write with precision and accuracy. His narrative contains every detail of his colloquies with Roosevelt, Cordell Hull, and Sumner Welles, and his frequent meetings with British and Soviet statesmen, while General Sikorski provided him with a summary of his conversations with Stalin and Molotov.

The contents of this volume, as has been noted, go far beyond the limits of the Polish problem. In retrospect, the Polish drama was not only lived by Poles but by all western political leaders. The entrance of the Soviet Union into the war posed the problem of preventing Stalin from negotiating a compromise peace with Hitler, that is, it presented the Allies with the alternative of sacrificing the integrity and independence of Poland—for the protection of which, at least formally, they had gone to war—or of running the risk of seeing the Soviet Union execute another about-face and effect a compromise with Hitler. The latter eventuality was not completely remote because the German government had made several offers on this subject, which perhaps did not receive a completely unfavorable reception in Moscow, where the fear of being abandoned by the western powers was strong. Thus, in addition to a political drama, it was also a psychological and human story that was unfolding in Washington and London in the face of a situation that seemed to supersede human will in order to assert

[263] *Defeat in Victory* (London: Gollancz, 1948).

itself as historical fate. Ciechanowski's account of this pageant is the most complete and vivid picture of it that has ever been produced.

The evolution of London's and Washington's attitude toward the Polish government in exile is described with remarkable clarity by Ciechanowski. The initial cordial frankness was gradually replaced by a growing reticence in dealing with the Polish government in exile, the climax of the change being the formal communication of the decisions taken as a result of the accords with the Soviets.

Obviously, the memoirs focus on the action of the Polish government in exile. On two occasions this government had the opportunity to reach agreements with the Soviet Union which, despite the fact that they presupposed a modification of Poland's eastern frontiers, were, under the circumstances, reasonably satisfactory. However, General Sikorski and his colleagues did not have the courage to make a decision that involved the loss of Polish territory. They believed that their mandate did not authorize them to do so, and in this belief they were legally correct. But, in so doing, they lost the opportunity offered by the momentary weakness of the Soviet Union in the face of the German armed threat, an opportunity that would not present itself again.

c. The Other Polish Memoir Sources.

The diary of Count Szembek,[264] Polish Undersecretary for Foreign Affairs from November, 1932, to September, 1939, presents some unique characteristics. Just as Ciano's diary had caused widespread comment in Rome, Szembek's diary has become famous among the members of the diplomatic corps accredited to Warsaw. On the other hand, Szembek made no secret of its existence. During his most important conversations, it was his practice to take notes, which he dictated to his secretary the following morning in order to have a clear record of the colloquies and to assemble the material for his memoirs. When Poland fell to the German forces Szembek was able to save his notes, but he died in 1945 before he was able to use them to write his memoirs. The diary was published some years later in its original form, a factor that tends to increase rather than reduce its importance as a source.

However, the diary is incomplete. All of those elements which, in the judgment of the publishers, were of secondary importance or of a technical nature were eliminated, while the pages for the first trimester of 1937 and for June of the same year were never located. Moreover, it can be assumed that other sections were suppressed as a matter of choice, and that the clearly polemical notes and references to living persons were eliminated.

[264] Comte Jan Szembek, *Journal 1933–1939* (Paris: Plon, 1952).

Despite these reservations, Szembek's diary remains a significant source. In fact, the label "diary" is not especially apropos in this case. It contains only indirect references to the author's daily activities and nothing in the way of comments or reflections on the diplomatic events of the period. It consists exclusively of brief summaries of Szembek's conversations with Polish and foreign statesmen and diplomats, so that, rather than a diary, it is a collection of minutes.

The volume contains no significant disclosures nor is it sufficiently complete to provide an accurate picture of certain events. Its real importance lies in its supplementary value. Among the major points of interest, mention should be made of the data provided on Franco-Polish relations. In effect, after the rise of Hitler to power in Germany, the Poles were convinced that a Nazi-Soviet understanding was impossible, a premise that would permit them greater independence of action in their relations with France, whose support appeared to have lost much of its value. This explains the negative position taken by the Poles on the question of the eastern pact of 1935, their undisguised impatience with the League of Nations, and the sympathy they showed for Italy during the Ethiopian war, symptoms of a break that was to become increasingly serious after the victory of the Popular Front in France, viewed as the *longa manus* of the Soviets. These differences became clearly evident during the Sudeten crisis. From the beginning, the Polish government manifested its desire to take advantage of the crisis to make good its claims to the Czechoslovak district of Teschen, but, as Szembek confirms in his diary, the French had been aware of Polish intentions in this matter since May, 1935, when Beck, during Laval's visit to Warsaw, made his designs on Teschen clear. It should also be noted that, toward the end of 1936, Beck considered the possibility of taking advantage of a probable Franco-Italian conflict following the Spanish Civil War in order to annex Teschen, leaving sub-Carpathian Ruthenia to the Hungarians and creating a buffer state in Slovakia, clearly a plan that anticipated the solution imposed by Hitler in March, 1939.

The other Polish memoir sources offer modest contributions and, as usual, they are limited to specific aspects of a problem. The former Ambassador to Paris, Lukasiewicz, has published a series of articles on the events of 1938 and 1939[265] which, despite the fact that they contain data worthy of consideration, leave some doubt as to their historical value.

Much more reliable are the memoirs of the former Ambassador to Berlin,

[265] Julius Lukasiewicz, "Memoirs and Reflections," twenty articles in Polish, appearing in *Dziennik Polski* of London from November 11, 1946, to April 29, 1947; "The Czechoslovak Problem in Franco-Polish Relations" (in Polish), *Sprawy Miedzynarodowe*, 1948, Nos. 2–3.

Lipski,[266] who focuses on the last phase of Polish-German relations before the war, while Ambassador Sokolnicki[267] has limited his comments to the Rhineland crisis, affirming that Beck was ready to take military measures against Germany if the signatories of the Locarno Pact had indicated their willingness to implement its terms.

Soviet-Polish relations between 1920 and 1945 have been examined by the former legal adviser of the Polish Foreign Ministry, Kulski,[268] in a historical synthesis containing valuable data, particularly for the war period, when the author was Counsellor to the Polish Embassy in London.

The book by the former Prime Minister of Poland, Mikolajczyk,[269] also treats Polish-Soviet relations, but for the more restricted period 1939–47. Its particular value lies in the author's description of the activity of the new government in Warsaw and in his report of the process by which the Communist party took over control of the government.

Recently, a further contribution to the Polish wartime story was made by Count Raczynski,[270] Ambassador to London from 1934 to 1945, who, after Zaleski's retirement in August, 1941, also served as Foreign Minister for the government in exile until July, 1943. Raczynski's testimony is almost completely limited to the war years and is based on an irregularly kept diary. For this reason, it is not possible to draw a complete picture of the activities of the Polish government in exile from this account, but the detail the author provides on certain specific points is extremely revealing, especially concerning relations with Great Britain and the controversies between the Polish leaders in exile, controversies which, on more than one occasion, affected the course of events.

While the following are not properly memoir sources as such, they contain important memoir characteristics and, therefore, may be cited as both documentary and memoir sources. The value of the Polish collection for the period September, 1941–July, 1942, is substantially increased by the addition of recently published dispatches between the Polish Ambassador to Kuibishev, Professor Kot, and the government in exile in London[271] and

[266] Joseph Lipski, "New Revelations on the Outbreak of the German-Polish Conflict in 1939" (in Polish), *Bellona*, 1950, fasc. I; "Further Revelations on the Origins of the Polish-German Non-Aggression Declaration" (in Polish), *Bellona*, 1951, fascs. I–II.

[267] The article by Michael Sokolnicki in *Wiadomosci Polskie*, 1946, No. 32.

[268] W. W. Kulski, "The lost opportunity for Russian-Polish Friendship," *Foreign Affairs*, fasc. July, 1947.

[269] Stanislaw Mikolajczyk, *The Rape of Poland* (New York: Whittlesey House, 1948).

[270] Count Edward Raczynski, *In Allied London* (London: Weidenfeld and Nicolson, 1962).

[271] Stanislaw Kot, *Listy z Rosji do Gen. Sikorskiego* [General Sikorski's Letters from Russia] (London: Jutro Polski, 1955).

the summaries of his conversations with the Kremlin leaders based on his personal notes, which have also been published.[272] His letters clarify, in a way that the documentary collection does not, the precarious bases for the Polish-Soviet Accord of July 30, 1941, not only because of the Kremlin's decision to re-draw Poland's eastern frontier, but also because of the Soviet intention to prevent the leaders of the government in exile in London from assuming control of postwar Poland. The Kremlin's aims did not elude either Kot or Sikorski—and their correspondence is significant on this point—but the best instrument with which to counter the Soviets was the Polish army, then being organized by General Anders from among Polish prisoners of war liberated by the Soviets. If, at the end of the conflict, these troops were to be found on Polish soil after having fought side by side with the Russians to liberate the country, the Polish leaders in London would have had, in this army, a powerful force with which to resume control of Poland's destiny. Instead, General Anders was obsessed with the single desire to remove his troops from the Soviet Union, where they had suffered imprisonment, privation, and humiliation even after July, 1941, in order to join them with the Anglo-American forces.

Kot exerted every conceivable pressure in an attempt to change General Anders' attitude, an attitude that was comprehensible from a psychological point of view but contrary to the wishes of the Polish government in London and to Kot's personal judgment of the situation. The controversy was finally resolved by Stalin, when he decided to remove the Polish army from the U.S.S.R. From this time on, the activity of the Polish Embassy in the Soviet Union was greatly limited by the Soviet authorities, who were already developing a new position on relations with Poland, which the incident created by the discovery of the evidence of the Katyn massacre would facilitate.

9. THE CZECHOSLOVAK MEMORIALISTS.

a. Beneš.

Twenty years after the publication of his memoirs concerning his work in creating the Czechoslovak Republic,[273] Beneš published another vol-

[272] *Rozmowy z Kremlem* [Conversations at the Kremlin] (London: Jutro Polski, 1959). Of the 274 dispatches comprising the volume of Sikorski's letters, 60 have been translated into English, along with all of the 34 minutes included in the second volume: Stanislaw Kot, *Conversations with the Kremlin and Dispatches from Russia* (London: Oxford University Press, 1963).

[273] See p. 426.

ume[274] intended as the first of a series of three summarizing his political activity as President of Czechoslovakia from December, 1935, to the end of World War II. Beneš had begun to work systematically on this project in 1945 and published the bulk of what he had written in 1947, more than a year after the national coalition government presided over by the Communist leader Gottwald had been created and the Communist penetration had made serious inroads in the country.

These memoirs were an attempt to explain to the people of Czechoslovakia those principles that had guided his policy after the Munich Agreements in order to emphasize their validity at a time when the internal situation raised grave doubts over the ability of Czechoslovak democratic freedoms to survive. The Communist *coup d'état* occurred on February 25, 1948, just a few months after Beneš had published his volume, and the following June he abandoned the presidency and retired to private life. The effects of this second major political failure hastened his death, which came in September of the same year.

The particular circumstances in which the book was written accented its defensive characteristics, which the author attempted to mask by his declarations of faith in the future and the conviction with which he supported the soundness of his political directives—a conviction that weakens only in the last chapter in the face of the distressing question mark about the country's future.

The volume opens with an account of the attempts made by Czechoslovakia in 1936–37 to block German expansion at Czechoslovakia's expense by a change in the *casus foederis* of the Little Entente (directed only against Hungary) or by renewed assurances from Paris regarding the application of the Franco-Czechoslovak mutual assistance treaty of June, 1924. Beneš reports very little regarding the attitude of the Soviet Union and the concrete measures taken to obtain the military assistance that Moscow had agreed to give in the treaty of May, 1935. To be sure, the Munich crisis was to be the subject of the second volume, but in one chapter of the first volume the author expresses the conviction that the U.S.S.R. would have fulfilled its obligations if France had done likewise. This thesis is supported by Communist historiography, but it has not yet been conclusively proved, not even by the volume of Soviet-Czechoslovak documents on Munich, already cited, which was designed for this specific purpose.

However, the motives leading Beneš to this conclusion are under-

---

[274] Edvard Beneš, *Pameti od Mnichova k nové válce a k novému vitežstvi* (Prague: Orbis, 1947); English translation, *Memoirs of Dr. Edward Beneš. From Munich to New War and New Victory* (London: Allen and Unwin, 1954).

standable. From the Czechoslovak point of view, the Soviet Union was the only friendly and allied power to emerge unblemished from the crisis beginning in September, 1938, and its obligation to come to the aid of Czechoslovakia was conditioned by French participation. Thus, in Beneš' eyes, the entire responsibility for the dismemberment of Czechoslovakia lay with Paris and London. These pages are indispensable for an understanding of the extent of Beneš' resentment and lack of faith in the western democracies induced by the conduct of these powers during the Sudeten crisis. Beneš regards the September, 1938, crisis as purely a Czechoslovak drama, outside of the European perspective and apart from the fundamental problem faced by Great Britain and France in German expansionist pressure. From the viewpoint of a Czechoslovak national, this attitude is entirely comprehensible, but from that of a statesman, it appears much less so. It indicates that Beneš did not fully understand that the appearance of Hitler's Reich had completely altered the European balance of power, recasting the little powers in the European drama from independent to supporting roles. In the twenty years during which Germany was virtually disarmed, the Czechoslovak alliance offered France the possibility of threatening her traditional enemy with war on two fronts in exchange for a similar guarantee to Prague regarding Germany and other revisionist states. Against a strong Germany, Czechoslovakia no longer offered France a guarantee commensurate with the aid that France would have to give Prague in return, and as Germany's power grew Czechoslovakia became increasingly dependent on outside support, and her ability to contribute effectively against Germany declined proportionately. Therefore, it was understandable that in this situation the western democracies would run the risk of challenging German power only when they were forced to do so to protect their own fundamental interests.

Perhaps, this is why Beneš regarded Munich not as an Anglo-French political blunder but as an open betrayal of Czechoslovakia which evoked his deep distrust of the western democracies. From that time on, the hope of winning the support of the Soviet Union, believed to be more trustworthy, conditioned Czechoslovak diplomacy. He refers to two meetings in London with the Soviet Ambassador, Maisky, on August 23 and September 19, 1939, which emerge as points of departure for Beneš' policy during the war. From the first meeting he concluded that the Soviet Union would seek to remain neutral as long as possible in the coming conflict, intervening only at the decisive moment. By so doing, the Soviets would control the peace conference. In the second meeting, he informed Maisky that one of the lessons learned from the Munich experience was that Czechoslovakia should share a frontier with the Soviet Union. He added, nevertheless, that the question of sub-Carpathian Ruthenia should be resolved between Prague and Moscow, a statement which should probably have been interpreted to mean that Czechoslovakia would not oppose an eventual Soviet annexation of this region.

The break in relations with Moscow following the latter's recognition of the Slovak state in the fall of 1939 did not discourage Beneš; after a time, he decided to establish confidential contacts with the Soviet government, and these were arranged without difficulty. Beneš affirms that, from the new information he was able to acquire through these contacts early in 1941, he became entirely convinced of the accuracy of his earlier political estimates and was certain now that the entry of the Soviet Union in the war against Germany was only a matter of time, as it proved to be.

Immediately after the German attack, the Soviets offered to reopen formal diplomatic relations with the Czechoslovak government through Beneš and to create Czechoslovak military units on Soviet soil, while at the same time they declared that they had no intention of interfering in the internal affairs of Czechoslovakia in any manner whatsoever. However, the accord signed on July 18, 1941, contained no mention of the last point. Nor does it appear to be confirmed in Beneš' emphatic statement that this accord was a mortal blow to Munich, in that the Soviet Union immediately recognized the Czechoslovak Republic in its pre-Munich form, since the Soviet Union refrained from committing itself on the problem of frontiers. Instead, the negotiations with Great Britain for an equivalent *de jure* recognition dragged on for some time, precisely because Beneš sought to link the recognition to the boundary question, a subject on which the British were not anxious to take a definite stand. Beneš attributed the failure to reach an accord with the British on this issue to the presence in the London government of several individuals held over from the Munich period.

During 1942 Beneš concluded the first phase of his program, that is, the annulment of the treaty of September 29, 1938, and its consequences. Molotov authorized him to announce publicly that the Soviet Union regarded its recognition of the Czechoslovak Republic in its pre-Munich territorial form as a "binding obligation." Several weeks later the London government also declared herself to be no longer bound by the agreements of 1938 regarding the boundaries of Czechoslovakia. De Gaulle made a similar announcement a short while later.

This phase of his program accomplished, President Beneš now sought to implement the second part, that is, the obtaining of guarantees that his country would never again be menaced by the grave problems that resulted in its dismemberment in 1938–39. Insofar as the external guarantees of

Czechoslovak liberties were concerned, he wrote, the lesson to be learned from Munich was that the U.S.S.R. could be trusted and, therefore, the Anglo-Saxon powers were not justified in their refusal to seek to compromise their differences with the Soviet Union. This, according to Beneš, was the fundamental reason for Munich. Germany was aware of this and had attacked the Soviet Union on the assumption that, at a given moment, it could conclude peace with the western powers in order to have a free hand against the U.S.S.R. A catastrophe of this magnitude had to be avoided, Beneš continues, and it could only be avoided by a firm and long-lasting agreement between the Anglo-Saxons and the Soviets. Meanwhile, he would provide the example by establishing the first keystone in this building, the conclusion of a treaty providing for mutual co-operation between Russia and Czechoslovakia and a mutual guarantee not to interfere in each other's internal affairs.

Moscow reacted favorably to the Beneš proposal. The same did not happen in London, however, where Eden, while agreeing in principle with Beneš' approach, made it known that it would be wiser to wait until the war was over and the general lines of Soviet policy became clear before signing any agreement. Beneš' reply was that he had complete faith in the word of the Soviets and that, as far as his experience was concerned, he had no reason to distrust the Kremlin.

During his stay in Moscow in December, 1943, for the signing of the Soviet-Czechoslovak treaty of co-operation, his beliefs were confirmed. The treaty, according to Beneš, provided a degree of security for Czechoslovak independence that it had never had before. Beneš has little to add concerning his conversations with Stalin and Molotov on this occasion, summarizing only the dispatches and impressions he sent to his colleagues in London. Moreover, he makes few references to his conversations with Czechoslovak Communists residing in Moscow. Nevertheless, it was on this occasion that, applying the new criteria of co-operation with the Soviets, arrangements were made for Communist participation in the government following liberation, and the major lines were agreed upon for the new social democratic organization of the state.

The Beneš memoirs terminate at this point. The material for 1944 and 1945 to the end of the war was to be included in the projected third volume. Even without this and the data on the Munich Pact, these memoirs cannot be considered incomplete, since he incorporates in this volume the crucial period of policy during his years as President. Furthermore, the last paragraphs of the volume furnish an appropriate conclusion to the work. In these, the author seeks to reply to the question that is raised in a note, that is, whether it was wise or unwise for him to have placed his faith in the Soviet Union. In spite of appearances, his reply reflects considerable doubt.

The western powers will have to prove their willingness to compromise with the Soviets, he writes; but the latter, he adds in his criticism of the other regimes, will have to demonstrate the same tolerance and comprehension. He emphasizes that the recognition of, and the total and definite respect for, the principle that every independent state has the right to choose the political system that best meets its needs are the necessary prerequisites for peaceful coexistence in the world. Otherwise, he continues, the course of events will lead to another war. The *coup d'état* in Prague in 1948 answered Beneš' question clearly and completely.

In an objective examination of the situation, it cannot be affirmed that Beneš' policy was the primary cause for the communization of Czechoslovakia. His grave error in judgment remains and should be kept in mind in order to evaluate properly his role as a statesman, beginning with his role as Masaryk's collaborator at the end of World War I and over the years immediately following. But the destiny of Czechoslovakia, like that of the rest of the eastern European states, did not depend on the decision made by the interested parties to co-operate with or to resist the Soviet Union. As noted elsewhere, it was entirely dependent on the military and political strategy determined by the Anglo-Americans during the middle and final phases of the conflict.

It should be noted, however, that Czechoslovakia was the last peaceful conquest by the Soviet Union, just as it had been Hitler's last peaceful acquisition. Both cases produced a reaction on the part of the western powers that was, perhaps, late, but decisive.

b. The Other Czechoslovak Memoir Sources.

The articles by Eduard Táborsky, Beneš' private secretary from 1938 to 1945, are very useful supplements to the latter's memoirs. In addition to keeping a diary on the events of the period, Táborsky came into possession of a number of Beneš' papers. Thus far, Táborsky has published only a part of the diary, the portion dealing with 1938 and the first half of 1939,[275] while the rest of the material has not appeared in book form, having been used as a basis for his articles[276] on fundamental aspects of Beneš' policy during World War II.

Regarding the assertion made by Beneš that the Soviet Union would

[275] Eduard Táborsky, *Pravda Zvítězila* (Prague: Práce, 1947).
[276] Eduard Táborsky, "Beneš and the Soviets," *Foreign Affairs*, January, 1949, pp. 302–14; "A Polish-Czechoslovak Confederation: A Story of the First Soviet Veto," *Journal of Central European Affairs*, January, 1950, pp. 379–95; "Beneš and Stalin—Moscow, 1943 and 1945," *Journal of Central European Affairs*, July, 1953, pp. 154–81; "The Triumph and Disaster of Eduard Beneš," *Foreign Affairs*, July, 1958, pp. 669–84.

definitely have come to the aid of Prague in September, 1938, if the French
had made this possible by fulfilling their obligations, Táborsky notes that
the President was completely aware of the fact that the communication
from Moscow to Prague of September 21, 1938, to this effect had only a
theoretical value. In fact, the Czechoslovak Ambassador to Moscow had
reported, toward the end of August, that the Soviets were convinced that
the French would not move to aid Czechoslovakia. During the Sudeten
crisis, Táborsky observes, the real difference in attitude between the Anglo-
French and the Soviets, which Beneš never forgot, was that while Daladier
and Chamberlain pressured the Czechoslovak government to accede to the
German demands, the Soviets alone made at least a gesture of good will.
However, this does not answer the question regarding the real Soviet desire
to aid Prague.

No less significant are Táborsky's comments regarding Beneš' journey to
Moscow in December, 1943. Concerning the preliminary negotiations, he
describes the energetic pressures applied to Beneš by Ambassador Bogomolov to convince him to ignore British opposition. This demonstrates that
Moscow set great store by the proposed treaty.

Táborsky then emphasizes Moscow's warm and enthusiastic reception to
Beneš, recalling that the atmosphere of friendship and cordiality created by
the Soviet leaders around the Bohemian President was an important factor
in determining the course of the conversations and in crystallizing Beneš'
great faith in the promises of his hosts.[277] This atmosphere was also
responsible, according to Táborsky, for Beneš' belief that the clauses of the
treaty simply re-emphasized the terms of the Anglo-Soviet treaty of May,
1942, a belief that was completely inaccurate. The author devotes particular
attention to the *casus foederis* as defined in the two treaties. The *casus
foederis* regarding Germany and her allies as defined in the Anglo-Soviet
treaty was strictly defensive in character, while in the Czechoslovak-Soviet
treaty the contracting parties were obliged to take common action "in the
event that one party became involved in hostilities in the postwar period"
against Germany "and against any other power siding with Germany in
such a war."[278] Therefore, the obligation was not limited to a war against
only one of her former Tripartite allies, as was established in the Anglo-

[277] In this context, Táborsky quotes the following excerpt from a letter written to
him by Beneš a few days before his death: "My greatest mistake was that, up to
the last moment, I refused to believe that Stalin had also lied to me, both in 1935
and later, and that his assurances to me and to Masaryk (jr.) were an intentional
deception."

[278] Here the author notes how closely this formula parallels that of the
Italo-German Pact of Steel, which, in effect, stated: "if one of the contracting parties
became involved in a war. . . ."

Soviet treaty, but also, for example, against France or the United States. In effect, Stalin, basing his argument on one of the clauses of this treaty, was able to justify Czechoslovakia's refusal to participate in the Marshall Plan.

Táborsky also offers useful data on another problem, that of sub-Carpathian Ruthenia. However, despite the fact that the author's material supplements Beneš' memoirs on this point, his observations are not wholly accurate. He states that Beneš' position may be summarized as follows: the President strongly desired to recover this region but he was disposed to sacrifice it if this was the price of good relations with the Soviet Union. It is true that, as Táborsky says, Stalin had confirmed Czechoslovakia's claims to the region, but it is equally true that as early as 1939, as has been noted, the Soviets were aware of Beneš' willingness to cede the area. This fact has not been properly evaluated by Táborsky. As is known, just as soon as the region was occupied by Soviet troops, the Czechoslovak government, still in London, on the basis of the general principles regarding the administration of liberated territories that had been established by the Soviet-Czechoslovak treaty of May, 1944, sent its representative to the area. When this representative arrived on the scene, he found it impossible to perform his functions because organized local groups, encouraged by the Soviet troops, proclaimed their desire to be annexed to the Soviet Union. Among the documents cited by Táborsky on the question that the Czechoslovaks sought to raise concerning Soviet practices in the region, there is one worthy of special note, that is, Zorin's reply (Zorin was an official of the Soviet Foreign Ministry at that time): "As we promised and as was established by the Soviet-Czechoslovak Treaty, we are neither authorized nor do we wish to intervene in your internal affairs. Therefore, it is difficult for us to help you resolve your problems in sub-Carpathian Ruthenia."

The final substantial contribution made by Táborsky concerns the question of the projected Polish-Czechoslovak federation, studied by Beneš and Sikorski from 1940 to 1942, at which time Stalin interposed his veto and the negotiations were abandoned. From the plentiful supply of material which he provides—although he is the major Czechoslovak source on the problem, Táborsky contributes little toward clarifying Beneš' position on the issue—it is still not clearly established whether, apart from the Soviet veto, Beneš sincerely desired to establish some form of union between Czechoslovakia and Poland or whether, in the beginning, he simply proposed to win Polish support in order to escape the isolation that had characterized his first year of exile, and then later to play the role of mediator in eastern European affairs, favoring a compromise between the Polish government in London and the Soviet Union.

This question is the central theme of the book by the former Czechoslovak Premier, Hodža.[279] He participated in the first phase of the negotiations, advancing the plan to form a tripartite federation in order to preserve an autonomous position for Slovakia (he was a Slovak) with respect to the Czechs in the proposed new arrangement.

Particular attention should be given to Nemec's and Moudry's well-documented book[280] on the question of sub-Carpathian Ruthenia. The author had been the Czechoslovak government's representative in the region immediately after the occupation by the Soviet forces.

Vlastimil Kybal offers an interesting contribution to the study of Italo-Czechoslovak relations during the early period of the Fascist regime.[281] Kybal had been Prague's Ambassador to Rome from 1920 to 1925, and in his article he reveals that immediately after Mussolini's rise to power there were good possibilities of strengthening the ties between the two countries, either on the basis of their having been allies in World War I or because of common interests on many problems. However, despite the author's repeated insistence, the opportunity was not exploited, largely because Beneš did not believe that Mussolini would last a month as Italy's Prime Minister. Kybal's detailed account not only clarifies these aspects of Italo-Czechoslovak relations but presents important data on the attitude of the other governments of the Little Entente toward Italy, as well as pertinent information on Mussolini's thinking on Danubian-Balkan problems.

Because of the chronological limits of his work, Ripka's memoirs[282] are of only marginal interest. He had been a member of the Czechoslovak government in exile and Minister of Foreign Trade from the liberation to the *coup d'état* of 1948. His narration focuses on the coup but also includes some important information concerning his work in London with the British Cabinet immediately after the departure of the Czechoslovak government for Prague in March, 1945.

Also to be noted are the memoirs of Fierlinger,[283] Ambassador to Moscow from 1937 to 1939 and from 1941, when Czechoslovak relations with the Soviet Union were re-established, to April, 1945, when, at the Communists'

---

[279] Milan Hodža, *Federation in Central Europe. Reflections and Reminiscences* (London: Yarrolds, 1942).

[280] F. Nemec and V. Moudry, *The Soviet Seizure of Subcarpathian Ruthenia* (Toronto: Anderson, 1955).

[281] "Czechoslovakia and Italy: My Negotiations with Mussolini 1922–1924," *Journal of Central European Affairs*, January and April, 1954.

[282] Hubert Ripka, *Le Coup de Prague: Une révolution préfabriquée. Souvenirs* (Paris: Plon, 1949).

[283] Zdenek Fierlinger, *Ve službách ČSR. Paměti z druheho zahraničniho odboje* [In the Service of the Czechoslovak Republic. Memoirs of the Second World War] (2 vols.; Prague: Svoboda, 1947–48).

suggestion, he became Prime Minister of the coalition government (National Front). His volumes are a rich source of information—as could be expected, since he occupied the most important diplomatic post from which to advance Beneš' policy during the war—not only on Beneš' directives but also on the attitude of the Czechoslovak exiles in Moscow and the plans for the reorganization of the Czechoslovak state. However, the fact that he was a left-wing Social Democrat who, during his mission to Moscow, had secretly embraced the Communist cause (the reason why Gottwald nominated him as Prime Minister) considerably reduces the historical value of his testimony.

10. THE AUSTRIAN MEMORIALISTS.

a. Schuschnigg.

The central theme of modern Austrian history is the *Anschluss,* the subject of the memoirs of Kurt von Schuschnigg,[284] the Austrian Chancellor at the time of the event. His contribution to a reconstruction of the events that led to Germany's annexation of Austria is a limited one because the volume gives a detailed account only of the final phase of the crisis, from the meeting at Berchtesgaden of February 18, 1938 (including the minutes of the meeting missing in the German documentary collection) to the dramatic events of March 11, 1938. The second part of the memoir is of greater value because it provides an insight into the author's ideas and the policies responsible for the program he put into effect upon assuming power in July, 1934. The third section of the memoir consists of the diary Schuschnigg kept during his seven-year imprisonment in the Reich.

The three parts indicate the logical division of the material, but the author's decision to retain the order of the chapters as he had written them results in a disorganized presentation. For example, the second part, laborious to read, is probably the most important. It contains an introductory chapter discussing historico-cultural considerations and others, not consecutive, devoted to a critical evaluation of earlier Austrian history, in which the author seeks to find the causes for the demise of Austria in 1938.

The first important conclusion to be drawn from this second section is that Schuschnigg did not believe that the Austria created by the Treaty of St. Germain had much prospect of survival. He regarded Austria as an

---

[284] *Ein Requiem in Rot-Weiss-Rot* (Zurich: Amstutz, 1946).

organism which the victorious powers had willed into being after removing its every means of independent existence.

The old Hapsburg Empire was a conglomeration of heterogeneous entities held together by several common elements: the dynasty, the state organization, the bureaucracy, and economic viability. Only these elements, according to Schuschnigg, which kept the Empire alive as something above the various nationalities that composed it, constituted the truly "Austrian" part of the Empire itself. The people, on the other hand, remained divided by nationality. Schuschnigg added that the "Austrian" prototype existed among the upper-class nobility, the ecclesiastical orders, the army, and among the elite of the *bourgeoisie,* but the process to transform the masses into Austrian citizens had failed. Instead, they were Germans, Magyars, Czechs, Slovaks, Ruthenians, Poles, Croatians, etc. Out of the ashes of this historico-politico-economic complex, states such as Czechoslovakia and Hungary could emerge, but a vibrant Austria such as that designed by the peace conference required a truly Austrian people, which still did not exist.

The new Austria, lacking the characteristics that had made it possible for the old Empire to survive, had inherited its worst feature: the lack of a "national consciousness." Reduced to a single ethnic group, the people had no awareness of being Austrian but remained German and, as such, responded to the appeal of Pan-Germanism. With the disappearance of the magnetic pole that held the Empire together, Imperial Vienna, it was no longer a question of *Grossedeutschtum* or *Kleindeutschtum,* as had been the case in the nineteenth century, but rather the Pan-German idea which meant *Anschluss,* union with Germany, to the Austrian Germans.

Schuschnigg confesses that he and others of his generation, while they recognized the realities of the situation, did not properly evaluate the practical appeal of the Pan-Germanic ideal. This is not surprising, considering that the author is revealed in this volume to be an example of what he defines as the "Austrian type," whose reaction to the destruction of the old Empire was different from that of the masses of Austrian Germans. In fact, while accepting the premise that postwar Austria was an artificial creation that had been ordered to survive, he refused to draw promptly the obvious conclusion that the independence of his country had been completely compromised. However, accepting the verdict of the peace treaty as an established fact, he sought to assign a function to the new Austria which was based on the old Austrian spirit. The author speaks of having dreamed of "a Reich composed of a confederation of central European states, economically self-sufficient, whose leadership, allowing for the safeguards of the sovereignty of the individual states, would logically be assumed by a

German state": an Austria, much reduced in size and strength, which would arouse no apprehension.

Of course, by the time that Schuschnigg became Chancellor, the realization of such a dream had long since demonstrated itself to be impossible. Therefore, there remained only the negative aspect of the prospects he had entertained for the future of Austria, that is, the grave difficulty of maintaining its independence. According to Schuschnigg, he concentrated his efforts toward this end because the maintenance of Austria as an independent state was a legal obligation, assumed and confirmed by Austria in the international order, and a moral obligation because of the absolute irreconcilability of his and his party's principles and National Socialist doctrine.

Schuschnigg observes that after the attempted *Anschluss,* resulting in the assassination of Chancellor Dollfuss, the question of Austria's survival became primarily a problem of foreign and economic policies vis-à-vis the Third Reich. Two instruments were available to Austria to ensure her independence. One was effective only in theory, that is, the League of Nations; and the other was of practical value, the Austrian agreement with Italy and Hungary, the Protocols of Rome of March 17, 1934. (It is interesting to note that the author fails to mention, even as an instrument of theoretical value, the Anglo-French-Italian declaration of February 17, 1934, renewed in September of the same year, perhaps because of the little assistance furnished by London and Paris during the July crisis.)

From the first meeting between Schuschnigg and Mussolini in Florence in August, 1934—reported by Schuschnigg from his notes of this and subsequent meetings with Mussolini in the years 1935–37—the Austrian Chancellor became convinced that Italian support could not go beyond a show of strength on the Brenner such as was displayed during the preceding crisis. He pointed out to Mussolini that the appearance of Italian troops on Austrian soil not only would prompt a similar action by Czechs and Yugoslavs but that it would also be politically "impossible" from an internal point of view because it would provoke a pro-German reaction in all of Austria. The other limitation to Italy's support, even if such support was restricted to a simple show of force, was the possibility of a change in Italo-German relations.

In such a situation, Schuschnigg was not able to justify a policy for the protection of Austria based exclusively on outside aid. Moreover, he adds, Austria was ethnically and economically a German state, and therefore it was not possible for it to join an anti-German coalition. There remained but one choice: a policy of appeasement toward Germany that would remove any pretext Hitler might have for justifying either a German invasion of

Austria or a policy of internal subversion that combined active support of the Austrian Nazis with a policy of economic strangulation of the country.

Schuschnigg concludes that, for these reasons, he was induced to sign the Austro-German Accord of July 11, 1936. In this accord, Hitler recognized the full sovereignty of the Austrian Republic and agreed to respect the principle of noninterference in Austrian internal affairs, while the Vienna government agreed to proceed with the "pacification" of the country by permitting the Austrian Nazis to enjoy full political rights. Shortly thereafter, the Ministry of Internal Affairs was entrusted to a man acceptable to Berlin, General Glaise-Horstenau.

If it is true, as Schuschnigg maintains, that this agreement was inevitable, then there is no doubt that it was Hitler's first successful step toward *Anschluss,* in that it annulled the consequences of the abortive attempt of 1934 and offered real prospects of Austrian Nazification.

Schuschnigg does not overlook other criticisms which might be made of his policy. To those who insist that he should have known that Hitler did not respect treaties, the author counters by saying that European powers concluded important treaties with the Third Reich even *after* Hitler violated the Austro-German treaty. After repeating the reasons which, according to Schuschnigg, made the accord with Germany necessary, he adds that he was aware that Hitler did not intend to keep his word. However, even a 10 per cent chance that he would was worth more to the Austrians than abandoning all hope.

Schuschnigg is well aware of other criticisms of his policy. To those who condemn him for not having reacted more energetically against the Austrian Nazis, he replies by adding to the reasons already mentioned the fact that the Austrian Nazi Party members were not the cause of Austria's collapse since they were always a minority, but that it should be ascribed to the large number of Nazi sympathizers who supported them because they were the champions of *Anschluss.* The observation is symptomatic, and perhaps it goes beyond the author's thinking on the matter. In fact, it might well serve as a more exhaustive reply than the one he presents to the criticism that the loss of Austria's independence was very likely facilitated, if not actually provoked, by the absence of a united front between Catholics and Social Democrats. Schuschnigg states that sixteen years of profound and radical contrasts between the two parties could not be overcome by his government. However, if we accept his preceding assertion as historically sound, we are led to conclude that their collaboration would have had little effect on the masses. As for the possibility of such a union's altering the course of events, the case of Czechoslovakia may serve as an example.

Schuschnigg terminates this portion of the account on an argumentative note. He asks his critics what would have happened if Austria had immediately bowed to the Nazi demands, that is, before the country was overcome by force and thus placed clearly in the right. In substance, this was the goal he had set for his policy in the event he found it impossible to preserve Austria's independence.

The author comments only briefly on Italo-Austrian relations. In addition to reporting his notes on his conversations with Mussolini, he offers useful particulars on Austria's position during the Ethiopian crisis and on the Italian efforts to force the dismissal of the Austrian Foreign Minister, Guido Schmidt, in the fall of 1937, for being guilty of criticizing Mussolini's policy.

b. The Other Austrian Memoir Sources.

Prince Starhemberg, Minister of the Interior in the second half of 1930, Vice-Chancellor from May, 1934, to May, 1936, and Minister of National Security from August, 1934, limited his memoirs to the events in which he played a role.[285] Aside from the offices he held, he was one of the major figures of recent Austrian history as Commandant of the National Guard (Heimwehr or Heimatschutz), one of the two paramilitary organizations that had emerged during the chaotic period immediately following World War I, which he transformed into a decisive force in Austrian political affairs in the years 1930–35.

Starhemberg's memoirs are a valuable source, not only for the numerous disclosures they contain, but primarily because they are, on the whole, reasonably objective. The author—a Hitler follower in the Munich *Putsch* of 1923, he became a pilot in the Free French Air Force during World War II—does not hesitate to narrate nearly all of the behind-the-scenes activities of his political life without reticence or concern for his errors and faults.

It was Hitler's idea to use the Heimwehr as an active force in Austrian internal politics, and in the spring of 1930 he advised Starhemberg to contact Mussolini for the purpose of obtaining Italian aid in reorganizing the National Guard. The plan was simple: Hitler believed that when the Heimwehr had become an efficient instrument of power, it would not be difficult for him to convince Starhemberg to use it in support of the Nazi cause. However, Hitler badly misjudged the Prince's character.

Starhemberg followed Hitler's advice and met with Mussolini in July, 1930. His requests were favorably received by the head of the Italian

[285] *Between Hitler and Mussolini. Memoirs of Ernst Rüdiger Prince Starhemberg* (London: Hodder and Stoughton, 1942).

government, who, naturally, outlined the precise terms governing Italian aid to the Heimwehr: Starhemberg was to try to make an efficient force of the National Guard to protect Austria's independence, a matter of primary concern to Italy. Mussolini insisted that not only must Austria reject any idea of *Anschluss* with Germany, but that Starhemberg should abandon any idea of an Austro-German accord because Germany was dominated by Prussians and a marked difference existed between them and the Austrians in character, tradition, and political systems. If it was true, as Starhemberg had stated, that the Austrian problem consisted of a dichotomy between the concepts of nationalism and patriotism, with the nationalists seeking the merger of Austria into a German fatherland, Austrian independence could only be preserved by developing a new spirit of nationalism among the people based on the above-mentioned differences between Germans and Austrians that would emphasize the concept of an Austrian fatherland, separate and distinct from the rest of the Germanic world.

After this colloquy, Starhemberg proceeded to reorganize and strengthen the Heimwehr. He succeeded in assuming its leadership and in entering the government for the sole purpose, as he admits, of immediately attempting a *coup d'état*, the objectives of which he does not make clear. However, this project was quickly abandoned because his movement found itself facing a serious problem in its relations with the Austrian Social Democrats.

On the eve of the political elections, Starhemberg was approached by Gregor Strasser, on behalf of Hitler, who proposed that the Heimwehr join with the National Socialists in offering a single list of candidates. Significant sums would be placed at Starhemberg's disposal for propaganda purposes for this "National Front" and for Starhemberg personally. After some hesitation, caused in part by the fact that a number of the Heimwehr leaders favored the proposal, Starhemberg finally decided to reject the offer. After an equally fruitless attempt the following year by Theo Habicht, a Nazi trustee for Austria, Hitler decided, in April, 1932, to deal personally with Starhemberg, but this attempt to win him to the Nazi cause also failed and Hitler was forced to abandon any hope of co-operation with the head of the Heimwehr.

With the accession of Dollfuss to the chancellorship in May, 1932, Prince Starhemberg, although not in the government, assumed a role of major importance because of his close ties with Italy, toward which Dollfuss was oriented for support in preserving Austria's independence. Starhemberg's visits to Rome became even more frequent, and his colloquies with Mussolini are amply reported in his memoirs.

Concerning his influence in changing the political structure of the state during the Dollfuss regime, Starhemberg readily admits that he strongly urged the Chancellor to suspend the functions of Parliament in March, 1933. He was convinced that the measure was necessary in order to prevent the National Socialists, now directly supported by Berlin, from winning an important number of parliamentary seats in the elections and thereby enabling them to repeat the tactics they had used in Germany to take over the government.

Starhemberg reports at length on the events stemming from the popular demonstrations of February 11–15, 1934, which terminated in the outlawing of the Social Democratic party (and the other parties as well), but his version of the affair has little in common with the recently developed thesis that Dollfuss acted at Mussolini's suggestion. Instead, Starhemberg attributes the responsibility for the demonstrations to the Vice-Chancellor and Minister of National Security, Major Fey, a member of the Heimwehr, who supposedly provoked the demonstrations and then violently crushed them in order to be acclaimed as the man who had saved Austria from a Marxist revolution.

Starhemberg also considers Fey to be one of those responsible for Dollfuss' assassination. Having been replaced as Vice-Chancellor by Starhemberg early in May, Major Fey, who was suspected of Nazi affiliations, was also removed from his post as Minister of National Security on July 1, 1934, although he was allowed to remain in the government in a minor position. Fey's relations with the new Minister were obviously not of the best. Therefore, Fey, who was informed by his aide-de-camp of the planned attempt on Dollfuss's life two days before it occurred, failed to communicate the information to his successor, intending to save the situation by intervening with the Viennese units of the Heimwehr. The speed with which the plotters moved frustrated Fey's plan: he not only arrived at the Chancellery after Dollfuss was killed, but was himself held as a hostage.

Starhemberg arrived at this recapitulation of the events from the inquest conducted by the Austrian courts, which he was in a position to examine, having taken over the Ministry of National Security in the new Schuschnigg government. He explains that these particulars were suppressed in the text of the inquiry published as a Brown Book (of which there are two versions, nevertheless) because, if they had been made public, the Nazis would have exploited them to involve Fey and the Heimwehr in the assassination of Dollfuss. It was also for this reason that Fey retained his post in the new government.

Starhemberg did not establish the degree of collaboration with Schuschnigg that he had had with Dollfuss. He is critical of the new Chancellor, emphasizing Schuschnigg's tendency to appease the internal opposition and, thereby, to appease Germany. However, at the same time, Starhemberg does not hide the fact that during this period the promises of aid received from Mussolini were becoming rather formal and nonspecific. As a result, the author's position was noticeably weakened, and his disagreements with Schuschnigg increased, beginning with his opposition to the accrediting of Von Papen as Germany's envoy extraordinary to Vienna. On May 13, 1936, Starhemberg was finally obliged to resign, finding himself in open conflict with Schuschnigg over the shift in the Ministry of Foreign Affairs. The Chancellor took over the post of Minister of Foreign Affairs and appointed Guido Schmidt as Undersecretary in that ministry. Starhemberg gives no other reasons for his resignation, beyond the fact that Von Papen had made several fruitless attempts to induce him to collaborate with the Reich.

It is from the volume by Zernatto,[286] the last Secretary-General of the Patriotic Front—the organization created by Dollfuss in February, 1934, after the dissolution of the political parties—that we learn some of the details surrounding this episode. According to Zernatto, it was Mussolini who, several weeks earlier, had suggested to Schuschnigg that it would be opportune to sacrifice Starhemberg in order to remove another cause of Hitler's resentment toward Austria. However, it is not improbable that Starhemberg's dismissal was directly requested by Von Papen during the course of the preliminary negotiations for the July 11 accord, following which the Heimwehr was dissolved. It appears from Schuschnigg's memoirs that Mussolini apparently only concurred with the German request. In this case, Schuschnigg may have interpreted Mussolini's reply to be a confirmation of the fact that Italy was no longer in a position to act as the guarantor of Austria's independence, a state of affairs in which the relations between Starhemberg and Mussolini were the most tangible expression. Zernatto's volume is not limited to this incident alone and constitutes an adequate source for a number of aspects of Austria's final crisis.

Austrian diplomatic memoirs are limited. The volume by George Franckenstein,[287] Austrian envoy to London from 1920 to 1938, provides some useful data only on the negotiations for an international loan which Austria obtained in 1922 from the League of Nations. A large part of his recollections refer to his earlier diplomatic experiences.

The memoirs of Lothar Wimmer[288] are somewhat more interesting. He

---

[286] Guido Zernatto, *Die Wahrheit über Österreich* (London: Longmans, 1938).

[287] *Diplomat of Destiny* (New York: Alliance Book Corporation, 1940).

[288] *Experience et tribulations d'un diplomate autrichien entre deux guerres 1929–1938* (Neuchâtel: La Baconnière, 1946). The author published a second volume of his memoirs covering the period from his departure from Belgrade to 1951: *Zwischen Ballhausplatz und Downing Street* (Vienna: Verlag George Fromme, 1958).

had been Embassy Counsellor in London from 1928 to 1934, in 1934 he became Minister to Athens, and in 1937, to Belgrade. The volume includes part of his London correspondence with Seipel, a personal friend, regarding the organization of the Austrian state. His notes on British policy toward Austria in 1934 are also noteworthy. However, the most important chapters concern his mission to Belgrade, from which, through his citations of the documents, it is possible to acquire important information relative to the Yugoslav internal situation and to Austro-Yugoslav relations during the year preceding the *Anschluss*.

Anton Rintelen was Austrian Minister to Rome from August, 1933, to July, 1934, but this mission is mentioned only in passing in his memoirs.[289] His diplomatic experience appears only as an occasional parenthesis in his political life, which extended from 1918 to 1938 and is the essence of this volume. He had been Governor of Styria for many years and was Minister of Public Instruction from 1926 until Dollfuss eliminated him from the government by packing him off to Rome. Two days prior to Dollfuss' assassination, Rintelen returned to Vienna, ready to assume the chancellorship in the event that the Nazi coup of July 25, 1934, proved successful. He was arrested and tried, but was freed by the amnesty for political crimes arranged in the Austro-German Accord of 1936. His testimony is valuable as an exposition of the viewpoint of those Austrians favoring the *Anschluss*.

The memoirs of Franz Winkler,[290] who was Vice-Chancellor in the Dollfuss Cabinet from the fall of 1933 and was accused of involvement in the July, 1934, *Putsch,* are informative. The author avoided arrest by fleeing abroad and was thus able to publish his account of the events within a year after they occurred.

The volume in which Julius Braunthal,[291] an Austrian Social Democrat, treats the Austrian problem after World War II from the external and internal points of view, based on his recollections of thirty years, is especially important for its Appendix. In it the historian Paul R. Sweet has included a number of letters exchanged between Mussolini and Dollfuss and other important documents taken from the Vienna state archives after World War II.

This material would seem to prove that it was Mussolini who urged Dollfuss to use force, if necessary, to get the Social Democrats to accept the authoritarian constitutional reforms. Mussolini added that if the Social

[289] *Erinnerungen an Österreichs Weg* (Munich: Verlag F. Bruckmann, 1941).
[290] *Die Diktatur in Österreich* (Zurich, 1935).
[291] *The Tragedy of Austria* (London: Gollancz, 1948), with an Appendix by Paul R. Sweet.

Democrats were not forced to accept the changes, there existed a greater and more concrete danger that the anti-Marxist Heimwehr would go over to the Nazis. Dollfuss agreed with this view and proposed to remove the Marxists from the positions of authority that they still retained just as soon as it was possible to do so. This is a significant documentation even though it is necessary to incorporate it with other data in order to explain adequately the causes of the incidents of February, 1934.

11. THE HUNGARIAN MEMORIALISTS.

a. Kállay.

The most important Hungarian memoir contribution is the recollections of Nicholas Kállay,[292] Prime Minister from March, 1942, to the German occupation of Hungary on March 19, 1944. Notwithstanding the fact that these memoirs are limited to this period of Hungarian foreign policy (Kállay had not held any major public office prior to March, 1942), they present a reasonably complete and, on the whole, objective account of the aims and activities of the Kállay government during its tenure in office. It should be noted, however, that the author wrote his memoirs during his exile in Italy and did not have his personal archive at his disposal, with the exception of some files of his correspondence with Hungarian diplomats abroad who were in contact with the West. At first, Kállay thought of publishing these documents in an appendix to the volume but later abandoned the idea, probably because of editorial reasons. Nevertheless, this correspondence, along with a great quantity of additional material gathered from other Hungarian political figures and diplomats, has been utilized by an expert in Magyar history in the preparation of an excellent volume on Hungary from 1929 to 1945.[293]

The Regent, Horthy, asked Kállay to form a government to replace Bárdossy because, among all the public figures in Hungary, Kállay was the most likely to succeed in giving Budapest's policy the purely "Hungarian character" which the Regent deemed necessary for the good of the country. Given the circumstances, Kállay had the best chance of success because he was the least prominent political personality, and the exact nature of his ideas was unknown outside of the small group of Bethlen conservatives.

---

[292] *Hungarian Premier. A Personal Account of a Nation's Struggle in the Second World War* (New York: Columbia University Press, 1954).

[293] C. A. Macartney, *October Fifteenth. A History of Modern Hungary, 1922–1945* (2 vols.; Edinburgh: The Edinburgh University Press, 1956–57).

Insofar as Germany was concerned, his appointment should not have aroused any unfavorable reactions because his only previous ministerial experience consisted of a stint as Minister of Agriculture in the government of the Radical-Nationalist Gömbös.

The basic conflict in political views (aside from personal differences) that led Horthy to ask for the resignation of the Bárdossy government was the fact that the latter believed that Hungary had already made an irrevocable choice in aligning with the Axis. Instead, the Regent was convinced, after the American entrance into the war, that the democracies would ultimately emerge victorious. He believed it to be necessary—and, what is more important, possible—for Hungary to break the tie with Germany and face the dreaded communist peril with the support of the western powers, since Horthy believed that London and Washington considered their alliance with the U.S.S.R. only a wartime necessity.

Horthy was convinced that Hungary's geographical position between the two powerful antagonists, Germany and the Soviet Union, was the best guarantee of its independence because the western powers would not permit it to fall under the domination of either one or the other.

Basing the future of Hungary on the presupposition that the defeat of Germany would not mean that the U.S.S.R. would be allowed a free hand in Europe, Kállay, during his two years in office, sought to put into effect a program designed to restore and defend Hungary's complete freedom of action in foreign affairs. This signified, first, a policy of resistance to Germany and the granting of only those concessions that would forestall occupation by German troops. Second, it meant restricting military collaboration with the Germans to the narrow limits to which it had been reduced by the Bárdossy government in the fall of 1941, while at the same time making every effort to strengthen Hungary's military potential. This attitude, known to the western democracies, should have made it clear that Hungary considered herself at war only with the Soviet Union and that as far as Hungary's relations with the western powers were concerned, rather than the existence of a state of war, there was a desire to reach a political agreement that would protect Hungary from the communist danger.

The first contact with the British was made in the summer of 1942 and led to the understanding that the Magyar government would send one of its representatives to Istanbul, armed with full powers to negotiate in the name of the Hungarian General Staff as well as the government. For varied reasons of a material nature, the envoy was unable to reach Istanbul until early January, 1943. He arrived with the information that, on the military level, Hungary was ready to assume two obligations: not to oppose the Anglo-American forces once they reached the Hungarian frontiers and to give active assistance in the struggle against Germany even before the arrival of the western allied forces if it were possible to develop a plan that would require an early intervention by the Hungarian armed forces in support of the Anglo-American advance. The British government replied by asking that two major Magyar military men be sent to Istanbul to detail these plans, but made no mention of any discussion of a political nature, which, of course, indicated that there was no change in the policy of unconditional surrender.

The British position greatly discouraged the Hungarian government because the latter had hoped to initiate negotiations for a political agreement and not for an armistice, which, insofar as Hungary was concerned, was considered to be already in effect with the western powers and because, in the proposed conversations, one of the British delegates slated to participate was known to Budapest to be a Kremlin informer. Therefore, the Hungarian attempts to arrive at a negotiated peace proved fruitless, and further Hungarian efforts to achieve the same ends were equally unproductive. Finally, in August, 1943, Kállay decided to accept the Anglo-American conditions and contacted the British Embassy in Turkey, announcing that this overture by Budapest signified acceptance of the principle of unconditional surrender and that Hungary was requesting to be informed of the preliminary conditions.

In September the British replied, asking for confirmation of the August 17 communication as a statement of surrender and acceptance of all of the conditions imposed by the Allies, that is, that the capitulation was to remain secret for a certain length of time but would be jointly announced publicly, however, not before the Allied forces reached Hungarian territory. Meanwhile, Hungary would withdraw her troops from the Russian front and would resist every German effort to occupy the country. And finally, an Allied mission would be parachuted into Hungary at the opportune moment to make the necessary arrangements for the capitulation.

The acceptance of these requests—leaving aside the formal aspect of the question, that is, the unconditional surrender, to which Kállay was still largely opposed—would have very soon led, in practice, to a German occupation of Hungary, forcing Magyar troops to fight a partisan war organized by an Allied military mission for the exclusive benefit of the Red army if the second front were not opened in the Balkans. However, aside from any other consideration, the principal reason for the dropping of the negotiations by Horthy and Kállay was that the Allies did not agree to erase Hungary from the list of enemy states, while the Magyar desire to change sides was being exploited by them for the purpose of gaining advantages of a purely military nature.

Notwithstanding the negative outcome of these negotiations, Kállay continued to search for a more favorable arrangement with the Allies, even though his child-like faith in the success of his policy had suffered a warning setback. If it would have been disastrous for Hungary to accept the conditions laid down by the Allies, at least in view of the objectives Kállay hoped to achieve, further delay did not improve his prospects. In the long run, the openly reticent attitude of the Kállay government regarding collaboration with the Germans, confirmed by information that reached Berlin of the Hungarian negotiations with the Allies, only served to induce Hitler to remove Kállay and to occupy the country when the military situation made it necessary.

In conclusion, if Kállay must be blamed for not having understood the political consequences of Soviet collaboration with the western democracies, it must also be recognized that his government did not have any real prospect of influencing the political destiny of Hungary, given the alignment of the major powers in the conflict. From a practical standpoint, the criticism voiced against the political class, of which Kállay was a prime example, that action was not taken early enough to modernize the structure of the Hungarian state, particularly in the area of agricultural reforms that would have destroyed the quasi-feudal land-holding system, is not justified. Two facts appear to support the contention that between this existing situation and the establishment of the Communist regime there is no direct relationship of cause and effect: the results of the only free elections held in Hungary in the immediate postwar period, in which the Communists won only 17 per cent of the votes, and the October, 1956, uprising, after nine years of Communist rule.

The chapter Kállay devotes to his visit to Rome early in April, 1943, is directly related to the history of Italy. At that time, the Hungarian Premier had only recently received the British reply to his overtures of January, in which London asked that two Magyar army officers be sent to Istanbul to negotiate the technical details of the proposed unconditional surrender. It was reasonable to suppose that the reply from the British would have been different if the plan to break with Germany had not been limited to Hungary alone. Therefore, in going to Rome, Kállay proposed to sound out Mussolini on the possibility of creating a unified front, including Finland, that would develop a common policy within the Axis with the ultimate goal, in effect, of returning to a nonbelligerent status.

According to Kállay's account, Mussolini believed that a separate peace was impossible: he noted, first of all, that it had been made impossible by the intransigence of the Anglo-Americans on the matter of unconditional surrender; and, second, even if the goal could be reached, Italy could not possibly benefit by it because the country would become a battlefield between the Anglo-American and German forces. However, Mussolini did not entirely reject the plan. He concluded that he would be able to consider it further only in the event that he was unable to convince Hitler, in his forthcoming colloquies with him, of the necessity of finding a way to end the war with the Soviet Union by late fall. From what is known from the Italian sources, Kállay's account is substantially correct, with the exception, perhaps, of the time limit (autumn, 1943) after which Mussolini would attempt to regain his freedom of action in the event that Hitler wanted to continue the war in the east. From the correspondence between the two dictators, it seems that Mussolini was intent on convincing Hitler to make a separate peace with the Soviet Union immediately because, with Tunisia considered lost, it was extremely likely that the Anglo-Americans would soon land on the Italian peninsula if the equilibrium between the two opposing forces was not substantially altered immediately.

b. The Other Hungarian Memoir Sources.

The brief sketch of his entire military and political career provided by Admiral Horthy in his volumes of memoirs[294] is of minor importance. In the narrative, Horthy touches on his service as aide-de-camp to Franz Joseph at the Imperial Court from 1909 to 1914; the troubled days of 1918–1919, when he took an active part in the overthrow of Béla Kun's Communist government and in the restoration of the monarchy, for which he was elected Regent on March 1, 1920; and the events of World War II and the surrender to the Red army, which he announced by proclamation on October 15, 1944, his last political act before being deposed and arrested by German authorities. Aside from the brevity of the observations in comparison to the length of his career, the fact that Horthy's references are only approximate on many points, as is the case in so many memoir accounts, limits the usefulness of the volume as a source. On the other hand, it was not expected that Horthy would make an outstanding contribution, since he wrote his memoirs at an advanced age and had only a few documents placed at his disposal by his colleagues. However, there are some noteworthy details in the section dealing with the final crisis of 1944.

Another of the attempts of the Kállay government to reach an accord with the Anglo-Americans in the winter of 1943–44 is narrated by a Magyar diplomat, Antal Ullein-Reviczky,[295] Hungarian Minister to Stockholm at that time. In December, 1943, Ullein was able to contact an

[294] Miklos Horthy, *Ein Leben für Ungarn* (Bonn: Athenäum-Verlag, 1953).
[295] *Guerre Allemande, Paix Russe. Le drame hongrois* (Neuchâtel: La Baconnière, 1947).

American representative of the Allied General Staff, to whom, on his own authority, he once again explained the Hungarian situation. Noting that the American seemed to react favorably to the Budapest approach to the problem, Ullein requested that Kállay send him concrete proposals which were, in effect, very similar to those that the Magyars had already presented during the negotiations with the British in Istanbul. The proposals reiterated the offer to surrender the moment the Anglo-American forces reached Hungarian territory and to join the Allies in the war against the Germans as soon as it was possible to do so. Meanwhile, the Americans were to ask the Soviets to restrict their operations in the Hungarian sector. Beyond that, the Budapest government put itself in the hands of the Allies and had no further reservations to make on the issue of unconditional surrender.

The reply of the American representative confirmed that the Allied General Staff was favorably disposed toward Hungary but that since 1943 the situation had changed considerably. Shortly, the second front would be opened in France, and, therefore, there was little chance that the Anglo-American troops would reach the Hungarian frontiers, while the Red army was moving rapidly toward them. However, the American informed Ullein that the British and the Americans were disposed to discuss the Hungarian surrender with the Soviets in order not to leave the Magyars alone to deal with them. This was the situation at the end of February, 1944, and the Hungarian government realized that it was highly unlikely that it could succeed in one of its aims, that is, the implementation of an operation that would prevent a German occupation of Hungarian territory, which would turn the country into a battleground between Soviet and German forces. As a result, Kállay decided to drop the negotiations and to accept the plan of the extremists of his political group to resist the Soviets with every means at Hungary's command.

Moreover, the Ullein volume contains a useful summary of Hungarian events during the period in which the author was chief of the Press Section of the Foreign Ministry, February, 1939, to August, 1943.

The work of Stephen Kertész[296] is more of a historical study than a memoir. Kertész was an official in the Foreign Ministry before and during the war and, ultimately, Secretary-General of the Hungarian delegation to the Paris peace conference in 1946. His account is a concise history of Hungary from the Treaty of Trianon of June 4, 1920, to 1946 and is significant for its accuracy and the documentary data it contains, as well as for the important references to the events in which he played a part during the war years.

[296] *Diplomacy in a Whirlpool. Hungary between Nazi Germany and Soviet Russia* (South Bend, Ind.: University of Notre Dame Press, 1953).

Politically, Kertész may be identified as an enlightened conservative with democratic tendencies—a position that may be termed somewhat critical of the Hungarian ruling class. However, he supports the thesis that the destiny of his country, like that of the rest of the small states, was largely determined by the decisions made by the Great Powers. Therefore, he writes, the democratic experiment attempted by Károlyi in Hungary in the winter of 1918–19 failed and Masaryk's in Czechoslovakia was successful because the latter was supported by the Allies, while the Magyar attempt was openly opposed by them. Concerning the events of World War II, the author maintains that there was little Hungary could do to prevent either German or Soviet occupation of its territory because, caught between these two giants, Budapest had little freedom of action. Moreover, he adds, the Anglo-Americans did nothing to encourage Hungarian resistance to the Reich, which would surely have developed if the Allies had promised their support for an equitable postwar territorial settlement. According to Kertész, it was natural, in the final analysis, that the Magyar population was not inclined to make major sacrifices when it knew in advance that these would lead to nothing more than a restoration of the frontiers defined by the Treaty of Trianon, which it considered to be completely unjust. And, it may be added, it should not be surprising that the Hungarian public did not demonstrate greater wisdom than that reflected in other countries, that is, of realizing that it was necessary to make sacrifices, not for territorial aggrandizement, but for the preservation of a blessing it already had, namely, its liberty.

Regarding the Horthy regime, the author is not critical, but he considers the Regent's policy only from the radical point of view of the revisionist sentiment of the Hungarians and refrains from discussing other aspects of the internal situation (the agrarian situation, for example). The author is of the opinion that these considerations played no determining role in the change of regimes in Hungary after World War II.

An opposing view is advanced by Mihaly Károlyi in his memoirs.[297] He had organized the first independent Hungarian government on October 31, 1918, and remained in power until he was overthrown by Béla Kun in March, 1919. However interesting these memoirs may be because, with the exception of Horthy's brief account, they are all that is available on those events, the volume contributes very little of importance to the study of the period. Nor is it possible to base strong arguments on the evidence presented, as the author does in insisting that if his Social Democratic experiment in government had been given time to develop and the agrarian

[297] *Memoirs of Michael Károlyi. Faith without Illusion* (London: Jonathan Cape, 1956).

reform and the other needed structural reforms required by the state had been implemented, the history of Hungary would have been very different. Furthermore, his narrative, like that of Admiral Horthy in an opposite sense, is too clearly polemical to offer substantive elements for judgment. However, Károlyi maintains that the assumption of power by Béla Kun was desired by the Hungarian conservatives because a Communist regime would surely have been overthrown by the Entente powers and the conservatives would have again inherited the country. Meanwhile, if he had been able to complete the basic reforms he had planned, the conservative class would have irremediably lost their dominant position. This is the argument advanced by Károlyi to counter the accusation that he had allowed the Communists to usurp his authority.

Károlyi returned to Hungary in 1946 and was appointed Ambassador to Paris the following year, a post he abandoned in 1949 after the complete Sovietization of Hungary and for the second time went into exile. He devotes the last part of his memoirs to his Paris mission.

Regarding the events in Hungary after the arrest of Horthy by the Germans, reference should be made to the volume by Ferenc Nagy,[298] one of the leaders of the Smallholders party and Prime Minister from February, 1946, to May, 1947. The emphasis of the volume is on the postwar period rather than on the period under consideration here.

Note should also be made of the memoirs of General Vilmos Nagy,[299] Minister of Defense in 1942–43, published in 1947. In the main, they concern his personal career, but, in addition to his tenure of office as Minister of Defense, they contain numerous references to the events of 1938–44 in which he played a role. Moreover, they contain an important summary of the tragic events of October 14–15, 1944, though other parts of his narrative are lacking in accuracy and objectivity.[300]

12. THE YUGOSLAV MEMORIALISTS.

a. Fotic.

The Yugoslav memoir sources, while also rather limited in number, are significant for the contribution the diplomats and statesmen of that country

[298] *The Struggle behind the Iron Curtain* (New York: Macmillan, 1948).

[299] *Végzetes Esztendök* [Fatal Years] (Budapest: Körmendy, 1947).

[300] For a complete bibliography of the Hungarian sources beginning in 1918, see Thomas Schreiber, "La Hongrie de 1918 à 1958. Etat des travaux," *Revue française de science politique,* 1958, No. 3; "Historiographie hongroise de la deuxième guerre mondiale," *Revue d'histoire de la deuxième guerre mondiale,* 1961, No. 44.

have made to the understanding of many unknown or little-known episodes pertinent to Belgrade's policy and to the activities of the Great Powers in the Balkans. Among these, attention is called to the volume published in 1948 by Constantin Fotic,[301] who was Yugoslavia's Minister to Washington from August, 1939, to the spring of 1945.

Fotic eventually found himself in the United States in a position similar to that of his Polish colleague, Ciechanowski, as a representative of a government that had been forced to abandon its national territory by the fortunes of war and whose destinies were linked to an Allied victory. Fotic's memoirs of this mission are, therefore, of great value, especially for the revelations they contain regarding the action taken by Washington and London in the Balkans, action which, according to the author, was marked by such inconsistency and lack of comprehension of Balkan problems as to result in a tragedy, not only for Yugoslavia, but for the entire free world.

There are many pages in the memoirs of the Yugoslav diplomat that attract the attention of scholars, and among these should be mentioned those relating to the part played by the United States in influencing Belgrade's policy toward Germany. According to Fotic, in this case Washington's suggestions carried great weight, but he laments that once war broke out with Germany, the Yugoslav government did not receive the support from the Allies that the situation required. As a case in point, attention is called to the details of the failure of the delivery of war materials sent by the United States to Yugoslavia, which were diverted elsewhere by the British command in the Mediterranean.

Elements of the greatest interest are to be found in these pages concerning subsequent Anglo-American policy in the Balkans. From the beginning, Roosevelt's reticent attitude toward the future disposition of Yugoslavia is indicative, nor should Fotic's analysis of the real reasons for Churchill's decision to support Tito over Mihaijlovic be ignored.

However, the most important part of the volume concerns the British Prime Minister's project to reach an accord with Stalin to divide Yugoslavia into two spheres of influence. The contributions made by Fotic's memoirs to an understanding of this important proposal are of fundamental significance, not only for the purposes of historical reconstruction, but also for a more exact evaluation of the policy later adopted by the Foreign Office on the Yugoslav problem.

Regarding Yugoslav internal developments and the discord between the ethnic and political groups which prevented the formation of a united front against the invader, Fotic's memoirs, while adding numerous details, must

[301] Constantin Fotitch, *The War We Lost—Jugoslavia's Tragedy and the Failure of the West* (New York: Viking Press, 1948).

be used with caution. Because of the author's Serbian origins and close ties to the monarchy, his writings are not the best source for an objective analysis of a situation whose facets must be subjected to a particularly rigid examination.

b. The Other Yugoslav Memoir Sources.

On the internal situation, the memoirs of Vladko Maček[302] are much more objective. Maček for many years had been the unchallenged leader of the Croatian Peasant party, and his volume focuses on the Yugoslav internal situation. It is precisely this aspect that is of keen interest to the student of diplomatic history, not only because the foreign policy of the Belgrade government was profoundly influenced by the internal struggle between the various ethnic groups—especially between Serbs and Croats— but also because this unique situation was exploited by other countries as a means of applying pressure to Belgrade. It is from this viewpoint that the Maček memoirs emerge as a source of great value. For example, Maček provides a detailed summary of his contacts with the Italian government during the spring of 1939 through an intermediary, the engineer Carne- lutti, an episode that was already known through Ciano's memoirs but which, in Maček's recollections, assumes a very different perspective. The part of the volume referring to the Italo-German occupation is equally important. After having proclaimed the independence of Croatia at the moment of the arrival of the German troops in Zagreb—according to Maček, the decision was made primarily to avoid a useless blood bath—the author firmly refused to collaborate with the invaders despite the pressures applied by the Germans, who planned to use him as an instrument against the Italian-supported Pavelic. The pages devoted to these events are especially interesting because, while they provide a vivid picture of the Croatian internal situation, they also clarify many aspects of the struggle that had developed between the German and Italian forces over the question of which was to have the dominant role in Croatia.

The Croatian Minister of Foreign Affairs, Perič, published a series of articles in a Croatian-language journal appearing in Argentina[303] on Zagreb's relations with Rome during the war. He has reported in detail on

[302] In the Struggle for Freedom (New York: Speller, 1957).

[303] Stijepo Perič, "Italo-Croatian Relations during the Second World War, I: The Prelude to the Pact of Rome, II: The Pact of Rome, III: The Genesis of the Pact of Rome according to the Memoirs of Filippo Anfuso" (in Croatian), Svovoda, I–III (1949).

those events in which he had a hand, and particularly noteworthy are the negotiations that led to the establishment of Croatia's Adriatic frontiers. However, his strong anti-Italian bias suggests that his version of the events be accepted with reservations.

An important source for the reconstruction of the position taken by Prince Paul and his attitude toward the Axis powers may be found in the memoirs of Stakič, one of the Regent's trusted advisors. He published his revelations[304] in a journal edited by Yugoslav exiles in South Africa, and through them we learn how, in September, 1939, Prince Paul had proposed to the British government that Yugoslavia align itself with the Allies by launching a preventive war against Italy, a proposal that was being seriously considered at the time in various French political and military circles.

London was opposed to the project because the British government still entertained hopes of preventing Italy's intervention in the war, but the episode is of interest, nevertheless, especially in the light of subsequent events. In the first place, Stakič justifies Yugoslavia's refusal to enter the war at the urging of the British some time later because Prince Paul pointed out that he had made the same proposal earlier and at a time when the war potential of the Allies was intact and Germany was involved in the Polish campaign. On the other hand, Prince Paul's intentions justify, in a certain sense, the Italian participation in the German operations against Yugoslavia in April, 1941. However, Stakič does not refer to any of his many missions undertaken before and during the conflict. Nevertheless, these can be reconstructed through the diary of the Minister of the Royal House, Milan Antic, which has been utilized in part by his successor, Knezevic.[305]

The latter notes that as soon as news reached Belgrade of the Italian ultimatum to Athens Prince Paul proposed to his advisers during the course of two meetings, on October 28 and 29, 1940, that Yugoslavia move to occupy Salonika, the traditional objective of Serbian expansionism toward the Aegean Sea. The proposal was not regarded with favor by the Yugoslav General Staff, but the Belgrade government continued to devote its attention to this project and began to sound out Berlin on the matter. The Germans advised that Belgrade should first seek an agreement with the Italians, and, with this, Stakič immediately left for Rome with a proposal for an Italo-Yugoslav alliance. On the very day (November 11) that he was

---

[304] Wladisla Stakič, "A Glance at Prince Paul's Internal and Foreign Policies" (in Serbo-Croatian), *Nasa Stvarnost*, Johannesburg, fasc. April, 1952.

[305] Rados Knezevic, "How Did It Happen?" (in Serbo-Croatian), *Poruka*, fasc. October, 1951. On this issue see also Knezevic, "Prince Paul, Hitler, and Salonika," *International Affairs*, I (1951).

received by Ciano, a strange episode occurred that was to affect the course of events dramatically. Several Italian aircraft bombed Bitolj (Monastir), the Yugoslav city on the Greek frontier, by mistake. This was purely and simply a case of an error in target identification, but in Belgrade it was interpreted as an indirect warning, a Roman roadblock on the road to Salonika, and, despite Mussolini's favorable reception of the Yugoslav idea, negotiations were interrupted and were later abandoned when the Greek campaign fared badly.

Negotiations were reopened in February, 1941, in two talks Stakič had with Mussolini. While Berlin was applying the strongest pressure to force Belgrade to join the Tripartite Pact, a thing that Yugoslavia was seeking by every means to avoid, Stakič came to Rome to examine the prospects for a military alliance with Italy, counting on Italian support in order to resist the German demands. This project was also received favorably by Mussolini, who made it clear, however, that it was imperative to resolve all of the problems outstanding between the two countries and particularly those concerning the ethnic minorities in the Venezia Giulia and in Albania by means of a transfer of populations. It is highly probable that, had an accord of this type been reached, the history of that area might have taken a different turn. However, while the conversations in Rome were continuing, German pressure on Belgrade became such as to force the Prime Minister, Czvetkovic, to sign the Tripartite Agreement and so put an end to the negotiations in Rome.

While the data on these events is provided by Knezevic, Czvetkovic has published a number of articles[306] on Yugoslavia's adhesion to the Tripartite Pact and on the *coup d'état* of March 27, 1941, that removed the Regent, Prince Paul, and brought King Peter to the throne. Concerning the first of these episodes, Czvetkovic writes—in denying Knezevic's assertions—that the Belgrade government never considered taking Salonika from Greece, but his assertions are contradicted by the recently published German diplomatic documents. These testify that the Salonika question was repeatedly discussed during the course of the conversations on Yugoslavia's adhesion to the Tripartite Pact, and on the occasion of the signing of the agreement, a secret accord was initialed guaranteeing Yugoslavia an outlet on the Aegean Sea. No less perplexing are his remarks concerning the events leading to the Simonovic coup. According to Czvetkovic, the Regent

[306] Dragudin Czvetkovic, *The Truth about March 25 and 27, 1941* (in Serbo-Croatian) (Paris, 1951); *March 27: National Uprising or Conspiracy against the State?* (in Serbo-Croatian) (Paris, 1951); "Prince Paul, Hitler, and Salonika," *International Affairs,* IV (1951). Another article on the same question appeared in *Le Figaro,* April 4, 1950.

was aware of the plot, but he offered no opposition because he saw it as the only way out of an unbearable situation.

To complete the references to the principal Yugoslav memoir sources, note should be made of the two significant articles published by the former Undersecretary for Foreign Affairs, Jukic.[307] These can be considered an important supplement to Fotic's volume in that they cast further light on British policy toward Yugoslavia, especially on those factors ignored by Fotic. Attention is also called to King Peter's memoirs.[308] This volume adds little to the account published by Fotic on developments in the Yugoslav question between 1941 and 1945, largely because Peter and Fotic shared identical views on the problems. However, the book has a certain useful-ness because King Peter was in exile in London and was in a position to report his relations with the British government. Concerning the conflict within the Yugoslav resistance movement between Mihajlovic and Tito, King Peter's account confirms what was revealed in the documents on the war of liberation,[309] especially regarding the very little support given to Tito by the Kremlin authorities in the early phases of the resistance. For example, this volume discloses the background to the recognition of Mihajlovic as head of the Yugoslav resistance movement by the Soviet radio and press toward the end of 1941.

There have been no significant contributions made by the Communists on this phase of Yugoslav history (almost all of the war diaries or the accounts of the principal exponents of the Tito movement are being published in previously mentioned collections) with the exception of Dedijer's volume on Tito[310] and the recently published brief account by Djilas[311] on his three missions to the U.S.S.R.

13. THE RUMANIAN MEMORIALISTS.

a. Gafencu.

In the present situation, in which two Great Powers are found confront-ing each other and all other states are reduced to the roles of recipients of political, economic, and military aid from one or the other of the two giants,

---

Ilija Jukic, "Yugoslavia Past and Present," *The New York Herald Tribune,* April 12, 13, 1949.

[308] Pierre II de Yougoslavie, *La vie d'un Roi. Mémoires* (Paris: Editions Denoël, 1955).

[309] See p. 295 *et seq.*

[310] Vladimir Dedijer, *Tito Speaks* (London: Weidenfeld and Nicolson, 1953).

[311] Milovan Djilas, *Conversazioni con Stalin* (Milan: Feltrinelli, 1962).

the study of the foreign policy of several of the Balkan states between the two world wars seems to have vital significance.

Great Britain, France, and Italy (limiting the reference to the western powers) are gradually becoming aware of the new position in which they find themselves, and they arrive at this bitter conclusion only through the realization that they are no longer in a position to affect international events decisively by unilateral decisions. For a long time, the knowledge that a nation was no longer a Great Power was considered humiliating, and before giving substance to a stronger movement for European political as well as military unification, it led, alternately, to displays of arrogance on the part of those who desired to play a role beyond their means or to that kind of inactivity characteristic of those who feel they have lost their autonomy.

In the end, this has led to a tendency to ignore the experience of others, particularly of such men as Titulescu, Gafencu, Beneš, and Venizelos, who were masters of the art of directing the policies of a satellite state. Obviously unable to change the material potential of their countries, they exploited their very weakness and converted it into an instrument such that it permitted them, in a certain sense, to dictate to the Great Powers. In this manner, French revisionist policy in the Balkans was destroyed at birth by Beneš, who was able to force Paléologue out of the Quai d'Orsay. The same may be said for British policy in the Near East, which was largely conditioned by the will of Venizelos, who is to be held responsible for the Liberals' political defeat in Great Britain.

Among the most outstanding personalities of the Balkan world we find Grigore Gafencu, who, after having been Rumanian Minister of Foreign Affairs from 1938 to 1940, was sent to Moscow as Minister Plenipotentiary and while at that post was able to see at close hand the dramatic events that led to Hitler's attack on the U.S.S.R.

He has left an extraordinarily valuable testimony on this period in his volume *Preliminaries to the War in the East*,[312] in which he not only reports the events that developed before his eyes, but he has also attempted to put them in their proper historical perspective and to recognize the motivating forces behind the actions of the antagonistic powers.

Gafencu's book is singularly penetrating and suggestive, going far beyond the usual limits of a memoir source. He draws frequent parallels between the evolution of Nazi-Soviet relations in 1939–41 and those of France under Napoleon I and Russia on the eve of the campaign of 1812, and the reader is struck by the remarkable similarity between the two

[312] Gregorio Gafencu, *Preliminari della guerra all'est* (Milan: Mondadori, 1946).

situations, which the author emphasizes by citing excerpts from the dispatches sent by Napoleon's ambassador, whose topicality is astonishing.

On the other hand, in examining the German action as a particular manifestation of the European policy of expansion toward the east, Gafencu has arrived at conclusions that are unique and profoundly significant. In effect, he has pointed out how the German *Drang nach Osten* was based on the erroneous presupposition that in the east there were extensive fertile and sparsely populated lands, lands where a crowded Germany with its high standard of living and its industriousness could find a natural outlet and a solution to all of its problems. According to Gafencu, this thesis was based on a fundamental misconception because in the east there are no vast, sparsely populated areas but, on the contrary, there are two hundred million Russians, and, behind them, even larger masses of people with a birth rate that is much higher than the European and who, with the strength created by this demographic pressure, always threaten to alter the existing situation.

Germany realized this only after attacking the Soviet Union. With a power based on her population of eighty million, Germany began her march to the east, only to encounter a population mass that was much greater than her own, and one that promptly applied the law of numbers. The German people only then realized that its eastern frontier was not a base for eastern expansion but, rather, a line of defense which could be held only with the support of the rest of Europe. This—Gafencu concludes—is the major development of modern times: it marks the end of the German dream of hegemony on the Continent and obliges Germany to find her place in an integrated Europe.

This book was written in 1942, when the documentation was extremely sparse and it was too early for the perspective necessary for an objective evaluation of the events. Consequently, Gafencu's work is to be admired for the author's clear understanding of the precedents leading to the conflict between Germany and the U.S.S.R., considered in the light of its dual aspect, the diplomatic game and the deep-seated causes for the conflict. Naturally, the sources appearing after the war make it possible now to add the finishing touches that complete the picture. However, the concept developed by Gafencu and based on the data in his possession—special reference should be made to his examination of the significance of the Soviet official communications—remains in essence fully valid, as do his conclusions regarding the methods and objectives of Soviet policy.

On the eve of the war, Gafencu, as Minister of Foreign Affairs, visited the principal capitals of Europe. He was able to confer with Daladier and Bonnet in Paris, Chamberlain and Halifax in London, Hitler and Von

Ribbentrop in Berlin, Beck in Warsaw, and Pius XII, Mussolini, and Ciano in Rome. He has left a detailed account of these conversations, along with his personal impressions and comments in the volume *The Last Days of Europe*.[313] It is the panorama of Europe just before the curtain was raised on the great drama: it is a view developed from the attitudes of the statesmen he visited, which he records, along with their fears, their hopes, and their illusions; that is, he sees them as men as well as representatives of a country or as exponents of a particular political trend.

Regarding Italy, Gafencu tells how he arrived in Rome as the bearer of a message from Bonnet urging peace and a reduction of tension, since Bonnet still hoped to arrive at a *modus vivendi* with the Fascist government. This was the eve of the signing of the alliance with Germany, and the Rumanian Foreign Minister notes that in his talks with Mussolini and Ciano the atmosphere of uncertainty was still dominant in Rome. If Ciano expressed his own doubts with sufficient clarity, Mussolini also appeared to be hesitant over a complete break with the western powers, and his statements tending to restrict Italy's claims against France to the colonial sphere appeared to Gafencu to be extremely revealing.

b. The Other Rumanian Memoir Sources.

The personal position of Nicolas P. Comnene, one-time Rumanian Minister to Berlin and Minister of Foreign Affairs from March to December, 1938, made it possible for him to follow closely the course of events in the Danube-Balkan area in the period preceding World War II.

Comnene settled in Florence and after the war published a number of volumes that are both memoirs and efforts at historical reconstruction. As a historian, Comnene may be criticized to some degree, but from the point of view of memoirs (often, the distinction is not easy to make) his volumes are worthy of the scholar's attention. The author was able to draw not only from his personal experiences but also from a vast quantity of unpublished material that, but for him, probably would have been irreparably lost.

The first of these volumes appeared in 1947 in Italian[314] and is, perhaps, the most interesting. The central theme of the work is the Munich crisis, which Comnene examines in its general development as well as from the point of view of Bucharest, which on this occasion had some importance.

---

[313] *Ultimi giorni dell'Europa. Viaggio diplomatico nel 1939* (Milan: Rizzoli, 1947).

[314] *Preludi del grande dramma. Ricordi e documenti di un diplomatico* (Rome: Leonardo, 1947).

Given the tension existing between Prague and Warsaw, there was little prospect of obtaining Poland's collaboration in facilitating eventual Soviet assistance to Czechoslovakia. Therefore, Soviet aid could only reach Czechoslovakia through Rumanian territory. Although Bucharest was anxious to aid Prague, the Rumanian government was not disposed to allow Soviet troops to enter Rumania for fear that the U.S.S.R. would use the occasion to effect a coup in Bessarabia. The Rumanians would have offered less resistance to Soviet aid to Prague via air because Soviet overflights of Rumania would have posed only a relative threat.

The problem was the subject of repeated conversations between Comnene, Bonnet, and Litvinov, without, however, any tangible results. The Soviets insisted on a formal authorization from Rumania, while the latter, obviously, could not take such a step. The problem was one of those that do not permit an explicit abandonment of positions of principle but that, on the basis of sufficiently long experience, is subject to tacit application in fact, contrary to formal declarations and dependent exclusively on the specific situation of the moment. This explains how, in a subject so rich in nuances, it was possible for the assertions of Comnene, Bonnet, and of the French Ambassador to Bucharest, Thierry, to differ and, therefore, for the Rumanian position to be interpreted in several different ways.

On the whole, this volume confirms the impression that Rumanian foreign policy up to 1940 was conducted with remarkable dignity and foresight. Without contradicting the letter or the spirit of its obligations, the Bucharest government displayed unusual acumen in meeting the new situation created by the collapse of the preceding diplomatic system, and, today, Rumania's position appears to be much more worthy of respect when compared to the general breakdown and the myopic concepts that determined the policies of other powers during the same period.

The second volume published by Comnene[315] is more a history than a memoir, even though the author frequently inserts his personal recollections as Rumania's delegate to the League of Nations, Minister to Berlin, and Minister of Foreign Affairs. The book is divided into five chapters, the first dealing with the events that led to the rise of National Socialism in Germany, based on an examination of the character of the German people and the atmosphere prevalent in Germany after World War I. The second chapter is devoted to Hitler—his temperament, his political development, and his program—and merits careful study for its clarity of exposition and for the acute observations it contains. The third chapter is, in substance, a

---

[315] I responsabili (Milan: Mondadori, 1949).

history of international relations, which today may be considered outdated but which is worth reading because of the personal elements introduced by the author. In fact, as a memoir, this chapter offers the richest and most original contribution. In the last two chapters, dealing with Hitler's German collaborators and with Mussolini and Ciano, Comnene draws a series of profiles based on his personal recollections.

A third volume by Comnene was published in 1957,[316] and, in part, it is patterned on the preceding one. Here, too, we find a gallery of personalities ably described by the author, accompanied by judgments and observations drawn from his own personal experience. Among the episodes to be recalled are Comnene's colloquies with Pius XI in 1931, in which the Pope expressed his opinion on the rights and prerogatives of the Holy See at a time when relations with the Italian government were particularly tense, and with Orlando, in which the latter commented on several aspects of the Paris peace negotiations.

A significant contribution is made by Alexander Cretzianu,[317] Secretary-General of the Rumanian Foreign Ministry from 1939 to 1941 and Minister to Ankara from September, 1943, to March, 1945. The first part of the volume describes several of the circumstances that led Rumania to enter the war against the Soviet Union. Rumania's position, observes Cretzianu, was consistently based on the accord with Paris and London, and, on the eve of the conflict, these ties were reconfirmed by the guarantee granted by the two western powers on April 13, 1939. There is no doubt, Cretzianu continues, that the effectiveness of this guarantee had been highly overestimated in Bucharest. Cretzianu had become aware of this when, in March, 1939, he met with Daladier and Halifax. Lord Halifax made it clear that effective aid to Rumania depended on the positions taken by Poland and the Soviet Union, while Daladier was convinced that a simple announcement of the guarantee would be sufficient to eliminate the danger of an aggression, and, therefore, he was not particularly concerned with studying the means for a practical realization of the assistance guaranteed by France and Great Britain.

After the outbreak of the war and the evidence of Soviet expansionism in Poland, the Baltic states, and in Finland, the Bucharest government asked whether the Franco-British guarantee was also valid against the Soviet Union. London replied that, in this case, the guarantee was dependent on Turkey's immediate assistance to Rumania and on the certainty that Italian opposition would not be encountered. From this one can deduce exactly

---

[316] *Luci e ombre sull'Europa* (*1914–1950*) (Milan: Bompiani, 1957).
[317] Alexandre Cretzianu, *The Lost Opportunity* (London: Cape, 1957).

what Italian intervention would have meant to Rumania in the event that the Rumanians found themselves alone facing the Soviet threat and the revisionist demands of both Sofia and Budapest.

Cretzianu contributes important data on the circumstances surrounding the presentation of the Soviet ultimatum of June 26, 1940, and on the cession of Bessarabia and northern Bukowina.[318] He emphasizes that this crisis was decisive for Rumania from several points of view. First of all, it made it possible for the pro-German elements in Rumania to exploit the country's isolation and the fear of new Soviet demands and to take over the government. Second, the desire to reconquer the territories taken by the Soviet Union lay at the roots of Rumania's decision to join in the war against the U.S.S.R. As a matter of fact, Cretzianu observes, no one, not even Marshal Antonescu, intended to embrace the German cause, and the intervention was conceived as a Rumanian war with limited objectives, so much so that every effort was made to avoid a declaration of war by Great Britain and, later, by the United States.

However, the most interesting pages of the volume are those referring to the Rumanian attempts to conclude a separate peace.[319] After resigning his office in October, 1941, Cretzianu established close contacts with the leaders of the opposition and particularly with Maniu, the leader of the Peasant party, and in July, 1943, he was sent by the Vice-Premier as Minister to Ankara for the specific purpose of contacting the Anglo-Americans. According to Cretzianu, conditions were still extremely favorable for a Rumanian withdrawal from the war—and, what is more important, for setting up a roadblock against Soviet penetration into the heart of the Balkans. Mihail Antonescu, who had tried to reach an agreement with Rome to this effect some time before,[320] had authorized him to state that the Rumanian government would remain in power to assure continuity but that it was ready to resign just as soon as a new government was organized and approved by the Allies. Antonescu, stating that he was certain of being able to handle the German reaction, seconded this plan, and, if his intentions were to be doubted, the Allies could count on the support of King Michael, whose popularity had increased considerably during the preceding months.

---

[318] "The Soviet Ultimatum to Roumania (26 June, 1940)," Journal of Central European Affairs, January, 1950. This article is based on the documents of the Rumanian Ministry of Foreign Affairs.

[319] "Roumanian Armistice Negotiations: Cairo 1944," Journal of Central European Affairs, October, 1951.

[320] In this context see the reference to the memoirs of the former Italian Minister to Bucharest, Bova Scoppa, pp. 464–65. For an over-all view of Rumanian policy from 1938 to 1944, see Andreas Hillgruber, Hitler, König Carol und Marschall Antonescu (Wiesbaden: Steiner Verlag, 1954).

Now, Cretzianu adds, not only Bucharest but Budapest and Sofia were also making desperate attempts to contact the Anglo-Americans and to conclude separate peace treaties, while in Greece and in Yugoslavia there existed resistance movements that were tying up a number of German divisions. Putting aside the possibility of a Turkish intervention, if the western Allies had opened a front in the Balkans, they would have been able to count on the support of the governments as well as the people of these countries, who were ready to risk everything in order to avoid falling under Soviet domination.

Arriving in Ankara with high hopes in September, 1943, Cretzianu soon realized that the situation was quite different from what he expected to find. His first contacts with the British were inconclusive, and, after the Inter-Allied Conference in Moscow in October, 1943, the British government made it known officially that the negotiations were to be conducted with the three principal allies and that they were to be limited to a discussion of the terms for unconditional surrender. Neither Cretzianu's efforts nor those of the mission led by the former Prime Minister, Barbu Stirbey, who was sent to Ankara by the Rumanian democratic parties with Antonescu's consent, produced the desired results, that is, convinced the Anglo-Americans to occupy Rumania before the arrival of the Soviet troops.

Cretzianu treats these negotiations in such detail that his testimony remains as a fundamental source for a study of the circumstances leading to the armistice of September 12, 1944. His narrative seeks to demonstrate that when the Allies abandoned the idea of a landing in the Balkans, the western powers committed one of the major blunders of the war: an important military error because they were unable to make use of the forces the Balkan states were ready to provide against Hitler; and, above all, a political blunder of incalculable import because the Soviets were permitted to extend their exclusive control over the peoples of southeastern Europe.

In this context it should be recalled that while the Anglo-Americans refused, after the Moscow Conference, to continue discussions with the Rumanians without Soviet participation, the latter opened negotiations with Bucharest without informing the Anglo-Americans. The details of this episode are narrated by Nano,[321] former Rumanian Minister to Stockholm, who was one of the participants, and they are interesting from several points of view.

These contacts were initiated in December, 1943, and were continued with greater emphasis in April, 1944. Therefore, the Soviets began these

[321] F. C. Nano, "The First Soviet Double Cross. A Chapter in the Secret History of World War II," *Journal of Central European Affairs*, October, 1952.

negotiations before the agreement on the spheres of influence in the Balkans, referred to in the comments on Hull's memoirs, was reached. In any event, that accord, despite its provisional nature, certainly could not justify separate negotiations with Bucharest.

It should also be stressed that during the course of the Stockholm negotiations the Soviets indicated that they were not opposed to dealing with the Antonescu government, ignoring the democratic opposition led by Maniu and Bratianu. Moreover, the conditions they offered Antonescu were considerably better than those that were offered to Stirbey at about the same time by the western powers. It does not appear that this was caused by any desire to reach an immediate accord with Bucharest without the participation of the Allies. Rather, the urgency appears to have derived from the projects the Kremlin had developed for the future of Rumania and from the development of a policy that, in the future, would be clearly antagonistic to Great Britain and the United States. Moscow was fully aware of the fact that Maniu and Bratianu represented an active force in Rumania (the Liberal party and the Peasant party had garnered 80 per cent of the vote in the last elections) and that they were anxious to retain close ties with the western democracies. Therefore, Maniu and Bratianu were serious obstacles to a Sovietization of Rumania—obviously already planned by Moscow despite solemn declarations to the contrary—while the Antonescu government, without any real popular support, seemed to be easy to maneuver because its very origins put it at the mercy of the Soviets. This is confirmed by the fact that the attitude maintained by the U.S.S.R. at the very end of the war toward the former German satellite governments was not determined by the previous actions of these governments or by their greater or lesser reflection of democratic principles, but by an evaluation of their capacities to resist future Sovietization.

Finally, reference should be made to the volume by Mihail Antonescu's former secretary, Barbul,[322] which includes several minutes of the meetings of the Rumanian Foreign Minister with Hitler and other Axis personalities; and the contributions of former Ambassador Gheorghe, who comments on his mission to Berlin as King Michael's last representative to that post,[323] and on the *coup d'état* of August 23, 1944, which toppled the Antonescu regime.[324]

[322] Georgiu Barbul, *Mémorial Antonescu; Le troisième homme de l'Axe* (Paris: La Couronne, 1950).
[323] Ion Gheorghe, *Rumänien Weg zum Stelliten Staat* (Heidelberg: Vowinckle, 1952).
[324] "Rumänien hätte das Los Europas zu Wenden Vermocht," *Nation Europa*, February, 1952.

14. THE FINNISH MEMORIALISTS.

a. Tanner.

The volumes by Väinö Tanner, leader of the Social Democratic party, frequently a member of the government, and Minister of Foreign Affairs from 1939–40, occupy a pre-eminent position among the Finnish memoir sources. At the end of the war, Tanner was tried and condemned as one of those responsible for the war against the Soviet Union. This explains the defensive character of his works and the bitterness with which he often judges both men and events. Although his contribution is limited to those events that in the over-all picture of World War II can be considered secondary, it is of indisputable importance on the basis of richness of detail and accuracy of data and, as such, has been received with great interest by scholars.

His most notable work concerns the "Winter War,"[325] the conflict provoked by the Soviet attack on Finland in November, 1939, and concluded by the Peace of Moscow of March 12, 1940, after a heroic resistance by the Finns. On this issue Tanner reveals that as early as 1938 the Soviet government, through its legation secretary in Finland, Yartsev, had begun negotiations with Helsinki for the purpose of obtaining guarantees that Finland would not become the base for a future attack against the Soviet Union. According to Yartsev, the U.S.S.R. feared that Germany might be planning just such an attack, and he therefore made it clear that the Soviet Union would not wait for the enemy to reach the Soviet frontiers but would stop him, fighting on Finnish soil. Consequently, in order to avoid such an eventuality, it was opportune for Finland to stop any attack and, if necessary, to accept Soviet assistance. This would have taken the form of a joint Soviet-Finnish operation for the fortification of the Aaland Islands, a right which would be granted the Soviets by agreement under these circumstances, in addition to Finnish consent for installation of an exclusive Soviet defensive base on another island. In exchange, the Soviets offered to guarantee the Finnish frontiers and also offered the Finns an extremely advantageous trade agreement.

Helsinki rejected these proposals on the grounds that they infringed on Finnish sovereignty and that they violated Finland's neutral policy. The

---

[325] *The Winter War. Finland against Russia, 1939–1940* (Stanford, Calif.: Stanford University Press, 1957).

Soviets then shifted their emphasis to the economic field, hoping to arrive at a favorable agreement by this approach, but this, too, was in vain. Several months later, in March, 1939, the U.S.S.R. renewed the offer with some modifications, proposing that Finland lease to the Soviet Union a group of islands facing Leningrad for defensive purposes. Later, Litvinov stated that the Soviet Union was disposed to exchange part of Soviet Karelia for these islands, but Helsinki's position did not change, and Moscow let the matter drop. The complete silence maintained on these negotiations, at Soviet insistence, deprived western diplomacy of a significant fact with which to evaluate the Soviet preoccupation with Germany and Moscow's objectives. This circumstance affected the attitude of the French and the British during the early stages of their negotiations with the Kremlin and offers startling analogies to the lack of information in London and Paris on the secret German-Polish negotiations on Danzig and the Polish Corridor prior to the guarantee given to Poland.

With the signing of the Nazi-Soviet Pact of August 23, 1939, in which the secret protocol recognized that Finland, along with Latvia and Estonia, were within the Soviet sphere of influence, Moscow lost interest in peaceful negotiations with Helsinki because now the Soviets would only have to wait for the opportune moment to realize their objectives without fear of opposition.

In examining these negotiations in retrospect, Tanner, who participated in them as a member of the Foreign Commission of the Diet, asks himself whether those who criticized the intransigence of the government during the preliminary phase of the negotiations were justified, considering the major amputations suffered by Finland in the Treaty of Moscow of March 12, 1940. In fact, he asserts, such reasoning does not take into account certain decisive considerations. In the first place, the Diet, unaware of the negotiations, would not have accepted so direct an infringement of Finnish sovereignty and so obvious an interference in Finnish foreign policy; second, he asks how one can be sure that once the Soviet Union found Helsinki disposed to compromise, it would not have added further demands for other concessions during the course of the negotiations.

Comparable analogies can be drawn in connection with the negotiations that took place in October and November, 1939, just before the Russo-Finnish War. A study of these negotiations is extremely pertinent to an understanding of the objectives sought by the U.S.S.R. at that time and to a comprehension of Soviet diplomatic methods. Tanner's volume—Tanner shared with Paasikivi the leadership of the Finnish delegation sent to Moscow—confirms the impression that Stalin really intended to reach a peaceful settlement with Finland. The Soviets were anxious to obtain bases in Finnish territory as well as to rectify the Karelian frontier, believed to be necessary for the defense of Leningrad against an eventual German attack, but, for the moment at least, Stalin had no plans for the Sovietization of Finland. His major concern was to resolve the question as soon as possible without provoking complications that could have had an adverse effect on relations with Berlin or that might have led to the outright involvement of the U.S.S.R. in the war then under way between Germany and the western powers. Only after he realized the absolute impossibility of arriving at a peaceful solution of the problem did Stalin consider resolving it by force, and then he was convinced that the overwhelming superiority of the Red army would quickly liquidate the crisis.

The Finnish government had published an important collection of documents on these negotiations in the Blue-White Book of 1940,[326] but Tanner offers a much more detailed and precise version of the events, basing it on a documentation of prime importance (official papers, minutes of the meetings, notes taken during official conversations, etc.), so that his memoirs, even if written in the first person, may be taken as a real diplomatic history of the Winter War. It abounds in significant revelations. The influence of the Finnish leaders on the course of the negotiations is clear. Their attitude contributed in large measure to maintaining the Helsinki government in a position of intransigence because not one of them felt that he could support a compromise that would provoke violent reactions among the people. In this context, the concern over the possible reactions of the public—in the era of open diplomacy—is one of the major problems of statesmen in democratic countries, who are normally given to overestimating the nationalistic drive of the public. The Italians had the same experience in the postwar period with regard to the Trieste question.

In the final phase of the negotiations, Stalin declared that he was disposed to forego his request for a base on the Hanko peninsula if Finland would lease to the Soviets a small group of islands nearby, but this proposal too, which was acceptable to the Finnish military, was rejected by the Helsinki government after consultation with parliamentary leaders.

Tanner's memoirs on the period of the Winter War, during which he was Minister of Foreign Affairs in the Ryti government, become an indispensable source for a study of Finnish relations with Germany, with Sweden, with the western powers, and, from the moment negotiations were begun for a peace treaty, with the Soviet Union. Among the more important data, note should be made of the long negotiations with London

[326] See p. 97.

and Paris for a Franco-British expeditionary force to be sent to the Finnish Front. These negotiations were seriously undertaken only in February, 1940, after the first unofficial contacts for an armistice with the Soviets had been made, and they were concluded without positive results, not only because of the opposition of Norway and Sweden to the transit of these troops across their territories, but also because the Finnish government believed that the acceptance of such an expeditionary force would make it extremely difficult to arrive at a compromise with the U.S.S.R. and, moreover, it would involve Finland in a war between the Great Powers.

Tanner is extremely critical of the Swedish attitude. He accuses the Swedish government of shielding itself behind a wall of rigid neutrality which later, and under other circumstances, it conveniently disregarded. Tanner is also very bitter about the Swedish public declaration that it did not intend to support Finland, a factor which may have induced the Soviets to increase their territorial demands in the negotiations for the treaty of March 12, 1940.

While the first criticism of Sweden does not appear to be wholly justified because Stockholm cannot be blamed for taking the steps necessary to preserve Swedish neutrality, the fact must also be recognized that, once it became apparent that there was a possibility of a compromise peace between Finland and the Soviet Union, the Swedes did their very best to terminate a situation that threatened their neutrality without demonstrating excessive concern over the price Finland would have to pay. During the final phases of the negotiations, Stockholm exerted great pressure on the Finns to accept the Soviet conditions, and, in those circumstances, it can be said that the Swedish attitude did not reflect any particularly friendly concern for Finnish interests.

Furthermore, at the time of publication Tanner's book contained important revelations on Finland's relations with Germany and on the repeated efforts made by Finland to induce Germany to act as mediator in the conflict. The question—which has elements of interest in the area of Soviet-German relations—may now be examined in the documents of the Wilhelmstrasse and in Blücher's memoirs, but Tanner's account retains its importance because it reflects the Finnish point of view and adds many important details. Moreover, it offers a useful comparison with the German documents.

Regarding the negotiations preceding the Peace of Moscow, Tanner's memoirs continue to be the most detailed and precise source available to scholars, both from the point of view of the diplomatic activity and the discussions between the political and military leaders in Helsinki.

Less well known because it has not been translated into a more generally understood language is another volume by Tanner, published in 1952.[327] The author, who, after the Treaty of Moscow, was forced to resign as Minister of Foreign Affairs (in August, 1940) and returned to the government only after the renewal of hostilities against the Soviet Union in June, 1941, devotes his attention in this work to the attempts made by Finland to leave the war once it became clear that there was no possible hope of a victory in the east. According to Tanner—and his assertions are confirmed in Mannerheim's memoirs—such a decision was reached in February, 1943. This decision was the basis for a whole series of initiatives, beginning in March, 1943, when Helsinki received the American offer to act as mediator to arrive at a compromise peace between Helsinki and Moscow. On that occasion the Foreign Minister, Ramsay, went to Berlin to sound out the German reaction, and he learned that there was not the slightest chance of Finland leaving the war with Germany's consent. Moreover, he was presented with a request to sign an agreement that would oblige the two countries not to sign a separate peace.

Only in November, 1943, did the first unofficial contacts take place with the Soviet Union. The Finnish desire for peace was strengthened not only by the disastrous outcome of the operations on the Russian Front but also—according to Tanner—by the Italian armistice, which was considered to be the clearest symptom of the imminent collapse of the Hitlerian system. However, it is significant that the Finns even in this situation established a return to the 1939 frontiers as a precondition to peace negotiations, a fact that led to the interruption of the negotiations. They were reopened in February, 1944, and this time in more precise form, first through the Minister of the U.S.S.R. in Stockholm, Madam Kollontay, and then through an envoy to Moscow, the former Finnish Minister to the Soviet Union, Paasikivi, who toward the end of March had two conferences with Molotov and received a list of the major conditions for peace.

This attempt also proved fruitless. According to Tanner, the Soviet demands, taken one by one, could have been regarded favorably, but in their entirety they were unacceptable. Apparently, the basic motives that led the Finnish leaders to reject the conditions can be reduced to two. First, the Finnish statesmen had no faith in Soviet promises and feared that, once the German forces were withdrawn and the Finnish army was reduced to a peacetime basis, the Red army would occupy the country, perhaps on some pretext such as an internal disorder fomented by the Communists themselves. Second, it was not difficult to foresee that the Germans would react to a separate peace by occupying the key positions in the country and

[327] *Suomen tie rauhaan 1943–1944* [Finland's Road toward Peace, 1943–1944] (Helsinki: Tammi, 1952).

installing a puppet government, just as they had done a few days earlier in Hungary when they became aware of the negotiations between Kállay and the Anglo-Americans. Again, according to Tanner, the Soviet demands were rejected not because Helsinki had any illusions about the outcome of the war, but because their acceptance, at that time, would have reduced the country to chaos. Nevertheless, the Finnish government would never have abandoned the intention of concluding peace with the Soviet Union as soon as possible.

Within certain limits, this thesis may be accepted as logical, but it leads Tanner to underestimate the importance that the Soviet offensive, launched in the summer of 1944, had on the decisions made by Helsinki, an offensive that was stopped only with great difficulty and with further German assistance. This attack had an important role in convincing the new government in Finland to ask for an armistice toward the end of August.

Tanner is responsible for other volumes, some published during his imprisonment and some appearing after his release in November, 1948. Two of these are especially noteworthy. The first[328] has the birth of Finnish independence as its subject and covers the period March, 1917–July, 1919. It also contains references to Finnish relations with Russia, although the emphasis is on internal problems, the struggle between the Whites and the Reds, and the institutional question. The second[329] is more directly pertinent to diplomatic history and includes numerous details based on an important documentation of the negotiations leading to the Peace of Tartu of October, 1920, between Finland and the Soviet Union, negotiations in which Tanner participated as a delegate.

b. The Other Finnish Memoir Sources.

Important testimony has been left by Marshal Mannerheim,[330] commander of the Finnish forces in the war of independence against the Bolsheviks in 1918, supreme commander during the two wars against the Soviet Union (1939–40 and 1941–44), and, in August, 1944, appointed President of the Republic. Thus the Mannerheim name is linked to all of the major events in modern Finnish history, and his memoirs covering his

[328] *Kuinka se oikein tapahtui?* [What Really Happened?] (Helsinki: Tammi, 1948).
[329] *Tarton rauha. Sen syntyvaiheet ja-vaikeudet* [The Peace of Tartu. Origins and Difficulties] (Helsinki: Tammi, 1949).
[330] Carl Gustav Mannerheim, *The Memoirs of Marshal Mannerheim* (New York: Dutton, 1954).

entire life must be considered, given the author's position, as an extremely valuable source.

The first part of the volume is devoted to the emergence of the Finnish state, and, notwithstanding the fact that it is essentially an account of internal and military developments, it includes pertinent data on diplomatic activity following the war. The fact that the struggle against the Bolsheviks was aided by a German expeditionary corps and that, later, a plan was advanced to offer the crown to a German prince put Finland in the difficult position of being considered by the victorious powers as a German creation. In turn, this situation created the urgent necessity of close Finnish rapport with Paris and London to gain immediate recognition for Finland in order to prevent the Finnish question from being discussed at the peace conference, where the whole issue of independence would have encountered the stiff opposition of the Russian exiles, led by Sazonov. Moreover, the situation was further complicated by difficulties with Sweden over the Aaland Islands. In this critical circumstance, Mannerheim was sent on missions to Stockholm, Paris, and London to resolve the problems, and his account of these diplomatic activities are the most important part of the volume.

However, scholars have shown keen interest in the chapters on World War II. Because of his personal prestige, Mannerheim was kept informed of the government's decisions and was consulted by the government—and his opinions often had a significant influence. His memoirs, although largely devoted to military matters, contain frequent references to political and diplomatic events. Therefore, it was to be expected that the memoirs would furnish useful data on the Finnish position in the war between the Great Powers, a position that was unique at best and foreign to the ideological basis of the conflict as described by the propaganda of the belligerents. In fact, the problem was not created by Finland's intervention in the war. It originated in the "strange alliance" concluded between Great Britain and the U.S.S.R. to resist the immediate peril. Nevertheless, the Finns have always insisted that the fact that they fought beside the Germans was purely accidental and that the war against the Soviet Union of June, 1941, was merely a "continuation" of the Winter War. This thesis, on which Mannerheim adds numerous details, is confirmed in that the Finnish High Command consistently refused to launch an offensive against Leningrad as the Germans requested and that, once the frontiers of 1939 or those positions deemed vital to Finland's defense were reached, the Finnish offensive was halted, despite the technical ability of the Finnish armed forces to extend it further.

Admittedly, the Finnish intervention had unique characteristics, not only because of the absence of a common ideological basis with Germany or because of the limited nature of its military operations but also because of the precedent established by the Winter War and the position taken by Finland toward the western powers, with whom Helsinki always sought to avoid a break in relations. However, it should be noted that the characteristics of a "parallel war," with respect to the German attack on the U.S.S.R., were progressively accentuated as the war went on, for the very obvious reason that it was necessary to differentiate between the Finnish and the German positions when it became apparent that a German victory was no longer possible.

Mannerheim's description of Finland's military-political situation during the summer of 1944 is one of the most interesting aspects of his memoirs. In contrast to Tanner, Mannerheim regards the Soviet offensive of that period as decisive. This offensive, Mannerheim observes, was not militarily justified because the Finnish front was clearly a secondary one and the outcome of operations in this sector would be determined by the results of the attack on Germany. The only possible explanation for it was that the Soviet Union intended to occupy all of Finland before the end of the war, that is, before a new world order could prevent it. It was precisely for this reason, Mannerheim affirms, that the Finnish leaders decided to sign the much discussed Ryti-Von Ribbentrop Accord of July, 1944. The Finns intended to arrive at a negotiated peace with the Soviets as soon as possible, but a preliminary condition to reopening these talks was resistance to the Soviet offensive. To be sure, the accord tied the Finns even more closely to the Reich because it included the obligation not to conclude a separate peace, but in return it assured Finland of the aid necessary to prevent a military collapse, which at that moment was the most pressing need. According to Mannerheim, at his suggestion it was decided to conclude the accord by a simple exchange of letters because these would commit only President Ryti and not the Finnish people. However, this thesis is not very convincing because Von Blücher's and Tanner's testimony indicate that the exchange of letters for the accord was suggested by the Germans in order to avoid the expected resistance of the Finnish Parliament to a formal accord. In any event, the fact remains that the majority of the Finns considered the Ryti-Von Ribbentrop Accord to be a contingent necessity for future negotiations with the U.S.S.R. This was confirmed in that as soon as the front was stabilized, the Finns requested an armistice.

This request was presented toward the end of August, 1944. On August 5 Mannerheim was elected President of the Republic, which gave him supreme control of both civil and military affairs and left him the authority to conclude an armistice. His account of the last phase of the war and of the conflict that developed when the German forces in Lapland refused to leave the country was expected to be of major importance, but the author's narrative on these events is rather general, certainly much less precise and detailed than those by Tanner and Erfurth.

On the Winter War of 1939–40, the memoirs of Juho Niukkanen[331] should also be noted. He was a member of the Agrarian party and Minister of Defense in the Ryti Cabinet, and in the government he represented the intransigents, refusing to the very end to agree to the acceptance of the Soviet demands, and, after the conclusion of the Treaty of Moscow, resigning in protest. His volume is entirely devoted to the Winter War and is a well-documented argument against Tanner, whom he accuses of failing to resist Soviet pressure with sufficient energy, mentioning in particular his failure to accept the aid offered by Great Britain and France to continue the war against the U.S.S.R.

Important elements of interest are to be found in the volume by Carl Olaf Frietsch,[332] a deputy representing the Swedish minority in the Diet, who during the "continuation of the war" was one of the most active supporters of the movement to end the war with the Soviets as soon as possible. His narrative ends with August, 1943, and emphasizes the Finnish politico-parliamentary situation rather than diplomacy (he was a member of the Diet's Commission on Foreign Affairs) and the activities of the so-called "opposition group favoring peace," the group that, in January, 1943, brought together those elements favoring an immediate peace with the Soviet Union.

15. THE SWEDISH AND NORWEGIAN MEMORIALISTS.

a. Dahlerus.

The Swedish industrialist Birger Dahlerus found himself playing a rather important role in the negotiations that took place during the summer of 1939 aimed at resolving the Polish-German crisis. A personal friend of Goering and well known in British political circles, he conducted a series of unofficial missions to London and Berlin in an attempt to find a basis for an agreement between the two countries. This episode was revealed during the

[331] *Talvisodan puolustusministeri kertoo* [The Minister of Defense during the Winter War Narrates] (Helsinki: Söderström, 1951).

[332] *Finlands Odesar 1939–1943* [Finland's Odyssey] (Helsinki: Söderström, 1945).

Nuremberg trials, and it immediately aroused considerable discussion on the effectiveness of the action taken with such good will by Dahlerus, who, unskilled in the techniques of diplomacy, sought to give the negotiations the qualities of a business deal. On the whole, it can be concluded that this interesting episode had little tangible effect on the decisions of Hitler and Von Ribbentrop, who probably regarded it only from the restricted viewpoint of its being a contribution to the action designed by them to isolate Poland diplomatically within the framework of the policy determined as early as May 23, 1939. However, even so circumscribed, Dahlerus' activity offers a number of interesting elements for a more exact historical evaluation of a series of important episodes, and the Swedish industrialist's memoirs,[333] from various points of view, are a source of considerable significance. The revelations they contain may be classified in three large categories: German policy toward Italy, the general crisis of the summer of 1939, and the attitudes of various groups in Germany on these matters.

Regarding the Reich's policy toward Italy, three points merit serious attention. On August 7, 1939, addressing a group of British leaders assembled in conference in Sönke Nissen Koog in an attempt to find a basis for an enduring Anglo-German understanding, Goering declared that at the time of the Italo-Ethiopian crisis Germany offered to support British sanctions against Italy in return for a free hand in Germany's relations with Austria; in other words, England should avoid blocking the Austro-German *Anschluss*. At the Chancellery, during the night of August 26, Hitler explained his project for an understanding with the British to Dahlerus, which, as is known, included an alliance between London and Berlin. During the course of the conversation, Goering added, with Hitler's consent, that the idea of the alliance also implied that Germany would aid England against Italy in the event that Great Britain became involved in a conflict with Italy over their interests in the Mediterranean or elsewhere. Goering was to return to the same subject the following day. On August 28, the Marshal made another declaration of extreme importance concerning Italy: "Whatever happens, Italy will remain neutral in such a conflict." This is a truly surprising statement. In order to understand its precise significance, it is necessary to conceive of it in terms of the policy of "raising," as in a poker game, employed by Von Ribbentrop in dealing with Great Britain, the success of which was dependent on London's believing, up to the last minute, that Italy would immediately enter the war on the side of Germany. For all practical purposes, Ciano's destiny was decided at that time when, after the French and British declaration of war, Von

---

[333] *The Last Attempt* (London: Hutchinson, 1948).

Ribbentrop openly accused the Fascist Foreign Minister of having informed the British of the Italian decision to remain neutral before the
outbreak of the war. Therefore, Goering's statements not only have the
value of proving that the Italians were not the only ones guilty of
indiscretions, but may also be decisively important to an evaluation of the
sincerity of his efforts for peace, in contrast to Von Ribbentrop's policy. This
leads to the very heart of the question of the various internal political
inclinations of the Nazi leaders. Goering struggled valiantly to avoid a new
military adventure. He acted with resolution toward this aim, without,
however, going beyond the limits of discipline and subordination to Hitler,
who listened principally to the advice of Von Ribbentrop, particularly after
the latter's success in the negotiations with Moscow.

Dahlerus' memoirs are especially worth while for a variety of points on
the general nature of the summer crisis of 1939. Among them are his
references to the meetings and messages of Halifax, Chamberlain, Hitler,
and Goering, and to concrete proposals made to London on the Polish-
German and British-German problems. Suffice it here to note that Dahlerus' volume offers, at last, the long-awaited explanation of the mystery
regarding the communication of Hitler's last proposals on Poland to the
British Foreign Office. As is known, Von Ribbentrop did no more than
hurriedly read these to Henderson, refusing to give the British Ambassador
a copy on the pretext that, since the Polish plenipotentiary failed to appear
by August 30, they were no longer applicable. Henderson did not understand more than three words of the text and yet was able to communicate its
exact tenor to London. It was Goering who authorized Dahlerus to
communicate the exact details of the text by telephone to the British
Embassy Counsellor, Forbes.

In conclusion, attention should be called to Beck's telegram to Lipski on
August 31, in which the Polish Foreign Minister authorized the Ambassador to contact Von Ribbentrop at the Wilhelmstrasse, without, however,
initiating any negotiations. This telegram was decoded and communicated
to Goering even before it was received by Lipski, and its text differs
noticeably from that published in the Polish White Book. It undoubtedly
had considerable effect on Hitler's decision to precipitate the action.

b. The Other Swedish and Norwegian Memoir Sources.

To another Swede, Count Folke Bernadotte, up to that time removed
from the world of politics, we owe our knowledge[334] of the attempt made *in*

---

[334] *La Fine. I miei negoziati in Germania nella primavera del 1945 e i loro sviluppi
politici* (Milan: Gentile, 1946).

extremis by Berlin to conclude a separate armistice with the western powers. In April, 1945, Bernadotte was in Germany on a mission for the Red Cross. Himmler, with whom Bernadotte had contacts for reasons pertaining to his mission, informed him that he was studying the possibilities of a capitulation on the western front, to be effected as soon as he was able to act without betraying his oath of loyalty to Hitler.

On April 23, convinced that the Führer's end was imminent, Himmler called in Bernadotte and officially informed him of his decision, urging him to get the Swedish Foreign Minister, Gunther, to act on the matter. He made it clear that he realized the great difficulties involved in reaching a successful solution but that he was firmly determined to spare millions of Germans from Soviet occupation. Bernadotte, while declaring himself convinced that Great Britain and the United States would reject the offer, agreed to transmit Himmler's message to the Swedish government, which in turn transmitted it to London and Washington. The Anglo-Americans replied that Germany's surrender must be complete and on all fronts. Otherwise the offensive would continue until total victory was achieved.

The episode was confirmed by the sixth volume of Churchill's memoirs, by a Swedish government publication,[335] and by the published Stalin correspondence with Churchill and Roosevelt (the latter had immediately informed Stalin of all of the details). The documents prove that Bernadotte's account is exact in all details, which is unusual for a memoir source, although it is less complete than Churchill's memoirs, since the latter had greater freedom in expressing himself on the action of the Swedish Foreign Minister and added an account of his own role in the matter.

Among the Swedish memoirs, mention should be made of the recollections of Erik Palmstierna,[336] Minister to London from 1920 to 1937, covering almost the entire period between the world wars, and of the memoirs of the Social Democrat Ernst Wigforss,[337] who was also a member of government. The latter are especially useful for the period 1932–49, covered in the third volume.

The memoirs of Norwegian statesmen are even more restricted. Both the volume by the Minister of Foreign Affairs, Halvdan Koht[338] and that of the President of Parliament, Carl J. Hambro,[339] refer to the April, 1940, German invasion of Norway and provide some data on the events during the months that followed. However, both books were published in the

[335] Kungl. Utrikesdepartementet, *Förhandlingarna 1945 om Svensk Intervention i Norge och Danmark* (Stockholm: Norstedt, 1958).
[336] *Atskelliga Egenheter* (Stockholm: Tidens Förlag, 1952).
[337] Ernst Wigforss, *Minnen* (3 vols.; Stockholm: Tidens Förlag, 1951–54).
[338] *Norway: Neutral and Invaded* (New York: Macmillan, 1941).
[339] *I Saw It Happen in Norway* (New York: Appleton-Century, 1940).

period 1940–41 primarily for reasons of propaganda, and they are of limited historical interest.

It should also be noted that among the Scandinavian countries, no memoirs have been published by Danish statesmen and diplomats.

16. THE BELGIAN AND DUTCH MEMORIALISTS.

a. Van Zuylen.

An essential source for the study of Belgian foreign policy between the two world wars is provided by the work of Ambassador van Zuylen.[340] This volume can be defined as a memoir source only with difficulty because, while it is evident that the author has drawn liberally from his personal recollections, the account is primarily a historical study based on the documents of the Foreign Ministry. On the other hand, the Belgian diplomat did not intend to trace the complete history of Belgian policy but preferred to focus his attention on several questions—and this is what underlines the personal character of the narrative—selected from among those he was best able to follow as Director of Political Affairs for the ministry.

Van Zuylen contributes much new information on the negotiations leading to the Franco-Belgian military alliance of 1920. At the end of World War I, Belgium had declared that it no longer considered itself bound to the perpetual neutrality assigned to it by the treaties of 1839, a unilateral action that remained even after the Paris peace conference, where no decision was taken on the matter. In that circumstance, it was Britain who insisted that Belgian neutrality be maintained, and the motives for this attitude are easy to understand. London feared that, once Belgium was released from her obligations, it would establish very close ties with France, thereby reinforcing French hegemony on the Continent. In any event, British opposition did not prevent Belgium from reconfirming the abrogation of the international statute of 1839, a fact that logically raised the problem of finding new methods to guarantee Belgium's independence through agreements with the interested powers.

For a time, the problem appeared to have been resolved by the conclusion of the Franco-American and the Franco-British treaties of guarantee of June 28, 1919, in which an attack against Belgium was considered an attack against France. However, the American Senate's failure to ratify the treaty

[340] Baron Pierre van Zuylen, *Les mains libres. Politique extérieure de la Belgique 1914–1940* (Brussels: L'Édition Universelle; Paris: Desclée de Brouwer, 1950).

destroyed this entire complex, and Brussels' successive requests that France and Great Britain reaffirm the guarantees given to Belgium by the treaties of 1839 encountered London's refusal, which insisted on Belgium's return to a policy of permanent neutrality as a prerequisite to any agreement.

Nevertheless, the possibility of an accord with France remained. According to Van Zuylen, the French had mentioned the possibility of such an accord as early as September, 1916, when Cambon, then Secretary-General of the Quai d'Orsay, made it known to the Belgian Minister, Hymans, that at the end of the war an economic and military union between the two countries would be desirable. From that time on, the subject was repeatedly raised by the diplomats of the Third Republic, who made it clear that only after Belgium had agreed to a military accord with Paris could it count on French support in resolving the problems that were of concern to Brussels. In the light of these precedents, the assertion that France was induced to seek an agreement with Belgium only after the failure to get the American and British treaties of guarantee is open to question. In fact, it seems that French security requirements were not the dominant factors in the matter and that the military accord was viewed by responsible French leaders as simply a means to reinforce and extend French supremacy on the Continent after the victory.

This interpretation appears to be further confirmed by the course taken by the negotiations. According to Van Zuylen, in a first plan developed by Marshal Foch in May, 1920, it was emphasized that a war with Germany was impossible as long as the Rhineland remained occupied but that during this period it was imperative to be prepared to "advance in order to enforce the terms of the Treaty of Versailles." In this statement, the aims of the French General Staff become clear; it was not a question of strengthening the Franco-Belgian defense system—a German attack was considered impossible for a long time to come—but, rather, of obtaining Belgian participation in coercive action against Germany in the event that the latter refused to observe the terms of the Versailles treaty. The military accords camouflaged, and not very effectively, French political aims: to bind Belgium to the intransigent policy adopted by Paris in direct defiance of London's moderate one.

Van Zuylen affirms that the Belgian government continued to reiterate that its aims were limited to the defense of the national territory. However, the fact remains that the treaty signed in September, 1920, was worded in such a way as to offer several interpretations. Without discussing the details of the treaty here, it should be noted that it could hardly be considered a simple technical accord because, if not in the letter, certainly in spirit, it contained obligations very similar to those of an alliance and it was considered as such by Paris where, from the beginning, it was evident that the French sought to give the treaty the widest possible interpretation. In fact, as confirmed by the memoirs of Reynaud, Flandin, and Gamelin, both the French government and the General Staff maintained that the alliance with Belgium was not to be considered effective only in the event of a German aggression but that it could also be invoked in a war against Germany in which France intervened on behalf of her eastern allies (Poland and Czechoslovakia). To be sure, this explanation is questionable, but the mere fact that it was so formulated demonstrated the dangerous implications contained in the treaty.

The motives that induced responsible Belgian leaders to accept the treaty remain to be clarified. Security requirements were not sufficient justification for the accord because the complete evacuation of the Rhineland was scheduled only for January, 1935. Against the treaty lay the fact that its acceptance meant that Belgium abandoned the position of equilibrium which Albert I's ministers always insisted should be maintained between London and Paris. Relations with London, in fact, became strained, especially after the Franco-Belgian occupation of the Ruhr, effected despite the opposition of Great Britain, and, therefore, Belgium saw herself precluded from the function of catalyst which she had heretofore been able to perform with efficacy between the two western powers.

Thus the accord appeared to have many negative features which were not offset by any appreciable advantages. Van Zuylen admits, after a careful examination of the documents in the archives of the Belgian Foreign Ministry, that the decision of the Belgian government is not easily explained. He suggests the hypothesis that Hymans was "looking for a success," a hypothesis that may contain some truth but that alone is insufficient as an explanation of what occurred. Indeed, on the basis of the French attitude during the negotiations, it seems, rather, that the decision of the Belgian ministers was determined by the fear of seeing France extend her exclusive influence over Luxemburg. To this factor should be added the Belgian hope for French support in the negotiations with Holland for a revision of the Escaut regime and in resisting the pressures of the Belgian General Staff, who saw in the treaty a good reason for seeking to block the reduction in military expenditures advocated by the Socialists.

Regardless of how often Brussels repeated that the accord did not limit Belgium's freedom of action, it was clearly evident that Albert I's ministers recognized the perils inherent in the new situation. This is borne out by the repeated attempts to arrive at a similar accord with the British and by the negotiations conducted with Paris to limit the implications of the 1920 treaty.

Concrete results were obtained from London only in 1934. The Brussels government had proposed a convention that would make the application of the guarantee contained in the Locarno Pacts more nearly automatic and more rapid. In substance, it was an attempt to eliminate any doubt about the fact that, in the event of an attack on Belgium, Great Britain would immediately come to its defense and, at the same time, to acquire indirectly a greater freedom of action with respect to France, from whom strong pressure was to be expected if Germany attacked either Poland or Czechoslovakia. But the British government refused to assume a formal obligation and limited itself to two public declarations, by Sir John Simon and Stanley Baldwin, that the independence and integrity of Belgium were of vital interest to Great Britain. It was not what the Belgians had hoped to gain. However, the firmness of the two statements constituted London's assumption of a position that could hardly be misunderstood.

Van Zuylen was one of the principal figures in these negotiations, and he comments on them in great detail. Among other things, he recalls that Sir John Simon frequently suggested that Belgium sign a nonaggression pact with Germany. According to the British Foreign Minister, such a pact would be extremely important because it would induce Hitler to reconfirm a number of obligations assumed by the pre-Nazi governments. But, Van Zuylen observes, the suggestion seemed to be inspired primarily by fear that the projected convention with Brussels would be interpreted as a hostile act toward Germany. London was disposed to assume new obligations toward Belgium, but only on condition that the latter would then reequilibrate her position by signing an accord with Germany. However, in practice this suggestion was impossible to realize, given the attitude of the Belgian public. Therefore, the Belgian government was obliged to refuse the terms, a refusal that, in all probability, had a considerable influence on the British decision to abandon the projected convention.

Conversations with the French were also undertaken for the purpose of clarifying the significance of the 1920 accord, which, after the Locarno Pacts, many demanded should be abrogated. A decisive push toward clarification was provided, Van Zuylen states, by Marshal Pétain's statements. In October, 1930, the Marshal told the Belgian Ambassador to Paris that, in case of war with Germany, the French army would cross Belgian territory with or without Belgian consent. After having informed the Belgian government of this colloquy, which apparently ended in a violent argument, Baron Gaffier warned that if the Marshal had expressed himself rather rudely, his thinking on the matter was shared by many in Paris and particularly by Poincaré, who affirmed that Belgium should join France in the event that the latter attacked Germany in defense of its eastern allies.

Thus, early in 1931, the Belgian government informed Paris that military co-operation between the two countries was regulated exclusively by the terms of Article 4 of the treaty of mutual assistance signed at Locarno, which was the equivalent of saying that the obligations of the military accord were considered to have been absorbed by the Locarno agreements.

The French reaction revealed that the ideas of Pétain and Poincaré were largely shared by the Quai d'Orsay. The Secretary-General of the Ministry, Léger, informed his Belgian colleague that the accords of 1920 contained three obligations not included in the Locarno Pacts: that of immediate mobilization in the event that Germany mobilized; that of entrusting the defense of the Belgian coasts to the French navy; and that of co-ordinating a joint defense of Luxemburg's eastern frontier. As Van Zuylen points out, the reference to these obligations was extremely significant. It involved two hypotheses: either German mobilization constituted a prelude to a German attack on France or Belgium, and in this case the Locarno agreements would be invoked, or German mobilization was a prelude to an attack against one of France's eastern allies, and in this event Belgium did not believe that it was committed to any specific action. This point was the source of brief but difficult negotiations which terminated in an exchange of letters containing a formula that is not entirely clear. However, the formula specified that the obligations assumed in the 1920 accords did not go beyond those specified in the Locarno treaties and in the League of Nations compact.

The Franco-Belgian military accord was finally abrogated in March, 1936, on the eve of Hitler's remilitarization of the Rhineland. The request for an increase in military spending, in view of the worsening international situation, met with the parliamentary opposition of the Socialists and the Flemish right wing, which blamed the need for further military expenditures on the existence of the treaty with France. In order to remove this obstacle, the Brussels government decided to ask France to join in a declaration terminating the 1920 agreement, a request to which France agreed early in March, only when it became clear that a refusal would mean that Belgium would denounce the pact unilaterally.

These factors should be kept in mind when we seek to consider the attitudes of the Belgian government and public in all of their nuances during the Rhineland crisis. Undoubtedly, the return to a completely independent policy of action announced by King Leopold in October, 1936, was essentially determined by the failure of the western powers to react to Hitler's *coup de force* and by the altered strategic situation following the remilitarization of the Rhineland, which, in case of a Franco-

German conflict, threatened to turn Belgium into the main theater of war. However, it should be kept in mind that before the crisis ever developed, Belgian public opinion had already manifested strong neutralist tendencies, and the campaign against the military alliance with France, at least during the last phase, was a clear illustration of this fact.

Van Zuylen's account provides important details on the negotiations entered into by the signatories of the Locarno Pacts in the aftermath of the Rhineland crisis. His account is especially significant concerning the talks that preceded the Franco-British declaration of April 24 and the German statement of October 13, 1937 (announcements that were in many ways parallel), whereby each of the three powers guaranteed to aid Belgium in the event that it was attacked, while the French and the British also absolved Belgium of her Locarno obligations, thus recognizing Brussels' new "independent position."

The memoirs assume a more personal tone when Van Zuylen refers to the events of the first phase of World War II, between September, 1939, and the beginning of the German offensive in the west, May 10, 1940. The data furnished by the author permit a reconstruction of the atmosphere in Brussels during those dramatic days and contribute to a better understanding of the various desperate attempts of the Belgian government to eliminate the aggression menacing Belgium. For example, Van Zuylen confirms that the offer of November 6, 1939, made by the Belgian and Dutch sovereigns to use their good offices was not aimed at facilitating a compromise peace, which no one in The Hague or Brussels believed possible, and for this reason a public appeal was to be avoided. Instead, its objective was to make it morally impossible for Hitler to attack the Low Countries at the very time when they were spearheading a peace move. On the other hand, the Belgian diplomat's account of the Belgian efforts in London and Paris to develop a plan of common action in the event of a German attack appears to be somewhat evasive. Perhaps the author preferred to avoid mentioning those facts that would reveal an aspect of Belgian policy that was not entirely neutral in character. On the other hand, it should be noted that such contacts were primarily of a military and technical nature and, therefore, largely handled by agencies other than the Ministry of Foreign Affairs.

b. The Other Belgian and Dutch Memoir Sources.

Chronologically, the first of the other Belgian memoir sources worthy of mention is the volume by Baron Beyens[341] on his mission to the Holy See

[341] *Quatre ans à Rome 1921–1926. Fin du Pontificat du Benôit XV. Pie XI. Le début du fascisme* (Paris: Plon, 1934).

from 1921 to 1926. The work, published in 1934, reflects the author's need to maintain the strictest reserve in his narrative, and with the exception of several references to the Pope, the emphasis is largely on Italian internal affairs during Fascism's early years rather than on the mission per se.

The drama of the Belgians is reflected in the memoirs of Ambassador Davignon,[342] who, on two occasions, in 1914 as a young attaché and in 1940 as Ambassador to Berlin, was compelled to witness the invasion of his country by the Germans. His account of his last mission to Berlin is a worthy companion of the François-Poncet and Henderson memoirs, not only for the value of his revelations—largely concentrated on the period between the outbreak of the war and the German offensive in the west—but also for the importance of the observations reconstructing the environment in the Third Reich and the roles of the German political leaders in Berlin's diplomatic spheres. Appointed Minister to Berlin immediately after the Rhineland crisis (the Belgian legation was raised to the rank of Embassy in November, 1938), Davignon was promptly called upon to handle the delicate Belgian-German negotiations culminating in the German announcement of October 13, 1937, referred to above. His version of these negotiations coincides almost exactly with that presented by Van Zuylen and is extremely useful for a comprehension of the negotiations and for an objective evaluation of the significance of the German declaration, whose tenor was to open the way to several critical judgments and to a number of debates on the action of the Belgian government. The most important revelations in the book concern the period immediately following the outbreak of the war, when the Belgian Embassy in Berlin found itself playing a major role, particularly for the information it garnered concerning German military plans. This information was unusually accurate, as was proved by the documents presented at the Nuremberg trials, and was to have a decisive effect on Belgian diplomatic activity during the winter of 1939–40.

A remarkably significant source is the memoirs of General van Overstraeten,[343] aide-de-camp to Albert I and to Leopold III. It is largely written in the form of a diary, and not only is the testimony of extraordinary value (often touching on elements rarely discussed in official documents), but the volume also contains a collection of unpublished documents of unparalleled importance. For example, it is the best source available for a study of the contacts between the French and Belgian general staffs during the "phoney war" and provides a full picture of the efforts of London and

---

[342] Vicomte Jacques Davignon, *Berlin 1936–1940. Souvenirs d'une mission* (Paris and Brussels: Les Éditions Universitaires, 1951).

[343] *Albert I, Léopold III. Vingt ans de politique militaire belge 1920–1940* (Paris: Desclée de Brouwer, 1949).

Paris to induce King Leopold's government to permit a concentration of British and French troops on Belgian soil as a defensive measure.

Insofar as the Dutch memoir sources are concerned, the most important contribution was made by the former Minister of Foreign Affairs, Van Kleffens,[344] who was appointed in August, 1939, and directed Dutch foreign policy throughout the war period as a member of the government in exile. However, his recollections are limited to the period preceding the German attack, and, having been published during the war, they princi pally reflect the propaganda needs of the moment.

17. THE SPANISH MEMORIALISTS.

a. Serrano Suñer.

Despite the very limited number of recent Spanish memoirs, there are two that are highly worthy of attention. Together they cover the entire period of World War II, although the volumes differ widely depending on the importance and the personalities of the authors.

The first of these is the volume by Ramon Serrano Suñer,[345] Minister of the Interior from 1937 to October, 1940, and then Foreign Minister until September, 1942. The work is openly apologetic but important, whether for an understanding of the author's beliefs and the politico-doctrinal premises on which he based his actions, or for what he reveals on various aspects of Spanish-German relations during the first phase of the conflict. The central theme of the narrative is the protracted negotiations during the summer and fall of 1940 for Spanish intervention on the side of the Axis. Serrano Suñer provides ample detail on only a part of these negotiations, limiting his references to his two journeys to Berlin in September and October and ignoring the other contacts between Spain and Germany, including the Hitler-Franco meeting at Hendaye. Therefore, the picture drawn is not nearly as accurate as that which can be reconstructed from the documents published in the German General Collection.

Regarding his trip to Germany in September, 1940, Serrano Suñer affirms that his purpose was to find out what Hitler's intentions were and to assure him that Spain would maintain a policy of benevolent neutrality toward the Axis. Thus, it was an exploratory mission, not designed as a

---

[344] Eelco Nicolaas van Kleffens, *The Rape of the Netherlands* (London: Hodder and Stoughton, 1940).

[345] *Entre Hendaya y Gibraltar. Noticia y reflexión, frente a una leyenda, sobre nuestra politica en dos guerras* (Madrid: Ediciones Españolas, 1947).

prelude to intervention but simply to promote a closer understanding between the two powers that would permit Spain to maintain her nonbelligerent status without provoking a dangerous crisis, given the presence of German divisions on the Pyrénées.

With this, Serrano Suñer elects to ignore the fact that on June 17, 1940, the Madrid government had approached Berlin and Rome with a proposal to begin negotiations leading to Spain's intervention and that, even after Berlin's negative reaction to this suggestion, Madrid continued to maintain an attitude clearly favorable toward participation in the conflict.

In effect, the Spanish leaders believed—along with almost everyone else —that Great Britain was on the verge of collapse, and, while they were fully aware of their country's weakness, they believed that an intervention *in extremis* was possible and thereby would guarantee Spain territorial advantages at the expense of Great Britain (Gibraltar) and France (Morocco).

While it is probably true that toward the middle of September the faith of the Spanish government in a quick German victory faded because of the German failure to effect a landing in England, it should not be forgotten that Serrano Suñer represented the element among the Falangist leaders who strongly supported Spain's intervention. This leads one to believe that, perhaps in partial contrast to Franco, Serrano Suñer went to Berlin with the idea of arranging the terms for Spain's intervention. It is certain that the request for Spain's immediate participation in the war, advanced by Von Ribbentrop from the very first meeting, did not come as a surprise to Germany, even less as an unpleasant surprise. However, Serrano Suñer's dilatory attitude during the course of the conversations, confirmed by the German minutes of the meeting, was obviously caused by something else: the disclosure of the extent of German aspirations in Morocco and in Central Africa and Hitler's request that Spain cede one of the Canary Islands to Germany.

The author makes no reference to the Hendaye meeting or to the successive talks aimed at the conclusion of a tripartite accord linking Spain to the Pact of Steel, by which Spain would promise to enter the war at a time to be determined by the Madrid government. The accord, whose essential lines were agreed upon at Hendaye, was initialed by Ciano on November 4 and by Serrano Suñer (who, in the meantime, had become Foreign Minister) on November 11. However, the Spanish resistance, based on the conviction that the war would now be a long one, the discontent manifested because the accord did not stipulate the exact areas to be ceded to Spain, and the reaction to Hitler's assertion that in any redistribution of African territories France's needs would have to be considered, in the event that it collaborated in the Axis victory, lead one to conclude that the Madrid government assumed these obligations for the sole purpose of avoiding a German coup against Spain. Moreover, by the same logic it may be added that the Spanish government was determined to treat developments in such a way as to avoid having to fulfill its obligations, especially since it would have been difficult for Spain to realize the advantages hoped for in the early stages of the negotiations.

During the course of these negotiations, Serrano Suñer met with Mussolini, first in Rome in September and later at Bordighera, during the Mussolini-Franco talks of February 12, 1941. From these contacts, he gained the impression that Mussolini opposed Spain's intervention, not only because the Italian had a much clearer idea of Spain's internal difficulties than did Hitler, but also because he feared losing his position as Hitler's only Mediterranean ally. Serrano Suñer's observations on this point have now been confirmed by various sources, demonstrating how well Madrid grasped Mussolini's thinking and the contrasting positions taken by Rome and Berlin in these negotiations.

From what has been said, it is evident that the attitude of the Spanish government underwent a substantial evolution during 1940. Its neutral position had remained firm until June, 1941. When the collapse of France seemed to indicate a quick end to the war, Spain moved to the very brink of intervention, only to gradually return to its neutral position when it became clear that the war would be a long one and that, in any event, Spanish territorial claims in Africa conflicted with German aspirations. The latter, if not a vital factor in the Spanish decision, was certainly one of no mean importance. On the details surrounding this evolution, on the factors that influenced it, and on the conflict in Madrid between those favoring and those opposing intervention, Serrano Suñer could have added a great deal. But this is an aspect of the Spanish diplomatic story on which the author maintains absolute silence. Thus, it is inevitable that from the point of view of diplomatic history his memoirs are of little importance, especially after the publication of the German documents, some of which were already known at the time the Serrano Suñer volume appeared.

b. Doussinague.

A completely different personality is revealed in the memoirs of Ambassador Doussinague,[346] a career diplomat who, from the fall of 1942 on, directed the political affairs section of the Spanish Foreign Ministry.

---

[346] José M. Doussinague, *España tenía razón* (Madrid: Espasa Calpe, 1950).

His volume is the work of a "technician," with all of the positive and negative features that this word implies. On the basis of his personal experience and a detailed documentation, the author has sought to trace an outline of Spanish policy during the war, and he has done so by citing numerous episodes in support of his theses rather than by defining Spanish policy. Consequently, the narrative is occasionally fragmentary and almost always limited to diplomatic maneuvers—the author delights in illustrating their effectiveness—but very rich in disclosures, many of which are of real interest.

Of course, some of the theses sustained in this volume are open to question. The assertion that the Spanish government consistently followed a policy of neutrality is unacceptable in the light of the facts now available on the negotiations between Madrid and Berlin during the second half of 1940. Yet Doussinague offers no comment of any kind on these talks, and, moreover, he has little to say on Serrano Suñer's subsequent activities. His detailed presentation of the peace proposal prepared by the Spanish government early in 1940 is followed by a very brief and general account of the period between the fall of France in 1940 and the replacement of Serrano Suñer by General Jordana in September, 1942. From here on, Doussinague's account regains its earlier detailed character, and his affirmations of the subsequent peaceful nature of Spanish policy are, of course, correct.

In effect, Doussinague does not take into account the changes in Spanish policy that had gradually developed, and he falls into the same error when he asserts that Serrano Suñer, despite his belief that it was necessary to establish closer ties with Germany for tactical reasons, did not contemplate an intervention on the side of the Axis. It is possible that this was the intention of the Spanish Foreign Minister during the summer of 1941, when Doussinague returned to Madrid from his mission to Greece and on various occasions discussed matters with Serrano Suñer. However, it should be noted that by mid-1941 the situation had altered considerably from what it had been the previous year and that, as a result, Serrano Suñer's views on the matter may have also undergone a considerable change. Doussinague is correct when he observes that, in evaluating the position of the Madrid government, it is necessary to ignore to a certain extent the rather frequent demonstrations of loyalty toward Germany by the Spanish leaders and the populace. These manifestations, the author notes, if partially expressions of real sympathy for the Axis cause, were also reflections of Spain's need of the moment: to assure Hitler that Spain would never be used as a base for the invasion of Europe, an assurance that was particularly important at the time when the bulk of Germany's armed forces were committed to the eastern front. Washington and London did not always understand this necessity.

In any case, as has been noted, with the appointment of Jordana as Foreign Minister in September, 1942, and with the author's transfer to the office of Director of Political Affairs in the same ministry in October, his account becomes increasingly accurate and detailed.

On the question of the new policy laid down by Jordana, a policy that clearly tended to return Spain to a position of strict neutrality between the two warring camps, Doussinague noted that it was established when the prospects of victory still favored Germany. This assertion is open to serious question. While it is true that until September, 1942, Germany had not suffered any serious setback on any of the military fronts, it is difficult to believe that Madrid had not detected the signs of the altered military situation. On the Russian Front, the German forces were experiencing great difficulty in reaching their objectives; in the Mediterranean, the British navy had successfully cut the supply lines to the Italo-German forces on the Egyptian Front; and, moreover, the Spanish government had been aware for some time (and Doussinague confirms it) of the prospect of an imminent Anglo-American landing in North Africa. Therefore, all indications suggested that the Germans were about to lose the strategic initiative on all major fronts, and the dismissal of Serrano Suñer could not be interpreted as anything less than the expression of a desire to adopt a policy more in line with the new requirements.

Shortly thereafter, the Anglo-American occupation of North Africa was to bind Spain even more closely to a policy of neutrality. Doussinague reveals that, a few days before the Allied landing in North Africa, the German Ambassador, Von Stohrer, urged that Spain extend its control to all of Morocco, promising full German support in the venture. The Spanish Minister rejected the suggestion, noting that it was in open contradiction to the aid given by the Reich to the Vichy government to assist the latter in defending its empire and that such an undertaking could not be discussed unless the future status of the French territories in Africa was clarified beforehand. Jordana's objection demonstrates how well the Spanish government was able to exploit Hitler's indecisiveness toward Madrid and Vichy, an attitude, Doussinague observed, that, while it sought to keep both governments tied to Germany, in fact resulted in making it impossible for the German Chancellor to achieve the full co-operation of either one of the two powers.

After the Allied landing in North Africa, the primary concern of the Spanish leaders was not fear of a German coup but, rather, the prospect of Anglo-American occupation of the Canary Islands. A warning about this possibility had been received in the summer of 1941; at that time Washington and London discussed the project, but ultimately the operation was considered necessary only in the event of German occupation of Spain. It is interesting to note that in that event, according to Doussinague, the Spanish government had decided to defend the archipelago, but only in a "parallel war" against the western Allies and not in alliance with Germany. In effect, this was the conception carried out by Italy until the failure of Italian military operations in Greece and North Africa obliged Mussolini to accept German aid. Moreover, in both cases this tendency toward a parallel war had similar origins: a matter of prestige and lack of faith in the intentions of the Nazi government, which, Spain feared, sought to intrude in areas where it desired to maintain an exclusive influence. Nor were the assurances given by the Allies at the time of the landings in North Africa sufficient to eliminate Spain's concern for the Canary Islands because threats to their security frequently appeared, nourished by the growing hostility of the American press and public toward Spain. It is probable that this fear influenced Spain's attitude toward Germany in that it drove the Spanish government to intensify its economic rapport with Berlin in order to obtain the military equipment necessary for defense.

Doussinague emphasizes the repeated attempts by Spain to launch negotiations that would lead to a compromise peace. The Madrid government was convinced that a continuation of the conflict to the point where one or the other of the belligerent groups was totally defeated would open the heart of a devastated Europe to communist penetration. This conviction was repeatedly brought to the attention of London, Berlin, and Washington, but without effect. Early in 1943 new soundings were made in Dublin, Buenos Aires, Stockholm, and Berne toward this end, with the idea that a group of neutral powers would have greater effect, but on this occasion the attempt also failed, largely because of the negative attitude of the Swiss, who had no intention of participating in an undertaking that was clearly anti-Soviet. Nor were the results of an offer of mediation contained in Jordana's speech of April 16, 1943, more auspicious. As Germany's defeat became more clearly apparent, Madrid increased its efforts to convince the western Allies that if Germany were completely destroyed, nothing could prevent the U.S.S.R. from dominating all of eastern Europe, even though it was unlikely that Soviet forces would cross the Rhine.

These Spanish initiatives were dictated by a fear of the repercussions of a total Axis defeat on the position of the Spanish Falangists and also by an evaluation, which coincided in many respects, of the postwar European situation. Thus, Doussinague concludes, Spain *tenía razón*. He was correct in considering communism as the gravest threat to western civilization; he was correct when he asserted that the destruction of Germany would leave Europe defenseless against communism and the Soviet Union; he was correct in assuming the anti-communist and anti-Soviet position which the western powers were also forced to adopt a very few years later.

18. THE MEMORIALISTS OF OTHER COUNTRIES.

a. The Swiss.

The Swiss memoir contribution is represented by the recollections of four diplomats: Wagnière, Frédéric Barbey, Stucki, and Burckhardt, and by the diary of a military man, Bernard Barbey.

Wagnière, Minister to Rome from April, 1918, to February, 1936, has utilized his experiences on this long mission to comment on Italian policy during those years.[347] While he reveals himself to be an attentive observer, although not always a shrewd and acute one, he devotes only a small part of his account to Italo-Swiss affairs of interest to the historian, emphasizing a facet of Fascist foreign policy of secondary importance.

Mussolini's advent to power aroused certain perplexities in Berne, stemming from one of his speeches in the Chamber the year before when he was only a deputy: Mussolini had challenged the statement made in the address of the Crown that Italy had achieved all of her Alpine frontier aspirations, noting that this was not true regarding the frontier north of Milan. After pointing out that the Canton Ticino was undergoing a continuous process of Germanization, Mussolini concluded his speech by referring to the Gothard as the natural and secure Italian frontier.

Swiss concern for an eventual Irridentist policy by the new government toward the Canton Ticino was completely assuaged by Mussolini when he received Wagnière for the first time on November 10, 1922. He explained that there were no territorial questions outstanding between Italy and Switzerland and that, insofar as the Germanization of the Ticino was concerned, his preoccupation came from the fact that, if the ethnic character of the region were altered, Italy would ultimately find an enemy people in the Canton in place of the friendly Ticinesi.

During the years of the Wagnière mission, Mussolini demonstrated his desire to maintain his commitment, frequently applying pressure to those newspapers that continued to stress the Italian character of the Canton

[347] Georges Wagnière, *Dix-huit ans à Rome* (Geneva: Jullien, 1944).

Ticino, even when the Swiss Socialist newspapers renewed their attacks on the Fascist regime.

Nor did the attitude of the Italian government change with the emergence, early in 1934, of a delicate problem that could have threatened the good relations existing between the two countries. In March of that year, Wagnière received instructions from Berne to advise Mussolini that the attempt to establish Fascist groups among the Swiss elements in Italy was not appreciated by the Federal Council. Mussolini did not reply immediately. However, a few days later, he informed Wagnière that he had sent a circular to all of the prefects urging them not to support the creation of these groups, while those already existing in Rome, Florence, and Milan would be placed under surveillance in order to prevent their taking any inopportune action. This decision, significant in itself, was accompanied by the announcement that the Italian government was ready to renew the Italo-Swiss Pact of 1924, which obliged both parties to submit all questions that might arise between the two countries to arbitration, and extending the period to ten years instead of the five provided by the agreement.

Frédéric Barbey, Minister to Brussels from 1918 to 1937, has also narrated in his volume[348] the developments, mainly internal, in the country to which he was accredited, but his account contains little of importance.

The volume by Walter Stucki[349] concerns only the last phase of his mission to Vichy. He offers numerous particulars on the arrest and deportation of Marshal Pétain and Laval and other members of the government by the Germans and on the delicate nature of his work in those exceptional circumstances, when he found himself seeking the means for a peaceful transfer of power from the survivors of the Vichy government to the French forces of liberation. Stucki comments in detail on these events, drawing heavily from his diary for those days (August 12–20 and 22–27, 1944). However, this narrative illustrates events that were purely episodic in character, with the exception of the references to the decision made by Laval and Pétain to refuse to continue in office outside of Vichy as a government in exile in Germany.

The memoirs of Carl Burckhardt[350] are rather unique. From 1937 to 1939 he had been the League of Nations High Commissioner in Danzig, and he reconstructs his activities from the reports he sent to the Secretary-General of the League. However, his account encompasses a much larger testimony

[348] *La Belgique d'Albert I et de Léopold III. Le témoignage d'un diplomat* (Paris: Perrin, 1950).

[349] *Von Pétain zur Vierten Republik: Vichy 1944* (Berne: Lang, 1947).

[350] *Ma mission à Dantzig* (Paris: Fayard, 1961).

because, owing to his office, he had numerous contacts with diplomats and statesmen and was often in a position to offer interesting information on several of the significant episodes that preceded the outbreak of the war, in particular on the Czechoslovak crisis and on German-Polish relations.

Finally, Bernard Barbey's diary[351] contains a few passages of political interest.[352] He was Chief of Staff to General Guisan, Commander of the Swiss army during the years of World War II.

b. The Greeks.

Greek memoirs are also few in number, and their contribution is generally restricted to the two decisive moments in Greek history during World War II: the Italian attack of October, 1940, and the civil war of 1944–45, following the liberation of the country.

On the first question, the volume by General Papagos,[353] Chief of the Greek General Staff, contains no revelations of major importance, although he devotes the first part of his memoir to the Greek diplomatic-military situation in the period prior to the Italian attack. Papagos discusses the negotiations undertaken during the initial phase of the conflict with Great Britain, France, and Turkey to define the nature of the assistance that the western powers would give to the Greek army in the event of a threat from either Italy or Bulgaria. However, the detailed documentation on which the General bases his account only demonstrates that no preliminary accord was reached with the Anglo-French and that he was vigorously opposed, at that time, to the request made by the commander of the French armed forces in the Levant, General Weygand, to base an Allied expeditionary force composed of four or five divisions in Salonika.

Regarding the questions that weighed heavily on the attitude of the Greek government, or at least on several of its members, with respect to

[351] *P. C. du Général. Journal du chef de l'Etat-Major particulier du Général Guisan (1940–1945)* (Neuchâtel: La Baconnière, 1948).

[352] Particular attention should be given to the volume by Jon Kimche, *Spying for Peace. General Guisan and Swiss Neutrality* (London: Weidenfeld and Nicolson, 1961), based largely on the papers of General Guisan. Special note should be taken of the Anglo-American negotiations with General Wolff for the surrender of the German forces in northern Italy, which are examined in an entirely new light, taking into account the knowledge Berlin had of the negotiations as well as the information the Soviets received from Switzerland directly by a radio that operated with the cognizance of the Swiss General Staff. The revelations contained in this volume suggest a substantial revision of the judgments previously rendered on this important episode that precipitated a serious crisis in the relations between Stalin, Roosevelt, and Churchill shortly before the death of the American President.

[353] Alexandros Papagos, *O Polemos tes Ellados* (Athens: Skazikis, 1945); Italian translation, *La Grecia in guerra (1940–1941)* (Milan: Garzanti, 1950).

Italy during the summer of 1940, nothing new is revealed in Papagos' account, and it is highly improbable that anything startlingly new will appear in the Metaxas diary,[354] whose publication has been initiated.

On the situation that developed in Greece after the liberation, reference is made to the memoirs of Papandreu,[355] Prime Minister at the time the government returned to Athens (October 18, 1944) and for the rest of that year, and to the Marcandonatos diary[356] (the latter was a functionary in the Foreign Ministry). Their versions of the events are in contrast to the memoirs of General Saraphis,[357] commander of the People's Army of National Liberation (ELAS), the military organization created by the Greek Communist party and by other minor leftist groups during the Italo-German occupation. The obvious polemical intent of these accounts renders their reliability highly problematical and limits their value to that of a revelation of the profound ideological cleavages created among the people by the civil war.

c. The Soviets.

Until recently, the contribution of Soviet memorialists was limited to the writings of two who fled the Soviet Union, Barmine and Butenko.[358] However, the particular motive that had prompted these diplomats to seek refuge abroad determined that their memoirs would focus primarily on the internal affairs of the U.S.S.R., permitting them to denounce the dictatorial regime of terror that characterized the Soviet system during the years preceding World War II. Above all, Barmine's thick volume, presenting detailed testimony on the situation, shocks the reader when he realizes that, as the author states in a laconic phrase, almost all of the personalities referred to were either executed or disappeared during the era of the "great purges."

Regarding his own diplomatic activity, Barmine has little to add because he had only been a Consul General in Resht in Iran from 1923 to 1924, and Chargé d'Affaires in Athens from 1936 to 1937, when he had fallen out of

---

[354] Joannes Metaxas, *To Prosopiko tou Emerologio* (Athens, 1951).

[355] George Papandreu, *E Apeleutherosis tes Ellados* [The Liberation of Greece] (Athens: Skazikis, 1945).

[356] Leon Marc (pseud.), *Les heures douloureuses de la Grèce libérée: Journal d'un témoin (octobre 1944–janvier 1945)* (Paris: Le François, 1947).

[357] Stephanos Saraphis, *Greek Resistance Army. The Story of Elas* (London: Birch Books, 1951).

[358] Alexandre Barmine, *Memoirs of a Soviet Diplomat* (London: Davies, 1938). The enlarged Italian edition is *Uno che sopravisse. La vita di un russo sotto il regime sovietico* (Bari: Laterza, 1948). Butenko's memoirs were published by various western newspapers at the time of the author's defection to the West.

favor with the party. Concerning Soviet policy toward Iran during his period of residence in Resht, Barmine reveals that Russo-Persian relations had not changed from the Czarist period because, particularly in northern Iran, the Soviet government in fact continued to exercise all of the economic privileges established by the Czarist government, notwithstanding their formal abolition in the treaty of 1921. He notes that in the struggle between the British and the Soviets to influence the Iranian Prime Minister, Reza Khan (who was later to overthrow the Quagiar dynasty and proclaim himself Shah), the Soviets erred in identifying the internal forces on which the Prime Minister's strength was based and dissipated their energies in pointless propaganda favoring a republic.

Regarding the effects of the "purge trials of 1937" on subsequent Soviet policy, Barmine's explanation should be noted, for it refutes the official view that the purge was a necessity posed by the discovery of a plot organized between commanders in the Red army and the German General Staff. The author maintains that Stalin decreed the sentences for the deliberate purpose of eliminating all those who would have opposed a direct Nazi-Soviet accord. According to Barmine, Stalin knew that Tukachevsky and the other military leaders were unalterably opposed to Nazi Germany and favored a united front with the democracies against Hitler, and that, therefore, Stalin had to eliminate them in order to proceed with his plans for the pact with Hitler. However, Barmine continues, Stalin did not realize that he was playing Hitler's game, the chief goal of which was the elimination of the best commanders of the army he soon proposed to attack. Barmine concludes that no faith should be placed in the Davies version of the affair, according to which Stalin, in executing the top commanders of the Red army, was freeing Russia of a fifth column in order to prepare for the war against Hitler. It is interesting to compare these versions with that presented by Hagen.

Only in 1961 did changes become apparent in the rigid reserve maintained by Soviet statesmen[359] and diplomats up to that time with the appearance, in serial form, of the memoirs of A. Y. Bogomolov[360] regarding his diplomatic missions during the war. However, after a short time the publication was interrupted, and for the time being only the part regarding his mission to Vichy is available. Bogomolov was Chargé d'Affaires there from November, 1940, to March, 1941, and Ambassador from that date

[359] The diary of the former Minister of Foreign Affairs, Litvinov, would constitute an exception, if it were regarded as authentic, a supposition that was questioned by the English historian E. Carr, who edited the publication (*Maxim Litvinov, Notes for a Journal* [London: Deutsch, 1955]).

[360] "Wartime Diplomatic Missions," *International Affairs*, Moscow, 1961, No. 6, pp. 70–79; No. 7, pp. 90–97; No. 8, pp. 69–76.

until the break in relations between the two countries, one week after the German attack on the U.S.S.R. Contrary to what was announced when publication was begun, the chapters have not yet appeared concerning his subsequent activities as Soviet representative to the governments in exile in London, to the French Committee at Algiers, and as Ambassador to Paris following the liberation of France.

While they do not contain any startling revelations, Bogomolov's memoirs are of some value. He begins his narrative by explaining that he was sent to Vichy in order to study the situation in occupied France and that of the workers in the areas under German control, to determine the extent of the collaborationist following and whether they or the opposition were the stronger, and, finally, to try to improve Franco-Soviet relations. However, he does not refer to the fact that during the period of Nazi-Soviet friendship, the Soviet government observed the practice of recognizing all of the politico-military changes effected by the Germans and thereby established diplomatic relations with Slovakia and with the Iraqi government of Ali el-Gailani, and requested the recall of the Norwegian, Belgian, Yugoslav, and Greek legations in Moscow.

Although he refers to various colloquies with the French leaders and with other members of the diplomatic corps, Bogomolov does not say much about his activity in Vichy. The only negotiation he treats in some detail concerns the repatriation of the "new" Soviet citizens (Estonians, Letts, Lithuanians, and Byelorussians) who served in the international brigades during the Spanish Civil War and who were still detained in France, not having been included in the previous negotiations for the repatriation of Soviet citizens. Bogomolov adds that, from the beginning of his mission, Laval expressed the desire to re-establish trade between the two countries but that this overture was not pursued further because the French Vice-Premier, and perhaps also Pétain, was not disposed to accept the preliminary conditions that Bogomolov had been told to request: the transfer of the gold and other assets of the states annexed by the U.S.S.R. in 1939–40 that were frozen in France. The conversations were reopened in February, 1941, with the new Vice-Premier, Darlan, who indicated his readiness to satisfy the preliminary Soviet requests, but these negotiations made little progress in the months that followed, until June, 1941.

Naturally, Bogomolov's judgment of Vichy's policy is a negative one, but while affirming his disbelief in Pétain's attempt to play a double game, he does not openly condemn the old Marshal. In recalling the last conversation he had with him on the day the Germans attacked the Soviet Union, Bogomolov narrates that Pétain, while bidding him farewell, expressed his hope for a Soviet victory. On leaving, Bogomolov was immediately aware that this would not have been the official attitude of the Vichy government and that Pétain had evidently not yet consulted anyone and the phrase simply reflected his own first impression.

The only substantial Soviet memoir contribution is the volume by Ivan Maisky[361] regarding his ambassadorial mission to London from 1932 to 1939. In addition to the usual comments on the environment, common to virtually every work of this kind, the author limits himself, in effect, to two issues: the Non-Intervention Committee, in which he was the Soviet representative, and the tripartite negotiations during the late spring and summer of 1939. On the first subject, omitted in the English translation, the author offers nothing new because it had been a well-known fact since the days of the Spanish Civil War that the declarations of the delegates on the Non-Intervention Committee had only a marginal relationship to the policies eventually pursued by the various powers. On the second question, Maisky's account does not vary from the interpretation given by Soviet historiography to the policy of appeasement and to the causes for the failure of the tripartite negotiations. The author often cites the German documents published by the Soviet government in 1948. Maisky's account also covers events in which he did not participate, such as the Nazi-Soviet Pact of August 23, 1939. And here, too, he does no more than repeat the well-known Soviet thesis concerning the motives that drove the U.S.S.R. to sign the accord with Germany.

However, in his conclusions, enumerating the advantages obtained by the Soviet Union from this agreement, Maisky recalls that the pact "freed 13,000,000 western Ukrainians and Byelorussians from the terrible fate of becoming slaves of Hitler, insured the national reunion of all Ukrainians and Byelorussians into single nations advancing rapidly on the path of Socialist development, and pushed forward the Soviet frontiers several hundred kilometers to the west. . . ."

d. The Turks, the South Africans, and the Argentines.

Concerning the other countries, reference should be made to the memoirs of the Turkish Minister, Mennan Tebelen;[362] the interesting

---

[361] *Who Helped Hitler?* (London: Hutchinson, 1964). The Italian edition, *Perchè scoppiò la Seconda guerra mondiale?* (Rome: Editori Riuniti, 1965), in contrast to the English edition, is complete with the exception of the pages of the conclusion reaffirming what had been reported in the text. The author had earlier published two other volumes of memoirs. The first, *Before the Storm* (London: Hutchinson, 1944), recalls the years of his youth; the second, *Journey into the Past* (London: Hutchinson, 1962), covers the five years (1912–17), he spent in London as an *émigré*.

[362] A. Mennan Tebelen, *Carnet d'un diplomate* (Paris: Denoël, 1951).

account by the former South African Minister of Defense, Pirow,[363] on his mission to Europe in November, 1938, in view of an Anglo-German *rapprochement;* and the testimony of the Argentine Ambassador, Escobar,[364] on his mission to Madrid from November, 1940, to the end of 1942. The latter account is especially important for its references to the Spanish internal situation and for its vivid description of the diplomatic world accredited to the Spanish capital.

[363] Oswald Pirow, "War der Zweite Welktkrieg unvermeidbar?," *Nation Europa,* April, 1952.

[364] Adrián C. Escobar, *Diálogo íntimo con España. Memorias de un embajador durante la tempestad europea* (Buenos Aires: Club de Lectores, 1950).

INDEX

Bismarck, Prince Otto von, 259, 347, 382, 392, 397, 398, 405, 406, 407, 408
Bissolati, Leonida, 357
Bitolj incident (1940), 615
Björkö treaty. *See* Treaties: Björkö
Black Cabinet, 108, 120, 122
Blücher, Wipert von, 520, 521, 628, 632
Blue Books. *See* Great Britain
Blue-White Books, Finnish. *See* Finland
Blum, Léon, 313
Boer War (1899–1901), 384, 399
Boghicevic (Boghitschewitsch), Milos, 156, 157, 158
Bogomolov, Alexander, 654–55
Bollati, Riccardo: Avarna correspondence, 32, 263, 284
Bompard, Maurice, 367
Bonar Law, Andrew, 501
Bonin Longare, Count Lelio, 345
Bonnet, Georges, 468, 469, 472, 473, 485, 618–19, 620
Bonnin, Georges, 107n
Bonomi, Ivanoe, 480, 481, 482
Bordighera meeting. *See* Meetings: Bordighera
Borges de Castro, Jose Ferreira, 82
Bosnia-Herzegovina, 125, 145, 153, 154, 159, 297, 353, 357, 378, 393, 400, 419, 439, 447, 516
Bourgeois, Leon, 367
Bouthillier, Yves, 474, 487
Bova Scoppa, Renato, 464, 465
Bowers, Claude, 544
Boxer Rebellion, 219, 332, 340, 453
Brancaccio, Nicola, 360
Bratianu, Dimitri, 116, 624
Braunthal, Julius, 603
Brenner Pass meeting. *See* Meetings: Brenner
Brest Litovsk: treaty of. *See* Treaties: Brest Litovsk
Briand, Aristide, 272, 363, 411, 511
Brinon, Ferdinand de: trial of, 315
Brockdorff-Rantzau, Ulrich von, 134
Bruns, Viktor, 75
Bryan, Mary Baird, 431
Bryan, William Jennings, 430
Bryans, J. Lonsdale, 507
Brybowski, 25n
Buchanan, Sir George, 380

Bucharest: peace of (1913), 145; peace of (1918), 117, 405, 441
Buchlau meeting. *See* Meetings: Buchlau
Buckle, George Earle, 384
Buftea, preliminaries to peace of (1918), 441
Bukowina, 185, 622
Bulgaria: Orange Books on Bulgaria's intervention in World War I, 96; Serbo-Bulgarian alliance (1912) negotiations, 394; relations with Entente powers (1914–15), 394; negotiations with Russia (1915), 185, 449
Bullitt, William C., 224, 542, 543
Bülow, Bernhard von, 172, 398, 399, 400, 401, 409, 410, 411, 423
Burckhardt, Carl, 650–51
Burian von Rajecz, Stephan, 414, 420
Burnet, Gilbert, 58
Busschère, Alphonse de, 78n
Butcher, Harry C., 553
Butenko, 653
Butler, Rohan, 196
Byo Ping, 336
Byrnes, James, 229, 230, 551, 552, 553

C

Cadorna, Luigi, 39; letter of November 3, 1917, 360, 361, 376
Cadorna, Raffaele, 258n
Cadwalader, John L., 83n
Caillaux, Joseph, 362, 411
Cairo conferences (1943), 230, 236, 541
Cairoli, Benedetto, 286, 344, 345
Calvo, Carlos, 73
Cambon, Jules, 150, 434, 638
Cambon, Paul, 368, 369: Grey-Cambon letters (1912), 146
Cammaerts, Emile, 437
Campbell, Sir Gerald, 474, 509
Canary Islands: Hitler's pretensions in, 645; eventuality of Anglo-American occupation during World War II, 648–49
Canevaro, Felice Napoleone, 261, 262
Canning, George, 89
Cantalupo, Roberto, 461
Cantillo, Alejandro del, 82n
Capmany y de Montpalau, Antonio de, 67n, 82
Caprivi, Leo von, 397, 407, 408

200, 203; Persian policy (1919), 200; Anglo-German relations (1920), 203; relations with U.S. (1919–20), 200; Belgian neutrality (1920), 200; Far Eastern policy (1920), 202, 203; eastern European policy (1920), 202, 203; negotiations for renewal of Anglo-Japanese Alliance (1920), 203; Baltic states policy (1920–21), 203; Polish policy (1920–21), 204; Chamberlain-Mussolini conversations (December 29, 1925), 272; Chamberlain-Mussolini conversations (September 30, 1926), 272; Far Eastern policy (1929–31), 207; Anglo-Soviet relations (1929–34), 207; Anglo-French-Italian declaration on Austria (1934), 597; Austrian policy (1934), 603; Anglo-German relations (1934), 205, 208; Simon-Baldwin declaration on Belgian independence (1934), 640; Eden's visit to Rome (June, 1935), 503, 504; Hoare-Laval proposal (1935), 500, 507; Anglo-French guarantee to Belgium (April 24, 1937), 641; Roosevelt-Chamberlain correspondence (January, 1938), 501; Anglo-German relations (1938), 173, 178; Polish policy (1938–39), 210; Anglo-Portuguese relations during Spanish Civil War, 299–304; Far Eastern policy (1938–39), 210; Rumanian guarantee (April, 1939), 621; Anglo-French-Soviet negotiations (1939), 210, 249, 280, 499, 580; Polish guarantee (1939), 621; activities of British Embassy in Rome (August, 1939), 280; Dahlerus negotiations (August, 1939), 634–35; German invasion plans, 192, 195; Anglo-French-Finnish negotiations (February, 1940), 626, 627; Eden's visit to Moscow (December, 1941), 531–32; Sikorski-U.S.S.R. relations, 303–4; Molotov's visit to London (May, 1942), 531; negotiations with Kállay (1942–43), 606–8; Hoare-Jordana notes (February, 1942), 499
Greece: White Books (1913–17), 443; White Book on Italian attack (1940), 98; relations with Entente powers during World War I, 118, 442; Corfu crisis, 268–69; Italian attack (1940), 287; background, 462–63

Green Books. See Italy
Gregory, Sir John Duncan, 382
Greiner, Helmuth, 193
Grew, Joseph, 546, 547
Grey, Sir Edward, 144, 146, 152, 199, 371, 372, 373, 375, 395, 411, 429: Grey-Cambon letters, 146, 147
Gromyko, Andrei, 237
Grozio, Ugo, 52, 60
Gruic, Slavko, 438
Guariglia, Raffaele, 252, 277, 458, 459, 460, 465, 470
Guderian, Heinz, 528
Guicciardini, Francesco, 350
Guiccioli, Alessandro, 344
Guichenon, Samuel, 56
Guisan, Henri, 652
Günther, Christian, 636
Gustav V (King of Sweden), 316: correspondence with Hitler (1940), 322
Gwyn, Stephen, 379

H

Haakon VII (King of Norway), 319, 320
Habicht, Max, 86n
Habicht, Theo, 600
Hagen, Walter, 528, 529
Hague Conference (1907), 388
Haile Selassie (King of Ethiopia), 480
Haldane, Richard, 144, 145, 373, 374, 383, 401
Halder, Franz: diaries, 195, 196
Halifax, Edward Wood, Lord, 210, 300, 314, 470n, 473, 479, 502, 507, 618, 621, 635
Hallendorf, Carl Jakob, 81n
Hamada, Kenji, 445
Hambro, Carl, 636
Hankey, Sir Maurice, 222, 360
Hanko peninsula, 627
Hanotaux, Gabriel, 151, 261
Harald (Prince of Norway), 320
Harding, Warren G., 200
Hardinge, Sir Arthur, 381
Hardinge of Penshurst, Lord, 382
Harriman, Averell, 533
Hartvig, Nicholas-Henrikovic, 394
Haskins, Charles Homer, 433
Hassell, Ulrich von, 179, 180, 183, 507, 530
Haswell, John H., 83n

Vopicka, J., 435
Voroschilov, Clemente Efremovic, 250

W

Wagnière, Georges, 650, 651
Wakatzuki, Reijiro, 569
Waldersee, Alfred von, 407, 413
Wang Ching-wei, 559, 575, 576, 577
War crimes, 164–67, 168, 193
World Wars I and II:
—World War I: Russian activity on
the eve of the war, 116, 117, 388;
formation of the Balkan League,
448–49; origins, 116–56, 362–441;
Poincaré's visit to St. Petersburg, 151;
Izvolski's policy after Bosnian crisis,
157; invasion of Belgium, 160;
Austro-Serbian crisis, 261, 353, 421,
438; crisis of 1914, 395, 401, 411,
414, 421, 422, 434; war responsibility, 115, 117, 131, 132, 134,
135, 152, 153, 155, 366, 372,
385, 391, 395, 396, 405, 447; submarine warfare, 402; Bulgarian intervention, 115, 381; negotiations for
Bulgarian intervention, 115, 116;
Japanese intervention, 142, 146; British intervention, 370–73; Greek neutrality, 442–44; Greek intervention,
113, 117, 358; Italian neutrality,
262–65, 353–59, 424, 425; Italo-Austrian negotiations (1914–15) to prevent Italian intervention on the Allied
side, 420; Italian intervention, 110–
22, 267, 352–58, 386; Rumanian
neutrality, 441; Rumanian intervention, 114, 119, 441; American
neutrality, 429, 434; American intervention, 380, 430; negotiations on
Turkish intervention, 117, 447–48;
War propaganda, 107–12, 141, 158–
59; wartime diplomacy, 137, 138,
358, 374; peace overtures, 138, 139,
220; Prince Sixtus affair, 364, 375,
419, 420; peace efforts by Holy See,
314, 375, 381, 430; Briand's peace
overture, 410; American mediation,
413; Austrian peace overtures, 390,
414–16; Burian's proposal, 420;
House mission (1915 and 1916),
429; Rumanian peace overture, 441;
armistices, 133, 134, 220, 383, 430,

490; negotiations for Italo-Austrian
armistice, 425
—World War II: responsibility, 164,
463; origins and the summer crisis of
1939, 375, 456, 463, 465, 470–71,
484, 490, 634–35; France and the
Polish guarantee, 501; the Rumanian
guarantee, 621; Italian intervention,
280–84, 456, 463, 465; proposal for
Portuguese intervention, 302; Finnish
intervention, 631; negotiations for
Spanish intervention, 644–46; Spanish neutrality, 645–50; Rumanian intervention against Soviet Union, 621;
peace initiatives (1939), 279; Russo-
Finnish War ("Winter War")
(1939–40), 320, 625, 627, 632, 633;
German invasion of Norway (1940),
636; Franco-German and Franco-
Italian armistices (June, 1940), 310,
314, 474, 476, 485, 491; Italo-Greek
War (1940), 652, 653; landing in
north Africa (Operation TORCH)
(1942), 540, 549, 647–49; Churchill's proposal for a landing in the
Balkans (1943), 229, 495; Trident
Conference (Washington, May,
1943), 540, 541; Quadrant Conference (Quebec, August, 1943), 541;
Spanish efforts to arrange a compromise peace (1943), 649–50; Japanese
offer to mediate the German-Soviet
conflict (spring, 1943), 560; Operation OVERLORD, 230; second front,
244; formulas for the military control
of Germany and Japan, 250–51; second Quebec Conference (September,
1944), 540; Finnish request for an
armistice (1944), 625; Rumanian armistice (September, 1944), 622;
Japanese request for Soviet mediation,
561, 562, 563, 564, 566; Soviet intervention against Japan, 551; the
atomic bomb, 551; dropping the
bomb, 565, 567; Japanese surrender
(1945), 561, 566; Moscow Conference (December, 1945), 552; London Conference (September–October,
1945), 552; Paris Conference
(April–May, June–July, 1946), 552
Washington Naval Disarmament Conference (1921–22), 200, 207
Watt, D. C., 181
Webster, Sir Charles, 16

THE HISTORY OF TREATIES AND INTERNATIONAL POLITICS

Mario Toscano

designer: Athena Blackorby
typesetter: Kingsport Press, Inc.
typefaces: Fairfield (text) and Electra Bold (display)
printer: Kingsport Press, Inc.
paper: Warren's 1854
binder: Kingsport Press, Inc.